# Jeep CJ Automotive Repair Manual

## by Larry Warren and John H Haynes Member of the Guild of Motoring Writers

### Models covered

CJ-2A, CJ-3A, CJ-3B, CJ-5, CJ-5A, CJ-6, CJ-7
Scrambler, Renegade, Laredo and Golden Eagle
Automatic and manual transmissions

ISBN 1 85010 357 7

Printed in the USA     *(11U6 – 412)*

**Haynes Publishing Group**
Sparkford Nr Yeovil
Somerset BA22 7JJ England

**Haynes North America, Inc.**
861 Lawrence Drive
Newbury Park
California 91320 USA

# Acknowledgments

Special thanks are due to American Motors Corporation for their supply of technical information and certain illustrations. Champion Spark Plug Company supplied the illustrations showing the various spark plug conditions.

# About this manual

## Its purpose

The purpose of this manual is to help you get the best value from your vehicle. It can do so in several ways. It can help you decide what work must be done, even if you choose to have it done by a dealer service department or a repair shop; it provides information and procedures for routine maintenance and servicing; and it offers diagnostic and repair procedures to follow when trouble occurs.

It is hoped that you will use the manual to tackle the work yourself. For many simpler jobs, doing it yourself may be quicker than arranging an appointment to get the vehicle into a shop and making the trips to leave it and pick it up. More importantly, a lot of money can be saved by avoiding the expense the shop must pass on to you to cover its labor and overhead costs. An added benefit is the sense of satisfaction and accomplishment that you feel after having done the job yourself.

## Using the manual

The manual is divided into Chapters. Each Chapter is divided into numbered Sections, which are headed in bold type between horizontal lines. Each Section consists of consecutively numbered paragraphs.

The two types of illustrations used (figures and photographs), are referenced by a number preceding their caption. Figure reference numbers denote Chapter and numerical sequence within the Chapter; (i.e. Fig. 3.4 means Chapter 3, figure number 4). Figure captions are followed by a Section number which ties the figure to a specific portion of the text. All photographs apply to the Chapter in which they appear and the reference number pinpoints the pertinent Section and paragraph; i.e., 3.2 means Section 3, paragraph 2.

Procedures, once described in the text, are not normally repeated. When it is necessary to refer to another Chapter, the reference will be given as Chapter and Section number i.e. Chapter 1/16). Cross references given without use of the word 'Chapter' apply to Sections and/or paragraphs in the same Chapter. For example, 'see Section 8' means in the same Chapter.

Reference to the left or right side of the vehicle is based on the assumption that one is sitting in the driver's seat, facing forward.

Even though extreme care has been taken during the preparation of this manual, neither the publisher nor the author can accept responsibility for any errors in, or omissions from, the information given.

# Introduction to the Jeep CJ

The Jeep CJ is available in an open utility body style with a folding windshield. Later models feature removable, folding tops or hardtops in both conventional and pick-up styles.

Power from the engine is passed through the transmission to a transfer case and then to the front and rear axles by driveshafts. Both manual and automatic transmissions are available on these vehicles.

Early models used a cam and lever type steering gear while later models featured a recirculating ball type steering gear with power assist as an option.

Suspension is by semi-elliptic springs with tubular shock absorbers. Both four-wheel drum and front disc/rear drum brakes are used on these vehicles, with power assist as an option.

# Contents

| | Page |
|---|---|
| Acknowledgements | 4 |
| About this manual | 4 |
| Introduction to the Jeep CJ | 4 |
| General dimensions | 6 |
| Vehicle identification numbers | 7 |
| Buying parts | 8 |
| Maintenance techniques, tools and working facilities | 9 |
| Booster battery (jump) starting | 15 |
| Jacking and towing | 15 |
| Automotive chemicals and lubricants | 16 |
| Safety first! | 17 |
| Troubleshooting | 18 |
| Chapter 1 Tune-up and routine maintenance | 25 | **1** |
| Chapter 2 Part A General engine overhaul procedures | 61 | **2A** |
| Chapter 2 Part B 151 cu in four-cylinder engine | 73 | **2B** |
| Chapter 2 Part C In-line six-cylinder engine | 86 | **2C** |
| Chapter 2 Part D V8 engine | 101 | **2D** |
| Chapter 2 Part E V6 engine | 111 | **2E** |
| Chapter 2 Part F L-and F-head four-cylinder engines | 122 | **2F** |
| Chapter 3 Cooling, heating and air-conditioning systems | 135 | **3** |
| Chapter 4 Fuel and exhaust systems | 146 | **4** |
| Chapter 5 Engine electrical systems | 177 | **5** |
| Chapter 6 Emissions control systems | 190 | **6** |
| Chapter 7 Part A Manual transmission | 204 | **7A** |
| Chapter 7 Part B Automatic transmission | 229 | **7B** |
| Chapter 7 Part C Transfer case | 234 | **7C** |
| Chapter 8 Driveline | 245 | **8** |
| Chapter 9 Brakes | 258 | **9** |
| Chapter 10 Chassis electrical system | 272 | **10** |
| Chapter 11 Suspension and steering systems | 300 | **11** |
| Chapter 12 Body | 311 | **12** |
| Chapter 13 Supplement: Revisions and information on 1984 through 1986 models | 317 | **13** |
| Conversion factors | 333 |
| Index | 334 |

1981 Jeep Renegade

Typical Jeep engine compartment (V8 engine)

# General dimensions

## Overall length

| | |
|---|---|
| CJ-2 . . . . . . . . . . . . . . . . . . . . . . . . . . . . . . . . . . . . . . . . . . | 130 in |
| CJ-3 . . . . . . . . . . . . . . . . . . . . . . . . . . . . . . . . . . . . . . . . . . | 130 in |
| CJ-5 . . . . . . . . . . . . . . . . . . . . . . . . . . . . . . . . . . . . . . . . . . | 139 in |
| CJ-6 . . . . . . . . . . . . . . . . . . . . . . . . . . . . . . . . . . . . . . . . . . | 159 in |
| CJ-7 | |
|   1975 through 1981 . . . . . . . . . . . . . . . . . . . . . . . . . . . . | 148 in |
|   1982 and 1983 . . . . . . . . . . . . . . . . . . . . . . . . . . . . . . | 153.2 in |

## Height

| | |
|---|---|
| CJ-2 . . . . . . . . . . . . . . . . . . . . . . . . . . . . . . . . . . . . . . . . . . | 66 in |
| CJ-3 . . . . . . . . . . . . . . . . . . . . . . . . . . . . . . . . . . . . . . . . . . | 66.4 in |
| CJ-5 . . . . . . . . . . . . . . . . . . . . . . . . . . . . . . . . . . . . . . . . . . | 68 in |
| CJ-6 . . . . . . . . . . . . . . . . . . . . . . . . . . . . . . . . . . . . . . . . . . | 68.4 in |
| CJ-7 . . . . . . . . . . . . . . . . . . . . . . . . . . . . . . . . . . . . . . . . . . | 69 in |

## Width

| | |
|---|---|
| CJ-2 . . . . . . . . . . . . . . . . . . . . . . . . . . . . . . . . . . . . . . . . . . | 59 in |
| CJ-3 . . . . . . . . . . . . . . . . . . . . . . . . . . . . . . . . . . . . . . . . . . | 59 in |
| CJ-5 . . . . . . . . . . . . . . . . . . . . . . . . . . . . . . . . . . . . . . . . . . | 59.9 in |
| CJ-6 . . . . . . . . . . . . . . . . . . . . . . . . . . . . . . . . . . . . . . . . . . | 59.9 in |
| CJ-7 . . . . . . . . . . . . . . . . . . . . . . . . . . . . . . . . . . . . . . . . . . | 59.9 in |

## Wheelbase

| | |
|---|---|
| CJ-2 and CJ-3 . . . . . . . . . . . . . . . . . . . . . . . . . . . . . . . . . . . | 80 in |
| CJ-5 | |
|   1954 through 1972 . . . . . . . . . . . . . . . . . . . . . . . . . . . . | 81 in |
|   1973 through 1983 . . . . . . . . . . . . . . . . . . . . . . . . . . . . | 84 in |
| CJ-6 | |
|   1959 through 1972 . . . . . . . . . . . . . . . . . . . . . . . . . . . . | 101 in |
|   1973 through 1976 . . . . . . . . . . . . . . . . . . . . . . . . . . . . | 104 in |
| CJ-7 . . . . . . . . . . . . . . . . . . . . . . . . . . . . . . . . . . . . . . . . . . | 93.5 in |

# Vehicle identification numbers

Modifications are a continuing and unpublicized process in vehicle manufacturing. Since spare parts manuals and lists are compiled on a numerical basis, the individual vehicle numbers are essential to identify the component required.

## Vehicle Identification Number (VIN)

This very important identification number is stamped on a plate which is located on the firewall under the hood. On later models the VIN is also attached to the dashboard next to the windshield on the driver's side.

## Safety certification label

Later models carry this sticker which certifies that federal safety standards are met. The sticker is located directly below the door opening on the driver's side. The label carries the VIN, gross vehicle weight and gross vehicle axle ratings.

## Engine identification numbers

Important information such as build codes, serial numbers and identification numbers can be found on the engines. On F- and L-head engines, the serial number is stamped on the boss just behind the water

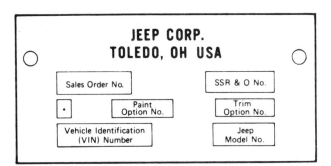

Typical vehicle identification plate

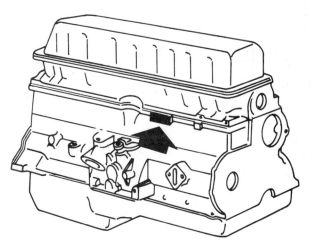

In-line six-cylinder engine build date code location

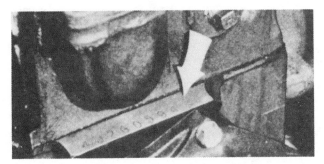

F- and L-head engine serial number location

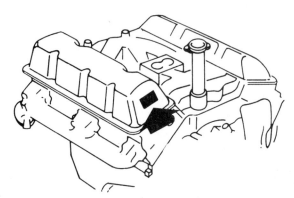

**V8 engine build date code location**

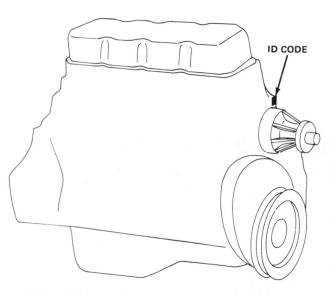

**151 cu in four-cylinder engine identification code location**

pump. On the V6, the code number is located on the right front face of the engine block, adjacent to the rocker arm cover. The in-line six-cylinder engine build date code is stamped on the machined surface between the number two and three cylinders on the right side. The V8 engine build date code is stamped on a plate affixed to the front surface of the right valve cover. The 151 cubic inch four-cylinder engine ID code is found on the front of the engine block or timing cover. In addition, engines built for use in Georgia have an additional two-digit number enclosed by asterisks. On six-cylinder engines the number is below the build date code, on V8 engines it is on the left side of the block next to the core plug and on four-cylinder engines it is on the left side of the flywheel housing.

### Manual transmission identification number

The transmission identification tag, which displays the vendor part and Jeep part number, is generally found on a tag attached to the upper left side of the transmission cover or shift control.

### Automatic transmission serial number

The automatic transmission serial number is found on a tag attached to the right side of the transmission case.

### Emissions control information label

Later models have an emissions control information label which is located in front of the radiator. This label contains information on engine application and tune-up specifications.

### Transfer case identification number

An identification tag featuring the vendor and Jeep numbers necessary to obtain the proper spare parts is affixed to the transfer case. On the Quadra-Trac transfer case, the tag is attached to the rear half of the case. On early model 18 and 20 transfer cases, the identification tag is fastened to the case, while on later model 20 and 300 cases it is held in place by the intermediate shaft lockplate bolt.

# Buying parts

Replacement parts are available from many sources, which generally fall into one of two categories – authorized dealer parts departments and independent retail auto parts stores. Our advice concerning these parts is as follows:

*Retail auto parts stores:* Good auto parts stores will stock frequently needed components which wear out relatively fast, such as clutch components, exhaust systems, brake parts, tune-up parts, etc. These stores often supply new or reconditioned parts on an exchange basis, which can save a considerable amount of money. Discount auto parts stores are often very good places to buy materials and parts needed for general vehicle maintenance such as oil, grease, filters, spark plugs, belts, touch-up paint, bulbs, etc. They also usually sell tools and general accessories, have convenient hours, charge lower prices and can often be found not far from home.

*Authorized dealer parts department:* This is the best source for parts which are unique to the vehicle and not generally available elsewhere (such as major engine parts, transmission parts, trim pieces, etc.).

*Warranty information:* If the vehicle is still covered under warranty, be sure that any replacement parts purchased – regardless of the source – do not invalidate the warranty!

To be sure of obtaining the correct parts, have engine and chassis numbers available and, if possible, take the old parts along for positive identification.

# Maintenance techniques, tools and working facilities

## Maintenance techniques

There are a number of techniques involved in maintenance and repair that will be referred to throughout this manual. Application of these techniques will enable the home mechanic to be more efficient, better organized and capable of performing the various tasks properly, which will ensure that the repair job is thorough and complete.

### Fasteners

Fasteners are nuts, bolts, studs and screws used to hold two or more parts together. There are a few things to keep in mind when working with fasteners. Almost all of them use a locking device of some type, either a lock washer, locknut, locking tab or thread adhesive. All threaded fasteners should be clean and straight, with undamaged threads and undamaged corners on the hex head where the wrench fits. Develop the habit of replacing all damaged nuts and bolts with new ones. Special locknuts with nylon or fiber inserts can only be used once. If they are removed, they lose their locking ability and must be replaced with new ones.

Rusted nuts and bolts should be treated with a penetrating fluid to ease removal and prevent breakage. Some mechanics use turpentine in a spout-type oil can, which works quite well. After applying the rust penetrant, let it ''work'' for a few minutes before trying to loosen the nut or bolt. Badly rusted fasteners may have to be chiseled or sawed off or removed with a special nut breaker, available at tool stores.

If a bolt or stud breaks off in an assembly, it can be drilled and removed with a special tool commonly available for this purpose. Most automotive machine shops can perform this task, as well as other repair procedures (such as repair of threaded holes that have been stripped out).

Flat washers and lock washers, when removed from an assembly, should always be replaced exactly as removed. Replace any damaged washers with new ones. Always use a flat washer between a lock washer and any soft metal surface (such as aluminum), thin sheet metal or plastic.

### Fastener sizes

For a number of reasons, automobile manufacturers are making wider and wider use of metric fasteners. Therefore, it is important to be able to tell the difference between standard (sometimes called U.S., English or SAE) and metric hardware, since they cannot be interchanged.

All bolts, whether standard or metric, are sized according to diameter, thread pitch and length. For example, a standard 1/2 — 13 x 1 bolt is 1/2 inch in diameter, has 13 threads per inch and is 1 inch long. An M12 — 1.75 x 25 metric bolt is 12 mm in diameter, has a thread pitch of 1.75 mm (the distance between threads) and is 25 mm long. The two bolts are nearly identical, and easily confused, but they are not interchangeable.

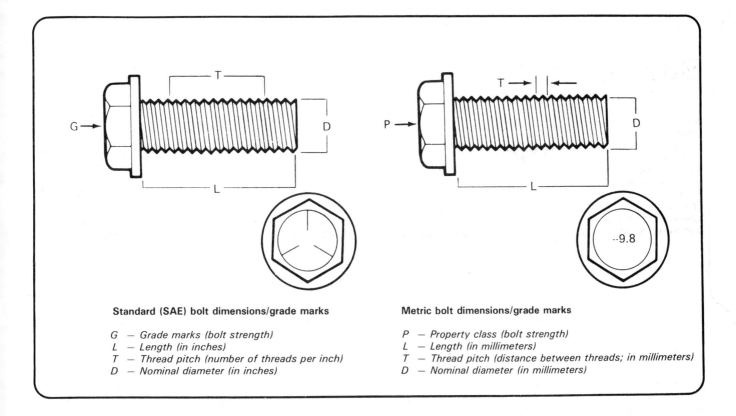

**Standard (SAE) bolt dimensions/grade marks**

G — Grade marks (bolt strength)
L — Length (in inches)
T — Thread pitch (number of threads per inch)
D — Nominal diameter (in inches)

**Metric bolt dimensions/grade marks**

P — Property class (bolt strength)
L — Length (in millimeters)
T — Thread pitch (distance between threads; in millimeters)
D — Nominal diameter (in millimeters)

In addition to the differences in diameter, thread pitch and length, metric and standard bolts can also be distinguished by examining the bolt heads. To begin with, the distance across the flats on a standard bolt head is measured in inches, while the same dimension on a metric bolt is measured in millimeters (the same is true for nuts). As a result, a standard wrench should not be used on a metric bolt and a metric wrench should not be used on a standard bolt. Also, standard bolts have slashes radiating out from the center of the head to denote the grade or strength of the bolt (which is an indication of the amount of torque that can be applied to it). The greater the number of slashes, the greater the strength of the bolt (grades 0 through 5 are commonly used on automobiles). Metric bolts have a property class (grade) number, rather than a slash, molded into their heads to indicate bolt strength. In this case, the higher the number, the stronger the bolt (property class numbers 8.8, 9.8 and 10.9 are commonly used on automobiles).

Strength markings can also be used to distinguish standard hex nuts from metric hex nuts. Standard nuts have dots stamped into one side, while metric nuts are marked with a number. The greater the number of dots, or the higher the number, the greater the strength of the nut.

Metric studs are also marked on their ends according to property class (grade). Larger studs are numbered (the same as metric bolts), while smaller studs carry a geometric code to denote grade.

It should be noted that many fasteners, especially Grades 0 through 2, have no distinguishing marks on them. When such is the case, the only way to determine whether it is standard or metric is to measure the thread pitch or compare it to a known fastener of the same size.

Since fasteners of the same size (both standard and metric) may have different strength ratings, be sure to reinstall any bolts, studs or nuts removed from your vehicle in their original locations. Also, when replacing a fastener with a new one, make sure that the new one has a strength rating equal to or greater than the original.

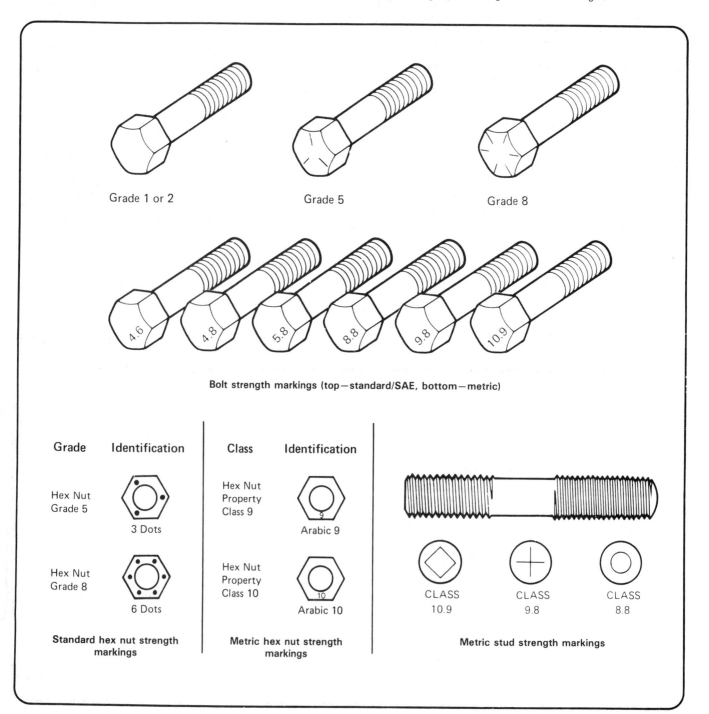

Grade 1 or 2          Grade 5          Grade 8

Bolt strength markings (top—standard/SAE, bottom—metric)

Grade          Identification

Hex Nut Grade 5          3 Dots

Hex Nut Grade 8          6 Dots

**Standard hex nut strength markings**

Class          Identification

Hex Nut Property Class 9          Arabic 9

Hex Nut Property Class 10          Arabic 10

**Metric hex nut strength markings**

CLASS 10.9          CLASS 9.8          CLASS 8.8

**Metric stud strength markings**

## Tightening sequences and procedures

Most threaded fasteners should be tightened to a specific torque value (torque is basically a twisting force). Over-tightening the fastener can weaken it and cause it to break, while under-tightening can cause it to eventually come loose. Bolts, screws and studs, depending on the material they are made of and their thread diameters, have specific torque values (many of which are noted in the Specifications at the beginning of each Chapter). Be sure to follow the torque recommendations closely. For fasteners not assigned a specific torque, a general torque value chart is presented here as a guide. As was previously mentioned, the size and grade of a fastener determine the amount of torque that can safely be applied to it. The figures listed here are approximate for Grade 2 and Grade 3 fasteners (higher grades can tolerate higher torque values).

Fasteners laid out in a pattern (i.e. cylinder head bolts, oil pan bolts, differential cover bolts, etc.) must be loosened or tightened in a sequence to avoid warping the component. This sequence will normally be shown in the appropriate Chapter. If a specific pattern is not given, the following procedures can be used to prevent warping. Initially, the bolts or nuts should be assembled finger-tight only. Next, they should be tightened one full turn each, in a criss-cross or diagonal pattern. After each one has been tightened one full turn, return to the first one and tighten them all one-half turn, following the same pattern. Finally, tighten each of them one-quarter turn at a time until each fastener has been tightened to the proper torque. To loosen and remove the fasteners, the procedure would be reversed.

## Component disassembly

Component disassembly should be done with care and purpose to help ensure that the parts go back together properly. Always keep track of the sequence in which parts are removed. Make note of special characteristics or marks on parts that can be installed more than one way (such as a grooved thrust washer on a shaft). It is a good idea to lay the disassembled parts out on a clean surface in the order that they were removed. It may also be helpful to make sketches or take instant photos of components before removal.

When removing fasteners from a component, keep track of their locations. Sometimes threading a bolt back in a part, or putting the washers and nut back on a stud, can prevent mix-ups later. If nuts and bolts cannot be returned to their original locations, they should be kept in a compartmented box or a series of small boxes. A cupcake or muffin tin is ideal for this purpose, since each cavity can hold the bolts and nuts from a particular area (i.e. oil pan bolts, valve cover bolts, engine mount bolts, etc.). A pan of this type is especially helpful when working on assemblies with very small parts, such as the carburetor, alternator, valve train or interior dash and trim pieces. The cavities can be marked with paint or tape to identify the contents.

Whenever wiring looms, harnesses or connectors are separated, it's a good idea to identify the two halves with numbered pieces of masking tape so they can be easily reconnected.

## Gasket sealing surfaces

Throughout any vehicle, gaskets are used to seal the mating surfaces between two parts and keep lubricants, fluids, vacuum or pressure contained in an assembly.

Many times these gaskets are coated with a liquid or paste-type gasket sealing compound before assembly. Age, heat and pressure can sometimes cause the two parts to stick together so tightly that they are very difficult to separate. Often, the assembly can be loosened by striking it with a soft-faced hammer near the mating surfaces. A regular hammer can be used if a block of wood is placed between the hammer and the part. Do not hammer on cast parts or parts that could be easily damaged. With any particularly stubborn part, always recheck to make sure that every fastener has been removed.

Avoid using a screwdriver or bar to pry apart an assembly, as they can easily mar the gasket sealing surfaces of the parts (which must remain smooth). If prying is absolutely necessary, use an old broom handle, but keep in mind that extra clean-up will be necessary if the wood splinters.

After the parts are separated, the old gasket must be carefully scraped off and the gasket surfaces cleaned. Stubborn gasket material can be soaked with rust penetrant or treated with a special chemical to soften it so it can be easily scraped off. A scraper can be fashioned from a piece of copper tubing by flattening and sharpening one end. Copper is recommended because it is usually softer than the surfaces to be scraped, which reduces the chance of gouging the part. Some gaskets can be removed with a wire brush, but regardless of the method used, the mating surfaces must be left clean and smooth. If for some reason the gasket surface is gouged, then a gasket sealer thick enough to fill scratches will have to be used during reassembly of the components. For most applications, a non-drying (or semi-drying) gasket sealer should be used.

## Hose removal tips

**Caution:** *If the vehicle is equipped with air conditioning, do not disconnect any of the A/C hoses without first having the system depressurized by a dealer service department or an air conditioning specialist.*

Hose removal precautions closely parallel gasket removal precautions. Avoid scratching or gouging the surface that the hose mates against or the connection may leak. This is especially true for radiator

| Metric thread sizes | Ft-lb | Nm |
|---|---|---|
| M-6 | 6 to 9 | 9 to 12 |
| M-8 | 14 to 21 | 19 to 28 |
| M-10 | 28 to 40 | 38 to 54 |
| M-12 | 50 to 71 | 68 to 96 |
| M-14 | 80 to 140 | 109 to 154 |
| **Pipe thread sizes** | | |
| 1/8 | 5 to 8 | 7 to 10 |
| 1/4 | 12 to 18 | 17 to 24 |
| 3/8 | 22 to 33 | 30 to 44 |
| 1/2 | 25 to 35 | 34 to 47 |
| **U.S. thread sizes** | | |
| 1/4 — 20 | 6 to 9 | 9 to 12 |
| 5/16 — 18 | 12 to 18 | 17 to 24 |
| 5/16 — 24 | 14 to 20 | 19 to 27 |
| 3/8 — 16 | 22 to 32 | 30 to 43 |
| 3/8 — 24 | 27 to 38 | 37 to 51 |
| 7/16 — 14 | 40 to 55 | 55 to 74 |
| 7/16 — 20 | 40 to 60 | 55 to 81 |
| 1/2 — 13 | 55 to 80 | 75 to 108 |

hoses. Because of various chemical reactions, the rubber in hoses can bond itself to the metal spigot that the hose fits over. To remove a hose, first loosen the hose clamps that secure it to the spigot. Then, with slip-joint pliers, grab the hose at the clamp and rotate it around the spigot. Work it back and forth until it is completely free, then pull it off. Silicone or other lubricants will ease removal if they can be applied between the hose and the outside of the spigot. Apply the same lubricant to the inside of the hose and the outside of the spigot to simplify installation.

As a last resort (and if the hose is to be replaced with a new one anyway), the rubber can be slit with a knife and the hose peeled from the spigot. If this must be done, be careful that the metal connection is not damaged.

If a hose clamp is broken or damaged, do not reuse it. Wire-type clamps usually weaken with age, so it is a good idea to replace them with screw-type clamps whenever a hose is removed.

## Tools

A selection of good tools is a basic requirement for anyone who plans to maintain and repair his or her own vehicle. For the owner who has few tools, if any, the initial investment might seem high, but when compared to the spiraling costs of professional auto maintenance and repair, it is a wise one.

To help the owner decide which tools are needed to perform the tasks detailed in this manual, the following tool lists are offered: *Maintenance and minor repair*, *Repair and overhaul* and *Special*. The newcomer to practical mechanics should start off with the *Maintenance and minor repair tool kit*, which is adequate for the simpler jobs performed on a vehicle. Then, as confidence and experience grow, the owner can tackle more difficult tasks, buying additional tools as they are needed. Eventually the basic kit will be expanded into the *Repair and overhaul tool set*. Over a period of time, the experienced do-it-yourselfer will assemble a tool set complete enough for most repair and overhaul procedures and will add tools from the *Special* category when it is felt that the expense is justified by the frequency of use.

### Maintenance and minor repair tool kit

The tools in this list should be considered the minimum required for performance of routine maintenance, servicing and minor repair work. We recommend the purchase of combination wrenches (box-end and open-end combined in one wrench); while more expensive than open-ended ones, they offer the advantages of both types of wrench.

*Combination wrench set (1/4 in to 1 in or 6 mm to 19 mm)*
*Adjustable wrench — 8 in*
*Spark plug wrench (with rubber insert)*
*Spark plug gap adjusting tool*
*Feeler gauge set*
*Brake bleeder wrench*
*Standard screwdriver (5/16 in x 6 in)*
*Phillips screwdriver (No. 2 x 6 in)*
*Combination pliers — 6 in*
*Hacksaw and assortment of blades*
*Tire pressure gauge*
*Grease gun*
*Oil can*
*Fine emery cloth*
*Wire brush*
*Battery post and cable cleaning tool*
*Oil filter wrench*
*Funnel (medium size)*
*Safety goggles*
*Jackstands (2)*
*Drain pan*

**Note:** *If basic tune-ups are going to be part of routine maintenance, it will be necessary to purchase a good quality stroboscopic timing light and combination tachometer/dwell meter. Although they are included in the list of Special tools, it is mentioned here because they are absolutely necessary for tuning most vehicles properly.*

### Repair and overhaul tool set

These tools are essential for anyone who plans to perform major repairs and are in addition to those in the *Maintenance and minor repair tool kit*. Included is a comprehensive set of sockets which, though expensive, are invaluable because of their versatility (especially when various extensions and drives are available). We recommend the 1/2-inch drive over the 3/8-inch drive. Although the larger drive is bulky and more expensive, it has the capacity of accepting a very wide range of large sockets (ideally, the mechanic would have a 3/8-inch drive set and a 1/2-inch drive set).

*Socket set(s)*
*Reversible ratchet*
*Extension — 10 in*
*Universal joint*
*Torque wrench (same size drive as sockets)*
*Ball peen hammer — 8 oz*
*Soft-faced hammer (plastic/rubber)*
*Standard screwdriver (1/4 in x 6 in)*
*Standard screwdriver (stubby — 5/16 in)*
*Phillips screwdriver (No. 3 x 8 in)*
*Phillips screwdriver (stubby — No. 2)*
*Pliers — vise grip*
*Pliers — lineman's*
*Pliers — needle nose*
*Pliers — snap-ring (internal and external)*
*Cold chisel — 1/2 in*
*Scriber*
*Scraper (made from flattened copper tubing)*
*Center punch*
*Pin punches (1/16, 1/8, 3/16 in)*
*Steel rule/straightedge — 12 in*
*Allen wrench set (1/8 to 3/8 in or 4 mm to 10 mm)*
*A selection of files*
*Wire brush (large)*
*Jackstands (second set)*
*Jack (scissor or hydraulic type)*

**Note:** *Another tool which is often useful is an electric drill motor (with a chuck capacity of 3/8-inch) and a set of good-quality drill bits.*

### Special tools

The tools in this list include those which are not used regularly, are expensive to buy, or which need to be used in accordance with their manufacturer's instructions. Unless these tools will be used frequently, it is not very economical to purchase many of them. A consideration would be to split the cost and use between yourself and a friend or friends. In addition, most of these tools can be obtained from a tool rental shop on a temporary basis.

This list primarily contains only those tools and instruments widely available to the public, and not those special tools produced by the vehicle manufacturer for distribution to dealer service departments. Occasionally, references to the manufacturer's special tools are included in the text of this manual. Generally, an alternative method of doing the job without the special tool is offered. However, sometimes there is no alternative to their use. Where this is the case, and the tool cannot be purchased or borrowed, the work should be turned over to the dealer service department or an automotive repair shop.

*Valve spring compressor*
*Piston ring groove cleaning tool*
*Piston ring compressor*
*Piston ring installation tool*
*Cylinder compression gauge*
*Cylinder ridge reamer*
*Cylinder surfacing hone*
*Cylinder bore gauge*
*Micrometer(s) and/or dial calipers*
*Hydraulic lifter removal tool*
*Balljoint separator*
*Universal-type puller*
*Impact screwdriver*
*Dial indicator set*
*Stroboscopic timing light (inductive pick-up)*
*Hand-operated vacuum/pressure pump*
*Tachometer/dwell meter*
*Universal electrical multimeter*
*Cable hoist*
*Brake spring removal and installation tools*
*Floor jack*

Valve spring compressor

Piston ring groove cleaning tool

Piston ring compressor

Piston ring removal/installation tool

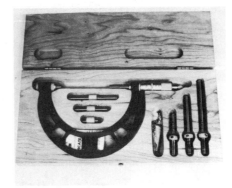

Cylinder ridge reamer

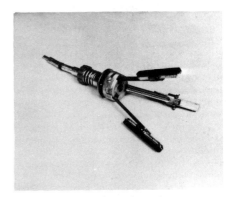

Cylinder surfacing hone

Telescoping gauge set

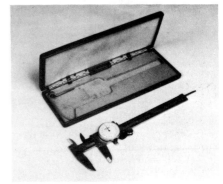

Micrometer set

Dial caliper

Universal-type puller

Dial indicator set

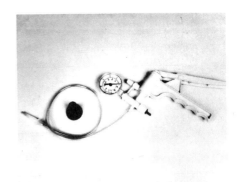

Hand-operated vacuum pump

## Buying tools

For the do-it-yourselfer who is just starting to get involved in vehicle maintenance and repair, there are a number of options available when purchasing tools. If maintenance and minor repair is the extent of the work to be done, the purchase of individual tools is satisfactory. If, on the other hand, extensive work is planned, it would be a good idea to purchase a modest tool set from one of the large retail chain stores. A set can usually be bought at a substantial savings over the individual tool prices (and they often come with a tool box). As additional tools are needed, add-on sets, individual tools and a larger tool box can be purchased to expand the tool selection. Building a tool set gradually allows the cost of the tools to be spread over a longer period of time and gives the mechanic the freedom to choose only those tools that will actually be used.

Tool stores will often be the only source of some of the special tools that are needed, but regardless of where tools are bought, try to avoid cheap ones (especially when buying screwdrivers and sockets) because they won't last very long. The expense involved in replacing cheap tools will eventually be greater than the initial cost of quality tools.

## Care and maintenance of tools

Good tools are expensive, so it makes sense to treat them with respect. Keep them clean and in usable condition and store them properly when not in use. Always wipe off any dirt, grease or metal chips before putting them away. Never leave tools lying around in the work area. Upon completion of a job, always check closely under the hood for tools that may have been left there (so they don't get lost during a test drive).

Some tools, such as screwdrivers, pliers, wrenches and sockets, can be hung on a panel mounted on the garage or workshop wall, while others should be kept in a tool box or tray. Measuring instruments, gauges, meters, etc. must be carefully stored where they cannot be damaged by weather or impact from other tools.

When tools are used with care and stored properly, they will last a very long time. Even with the best of care, tools will wear out if used frequently. When a tool is damaged or worn out, replace it; subsequent jobs will be safer and more enjoyable if you do.

## Working facilities

Not to be overlooked when discussing tools is the workshop. If anything more than routine maintenance is to be carried out, some sort of suitable work area is essential.

It is understood, and appreciated, that many home mechanics do not have a good workshop or garage available and end up removing an engine or doing major repairs outside. It is recommended, however, that the overhaul or repair be completed under the cover of a roof.

A clean, flat workbench or table of comfortable working height is an absolute necessity. The workbench should be equipped with a vise that has a jaw opening of at least four inches.

As mentioned previously, some clean, dry storage space is also required for tools, as well as the lubricants, fluids, cleaning solvents, etc. which soon become necessary.

Sometimes waste oil and fluids, drained from the engine or cooling system during normal maintenance or repairs, present a disposal problem. To avoid pouring them on the ground or into a sewage system, simply pour the used fluids into large containers, seal them with caps and take them to an authorized disposal site or recycling center. Plastic jugs (such as old antifreeze containers) are ideal for this purpose.

Always keep a supply of old newspapers and clean rags available. Old towels are excellent for mopping up spills. Many mechanics use rolls of paper towels for most work because they are readily available and disposable. To help keep the area under the vehicle clean, a large cardboard box can be cut open and flattened to protect the garage or shop floor.

Whenever working over a painted surface (such as when leaning over a fender to service something under the hood), always cover it with an old blanket or bedspread to protect the finish. Vinyl covered pads, made especially for this purpose, are available at auto parts stores.

# Booster battery (jump) starting

Certain precautions must be observed when using a booster battery to jump start a vehicle.

a) Before connecting the booster battery, make sure that the ignition switch is in the Off position.
b) Turn off the lights, heater and other electrical loads.
c) The eyes should be shielded. Safety goggles are a good idea.
d) Make sure the booster battery is the same voltage as the dead one in the vehicle.
e) The two vehicles must not touch each other.
f) Make sure the transaxle is in Neutral (manual transaxle) or Park (automatic transaxle).
g) If the booster battery is not a maintenance-free type, remove the vent caps and lay a cloth over the vent holes.

Connect the red jumper cable to the *positive* (+) terminals of each battery.

Connect one end of the black jumper cable to the *negative* (–) terminal of the booster battery. The other end of this cable should be connected to a good ground on the vehicle to be started, such as a bolt or bracket on the engine block. Use caution to insure that the cable will not come into contact with the fan, drivebelts or other moving parts of the engine.

Start the engine using the booster battery, then, with the engine running at idle speed, disconnect the jumper cables in the reverse order of connection.

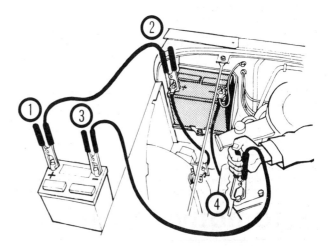

**Make the booster battery cable connections in the numerical order shown (note that the negative cable of the booster battery is not attached to the negative terminal of the dead battery)**

# Jacking and towing

## Jacking

Two types of jacks are used: a screw-type on earlier models and a scissors-type on later models. On earlier models the jack is located in a compartment under the passenger seat and on later models in the engine compartment below the battery or next to the driver's seat.

The jack should be used only for raising the vehicle for the purpose of changing a tire or placing jackstands under the frame. **Caution:** *Never, under any circumstances, perform work under the vehicle or start the engine while the jack is being used as the only means of support.*

The vehicle should be on level ground with the wheels blocked and the transmission in Park (automatic) or Reverse (manual). Pry off the wheel cover (if so equipped) using the tapered end of the lug wrench. Loosen the lug nuts one-half turn and leave them in place until the wheel is raised off the ground.

**The jack should be placed under the spring pivot**

From the side of the vehicle, place the jack under either front or rear spring hanger, depending on the wheel to be lifted. Raise the vehicle with the jack, remove the lug nuts, pull off the wheel and replace it with the spare.

With the beveled side in, replace the lug nuts and tighten them until snug. Lower the vehicle, remove the jack and tighten the nuts in a crisscross pattern. Replace the wheel cover by placing it in position and using the heel of your hand or a rubber mallet to seat it.

## Towing

These vehicles can be towed at freeway speeds with all four wheels on the ground and the ignition key in the Off position (if equipped with locking column) by using the following procedures.

**Manual transmission**

Shift the transmission and transfer case into Neutral on models built through 1979. On 1980 through 1983 models, the transmission should be placed in gear and the transfer case in Neutral. If equipped with locking hubs, they should be in the free-wheeling position on models built through 1976 and locked (to ensure axle lubrication) on 1977 through 1983 models. On 1980 through 1983 models, it will be necessary to stop every 200 miles, start the engine and run it for one minute with the transmission in gear and the transfer case in Neutral to circulate the transfer case oil.

**Automatic transmission**

On models equipped with Quadra-Trac and an automatic transmission, but without the low range reduction unit, the vehicle can be towed with the transmission in Neutral and the front and rear driveshafts removed (Chapter 8). If equipped with the reduction unit, shift the transmission into Park and shift the reduction unit into Neutral. The Emergency Drive control located in the glovebox must be in the Normal position. If the engine was shut off with this control in the Emergency Drive position, restart it and turn the knob to Normal before towing the vehicle.

On 1980 through 1983 models, shift the transmission into Park and the transfer case into Neutral. Stop every 200 miles, start the engine and run it for approximately one minute with the transmission in Park and the transfer case in Neutral to circulate the transfer case oil.

# Automotive chemicals and lubricants

A number of automotive chemicals and lubricants are available for use during vehicle maintenance and repair. They include a wide variety of products ranging from cleaning solvents and degreasers to lubricants and protective sprays for rubber, plastic and vinyl.

*Contact point/spark plug cleaner* is a solvent used to clean oily film and dirt from points, grime from electrical connectors and oil deposits from spark plugs. It is oil free and leaves no residue. It can also be used to remove gum and varnish from carburetor jets and other orifices.

*Carburetor cleaner* is similar to contact point/spark plug cleaner but it is a stronger solvent and may leave a slight oily residue. It is not recommended for cleaning electrical components or connections.

*Brake system cleaner* is used to remove grease or brake fluid from brake system components where clean surfaces are absolutely necessary and petroleum-based solvents cannot be used. It also leaves no residue.

*Silicone-based lubricants* are used to protect rubber parts such as hoses, weatherstripping and grommets, and are used as lubricants for hinges and locks.

*Multi-purpose grease* is an all-purpose lubricant used wherever grease is more practical than a liquid lubricant such as oil. Some multi-purpose grease is white and specially formulated to be more resistant to water than ordinary grease.

*Bearing grease/wheel bearing grease* is a heavy grease used where increased loads and friction are encountered (i.e. wheel bearings, universal joints, etc.).

*High-temperature wheel bearing grease* is designed to withstand the extreme temperatures encountered by wheel bearings in disc-brake equipped vehicles. It usually contains molybdenum disulfide, which is a 'dry' type lubricant.

*Gear oil* (sometimes called gear lube) is a specially designed oil used in differentials, manual transmissions and transfer cases, as well as other areas where high-friction, high-temperature lubrication is required. It is available in a number of viscosities (weights) for various applications.

*Motor oil,* of course, is the lubricant specially formulated for use in engines. It normally contains a wide variety of additives to prevent corrosion and reduce foaming and wear. Motor oil comes in various weights (viscosity ratings) of from 5 to 80. The recommended weight of the oil depends on the seasonal temperature and the demands on the engine. Light oil is used in cold climates and under light load conditions; heavy oil is used in hot climates and where high loads are encountered. Multi-viscosity oils are designed to have characteristics of both light and heavy oils and are available in a number of weights from 5W-20 to 20W-50.

*Oil additives* range from viscosity index improvers to slick chemical treatments that purportedly reduce friction. It should be noted that most oil manufacturers caution against using additives with their oils.

*Gas additives* perform several functions, depending on their chemical makeup. They usually contain solvents that help dissolve gum and varnish that build up on carburetor and intake parts. They also serve to break down carbon deposits that form on the inside surfaces of the combustion chambers. Some additives contain upper cylinder lubricants for valves and piston rings.

*Brake fluid* is a specially formulated hydraulic fluid that can withstand the heat and pressure encountered in brake systems. Care must be taken that this fluid does not come in contact with painted surfaces or plastics. An opened container should always be resealed to prevent contamination by water or dirt.

*Undercoating* is a petroleum-based, tar-like substance that is designed to protect metal surfaces on the underside of a vehicle from corrosion. It also acts as a sound-deadening agent by insulating the bottom of the vehicle.

*Weatherstrip cement* is used to bond weatherstripping around doors, windows and trunk lids. It is sometimes used to attach trim pieces as well.

*Degreasers* are heavy-duty solvents used to remove grease and grime that may accumulate on engine and chassis components. They can be sprayed or brushed on and, depending on the type, are rinsed off with either water or solvent.

*Solvents* are used alone or in combination with degreasers to clean parts and assemblies during repair and overhaul. The home mechanic should use only solvents that are non-flammable and that do not produce irritating fumes.

*Gasket sealing compounds* may be used in conjunction with gaskets, to improve their sealing capabilities, or alone, to seal metal-to-metal joints. Many gasket sealers can withstand extreme heat, some are impervious to gasoline and lubricants, while others are capable of filling and sealing large cavities. Depending on the intended use, gasket sealers either dry hard or stay relatively soft and pliable. They are usually applied by hand, with a brush, or are sprayed on the gasket sealing surfaces.

*Thread cement* is an adhesive locking compound that prevents threaded fasteners from loosening because of vibration. It is available in a variety of types for different applications.

*Moisture dispersants* are usually sprays that can be used to dry out electrical components such as the distributor, fuse block and wiring connectors. Some types can also be used as treatment for rubber and as a lubricant for hinges, cables and locks.

*Waxes and polishes* are used to help protect painted and plated surfaces from the weather. Different types of paint may require the use of different types of wax polish. Some polishes utilize a chemical or abrasive cleaner to help remove the top layer of oxidized (dull) paint on older vehicles. In recent years many non-wax polishes that contain a wide variety of chemicals such as polymers and silicones have been introduced. These non-wax polishes are usually easier to apply and last longer than conventional waxes and polishes.

# Safety first!

Regardless of how enthusiastic you may be about getting on with the job at hand, take the time to ensure that your safety is not jeopardized. A moment's lack of attention can result in an accident, as can failure to observe certain simple safety precautions. The possibility of an accident will always exist, and the following points should not be considered a comprehensive list of all dangers. Rather, they are intended to make you aware of the risks and to encourage a safety conscious approach to all work you carry out on your vehicle.

## Essential DOs and DON'Ts

**DON'T** rely on a jack when working under the vehicle. Always use approved jackstands to support the weight of the vehicle and place them under the recommended lift or support points.

**DON'T** attempt to loosen extremely tight fasteners (i.e. wheel lug nuts) while the vehicle is on a jack — it may fall.

**DON'T** start the engine without first making sure that the transmission is in Neutral (or Park where applicable) and the parking brake is set.

**DON'T** remove the radiator cap from a hot cooling system — let it cool or cover it with a cloth and release the pressure gradually.

**DON'T** attempt to drain the engine oil until you are sure it has cooled to the point that it will not burn you.

**DON'T** touch any part of the engine or exhaust system until it has cooled sufficiently to avoid burns.

**DON'T** siphon toxic liquids such as gasoline, antifreeze and brake fluid by mouth, or allow them to remain on your skin.

**DON'T** inhale brake lining dust — it is potentially hazardous (see Asbestos below).

**DON'T** allow spilled oil or grease to remain on the floor — wipe it up before someone slips on it.

**DON'T** use loose fitting wrenches or other tools which may slip and cause injury.

**DON'T** push on wrenches when loosening or tightening nuts or bolts. Always try to pull the wrench toward you. If the situation calls for pushing the wrench away, push with an open hand to avoid scraped knuckles if the wrench should slip.

**DON'T** attempt to lift a heavy component alone — get someone to help you.

**DON'T** rush or take unsafe shortcuts to finish a job.

**DON'T** allow children or animals in or around the vehicle while you are working on it.

**DO** wear eye protection when using power tools such as a drill, sander, bench grinder, etc. and when working under a vehicle.

**DO** keep loose clothing and long hair well out of the way of moving parts.

**DO** make sure that any hoist used has a safe working load rating adequate for the job.

**DO** get someone to check on you periodically when working alone on a vehicle.

**DO** carry out work in a logical sequence and make sure that everything is correctly assembled and tightened.

**DO** keep chemicals and fluids tightly capped and out of the reach of children and pets.

**DO** remember that your vehicle's safety affects that of yourself and others. If in doubt on any point, get professional advice.

## Asbestos

Certain friction, insulating, sealing, and other products — such as brake linings, brake bands, clutch linings, torque converters, gaskets, etc. — contain asbestos. *Extreme care must be taken to avoid inhalation of dust from such products since it is hazardous to health.* If in doubt, assume that they *do* contain asbestos.

## Fire

Remember at all times that gasoline is highly flammable. Never smoke or have any kind of open flame around when working on a vehicle. But the risk does not end there. A spark caused by an electrical short circuit, by two metal surfaces contacting each other, or even by static electricity built up in your body under certain conditions, can ignite gasoline vapors, which in a confined space are highly explosive. Do not, under any circumstances, use gasoline for cleaning parts. Use an approved safety solvent.

Always disconnect the battery ground (−) cable *at the battery* before working on any part of the fuel system or electrical system. Never risk spilling fuel on a hot engine or exhaust component.

It is strongly recommended that a fire extinguisher suitable for use on fuel and electrical fires be kept handy in the garage or workshop at all times. Never try to extinguish a fuel or electrical fire with water.

## Torch (flashlight in the US)

Any reference to a "torch" appearing in this manual should always be taken to mean a hand-held, battery-operated electric light or flashlight. It DOES NOT mean a welding or propane torch or blowtorch.

## Fumes

Certain fumes are highly toxic and can quickly cause unconsciousness and even death if inhaled to any extent. Gasoline vapor falls into this category, as do the vapors from some cleaning solvents. Any draining or pouring of such volatile fluids should be done in a well ventilated area.

When using cleaning fluids and solvents, read the instructions on the container carefully. Never use materials from unmarked containers.

Never run the engine in an enclosed space, such as a garage. Exhaust fumes contain carbon monoxide, which is extremely poisonous. If you need to run the engine, always do so in the open air, or at least have the rear of the vehicle outside the work area.

If you are fortunate enough to have the use of an inspection pit, never drain or pour gasoline and never run the engine while the vehicle is over the pit. The fumes, being heavier than air, will concentrate in the pit with possibly lethal results.

## The battery

Never create a spark or allow a bare light bulb near a battery. They normally give off a certain amount of hydrogen gas, which is highly explosive.

Always disconnect the battery ground (−) cable *at the battery* before working on the fuel or electrical systems.

If possible, loosen the filler caps or cover when charging the battery from an external source (this does not apply to sealed or maintenance-free batteries). Do not charge at an excessive rate or the battery may burst.

Take care when adding water to a non maintenance-free battery and when carrying a battery. The electrolyte, even when diluted, is very corrosive and should not be allowed to contact clothing or skin.

Always wear eye protection when cleaning the battery to prevent the caustic deposits from entering your eyes.

## Mains electricity (household current in the US)

When using an electric power tool, inspection light, etc., which operates on household current, always make sure that the tool is correctly connected to its plug and that, where necessary, it is properly grounded. Do not use such items in damp conditions and, again, do not create a spark or apply excessive heat in the vicinity of fuel or fuel vapor.

## Secondary ignition system voltage

A severe electric shock can result from touching certain parts of the ignition system (such as the spark plug wires) when the engine is running or being cranked, particularly if components are damp or the insulation is defective. In the case of an electronic ignition system, the secondary system voltage is much higher and could prove fatal.

# Troubleshooting

## Contents

| Symptom | Applicable Section |
|---|---|
| *Engine mechanical* | |
| Engine backfires | 13 |
| Engine 'diesels' (continues to run) after switching off | 15 |
| Engine hard to start when cold | 4 |
| Engine hard to start when hot | 5 |
| Engine lacks power | 12 |
| Engine lopes while idling or idles erratically | 8 |
| Engine misses at idle speed | 9 |
| Engine misses throughout driving speed range | 10 |
| Engine rotates but will not start | 2 |
| Engine stalls | 11 |
| Engine starts but stops immediately | 7 |
| Engine will not rotate when attempting to start | 1 |
| Pinging or knocking engine sounds during acceleration or uphill | 14 |
| Starter motor noisy or excessively rough in engagement | 6 |
| Starter motor operates without rotating engine | 3 |
| *Engine electrical* | |
| Battery will not hold a charge | 16 |
| Charge light fails to come on when key is turned on | 18 |
| Charge light fails to go out | 17 |
| *Fuel system* | |
| Excessive fuel consumption | 19 |
| Fuel leakage and/or fuel odor | 20 |
| *Cooling system* | |
| External coolant leakage | 23 |
| Internal coolant leakage | 24 |
| Overcooling | 22 |
| Overheating | 21 |
| Poor coolant circulation | 26 |
| Coolant loss | 25 |
| *Clutch* | |
| Clutch slips (engine speed increases with no increase in vehicle speed) | 28 |
| Clutch pedal stays on floor when disengaged | 32 |
| Fails to release (pedal pressed to the floor — shift lever does not move freely in and out of Reverse) | 27 |
| Grabbing (chattering) as clutch is engaged | 29 |
| Squeal or rumble with clutch fully disengaged (pedal depressed) | 31 |
| Squeal or rumble with clutch fully engaged (pedal released) | 30 |
| *Manual transmission* | |
| Difficulty in engaging gears | 37 |
| Noisy in all gears | 34 |
| Noisy in Neutral with engine running | 33 |
| Noisy in one particular gear | 35 |
| Oil leakage | 38 |
| Slips out of high gear | 36 |
| *Automatic transmission* | |
| Engine will start in gears other than Park or Neutral | 42 |
| Fluid leakage | 39 |
| General shift mechanism problems | 40 |
| Transmission slips, shifts rough, is noisy or has no drive in forward or reverse gears | 43 |
| Transmission will not downshift with accelerator pedal pressed to the floor | 41 |
| *Transfer case* | |
| Lubricant leaks from the vent or output shaft seals | 48 |

| Symptom | Applicable Section |
|---|---|
| Noisy or jumps out of 4-wheel drive Low range | 46 |
| Rasping, pulsating noise, particularly at low speeds (Quadra-Trac) | 47 |
| Transfer case difficult to shift into the desired range | 44 |
| Transfer case noisy in all gears | 45 |
| *Driveshaft* | |
| Knock or clunk when the transmission is under initial load (just after transmission is put into gear) | 50 |
| Leakage of fluid at front of driveshaft | 49 |
| Metallic grating sound consistent with vehicle speed | 51 |
| Vibration | 52 |
| *Axles* | |
| Noise (same when in drive as when vehicle is coasting) | 53 |
| Oil leakage | 55 |
| Vibration | 54 |
| *Brakes* | |
| Brake pedal feels spongy when depressed | 59 |
| Brake pedal pulsates during brake application | 62 |
| Excessive brake pedal travel | 58 |
| Excessive effort required to stop vehicle | 60 |
| Noise (high-pitched squeal without brake applied) | 57 |
| Pedal travels to floor with little resistance | 61 |
| Vehicle pulls to one side during braking | 56 |
| *Suspension and steering* | |
| Vehicle pulls to one side | 63 |
| Excessive pitching and/or rolling around corners or during braking | 65 |
| Excessive play in steering | 67 |
| Excessive tire wear (not specific to one area) | 69 |
| Excessive tire wear on inside edge | 71 |
| Excessive tire wear on outside edge | 70 |
| Excessively stiff steering | 66 |
| Lack of power assistance | 68 |
| Shimmy, shake or vibration | 64 |
| Tire tread worn in one place | 72 |

This section provides an easy-reference guide to the more common problems which may occur during the operation of your vehicle. These problems and possible causes are grouped under various components or systems i.e. Engine, Cooling system, etc., and also refer to the Chapter and/or Section which deals with the problem.

Remember that successful troubleshooting is not a mysterious 'black art' practiced only by professional mechanics, it's simply the result of a bit of knowledge combined with an intelligent, systematic approach to the problem. Always work by a process of elimination, starting with the simplest solution and working through to the most complex — and never overlook the obvious. Anyone can forget to fill the gas tank or leave the lights on overnight, so don't assume that you are above such oversights.

Finally, always get clear in your mind why a problem has occurred and take steps to ensure that it doesn't happen again. If the electrical system fails because of a poor connection, check all other connections in the system to make sure that they don't fail as well; if a particular fuse continues to blow, find out why — don't just go on replacing fuses. Remember, failure of a small component can often be indicative of potential failure or incorrect functioning of a more important component or system.

*Engine mechanical*

### 1 Engine will not rotate when attempting to start

1 Battery terminal connections loose or corroded. Check the cable terminals at the battery; tighten the cable or remove corrosion as necessary.
2 Battery discharged or faulty. If the cable connections are clean and tight on the battery posts, turn the key to the On position and switch on the headlights and/or windshield wipers. If they fail to function, the battery is discharged.
3 Automatic transmission not fully engaged in Park.
4 Broken, loose or disconnected wiring in the starting circuit. Inspect all wiring and connectors at the battery, starter solenoid and ignition switch.
5 Starter motor pinion jammed on flywheel ring gear. If manual transmission, place in gear and rock the vehicle to manually turn the engine. Remove starter (Chapter 5) and inspect pinion and flywheel at earliest convenience.
6 Starter solenoid faulty (Chapter 5).
7 Starter motor faulty (Chapter 5).
8 Ignition switch faulty (Chapter 10).

### 2 Engine rotates but will not start

1 Fuel tank empty.
2 Battery discharged (engine rotates slowly). Check the operation of electrical components as described in previous Section (Chapter 5).
3 Battery terminal connections loose or corroded. See previous Section.
4 Carburetor flooded and/or fuel level in carburetor incorrect. This will usually be accompanied by a strong fuel odor from under the hood. Wait a few minutes, depress the accelerator pedal all the way to the floor and attempt to start the engine.
5 Choke control inoperative (Chapter 4).
6 Fuel not reaching carburetor. With ignition switch in Off position, open hood, remove the top plate of air cleaner assembly and observe the top of the carburetor (manually move choke plate back if necessary). Have an assistant depress accelerator pedal fully and check that fuel spurts into carburetor. If not, check fuel filter (Chapter 1), fuel lines and fuel pump (Chapter 4).
7 Excessive moisture on, or damage to, ignition components (Chapter 5).
8 Worn, faulty or incorrectly adjusted breaker points or spark plugs (Chapter 1).
9 Broken, loose or disconnected wiring in the starting circuit (see previous Section).
10 Distributor loose (which changes ignition timing). Turn the distributor as necessary to start the engine, then set ignition timing as soon as possible (Chapter 1).
11 Ignition condenser faulty (Chapter 1).
12 Broken, loose or disconnected wires at the ignition coil or distributor or faulty coil (Chapter 5).

### 3 Starter motor operates without rotating engine

1 Starter pinion sticking. Remove the starter (Chapter 5) and inspect.
2 Starter pinion or engine flywheel teeth worn or broken. Remove the inspection cover at the rear of the engine (if so equipped) and inspect.

### 4 Engine hard to start when cold

1 Battery discharged or low. Check as described in Section 1.
2 Choke control inoperative or out of adjustment (Chapter 1).
3 Carburetor flooded (see Section 2).
4 Fuel supply not reaching the carburetor (see Section 4).
5 Carburetor worn and in need of repair (Chapter 4).

### 5 Engine hard to start when hot

1 Choke sticking in the closed position (Chapter 1).
2 Carburetor flooded (see Section 2).
3 Air filter clogged (Chapter 1).
4 Fuel not reaching the carburetor (see Section 4).

### 6 Starter motor noisy or excessively rough in engagement

1 Pinion or flywheel gear teeth worn or broken. Remove the inspection cover at the rear of the engine (if so equipped) and inspect.
2 Starter motor mounting bolts loose or missing.

### 7 Engine starts but stops immediately

1 Loose or faulty electrical connections at distributor, coil or alternator.
2 Insufficient fuel reaching the carburetor. Disconnect the fuel line at the carburetor and remove the filter (Chapter 1). Place a container under the disconnected fuel line. Observe the flow of fuel from the line. If little or none at all, check for blockage in the lines and/or replace the fuel pump (Chapter 4).
3 Vacuum leak at the gasket surfaces of the intake manifold and/or carburetor. Check that all mounting bolts (nuts) are tightened securely and that all vacuum hoses conencted to the carburetor and manifold are positioned properly and in good condition.
4 Faulty ignition ballast resistor (Chapter 5).

### 8 Engine lopes while idling or idles erratically

1 Vacuum leakage. Check mounting bolts (nuts) at the carburetor and intake manifold for tightness. Check that all vacuum hoses are connected and in good condition. Use a doctor's stethoscope or a length of fuel hose held against your ear to listen for vacuum leaks while the engine is running. A hissing sound will be heard. A soapy water solution will also detect leaks. Check the carburetor and intake manifold gasket surfaces.
2 Leaking EGR valve or plugged PCV valve (see Chapter 6).
3 Air cleaner clogged and in need of replacement (Chapter 1).
4 Fuel pump not delivering sufficient fuel to the carburetor (see Section 7).
5 Carburetor out of adjustment (Chapter 4).
6 Leaking head gasket. If this is suspected, take the vehicle to a repair shop or dealer where it can be pressure checked without the need to remove the head(s).
7 Timing chain and/or gears worn (Chapter 2).
8 Camshaft lobes worn, necessitating the removal of the camshaft for inspection (Chapter 2).

### 9 Engine misses at idle speed

1 Spark plugs faulty or not gapped properly (Chapter 1).
2 Faulty spark plug wires (Chapter 1).
3 Carburetor choke not operating properly (Chapter 1).
4 Sticking or faulty emissions system components (Chapter 6).
5 Clogged fuel filter and/or foreign matter in fuel. Remove the fuel filter (Chapter 1) and inspect.
6 Vacuum leaks at carburetor, intake manifold or at hose connections. Check as described in Section 8.
7 Incorrect idle speed or idle mixture (Chapter 1).
8 Incorrect ignition timing (Chapter 1).
9 Uneven or low cylinder compression. Check compression as described in Chapter 1.

### 10 Engine misses throughout driving speed range

1 Fuel filter clogged and/or impuities in the fuel system (Chap-

ter 1). Also check fuel output at the carburetor (see Section 7).
2   Faulty or incorrectly gapped spark plugs (Chapter 1).
3   Incorrect ignition timing (Chapter 1).
4   Check for cracked distributor cap, disconnected distributor wires or damage to the ignition system components (Chapter 5).
5   Leaking spark plug wires (Chapter 1).
6   Faulty emissions system components (Chapter 6).
7   Low or uneven cylinder compression pressures. Check as described in Chapter 1.
8   Faulty breaker points or condenser (Chapter 1).
9   Vacuum leaks at carburetor, intake manifold or vacuum hoses (see Section 8).

### 11   Engine stalls

1   Carburetor idle speed incorrectly set (Chapter 1).
2   Fuel filter clogged and/or water and impurities in the fuel system (Chapter 1).
3   Choke improperly adjusted or sticking (Chapter 1).
4   Distributor components damp, points out of adjustment or damage to distributor cap, rotor etc. (Chapter 5).
5   Faulty emissions system components (Chapter 6).
6   Faulty or incorrectly gapped spark plugs. Also check spark plug wires (Chapter 1).
7   Vacuum leak at the carburetor, intake manifold or vacuum hoses. Check as described in Section 8.
8   Valve clearance incorrectly set (Chapter 1).

### 12   Engine lacks power

1   Incorrect ignition timing (Chapter 1).
2   Exxcessive play in distributor shaft. At the same time, check for worn or out-of-adjustment points, faulty distributor cap, wires, etc. (Chapter 1).
3   Faulty or incorrectly gapped spark plugs (Chapter 1).
4   Carburetor not adjusted properly or excessively worn (Chapter 4).
5   Weak condenser (Chapter 5).
6   Faulty coil (Chapter 5).
7   Brakes binding (Chapter 1).
8   Automatic transmission fluid level incorrect, causing slippage (Chapter 1).
9   Manual transmission clutch slipping (Chapter 8).
10  Fuel filter clogged and/or impurities in the fuel system (Chapter 1).
11  Emissions control system not functioning properly (Chapter 6).
12  Use of sub-standard fuel. Fill tank with proper octane fuel.
13  Low or uneven cylinder compression pressures. Check as described in Chapter 1.

### 13   Engine backfires

1   Emission system not functioning properly (Chapter 6).
2   Ignition timing incorrect (Chapter 1).
3   Carburetor in need of adjustment or worn excessively (Chapter 4).
4   Vacuum leak at carburetor, intake manifold or vacuum hoses. Check as described in Section 8.
5   Valve clearance incorrectly set, and/or valves sticking (Chapter 1).

### 14   Pinging or knocking engine sounds during acceleration or uphill

1   Incorrect grade of fuel. Fill tank with fuel of the proper octane rating.
2   Ignition timing incorrect (Chapter 1).
3   Carburetor in need of adjustment (Chapter 4).
4   Improper spark plugs. Check plug type with that specified on label located inside engine compartment. Also check plugs and wires for damage (Chapter 1).
5   Worn or damaged distributor components (Chapter 5).
6   Faulty emissions system (Chapter 6).
7   Vacuum leak. Check as described in Section 8.

### 15   Engine 'diesels' (continues to run) after switching off

1   Idle speed too high (Chapter 1).
2   Electrical solenoid at side of carburetor not functioning properly (not all models, see Chapter 4).
3   Ignition timing incorrectly adjusted (Chapter 1).
4   Air cleaner heat valve not operating properly (Chapter 1).
5   Excessive engine operating temperature. Probable causes of this are malfunctioning thermostat, clogged radiator, faulty water pump (Chapter 3).

## Engine electrical

### 16   Battery will not hold a charge

1   Alternator drivebelt defective or not adjusted properly (Chapter 1).
2   Electrolyte level low or electrolyte too weak (Chapter 1).
3   Battery terminals loose or corroded (Chapter 1).
4   Alternator not charging properly (Chapter 5).
5   Loose, broken or faulty wiring in the charging circuit (Chapter 5).
6   Short in vehicle circuitry causing a continual drain on battery.
7   Battery defective internally.

### 17   Charge light fails to go out

1   Fault in alternator or charging circuit (Chapter 5).
2   Alternator drivebelt defective or not properly adjusted (Chapter 1).

### 18   Charge light fails to come on when key is turned on

1   Warning light bulb faulty (Chapter 10).
2   Alternator faulty (Chapter 5).
3   Fault in the printed circuit, dash wiring or bulb holder (Chapter 10).

## Fuel system

### 19   Excessive fuel consumption

1   Clogged air filter element (Chapter 1).
2   Incorrect ignition timing (Chapter 1).
3   Choke sticking or improperly adjusted (Chapter 1).
4   Emissions system not functioning properly (not all vehicles, see Chapter 6).
5   Carburetor idle speed and/or mixture not adjusted properly (Chapter 1).
6   Carburetor internal parts excessively worn or damaged (Chapter 4).
7   Low tire pressure or incorrect tire size (Chapter 1).

### 20   Fuel leakage and/or fuel odor

1   Leak in a fuel feed or vent line (Chapter 4).
2   Tank overfilled. Fill only to automatic shut-off.
3   Emissions system filter in need of replacement (Chapter 6).
4   Vapor leaks from system lines (Chapter 4).
5   Carburetor internal parts excessively worn or damaged (Chapter 4).

## Cooling system

### 21   Overheating

1   Insufficient coolant in system (Chapter 1).
2   Fan belt defective or not adjusted properly (Chapter 1).
3   Radiator core blocked or radiator grille dirty and restricted (Chapter 3).
4   Thermostat faulty (Chapter 3).
5   Fan blades broken or cracked (Chapter 3).
6   Radiator cap not maintaining proper pressure. Have cap pressure

tested by gas station or repair shop.
7   Ignition timing incorrect (Chapter 1).

## 22   Overcooling

1   Thermostat faulty (Chapter 3).
2   Inaccurate temperature gauge (Chapter 10)

## 23   External coolant leakage

1   Deteriorated or damaged hoses. Loosen clamps at hose connections (Chapter 1).
2   Water pump seals defective. If this is the case, water will drip from the 'weep' hole in the water pump body (on some models) (Chapter 3).
3   Leakage from radiator core or header tank. This will require the radiator to be professionally repaired (see Chapter 3 for removal procedures).
4   Engine drain plugs or water jacket core plugs leaking (see Chapters 2 and 3).

## 24   Internal coolant leakage

**Note:** *Internal coolant leaks can usually be detected by examining the oil. Check the dipstick and inside of the rocker arm cover(s) for water deposits and an oil consistency like that of a milkshake.*
1   Faulty cylinder head gasket. Have the system pressure-tested or remove the cylinder head(s) (Chapter 2) and inspect.
2   Cracked cylinder bore or cylinder head. Dismantle engine and inspect (Chapter 2).

## 25   Coolant loss

1   Overfilling system (Chapter 1).
2   Coolant boiling away due to overheating (see Section 21).
3   Internal or external leakage (see Sections 23 and 24).
4   Faulty radiator cap. Have the cap pressure tested.

## 26   Poor coolant circulation

1   Inoperative water pump. A quick test is to pinch the top radiator hose closed with your hand while the engine is idling, then let it loose. You should feel the surge of coolant if the pump is working properly (Chapter 3).
2   Restriction in cooling system. Drain, flush and refill the system (Chapter 1). If it appears necessary, remove the radiator (Chapter 3) and have it reverse-flushed or professionally cleaned.
3   Fan drivebelt defective or not adjusted properly (Chapter 1).
4   Thermostat sticking (Chapter 3).

## *Clutch*

## 27   Fails to release (pedal pressed to the floor — shift lever does not move freely in and out of Reverse)

1   Improper linkage free play adjustment (Chapter 1).
2   Clutch fork off ball stud. Look under the vehicle, on the left side of transmission.
3   Clutch disc warped or damaged (Chapter 8).

## 28   Clutch slips (engine speed increases with no increase in vehicle speed)

1   Linkage in need of adjustment (Chapter 1).
2   Clutch disc oil soaked or facing worn. Remove disc (Chapter 8) and inspect.

3   Clutch disc not seated. It may take 30 or 40 normal starts for a new disc to seat.

## 29   Grabbing (chattering) as clutch is engaged

1   Oil on clutch disc. Remove disc (Chapter 8) and inspect. Correct any leakage source.
2   Worn or loose engine or transmission mounts. These units move slightly when clutch is released. Inspect mounts and bolts.
3   Worn splines on clutch disc. Remove clutch components (Chapter 8) and inspect.
4   Warped pressure plate or flywheel. Remove clutch components and inspect.

## 30   Squeal or rumble with clutch fully engaged (pedal released)

1   Inproper adjustment; no free play (Chapter 1).
2   Release bearing binding on transmission bearing retainer. Remove clutch components (Chapter 8) and check bearing. Remove any burrs or nicks, clean and relubricate before reinstallation.
3   Weak linkage or pedal return spring. Replace the spring.

## 31   Squeal or rumble with clutch fully disengaged (pedal depressed)

1   Worn, faulty or broken release bearing (Chapter 8).
2   Worn or broken pressure plate springs (or diaphragm fingers) (Chapter 8).
3   Crankshaft pilot bushing worn. Replace bushing (Chapter 8).

## 32   Clutch pedal stays on floor when disengaged

1   Bind in linkage or release bearing. Inspect linkage or remove clutch components as necessary.
2   Linkage springs being over-traveled. Adjust linkage for proper free play. Make sure proper pedal stop (bumper) is installed.

## *Manual transmission*
**Note:** *All the following references are to Chapter 7, unless noted.*

## 33   Noisy in Neutral with engine running

1   Input shaft bearing worn.
2   Damaged main drivegear bearing.
3   Worn countergear bearings.
4   Worn or damaged countergear anti-lash plate.

## 34   Noisy in all gears

1   Any of the above causes, and/or:
2   Insufficient lubricant (see checking procedures in Chapter 1).

## 35   Noisy in one particular gear

1   Worn, damaged or chipped gear teeth for that particular gear.
2   Worn or damaged synchronizer for that particular gear.

## 36   Slips out of high gear

1   Transmission mounting bolts loose.
2   Shift rods interfering with engine mounts or clutch lever.
3   Shift rods not working freely.
4   Damaged mainshaft pilot bearing.

5   Dirt between transmission case and engine or misalignment of transmission.
6   Worn or improperly adjusted linkage.

### 37   Difficulty in engaging gears

1   Clutch not releasing completely (see clutch adjustment, Chapter 1).
2   Loose, damaged or maladjusted shift linkage. Make a thorough inspection, replacing parts as necessary. Adjust as described in Chapter 7.

### 38   Oil leakage

1   Excessive amount of lubricant in transmission (see Chapter 1 for correct checking procedures; drain lubricant as required).
2   Side cover loose or gasket damaged.
3   Rear oil seal or speedometer oil seal in need of replacement.

## Automatic transmission

**Note:** *Due to the complexity of the automatic transmission, it is difficult for the home mechanic to properly diagnose and service this component. For problems other than the following, the vehicle should be taken to a reputable mechanic.*

### 39   Fluid leakage

1   Automatic transmission fluid is a deep red color and fluid leaks should not be confused with engine oil, which can easily be blown by air flow to the transmission.
2   To pinpoint a leak, first remove all built-up dirt and grime from around the transmission. Degreasing agents and/or steam cleaning will achieve this. With the underside clean, drive the vehicle at low speeds so air flow will not blow the leak far from its source. Raise the vehicle and determine where the leak is coming from. Common areas of leakage are:
   a)   Fluid pan: tighten mounting bolts and/or replace pan gasket as necessary (see Chapter 7).
   b)   Rear extension: tighten bolts and/or replace oil seal as necessary (Chapter 7).
   c)   Filler pipe: replace the rubber seal where pipe enters transmission case.
   d)   Transmission oil lines: tighten connectors where lines enter transmission case and/or replace lines.
   e)   Vent pipe: transmission over-filled and/or water in fluid (see checking procedures, Chapter 1).
   f)   Speedometer connector: replace the O-ring where speedometer cable enters transmission case.

### 40   General shift mechanism problems

1   Chapter 7 deals with checking and adjusting the shift linkage on automatic transmissions. Common problems which may be attributed to poorly adjusted linkage are:
   a)   Engine starting in gears other than Park or Neutral.
   b)   Indicator on quadrant pointing to a gear other than the one actually being selected.
   c)   Vehicle will not hold firm when in Park position.
2   Refer to Chapter 7 to adjust the manual linkage.

### 41   Transmission will not downshift with accelerator pedal pressed to the floor

Chapter 7 deals with adjusting the downshift cable or downshift switch to enable the transmission to downshift properly.

### 42   Engine will start in gears other than Park or Neutral

Chapter 7 deals with adjusting the various linkages used with automatic transmissions.

### 43   Transmission slips, shifts rough, is noisy or has no drive in forward or reverse gears

1   There are many probable causes for the above problems, but the home mechanic should concern himself with only one possibility: fluid level.
2   Before taking the vehicle to a repair shop, check the level and condition of the fluid as described in Chapter 1. Correct fluid level as necessary or change the fluid and filter if needed. If problem persists, have a professional diagnose the probable cause.

## Transfer case

### 44   Transfer case difficult to shift into the desired range

1   Speed may be too great to permit engagement. Stop the vehicle and shift into the desired range.
2   Shift linkage loose, bent or binding. Check the linkage for damage or wear and replace or lubricate as necessary (Chapter 7).
3   If the vehicle has been driven on a paved surface for some time, the driveline torque can make shifting difficult. Stop and shift into 2-wheel drive on paved or hard surfaces.
4   Insufficient or incorrect grade or lubricant. Drain and refill the transfer case with the specified lubricant (Chapter 1).
5   Worn or damaged internal components. Disassembly and overhaul of the transfer case may be necessary (Chapter 7).

### 45   Transfer case noisy in all gears

Insufficient or incorrect grade of lubricant. Drain and refill (Chapter 1).

### 46   Noisy or jumps out of 4-wheel drive Low range

1   Transfer case not fully engaged. Stop the vehicle, shift into Neutral and then engage 4L.
2   Shift linkage loose, worn or binding. Tighten, repair or lubricate linkage as necessary.
3   Shift fork cracked, inserts worn or fork binding on the rail. Disassemble and repair as necessary (Chapter 7).

### 47   Rasping, pulsating noise, particularly at low speeds (Quadra-Trac)

Quadra-Trac stick-slip condition caused by improper lubrication or mismatched tire sizes. Drain and refill the transfer case (Chapter 1) and check the tire size and inflation.

### 48   Lubricant leaks from the vent or output shaft seals

1   Transfer case is overfilled. Drain to the proper level (Chapter 1).
2   Vent is clogged or jammed closed. Clear or replace the vent.
3   Output shaft seal incorrectly installed or damaged. Replace the seal and check the seal contact surfaces for nicks and scoring.

## Driveshaft

### 49   Leakage of fluid at front of driveshaft

Defective transmission or transfer case oil seal. See Chapter 7 for replacement procedures.

### 50   Knock or clunk when transmission is under initial load (just after transmission is put into gear)

1   Loose or disconnected rear suspension components. Check all

mounting bolts and bushings (Chapter 11).
2   Loose driveshaft bolts. Inspect all bolts and nuts and tighten to the specified torque (Chapter 8).
3   Worn or damaged universal joint bearings. Test for wear (Chapter 8).

### 51   Metallic grating sound consistent with vehicle speed

Pronounced wear in the universal joint bearings. Test for wear (Chapter 8).

### 52   Vibration

**Note:** *Before it can be assumed that the driveshaft is at fault, make sure the tires are perfectly balanced and perform the following test.*
1   Install a tachometer inside the vehicle to monitor engine speed as the vehicle is driven. Drive the vehicle and note the engine speed at which the vibration (roughness) is most pronounced. Now shift the transmission to a different gear and bring the engine speed to the same point.
2   If the vibration occurs at the same engine speed (rpm) regardless of which gear the transmission is in, the driveshaft is NOT at fault since the driveshaft speed varies.
3   If the vibration decreases or is eliminated when the transmission is in a different gear at the same engine speed, refer to the following probable causes.
4   Bent or dented driveshaft. Inspect and replace as necessary (Chapter 8).
5   Undercoating or build-up dirt, etc. on the driveshaft. Clean the shaft thoroughly and recheck.
6   Worn universal joint bearings. Remove and inspect (Chapter 8).
7   Driveshaft and/or companion flange out of balance. Check for missing weights on the shaft. Remove driveshaft (Chapter 8) and reinstall 180° from original position. Retest. Have driveshaft professionally balanced if problem persists.

## Axles

### 53   Noise (same when in drive as when vehicle is coasting)

1   Road noise. No corrective procedures available.
2   Tire noise. Inspect tires and tire pressures (Chapter 1).
3   Front wheel bearings loose, worn or damaged (Chapter 1).

### 54   Vibration

See probable causes under *Driveshaft*. Proceed under the guidelines listed for the driveshaft. If the problem persists, check the rear wheel bearings by raising the rear of the vehicle and spinning the wheels by hand. Listen for evidence of rough (noisy) bearings. Remove and inspect (Chapter 8).

### 55   Oil leakage

1   Pinion seal damaged (Chapter 8).
2   Axle shaft oil seals damaged (Chapter 8).
3   Differential inspection cover leaking. Tighten mounting bolts or replace the gasket as required (Chapter 8).

## Brakes

**Note:** *Before assuming that a brake problem exists, make sure that the tires are in good condition and inflated properly (see Chapter 1), the front end alignment is correct and that the vehicle is not loaded with weight in an unequal manner.*

### 56   Vehicle pulls to one side during braking

1   Defective, damaged or oil contaminated brake shoes or pads on

one side. Inspect as described in Chapter 1.
2   Excessive wear of brake shoe pad material or drum/disc on one side. Inspect and correct as necessary.
3   Loose or disconnected front suspension components. Inspect and tighten all bolts to the specified torque (Chapter 1).
4   Defective wheel cylinder or caliper assembly. Remove and inspect for stuck piston or damage (Chapter 9).

### 57   Noise (high-pitched squeal without brake applied)

Front brake pads worn out. The noise comes from the wear sensor rubbing against the disc (does not apply to all vehicles). Replace pads with new ones immediately (Chapter 9).

### 58   Excessive brake pedal travel

1   Partial brake system failure. Inspect entire system (Chapter 9) and correct as required.
2   Insufficient fluid in master cylinder. Check (Chapter 1), add fluid and bleed system if necessary.
3   Rear brakes not adjusting properly. Make a series of starts and stops while the vehicle is in Reverse. If this does not correct the situation, remove drums and inspect self-adjusters (Chapter 9).
4   On early models, adjust the brakes (Chapter 9).

### 59   Brake pedal feels spongy when depressed

1   Air in hydraulic lines. Bleed the brake system (Chapter 9).
2   Faulty flexible hoses. Inspect all system hoses and lines. Replace parts as necessary.
3   Master cylinder mounting nuts loose. Inspect master cylinder (nuts) and tighten to specified torque.
4   Master cylinder faulty (Chapter 9).

### 60   Excessive effort required to stop vehicle

1   Power break servo not operating properly (Chapter 9).
2   Excessively worn shoes or pads. Inspect and replace if necessary (Chapter 9).
3   One or more caliper pistons or wheel cylinders seized or sticking. Inspect and rebuild as required (Chapter 9).
4   Brake shoes or pads contaminated with oil or grease. Inspect and replace as required (Chapter 9).
5   New pads or shoes installed and not yet seated. It will take awhile for the new material to seat against the drum (or rotor).

### 61   Pedal travels to floor with little resistance

Little or no fluid in the master cylinder reservoir (caused by leaking wheel cylinder(s), leaking caliper piston(s), loose, damaged or disconnected brake lines). Inspect entire system and correct as necessary.

### 62   Brake pedal pulsates during brake application

1   Wheel bearings not adjusted properly or in need of replacement (Chapter 11).
2   Caliper not sliding properly due to improper installation or obstructions. Remove and inspect (Chapter 9).
3   Rotor not within specifications. Remove the rotor (Chapter 9) and check for excessive lateral runout and parallelism. Have the rotor machined or replace it with a new one.
4   Out-of-round brake drums. Remove the drums and have them resurfaced or replace them with new ones.

*Suspension and steering*

#### 63   Vehicle pulls to one side

1   Tire pressures uneven (Chapter 1).
2   Defective tire (Chapter 1).
3   Excessive wear in suspension or steering components (Chapter 1).
4   Front end in need of alignment. Take vehicle to a qualified specialist.
5   Front brakes dragging. Inspect brakes as described in Chapter 1.

#### 64   Shimmy, shake or vibration

1   Tire or wheel out-of-balance or out-of-round. Have professionally balanced.
2   Loose, worn or out-of-adjustment wheel bearings (Chapter 1).
3   Shock absorbers and/or suspension components worn or damaged (Chapter 1).

#### 65   Excessive pitching and/or rolling around corners or during braking

1   Defective shock absorbers. Replace as a set (Chapter 11).
2   Broken or weak springs and/or suspension components. Inspect as described in Chapter 11.

#### 66   Excessively stiff steering

1   Lack of lubricant in steering box (manual) or power steering fluid reservoir (Chapter 1).
2   Incorrect tire pressures (Chapter 1).
3   Lack of lubrication at steering joints (Chapter 1).
4   Front end out of alignment.
5   See also Section 68, *Lack of power assistance*.

#### 67   Excessive play in steering

1   Loose wheel bearings (Chapter 1).

2   Excessive wear in suspension or steering components (Chapter 1).
3   Steering gear out of adjustment (Chapter 11).

#### 68   Lack of power assistance

1   Steering pump drivebelt faulty or not adjusted properly (Chapter 1).
2   Fluid level low (Chapter 1).
3   Hoses or lines restricting the flow. Inspect and replace parts as necessary.
4   Air in power steering system. Bleed system (Chapter 11).

#### 69   Excessive tire wear (not specific to one area)

1   Incorrect tire pressures (Chapter 1).
2   Tires out of balance. Have professionally balanced.
3   Wheels damaged. Inspect and replace as necessary.
4   Suspension or steering components excessively worn (Chapter 1).

#### 70   Excessive tire wear on outside edge

1   Inflation pressures not correct (Chapter 1).
2   Excessive speed on turns.
3   Front end alignment incorrect (excessive toe-in). Have professionally aligned.
4   Suspension arm bent or twisted.

#### 71   Excessive tire wear on inside edge

1   Inflation pressures incorrect (Chapter 1).
2   Front end alignment incorrect (toe-out). Have professionally aligned.
3   Loose or damaged steering components (Chapter 11).

#### 72   Tire tread worn in one place

1   Tires out of balance.
2   Damaged or buckled wheel. Inspect and replace if necessary.
3   Defective tire.

# Chapter 1 Tune-up and routine maintenance

*Refer to Chapter 13 for Specifications and information related to 1984 through 1986 models*

## Contents

Air filter and PCV filter replacement . . . . . . . . . . . . . . . . . . . 17
Automatic transmission fluid change . . . . . . . . . . . . . . . . . . . 27
Battery — check and maintenance . . . . . . . . . . . . . . . . . . . . . 38
Brake check . . . . . . . . . . . . . . . . . . . . . . . . . . . . . . . . . . . . . 31
Carburetor choke check (late models only) . . . . . . . . . . . . 19
Carburetor mounting torque check . . . . . . . . . . . . . . . . . . . 20
Chassis lubrication . . . . . . . . . . . . . . . . . . . . . . . . . . . . . . . . . 7
Clutch pedal free play check . . . . . . . . . . . . . . . . . . . . . . . . 24
Cooling system check . . . . . . . . . . . . . . . . . . . . . . . . . . . . . . . 8
Cooling system servicing (draining, flushing
    and refilling) . . . . . . . . . . . . . . . . . . . . . . . . . . . . . . . . . . . 39
Contact points and condenser — replacement and adjustment
    (1953 through 1974 models) . . . . . . . . . . . . . . . . . . . . . . 34
Cylinder compression check . . . . . . . . . . . . . . . . . . . . . . . . 37
Differential lubricant change . . . . . . . . . . . . . . . . . . . . . . . . 30
Drivebelt check and adjustment . . . . . . . . . . . . . . . . . . . . . 11
Engine idle speed adjustment . . . . . . . . . . . . . . . . . . . . . . . 21
Engine oil and filter change . . . . . . . . . . . . . . . . . . . . . . . . . . 5
Evaporative Control System (ECS) filter replacement . . . . . . . 36
Exhaust Gas Recirculation (EGR) valve check . . . . . . . . . . . 23
Exhaust system check . . . . . . . . . . . . . . . . . . . . . . . . . . . . . . . 9
Exhaust heat valve check . . . . . . . . . . . . . . . . . . . . . . . . . . . 22
Fluid level checks . . . . . . . . . . . . . . . . . . . . . . . . . . . . . . . . . . . 4
Fuel filter replacement . . . . . . . . . . . . . . . . . . . . . . . . . . . . . 14
Fuel system check . . . . . . . . . . . . . . . . . . . . . . . . . . . . . . . . 13
Ignition timing check and adjustment . . . . . . . . . . . . . . . . . 35
Introduction to routine maintenance . . . . . . . . . . . . . . . . . . . 1
Manual transmission lubricant change . . . . . . . . . . . . . . . . . 28
Oil bath-type air cleaner service . . . . . . . . . . . . . . . . . . . . . . 16
Positive Crankcase Ventilation (PCV) valve replacement . . . . . 15
Routine maintenance schedule . . . . . . . . . . . . . . . . . . . . . . . . 3
Spark plug replacement . . . . . . . . . . . . . . . . . . . . . . . . . . . . 32
Spark plug wires, distributor cap and rotor — check
    and replacement . . . . . . . . . . . . . . . . . . . . . . . . . . . . . . . 33
Suspension and steering check . . . . . . . . . . . . . . . . . . . . . . 10
Thermo-controlled Air Cleaner (TAC) check . . . . . . . . . . . . 18
Tire and tire pressure checks . . . . . . . . . . . . . . . . . . . . . . . . . 6
Tire rotation . . . . . . . . . . . . . . . . . . . . . . . . . . . . . . . . . . . . . 25
Transfer case lubricant change . . . . . . . . . . . . . . . . . . . . . . 29
Tune-up sequence . . . . . . . . . . . . . . . . . . . . . . . . . . . . . . . . . . 2
Underhood hoses — check and replacement . . . . . . . . . . . . 12
Valve clearance adjustment (F- and L-head engines only) . . . . 40
Wheel bearing check . . . . . . . . . . . . . . . . . . . . . . . . . . . . . . 26
Windshield wipers — inspection and blade replacement . . . . . 41

**1**

## Specifications

**Note:** *Additional specifications can be found in the appropriate Chapters.*

## Recommended lubricants and fluids

Engine oil type . . . . . . . . . . . . . . . . . . . . . . . . . . . . . . . . . . . . API SF rating
Single viscosity
    Above +40ºF (15º C) . . . . . . . . . . . . . . . . . . . . . . . . . . . SAE 30 or 40W
    Above 0ºF (-18º C) . . . . . . . . . . . . . . . . . . . . . . . . . . . . SAE 20W
    Below 0ºF (-18º C) . . . . . . . . . . . . . . . . . . . . . . . . . . . . SAE 10W*
Multi-viscosity
    Above +40ºF (15º C) . . . . . . . . . . . . . . . . . . . . . . . . . . . SAE 10W-30, 20W-30 or 10W-40
    Above 0º (-18º C) . . . . . . . . . . . . . . . . . . . . . . . . . . . . . SAE 10W-30 or 10W-40
    Below 0º F (-18º C) . . . . . . . . . . . . . . . . . . . . . . . . . . . . SAE 5W-20 or 5W-30

*\*Do not operate at speeds above 55 mph with SAE 10W oil*

Engine coolant type . . . . . . . . . . . . . . . . . . . . . . . . . . . . . . 50/50 mix of water and ethlene glycol based antifreeze
Automatic transmission fluid type . . . . . . . . . . . . . . . . . . . . DEXRON II
Manual transmission lubricant type and viscosity
    1982 and 1983 T4 and T5 4- and 5-speed only . . . . . . . . DEXRON II ATF
    All others . . . . . . . . . . . . . . . . . . . . . . . . . . . . . . . . . . . API GL-4, SAE 80W-90
Transfer case lubricant type and viscosity
    Spicer 18 and 20 . . . . . . . . . . . . . . . . . . . . . . . . . . . . . . API GL-5, SAE 80W-90
    Model 300 . . . . . . . . . . . . . . . . . . . . . . . . . . . . . . . . . . API GL-5, SAE 85W-90
    Quadra-Trac . . . . . . . . . . . . . . . . . . . . . . . . . . . . . . . . . Jeep Quadra-Trac lubricant or SAE 30W non-detergent motor oil
Front and rear differential lubricant type and viscosity
    Conventional . . . . . . . . . . . . . . . . . . . . . . . . . . . . . . . . . API GL-5, SAE 80W-90
    Trac-Loc . . . . . . . . . . . . . . . . . . . . . . . . . . . . . . . . . . . API GL-5 SAE 80W-90 limited slip lubricant
Brake fluid type . . . . . . . . . . . . . . . . . . . . . . . . . . . . . . . . . DOT type 3 (SAE J1703)
Steering gear lubricant . . . . . . . . . . . . . . . . . . . . . . . . . . . . Lithium based chassis lube
Power steering system fluid . . . . . . . . . . . . . . . . . . . . . . . . . DEXRON II
Suspension and steering component grease . . . . . . . . . . . . . NLGI No. 2 lithium based grease
Wheel bearing grease . . . . . . . . . . . . . . . . . . . . . . . . . . . . . NLGI No. 2 lithium based grease

## Capacities

Engine oil (with filter change)
| | |
|---|---|
| F- and L-head four-cylinder engine | 5 US qts |
| Six-cylinder engine | 6 US qts |
| V6 engine | 5 US qts |
| V8 engine | 5 US qts |
| 151 cu in four-cylinder engine | 3 US qts |

Cooling system
| | |
|---|---|
| F- and L-head four-cylinder engine | 12 US qts |
| Six-cylinder engine | 10.5 US qts |
| V6 engine | 10 US qts |
| V8 engine | |
|     1972 through 1976 | 14 US qts |
|     1977 through 1983 | 12 US qts |
| 151 cu in four-cylinder engine | 7.8 US qts |

Automatic transmission
| | |
|---|---|
| Through 1979 | 5 US qts |
| 1980 through 1983 | 4.25 US qts |

Manual transmission
| | |
|---|---|
| 3-speed (F- and L-head and V6 engines) | 2.5 US pts |
| 4-speed (F- and L-head and V6 engines) | 6.75 US pts |
| 3-speed (six-cylinder engine) | |
|     1972 through 1975 | 2.5 US pts |
|     1976 through 1979 | 2.8 US pts |
| 3-speed (V8) | 2.75 US pts |
| 4-speed | |
|     1972 through 1979 | 6.5 US pts |
|     1980 through 1983 | |
|         SR-4 | 3.0 US pts |
|         T-176 | 3.5 US pts |
| T-5 5-speed | 4.0 US pts |

Transfer case
| | |
|---|---|
| Model 18 | 3.25 US pts |
| Model 20 | 3.25 US pts |
| Model 300 | 4 US pts |
| Quadra-Trac (1976 only) | |
|     With reduction unit | 4.5 US pts |
|     All others | 3.5 US pts |
| Quadra-Trac (1977 through 1979) | |
|     With reduction unit | 2.5 US pts |
|     All others | 2.0 US pts |

Differential
| | |
|---|---|
| Through 1971 (front and rear) | 2.5 US pts |
| 1972 through 1975 | |
|     Front | 2.5 US pts |
|     Rear | 3.0 US pts |
| 1976 and 1977 | |
|     Front | 2.5 US pts |
|     Rear | 4 US pts |
| 1978 through 1983 | |
|     Front | 2.5 US pts |
|     Rear | 4.8 US pts |

## Spark plug type *(Check the Emissions Control Information label Specifications for your vehicle)*

| | |
|---|---|
| F-head four-cylinder engine | AC-45 or Champion J-8 |
| L-head four-cylinder engine | Champion J-8 |
| In-line six-cylinder engine | N12Y, RN12Y, N13L or RN13L |
| V6 engine | AC-44S or Champion UJ12Y |
| V8 engine | N12Y or RN13L |
| 151 cu in four-cylinder engine | R44TSX |

## Spark plug gap

| | |
|---|---|
| F-head four-cylinder engine | 0.030 in |
| L-head four-cylinder engine | 0.030 in |
| In-line six-cylinder engine | 0.033 to 0.037 in |
| V6 engine | 0.035 in |
| V8 engine | 0.033 to 0.038 in |
| 151 cu in four-cylinder engine | 0.060 in |

## Spark plug firing order

| | |
|---|---|
| F- and L-head four cylinder engine | 1-3-4-2 |
| Six-cylinder in-line engine | 1-5-3-6-2-4 |
| V6 engine | 1-6-5-4-3-2 |
| V8 engine | 1-8-4-3-6-5-7-2 |
| 151 cu in four-cylinder engine | 1-2-3-4 |

## Distributor direction of rotation
F- and L-head four cylinder engines . . . . . . . . . . . . . . . . . .    Counterclockwise
All others . . . . . . . . . . . . . . . . . . . . . . . . . . . . . . . . . .    Clockwise

## Battery specific gravity (fully charged)
F- and L-head four-cylinder and V6 engines . . . . . . . . . . . . .    1.260
All others . . . . . . . . . . . . . . . . . . . . . . . . . . . . . . . . . .    1.265

## Distributor point gap
L-head engine
   Autolite distributor . . . . . . . . . . . . . . . . . . . . . . . . . .    0.020 in
   Delco-Remy distributor . . . . . . . . . . . . . . . . . . . . . . . .    0.022 in
F-head engine (Prestolite distributor) . . . . . . . . . . . . . . . . .    0.020 in
All six-cylinder and V8 engines . . . . . . . . . . . . . . . . . . . . .    0.016

## Dwell angle
L-head engine . . . . . . . . . . . . . . . . . . . . . . . . . . . . . . . .    25 to 34°
F-head engine . . . . . . . . . . . . . . . . . . . . . . . . . . . . . . . .    42°
In-line six-cylinder engines . . . . . . . . . . . . . . . . . . . . . . . .    31 to 34°
V-6 engine
   Prestolite distributor . . . . . . . . . . . . . . . . . . . . . . . . .    32°
   Delco-Remy distributor . . . . . . . . . . . . . . . . . . . . . . . .    30°
V8 engine . . . . . . . . . . . . . . . . . . . . . . . . . . . . . . . . . .    29 to 31°

## Ignition timing
F- and L-head non-emission controlled engines . . . . . . . . . .    5° BTDC
F-head emission controlled engines . . . . . . . . . . . . . . . . . .    0° (TDC)
V6 engine
   Delco-Remy distributor . . . . . . . . . . . . . . . . . . . . . . . .    5° BTDC
   Prestolite distributor . . . . . . . . . . . . . . . . . . . . . . . . .    0° (TDC)
In-line six-cylinder engines
  1973 and 1974
    232 cu in engine . . . . . . . . . . . . . . . . . . . . . . . . . . . .    5° BTDC
    258 cu in engine . . . . . . . . . . . . . . . . . . . . . . . . . . . .    3° BTDC
  1975
    232 cu in engine (without EGR) . . . . . . . . . . . . . . . . .    3° to 7° BTDC
    258 cu in engine (with EGR) . . . . . . . . . . . . . . . . . . .    1° to 5° BTDC
  1976
    232 and 258 cu in engine (manual transmission) . . . . . .    6° to 10° BTDC
    258 cu in engine (automatic transmission) . . . . . . . . . .    4° to 8° BTDC
  1977
    232 cu in engine with 49-state emission (YF carburetor) .    5° BTDC
    232 cu in engine with altitude compensator (YF
     carburetor)
      Above 4000 ft . . . . . . . . . . . . . . . . . . . . . . . . . . .    10°
      Below 4000 ft . . . . . . . . . . . . . . . . . . . . . . . . . . .    8°
    258 cu in engine (YF carburetor)
      Manual transmission and 49-state emissions . . . . . . .    1° to 5° BTDC
      Manual transmission and altitude compensator . . . . . .    8° to 12° BTDC
      Manual transmission and California emissions . . . . . .    4° to 8° BTDC
      Automatic transmission and 49-state emissions . . . . .    8° to 12° BTDC
      Automatic transmission and California emissions . . . . .    6° to 10° BTDC
    258 cu in engine (BBD carburetor) . . . . . . . . . . . . . . .    4° to 8° BTDC
  1978
    232 cu in engine (YF carburetor)
      Manual transmission and 49-state emissions . . . . . . . .    3° to 7° BTDC
      Manual transmission and altitude compensator
        Above 4000 ft . . . . . . . . . . . . . . . . . . . . . . . . .    8° to 12° BTDC
        Below 4000 ft . . . . . . . . . . . . . . . . . . . . . . . . .    5° BTDC
    258 cu in engine (YF carburetor)
      Manual transmission and 49-state emissions . . . . . . . .    1° to 5° BTDC
      Manual transmission and California emissions . . . . . . .    6° to 10° BTDC
      Automatic transmission and 49-state emissions . . . . . .    8° to 10° BTDC
      Automatic transmission and California emissions . . . . .    6° to 10° BTDC
    258 cu in engine (BBD carburetor — all) . . . . . . . . . . .    4° to 8° BTDC
  1979
    258 cu in (YF carburetor)
      Manual transmission . . . . . . . . . . . . . . . . . . . . . . . .    4° to 8° BTDC
      Automatic transmission . . . . . . . . . . . . . . . . . . . . . .    2° to 6° BTDC
    258 cu in (BBD carburetor)
      Manual transmission . . . . . . . . . . . . . . . . . . . . . . . .    6° to 8° BTDC
      Automatic transmission . . . . . . . . . . . . . . . . . . . . . .    8° to 10° BTDC

## Ignition timing (continued)

V8 engine
  1973 and 1974 ................................... 4° to 6° BTDC
  1975 (manual transmission) ........................ 3° to 7° BTDC
  1976
    Automatic transmission and 49-state emissions ....... 8° to 12° BTDC
    Manual transmission and 49-state emissions ......... 3° to 7° BTDC
    Manual and automatic transmission and California
      emissions ................................... 3° to 7° BTDC
  1977
    49 state emissions ............................. 8° to 12° BTDC
    California emissions ........................... 3° to 7° BTDC
  1978
    Manual transmission ........................... 3° to 7° BTDC
    Automatic transmission ......................... 8° to 12° BTDC
    Automatic transmission and California emissions ....... 3° to 7° BTDC
  1979
    Manual transmission ........................... 3° to 7° BTDC
    Automatic transmission ......................... 6° to 10° BTDC
  1980
    Manual transmission and 49-state emissions ......... 6° to 10° BTDC
    Manual transmission and California emissions ........ 3° to 7° BTDC
    Manual transmission hilly terrain operation .......... 10° to 14° BTDC
    Automatic transmission and 49-state emissions ....... 8° to 12° BTDC
    Automatic transmission and California emissions ...... 3° to 7° BTDC
  1981
    Manual transmission and 49-state emissions ......... 8° BTDC
    Manual transmission hilly terrain operation .......... 12° BTDC
    Automatic transmission and 49-state emissions ....... 10° BTDC
151 cu in four-cylinder in-line engine
  1980 and 1981 (with vacuum advance hose disconnected)
    Manual transmission and 49-state emissions .......... 10° BTDC
    Manual transmission and California emissions ........ 12° BTDC
    Automatic transmission and 49-state emissions ....... 12° BTDC
    Automatic transmission and California emissions ...... 10° BTDC
  1982 (with vacuum advance hose disconnected)
    Manual transmission and 49-state emissions .......... 12° BTDC
    Manual transmission and California emissions ........ 8° BTDC
    Manual transmission high altitude operation
      (above 4000 ft) ............................ 17° BTDC
  1983 (with vacuum advance hose disconnected) (all) ..... 12° BTDC

## Valve clearances

F-head engine
  Intake ...................................... 0.016 in
  Exhaust ..................................... 0.018 in
L-head engine (intake and exhaust) .................. 0.016 in

## Curb idle speed settings

L-head engine ................................... 600 rpm
F-head engine
  YF-938-SD carburetor ......................... 600 rpm
  YF-4002-S carburetor ......................... 650 to 700 rpm
  YF-4366-S, YF-4941-S and YF-6115-S carburetors
    With distributor IAY-4401A ..................... 650 to 700 rpm
    With distributor IAY-4401B ..................... 700 to 750 rpm
V6 engine (all models) ............................ 650 to 750 rpm
In-line six-cylinder engines
  1972 and 1973
    Automatic transmission ........................ 550 rpm
    Manual transmission *with* EGR ................. 600 rpm
    Manual transmission *without* EGR .............. 700 rpm
  1974
    Automatic transmission ........................ 550 rpm
    Manual transmission .......................... 600 rpm
  1975
    232 and 258 cu in engine *without* EGR ............ 700 rpm
    258 cu in engine *with* EGR
      Manual transmission ....................... 450 to 650 rpm
      Automatic transmission ..................... 550 to 750 rpm
    232 and 258 cu in California engines ............. 500 to 700 rpm
  1976
    232 cu in engine (manual transmission) ........... 500 to 700 rpm

258 cu in engine
    Automatic transmission . . . . . . . . . . . . . . . . . . . . . . . .    450 to 650 rpm
    Automatic transmission and California emissions . . . . .    600 to 800 rpm
    Manual transmission . . . . . . . . . . . . . . . . . . . . . . . . . .    500 to 700 rpm
    Manual transmission and California emissions . . . . . . .    500 to 700 rpm
1977 without altitude compensation device
    Manual transmission . . . . . . . . . . . . . . . . . . . . . . . . . .    850 rpm
    Automatic transmission . . . . . . . . . . . . . . . . . . . . . . . .    550 rpm
1977 with altitude compensation device
    Manual transmission . . . . . . . . . . . . . . . . . . . . . . . . . .    600 rpm
    Automatic transmission . . . . . . . . . . . . . . . . . . . . . . . .    550 rpm
    Manual transmission and California emissions . . . . . . . .    850 rpm
    Automatic transmission and California emissions . . . . . . .    700 rpm
1978
    232 cu in engine
        Manual transmission . . . . . . . . . . . . . . . . . . . . . . . . . .    750 to 950 rpm
        Automatic transmission/altitude compensation device . .    500 to 700 rpm
    258 cu in engine
        Manual transmission . . . . . . . . . . . . . . . . . . . . . . . . . .    750 to 950 rpm
        Manual transmission/altitude compensation device . . . .    500 to 700 rpm
        Automatic transmission . . . . . . . . . . . . . . . . . . . . . . . .    450 to 650 rpm
1979 and 1980
    Manual transmission . . . . . . . . . . . . . . . . . . . . . . . . . .    600 to 800 rpm
    Automatic transmission . . . . . . . . . . . . . . . . . . . . . . . .    500 to 700 rpm
1981 and 1982
    Manual transmission . . . . . . . . . . . . . . . . . . . . . . . . . .    650 rpm
    Automatic transmission . . . . . . . . . . . . . . . . . . . . . . . .    550 rpm
1983
    Manual transmission and 49-state emissions . . . . . . . . .    600 rpm
    Automatic transmission and 49-state emissions . . . . . . .    500 rpm
    Manual transmission and California emissions . . . . . . . .    650 rpm
    Automatic transmission and California emissions . . . . . .    550 rpm
    Manual transmission and altitude compensation device . .    700 rpm
    Automatic transmission and altitude compensation device    650 rpm
V8 engine
1972 through 1974 . . . . . . . . . . . . . . . . . . . . . . . . . . . . . .    700 to 800 rpm
1975 and 1976
    Manual transmission . . . . . . . . . . . . . . . . . . . . . . . . . .    650 to 850 rpm
    Automatic transmission . . . . . . . . . . . . . . . . . . . . . . . .    600 to 800 rpm
1977
    Manual transmission . . . . . . . . . . . . . . . . . . . . . . . . . .    700 to 750 rpm
    Automatic transmission . . . . . . . . . . . . . . . . . . . . . . . .    700 rpm
1978
    Manual transmission . . . . . . . . . . . . . . . . . . . . . . . . . .    650 to 850 rpm
    Automatic transmission . . . . . . . . . . . . . . . . . . . . . . . .    600 to 800 rpm
1979
    Manual transmission . . . . . . . . . . . . . . . . . . . . . . . . . .    600 to 800 rpm
    Manual transmission and California emissions . . . . . . . .    650 to 850 rpm
    Automatic transmission . . . . . . . . . . . . . . . . . . . . . . . .    550 to 750 rpm
1980
    Manual transmission . . . . . . . . . . . . . . . . . . . . . . . . . .    600 to 800 rpm
    Automatic transmission and 49-state emissions . . . . . . .    550 to 750 rpm
    Automatic transmission and California emissions . . . . . . .    500 to 700 rpm
1981
    Manual transmission and 49-state emissions . . . . . . . . .    500 to 700 rpm
    Manual transmission and hilly terrain operation . . . . . . . .    700 rpm
    Automatic transmission . . . . . . . . . . . . . . . . . . . . . . . .    550 to 650 rpm
151 cu in four-cylinder engine
    1980 and 1981
        Manual transmission . . . . . . . . . . . . . . . . . . . . . . . . . .    900 rpm
        Automatic transmission . . . . . . . . . . . . . . . . . . . . . . . .    700 rpm
    1982 and 1983 (all models) . . . . . . . . . . . . . . . . . . . . . .    900 rpm

## Compression pressure

F- and L-head four-cylinder engines . . . . . . . . . . . . . . . . . . . .    120 to 130 psi
V6 engine . . . . . . . . . . . . . . . . . . . . . . . . . . . . . . . . . . . . . . . .    Lowest reading cyl. must be at least 75% of highest reading cyl.
In-line six-cylinder engines
    232 cu in engine . . . . . . . . . . . . . . . . . . . . . . . . . . . . . . .    140 psi
    258 cu in engine . . . . . . . . . . . . . . . . . . . . . . . . . . . . . . .    150 psi
V8 engine . . . . . . . . . . . . . . . . . . . . . . . . . . . . . . . . . . . . . . . .    140 psi
151 cu in four-cylinder engine . . . . . . . . . . . . . . . . . . . . . . . .    140 psi

## Clutch pedal free play

1953 through 1972 . . . . . . . . . . . . . . . . . . . . . . . . . . . . . . . . .    3/4 to 1-1/4 in
1973 through 1975 . . . . . . . . . . . . . . . . . . . . . . . . . . . . . . . . .    1/2 to 3/4 in

## Clutch pedal free play (continued)

1976 and 1977 . . . . . . . . . . . . . . . . . . . . . . . . . . . . . . . . .          3/4 to 1 in
1978 through 1983 . . . . . . . . . . . . . . . . . . . . . . . . . . . . . .          1 to 1-1/4 in

## Brakes

Disc brake pad lining service limit . . . . . . . . . . . . . . . . . . .          When worn to approximately the thickness of the pad backing plate
Drum brake shoe lining service limit
   Bonded . . . . . . . . . . . . . . . . . . . . . . . . . . . . . . . . . . . .          1/16 in
   Riveted . . . . . . . . . . . . . . . . . . . . . . . . . . . . . . . . . . . .          1/32 in above rivet head

## Torque specifications

| | Ft-lb | Nm |
| --- | --- | --- |
| Automatic transmission oil pan bolts . . . . . . . . . . . . . . . . . . | 12 | 16 |
| Manual transmission drain and fill plugs . . . . . . . . . . . . . . | 15 to 20 | 20 to 27 |
| Transfer case drain and fill plugs . . . . . . . . . . . . . . . . . . . . | 15 to 25 | 20 to 34 |
| Axle housing drain and fill plugs . . . . . . . . . . . . . . . . . . . . | 15 to 25 | 20 to 34 |
| Spark plugs | | |
|    F- and L-head four-cylinder engines . . . . . . . . . . . . . . . . | 25 to 33 | 34 to 44 |
|    V6 engine . . . . . . . . . . . . . . . . . . . . . . . . . . . . . . . . . . . . | 25 to 35 | 34 to 45 |
|    All others . . . . . . . . . . . . . . . . . . . . . . . . . . . . . . . . . . . . | 22 to 33 | 17 to 44 |

## 1  Introduction to routine maintenance

This Chapter was designed to help the home mechanic maintain his (or her) vehicle for peak performance, economy, safety and long life.

On the following pages you will find a maintenance schedule along with Sections which deal specifically with each item on the schedule. Included are visual checks, adjustments and item replacements.

Servicing your vehicle using the time/mileage maintenance schedule and the sequenced Sections will give you a planned program of maintenance. Keep in mind that it is a comprehensive plan; maintaining only a few items at the specified intervals will not produce the same results.

As you service your vehicle you will find that, due to the nature of the job, many of the procedures can and should be grouped together. Examples of this are:

*If the vehicle is raised* for chassis lubrication, it is an ideal time for the manual transmission oil, exhaust system, suspension, steering and fuel system checks.

*If the tires and wheels are removed,* as during a routine tire rotation, go ahead and check the brakes and wheel bearings at the same time.

*If you must borrow or rent a torque wrench,* it is a good idea to replace the spark plugs and/or repack (or replace) the wheel bearings all in the same day to save time and money.

The first step in this or any maintenance plan is to prepare yourself before the actual work begins. Read through the appropriate Sections for all work that is to be performed before you begin. Gather together all necessary parts and tools. If it appears that you could have a problem during a particular job, don't hesitate to ask advice from your local parts man or dealer service department.

## 2  Tune-up sequence

The term 'tune-up' is loosely applied to any general operation that puts the engine back into proper running condition. A tune-up is not a specific operation, but rather a combination of individual operations, such as replacing the spark plugs, adjusting the idle speed, setting the ignition timing, etc.

If, from the time the vehicle is new, the routine maintenance schedule (Section 3) is followed closely and frequent checks are made of fluid levels and high wear items, as suggested throughout this manual, the engine will be kept in relatively good running condition and the need for all inclusive tune-ups will be minimized.

More likely than not, however, there will be times when the engine is running poorly due to lack of regular maintenance. This is even more likely if a used vehicle which has not received regular and frequent maintenance checks is bought. In such cases an engine tune-up will be needed outside of the regular routine maintenance intervals.

The following series of operations are those most often needed to bring a generally poor running engine back into a proper state of tune.

### Minor tune-up

Clean, inspect and test battery (Sec 38)
Check all engine-related fluids (Sec 4)
Check cylinder compression (Sec 37)
Check and adjust drivebelts (Sec 11)
Replace spark plugs (Sec 32)
Inspect distributor cap and rotor (Sec 32)
Check and/or replace breaker points and adjust dwell angle (Sec 34)
Inspect and/or replace spark plug and coil wires (Sec 33)
Change oil and filter (Sec 5)
Check and adjust idle speed (Sec 21)
Check and adjust timing (Sec 35)
Check and adjust fuel/air mixture (Chapter 4)
Replace fuel filter (Sec 14)
Replace PCV valve (Sec 15)
Adjust valve clearances (Sec 40)
Check cooling system (Sec 8)

### Major tune-up

Perform all operations listed under *Minor tune-up*
Check ignition advance systems (Chapter 5)
Check EGR system (Chapter 6)
Test alternator and regulator (Chapter 5)
Test ignition system (Chapter 5)
Test charging system (Chapter 5)
Check fuel system (Chapter 4)

## 3  Routine maintenance schedule

This maintenance schedule covers all of the service procedures recommended by the manufacturer. In some instances the intervals have been altered where additional or more frequent checks are advisable. **Note:** *Not all maintenance checks or operations are applicable to every model.*

### Every 250 miles, weekly or before a long trip

Check the tire pressures (when cold)
Inspect the tires for wear and damage (Sec 6)
Check the steering for smooth and accurate operation (Sec 10)
Check the power steering fluid level, refilling as necessary (Sec 4)
Check the brake fluid level and , if it has dropped noticeably, inspect the system for leaks (add fluid if necessary) (Sec 4)
Check the operation of the brakes (Sec 31)
Check the automatic transmission fluid level (Sec 4)

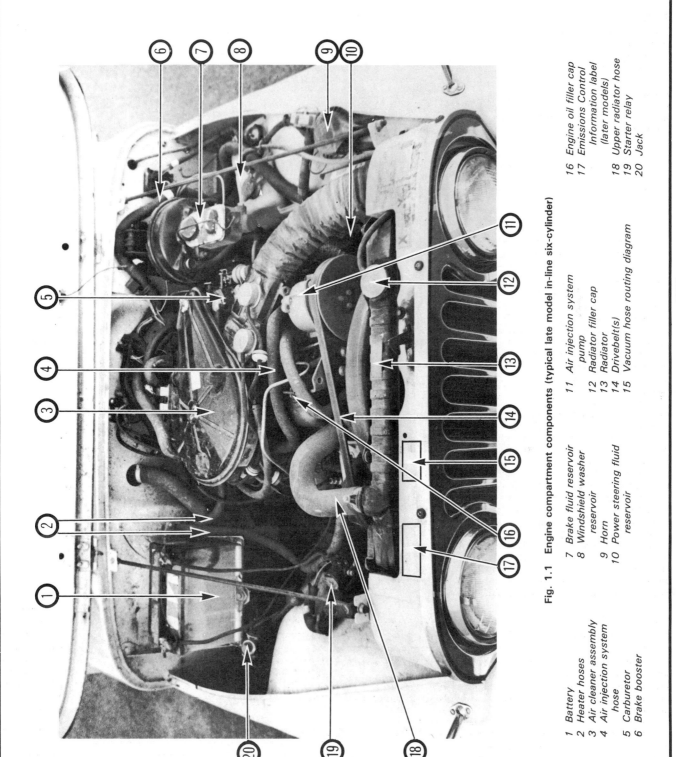

Fig. 1.1  Engine compartment components (typical late model in-line six-cylinder)

1  Battery
2  Heater hoses
3  Air cleaner assembly
4  Air injection system hose
5  Carburetor
6  Brake booster

7  Brake fluid reservoir
8  Windshield washer reservoir
9  Horn
10 Power steering fluid reservoir

11 Air injection system pump
12 Radiator filler cap
13 Radiator
14 Drivebelt(s)
15 Vacuum hose routing diagram

16 Engine oil filler cap
17 Emissions Control Information label (later models)
18 Upper radiator hose
19 Starter relay
20 Jack

1

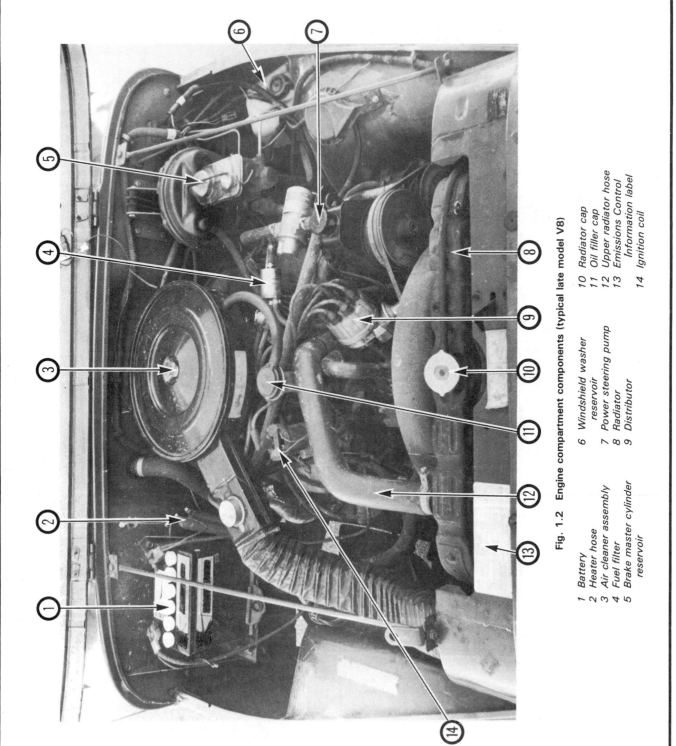

Fig. 1.2 Engine compartment components (typical late model V8)

1  Battery
2  Heater hose
3  Air cleaner assembly
4  Fuel filter
5  Brake master cylinder
   reservoir
6  Windshield washer
   reservoir
7  Power steering pump
8  Radiator
9  Distributor
10 Radiator cap
11 Oil filler cap
12 Upper radiator hose
13 Emissions Control
   Information label
14 Ignition coil

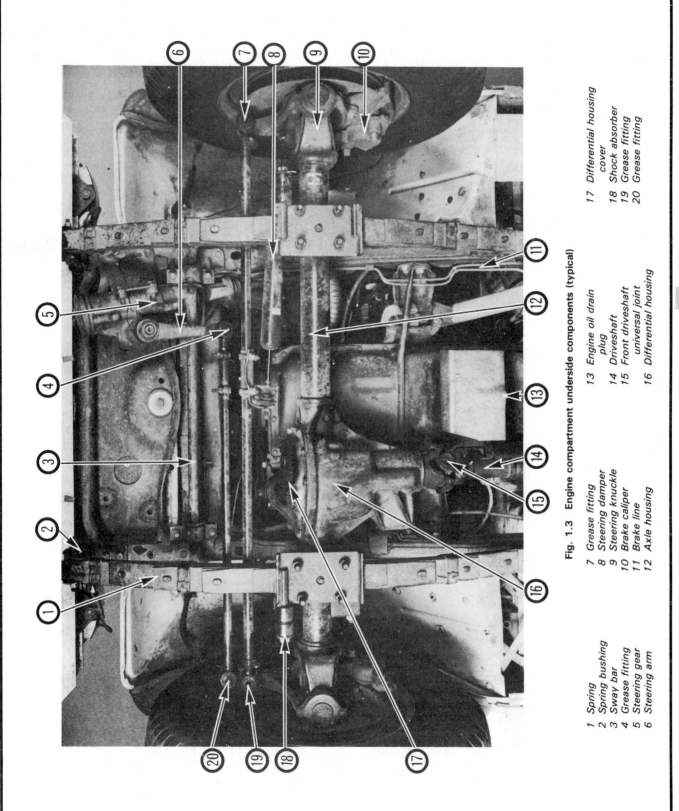

**Fig. 1.3  Engine compartment underside components (typical)**

1  Spring
2  Spring bushing
3  Sway bar
4  Grease fitting
5  Steering gear
6  Steering arm

7  Grease fitting
8  Steering damper
9  Steering knuckle
10  Brake caliper
11  Brake line
12  Axle housing

13  Engine oil drain plug
14  Driveshaft
15  Front driveshaft universal joint
16  Differential housing

17  Differential housing cover
18  Shock absorber
19  Grease fitting
20  Grease fitting

1

Fig. 1.4  Rear axle and related components (typical)

1  Brake hose
2  Rear universal joint
3  Rear driveshaft
4  Muffler

5  Spring
6  Parking brake cable
7  Shock absorber
8  Exhaust pipe

9  Fuel tank
10  Axle housing
11  Spring bushing
12  Rear drum brake

Check the operation of all lights
Check the operation of the windshield wipers and washers
Check the wiper mechanism and blades (Sec 41)
Fill the washer reservoir as necessary (Sec 4)
Check the horn operation
Check the operation of all gauges and instruments
Check the radiator coolant level (Sec 4)
Check the battery electrolyte level (Sec 4)

**Every 3000 miles or 3 months, whichever comes first**

Change engine oil and filter (heavy-duty operation) (Sec 5)
Check and service the oil bath-type air cleaner (Sec 16)
Lubricate the clutch lever and linkage (heavy-duty operation) (Sec 7)
Lubricate the suspension and steering components (heavy-duty operation) (Sec 7)

**Every 5000 miles or 5 months, whichever comes first**

Lubricate the suspension and steering components (Sec 7)
Check the PCV valve for proper operation (Sec 15)
Change the engine oil and filter (Sec 5)
Check and lubricate the clutch lever and linkage (Sec 7)
Check the transfer case lubricant level (Sec 4)
Check and adjust the engine idle speed (Sec 21)
Check the manual transmission lubricant level (Sec 4)
Lubricate the rear wheel bearings *on 1953 through 1971 models with* grease fittings (Sec 7)
Check the front and rear axle lubricant level (Sec 4)
Inspect the exhaust system (Sec 9)
Check and adjust the F- and L-head valve clearances (Sec 40)
Inspect the brake lines and hoses (Chapter 9)
Inspect the brake discs and pads (Sec 31)
Check the steering box lubricant level (Sec 7)

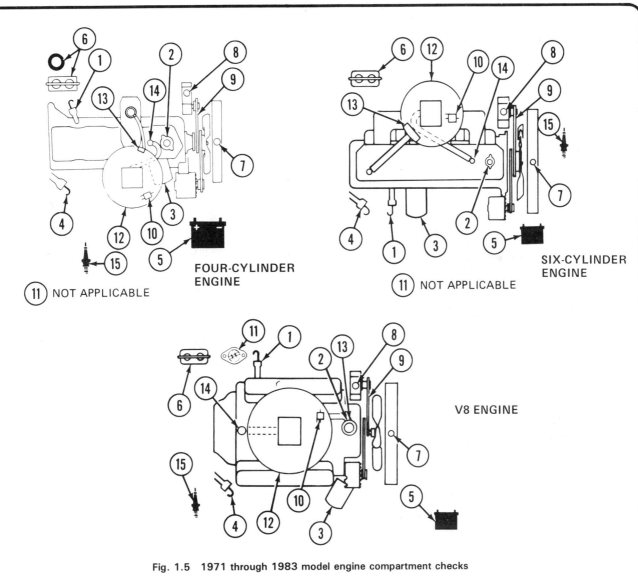

**Fig. 1.5   1971 through 1983 model engine compartment checks**

1   Engine oil level
2   Oil filler
3   Oil filter
4   Automatic transmission fluid level
5   Battery electrolyte level
6   Brake master cylinder fluid level
7   Coolant level and condition
8   Power steering fluid level
9   Drivebelt tension
10  Fuel filter
11  Exhaust heat valve check and lubrication
12  Air cleaner filter element
13  PCV filter
14  PCV valve and hose connections
15  Spark plug replacement

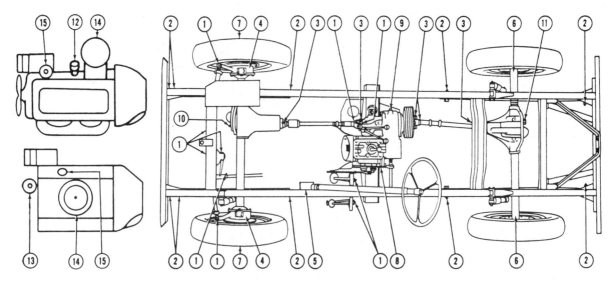

Fig. 1.6   1953 through 1971 chassis lubrication and check points

1  Chassis bearing
   grease fittings
2  Spring shackle and
   pivot bushings
3  Universal joints and
   driveshaft
4  Front axle bearings

5  Steering gear housing
6  Rear wheel bearings
7  Front wheel bearings
8  Transmission
9  Transfer case
10 Front differential

11 Rear differential
12 Distributor
13 V6 engine distributor
   cam
14 Air cleaner
15 Engine oil

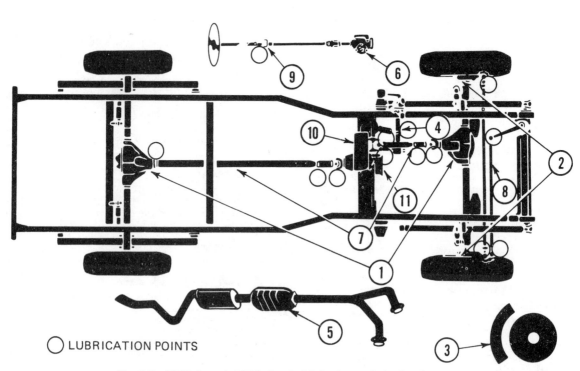

○ LUBRICATION POINTS

BRAKES

Fig. 1.7   1972 through 1983 chassis lubrication and check points

1  Front and rear
   differentials
2  Front wheel bearings
   and manual locking hub
3  Brake operation
   and fluid level

4  Clutch lever and
   linkage
5  Exhaust system
   check
6  Manual steering
   gear
7  Driveshaft

Check the deflection of all drivebelts (Sec 11)
Check the operation of the brake booster (Chapter 9)
Check the steering wheel for excessive free play (more
  than an inch) (Chapter 11)
Inspect and lubricate the exhaust manifold heat valve (Sec 22)
Drain and replace the transfer case lubricant (heavy-duty operation)
  (Sec 29)
Lubricate the F- and L-head engine distributor (Sec 34)
Check and replace (if necessary) the air cleaner
  filter element (Sec 17)
Inspect the distributor cap and rotor (Sec 33)
Lubricate the driveshaft universal joints (Sec 7)

## Every 10 000 miles or 10 months, whichever comes first

Replace the automotic transmission fluid and filter (heavy-duty
  operation) (Sec 27)
Inspect the brake linings and drums (Sec 31)
Check the emissions system air injection hoses (Chapter 6)
Replace the fuel filter (Sec 14)
Check the radiator hoses for cracks and leaks (Sec 12)
Check the shock absorbers, bushings and mounts for wear and
  damage (replace components as necessary) (Sec 10)
Lubricate the rear wheel bearings on early model CJ-2 with full-
  floating axleshafts (Chapter 11)

## Every 15 000 miles or 15 months, whichever comes first

Check and adjust the automatic transmission linkage (Chapter 7)
Lubricate all latches, hinges, seat tracks and lock
  cylinders (Chapter 12)
Check and adjust, if necessary, the clutch pedal height (Chapter 8)
Have the front end alignment checked and adjusted as necessary
Replace the spark plugs (Sec 32)
Perform a minor or major tune-up as necessary (Sec 2)
Check the choke linkage for free movement, lubricating
  as necessary (Sec 19)
Inspect all vacuum hoses and connections (Sec 12)
Inspect the ECS charcoal canister and replace the filter, if so
  equipped (Sec 36)
Lubricate the front wheel bearings (Chapter 11)
Replace the distributor cam lubricator, if so equipped (Chapter 5)
Check the EGR system (Sec 23)
Check the PCV valve and hoses (Sec 15)
Check the Thermo-controlled Air Cleaner (TAC) system (Sec 18)
Check the Transmission Controlled Spark (TCS) system (Chapter 6)
Inspect the fuel system hoses, connections, fuel tank
  and cap (Sec 13)
Check and adjust, as necessary, the transfer case
  shift linkage (Chapter 7)

## Every 20 000 miles or 20 months, whichever comes first

Check the operation of the high-altitude compensation system, if
  so equipped (Chapter 4)

## Every 25 000 miles or 25 months, whichever comes first

Drain and refill the automatic transmission (Sec 27)
Replace all drivebelts (Sec 11)
Drain and refill the cooling system with the specified
  coolant (Sec 39)

## Every 30 000 miles or 30 months, whichever comes first

Drain and refill the differentials (Sec 30)
Drain and refill the manual transmission (Sec 28)

Check the tightness of the cylinder head bolts (Chapter 2)
Drain and refill the transfer case (Sec 29)

### Heavy-duty operation

Heavy-duty operation is defined as off-road operation (see below),
extended idling, towing heavy trailers (2000 lbs), operating in dusty
conditions or excessive short run use (6 to 8 mile trips constituting
30 percent of the vehicle's use). Shorter maintenance intervals are
recommended in these instances.

### Off-road operation

After driving off road through mud, sand or water, check the following
daily:

  *Brake discs and pads*
  *Brake drums and shoes*
  *Brake lines and hoses*
  *Transmission, transfer case and differential oil*
  *Air filter*

Also, lubricate the following daily or as soon as practical:

  *Steering linkage and knuckles*
  *Driveshaft universal joints*

### 4  Fluid level checks

1    There are a number of components on a vehicle which rely on the
use of fluids to perform their job. During the normal operation of the
vehicle, the fluids are used up and must be replenished before damage
occurs. See the *Recommended lubricants and fluids* Section at the front
of this Chapter for the specific fluid to be used when additions are required. When checking fluid levels it is important to have the vehicle
on a level surface.

### *Engine oil*
2    The engine oil level is checked with a dipstick which is located at
the side of the engine block. The dipstick extends through a tube and
into the oil pan at the bottom of the engine.
3    Preferably, the oil level should be checked before the vehicle has
been driven, or about 15 minutes after the engine has been shut off.
If the oil is checked immediately after driving the vehicle, some of the
oil will remain in the upper engine components, resulting in an inaccurate reading on the dipstick.
4    Pull the dipstick from the tube and wipe all the oil from the end
with a clean rag (photo). Insert the clean dipstick all the way back into
the oil pan and pull it out again. Observe the oil at the end of the dipstick.
At its highest point, the level should be between the Add and Full marks
(photo).
5    It takes approximately one (1) quart of oil to raise the level from
the Add mark to the Full mark on the dipstick. Do not allow the level
to drop below the Add mark since engine damage due to oil starvation
may result. On the other hand, do not overfill the engine by adding oil
above the Full mark as oil-fouled spark plugs, oil leaks or oil seal failures
may occur.
6    Oil is added to the engine after removing a twist-off cap located
either on the rocker arm cover or a raised tube near the front of the
engine. The cap should be marked *Engine oil* or something similar
(photo). An oil can spout or funnel will reduce spills as the oil is poured
in.
7    Checking the oil level can also be an important preventative
maintenance step. If you find the oil level dropping abnormally, it is an
indication of oil leakage or internal engine wear, which should be corrected. If there are water droplets in the oil, or if it is milky looking,
this also indicates component failure (the engine should be checked
immediately). The condition of the oil should also be checked along
with the level. With the dipstick removed from the engine, wipe your
thumb and index finger up the dipstick, looking for small dirt and metal
particles, which will cling to the dipstick. Their presence is an indication that the oil should be changed (Sec 5).

*Engine coolant*

8    Many vehicles are equipped with a pressurized coolant recovery system which makes coolant level checks very easy. A clear or white coolant reservoir attached to the inner fender panel is connected by a hose to the radiator neck. As the engine heats up during operation, coolant is forced from the radiator through the connecting tube and into the reservoir. As the engine cools, coolant is automatically drawn back into the radiator to maintain the correct level.

9    The coolant level should be checked when the engine is cold. Merely observe the level of fluid in the reservoir, which should be at or near the Full cold mark on the side of the reservoir. If the system is completely cooled, also check the level in the radiator by removing the cap. Some systems also have a Full hot mark to check the level when the engine is hot.

10   If your particular vehicle is not equipped with a coolant recovery system, the level should be checked by removing the radiator cap. **Warning:** *The cap should not, under any circumstances, be removed while the system is hot as escaping steam could cause serious injury.*

*Wait until the engine has completely cooled, then wrap a thick cloth around the cap and turn it to its first stop. If any steam escapes from the cap, allow the engine to cool further, then remove the cap and check the level in the radiator. It should be about one (1) inch below the bottom of the filler neck (photo).*

11   If only a small amount of coolant is required to bring the system up to the proper level, regular water can be used. However, to maintain the proper antifreeze/water mixture in the system, both should be mixed together to replenish a low level. High-quality antifreeze offering protection to −20°F should be mixed with water in the proportion specified on the container. Do not allow antifreeze to come in contact with your skin or painted surfaces of the vehicle. Flush contacted areas immediately with plenty of water. **Caution:** *Antifreeze can be fatal to children and pets. They like it because it is sweet. Just a few drops can cause death. Wipe up garage floor and drip pan coolant spills immediately.*

12   On systems with a recovery tank, coolant should be added to the reservoir after removing the reservoir cap. Coolant should be added

4.4A  Withdrawing the oil dipstick (V8 engine shown)

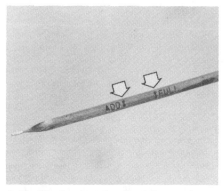

4.4B  The level on the dipstick must be between the Add and Full marks (arrows)

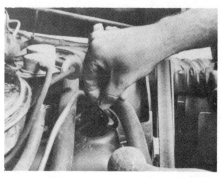

4.6  Remove the engine oil filler cap by rotating it and lifting it away from the rocker arm cover (later model in-line six-cylinder shown)

4.10  Checking the coolant level in the radiator (in this example the level is low)

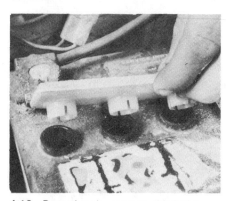

4.18  Removing the caps to check the battery electrolyte level

4.19  Carefully add distilled water to the battery cells to avoid splattering electrolyte

4.24  Checking the brake master cylinder fluid level

4.43  Dana Model 300 transfer case filler plug location (arrow)

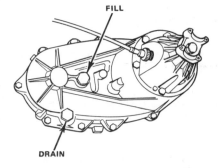

Fig. 1.8  Quadra-Trac transfer case fill and drain plugs (Sec 4 and 29)

directly to the radiator on systems without a coolant recovery tank.

13  As the coolant level is checked, note the condition of the coolant. It should be relatively clear. If it is brown or a rust color, the system should be drained, flushed and refilled (Sec 39).

14  If the cooling system requires repeated additions to maintain the proper level, have the radiator cap checked for proper sealing ability. Also, check for leaks in the system (cracked hoses, loose hose connections, leaking gaskets, etc.) (Sec 12).

### Windshield washer fluid

15  The fluid for the windshield washer system is located in a plastic reservoir. The level inside the reservoir should be maintained at the Full mark.

16  A good quality washer solvent should be added to the reservoir whenever replenishing is required. Do not use plain water alone in this system, especially in cold climates where the water could freeze.

### Battery electrolyte

**Note:** *There are certain precautions to be taken when working on or near the battery: a) never expose a battery to open flame or sparks which could ignite the hydrogen gas given off by the battery; b) wear protective clothing and eye protection to reduce the possibility of the corrosive sulfuric acid solution inside the battery harming you (if the fluid is splashed or spilled, flush the contacted area immediately with plenty of water); c) remove all metal jewelry which could contact the positive terminal and another grounded metal source, causing a short circuit; d) always keep batteries and battery acid out of the reach of children.*

17  Vehicles equipped with maintenance-free batteries require no maintenance because the battery case is sealed and has no removeable caps for adding water.

18  If a maintenance-type battery is installed, the caps on the top of the battery should be removed periodically to check for a low electrolyte level (photo). This check will be more critical during the warm summer months.

19  Remove each of the caps and add *distilled* water to bring the level of each cell to the split ring in the filler opening (photo).

20  At the same time the battery electrolyte level is checked, the overall condition of the battery and its related components should be inspected. If corrosion is present on the cable ends or battery terminals, remove the cables and clean away all corrosion using a baking soda/water solution or a wire brush cleaning tool designed for this purpose. See Section 38 for complete battery care and servicing procedures.

### Brake fluid

21  The brake master cylinder is located on the left side of the engine compartment firewall and has a cap which must be removed to check the fluid level.

22  Before removing the cap, use a rag to clean all dirt, grease, etc. from around the cap area. If any foreign matter enters the master cylinder with the cap removed, blockage of the brake system lines can occur. Also, make sure all painted surfaces around the master cylinder are covered, as brake fluid will ruin paint.

23  Release the clip(s) securing the cap to the top of the master cylinder. In most cases, a screwdriver can be used to pry the wire clip(s) free.

24  Carefully lift the cap off the cylinder and note the fluid level (photo). It should be approximately 1/4-inch below the top edge of each reservoir (photo).

25  If additional fluid is necessary to bring the level up to the proper height, carefully pour the specified brake fluid into the master cylinder. Be careful not to spill the fluid on painted surfaces. Be sure the specified fluid is used, as mixing different types of brake fluid can cause damage to the system. See *Recommended lubricants and fluids* or your owner's manual.

26  At this time the fluid and master cylinder can be inspected for contamination. Normally, the hydraulic system will not require periodic draining and refilling, but if rust deposits, dirt particles or water droplets are seen in the fluid, the system should be drained and refilled with fresh fluid.

27  Reinstall the master cylinder cap and secure it with the clip(s). Make sure the cap is properly seated to prevent fluid loss.

28  The brake fluid level in the master cylinder will drop slightly as the brake shoes or pads at each wheel wear down during normal operation. If the master cylinder requires repeated replenishing to keep it at

the proper level, it is an indication of leakage in the brake system which should be corrected immediately. Check all brake lines and connections, along with the wheel cylinders and booster (see Chapter 9 for more information).

29  If upon checking the master cylinder fluid level you discover one or both reservoirs empty or nearly empty, the system should be bled (Chapter 9). When the fluid level gets low, air can enter the system and should be removed by bleeding the brakes.

### Manual transmission lubricant

30  Manual transmissions do not have a dipstick. The oil level is checked by removing a plug in the side of the transmission case. Locate the plug and use a rag to clean the plug and the area around it.

31  With the engine cold, remove the plug. If oil immediately starts leaking out, thread the plug back into the transmission because the level is all right. If there is no oil flow, completely remove the plug and place your little finger inside the hole. The oil level should be just at the bottom of the plug hole.

32  If the transmission requires more oil, use a syringe to squeeze the appropriate lubricant into the plug hole to bring the oil up to the proper level.

33  Thread the plug back into the transmission and tighten it securely. Drive the vehicle and check for leaks around the plug.

### Automatic transmission fluid

34  The fluid inside the transmission must be at normal operating temperature to get an accurate reading on the dipstick. This is done by driving the vehicle for several miles, making frequent starts and stops to allow the transmission to shift through all gears.

35  Park the vehicle on a level surface, place the selector in Park and leave the engine running at an idle.

36  Remove the transmission dipstick and wipe all the fluid from the end with a clean rag.

37  Push the dipstick back into the transmission until the cap seats firmly on the dipstick tube. Now remove the dipstick again and observe the fluid on the end. The highest point of fluid should be between the Full mark and ¼-inch below the Full mark.

38  If the fluid level is at or below the Add mark on the dipstick, add sufficient fluid to raise the level to the Full mark. One pint of fluid will raise the level from Add to Full. Fluid should be added directly into the dipstick guide tube, using a funnel to prevent spills.

39  It is important that the transmission is not overfilled. Under no circumstances should the fluid level be above the Full mark on the dipstick, as this could cause internal damage to the transmission. The best way to prevent overfilling is to add fluid a little at a time, driving the vehicle and checking the level between additions.

40  Use only transmission fluid specified by the manufacturer. This information can be found in the *Recommended lubricants and fluids* Section.

41  The condition of the fluid should also be checked along with the level. If the fluid at the end of the dipstick is a dark reddish-brown color, or if it has a 'burnt' smell, the fluid should be changed. If you are in doubt about the condition of the fluid, purchase some new fluid and compare the two for color and smell.

### Transfer case lubricant

42  The transfer case lubricant level should be checked at the same time as the manual transmission and differentials.

43  Remove the filler plug and determine whether or not the lubricant level is even with the bottom of the filler hole (photo). On Quadra-Trac transfer cases with reduction units, the reduction units have a separate lubricant supply which must be checked also.

44  Fill the transfer case and, if so equipped, the reduction unit to the proper level with the specified lubricant. Replace the filler plugs, drive the vehicle and check for leaks.

### Differential lubricant

45  Like the manual transmission and transfer case, the front and rear differentials have an inspection and fill plug which must be removed to check the level.

46  Remove the plug, which is located either in the removable cover plate or on the side of the differential carrier. Use your little finger to reach inside the housing to feel the level of the oil. It should be at the bottom of the plug hole (photos).

47  If such is not the case, add the proper lubricant to the carrier

1

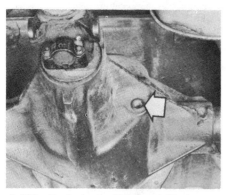

4.46A  Typical axle differential fill plug (arrow)

4.46B  Some models have the fill plug (arrow) in the removable differential cover

4.54  Checking the power steering pump fluid level

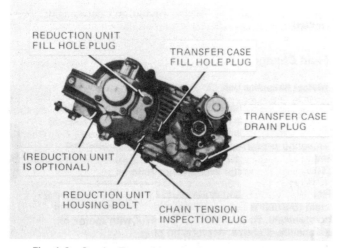

Fig. 1.9  Quadra-Trac with reduction unit (Sec 4 and 29)

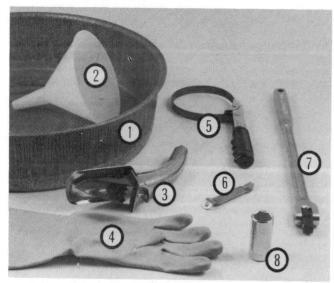

5.3  Typical oil change tools

| | |
|---|---|
| 1  Drain pan | 5  Filter wrench |
| 2  Funnel | 6  Can opener |
| 3  Oil can spout | 7  Breaker bar |
| 4  Rubber glove(s) | 8  Socket (6-point) |

through the plug hole. A syringe or a small funnel can be used for this.
48  Make certain the correct lubricant is used, as regular and Trak-Lok rear axles require different lubricants. A Trak-Lok axle with the wrong lubricant will make a chattering noise and must be drained and refilled with the proper lubricant.
49  Tighten the plug securely and check for leaks after the first few miles of driving.

*Power steering fluid*

50  Unlike manual steering, the power steering system relies on fluid which may, over a period of time, require replenishing.
51  The reservoir for the power steering pump will be located near the front of the engine, and can be mounted on either the left or right side.
52  The power steering fluid level should be checked only after the vehicle has been driven, with the fluid at operating temperature. The front wheels should be pointed straight ahead.
53  With the engine shut off, use a rag to clean the reservoir cap and the areas around the cap. This will help prevent foreign material from falling into the reservoir when the cap is removed.
54  Twist off the reservoir cap, which has a built-in dipstick attached to it. Pull off the cap and remove the fluid at the bottom of the dipstick with a clean rag. Now reinstall the dipstick/cap assembly to get a fluid level reading. Remove the dipstick/cap and note the fluid level. It should be at the Full hot mark on the dipstick (photo).
55  If additional fluid is required, pour the specified type directly into the reservoir using a funnel to prevent spills.
56  If the reservoir requires frequent fluid additions, all power steering hoses, hose connections, the power steering pump and the steering box should be checked carefully for leaks.

## 5  Engine oil and filter change

1  Frequent oil changes may be the best form of preventative maintenance available to the home mechanic. When engine oil is old, it gets diluted and contaminated, which ultimately leads to premature engine wear.
2  Although some sources recommend oil filter changes every other oil change, we feel that the minimal cost of an oil filter and the relative ease with which it is installed dictate that a new filter be used whenever the oil is changed.
3  The tools necessary for a normal oil and filter change are a wrench to fit the drain plug at the bottom of the oil pan, an oil filter wrench to remove the old filter, a container with a six-quart capacity to drain the old oil into and a funnel or oil can spout to help pour fresh oil into the engine (photo).
4  In addition, you should have plenty of clean rags and newspapers handy to mop up any spills. Access to the underside of the vehicle is greatly improved if it can be lifted on a hoist, driven onto ramps or supported by jackstands. **Caution:** *Do not work under a vehicle which is supported only by a bumper, hydraulic or scissors-type jack.*
5  If this is your first oil change on the vehicle, it is a good idea to crawl underneath and familiarize yourself with the locations of the oil

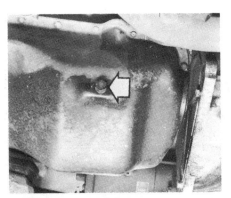

5.9   Typical oil drain plug location (arrow)

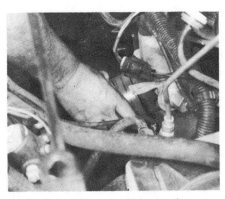

5.20   The oil filter should be *hand-tightened* only

5.24   Pouring oil into the filler opening (V8 engine shown)

**1**

drain plug and the oil filter. Since the engine and exhaust components will be warm during the actual work, it is a good idea to figure out any potential problems before the engine and exhaust pipes are hot.

6   Allow the engine to warm up to normal operating temperature. If new oil or any tools are needed, use the warm-up time to locate everything necessary for the job. The correct type of oil to buy for your application can be found in *Recommended lubricants and fluids* near the front of this Chapter.

7   With the engine oil warm (warm engine oil will drain better and more built-up sludge will be removed with the oil), raise the vehicle for access beneath it. Make sure the vehicle is firmly supported. If jackstands are used, they should be placed toward the front of the frame rails which run the length of the vehicle.

8   Move all necessary tools, rags and newspapers under the vehicle. Position the drain pan under the drain plug. Keep in mind that the oil will initially flow from the pan with some force, so position the pan accordingly.

9   Use the wrench to remove the drain plug near the bottom of the oil pan but be careful not to touch any of the hot exhaust pipe components. Depending on how hot the oil has become, you may want to wear gloves while unscrewing the plug the final few turns (photo).

10   Allow the old oil to drain into the pan. It may be necessary to move the pan farther under the engine as the oil flow reduces to a trickle.

11   After all the oil has drained, clean the drain plug thoroughly with a clean rag. Small metal particles may cling to the plug and immediately contaminate the new oil.

12   Clean the area around the drain plug opening and reinstall the plug. Tighten it securely.

13   Move the drain pan into position under the oil filter.

14   Now use the filter wrench to loosen the oil filter. Chain or metal band-type filter wrenches may distort the filter canister, but don't worry about it because the filter will be discarded.

15   Sometimes the oil filter is on so tight it cannot be loosened, or it is positioned in an area which is inaccessible with a filter wrench. As a last resort, you can punch a metal bar or long screwdriver directly through the **bottom** of the canister and use it as a T-bar to turn the filter. If this must be done, be prepared for oil to spurt out of the canister as it is punctured.

16   Completely unscrew the old filter. Be careful, it is full of oil. Empty the old oil inside the filter into the drain pan.

17   Compare the old filter with the new one to make sure they are the same type.

18   Use a clean rag to remove all oil, dirt and sludge from the area where the oil filter mounts to the engine. Check the old filter to make sure the rubber gasket is not stuck to the engine mounting surface. If the gasket is stuck to the engine (use a flashlight to check), remove it.

19   Open one of the cans of new oil and fill the new filter about half full of oil. Also apply a light coat of fresh oil to the rubber gasket of the new oil filter.

20   Attach the new filter to the engine following the tightening directions printed on the filter canister or packing box (photo). Most filter manufacturers recommend against using a filter wrench due to the possibility of overtightening and damaging the canister.

21   Remove all tools, rags, etc. from under the vehicle, being careful not to spill the oil in the drain pan. Lower the vehicle.

22   Move to the engine compartment and locate the oil filler cap on the engine. In most cases there will be a screw-off cap on the rocker arm cover or a cap at the end of a fill tube at the front of the engine. In any case, the cap will most likely be labeled *Engine Oil* or something similar.

23   If an oil can spout is used, push the spout into the top of the oil can and pour the fresh oil through the filler opening. A funnel placed in the opening may also be used.

24   Pour about three (3) quarts of fresh oil into the engine (photo). Wait a few minutes to allow the oil to drain to the pan, then check the level on the oil dipstick (see Sec 4 if necessary). If the oil level is above the Add mark, start the engine and allow the new oil to circulate.

25   Run the engine for only about a minute and then shut it off. Immediately look under the vehicle and check for leaks at the oil pan drain plug and around the oil filter. If either is leaking, tighten with a bit more force.

26   With the new oil circulated and the filter now completely full, recheck the level and add enough oil to bring the level to the Full mark on the dipstick.

27   During the first few trips after an oil change, make it a point to check frequently for leaks and correct oil level.

28   The old oil drained from the engine cannot be reused in its present state and should be disposed of. Oil reclamation centers, auto repair shops and gas stations will normally accept the oil, which can be refined and used again. After the oil has cooled, it can be drained into a suitable container (capped plastic jugs, topped bottles, milk cartons, etc.) for transportation to a disposal site.

**6   Tire and tire pressure checks**

1   Periodically inspecting the tires may not only prevent you from being stranded with a flat tire, but can also give you clues as to possible problems with the steering and suspension systems before major damage occurs.

2   Proper tire inflation adds miles to the lifespan of the tires, allows the vehicle to achieve maximum miles per gallon figures and contributes to overall ride quality.

3   When inspecting the tires, first check the wear of the tread. Irregularities in the tread pattern (cupping, flat spots, more wear on one side than the other) are indications of front end alignment and/or balance problems. If any of these conditions are noted, take the vehicle to a reputable repair shop to correct the problem.

4   Also check the tread area for cuts and punctures. Many times a nail or tack will embed itself into the tire tread and yet the tire will hold its air pressure for a short time. In most cases, a repair shop or gas station can repair the punctured tire.

5   It is also important to check the sidewalls of the tires, both inside and outside. Check for deteriorated rubber, cuts, and punctures. Also inspect the inboard side of the tire for signs of brake fluid leakage, indicating that a thorough brake inspection is needed immediately.

6   Incorrect tire pressure cannot be determined merely by looking at the tire. This is especially true for radial tires. A tire pressure gauge must be used. If you do not already have a reliable gauge, it is a good

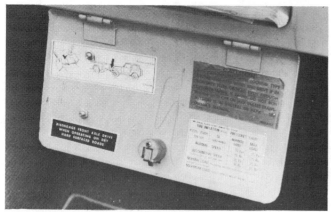

6.8   The tire pressure placard is located on the glovebox door

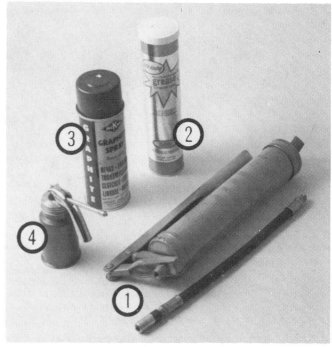

7.1   Tools required for chassis lubrication

1   *Grease gun and flexible nozzle*
2   *Grease cartridge*
3   *Multi-purpose spray lubricant*
4   *Oil can*

idea to purchase one and keep it in the glove box. Built-in pressure gauges at gas stations are often unreliable.

7   Always check tire inflation when the tires are cold. Cold, in this case, means the vehicle has not been driven more than one mile after sitting for three hours or more. It is normal for the pressure to increase 4 to 8 pounds or more when the tires are hot.

8   Unscrew the valve cap protruding from the wheel or hubcap and firmly press the gauge onto the valve stem. Observe the reading on the gauge and compare the figure to the recommended tire pressure listed on the tire placard. The tire placard is usually attached to the glove box door (photo).

9   Check all tires and add air as necessary to bring them up to the recommended pressure levels. Do not forget the spare tire. Be sure to reinstall the valve caps (which will keep dirt and moisture out of the valve stem mechanism).

## 7   Chassis lubrication

1   A grease gun and a cartridge filled with the proper grease (see *Recommended lubricants and fluids*) are necessary to lubricate most chassis components (photo).

2   Using the accompanying illustrations, locate the various grease fittings (photo).

3   For easier access under the vehicle, raise it with a jack and place jackstands under the frame. *Make sure the vehicle is firmly supported by the stands.*

4   Before proceeding, force a little of the grease out of the nozzle to remove any dirt from the end of the gun. Wipe the nozzle clean with a rag.

5   Wipe the grease fitting clean and push the grease gun nozzle firmly over it. Squeeze the trigger on the grease gun to force grease into the component. The tie-rods and balljoints should be lubricated until the rubber reservoir is firm to the touch. Do not pump too much grease into the fittings as it could rupture the reservoir. If the grease seeps out around the grease gun nozzle, the fitting is clogged or the nozzle is not fully seated on the fitting. Resecure the gun nozzle to the fitting and try again. If necessary, replace the fitting with a new one.

6   Wipe any excess grease from the components and the grease fitting.

7   Early models feature different types of rear wheel bearing lubrication. *On models with grease fittings,* carefully lubricate the fitting with wheel bearing grease until the grease flows from the vent opening. Make sure this vent is kept open or the grease will eventually back up onto the brake shoes. *On models without grease fittings,* it will be necessary to remove the rear wheel bearings and lubricate them as described in Chapter 8.

8   On later models, the clutch lever shaft should be carefully lubricated using chassis grease (photo).

9   While you are under the vehicle, clean and lubricate the brake cable.

10  Lower the vehicle to the ground for the remaining lubrication procedures.

11  Open the hood and smear a little chassis grease on the latch mechanism.

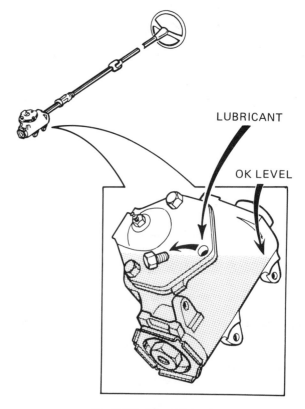

LUBRICANT

OK LEVEL

Fig. 1.10   Manual steering gear lubrication check (Sec 7)

7.2 Steering arm grease fitting location (arrow)

7.8 Clutch lever shaft grease fitting location (arrow)

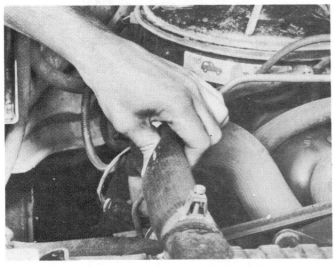

8.4 Squeezing the radiator hose to check for cracks and deterioration

9.2 Check the area around the exhaust pipe connections (arrow) for cracks and evidence of leaks

12 Remove the bolt opposite the steering gear adjuster and check the lubricant level. If it is not even with the bottom of the bolt hole, add chassis lubricant to the proper level and replace the bolt.

13 Lubricate all hinges (door, glove box door, hood and lift gate) with light engine oil, multi-purpose oil or spray lubricant, which is available at auto parts stores.

14 Finally, the key lock cylinders should be lubricated with spray graphite or silicone, also available at auto parts stores.

## 8 Cooling system check

1 Many major engine failures can be attributed to a faulty cooling system. If the vehicle is equipped with an automatic transmission, the cooling system also plays an important role in prolonging transmission life.

2 The cooling system should be checked with the engine cold. Do this before the vehicle is driven for the day or after it has been shut off for at least three hours.

3 Remove the radiator cap and thoroughly clean the cap (inside and out) with clean water. Also clean the filler neck on the radiator. All traces of corrosion should be removed.

4 Carefully check the upper and lower radiator hoses along with the smaller diameter heater hoses. Inspect each hose along its entire length, replacing any hose which is cracked, swollen or shows signs of deterioration (photo). Make sure that all hose connections are tight. A leak in the

cooling system will usually show up as white or rust colored deposits on the areas adjoining the leak.

6 Use compressed air or a soft brush to remove bugs, leaves, etc. from the front of the radiator or air-conditioning condenser. Be careful not to damage the delicate cooling fins or cut yourself on them.

7 Finally, have the cap and system pressure tested. If you do not have a pressure tester, most gas stations and repair shops will do this for a minimal charge.

## 9 Exhaust system check

1 With the engine cold (at least three hours after the vehicle has been driven), check the complete exhaust system from its starting point at the engine to the end of the tailpipe. This should be done on a hoist where unrestricted access is available.

2 Check the pipes and connections for signs of leakage and/or corrosion indicating a potential failure. Make sure that all brackets and hangers are tight and in good condition (photo).

3 At the same time, inspect the underside of the body for holes, corrosion, open seams, etc. which may allow exhaust gases to enter the passenger compartment. Seal all body openings with silicone or body putty.

4 Rattles and other noises can often be traced to the exhaust system, especially the mounts and hangers. Try to move the pipes, muffler and catalytic converter (if so equipped). If the components come into contact with the body or driveline parts, secure the exhaust system with

11.3  Twist the drivebelt to check the underside (arrow) for cracks and deterioration

14.5  Removing the fuel filter screw-type clamp with a screwdriver (in-line six-cylinder engine shown)

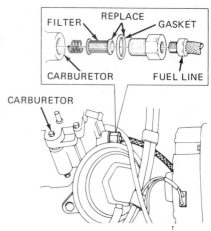

Fig. 1.11  Carburetor mounted fuel filter — exploded view (Sec 14)

new mounts.

5    This is also an ideal time to check the running condition of the engine by inspecting inside the very end of the tailpipe. The exhaust deposits here are an indication of engine state-of-tune. If the pipe is black and sooty or coated with white deposits, the engine is in need of a tune-up (including a thorough carburetor inspection and adjustment).

## 10  Suspension and steering check

1    Whenever the front of the vehicle is raised for service, it is a good idea to visually check the suspension and steering components for wear.
2    Indications of a fault in these systems are excessive play in the steering wheel before the front wheels react, excessive sway around corners, body movement over rough roads or binding at some point as the steering wheel is turned.
3    Before the vehicle is raised for inspection, test the shock absorbers by pushing down to rock the vehicle at each corner. If you push the vehicle down and it does not come back to a level position within one or two bounces, the shocks are worn and must be replaced. As this is done, check for squeaks and strange noises from the suspension components. Information on shock absorber and suspension components can be found in Chapter 11.
4    Now raise the front end of the vehicle and support it firmly on jackstands placed under the frame rails. Because of the work to be done, make sure the vehicle cannot fall from the stands.
5    Grab the top and bottom of the front tire with your hands and rock the tire/wheel on the spindle. If there is movement of more than 0.005-inch, the wheel bearings should be serviced (see Chapter 11).
6    Crawl under the vehicle and check for loose bolts, broken or disconnected parts and deteriorated rubber bushings on all suspension and steering components. Look for grease or fluid leaking from around the steering box. Check the power steering hoses and connections for leaks. Check the balljoints for wear.
7    Have an assistant turn the steering wheel from side-to-side and check the steering components for free movement, chafing and binding. If the steering does not react with the movement of the steering wheel, try to determine where the slack is located.

## 11  Drivebelt check and adjustment

1    The drivebelts, or V-belts as they are sometimes called, are located at the front of the engine and play an important role in the overall operation of the vehicle and its components. Due to their function and material make-up, the belts are prone to failure after a period of time and should be inspected and adjusted periodically to prevent major engine damage.
2    The number of belts used on a particular vehicle depends on the accessories installed. Drivebelts are used to turn the generator/alternator, smog pump, power steering pump, water pump, fan and air conditioning compressor. A single belt may be used for more than one of these components and the wide ribbed serpentine belt is used for all

of them.
3    With the engine off, open the hood and locate the various belts at the front of the engine. Using your fingers (and a flashlight if necessary), move along the belts checking for cracks and separation of the belt plies. Also check for fraying and glazing, which gives the belt a shiny appearance. Both sides of the belts should be inspected, which means you will have to twist the belt to check the underside (photo).
4    The tension of each belt is checked by pushing on the belt at a distance halfway between the pulleys. A special tension gauge is required to check the serpentine belt. On standard belts, push firmly with your thumb and see how much the belt moves down (deflects). Generally, if the distance (pulley center-to-pulley center) is between 7 and 11 inches, the belt should deflect ¼ -inch. If the belt is longer and travels between pulleys spaced 12 to 16 inches apart, the belt should deflect ½ -inch. On the serpentine belt, the gauge should read between 180 and 200 lbs on a new belt and 140 and 160 lbs on a used belt.
5    If it is necessary to adjust the belt tension, either to make the belt tighter or looser, it is done by moving the belt-driven accessory on the bracket.
6    For each component there will be an adjustment or strap bolt and a pivot bolt. Both bolts must be loosened slightly to enable you to move the component.
7    After the two bolts have been loosened, move the component away from the engine (to tighten the belt) or toward the engine (to loosen the belt). Hold the accessory in position and check the belt tension. If it is correct, tighten the two bolts until snug, then recheck the tension. If it is all right, tighten the two bolts completely.
8    If it is necessary to use a pry bar to move the accessory while the belt is adjusted, be very careful not to damage the component being moved or the part being pried against.

## 12  Underhood hoses — check and replacement

**Caution:** *Replacement of air-conditioner hoses should be left to a dealer or air-conditioning specialist who can depressurize the system and perform the work safely.*

1    The high temperatures present under the hood can cause deterioration of the numerous rubber and plastic hoses.
2    Periodic inspection should be made for cracks, loose clamps and leaks because some of the hoses are part of the emission control system and can affect the engine's performance.
3    Remove the air cleaner if necessary and trace the entire length of each hose. Squeeze each hose to check for cracks and look for swelling, discoloration and leaks.
4    If the vehicle has considerable mileage or if one or more of the hoses is suspect, it is a good idea to replace all of the hoses at one time.
5    Measure the length and inside diameter of each hose and obtain and cut the replacement to size. Since original equipment hose clamps are often good for only one or two uses, it is a good idea to replace them with screw-type clamps.

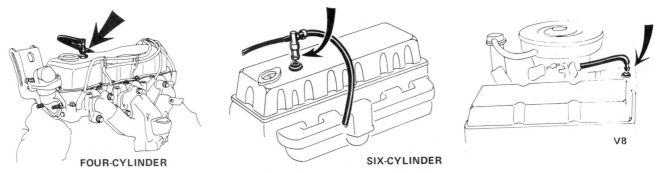

FOUR-CYLINDER                    SIX-CYLINDER                    V8

Fig. 1.12   1971 through 1983 model engine PCV valve locations (Sec 15)

6   Replace each hose one at a time to eliminate the possibility of confusion. Hoses attached to the heater and radiator contain coolant, so newspapers or rags should be kept handy to catch the spills when they are disconnected.

7   After installation, run the engine until it reaches operating temperature, shut it off and check for leaks. After the engine has cooled, retighten all of the screw-type clamps.

## 13   Fuel system check

**Caution:** *There are certain precautions to take when inspecting or servicing the fuel system components. Work in a well-ventilated area and do not allow open flames (cigarettes, appliance pilot lights, etc.) to get near the work area. Mop up spills immediately and do not store fuel-soaked rags where they could ignite.*

1   The fuel system is under a small amount of pressure, so if any fuel lines are disconnected for servicing, be prepared to catch the fuel as it spurts out. Plug all disconnected fuel lines immediately after disconnection to prevent the tank from emptying itself.

2   The fuel system is most easily checked with the vehicle raised on a hoist where the components underneath are readily visible and accessible.

3   If the smell of gasoline is noticed while driving, or after the vehicle has been in the sun, the system should be thoroughly inspected immediately.

4   Remove the gas filler cap and check for damage, corrosion and a proper sealing imprint on the gasket. Replace the cap with a new one if necessary.

5   With the vehicle raised, inspect the gas tank and filler neck for punctures, cracks and other damage. The connection between the filler neck and the tank is especially critical. Sometimes a rubber filler neck will leak due to loose clamps or deteriorated rubber; problems a home mechanic can usually rectify. **Caution:** *Do not, under any circumstances, try to repair a fuel tank youself (except rubber components) unless you have considerable experience. A welding torch or any open flame can easily cause the fuel vapors to explode if the proper precautions are not taken.*

6   Carefully check all rubber hoses and metal lines leading away from the fuel tank. Check for loose connections, deteriorated hoses, crimped lines and other damage. Follow the lines up to the front of the vehicle, carefully inspecting them all the way. Repair or replace damaged sections as necessary.

7   If a fuel odor is still evident after the inspection, refer to Section 36 on the evaporative emissions system.

## 14   Fuel filter replacement

**Caution:** *Gasoline is extremely flammable so extra safety precautions must be observed when working on any part of the fuel system. Do not smoke and do not allow bare light bulbs or open flames near the vehicle. Also, do not perform this maintenance procedure in a garage if a natural gas-type water heater or dryer is located in the garage.*

1   These models use a variety of fuel filters. Earlier model F- and L-head four-cylinder engines use a non-replaceable filter screen located in the fuel pump bowl. The screen and bowl should be removed and

thoroughly cleaned at the recommended intervals. Later models are equipped with replaceable filters located in the fuel line. The 151 cubic inch four-cylinder and the V6 engine have screw-in type filters located at the carburetor.

2   This job should be done with the engine cold (after sitting for at least three hours). The necessary tools are pliers for the in-line filter or open-end wrenches to fit the fuel line nuts of the screw-in type filter. Flare-nut wrenches which wrap around the nut should be used if available. In addition, you will have to obtain a replacement filter (make sure it is correct for your specific vehicle and engine) and some clean rags.

3   Remove the air cleaner assembly. If vacuum hoses must be disconnected, make sure you note their positions and/or tag them to help during installation.

4   Place some rags under the filter to catch any spilled fuel.

### In-line filter

5   Remove the retaining clips or screw-type clamps from the fuel lines and pull the filter free (photo).

6   Install the new filter in the same position as the old one and push the fuel hoses into place, securing them with the clips or clamps. Later models have a breather fitting and hose which is part of the ECS system; it must be at the top.

### Screw-in type filter

7   With the proper size wrench, hold the nut next to the carburetor body. Now loosen the nut fitting and the end of the metal fuel line. A flare-nut wrench on this fitting will prevent slipping and possible damage. However, an open-end wrench should do the job. Make sure the larger nut next to the carburetor is held firmly while the fuel line is disconnected.

8   With the fuel line disconnected, move it to the side slightly for better access to the inlet filter nut. *Do not crimp the fuel line.*

9   Now unscrew the fuel inlet filter nut which was previously held steady. As this fitting is drawn away from the carburetor body, be careful not to lose the thin washer-type gasket or the spring located behind the fuel filter. Also, pay close attention to how the filter was installed.

10   Compare the old filter with the new one to make sure they are of the same length and design.

11   Reinstall the spring in the carburetor body, after inspecting it for damage and defects.

12   Place the new filter into position behind the spring.

13   Install a new washer-type gasket on the fuel inlet filter nut (a new gasket is usually supplied with the new filter) and tighten the nut in the carburetor. Make sure it is not cross-threaded or over-tightened as fuel leaks could result.

14   On all models, reinstall the air cleaner assembly and return all hoses to their original positions. Start the engine and check for fuel leaks.

## 15   Positive Crankcase Ventilation (PCV) valve replacement

1   The PCV valve is located in the rocker arm cover on in-line and V6 engines and in the intake manifold on V8 engines. A hose connected to the valve runs to either the carburetor or intake manifold.

2   When purchasing a replacement PCV valve, make sure it is for your

Fig. 1.13   F- and L-head engine oil bath air cleaner
components — exploded view (Sec 16)

| | | | |
|---|---|---|---|
| 1 | Horn | 7 | Clamp |
| 2 | Flexible connector | 8 | Oil cup |
| 3 | Hose clamp | 9 | Clamp |
| 4 | Carburetor vent tube | 10 | Hose |
| 5 | Body | 11 | Clamp |
| 6 | Screw and lock washer | 12 | Gasket |

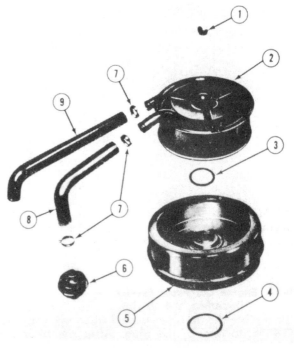

Fig. 1.14   V6 engine oil bath air cleaner
components — exploded view (Sec 16)

| | | | |
|---|---|---|---|
| 1 | Wing nut | 6 | Breather |
| 2 | Cover | 7 | Clamp |
| 3 | Rubber gasket | 8 | Vent tube |
| 4 | Cork gasket | 9 | Air pump hose |
| 5 | Oil cap | | |

particular vehicle, model year and engine size.

3    Pull the valve (with the hose attached) from the rubber grommet in the rocker arm cover or manifold.

4    Loosen the retaining clamp and pull the PCV valve from the end of the hose, noting its installed position and direction.

5    Compare the old valve with the new one to make sure they are the same.

6    Push the new valve into the end of the hose until it is fully seated and reinstall the clamp.

7    Inspect the rubber grommet for damage and replace it with a new one, if faulty.

8    Push the PCV valve and hose securely into position.

9    More information on the PCV system can be found in Chapter 6.

## 16   Oil bath-type air cleaner service

1    Early model F- and L-head and V6 engines are equipped with oil bath-type air cleaners. They must be drained, cleaned and re-filled at the specified intervals.

### F- and L-head engines

2    Remove the retaining bolt and lift the oil cup from the body of the air cleaner assembly.

3    Pour the oil into a suitable container and wash the cup thoroughly with solvent.

4    Detach the breather hose, remove the two wing nut screws and lift the air cleaner assembly from the engine. Wash the assembly thoroughly with solvent, particularly in the area of the filtering element. Dry the assembly with clean, lint-free cloths or compressed air.

5    Reinstall the air cleaner assembly.

6    Fill the oil cup with clean engine oil, using SAE 40 or 50 weight in warm weather and SAE 20 in cold weather. Install the oil cup in the air cleaner assembly.

### V6 engine

7    Remove the wing nut at the top of the carburetor and lift the air cleaner assembly off.

8    Remove the oil cup and pour the old oil into a suitable container.

9    Wash the cup and filter element thoroughly with solvent and dry with compressed air or clean, lint-free cloths. The filter element must be dry after cleaning, with no solvent residue or oil.

10   Check the air cleaner assembly hoses, clamps and connections, replacing defective or damaged parts as necessary.

11   Fill the oil cup with clean oil (SAE 40 or 50 weight in warm weather and SAE 20 in cold weather) and install it in the filter element, making sure the gasket is in position.

12   Attach the air cleaner assembly and gasket to the carburetor, securing it with the wing nut.

## 17   Air filter and PCV filter replacement

1    At the specified intervals, the air filter and PCV filter should be replaced with new ones. A thorough program of preventative maintenance would call for the two filters to be inspected between changes.

2    The air filter is located inside the air cleaner housing on the top of the engine. The filter is generally replaced by removing the wing nut at the top of the air cleaner assembly and lifting off the top plate. If vacuum hoses are connected to the plate, note their positions and disconnect them.

3    While the top plate is off, be careful not to drop anything down into the carburetor.

4    Lift the air filter element out of the housing (photo).

5    To check the filter, hold it up to strong sunlight, or place a flashlight or droplight on the inside of the filter. On filters with a foam cover, first remove the cover. If you can see light coming through the paper element, the filter is all right. Check all the way around the filter.

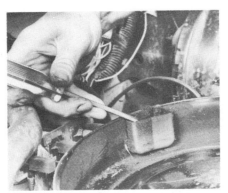

17.4 Lifting the air filter element from the housing

17.11 Using a screwdriver to remove the PCV filter element (later model in-line six-cylinder engine shown)

19.3 Typical carburetor choke plate location (arrow)

**FOUR- and SIX-CYLINDER**

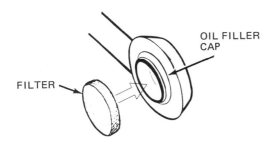

OIL FILLER CAP

FILTER

**OIL FILLER CAP FILTER (V8)**

**Fig. 1.15 Typical PCV air filter installation (Sec 17)**

6 Wipe out the inside of the air cleaner housing with a clean rag.
7 On new filter elements with removable foam covers, remove the cover, soak it in clean engine oil, wring it out and install it on the element. If the element is being reused, first wash the cover thoroughly in solvent and squeeze it dry.
8 Place the old filter (if in good condition) or the new filter (if the specified interval has elapsed) back into the air cleaner housing. Make sure it seats properly in the bottom of the housing.
9 Connect any disconnected vacuum hoses to the top plate and reinstall the plate.
10 On later models, the PCV filter is located inside the air cleaner housing or in the oil filler cap. Remove the top plate as described previously and locate the filter on the side of the housing or remove the filler cap.
11 Remove the filter element from the retainer or filler cap (photo).
12 Wash the filter element thoroughly with kerosene or solvent and reinstall it. On some filler caps, the element is not removable and the assembly should be cleaned by blowing compressed air through the filler tube opening (in the reverse direction of normal air flow) in the cap. If the element is badly clogged or contaminated, replace the complete cap assembly with a new one.

## 18 Thermo-controlled Air Cleaner (TAC) check

1 Later models are equipped with a thermostatically controlled air cleaner which draws air to the carburetor from different locations depending upon engine temperature.
2 This is a simple visual check; however, if access is tight, a small mirror may have to be used.
3 Open the hood and locate the baffle inside the air cleaner assembly. It will be located inside the long snorkel of the metal air cleaner housing. Make sure that the flexible air hose(s) are securely attached and undamaged.
4 If there is a flexible air duct attached to the end of the snorkel leading to an area behind the grille, disconnect it at the snorkel. This will enable you to look through the end of the snorkel and see the baffle inside.
5 The check should be done when the engine and outside air are cold. Start the engine and look through the snorkel at the baffle, which should move to a closed position. With the baffle closed, air cannot enter through the end of the snorkel, but instead enters the air cleaner through the flexible duct attached to the exhaust manifold.
6 As the engine warms up to operating temperature, the baffle should open to allow air through the snorkel end. Depending on ambient temperature, this may take 10 to 15 minutes. To speed up this check you can reconnect the snorkel air duct, drive the vehicle and then check to see if the baffle is completely open.
7 If the thermo-controlled air cleaner is not operating properly, see Chapter 6 for more information.

## 19 Carburetor choke check (late models only)

1 The choke only operates when the engine is cold, so this check should be performed before the vehicle has been started for the day.
2 Open the hood and remove the top plate of the air cleaner assembly. It is usually held in place by a wing nut at the center. If any vacuum hoses must be disconnected, make sure you tag them to ensure reinstallation in their original positions. Place the top plate and wing nut aside, out of the way of moving engine components.
3 Look at the top of the carburetor at the center of the air cleaner housing. You will notice a flat plate at the carburetor opening (photo).
4 Have an assistant press the accelerator pedal to the floor. The plate should close completely. Start the engine while you observe the plate at the carburetor. **Caution:** *Do not position your face directly over the carburetor, as the engine could backfire, causing serious burns.* When the engine starts, the choke plate should open slightly.
5 Allow the engine to continue running at an idle speed. As the engine warms up to operating temperature, the plate should slowly open, allowing more air to enter through the top of the carburetor.
6 After a few minutes, the choke plate should be fully open to the vertical position.
7 You will notice that the engine speed corresponds with the plate opening. With the plate completely closed, the engine should run at a fast idle speed. As the plate opens, the engine speed will decrease.

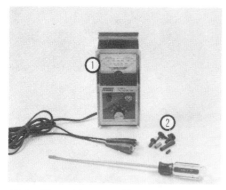

21.2   The tachometer (1), screwdriver and assorted vacuum hose plugs (2) used when adjusting the engine idle speed

21.4   Typical idle speed adjustment screw locations (arrows)

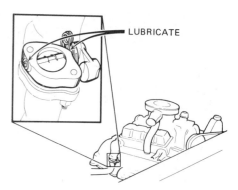

Fig. 1.16   Typical heat valve location and lubrication points (Sec 22)

8   If a fault is detected during the above checks, refer to Chapter 4 for specific information related to adjusting and servicing the choke components.

## 20   Carburetor mounting torque check

1   The carburetor is attached to the top of the intake manifold by two or four nuts. These fasteners can sometimes work loose from vibration and temperature changes during normal engine operation and cause a vacuum leak.
2   To properly tighten the carburetor mounting nuts, a torque wrench is necessary. If you do not own one, they can usually be rented on a daily basis.
3   Remove the air cleaner assembly, tagging each hose to be disconnected with a piece of numbered tape to make reassembly easier.
4   Locate the mounting nuts at the base of the carburetor. Decide what special tools or adapters will be necessary, if any, to tighten the nuts with a properly sized socket and the torque wrench.
5   Tighten the nuts to a torque of about 12 ft-lbs. Do not overtighten the nuts, as the threads may strip.
6   If you suspect that a vacuum leak exists at the bottom of the carburetor, obtain a length of hose about the diameter of fuel hose. Start the engine and place one end of the hose next to your ear as you probe around the base of the carburetor with the other end. You will hear a hissing sound if a leak exists.
7   If, after the nuts are properly tightened, a vacuum leak still exists, the carburetor must be removed and a new gasket installed. See Chapter 4 for more information.
8   After tightening the nuts, reinstall the air cleaner and return all hoses to their original positions.

## 21   Engine idle speed adjustment

1   Engine idle speed is the speed at which the engine operates when no accelerator pedal pressure is applied. This speed is critical to the performance of the engine itself, as well as many engine sub-systems.
2   A hand-held tachometer (photo) must be used when adjusting the idle speed to get an accurate reading. The exact hook-up for these meters varies with the manufacturer, so follow the particular directions included.
3   Since these models were equipped with many different carburetors in the time period covered by this manual, and each has its own peculiarities when setting idle speed, it would be impractical to cover all types in this Section. Chapter 4 contains information on each individual carburetor used. The carburetor used on your particular engine can be found in the Specifications Section of Chapter 4. However, all vehicles covered in this manual should have a tune-up decal or Emission Control Information label in the engine compartment, usually placed near the top of the radiator. The printed instructions for setting idle speed can be found on this decal or label, and should be followed since they are for your particular engine.

4   Basically, for most applications, the idle speed is set by turning an adjustment screw located at the side of the carburetor (photo). Turning the screw changes the position of the throttle valve in the carburetor. This screw may be on the linkage itself or may be part of the idle stop solenoid. Refer to the tune-up decal or Chapter 4.
5   Once you have located the idle speed screw, experiment with different length screwdrivers until the adjustments can easily be made without coming into contact with hot or moving engine components.
6   Follow the instructions on the tune-up decal or Emission Control Information label, which may include disconnecting certain vacuum or electrical connections. To plug a vacuum hose after disconnecting it, insert a properly sized metal rod into the opening or thoroughly wrap the open end with tape to prevent any vacuum loss through the hose.
7   If the air cleaner is removed, the vacuum hose to the snorkel should be plugged.
8   Make sure the parking brake is firmly set and the wheels blocked to prevent the vehicle from rolling. This is especially true if the transmission is to be in Drive. An assistant inside the vehicle pushing on the brake pedal is the safest method.
9   For all applications, the engine must be completely warmed-up to operating temperature, which will automatically render the choke fast idle inoperative.
10   Turn the idle speed screw in or out, as required, until the idle speed listed in the Specifications is obtained.

## 22   Exhaust heat valve check

1   The exhaust heat valve is located at the junction of the exhaust pipe and manifold. It can be identified by an external weight and spring.
2   With the engine and exhaust pipe cold, try moving the weight by hand. It should move freely. Lubricate the valve with graphite at the time of inspection and at the specified intervals.
3   With the engine cold, start it and observe the heat valve. Upon starting, the weight should move to the closed position. As the engine warms to normal operating temperature, the weight should move the valve to the open position, allowing a free flow of exhaust gas through the tailpipe. Since it could take several minutes for the system to heat up, you could mark the position of the weight when cold, drive the vehicle and then recheck the position of the weight.

## 23   Exhaust Gas Recirculation (EGR) valve check

1   The EGR valve is located on a spacer plate located below the carburetor on four-cylinder engines, on the side of the intake manifold on six-cylinder engines and on a machined surface at the rear of the intake manifold on V8 engines. Most of the time when a fault develops in this emissions system, it is due to a stuck or corroded EGR valve.
2   With the engine cold to prevent burns, reach under the EGR valve and manually push on the diaphragm. Using moderate pressure, you should be able to move the diaphragm up and down within the housing.
3   If the diaphragm does not move or moves only with much effort,

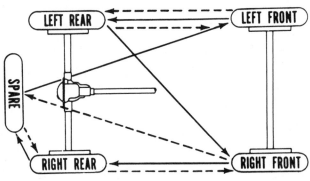

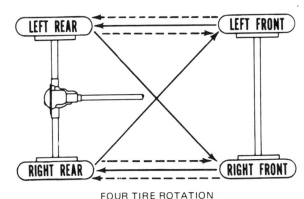

FIVE TIRE ROTATION

FOUR TIRE ROTATION
- - - - - RADIAL TIRE ROTATION
————— - BIAS/BIAS BELTED TIRE ROTATION

**Fig. 1.17  Tire rotation diagram (Sec 25)**

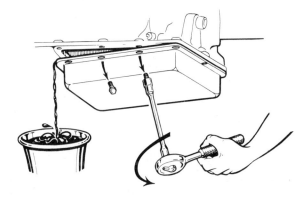

**Fig. 1.18  Automatic transmission oil pan removal (Sec 27)**

replace the EGR valve with a new one. If you are in doubt about the condition of the valve, go to your local parts store and compare the free movement of your EGR valve with a new valve.
4    Further testing of the EGR system and component replacement procedures can be found in Chapter 6.

## 24   Clutch pedal free play check

1    Proper clutch pedal free play is very important for proper clutch operation and to ensure normal clutch service life.
2    Clutch pedal free play is the distance the clutch pedal moves before

the mechanical linkage actually begins to disengage the clutch disc from the flywheel and pressure plate.
3    To check the free play, slowly depress the clutch pedal until the resistance offered by the clutch release mechanism is felt (the pedal will suddenly become much more difficult to move).
4    Measure the distance the clutch pedal has travelled and compare it to the Specifications. If adjustment is required, refer to Chapter 8 for the step-by-step procedure to follow.

## 25   Tire rotation

1    The tires should be rotated at the specified intervals and whenever uneven wear is noticed. Since the vehicle will be raised and the tires removed anyway, this is a good time to check the brakes (Sec 31) and/or repack the wheel bearings (Chapter 11). Read over these Sections before beginning.
2    The location for each tire in the rotation sequence depends on the type of tire used on your vehicle. Tire type can be determined by reading the raised printing on the sidewall of the tire. The accompanying illustration shows the rotation sequence for each type of tire.
3    See the information in *Jacking and towing* at the front of this manual for the proper procedures to follow when raising the vehicle and changing a tire; however, if the brakes are to be checked, do not apply the parking brake as stated. Make sure the tires are blocked to prevent the vehicle from rolling.
4    Preferably, the entire vehicle should be raised at the same time. This can be done on a hoist or by jacking up each corner and then lowering the vehicle onto jackstands placed under the frame rails. Always use four jackstands and make sure the vehicle is firmly supported all around.
5    After rotation, check and adjust the tire pressures as necessary and be sure to check wheel lug nut tightness.

## 26   Wheel bearing check

1    In most cases, the front wheel bearings will not need servicing until the brake pads are changed. However, these bearings should be checked whenever the front wheels are raised for any reason. Also, it is very important to adjust and lubricate the bearings at the specified intervals (Chapter 11).
2    With the vehicle securely supported on jackstands and the transfer case in Neutral with the hubs unlocked, spin the wheel and check for noise, rolling resistance and free play. Now grasp the top of the tire with one hand and the bottom of the tire with the other. Move the tire in-and-out on the spindle. If it moves more than 0.005-inch, the bearings should be adjusted as described in Chapter 11. The bearings should be packed with grease at the specified intervals.

## 27   Automatic transmission fluid change

1    At the specified time intervals, the transmission fluid should be changed and the filter replaced with a new one. Since there is no drain plug, the transmission oil pan must be removed from the bottom of the transmission to drain the fluid.
2    Before draining, purchase the specified transmission fluid (see *Recommended lubricants and fluids*) and a new filter. The necessary gaskets should be included with the filter; if not, purchase an oil pan gasket and an O-ring seal.
3    Other tools necessary for this job include:

*Jackstands to support the vehicle in a raised position*
*A wrench to remove the oil pan bolts*
*A drain pan capable of holding at least six quarts*
*Newspapers and clean rags*

4    The fluid should be drained immediately after the vehicle has been driven. This will remove any built-up sediment better then if the fluid were cold. Because of this, it may be wise to wear protective gloves (fluid temperature can exceed 350° F in a hot transmission).
5    After the vehicle has been driven to warm up the fluid, raise and place it on jackstands for access underneath. Make sure the vehicle is firmly supported by the four stands placed under the frame rails.

1

6    Move the necessary equipment under the vehicle, being careful not to touch any of the hot exhaust components.
7    Place the drain pan under the transmission oil pan and remove the oil pan bolts along the rear and sides of the pan. *Loosen, but do not remove, the bolts at the front of the pan.*
8    Carefully pry the oil pan down at the rear, allowing the hot fluid to drain into the pan. If necessary, use a screwdriver to break the gasket seat at the rear of the pan; however, do not damage the pan or transmission gasket surfaces in the process.
9    Support the pan and remove the remaining bolts at the front. Lower the pan and drain the remaining fluid into the container. As this is done, check the fluid for metal particles, which may be an indication of internal transmission failure.
10    Now visible on the bottom of the transmission is the filter/strainer held in place by three screws.
11    Remove the three screws, the filter and the O-ring seal from the pick-up pipe.
12    Thoroughly clean the transmission oil pan with solvent. Inspect it for metal particles and foreign matter. Dry it with compressed air (if available).
13    Clean the filter mounting surface on the valve body. This surface should be smooth and free of damage and nicks.
14    Place the new O-ring in position on the pick-up pipe and install the strainer and pipe assembly.
15    Place the new gasket in position and retain it with petroleum jelly.
16    Lift the pan up to the bottom of the transmission and install the mounting bolts. Tighten the bolts in a diagonal fashion, working around the pan.
17    Lower the vehicle.
18    Open the hood and remove the transmission fluid dipstick from the guide tube.
19    Since fluid capacities vary between the various transmission types, it is best to add a little fluid at a time, continually checking the level with the dipstick. Allow the fluid time to drain into the pan. Add fluid until the level just registers on the end of the dipstick. In most cases, a good starting point will be four (4) quarts added to the transmission through the filler tube (use a funnel to prevent spills).
20    With the selector lever in Park, apply the parking brake and start the engine without depressing the accelerator pedal (if possible). Allow the engine to run at a slow idle for a few minutes.
21    With the brake pedal depressed and the parking brake applied, shift the transmission through all gear positions and then place it in Park.
22    Check the fluid level on the dipstick, adding as necessary to bring the level up to the Full mark. Do not allow the fluid level to go above this point, as the transmission would then be overfull, necessitating the removal of the oil pan to drain out the excess fluid.
23    Look under the vehicle for leaks around the oil pan mating surface.
24    Push the dipstick firmly back into the tube and drive the vehicle to reach normal operating temperature (15 miles of highway driving or its equivalent in the city). Park the vehicle on a level surface and check the fluid level on the dipstick with the engine idling and the transmission in Park. The level should now be at the Full mark on the dipstick. If not, add more fluid as necessary to bring the level up to this point. Again, do not overfill.

## 28   Manual transmission lubricant change

1    The manual transmission lubricant should be drained and replaced at the specified intervals. Drive the vehicle to bring the transmission lubricant to operating temperature.
2    Raise the vehicle and support it securely. Before beginning this job, you will need:

*A wrench to remove the transmission plug*
*A drain pan of at least six-quart capacity*
*An adequate supply of the specified lubricant*
*Jackstands to support the vehicle in a raised position*
*Newspapers and clean rags*

3    Place the drain pan under the drain plug and remove the fill plug.
4    Remove the drain plug (photo) and allow the transmission lubricant to drain into the pan. Inspect the lubricant for signs of contamination and metal particles, which could indicate a malfunction in the transmission.
5    Install the fill plug and fill the transmission with the specified lubricant (see *Recommended lubricants and fluids*) to the bottom of the fill plug hole. Install the fill plug and tighten it securely.
6    Lower the vehicle, drive it and check for leaks.

## 29   Transfer case lubricant change

1    The transfer case lubricant should be drained and replaced at the same time as the manual transmission (Sec 28).
2    Follow the procedures in Steps 2 and 3 of Section 28.
3    Remove the drain plug and allow the lubricant to run into the pan (photo). On Quadra-Trac models equipped with reduction units, loosen the five retaining bolts and pull the unit forward sufficiently to permit draining.
4    Inspect the lubricant for clues as to the condition of the transfer

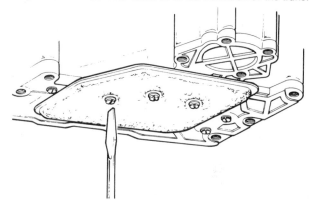

Fig. 1.19   Removing the automatic transmission fluid filter (Sec 27)

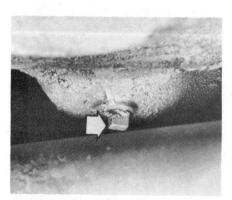

28.4   Typical transmission drain plug location (arrow)

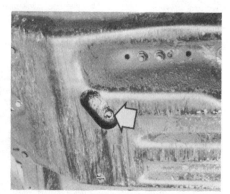

29.3   On later models, the transfer case drain plug (arrow) is accessible through an opening in the skid plate

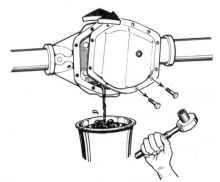

Fig. 1.20   Removing the differential cover to drain the lubricant (Sec 30)

case, such as metal particles, water and other contamination.
5   Install the drain plug. Push the Quadra-Trac reduction unit back into position and tighten the retaining bolts.
6   Fill the transfer case to just below the filler hole with the specified lubricant and install the plug. Tighten it securely.
7   Lower the vehicle, test drive it and check for leaks.

## 30  Differential lubricant change

1   Some differentials can be drained by removing a drain plug, while on others it is necessary to remove the cover plate on the differential housing. Because of this, be sure to buy a new gasket at the same time the gear lubricant is purchased.
2   Move a drain pan (at least five-pint capacity), rags, newspapers and wrenches under the vehicle.
3   On drain plug-equipped differentials, remove the fill plug, followed by the drain plug, and allow the lubricant to drain into the pan. When it is completely drained, replace the drain plug and refill the differential with the specified lubricant to the base of the fill plug hole. Install the fill plug and tighten it securely.
4   On differentials without drain plugs, remove the bolts on the lower half of the differential cover plate. Use the upper bolts to keep the cover loosely attached to the differential. Allow the lubricant to drain into

the drain pan, then completely remove the cover.
5   Using a lint-free rag, clean the inside of the cover and accessible areas of the differential housing. As this is done, check for chipped gears and metal particles in the lubricant, indicating the differential should be more thoroughly inspected and/or repaired (see Chapter 8 for more information.)
6   Thoroughly clean the gasket mating surface on the cover and the differential housing. Use a gasket scraper or putty knife to remove all traces of the old gasket.
7   Apply a thin film of RTV-type gasket sealant to the cover flange and then press a new gasket into position on the cover. Make sure the bolt holes align properly.
8   Place the cover on the differential housing and install the bolts. Tighten the bolts a little at a time, working across the cover in a diagonal fashion until all bolts are tight.
9   Remove the fill plug on the side of the differential housing or cover and fill the housing with the proper lubricant until the level is at the bottom of the plug hole.
10  Securely install the plug.

## 31  Brake check

1   The brakes should be inspected every time the wheels are removed or whenever a problem is suspected. Indications of a potential brake system fault are: the vehicle pulls to one side when the brake pedal is depressed, noises coming from the brakes when they are applied, excessive brake pedal travel, pulsating pedal and leakage of fluid (which is usually seen on the inside of the tire or wheel).

### Disc brakes
2   Disc brakes can be visually checked without removing any parts except the wheels.
3   Raise the vehicle and place it securely on jackstands. Remove the front wheels (See *Jacking and towing* at the front of this manual, if necessary).
4   Now visible is the disc brake caliper, which contains the pads. There is an outer brake pad and an inner pad. Both should be inspected.
5   Most later model vehicles come equipped with a wear sensor attached to the inner pad. This is a small, bent piece of metal which is visible from the inboard side of the brake caliper. When the pads wear to a danger limit, the metal sensor rubs against the disc and makes a screeching sound.
6   Inspect the pad thickness by looking at each end of the caliper and through the inspection hole in the caliper body (photo). If the wear

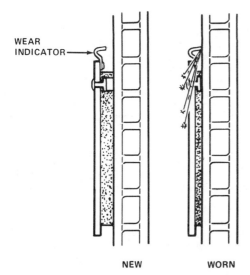

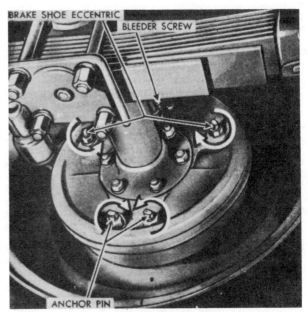

Fig. 1.21  Disc brake wear indicators (Sec 31)

NEW          WORN

31.6   The brake pad lining (arrow) can be seen through the inspection hole in the caliper

Fig. 1.22   Early model CJ 2A and 3A brake adjustment points (Sec 31)

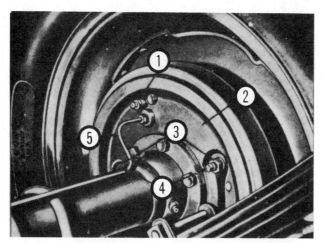

**Fig. 1.23  Early model CJ 3B, CJ 5 and CJ 6 brake
adjustment components (Sec 31)**

1  *Bleeder screw*                    4  *Eccentric adjusting*
2  *Brake backing plate*                 *screw*
3  *Eccentric locknut*                5  *Brake line*

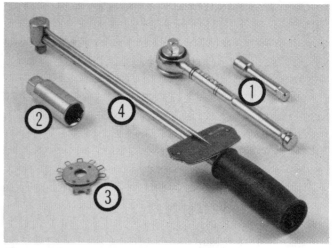

32.2  Tools required for spark plug replacement

1  *Ratchet/extension*       3  *Spark plug gap tool*
2  *Spark plug socket*       4  *Torque wrench*

sensor clip is very close to the rotor, or if the lining material is 1/8-inch or less in thickness, the pads should be replaced. Keep in mind that the lining material is riveted or bonded to a metal backing shoe and the metal portion is not included in this measurement. If the lining material is worn to a point where it is thinner than the backing plate, new pads are required.

7    It will be difficult, if not impossible, to measure the exact thickness of the remaining lining material. If you are in doubt as to the pad quality, remove the pads for further inspection or replacement. See Chapter 9 for disc brake pad replacement.

8    Before installing the wheels, check for leakage and damage to the brake hose (cracking, splitting, etc.) around the brake hose connections. Replace the hoses or fittings as necessary, referring to Chapter 9.

9    Also check the disc for scoring, gouging or burnt spots. If these conditions exist, the hub/rotor assembly should be removed for servicing (Chapter 9).

### Drum brakes

**Inspection**

10   Raise the vehicle and support it securely on jackstands.
11   Remove the wheels, referring to *Jacking and towing* at the front of this manual, if necessary.
12   Remove the hub and brake drum as described in Chapter 9.
13   With the drum removed, carefully brush away any accumulations of dirt and dust. **Caution:** *Do not blow the dust out with compressed air. Make an effort not to inhale the dust because it contains asbestos and is harmful to your health.*
14   Observe the thickness of the lining material on both the front and rear brake shoes. Measure the amount of remaining lining and compare this to the Specifications. If the linings look worn, but you are unable to determine their exact thickness, compare them with a new set at an auto parts store. The shoes should also be replaced if they are cracked, glazed (shiny surface) or contaminated with brake fluid.
15   Make sure that all the brake assembly springs are connected and in good condition.
16   Inspect the brake components for signs of fluid leakage. With your finger, carefully pry back the rubber cups on the wheel cylinder located at the top of the brake shoes. Any leakage is an indication that the wheel cylinders should be overhauled immediately (Chapter 9). Also check the hoses and connections for signs of leakage.
17   Wipe the inside of the drum with a clean rag and denatured alcohol or brake system cleaner. Again, be careful not to breathe the dangerous asbestos dust.
18   Check the inside of the drum for cracks, scoring, deep scratches and hard spots (which will appear as small discolorations).
19   If all parts are found in good condition after the inspection process, reinstall the brake drum (Chapter 9). Adjust the brakes (see below) and lower the vehicle to the ground.

**Brake adjustment**

20   On models without self-adjusting brakes, the brakes must be adjusted periodically to compensate for wear. With the vehicle raised and supported securely, locate the adjusting screws.
21   On early models, loosen the brake shoe adjusting eccentric locknuts. Rotate the wheel while turning the forward brake shoe eccentric toward the front of the vehicle until the shoe contacts the drum. Continue rotating the wheel while backing off the eccentric until the wheel rotates freely. Tighten the locknut and repeat the procedure for the rear shoe, turning the eccentric toward the rear of the vehicle.
22   Further adjustment can be made on some early models by turning the eccentric anchor pins toward each other until the shoe-to-drum clearance is approximately 0.005-inch at the lower end and 0.008-inch at the upper end of the brake shoe lining. This can be checked with a feeler gauge inserted through a slot in the brake drum on early models.

### *Parking brake*

23   The easiest way to check the operation of the parking brake is to park the vehicle on a steep hill, with the parking brake set and the transmission in Neutral. If the parking brake cannot prevent the vehicle from rolling, it should be adjusted (see Chapter 9).

### 32   Spark plug replacement

1    The spark plugs are located on each side of the engine on a V8 or V6 and may or may not be easily accessible for removal. In-line engines generally have fewer spark plug accessibility problems. If the vehicle is equipped with air conditioning or power steering, some of the plugs may be difficult to remove (in which case special extension or swivel tools will be necessary). Make a survey under the hood to determine if special tools will be needed.
2    In most cases the tools necessary for a spark plug replacement job include a plug wrench or spark plug socket which fits onto a ratchet wrench (this special socket will be insulated inside to protect the procelain insulator) and a wire-type feeler gauge to check and adjust the spark plug gap (photo). If the vehicle is equipped with HEI or BID (electronic) ignition, a special spark plug wire removal tool is available for separating the wire boot from the spark plug.
3    The best procedure to follow when replacing the spark plugs is to purchase the new spark plugs beforehand, adjust them to the proper gap and then replace each plug one at a time. When buying the new spark plugs it is important to obtain the correct plugs for your specific engine. This information can be found in the Specifications Section but should be checked against the information found on the tune-up decal or Emission Control Information label located under the hood or in the factory owner's manual. If differences exist between these sources, purchase the spark plug type specified on the tune-up

Fig. 1.24  Typical contact breaker point components (Sec 34)

1  Point mounting screw
2  Condenser lead wire
3  Primary lead wire
4  Condenser
5  Point cam
6  Point rubbing block
7  Adjustment slot

decal or emission label as it was printed for your specific engine.

4   With the new spark plugs on hand, allow the engine to cool thoroughly before attempting removal. During this time, each of the new spark plugs can be inspected for defects and the gap can be checked/adjusted.

5   The gap is checked by inserting the proper thickness gauge between the electrodes at the tip of the plug. The gap between these electrodes should be the same as that given in the Specifications or on the tune-up decal/emissions label. The wire should just touch each of the electrodes. If the gap is incorrect, use the notched adjuster on the feeler gauge body to bend the curved side electrode slightly until the proper gap is obtained. Also at this time check for cracks in the spark plug body, indicating the spark plug should not be used. If the side electrode is not exactly over the center one, use the notched adjuster to align them.

6   Cover the fenders of the vehicle to prevent damage to the exterior paint.

7   With the engine cool, remove the spark plug wire from one spark plug. Do this by grabbing the boot at the end of the wire, not the wire itself. Sometimes it is necessary to use a twisting motion while the boot and plug wire are pulled free. Use of a plug wire removal tool is recommended.

8   If compressed air is available, use it to blow any dirt or foreign material away from the spark plug area. A common bicycle pump will also work. The idea here is to eliminate the possibility of material falling into the engine cylinder as the spark plug is removed.

9   Now place the spark plug wrench or socket over the plug and remove it from the engine by turning in a *counterclockwise* direction.

10   Compare the spark plug with those shown in the accompanying color photos to get an indication of the overall running condition of the engine.

11   Carefully insert one of the new plugs into the spark plug hole and tighten it as much as possible by hand. The spark plug should screw easily into the engine. If it doesn't, change the angle of the spark plug slightly, as chances are the threads are not matched (cross-threaded).

12   Finally, tighten the spark plug with the wrench or socket. It is a good idea to use a torque wrench for this to ensure that the plug is seated correctly. The correct torque figure is given in the Specifications.

13   Before pushing the spark plug wire onto the end of the plug, inspect it following the procedures outlined in Section 33.

14   Attach the plug wire to the new spark plug, again using a twisting motion on the boot until it is firmly seated. Make sure the wire is routed away from the exhaust manifold.

15   Repeat the procedure for the remaining spark plugs, replacing them one at a time to prevent mixing up the plug wires.

34.1   Although it is possible to clean contact points that are pitted, burned and corroded (as shown here), they *should* be replaced instead

## 33   Spark plug wires, distributor cap and rotor — check and replacement

1   The spark plug wires should be checked at the recommended intervals and whenever new spark plugs are installed in the engine.

2   The wires should be inspected one at a time to prevent mixing up the order, which is essential for proper engine operation.

3   Disconnect the plug wire from the spark plug. A removal tool can be used for this purpose or you can grab the rubber boot, twist slightly and pull the wire free. *Do not pull on the wire itself, only on the rubber boot.*

4   Inspect inside the boot for corrosion, which will look like a white crusty powder. Push the wire and boot back onto the end of the spark plug. It should be a tight fit on the plug end. If it is not, remove the wire and use pliers to carefully crimp the metal connector inside the wire boot until it fits securely on the end of the spark plug.

5   Using a clean rag, wipe the entire length of the wire to remove any built-up dirt and grease. Once the wire is clean, check for burns, cracks and other damage. Do not bend the wire, since the conductor might break.

6   Disconnect the wire from the distributor. Again, pull only on the rubber boot. Check for corrosion and a tight fit in the same manner as the spark plug end. Replace the wire in the distributor.

7   Check the remaining spark plug wires, making sure they are securely fastened at the distributor and spark plug when the check is complete.

8   If new spark plug wires are required, purchase a set for your specific engine model. Wire sets are available pre-cut, with the rubber boots already installed. Remove and replace the wires one at a time to avoid mix-ups in the firing order.

9   Check the distributor cap and rotor for wear. Look for cracks, carbon tracks and worn, burned or loose contacts. Replace the cap and rotor with new parts if defects are found. It is common practice to install a new cap and rotor whenever new spark plug wires are installed. When installing a new cap, remove the wires from the old cap one at a time and attach them to the new cap in the exact same location — do not simultaneously remove all the wires from the old cap or firing order mix-ups may occur.

## 34   Contact points and condenser — replacement and adjustment (1953 through 1974 models)

1   Although the contact points can be cleaned and dressed with a fine-cut file, it is recommended that the home mechanic replace them with new ones instead (photo).

2   The contact point set and condenser should be replaced as a set. Point alignment and spring tension are factory set and should not require further adjustment (if they do, bend the *stationary* contact only).

3   Whenever contact point replacement is done, it is a good idea to

use magnetized tools to prevent screws or nuts from falling down into the distributor (which would require distributor disassembly to retrieve them).

### Contact point removal and installation

4   Remove the distributor cap (Chapter 5).
5   Position the cap (with the spark plug wires still attached) out of the way. Use a length of wire or string to restrain it if necessary.
6   Remove the rotor, which is now visible at the top of the distributor

shaft. On some models the rotor is held in position with screws (photo), while on others it is a push fit on the shaft and can be pulled off. Place the rotor in a safe place where it cannot be damaged.
7   Disconnect the primary and condenser wire leads at the contact point set. The wires may be attached with a small nut (which should be loosened, but not removed), a small screw or a quick-disconnect fitting (photos).
8   Remove the screw(s) which secure the contact point set to the breaker plate (photo). *Do not completely remove the screws securing*

34.6   Some rotors are attached with screws, which must be removed before the rotor can be separated from the distributor shaft

34.7A   On some models, the primary and condenser wires are attached to the points by a small nut or screw, which must be loosened to detach the wires

34.7B   On other models, the wires can simply be pulled off the points (pliers may be required — pull only on the terminals, not the wires)

34.8   Removing the point-mounting screw (on models with slotted mounting holes, the screw(s) should be loosened only)

34.15   Before adjusting the point gap, the rubbing block must be resting on one of the cam lobes (which should open the points)

34.16A   On some models, the point gap is adjusted by inserting a screwdriver into the slot and twisting it to move the stationary point (you should feel a very slight drag on the gauge as it is withdrawn from between the point contacts)

34.16B   Some models have an adjusting screw which must be turned with an Allen wrench to change the point gap (you should feel a very slight drag on the gauge as it is withdrawn from between the point contacts)

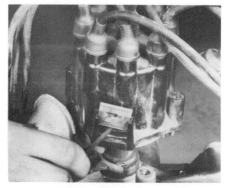

34.29   On some models, the dwell can be adjusted with the engine running by opening the window in the distributor cap and turning the point-adjusting screw with an Allen wrench

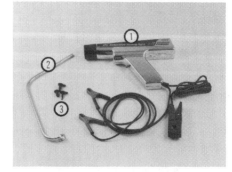

35.5   The timing light (1), special curved distributor bolt wrench (2) and vacuum hose plugs (3) used for ignition timing adjustment

point sets that have slots at these locations. Separate the point set from the breaker plate.

9   The condenser can now be removed from the distributor. Loosen the mounting strap screw and slide the condenser out of the bracket, or completely remove the condenser and strap, depending on the particular mounting arrangement.

10   Before installing the new points and condenser, remove all old lubricant, dirt, etc. from the breaker plate and the point cam surface of the distributor shaft.

11   Lubricate the point cam with the special grease supplied with the new points or commercially available point cam lube (do not use multipurpose grease). Some models have a cam lubricator wick mounted on the breaker plate. The wick can be rotated to provide lubrication if it is still in good condition, but if in doubt, replace the wick with a new one to provide adequate lubrication of the cam surface. It is removed by squeezing together the base of the retainer with long-nosed pliers and then lifting the unit out of the breaker plate. It is important that the cam lubricator wick be adjusted so the end of the wick just touches the cam lobes. Note: On early L- and F-head four-cylinder engines, place one drop of engine oil on the lubricator wick at the top of the distributor shaft and four or five drops in the oiler located on the side of the housing.

12   Place the new condenser in position and tighten the mounting screw.

13   Attach the new contact point set to the breaker plate and tighter the mounting screw(s) until just snug.

14   Connect the primary and condenser wire leads to the new point assembly. Make sure the condenser lead is positioned the same way it was before removal.

15   Although the gap between the contact points will be set when the dwell angle is adjusted, it is a good idea to adjust the initial gap to start the engine. With the points in position and the mounting screw(s) snug, but not completely tight, make sure that the point rubbing block is resting on one of the lobes of the cam (photo). To move the cam, turn the crankshaft by placing a wrench over the large bolt at the front of the crankshaft.

16   With the rubbing block on a cam lobe (points fully open), place a blade-type feeler gauge between the contacts. The gap should be as specified. On some models, the gap can be changed with a screwdriver. Insert the screwdriver into the adjustment slot and twist it slightly to move the stationary point (photo). On other models, the gap is changed by turning the adjusting screw with an Allen wrench (photo). When the gap is correct, tighten the mounting screw(s) securely.

17   Before installing the rotor, inspect it for cracks and damage. Carefully check the condition of the metal contact at the top of the rotor. If in doubt as to its condition, replace it with a new one.

18   Install the rotor. It is keyed to fit on the shaft only one way. Make sure it is completely seated.

19   Before installing the distributor cap, inspect it for cracks and damage. Closely examine the contacts on the inside of the cap for excessive corrosion. If in doubt as to the quality of the cap, replace it with a new one.

20   Install the distributor cap.

21   Start the engine and check the dwell angle and the ignition timing.

### Dwell angle adjustment

22   Whenever new contact points are installed or the original points are cleaned, the dwell angle must be checked and adjusted.

23   Setting the dwell angle is actually quite easy; however, a dwell meter must be used for precise adjustment. Combination tach/dwell meters are common tune-up instruments which can be purchased at a reasonable cost.

24   Connect the dwell meter according to the manufacturer's instructions. Usually, one lead is attached to the primary wire at the distributor and the other lead is attached to a good ground on the engine. Make sure the engine selector switch on the meter is in the correct position.

25   Start the engine and allow it to idle until it has reached normal operating temperature. The engine must be warm to achieve an accurate reading.

26   Note the dwell meter reading. If it is within the specified range, shut off the engine and disconnect the meter. If it is not within the specified range, shut off the engine and remove the distributor cap and rotor. Some models have a distributor cap equipped with a metal 'window' which can be raised (and held up with tape, if necessary) for dwell adjustment, instead of having to remove the distributor cap.

27   On non window-type distributors, loosen the breaker point mounting screw slightly, then move the stationary point (Step 16) to change the point gap (dwell). Increasing the point gap will decrease the dwell reading, while decreasing the point gap will increase the dwell reading. Tighten the point mounting screw, install the rotor and distributor cap and recheck the dwell.

28   Repeat the procedure until the dwell reading is within the specified range (see Step 34).

29   On window-type distributors, insert a proper size Allen wrench through the window and into the adjusting screw socket (photo).

30   Start the engine and turn the adjusting screw as required to obtain the specified dwell reading on the meter. Remove your hand and recheck the reading.

31   Remove the Allen wrench and close the window. Shut off the engine and disconnect the dwell meter.

32   If you cannot obtain a dwell meter, you can get an approximate dwell setting on window-type distributors without one by using the following method.

33   With the engine at normal operating temperature, raise the window and insert the Allen wrench. Start the engine and turn the wrench clockwise until the engine starts to misfire. Then turn the screw one-half turn counterclockwise. Remove the Allen wrench and close the window. Have the dwell angle checked and/or adjusted with a meter as soon as possible.

34   Note: On all models, try to obtain a dwell setting that is toward the lower end of the specified range. Then, as the points wear (which increases dwell), the dwell will remain within the specified range for a longer period of time.

### 35   Ignition timing — check and adjustment

1   All later model vehicles are equipped with a tune-up or Emissions Control Information label inside the engine compartment. This label contains important ignition timing specifications and procedures to be followed specific to that vehicle. If information on the label differs from the information given in this Section, the label should be followed.

2   At the specified intervals, whenever the contact points have been replaced, the distributor removed or a change made in the fuel type, the ignition timing must be checked and adjusted if necessary.

3   Before attempting to check the timing, make sure the contact point dwell angle is correct (Section 34; 1953 through 1974 models only), and the idle speed is as specified (Section 21).

4   Disconnect the vacuum hose from the distributor and plug the now-open end of the hose with a rubber plug, rod or bolt of the proper size. Make sure the idle speed remains correct; adjust as necessary.

5   Connect a timing light in accordance with the manufacturer's instructions (photo). Generally, the light will be connected to the battery terminals and to the number one (1) spark plug in some fashion. On V-type engines, the number one spark plug is the first one on the right as you are facing the engine from the front. On in-line engines,

Fig. 1.25   Early model L-head engine timing mark location (Sec 35)

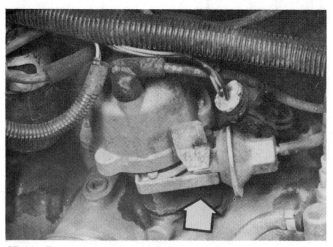

35.11  Typical late model distributor bolt location (arrow)

Fig. 1.26  Later model F- and L-head engine timing mark location (Sec 35)

it is the front spark plug.

6    Locate the numbered timing tag on the front cover of the engine. It is just behind the lower crankshaft pulley. Clean it off with solvent, if necessary, to reveal the printing and small grooves.

7    Locate the notched groove across the crankshaft pulley. It may be necessary to have an assistant temporarily turn the ignition off and on in short bursts without starting the engine to bring this groove into a position where it can easily be cleaned and marked. Stay clear of all moving engine components if the engine is turned over in this manner.

8    Use white soapstone, chalk or paint to mark the groove on the crankshaft pulley. Also put a mark on the timing tag in accordance with the number of degrees called for in the Specifications or on the label in the engine compartment. Each peak or notch on the timing tab represents 2º. The word *Before* or the letter A indicates advance and the letter O indicates Top Dead Center (TDC). As an example, if your vehicle specifications call for 8º BTDC (Before Top Dead Center), you will make a mark on the timing tag 4 notches *before* the O. Some models have a T or TDC mark.

9    Make sure that the wiring for the timing light is clear of all moving engine components, then start the engine.

10   Point the flashing timing light at the timing marks, again being careful not to come in contact with moving parts. The marks you made

Fig. 1.27  V6 engine timing mark location (Sec 35)

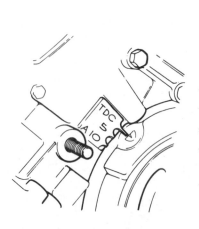

Fig. 1.28  V8 engine timing mark location (Sec 35)

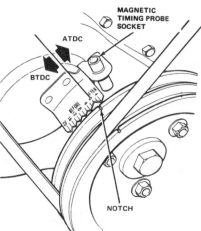

Fig. 1.29  151 cu in four-cylinder timing scale and mark location (Sec 35)

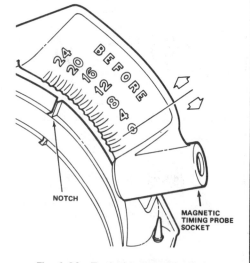

Fig. 1.30  Typical in-line six-cylinder engine timing marks (Sec 35)

## CARBON DEPOSITS

*Symptoms:* Dry sooty deposits indicate a rich mixture or weak ignition. Causes misfiring, hard starting and hesitation.

*Recommendation:* Check for a clogged air cleaner, high float level, sticky choke and worn ignition points. Use a spark plug with a longer core nose for greater anti-fouling protection.

## OIL DEPOSITS

*Symptoms:* Oily coating caused by poor oil control. Oil is leaking past worn valve guides or piston rings into the combustion chamber. Causes hard starting, misfiring and hesition.

*Recommendation:* Correct the mechanical condition with necessary repairs and install new plugs.

## TOO HOT

*Symptoms:* Blistered, white insulator, eroded electrode and absence of deposits. Results in shortened plug life.

*Recommendation:* Check for the correct plug heat range, over-advanced ignition timing, lean fuel mixture, intake manifold vacuum leaks and sticking valves. Check the coolant level and make sure the radiator is not clogged.

## PREIGNITION

*Symptoms:* Melted electrodes. Insulators are white, but may be dirty due to misfiring or flying debris in the combustion chamber. Can lead to engine damage.

*Recommendation:* Check for the correct plug heat range, over-advanced ignition timing, lean fuel mixture, clogged cooling system and lack of lubrication.

## HIGH SPEED GLAZING

*Symptoms:* Insulator has yellowish, glazed appearance. Indicates that combustion chamber temperatures have risen suddenly during hard acceleration. Normal deposits melt to form a conductive coating. Causes misfiring at high speeds.

*Recommendation:* Install new plugs. Consider using a colder plug if driving habits warrant.

## GAP BRIDGING

*Symptoms:* Combustion deposits lodge between the electrodes. Heavy deposits accumulate and bridge the electrode gap. The plug ceases to fire, resulting in a dead cylinder.

*Recommendation:* Locate the faulty plug and remove the deposits from between the electrodes.

## NORMAL

*Symptoms:* Brown to grayish-tan color and slight electrode wear. Correct heat range for engine and operating conditions.

*Recommendation:* When new spark plugs are installed, replace with plugs of the same heat range.

## ASH DEPOSITS

*Symptoms:* Light brown deposits encrusted on the side or center electrodes or both. Derived from oil and/or fuel additives. Excessive amounts may mask the spark, causing misfiring and hesitation during acceleration.

*Recommendation:* If excessive deposits accumulate over a short time or low mileage, install new valve guide seals to prevent seepage of oil into the combustion chambers. Also try changing gasoline brands.

## WORN

*Symptoms:* Rounded electrodes with a small amount of deposits on the firing end. Normal color. Causes hard starting in damp or cold weather and poor fuel economy.

*Recommendation:* Replace with new plugs of the same heat range.

## DETONATION

*Symptoms:* Insulators may be cracked or chipped. Improper gap setting techniques can also result in a fractured insulator tip. Can lead to piston damage.

*Recommendation:* Make sure the fuel anti-knock values meet engine requirements. Use care when setting the gaps on new plugs. Avoid lugging the engine.

## SPLASHED DEPOSITS

*Symptoms:* After long periods of misfiring, deposits can loosen when normal combustion temperature is restored by an overdue tune-up. At high speeds, deposits flake off the piston and are thrown against the hot insulator, causing misfiring.

*Recommendation:* Replace the plugs with new ones or clean and reinstall the originals.

## MECHANICAL DAMAGE

*Symptoms:* May be caused by a foreign object in the combustion chamber or the piston striking an incorrect reach (too long) plug. Causes a dead cylinder and could result in piston damage.

*Recommendation:* Remove the foreign object from the engine and/or install the correct reach plug.

should appear stationary. If the marks are in alignment, the timing is correct. If the marks are not aligned, turn off the engine.

11  Loosen the bolt at the base of the distributor (photo). On some vehicles this task is made much easier with a special curved distributor wrench. Loosen the bolt only slightly, just enough to turn the distributor. (See Chapter 5 for further details, if necessary.)

12  Now restart the engine and turn the distributor until the timing marks coincide.

13  Shut off the engine and tighten the distributor bolt, being careful not to move the distributor.

14  Start the engine and recheck the timing to make sure the marks are still in alignment.

15  Disconnect the timing light, unplug the distributor vacuum hose and connect the hose to the distributor.

16  Drive the vehicle and listen for pinging noises. They will be most noticeable when the engine is hot and under a load (climbing a hill, accelerating from a stop). If you hear engine pinging, the ignition timing is too far advanced (Before Top Dead Center). Reconnect the timing light and turn the distributor to move the mark 1° or 2° in the retard direction. Road test the vehicle again to check for proper operation.

17  To keep pinging at a minimum yet still allow you to operate the vehicle at the specified timing setting, it is a good idea to use gasoline of the same octane at all times. Switching fuel brands and octane levels can decrease performance and economy and possibly damage the engine.

### 36  Evaporative Control System (ECS) filter replacment

1  The function of the ECS emissions system is to draw fuel vapors from the tank and carburetor, store them in a charcoal canister, and then burn them during normal engine operation.

2  The filter at the bottom of the charcoal canister should be replaced at the specified intervals. If, however, a fuel odor is detected, the canister, filter and system hoses should be immediately inspected.

3  To replace the filter, locate the canister at the front of the engine compartment. It will have several hoses running out the top of it.

4  Remove the two bolts which secure the bottom of the canister to the body.

5  Turn the canister upside-down and pull out the old filter. If you

cannot turn the canister enough, due to the short length of the hoses, the hoses must be marked with pieces of tape and then disconnected from the top.

6  Push the new filter into the bottom of the canister, making sure it is seated all the way around.

7  Place the canister back into position and tighten the two mounting bolts. Connect the various hoses if they were disconnected.

8  The ECS system is explained in more detail in Chapter 6.

### 37  Cylinder compression check

1  A compression check will tell you what mechanical condition the engine is in. Specifically, it can tell you if the compression is down due to leakage caused by worn piston rings, defective valves and seats or a blown head gasket.

2  Begin by cleaning the area around the spark plugs before you remove then. This will keep dirt from falling into the cylinders while you are performing the compression test.

3  Remove the coil high-tension lead from the distributor and ground it on the engine block. Block the throttle and choke valves wide open.

4  With the compression gauge in the number one cylinder's spark plug hole, crank the engine over at least four compression strokes and observe the gauge. The compression should build up quickly in a healthy engine. Low compression on the first stroke, followed by gradually increasing pressure on successive strokes, indicates worn piston rings. A low compression reading on the first stroke, which does not build up during successive strokes, indicates leaking valves or a defective head gasket. Record the highest gauge reading obtained.

5  Repeat the procedure for the remaining cylinders and compare the results to the Specifications. Compression readings 10% above or below the specified amount can be considered normal.

6  Pour a couple of teaspoons of engine oil (a squirt can works great for this) into each cylinder, through the spark plug hole, and repeat the test.

7  If the compression increases after the oil is added, the piston rings are definitely worn. If the compression does not increase significantly, the leakage is occurring at the valves or head gasket. Leakage past the valves may be caused by burned valve seats/faces, warped, bent or cracked valves, valves that are out of adjustment, incorrect valve timing and broken valve springs.

8  If two adjacent cylinders have equally low compression, there is a strong possibility that the head gasket between them is blown. The appearance of coolant in the combustion chambers or the crankcase would verify this condition.

9  If the compression is higher than normal, the combustion chambers are probably coated with carbon deposits. If that is the case, the cylinder head(s) should be removed and decarbonized.

10  If compression is way down, or varies greatly between cylinders, it would be a good idea to have a leak-down test performed by a reputable automotive repair shop. This test will pinpoint exactly where the leakage is occurring and how severe it is.

### 38  Battery — check and maintenance

**Caution:** *Certain precautions must be followed when checking or servicing the battery. Hydrogen gas, which is highly flammable, is always present in the battery cells so keep lighted tobacco and any other open flames or sparks away from the battery. The electrolyte inside the battery is actually dilute sulfuric acid, which can be hazardous to your skin and cause injury if splashed in the eyes. It will also ruin clothes and painted surfaces.*

1  Tools and materials required for battery maintenance include eye and hand protection, baking soda, petroleum jelly, a battery cable puller, cable/terminal post cleaning tools and a hydrometer (photo).

*Checking*

2  Check the battery for cracks and evidence of leakage.

3  To check the electrolyte level in the battery, remove all vent caps. If the battery level is low, add distilled water until the level is above the cell plates. There is an indicator in each cell to help you judge when enough water has been added. Do not overfill. **Note:** *Some models may be equipped with maintenance-free batteries which have no provision*

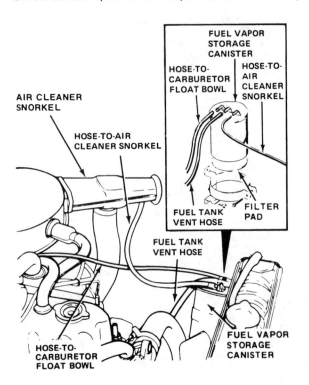

Fig. 1.31  Evaporative Control System (ECS) canister installation (Sec 36)

*(or need) for adding water. Also, some models may be equipped with translucent batteries so the electrolyte level can be observed without removing any vent caps. On these batteries, the level should be between the upper and lower lines.*

4   Periodically check the specific gravity of the electrolyte with an hydrometer. This is especially important during cold weather. If the reading is below the specified range, the battery should be recharged. Maintenance-free batteries have a built-in hydrometer which indicates the battery state-of-charge.

5   Check the tightness of the battery cable clamps to ensure good electrical connections. If corrosion is evident, remove the cables from the battery terminals (a puller may be required), clean them with a battery terminal brush, then reinstall them (photos). Corrosion can be kept to a minimum by applying a layer of petroleum jelly or grease to the terminal and cable clamps after they are assembled.

6   Inspect the entire length of each battery cable for corrosion, cracks and frayed conductors. Replace the cables with new ones if they are damaged (Chapter 5).

7   Make sure that the rubber protector over the positive terminal is not torn or missing. It should completely cover the terminal.

8   Make sure that the battery is securely mounted, but do not over-tighten the clamp bolts.

9   The battery case and caps should be kept clean and dry. If corrosion is evident, clean the battery as explained in Step 12.

10   If the vehicle is not being used for an extended period, disconnect the battery cables and have the battery charged approximately every six weeks.

### Cleaning

11   Corrosion on the battery hold-down components and inner fender panels can be removed by washing with a solution of water and baking soda. Once the area has been thoroughly cleaned, rinse it with clean water.

12   Corrosion on the battery case and terminals can also be removed with a solution of water and baking soda and a stiff brush. Be careful that none of the solution is splashed into your eyes or onto your skin

(wear protective gloves). Do not allow any of the baking soda and water solution to get into the battery cells. Rinse the battery thoroughly once it is clean.

13   Metal parts of the vehicle which have been damaged by spilled battery acid should be painted with a zinc-based primer and paint. Do this only after the area has been thoroughly cleaned and dried.

### Charging

14   As mentioned before, if the battery's specific gravity is below the specified amount, the battery must be recharged.

15   If the battery is to remain in the vehicle during charging, disconnect the cables from the battery to prevent damage to the electrical system.

16   When batteries are being charged, hydrogen gas (which is very explosive and flammable) is produced. *Do not smoke or allow an open flame near a charging or a recently charged battery. Also, do not plug in the battery charger until the connections have been made at the battery posts.*

17   The average time necessary to charge a battery at the normal rate is from 12 to 16 hours (sometimes longer). Always charge the battery slowly. A quick charge or boost charge is hard on a battery and will shorten its life. Use a battery charger that is rated at no more than 1/10 the amp/hour rating of the battery.

18   Remove all of the vent caps and cover the holes with a clean cloth to prevent the spattering of electrolyte. Hook the battery charger leads to the battery posts (positive to positive, negative to negative), then plug in the charger. Make sure it is set at 12 volts (6 volts on early models) if it has a selector switch.

19   Watch the battery closely during charging to make sure that it does not overheat.

20   The battery can be considered fully charged when it is gassing freely and there is no increase in specific gravity during three successive readings taken at hourly intervals. Overheating of the battery during charging at normal charging rates, excessive gassing and continual low specific gravity readings are an indication that the battery should be replaced with a new one.

38.1   Eye and hand protection, baking soda, petroleum jelly and tools required for battery maintenance

38.5A   Battery terminal corrosion usually appears as a white fluffy powder

38.5B   Removing the cable from the battery terminal post (always remove the ground cable first and hook it up last)

38.5C   Cleaning the battery terminal post with a special tool

38.5D   Cleaning the battery cable clamp

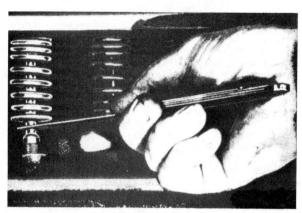

Fig. 1.32  Checking the valve lifter-to-valve stem clearance
(Sec 40)

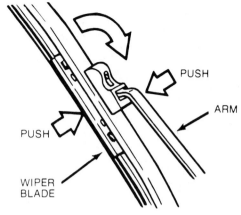

Fig. 1.33  Wiper blade replacement (Sec 41)

## 39  Cooling system servicing (draining, flushing and refilling)

1    Periodically, the cooling system should be drained, flushed and refilled to replenish the antifreeze mixture and prevent the formation of rust and corrosion which can impair the performance of the cooling system and ultimately cause engine damage.
2    At the same time the cooling system is serviced, all hoses and the radiator cap should be inspected and replaced if faulty.
3    Since antifreeze is a poisonous solution, be careful not to spill any of the coolant mixture on the vehicle's paint or your own skin. If this happens, rinse immediately with plenty of clear water. Also, consult your local authorities about the dumping of antifreeze before draining the cooling system. In many areas, reclamation centers have been set up to collect automobile oil and drained antifreeze/water mixtures rather than allowing these liquids to be added to the sewage system.
4    With the engine cold, remove the radiator cap.
5    Move a large container under the radiator to catch the coolant mixture as it is drained.
6    Drain the radiator. Most models are equipped with a drain plug at the bottom of the radiator, which can be opened using a wrench to hold the fitting while the petcock is turned to the open position. If the drain has excessive corrosion and cannot be turned easily, or if the radiator is not equipped with a drain, disconnect the lower radiator hose to drain the coolant. Be careful that none of the solution is splashed onto your skin or into your eyes.
7    If so equipped, remove the engine block drain plugs.
8    On systems with a coolant reservoir, disconnect the overflow hose and remove the reservoir. Flush it out with clean water.
9    Place a water hose (a common garden hose is fine) in the radiator filler neck at the top of the radiator and flush the system until the water runs clear at all drain points.
10   In severe cases of contamination or clogging of the radiator, remove it (see Chapter 3) and reverse flush it. This involves simply inserting the hose in the bottom radiator outlet to allow the clear water to run against the normal flow, draining through the top. A radiator repair shop should be consulted if further cleaning or repair is necessary.
11   If the coolant is regularly drained and the system refilled with the correct antifreeze mixture, there should be no need to employ chemical cleaners or descalers.
12   To refill the system, reconnect the radiator hose(s) and install the drain plugs securely in the engine. Special thread-sealing tape (available at auto parts stores) should be used on the drain plugs installed in the engine block. Install the coolant reservoir and the overflow hose where applicable.
13   On vehicles without a coolant reservoir, refill the system through the radiator filler cap until the coolant level is about one (1) inch below the filler neck.
14   On vehicles with a reservoir, fill the radiator to the base of the filler neck and then add more coolant to the reservoir.
15   Run the engine until normal operating temperature is reached, then with the engine idling, add coolant up to the correct level.
16   Always refill the system with a mixture of high-quality antifreeze and water in the proportion called for on the antifreeze container or in your owner's manual. Chapter 3 also contains information on anti-

freeze mixtures.
17   Keep a close watch on the coolant level and the various cooling hoses during the first few miles of driving. Tighten the hose clamps and/or add more coolant mixture as necessary.

## 40  Valve clearance adjustment (F- and L-head engines only)

**Note:** *The F- and L-head engines are the only engines that require periodic valve adjustments. All other engines used in the Jeep CJ series are equipped with hydraulic lifters, which are self-adjusting.*

1    The valves on F- and L-head engines must be adjusted at the specified intervals with the engine *cold* (at room temperature).
2    Prior to adjustment, remove the valve cover on the side of the engine (F- and L-head) and the rocker arm cover (F-head).
3    Valve clearance is measured by inserting a feeler gauge between the valve stem and lifter (F- and L-head) and rocker arm and pushrod (F-head) with the lifter on the heel or low portion of the camshaft.
4    Rotate the engine with a wrench on the crankshaft pulley until the valve is closed, then continue to rotate it approximately 90° further to make sure the lifter is on the heel of the cam lobe.
5    Insert a feeler gauge between the lifter and valve stem or pushrod and rocker arm to determine the clearance. Compare the measured clearance to the Specifications.
6    To adjust, loosen the lifter or rocker arm locknut and turn the adjusting nut in or out to obtain the specified clearance. Tighten the locknut while holding the adjusting screw so it won't turn.
7    Begin the checking and adjustment procedure at the number one cylinder and work back to the number four cylinder. After all the valves are adjusted, it is a good idea to go back and double-check the clearances to make sure that they have not changed during the tightening of the adjustment screw.
8    Inspect the valve and rocker arm cover gasket surfaces to make sure they are in good condition. If there is any doubt, install a new gasket after cleaning the surface, to preclude the possibility of leaks.

## 41  Windshield wipers — inspection and replacement

1    The windshield wiper and blade assembly should be inspected periodically for damage, loose components and cracked or worn blade elements.
2    Road film can build up on the wiper blades and affect their efficiency so they should be washed regularly with a mild detergent solution.
3    The action of the wiping mechanism can loosen the bolts, nuts and fasteners so they should be checked and tightened, as necessary, at the same time the wiper blades are checked.
4    If the wiper blade elements are cracked, worn or warped, they should be replaced with new ones. Raise the wiper arm away from the windshield, push the arm end into the wiper blade and rotate the blade around the tip of the arm. Attach the new blade to the arm tip and rotate it into position.

# Chapter 2 Part A
# General engine overhaul procedures

*Refer to Chapter 13 for Specifications and information related to 1984 through 1986 models*

## Contents

Crankshaft — inspection . . . . . . . . . . . . . . . . . . . . . . . . . . . 16
Crankshaft — removal . . . . . . . . . . . . . . . . . . . . . . . . . 12
Cylinder head — cleaning and inspection . . . . . . . . . . . . . . 8
Cylinder head — disassembly . . . . . . . . . . . . . . . . . . . . . 7
Cylinder head — reassembly . . . . . . . . . . . . . . . . . . . . . . 10
Engine block — cleaning . . . . . . . . . . . . . . . . . . . . . . 13
Engine block — inspection . . . . . . . . . . . . . . . . . . . . . 14
Engine disassembly — general information . . . . . . . . . . . 6
Engine overhaul — general information . . . . . . . . . . . . . . 3
Engine rebuilding alternatives . . . . . . . . . . . . . . . . . . . . . 4
Engine removal — methods and precautions . . . . . . . . . . . 5

General information . . . . . . . . . . . . . . . . . . . . . . . . . . . . . 1
Initial start-up and break-in after overhaul . . . . . . . . . . . . . 20
Main and connecting rod bearings — inspection . . . . . . . . . 17
Piston/connecting rod assembly — inspection . . . . . . . . . . . 15
Piston/connecting rod assembly — installation and bearing oil
   clearance check . . . . . . . . . . . . . . . . . . . . . . . . . . . . . 19
Piston/connecting rod assembly — removal . . . . . . . . . . . . 11
Piston rings — installation . . . . . . . . . . . . . . . . . . . . . . . 18
Repair operations possible with the engine in the vehicle . . . . 2
Valves — servicing . . . . . . . . . . . . . . . . . . . . . . . . . . . . . 9

## 1  General information

Included in this portion of Chapter 2 are general overhaul procedures common to all engines used in the vehicles covered by this manual. The material ranges from advice concerning how to prepare for and approach an engine overhaul to detailed, step-by-step procedures covering removal and installation of internal engine components and the inspection of parts.

Keep in mind that the information here should be used in conjunction with one of the other Parts of Chapter 2 (depending on the particular engine involved). To accomplish a typical engine overhaul, refer to the procedures in the appropriate Part of Chapter 2 to remove the engine from the vehicle and begin engine disassembly. Once the external components have been removed, proceed to Chapter 2, Part A, for the the remainder of the engine teardown, certain cleaning and inspection procedures and the installation of internal parts. Return to the appropriate Part of Chapter 2 to complete engine reassembly and install it in the vehicle.

In order to avoid confusion and reduce the possibility of errors, all specifications and clearances for each particular engine are included in the appropriate Part of Chapter 2 — not Part A.

## 2  Repair operations possible with the engine in the vehicle

Many major repair operations can be accomplished without removing the engine from the vehicle.

It is a very good idea to clean the engine compartment and the exterior of the engine with some type of pressure washer before any work is begun. A clean engine will make the job easier and will prevent the possibility of getting dirt into internal areas of the engine.

Remove the hood (Chapter 12) and cover the fenders to provide as much working room as possible and to prevent damage to the painted surface.

If oil or coolant leaks develop, indicating a need for gasket or seal replacement, the repairs can generally be made with the engine in the vehicle. The oil pan gasket, the cylinder head gasket(s), intake and exhaust manifold gaskets, timing chain cover gaskets and the front and rear crankshaft oil seals are accessible with the engine in place. In the case of the rear crankshaft oil seal on the 151-cubic-inch four-cylinder engine, the transmission, the clutch components and the flywheel/driveplate must be removed first.

Exterior engine components, such as the water pump, the starter motor, the alternator, the distributor, the fuel pump and the carburetor, as well as the intake and exhaust manifolds, are quite easily removed for repair with the engine in place.

Since the cylinder head(s) can be removed without pulling the engine, valve component servicing can also be accomplished with the engine in the vehicle.

Replacement, repairs to or inspection of the timing gears or sprockets and chain and the oil pump are all possible with the engine in place.

In extreme cases caused by a lack of necessary equipment, repair or replacement of piston rings, pistons, connecting rods and rod bearings and reconditioning of the cylinder bores is possible with the engine in the vehicle. However, this practice is not recommended because of the cleaning and preparation work that must be done to the components involved.

Detailed removal, inspection, repair and installation procedures for the above mentioned components can be found in the appropriate Part of Chapter 2 or the other Chapters in this manual.

## 3   Engine overhaul — general information

It is not always easy to determine when, or if, an engine should be completely overhauled, since a number of factors must be considered.

High mileage is not necessarily an indication that an overhaul is needed while low mileage, on the other hand, does not preclude the need for an overhaul. Frequency of servicing is probably the single most important consideration. An engine that has regular (and frequent) oil and filter changes, as well as other required maintenance, will most likely give many thousands of miles of reliable service. Conversely, a neglected engine may require an overhaul very early in its life.

Excessive oil consumption is an indication that piston rings and/or valve guides are in need of attention (make sure that oil leaks are not responsible before deciding that the rings and guides are bad). Have a cylinder compression or leak-down test performed by an experienced tune-up mechanic to determine for certain the extent of the work required.

If the engine is making obvious knocking or rumbling noises, the connecting rod and/or main bearings are probably at fault. Check the oil pressure with a gauge (installed in place of the oil pressure sending unit) and compare it to the Specifications. If it is extremely low, the bearings and/or oil pump are probably worn out.

Loss of power, rough running, excessive valve train noise and high fuel consumption rates may also point to the need for an overhaul (especially if they are all present at the same time). If a complete tune-up does not remedy the situation, major mechanical work is the only solution.

An engine overhaul generally involves restoring the internal parts to the specifications of a new engine. During an overhaul, the piston rings are replaced and the cylinder walls are reconditioned (rebored and/or honed). If a rebore is done, then new pistons are also required. The main and connecting rod bearings are replaced with new ones and, if necessary, the crankshaft may be reground to restore the journals. Generally, the valves are serviced as well, since they are usually in less-than-perfect condition at this point. While the engine is being overhauled, other components such as the carburetor, the distributor, the starter and the alternator can be rebuilt also. The end result should be a like-new engine that will give as many trouble-free miles as the original.

Before beginning the engine overhaul, read through the entire procedure to familiarize yourself with the scope and requirements of the job. Overhauling an engine is not that difficult, but it is time consuming. Plan on the vehicle being tied up for a minimum of two weeks, especially if parts must be taken to an automotive machine shop for repair or reconditioning. Check on availability of parts and make sure that any necessary special tools and equipment are obtained in advance. Most work can be done with typical shop hand tools, although a number of precision measuring tools are required for inspecting parts to determine if they must be replaced. Often a reputable automotive machine shop will handle the inspection of parts and offer advice concerning reconditioning and replacement. **Note:** *Always wait until the engine has been completely disassembled and all components, especially the engine block, have been inspected before deciding what service and repair operations must be performed by an automotive machine shop.* Since the block's condition will be the major factor to consider when determining whether to overhaul the original engine or buy a rebuilt one, never purchase parts or have machine work done on other components until the block has been thoroughly inspected. As a general rule, time is the primary cost of an overhaul, so it does not pay to install worn or sub-standard parts.

As a final note, to ensure maximum life and minimum trouble from a rebuilt engine, everything must be assembled with care in a spotlessly clean environment.

## 4   Engine rebuilding alternatives

The home mechanic is faced with a number of options when performing an engine overhaul. The decision to replace the engine block, piston/rod assemblies and crankshaft depends on a number of factors, with the number one consideration being the condition of the block. Other considerations are cost, access to machine shop facilities, parts availability, time required to complete the project and experience.

Some of the rebuilding alternatives include:   **Individual parts** — *If the inspection procedures reveal that the engine block and most engine components are in reusable condition, purchasing individual parts may be the most economical alternative. The block, crankshaft and piston/rod assemblies should all be inspected carefully. Even if the block shows little wear, the cylinder bores should receive a finish hone; a job for an automotive machine shop.*

**Master kit** *(crankshaft kit)* — *This rebuild package usually consists of a reground crankshaft and a matched set of pistons and connecting rods. The pistons will already be installed on the connecting rods. Piston rings and the necessary bearings may or may not be included in the kit. These kits are commonly available for standard cylinder bores, as well as for engine blocks which have been bored to a regular oversize.*

**Short block** — *A short block consists of an engine block with a crankshaft and piston/rod assemblies already installed. All new bearings are incorporated and all clearances will be correct. Depending on where the short block is purchased, a guarantee may be included. The existing camshaft, valve train components, cylinder head(s) and external parts can be bolted to the short block with little or no machine shop work necessary.*

**Long block** — *A long block consists of a short block plus oil pump, oil pan, cylinder head(s), rocker arm cover(s), camshaft and valve train components, timing gears or sprockets and chain and timing gear/chain cover. All components are installed with new bearings, seals and gaskets incorporated throughout. The installation of manifolds and external parts is all that is necessary. Some form of guarantee is usually included with the purchase.*

Give careful thought to which alternative is best for you and discuss the situation with local automotive machine shops, auto parts dealers or dealership partsmen before ordering or purchasing replacement parts.

## 5   Engine removal — methods and precautions

If it has been decided that an engine must be removed for overhaul or major repair work, certain preliminary steps should be taken.

Locating a suitable work area is extremely important. A shop is, of course, the most desirable place to work. Adequate work space along with storage space for the vehicle is very important. If a shop or garage is not available, at the very least a flat, level, clean work surface made of concrete or asphalt is required.

Cleaning the engine compartment and engine prior to removal will help keep tools clean and organized.

An engine hoist or A-frame will also be necessary. Make sure that the equipment is rated in excess of the combined weight of the engine and its accessories. Safety is of primary importance, considering the potential hazards involved in lifting the engine out of the vehicle.

If the engine is being removed by a novice, a helper should be available. Advice and aid from someone more experienced would also be helpful. There are many instances when one person cannot simultaneously perform all of the operations required when lifting the engine out of the vehicle.

Plan the operation ahead of time. Arrange for or obtain all of the tools and equipment you will need prior to beginning the job. Some of the equipment necessary to perform engine removal and installation safely and with relative ease are (in addition to an engine hoist) a heavy-duty floor jack, complete sets of wrenches and sockets as described in the front of this manual, wooden blocks and plenty of rags and cleaning solvent for mopping up the inevitable spills. If the hoist is to be rented, make sure that you arrange for it in advance and perform beforehand all of the operations possible without it. This will save you money and time.

Plan for the vehicle to be out of use for a considerable amount of time. A machine shop will be required to perform some of the work which the home mechanic cannot accomplish due to a lack of special equipment. These shops often have a busy schedule so it would be wise to consult them prior to removing the engine in order to accurately estimate the amount of time required to rebuild or repair components that may need work.

Always use extreme caution when removing and installing the engine; serious injury can result from careless actions. Plan ahead. Take your time and a job of this nature, although major, can be accomplished successfully.

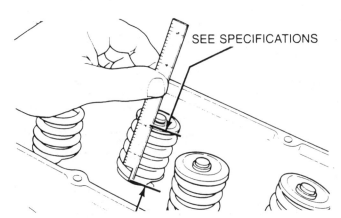

Fig. 2.1  Measuring the installed valve spring height with a
steel rule (Sec 7)

7.3  Use a valve spring compressor to compress the springs,
then remove the keepers from the valve stem

**2A**

## 6  Engine disassembly — general information

It is much easier to dismantle and repair the engine if it is mounted
on a portable-type engine stand. For a reasonable fee, these stands
can often be rented from an equipment rental yard. Before the engine
is mounted on a stand, the flywheel/driveplate should be removed from
the engine (refer to the appropriate Section).

If a stand is not available, it is possible to dismantle the engine with
it blocked up on a sturdy workbench or on the floor. Be extra careful
not to tip or drop the engine when working without a stand.

If you are obtaining a factory replacement or reconditioned engine,
all external components must come off first — just as they will if you
are doing a complete engine overhaul yourself. These include:

*Alternator and brackets*
*Distributor and spark plug wires*
*Thermostat and cover*
*Oil filter*
*Carburetor*
*Intake and exhaust manifolds*
*Water pump*
*Engine mount brackets*
*Clutch and flywheel or driveplate*

**Note:** *When removing the external components from the engine, pay
close attention to details that may be helpful or important during installation. Look for the correct positioning of gaskets, seals, spacers,
pins, washers, bolts and other small items.*

If you are obtaining what is termed a short block, which consists
of the block, crankshaft, pistons and connecting rods all assembled, then the cylinder head(s), oil pan and oil pump will have to be
removed also.

Remove all of the components according to the procedures described in the appropriate Chapters of this manual.

## 7  Cylinder head — disassembly

**Note:** *New and rebuilt cylinder heads are commonly available for most
engines at dealerships and auto parts stores. Due to the fact that some
specialized tools are necessary for the disassembly and inspection procedures, and replacement parts may not be readily available, it may be
more practical and economical for the home mechanic to purchase a
replacement head (or heads) rather than taking the time to disassemble, inspect and recondition the original head(s).*

1   Cylinder head disassembly involves removal and disassembly of
the intake and exhaust valves and their related components. If so equipped, remove the rocker arm nuts/bolts, balls (or pivots) and rocker arms.
Label the parts or store them separately so they can be reinstalled in
their original locations.

2   Before the valves are removed, arrange to label and store them,
along with their related components, so they can be kept separate and
reinstalled in the same valve guides they are removed from. Also,
measure the valve spring installed height (for each valve) and compare
it to the Specifications. If it is greater than specified, the valve seats
and valve faces need attention.

3   Compress the valve spring on the first valve with a spring compressor and remove the keepers (photo). Carefully release the valve
spring compressor and remove the retainer (or rotator), the shield (if
so equipped), the springs, the seal (or oil deflector), the spring seat
and the valve from the head. If the valve binds in the guide (won't pull
through), push it back into the head and deburr the area around the
keeper groove with a fine file or whetstone.

4   Repeat the procedure for the remaining valves. Remember to keep
all the parts for each valve together so they can be reinstalled in the
same locations.

5   Once the valves have been removed and safely stored, the head
should be thoroughly cleaned and inspected. If a complete engine
overhaul is being done, finish the engine disassembly procedures before
beginning the cylinder head cleaning and inspection process.

## 8  Cylinder head — cleaning and inspection

1   Thorough cleaning of the cylinder head and related valve train components, followed by a detailed inspection, will enable you to decide
how much valve service work must be done during the engine overhaul.

### Cleaning

2   Scrape away all traces of old gasket material and sealing compound from the head gasket, intake manifold and exhaust manifold sealing surfaces.

3   Remove any built-up scale from around the coolant passages.

4   Run a stiff wire brush through the oil holes to remove any deposits
that may have formed in them.

5   It is a good idea to run an appropriate size tap into each of the
threaded holes to remove any corrosion or thread sealant that may be
present. If compressed air is available, use it to clear the holes of debris
produced by this operation.

6   Clean the exhaust and intake manifold stud threads in a similar
manner with an appropriate size die. Clean the rocker arm pivot bolt
or stud threads with a wire brush.

7   Next, clean the cylinder head with solvent and dry it thoroughly.
Compressed air will speed the drying process and ensure that all holes
and recessed areas are clean. **Note:** *Decarbonizing chemicals are
available and may prove very useful when cleaning cylinder heads and
valve train components. They are very caustic and should be used with
caution. Be sure to follow the instructions on the container.*

8   Clean the rocker arms, pivots and pushrods with solvent and dry
them thoroughly. Compressed air will speed the drying process and
can be used to clean out the oil passages.

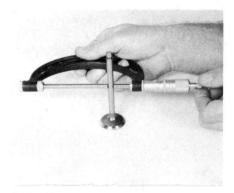

8.20   Measure the valve stem diameter at three points

8.21A   Measure the free length of each valve spring with a dial or Vernier caliper

8.21B   Check each valve spring for squareness

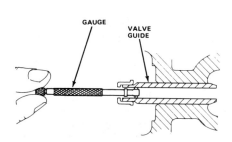

Fig. 2.2   Use a small hole gauge to determine the inside diameter of the valve guides (the gauge is then measured with a micrometer) (Sec 8)

Fig. 2.3   A dial indicator can also be used to determine the valve stem-to-guide clearance (Sec 8)

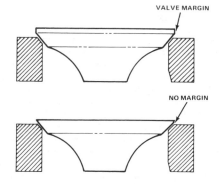

Fig. 2.4   The margin width on each valve must be as specified (if no margin exists, the valve must be replaced) (Sec 8)

9   Clean all the valve springs, keepers, retainers, rotators, shields and spring seats with solvent and dry them thoroughly. Do the parts from one valve at a time so no mixing of parts between valves occurs.
10   Scrape off any heavy deposits that may have formed on the valves, then use a motorized wire brush to remove deposits from the valve heads and stems. Again, make sure the valves do not get mixed up.

*Inspection*
**Cylinder head**
11   Inspect the head very carefully for cracks, evidence of coolant leakage and other damage. If cracks are found, a new cylinder head should be obtained.
12   Using a straightedge and feeler gauges, check the head gasket mating surface for warpage. If the head is warped beyond the limits given in the Specifications, it can be resurfaced at an automotive machine shop.
13   Examine the valve seats in each of the combustion chambers. If they are pitted, cracked or burned, the head will require valve service that is beyond the scope of the home mechanic.
14   Measure the inside diameters of the valve guides (at both ends and the center of each guide) with a small hole gauge and a 0-to-1-inch micrometer. Record the measurements for future reference. These measurements, along with the valve stem diameter measurements, will enable you to compute the valve stem-to-guide clearances. These clearances, when compared to the Specifications, will be one factor that will determine the extent of valve service work required. The guides are measured at the ends and at the center to determine if they are worn in a bell-mouth pattern (more wear at the ends). If they are, guide reconditioning or replacement is necessary. As an alternative, use a dial indicator to measure the lateral movement of each valve stem with the valve in the guide and approximately 1/16-inch off the seat (see the accompanying illustration).

**Rocker arm components**
15   Check the rocker arm faces (that contact the pushrod ends and valve stems) for pits, wear and rough spots. Check the pivot contact areas as well.
16   Inspect the pushrod ends for scuffing and excessive wear. Roll the pushrod on a flat surface, such as a piece of glass, to determine if it is bent.
17   Any damaged or excessively worn parts must be replaced with new ones.
**Valves**
18   Carefully inspect each valve face for cracks, pits and burned spots. Check the valve stem and neck for cracks. Rotate the valve and check for any obvious indication that it is bent. Check the end of the stem for pits and excessive wear. The presence of any of these conditions indicates the need for valve service by a properly equipped professional.
19   Measure the width of the valve margin (on each valve) and compare it to the Specifications. Any valve with a margin narrower than specified will have to be replaced with a new one.
20   Measure the valve stem diameter (photo). **Note:** *The exhaust valves used in the GM 151 cu in four-cylinder engine have tapered stems and are approximately 0.001-inch larger at the tip end than at the head end.* By subtracting the stem diameter from the corresponding valve guide diameter, the valve stem-to-guide clearance is obtained. Compare the results to the Specifications. If the stem-to-guide clearance is greater than specified, the guides will have to be reconditioned and new valves may have to be installed, depending on the condition of the old ones.
**Valve components**
21   Check each valve spring for wear (on the ends) and pits. Measure the free length (photo) and compare it to the Specifications. Any springs that are shorter than specified have sagged and should not be reused. Stand the spring on a flat surface and check it for squareness (photo).

10.6  Checking the valve stem seals
(GM 151 cu in four-cylinder engine only)
for leakage

11.2  A special tool is required to
remove the ridge from the top of each
cylinder

11.6  Checking connecting rod end play
with a feeler gauge

22  Check the spring retainers (or rotators) and keepers for obvious wear and cracks. Any questionable parts should be replaced with new ones, as extensive damage will occur in the event of failure during engine operation.
23  If the inspection process indicates that the valve components are in generally poor condition and worn beyond the limits specified, which is usually the case in an engine that is being overhauled, reassemble the valves in the cylinder head and refer to Section 9 for valve servicing recommendations.
24  If the inspection turns up no excessively worn parts, and if the valve faces and seats are in good condition, the valve train components can be reinstalled in the cylinder head without major servicing. Refer to the appropriate Section for cylinder head reassembly procedures.

## 9  Valves — servicing

1  Because of the complex nature of the job and the special tools and equipment needed, servicing of the valves, the valve seats and the valve guides (commonly known as a 'valve job') is best left to a professional.
2  The home mechanic can remove and disassemble the head, do the initial cleaning and inspection, then reassemble and deliver the head to a dealer service department or a reputable automotive machine shop for the actual valve servicing. In the case of an F- or L-head engine, the block will also have to be taken to the machine shop for valve service work. Refer to Chapter 2F for the procedure to follow when removing the valves from the block.
3  The dealer service department, or automotive machine shop, will remove the valves and springs, recondition or replace the valves and valve seats, recondition the valve guides, check and replace the valve springs, spring retainers or rotators and keepers (as necessary), replace the valve seals with new ones, reassemble the valve components and make sure the installed spring height is correct. The cylinder head gasket surface will also be resurfaced if it is warped.
4  After the valve job has been performed by a professional, the head will be in like-new condition. When the head is returned, be sure to clean it again, very thoroughly (before installation on the engine), to remove any metal particles and abrasive grit that may still be present from the valve service or head resurfacing operations. Use compressed air, if available, to blow out all the oil holes and passages.

## 10  Cylinder head — reassembly

1  Regardless of whether or not the head was sent to an automotive machine shop for valve servicing, make sure it is clean before beginning reassembly.
2  If the head was sent out for valve servicing, the valves and related components will already be in place.
3  Lay all the spring seats in position, then lubricate and install new seals (or deflectors) on each of the valve guides (*six-cylinder and V8 engines only*). On all four-cylinder engines the seals are installed in the lower grooves in the valves after the springs are compressed (lubricate the seals before installation). *V6 engines are not*

equipped with seals.
4  Next, install the valves (taking care not to damage the new seals), the springs, the shields (if so equipped), the retainers (or rotators) and the keepers. **Note:** *On V6 engines, the spring must be installed with the closely spaced coils next to the head.* Coat the valve stems with clean moly-based grease (or engine assembly lube) before slipping them into the guides. When compressing the springs with the valve spring compressor, do not let the retainers contact the valve guide seals or deflectors (*six-cylinder and V8 engines only*). Make certain that the keepers are securely locked in their retaining grooves.
5  Double check the installed valve spring height. If it was correct before disassembly, it should still be within the specified limits.
6  *On four-cylinder engines only*, check the valve stem seals with a vacuum pump and adapter (photo). A properly installed seal should not leak.
7  Install the rocker arms and tighten the bolts/nuts to the specified torque. Be sure to lubricate the pivots with moly-based grease or engine assembly lube.

## 11  Piston/connecting rod assembly — removal

1  Prior to removing the piston/connecting rod assemblies, remove the cylinder head(s) and the oil pan by referring to the appropriate Sections.
2  Using a ridge reamer, completely remove the ridge at the top of each cylinder (follow the manufacturer's instructions provided with the ridge reaming tool) (photo). Failure to remove the ridge before attempting to remove the piston/connecting rod assemblies will result in piston breakage.
3  With the engine in the upside-down position, remove the oil pick-up tube and oil pump from the bottom of the engine block.
4  Before the connecting rods are removed, check the end play as follows. Mount a dial indicator with its stem in line with the crankshaft and touching the side of the number one cylinder connecting rod cap.
5  Push the connecting rod forward, as far as possible, and zero the dial indicator. Next, push the connecting rod all the way to the rear and check the reading on the dial indicator. The distance that it moves is the end play. If the end play exceeds the service limit, a new connecting rod will be required. Repeat the procedure for the remaining connecting rods.
6  An alternative method is to slip feeler gauges between the connecting rod and the crankshaft throw until the play is removed (photo). The end play is then equal to the thickness of the feeler gauge(s).
7  Check the connecting rods and connecting rod caps for identification marks. If they are not plainly marked, identify each rod and cap using a small punch to make the appropriate number of indentations to indicate the cylinders they are associated with.
8  Loosen each of the connecting rod cap nuts approximately 1/2 turn each. **Note:** *On F- and L-head engines, first remove the stamped locking nuts and discard them.* Remove the number one connecting rod cap and bearing insert. Do not drop the bearing insert out of the cap. Slip a short length of plastic or rubber hose over each connecting rod cap bolt (to protect the crankshaft journal and cylinder wall when the piston is removed) (photo) and push the connecting rod/piston

**2A**

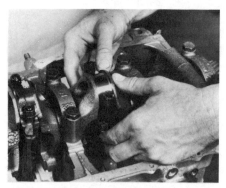

11.8   To prevent damage to the crankshaft journals and cylinder walls, slip sections of hose over the rod bolts before removing the pistons

12.5   Checking crankshaft end play with a feeler gauge (GM 151 cu in four-cylinder engine shown)

12.6   Mark the bearing caps with a center punch before removing them

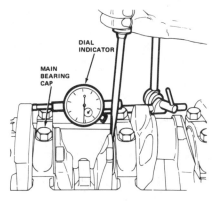

Fig. 2.5   Checking crankshaft end play with a dial indicator (Sec 12)

13.1   Using pliers to remove a soft plug from the block

14.4A   A telescoping gauge can be used to determine the cylinder bore diameter

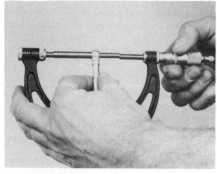

14.B   The gauge is then measured with a micrometer to determine the bore size in inches

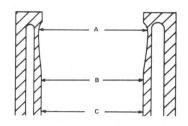

Fig. 2.6   Measure the diameter of each cylinder just under the wear ridge (A), at the center (B) and at the bottom (C) (Sec 14)

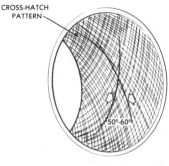

Fig. 2.7   The cylinder hone should leave a cross-hatch pattern with the lines intersecting at approximately a 60° angle (Sec 14)

assembly out through the top of the engine. Use a wooden tool to push on the upper bearing insert in the connecting rod. If resistance is felt, double-check to make sure that all of the ridge was removed from the cylinder.

9    Repeat the procedure for the remaining cylinders. After removal, reassemble the connecting rod caps and bearing inserts in their respective connecting rods and install the cap nuts finger tight. Leaving the old bearing inserts in place until reassembly will help prevent the connecting rod bearing surfaces from being accidentally nicked or gouged.

## 12   Crankshaft — removal

1    Before beginning this procedure, the preliminary steps outlined in Chapters 2B, 2C, 2D, 2E or 2F (as appropriate) must be completed.
2    If not already done, remove the piston assemblies from the engine

block, as described in Section 11. Be sure to mark each connecting rod and bearing cap so they will be properly mated during reassembly.
3    Before the crankshaft is removed, check the end play as follows. Mount a dial indicator with the stem in line with the crankshaft and just touching one of the crank throws (see accompanying illustration).
4    Push the crankshaft all the way to the rear and zero the dial indicator. Next, pry the crankshaft to the front as far as possible and check the reading on the dial indicator. The distance that it moves is the end play. If it is greater than specified, check the crankshaft thrust surfaces for wear. If no wear is apparent, new main bearings should correct the end play.
5    If a dial indicator is not available, feeler gauges can be used. Gently pry or push the crankshaft all the way to the front of the engine. Slip feeler gauges between the crankshaft and the front face of the thrust main bearing (photo) to determine the clearance (which is equivalent to crankshaft end play).

14.7   Honing a cylinder with a surfacing hone

15.4   Cleaning the piston ring grooves with a piston ring groove cleaning tool

15.10   Checking the piston ring side clearance with a feeler gauge

6   Loosen each of the main bearing cap bolts 1/4 of a turn at a time, until they can be removed by hand. Check the main bearing caps to see if they are marked as to their locations. They are usually numbered consecutively (beginning with 1) from the front of the engine to the rear. If they are not, mark them with number stamping dies or a center punch (photo). Most main bearing caps have a cast-in arrow, which points to the front of the engine.
7   Gently tap the caps with a soft-faced hammer, then separate them from the engine block. If necessary, use the main bearing cap bolts as levers to remove the caps. Try not to drop the bearing insert if it comes out with the cap.
8   Carefully lift the crankshaft out of the engine. It is a good idea to have an assistant available, since the crankshaft is quite heavy. With the bearing inserts in place in the engine block and in the main bearing caps, return the caps to their respective locations on the engine block and tighten the bolts finger tight.

### 13   Engine block — cleaning

1   Remove the soft plugs from the engine block. To do this, knock the plugs into the block (using a hammer and punch), then grasp them with large pliers and pull them back through the holes (photo).
2   Using a gasket scraper, remove all traces of gasket material from the engine block. Be very careful not to nick or gouge the gasket sealing surfaces.
3   Remove the main bearing caps and separate the bearing inserts from the caps and the engine block. Tag the bearings according to which cylinder they removed from (and whether they were in the cap or the block) and set them aside.
4   Using a hex wrench of the appropriate size, remove the threaded oil gallery plugs from the front and back of the block.
5   If the engine is extremely dirty, it should be taken to an automotive machine shop to be steam cleaned or hot tanked. Any bearings left in the block (such as the camshaft bearings) will be damaged by the cleaning process, so plan on having new ones installed while the block is at the machine shop.
6   After the block is returned, clean all oil holes and oil galleries one more time (brushes for cleaning oil holes and galleries are available at most auto parts stores). Flush the passages with warm water until the water runs clear, dry the block thoroughly and wipe all machined surfaces with a light, rust-preventative oil. If you have access to compressed air, use it to speed the drying process and to blow out all the oil holes and galleries.
7   If the block is not extremely dirty or sludged up, you can do an adequate cleaning job with warm soapy water and a stiff brush. Take plenty of time and do a thorough job. Regardless of the cleaning method used, be very sure to thoroughly clean all oil holes and galleries, dry the block completely and coat all machined surfaces with light oil.
8   The threaded holes in the block must be clean to ensure accurate torque readings during reassembly. Run the proper size tap into each of the holes to remove any rust, corrosion, thread sealant or sludge and to restore any damaged threads. If possible, use compressed air to clear the holes of debris produced by this operation. Now is a good time to thoroughly clean the threads on the head bolts and the main bearing cap bolts as well.

9   Reinstall the main bearing caps and tighten the bolts finger tight.
10   After coating the sealing surfaces of the new soft plugs with a good quality gasket sealer, install them in the engine block. Make sure they are driven in straight and seated properly or leakage could result. Special tools are available for this purpose, but equally good results can be obtained using a large socket (with an outside diameter slightly larger than the outside diameter of the soft plug) and a large hammer.
11   If the engine is not going to be reassembled right away, cover it with a large plastic trash bag to keep it clean.

### 14   Engine block — inspection

1   Thoroughly clean the engine block as described in Section 13 and double-check to make sure that the ridge at the top of each cylinder has been completely removed.
2   Visually check the block for cracks, rust and corrosion. Look for stripped threads in the threaded holes. It is also a good idea to have the block checked for hidden cracks by an automotive machine shop that has the special equipment to do this type of work. If defects are found, have the block repaired, if possible, or replaced.
3   Check the cylinder bores for scuffing and scoring.
4   Using the appropriate precision measuring tools, measure each cylinder's diameter at the top (just under the ridge), center and bottom of the cylinder bore, *parallel* to the crankshaft axis (photos). Next, measure each cylinder's diameter at the same locations *across* the crankshaft axis. Compare the results to the Specifications. If the cylinder walls are badly scuffed or scored, or if they are out-of-round or tapered beyond the limits given in the Specifications, have the engine block rebored and honed at an automotive machine shop. If a rebore is done, oversize pistons and rings will be required as well.
5   If the cylinders are in reasonably good condition and not worn to the outside of the limits, and if the piston-to-cylinder clearances can be maintained properly, then they do not have to be rebored; honing is all that is necessary.
6   Before honing the cylinders, install the main bearing caps (without the bearings) and tighten the bolts to the specified torque.
7   To perform the honing operation, you will need the proper size flexible hone (with fine stones), plenty of light oil or honing oil, some rags and an electric drill motor. Mount the hone in the drill motor, compress the stones and slip the hone into the first cylinder (photo). Lubricate the cylinder thoroughly, turn on the drill and move the hone up and down in the cylinder at a pace which will produce a fine cross-hatch pattern on the cylinder walls (with the cross-hatch lines intersecting at approximately a 60° angle). Be sure to use plenty of lubricant and do not take off any more material than is absolutely necessary to produce the desired finish. Do not withdraw the hone from the cylinder while it is running. Instead, shut off the drill and continue moving the hone up and down in the cylinder until it comes to a complete stop, then compress the stones and withdraw the hone. Wipe the oil out of the cylinder and repeat the procedure on the remaining cylinders. Remember, do not remove too much material from the cylinder wall. If you do not have the tools or do not desire to perform the honing operation, most automotive machine shops will do it for a reasonable fee.

2A

8    After the honing job is complete, chamfer the top edges of the cylinder bores with a small file so the rings will not catch when the pistons are installed.

9    Next, the entire engine block must be thoroughly washed again with warm, soapy water to remove all traces of the abrasive grit produced during the honing operation. Be sure to run a brush through all oil holes and galleries and flush them with running water. After rinsing, dry the block and apply a coat of light rust preventative oil to all machined surfaces. Wrap the block in a plastic trash bag to keep it clean and set it aside until reassembly.

## 15   Piston/connecting rod assembly — inspection

1    Before the inspection process can be carried out, the piston/connecting rod assemblies must be cleaned and the original piston rings removed from the pistons. **Note:** *Always use new piston rings when the engine is reassembled.*

2    Using a piston ring installation tool, carefully remove the rings from the pistons. Do not nick or gouge the pistons in the process.

3    Scrape all traces of carbon from the top (or crown) of the piston. A hand-held wire brush or a piece of fine emery cloth can be used once the majority of the deposits have been scraped away. Do not, under any circumstances, use a wire brush mounted in a drill motor to remove deposits from the pistons. The piston material is soft and will be eroded away by the wire brush.

4    Use a piston ring groove cleaning tool to remove any carbon deposits from the ring grooves. If a tool is not available, a piece broken off the old ring will do the job. Be very careful to remove only the carbon deposits. Do not remove any metal and do not nick or scratch the sides of the ring grooves (photo).

5    Once the deposits have been removed, clean the piston/rod assemblies with solvent and dry them thoroughly. Make sure that the oil hole in the big end of the connecting rod and the oil return holes in the back sides of the ring grooves are clear.

6    If the pistons are not damaged or worn excessively, and if the engine block is not rebored, new pistons will not be necessary. Normal piston wear appears as even vertical wear on the piston thrust surfaces and slight looseness of the top ring in its groove. New piston rings, on the other hand, should always be used when an engine is rebuilt.

7    Carefully inspect each piston for cracks around the skirt, at the pin bosses and at the ring lands.

8    Look for scoring and scuffing on the thrust faces of the skirt, holes in the piston crown and burned areas at the edge of the crown. If the skirt is scored or scuffed, the engine may have been suffering from overheating and/or abnormal combustion, which caused excessively high operating temperatures. The cooling and lubrication systems should be checked thoroughly. A hole in the piston crown, an extreme to be sure, is an indication that abnormal combustion (preignition) was occurring. Burned areas at the edge of the piston crown are usually evidence of spark knock (detonation). If any of the above problems exist, the causes must be corrected or the damage will occur again.

9    Corrosion of the piston (evidenced by pitting) indicates that coolant is leaking into the combustion chamber and/or the crankcase. Again, the cause must be corrected or the problem may persist in the rebuilt engine.

10   Measure the piston ring side clearance by laying a new piston ring in each ring groove and slipping a feeler gauge in beside it (photo). Check the clearance at three or four locations around each groove. Be sure to use the correct ring for each groove; they are different. If the side clearance is greater than specified, new pistons and/or rings will have to be used.

11   Check the piston-to-bore clearance by measuring the bore (see Section 14) and the piston diameter (photo). Make sure that the pistons and bores are correctly matched. Measure the piston across the skirt, on the thrust faces (at a 90° angle to the piston pin), directly in line with the center of the pin hole. **Note:** *On V6 engines, make the measurement 1/4-inch below the oil ring groove.* Subtract the piston diameter from the bore diameter to obtain the clearance. In the case of an F- or L-head engine, the manufacturer also recommends the following alternative method of determining piston-to-bore clearance. Obtain a piece of 0.003-inch thick feeler gauge stock which is 3/4-inch

wide. Feeler gauge stock comes in 12-inch lengths and is generally available at automotive parts stores. Insert the piston into the cylinder bore upside-down with the feeler gauge extending the full length of the piston on the thrust side (opposite the slot). Attach a suitable scale to the feeler gauge and measure the amount of force necessary to remove it from between the piston and bore. The scale should register between five and ten pounds. If the pull is excessive, a slightly smaller piston or additional honing of the cylinder bore is necessary. Too little pull indicates the need for a larger piston. If it is greater than specified, the block will have to be rebored and new pistons and rings installed. Check the piston-to-rod clearance by twisting the piston and rod in opposite directions. Any noticeable play indicates that there is excessive wear, which must be corrected. The piston/connecting rod assemblies should be taken to an automotive machine shop to have new piston pins installed and the pistons and connecting rods rebored.

12   If the pistons must be removed from the connecting rods, such as when new pistons must be installed, or if the piston pins have too much play in them, they should be taken to an automotive machine shop. While they are there, it would be convenient to have the connecting rods checked for bend and twist, as automotive machine shops have special equipment for this purpose. *Unless new pistons or connecting rods must be installed, do not disassemble the pistons from the connecting rods.*

13   Check the connecting rods for cracks and other damage. Temporarily remove the rod caps, lift out the old bearing inserts, wipe the rod and cap bearing surfaces clean and inspect them for nicks, gouges and scratches. After checking the rods, replace the old bearings, slip the caps into place and tighten the nuts finger tight.

## 16   Crankshaft — inspection

1    Clean the crankshaft with solvent and dry it thoroughly. Be sure to clean the oil holes with a stiff brush and flush them with solvent. Check the main and connecting rod bearing journals for uneven wear, scoring, pitting and cracks. Check the remainder of the crankshaft for cracks and damage.

2    Using an appropriate size micrometer, measure the diameter of the main and connecting rod journals (photo) and compare the results to the Specifications. By measuring the diameter at a number of points around the journal's circumference, you will be able to determine whether or not the journal is worn out-of-round. Take the measurement at each end of the journal, near the crank throw, to determine whether the journal is tapered.

3    If the crankshaft journals are damaged, tapered, out-of-round or worn beyond the limits given in the Specificatioins, have the crankshaft reground by a reputable automotive machine shop. Be sure to use the correct undersize bearing inserts if the crankshaft is reconditioned.

4    Refer to Section 17 and examine the main and rod bearing inserts. If the bearing inserts and journals are all in good condition, do not decide to reuse the bearings until the oil clearances have been checked.

## 17   Main and connecting rod bearings — inspection

1    Even though the main and connecting rod bearings should be replaced with new ones during the engine overhaul, the old bearings should be retained for close examination, as they may reveal valuable information about the condition of the engine.

2    Bearing failure occurs mainly because of lack of lubrication, the presence of dirt or other foreign particles, overloading the engine and corrosion. Regardless of the cause of bearing failure, it must be corrected before the engine is reassembled to prevent it from happening again.

3    When examining the bearings, remove them from the engine block, the main bearing caps, the connecting rods and the rod caps and lay them out on a clean surface in the same general position as their location in the engine. This will enable you to match any noted bearing problems with the corresponding crankshaft journal.

4    Dirt and other foreign particles get into the engine in a variety of ways. If may be left in the engine during assembly, or it may pass through filters or breathers. It may get into the oil, and from there into the bearings. Metal chips from machining operations and normal engine wear are often present. Abrasives are sometimes left in engine com-

15.11  Measure the piston diameter directly in line with the piston pin hole *(except on V6 engines)*

16.2  Measure the diameter of each crankshaft journal at several points to detect taper and out-of-round conditions

18.3A  Use the piston to square up the ring in the cylinder prior to checking the ring end gap

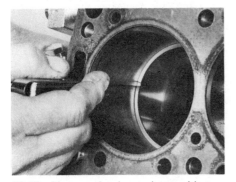

18.3B  Measure the ring end gap with a feeler gauge

18.9A  Installing the spacer/expander in the oil control ring groove

18.9B  *Do not* use a piston ring tool when installing the oil ring side rails

2A

ponents after reconditioning, especially when parts are not thoroughly cleaned using the proper cleaning methods. Whatever the source, these foreign objects often end up embedded in the soft bearing material and are easily recognized. Large particles will not embed in the bearing and will score or gouge the bearing and shaft. The best prevention for this cause of bearing failure is to clean all parts thoroughly and keep everything spotlessly clean during engine assembly. Frequent and regular engine oil and filter changes are also recommended.

5    Lack of lubrication (or lubrication breakdown) has a number of interrelated causes. Excessive heat (which thins the oil), overloading (which squeezes the oil from the bearing face) and oil leakage or throw-off (from excessive bearing clearances, worn oil pump or high engine speeds) all contribute to lubrication breakdown. Blocked oil passages, which usually are the result of misaligned oil holes in a bearing shell, will also oil-starve a bearing and destroy it. When lack of lubrication is the cause of bearing failure, the bearing material is wiped or extruded from the steel backing of the bearing. Temperatures may increase to the point where the steel backing turns blue from overheating.

6    Driving habits can have a definite effect on bearing life. Full-throttle, low-speed operation (or 'lugging' the engine) puts very high loads on bearings, which tends to squeeze out the oil film. These loads cause the bearings to flex, which produces fine cracks in the bearing face (fatigue failure). Eventually the bearing material will loosen in pieces and tear away from the steel backing. Short-trip driving leads to corrosion of bearings because insufficient engine heat is produced to drive off the condensed water and corrosive gases. These products collect in the engine oil, forming acid and sludge. As the oil is carried to the engine bearings, the acid attacks and corrodes the bearing material.

7    Incorrect bearing installation during engine assembly will lead to bearing failure as well. Tight-fitting bearings leave insufficient bearing oil clearance and will result in oil starvation. Dirt or foreign particles trapped behind a bearing insert result in high spots on the bearing which lead to failure.

## 18   Piston rings — installation

1    Before installing the new piston rings, the ring end gaps must be

checked. It is assumed that the piston ring side clearance has been checked and verified correct (Section 15).

2    Lay out the piston/connecting rod assemblies and the new ring sets so the ring sets will be matched with the same piston and cylinder during the end gap measurement and engine assembly.

3    Insert the top (number one) ring into the first cylinder and square it up with the cylinder walls by pushing it in with the top of the piston (photo). The ring should be near the bottom of the cylinder at the lower limit of ring travel. To measure the end gap, slip a feeler gauge between the ends of the ring (photo). Compare the measurement to the Specifications.

4    If the gap is larger or smaller than specified, double-check to make sure that you have the correct rings before proceeding.

5    If the gap is too small, it must be enlarged or the ring ends may come in contact with each other during engine operation, which can cause serious damage to the engine. The end gap can be increased by filing the ring ends very carefully with a fine file. Mount the *file* in a vise equipped with soft jaws, slip the ring over the file with the ends contacting the file face and slowly move the ring to remove material from the ends. *When performing this operation, file only from the outside in.*

6    Excess end gap is not critical unless it is greater than 0.040-inch (1 mm). Again, double-check to make sure you have the correct rings for your engine.

7    Repeat the procedure for each ring that will be installed in the first cylinder and for each ring in the remaining cylinders. Remember to keep rings, pistons and cylinders matched up.

8    Once the ring end gaps have been checked/corrected, the rings can be installed on the pistons.

9    The oil control ring (lowest one on the piston) is installed first. It is composed of three separate components. Slip the spacer expander into the groove (photo), then install the upper side rail. *Do not use a piston ring installation tool on the oil ring side rails, as they may be damaged.* Instead, place one end of the side rail into the groove between the space expander and the ring land, hold it firmly in place and slide a finger around the piston while pushing the rail into the groove (photo). Next, install the lower side rail in the same manner.

10  After the three oil ring components have been installed, check to

make sure that both the upper and lower side rails can be turned smoothly in the ring groove.

11  The number two (middle) ring is installed next. It is stamped with a mark so it can be readily distinguished from the top ring (the top ring is marked Top or T). **Note:** *Do not mix up the top and middle rings since they have different cross sections. On F- and L-head four-cylinder engines, the top ring can be distinguished by the bevel on the inside edge, while the middle ring has a slightly tapered face only. On these engines, the T or Top stamped on the rings indicates only how the ring is to be installed, not the groove it is installed in.*

12  Use a piston ring installation tool and *make sure that the identification mark is facing up,* then slip the ring into the middle groove on the piston (photo). Do not expand the ring any more than is necessary to slide it over the piston.

13  Finally, install the number one (top) ring in the same manner. Make sure the identifying mark is facing up.

14  Repeat the procedure for the remaining pistons and rings. Be careful not to confuse the number one and number two rings.

---

**19  Piston/connecting rod assembly — installation and bearing oil clearance check**

---

1  Before installing the piston/connecting rod assemblies, the cylinder walls must be perfectly clean, the top edge of each cylinder must be chamfered, and the crankshaft must be in place.

2  Remove the connecting rod cap from the end of the number one connecting rod. Remove the old bearing inserts and wipe the bearing surfaces of the connecting rod and cap with a clean, lint-free cloth (they must be kept spotlessly clean).

3  Clean the back side of the new upper bearing half, then lay it in

**Fig. 2.8   Typical piston ring marks (always install the rings with the marks facing *up*) (Sec 18)**

place in the connecting rod. Make sure that the tab on the bearing fits into the recess in the rod. Also, the oil holes in each rod and upper bearing insert must line up. Do not hammer the bearing insert into place and be very careful not to nick or gouge the bearing face. *Do not lubricate the bearing at this time.*

4  Clean the back side of the other bearing insert and install it in the rod cap. Again, make sure the tab on the bearing fits into the recess in the cap, and do not apply any lubricant. It is critically important that the mating surfaces of the bearing and connecting rod are perfectly clean and oil-free when they are assembled.

5  Position the piston ring gaps as shown in the accompanying illustrations, then slip a section of plastic or rubber hose over the connecting rod cap bolts. **Note:** *On F- and L-head four-cylinder engines only, position the rings so that none of the gaps are aligned with each other or the T-slot in the piston skirt.*

6  Lubricate the piston and rings with clean engine oil and attach a piston ring compressor to the piston. Leave the skirt protruding about 1/4-inch to guide the piston into the cylinder. The rings must be compressed as far as possible.

7  Rotate the crankshaft until the number one connecting rod journal is as far from the number one cylinder as possible (bottom dead

18.12   Installing the compression rings (note the special tool)

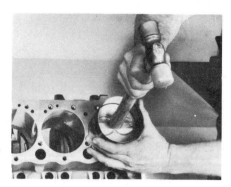

19.10   If resistance is encountered when tapping the piston/connecting rod assembly into the block, *stop immediately* and make sure the rings are fully compressed

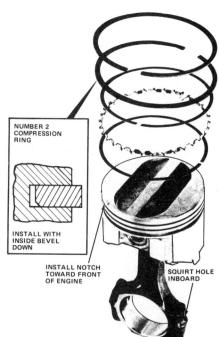

Fig. 2.9   Piston ring gap positions (V6 and V8 engines) (Sec 19)

19.12   Position the Plastigage strip on the bearing journal, parallel to the journal axis

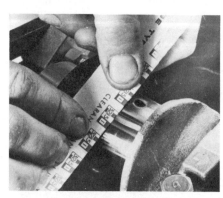

19.14   The crushed Plastigage is compared to the scale printed on the container to obtain the bearing oil clearance

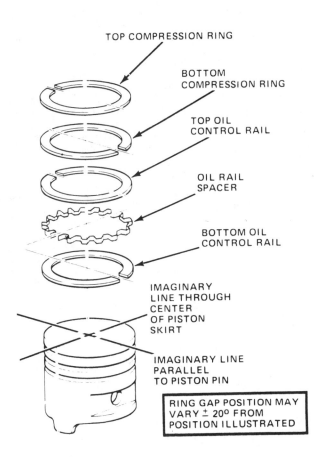

TOP COMPRESSION RING

BOTTOM COMPRESSION RING

TOP OIL CONTROL RAIL

OIL RAIL SPACER

BOTTOM OIL CONTROL RAIL

IMAGINARY LINE THROUGH CENTER OF PISTON SKIRT

IMAGINARY LINE PARALLEL TO PISTON PIN

RING GAP POSITION MAY VARY ± 20° FROM POSITION ILLUSTRATED

**Fig. 2.10  Piston ring gap positions (in-line six-cylinder engines) (Sec 19)**

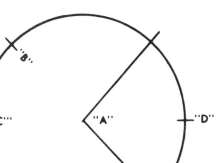

ENGINE FRONT

"B"

"C"        "A"        "D"

"B"

**Fig. 2.11  Piston ring end gap positions (GM 151 cu in four-cylinder engines) (Sec 19)**

A  Oil ring spacer gap
B  Oil ring side rail gaps
C  Second compression ring gap
D  Top compression ring gap

center), and apply a uniform coat of engine oil to the cylinder walls.

8   With the notch or arrow on top of the piston (or the F on the skirt) facing to the front of the engine, gently place the piston/connecting rod assembly into the number one cylinder bore and rest the bottom edge of the ring compressor on the engine block. Tap the top edge of the ring compressor to make sure it is contacting the block around its entire circumference. **Note:** *On in-line six-cylinder engines, the oil holes in the connecting rods must face the camshaft. On GM four-cylinder engines, the projections on the rods must face the front of the engine. On V8s, the numbers on the rods and caps must face out and the oil holes must face in. On F- and L-head four-cylinder engines, the connecting rod identification number must face the camshaft side of the block. On V6 engines, the right bank piston/connecting rod assemblies must be installed with the bosses on the rods and caps facing forward. On the left bank, the bosses must face to the rear. In both cases, the connecting rod oil holes will face the camshaft (up).*

9   Clean the number one connecting rod journal on the crankshaft and the bearing faces in the rod.

10  Carefully tap on the top of the piston with the end of a wooden hammer handle (photo) while guiding the end of the connecting rod into place on the crankshaft journal. The piston rings may try to pop out of the ring compressor just before entering the cylinder bore, so keep some downward pressure on the ring compressor. Work slowly, and if any resistance is felt as the piston enters the cylinder, stop immediately. Find out what is hanging up and fix it before proceeding. *Do not, for any reason, force the piston into the cylinder, as you will break a ring and/or the piston.*

11  Once the piston/connecting rod assembly is installed, the connecting rod bearing oil clearance must be checked before the rod cap is permanently bolted in place.

**2A**

12  Cut a piece of the the appropriate type Plastigage slightly shorter than the width of the connecting rod bearing and lay it in place on the number one connecting rod journal, parallel with the journal axis (it must not cross the oil hole in the journal) (photo).

13  Clean the connecting rod cap bearing face, remove the protective hoses from the connecting rod bolts and gently install the rod cap in place. Make sure the mating mark on the cap is on the same side as the mark on the connecting rod. Install the nuts and tighten them to the specified torque, working up to it in three steps. *Do not rotate the crankshaft at any time during this operation.*

14  Remove the rod cap, being very careful not to disturb the Plastigage. Compare the width of the crushed Plastigage to the scale printed on the Plastigage container to obtain the oil clearance (photo). Compare it to the Specifications to make sure the clearance is correct. If the clearance is not correct, double-check to make sure that you have the correct size bearing inserts. Also, recheck the crankshaft connecting rod journal diameter and make sure that no dirt or oil was between the bearing inserts and the connecting rod or cap when the clearance was measured.

15  Carefully scrape all traces of the Plastigage material off the rod journal and/or bearing face (be very careful not to scratch the bearing — use your fingernail or a piece of hardwood). Make sure the bearing faces are perfectly clean, then apply a uniform layer of clean, high-quality moly-based grease or engine assembly lube to both of them. You will have to push the piston into the cylinder to expose the face of the bearing insert in the connecting rod; be sure to slip the protective hoses over the rod bolts first.

16  Slide the connecting rod back into place on the journal, remove the protective hoses from the rod cap bolts, install the rod cap and tighten the nuts to the specified torque. Again, work up to the torque in three steps.

17  Repeat the entire procedure for the remaining piston/connecting rod assemblies. Keep the back sides of the bearing inserts and the inside of the connecting rod and cap perfectly clean when assembling them. Make sure you have the correct piston for the cylinder and that the notch, arrow or F on the piston faces to the front of the engine when the piston is installed. Remember, use plenty of oil to lubricate the piston before installing the ring compressor and cap. Also, when installing the rod caps for the final time, be sure to lubricate the bearing faces adequately. **Note:** *On F- and L-head four-cylinder engines, the connecting rod cap nuts are locked with stamped nuts. Used stamped nuts should be discarded and replaced with new ones. These locking stamped nuts should be installed with the flat face against the connecting rod nut. Turn each locking nut finger tight, then 1/3-turn more with a wrench.*

## 20　Initial start-up and break-in after overhaul

1　Once the engine has been properly installed in the vehicle, double-check the engine oil and coolant levels.
2　With the spark plugs out of the engine and the coil high-tension lead grounded to the engine block, crank the engine over until oil pressure registers on the gauge (if so equipped) or until the oil light goes off.
3　Install the spark plugs, hook up the plug wires and the coil high-tension lead.
4　Make sure the carburetor choke plate is closed, then start the engine. It may take a few moments for the gasoline to reach the carburetor, but the engine should start without a great deal of effort.
5　As soon as the engine starts, it should be set at a fast idle (to ensure proper oil circulation) and allowed to warm up to normal operating temperature. While the engine is warming up, make a thorough check for oil and coolant leaks.

6　Shut the engine off and recheck the engine oil and coolant levels. Also, check the ignition timing and the engine idle speed (refer to Chapter 1) and make any necessary adjustments.
7　Drive the vehicle to an area with minimum traffic, accelerate at full throttle from 30 to 50 mph, then allow the vehicle to slow to 30 mph with the throttle closed. Repeat the procedure 10 or 12 times. This will load the piston rings and cause them to seat properly against the cylinder walls. Check again for oil and coolant leaks.
8　Drive the vehicle gently for the first 500 miles (no sustained high speeds) and keep a constant check on the oil level. It is not unusual for an engine to use oil during the break-in period.
9　At approximately 500 to 600 miles, change the oil and filter, re-torque the cylinder head bolts and recheck the valve clearances (if applicable).
10　For the next few hundred miles, drive the vehicle normally. Do not pamper it or abuse it.
11　After 2000 miles, change the oil and filter again and consider the engine fully broken in.

# Chapter 2 Part B
# 151 cu in four-cylinder engine

## Contents

Camshaft and bearings — removal and installation . . . . . . . .  38
Crankshaft pulley hub and front oil seal — removal
  and installation . . . . . . . . . . . . . . . . . . . . . . . . . . . . . . . .  31
Crankshaft — inspection . . . . . . . . . . . . . . . . . .  Chapter 2A
Crankshaft — installation and main bearing
  oil clearance check . . . . . . . . . . . . . . . . . . . . . . . . . . . .  40
Crankshaft — removal . . . . . . . . . . . . . . . . . . . . . . . . . . . .  39
Cylinder head — reassembly . . . . . . . . . . . . . . . .  Chapter 2A
Cylinder head — disassembly . . . . . . . . . . . . . . .  Chapter 2A
Cylinder head — cleaning and inspection . . . . . . . .  Chapter 2A
Cylinder head — installation . . . . . . . . . . . . . . . . . . . . . .  30
Cylinder head — removal . . . . . . . . . . . . . . . . . . . . . . . . .  29
Engine block — cleaning . . . . . . . . . . . . . . . . . . .  Chapter 2A
Engine block — inspection . . . . . . . . . . . . . . . . . .  Chapter 2A
Engine disassembly — general information . . . . . . .  Chapter 2A
Engine — installation . . . . . . . . . . . . . . . . . . . . . . . . . . . .  41
Engine overhaul — general information . . . . . . . . .  Chapter 2A
Engine rebuilding alternatives . . . . . . . . . . . . . . . .  Chapter 2A
Engine — removal . . . . . . . . . . . . . . . . . . . . . . . . . . . . . . .  22
Engine removal — methods and precautions . . . . . .  Chapter 2A
Exhaust manifold — removal and installation . . . . . . . . . . .  28
Flywheel and rear main oil seal — removal and installation . . .  37
General information . . . . . . . . . . . . . . . . . . . . . . . . . . . . . .  21
Hydraulic lifters — removal, inspection and
  installation . . . . . . . . . . . . . . . . . . . . . . . . . . . . . . . . . . .  26
Initial start-up and break-in after overhaul . . . . . . .  Chapter 2A
Intake manifold — removal and installation . . . . . . . . . . . . .  27
Main and connecting rod bearings — inspection . . .  Chapter 2A
Oil pan — removal and installation . . . . . . . . . . . . . . . . . . .  34
Oil pump — disassembly, inspection and reassembly . . . . . . .  36
Oil pump driveshaft — removal and installation . . . . . . . . . . .  33
Oil pump — removal and installation . . . . . . . . . . . . . . . . . .  35
Piston/connecting rod assembly — inspection . . . . .  Chapter 2A
Piston/connection rod assembly — installation
  and bearing oil clearance check . . . . . . . . . . . . .  Chapter 2A
Piston/connecting rod assembly — removal . . . . . . .  Chapter 2A
Piston rings — installation . . . . . . . . . . . . . . . . . .  Chapter 2A
Pushrod cover — removal and installation . . . . . . . . . . . . . .  25
Repair operations possible with the engine in the
  vehicle . . . . . . . . . . . . . . . . . . . . . . . . . . . . . . .  Chapter 2A
Rocker arm cover — removal and installation . . . . . . . . . . . .  23
Rocker arms, pushrods and valve springs — removal
  and installation (engine in vehicle) . . . . . . . . . . . . . . . . . .  24
Timing gear cover — removal and installation . . . . . . . . . . . .  32
Valves — servicing . . . . . . . . . . . . . . . . . . . . . . . .  Chapter 2A

## Specifications

### General
Displacement . . . . . . . . . . . . . . . . . . . . . . . . . . . . . . .  151 cu in
Bore and stroke . . . . . . . . . . . . . . . . . . . . . . . . . . . . .  4.0 x 3.0 in
Compression ratio . . . . . . . . . . . . . . . . . . . . . . . . . . .  8.24 : 1
Oil pressure . . . . . . . . . . . . . . . . . . . . . . . . . . . . . . . .  36 to 41 psi at 2000 rpm

### Cylinder bores
Taper limit
  1980 . . . . . . . . . . . . . . . . . . . . . . . . . . . . . . . . . . .  0.0005 in max.
  1981 through 1983 . . . . . . . . . . . . . . . . . . . . . . . . . .  0.002 in max.
Out-of-round limit
  1980 . . . . . . . . . . . . . . . . . . . . . . . . . . . . . . . . . . .  0.0005 in max.
  1981 through 1983 . . . . . . . . . . . . . . . . . . . . . . . . . .  0.0015 in max.

### Pistons and rings
Piston diameter . . . . . . . . . . . . . . . . . . . . . . . . . . . . .  3.9968 to 3.992 in
Piston-to-cylinder bore clearance
  Top . . . . . . . . . . . . . . . . . . . . . . . . . . . . . . . . . . . .  0.0025 to 0.0033 in
  Bottom . . . . . . . . . . . . . . . . . . . . . . . . . . . . . . . . . .  0.0017 to 0.0041
Piston ring side clearance . . . . . . . . . . . . . . . . . . . . .  0.0030 in
Piston ring end gap
  Top ring . . . . . . . . . . . . . . . . . . . . . . . . . . . . . . . . .  0.010 to 0.022 in
  2nd ring . . . . . . . . . . . . . . . . . . . . . . . . . . . . . . . . .  0.010 to 0.028 in
  Oil ring side rails . . . . . . . . . . . . . . . . . . . . . . . . . . .  0.015 to 0.055 in
Piston pin diameter . . . . . . . . . . . . . . . . . . . . . . . . . .  0.92705 to 0.92745 in
Piston pin-to-piston clearance
  Standard . . . . . . . . . . . . . . . . . . . . . . . . . . . . . . . . .  0.0003 in
  Service limit . . . . . . . . . . . . . . . . . . . . . . . . . . . . . .  0.0005 in
Piston pin-to-connecting rod clearance . . . . . . . . . . . .  Press fit

## Crankshaft and connecting rods

Main journal
  Diameter . . . . . . . . . . . . . . . . . . . . . . . . . . . . . . . . . . . . . . . .   2.2988 in
  Taper limit . . . . . . . . . . . . . . . . . . . . . . . . . . . . . . . . . . . . . .   0.0005 in max.
  Out-of-round limit . . . . . . . . . . . . . . . . . . . . . . . . . . . . . . . .   0.0005 in max.
Main bearing oil clearance
  Standard . . . . . . . . . . . . . . . . . . . . . . . . . . . . . . . . . . . . . . . .   0.0005 in
  Service limit . . . . . . . . . . . . . . . . . . . . . . . . . . . . . . . . . . . . .   0.0022 in
Connecting rod journal
  Diameter . . . . . . . . . . . . . . . . . . . . . . . . . . . . . . . . . . . . . . . .   2.000 in
  Taper limit . . . . . . . . . . . . . . . . . . . . . . . . . . . . . . . . . . . . . .   0.0005 in max.
  Out-of-round limit . . . . . . . . . . . . . . . . . . . . . . . . . . . . . . . .   0.0005 in max.
Connecting rod bearing oil clearance
  Standard . . . . . . . . . . . . . . . . . . . . . . . . . . . . . . . . . . . . . . . .   0.0005 in
  Service limit . . . . . . . . . . . . . . . . . . . . . . . . . . . . . . . . . . . . .   0.0026 in
Connecting rod end play . . . . . . . . . . . . . . . . . . . . . . . . . . . . .   0.017 in
Crankshaft end play . . . . . . . . . . . . . . . . . . . . . . . . . . . . . . . . .   0.0035 to 0.0085 in

## Camshaft

Bearing journal diameter . . . . . . . . . . . . . . . . . . . . . . . . . . . . .   1.869 in
Bearing oil clearance
  Standard . . . . . . . . . . . . . . . . . . . . . . . . . . . . . . . . . . . . . . . .   0.0007 in
  Service limit . . . . . . . . . . . . . . . . . . . . . . . . . . . . . . . . . . . . .   0.0027 in
Lobe lift . . . . . . . . . . . . . . . . . . . . . . . . . . . . . . . . . . . . . . . . . .   0.230 in
End play . . . . . . . . . . . . . . . . . . . . . . . . . . . . . . . . . . . . . . . . . .   0.0015 to 0.0050 in

## Cylinder head and valve train

Cylinder head warpage limit . . . . . . . . . . . . . . . . . . . . . . . . . .   0.008 in max.
Valve seat angle . . . . . . . . . . . . . . . . . . . . . . . . . . . . . . . . . . . .   46º
Valve seat width
  Intake . . . . . . . . . . . . . . . . . . . . . . . . . . . . . . . . . . . . . . . . . . .   0.0353 to 0.0747 in
  Exhaust . . . . . . . . . . . . . . . . . . . . . . . . . . . . . . . . . . . . . . . . .   0.058 to 0.097 in
Valve face angle . . . . . . . . . . . . . . . . . . . . . . . . . . . . . . . . . . . .   45º
Valve margin minimum width . . . . . . . . . . . . . . . . . . . . . . . . .   1/32 in
Valve stem-to-guide clearance
  Standard
    1982 and 1983 *exhaust* only . . . . . . . . . . . . . . . . . . . . .   0.020 in
    All others . . . . . . . . . . . . . . . . . . . . . . . . . . . . . . . . . . . . . .   0.010 in
  Service limit . . . . . . . . . . . . . . . . . . . . . . . . . . . . . . . . . . . . .   0.0027 in
Valve spring pressure (lbs at specified length)
  Closed . . . . . . . . . . . . . . . . . . . . . . . . . . . . . . . . . . . . . . . . . .   78 to 86 at 1.66 in
  Open . . . . . . . . . . . . . . . . . . . . . . . . . . . . . . . . . . . . . . . . . . .   172 to 180 at 1.254 in
Valve lash adjustment . . . . . . . . . . . . . . . . . . . . . . . . . . . . . . .   Zero
Lifter leakdown rate . . . . . . . . . . . . . . . . . . . . . . . . . . . . . . . . .   12 to 90 seconds with a 50-lb load
Lifter diameter . . . . . . . . . . . . . . . . . . . . . . . . . . . . . . . . . . . . .   0.8120 to 0.8427 in
Lifter bore diameter . . . . . . . . . . . . . . . . . . . . . . . . . . . . . . . . .   0.8435 to 0.8445 in
Lifter-to-bore clearance . . . . . . . . . . . . . . . . . . . . . . . . . . . . . .   0.0025 in
Pushrod length . . . . . . . . . . . . . . . . . . . . . . . . . . . . . . . . . . . . .   8.927 in

## Torque specifications

| | Ft-lb | Nm |
|---|---|---|
| Adapter-to-intake manifold . . . . . . . . . . . . . . . . . . . . . . . . . . . . | 10 to 16 | 14 to 20 |
| Camshaft thrust plate-to-block screws . . . . . . . . . . . . . . . . . | 4.4 to 9 | 6 to 12 |
| Carburetor-to-manifold nuts . . . . . . . . . . . . . . . . . . . . . . . . . . | 10 to 16 | 14 to 20 |
| Connecting rod nuts . . . . . . . . . . . . . . . . . . . . . . . . . . . . . . . . . | 30 | 40 |
| Crankshaft pulley hub bolt . . . . . . . . . . . . . . . . . . . . . . . . . . . | 157 to 163 | 217 to 223 |
| Cylinder head bolts . . . . . . . . . . . . . . . . . . . . . . . . . . . . . . . . . | 92 | 125 |
| Distributor clamp bolt . . . . . . . . . . . . . . . . . . . . . . . . . . . . . . . | 6 to 12 | 9 to 15 |
| Distributor clamp pivot bolt . . . . . . . . . . . . . . . . . . . . . . . . . . | 9 to 15 | 14 to 21 |
| Driveplate-to-crankshaft bolts . . . . . . . . . . . . . . . . . . . . . . . . | 42 to 48 | 57 to 63 |
| Driveplate-to-converter bolts . . . . . . . . . . . . . . . . . . . . . . . . . | 40 | 54 |
| EGR valve-to-manifold . . . . . . . . . . . . . . . . . . . . . . . . . . . . . . | 6.6 to 11 | 9 to 15 |
| Exhaust manifold bolts . . . . . . . . . . . . . . . . . . . . . . . . . . . . . . | 36 to 42 | 47 to 53 |
| Exhaust pipe-to-manifold nuts . . . . . . . . . . . . . . . . . . . . . . . . | 34 to 40 | 49 to 55 |
| Fan and pulley-to-water pump . . . . . . . . . . . . . . . . . . . . . . . . | 15 to 21 | 21 to 27 |
| Flywheel-to-crankshaft bolts . . . . . . . . . . . . . . . . . . . . . . . . . | 65 to 71 | 90 to 96 |
| Fuel pump-to-block . . . . . . . . . . . . . . . . . . . . . . . . . . . . . . . . . | 12 to 18 | 17 to 23 |
| Intake manifold . . . . . . . . . . . . . . . . . . . . . . . . . . . . . . . . . . . . | 34 to 40 | 47 to 53 |
| Main bearing cap bolts . . . . . . . . . . . . . . . . . . . . . . . . . . . . . . | 65 | 88 |
| Oil filter adapter-to-block . . . . . . . . . . . . . . . . . . . . . . . . . . . . | 32 to 38 | 44 to 50 |
| Oil pan drain plug . . . . . . . . . . . . . . . . . . . . . . . . . . . . . . . . . . | 23 to 28 | 31 to 37 |
| Oil pan bolts . . . . . . . . . . . . . . . . . . . . . . . . . . . . . . . . . . . . . . | 45 to 48 | 53 to 59 |
| Oil pump cover bolts . . . . . . . . . . . . . . . . . . . . . . . . . . . . . . . . | 6 to 12 | 14 to 20 |
| Oil pump-to-block bolts . . . . . . . . . . . . . . . . . . . . . . . . . . . . . . | 15 to 21 | 22 to 28 |
| Oil pump-to-driveshaft plate . . . . . . . . . . . . . . . . . . . . . . . . . | 7 to 13 | 11 to 17 |
| Oil screen support nut . . . . . . . . . . . . . . . . . . . . . . . . . . . . . . . | 25 to 31 | 35 to 41 |

| | | |
|---|---|---|
| Air injection bracket | 34 to 40 | 47 to 54 |
| Pressure plate-to-flywheel bolts | 15 to 22 | 20 to 30 |
| Crankshaft pulley bolt | 22 to 28 | 31 to 37 |
| Pushrod cover bolts | 4.4 to 9 | 6 to 12 |
| Rocker arm cover bolts | 4 to 10 | 7 to 13 |
| Rocker arm stud | 57 to 63 | 73 to 79 |
| Rocker arm-to-stud nuts | 17 to 23 | 24 to 30 |
| Starter bolts | 14 to 20 | 21 to 27 |
| Thermostat housing bolts | 19 to 25 | 27 to 33 |
| Timing cover | 5 | 2 to 8 |
| Timing cover-to-block | 9 | 6 to 12 |
| Water outlet housing | 14 to 20 | 20 to 26 |
| Water pump | 14 to 20 | 20 to 26 |

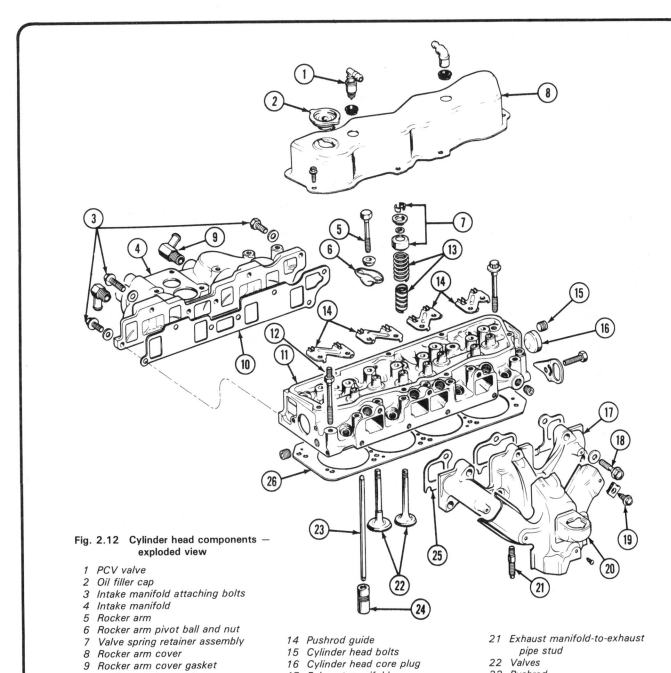

**2B**

Fig. 2.12 Cylinder head components —
exploded view

1  PCV valve
2  Oil filler cap
3  Intake manifold attaching bolts
4  Intake manifold
5  Rocker arm
6  Rocker arm pivot ball and nut
7  Valve spring retainer assembly
8  Rocker arm cover
9  Rocker arm cover gasket
10  Intake manifold gasket
11  Cylinder head
12  Rocker arm stud
13  Valve spring

14  Pushrod guide
15  Cylinder head bolts
16  Cylinder head core plug
17  Exhaust manifold
18  Exhaust manifold bolt
19  Dipstick tube attaching screw
20  Exhaust manifold heat shield

21  Exhaust manifold-to-exhaust
       pipe stud
22  Valves
23  Pushrod
24  Valve lifter
25  Exhaust manifold gasket
26  Cylinder head gasket

## 21   General information

The 151 cubic-inch four-cylinder engine features a crossflow cylinder head, hydraulic valve lifters and ball and socket-type rocker arms. The camshaft is mounted in the engine block and is gear driven by the crankshaft.

The oil pump is mounted in the crankcase and is driven by a shaft actuated by the crankshaft. The crankshaft is supported by five replaceable main bearings.

## 22   Engine removal

**Note:** *The following sequence of operations does not necessarily need to be performed in the order given. It is, rather, a checklist of everything that must be disconnected or removed before the engine can be lifted out of the vehicle. If your vehicle is equipped with an automatic transmission, the engine removal procedure will be slightly different from the procedure for vehicles equipped with a manual transmission. It is very important that all linkages, electrical wiring, hoses and cables be removed or disconnected before attempting to lift the engine clear of the vehicle, so double-check everything thoroughly.*

1   Open the hood and tilt it all the way back to provide clearance.
2   Disconnect the negative cable from the battery and the body ground wire from the dash panel.
3   Remove the air cleaner assembly.
4   Raise the vehicle and support it securely on jackstands.
5   Unbolt the exhaust pipe from the manifold and disconnect the oxygen sensor (if so equipped).
6   Remove the starter motor.
7   Disconnect the distributor and oil pressure sending unit wires.
8   *On manual transmission-equipped models,* disconnect the clutch hydraulic slave cylinder and remove the flywheel inspection plate. Remove the bellhousing-to-engine bolts.
9   *On automatic transmission-equipped models,* mark the torque converter-to-driveplate relative position, then remove the attaching bolts. Remove the torque converter housing-to-engine bolts.
10   Lower the vehicle and support the transmission with a jack.
11   Tag or mark all of the vacuum hoses and disconnect them.
12   Disconnect the bowl vent hose and mixture control solenoid wire from the carburetor (not all vehicles).
13   Disconnect the wires from the alternator.
14   Disconnect the throttle cable and the choke and solenoid wires from the carburetor.
15   Disconnect the coolant temperature sending unit wire from the engine.
16   Drain the coolant into a suitable container and remove the lower radiator hose. Remove the heater hoses.
17   Remove the fan shroud, upper radiator hose, radiator and shroud.
18   Disconnect and plug the power steering hoses.
19   Remove the engine mount nuts.
20   Attach a suitable lifting device to the engine. Raise the engine and move it carefully forward to disengage it from the transmission. It may be necessary to raise and lower the transmission with the jack to separate the engine from the transmission. Lift the engine from the engine compartment.

## 23   Rocker arm cover — removal and installation

**Note:** *If the engine has been removed from the vehicle, disregard the following steps which do not apply.*

1   Remove the air cleaner.
2   Remove the PCV valve and hose.
3   If so equipped, remove the PULSAIR air hose from the air valve.
4   Remove the spark plug wires from the plugs and mounting clips, labeling each wire as to its proper position.
5   Remove the rocker arm cover bolts.
6   Remove the rocker arm cover. To break the gasket seal, it may be necessary to tap the cover with your hand or a rubber mallet. Do not pry on the cover.
7   Prior to installation, clean all dirt, oil and old gasket material from

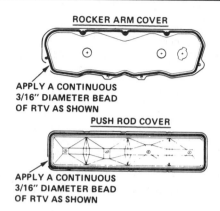

ROCKER ARM COVER

APPLY A CONTINUOUS
3/16" DIAMETER BEAD
OF RTV AS SHOWN

PUSH ROD COVER

APPLY A CONTINUOUS
3/16" DIAMETER BEAD
OF RTV AS SHOWN

**Fig. 2.13   Recommended sealant application for installation of the rocker arm and pushrod covers (Sec 23 and 25)**

the sealing surfaces of the cover and cylinder head with a degreaser.
8   Place a continuous 3/16-inch (5 mm) diameter bead of RTV-type sealant or equivalent around the sealing lip of the cover. Be sure to apply the sealant to the inside of the mounting bolt holes.
9   Place the rocker arm cover on the cylinder head while the sealant is still wet, install the mounting bolts and tighten them to the specified torque.
10   Complete the installation by reversing the removal procedure.

## 24   Rocker arms, pushrods and valve springs — removal and installation (engine in vehicle)

**Note:** *Valve mechanism components must be reinstalled in their original positions. Place all removed components in a compartmented box to aid in identification.*

1   Remove the rocker arm cover as described in Section 23.
2   If only the pushrod is to be replaced, loosen the rocker nut enough so the rocker arm can be rotated away from the pushrod. If the rocker arm or valve spring is to be replaced, remove the rocker arm nut and ball and lift off the rocker arm.
3   Pull the pushrod out of the hole.
4   If the valve spring is to be removed, remove the spark plug from the cylinder being serviced.
5   There are two methods of keeping the valve in place while the valve spring is removed. If you have access to compressed air, attach an air hose adapter to your air hose and insert it into the spark plug hole. When air pressure is applied, the valves will be held in place by the pressure.
6   If you do not have access to compressed air, bring the piston to top dead center (TDC) on the compression stroke. Feed a long piece of 1/4-inch nylon cord in through the spark plug hole until it fills the combustion chamber. Be sure to leave the end of the cord hanging out of the spark plug hole so it can be removed easily.
7   Thread the rocker arm nut onto the rocker arm stud. Position a valve spring compressor tool over the spring and hook it under the rocker arm nut. Using the nut to secure the tool, apply downward pressure to the valve spring. If care is taken, a screwdriver can also be used in this manner to compress the spring. Compress the spring just enough to allow the removal of the keepers, then let up on the spring.
8   Remove the valve spring retainer, cup shield, valve spring and valve stem oil seal. The valve stem oil seal must be replaced with a new one whenever the keepers have been disturbed.
9   Inspection procedures for the various valve components are detailed in Chapter 2A.
10   Installation is the reverse of the removal procedure. Prior to installing the rocker arms, coat the bearing surfaces of the arms and rocker arm balls with engine assembly lube or moly-based grease. The valve mechanisms require no special lash adjustment.

## 25   Pushrod cover — removal and installation

1   Remove the intake manifold as described in Section 27.

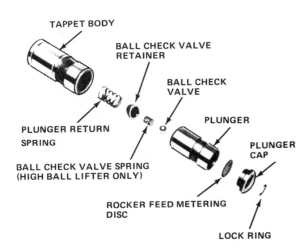

Fig. 2.14  Exploded view of the hydraulic valve lifter (Sec 26)

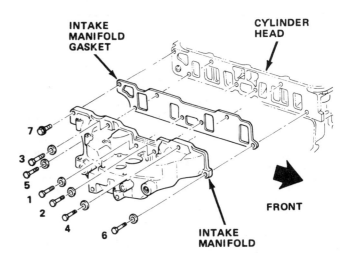

Fig. 2.15  Recommended tightening sequence for the intake
manifold mounting bolts (Sec 27)

2   Remove the pushrod cover bolts and lift off the cover. If the gasket seal is difficult to break, tap lightly on the cover with a rubber mallet. Do not pry on the cover.
3   Using a degreaser, thoroughly clean the sealing surfaces on the cover and engine block to remove all oil and old gasket material.
4   Prior to installation of the cover, place a continuous 3/16-inch (5 mm) bead of RTV-type sealant or equivalent to the sealing lip of the pushrod cover.
5   With the sealant still wet, place the cover in position on the block, install the cover bolts and tighten them to the specified torque.
6   Install the intake manifold and related components.

## 26  Hydraulic lifters — removal, inspection and installation

1   A noisy valve lifter is easiest to detect when the engine is idling. Place a length of hose or tubing near the position of each intake and exhaust valve while listening at the other end of the tube. Another method is to remove the rocker arm cover and, with the engine idling, place a finger on each of the valve spring retainers, one at a time. If a valve lifter is defective, it will be evident from the shock felt at the retainer as the valve seats.
2   Provided that adjustment is correct, the most likely cause of a noisy valve lifter is a piece of dirt trapped between the plunger and lifter body.
3   Remove the rocker arm cover as described in Section 23.
4   Remove the intake manifold as described in Section 27.
5   Remove the pushrod cover as described in Section 25.
6   Loosen the rocker arm nut and rotate the rocker arm away from the pushrod.
7   Remove the pushrod.
8   To remove the lifters, a special hydraulic lifter removal tool can be used, or a sharp scribe can be positioned at the top of the lifter and used to force the lifter up. Do not use pliers or other tools on the outside of the lifter body, as they will damage the machined surface and render the lifter useless.
9   The lifters should be kept separate for reinstallation in their original positions.
10   To dismantle a valve lifter, hold the plunger down with a pushrod and then extract the pushrod seat retainer using a small screwdriver.
11   Remove the pushrod seat and the metering valve.
12   Remove the plunger, ball check valve and plunger spring. Remove the ball check valve and spring by prying with a small screwdriver.
13   Examine all components for wear. Check the ball for flat spots. If any are noted, replace the complete lifter assembly.
14   Examine each lifter for scoring, wear and erosion of the camshaft lobe mating surface. Any imperfections on the lifter body surface is cause for replacement. Wear in the lifter bore in the block is rare.
15   Reassembly should be performed in the following manner:

a)   Place the check ball on the small hole in the bottom of the plunger.

b)   Insert the check ball spring in the seat in the ball retainer and place the retainer over the ball so that the spring rests on the ball. Using a small screwdriver, carefully press the retainer into position in the plunger.
c)   Place the plunger spring over the ball retainer, invert the lifter body and slide it over the spring and plunger. Make sure the oil holes in the body and plunger line up.
d)   Fill the assembly with SAE 10W oil. Place the metering valve and pushrod seat into position, press down on the seat and install the pushrod seat retainer.

16   When installing the lifters, make sure they are replaced in their original bores and coat them with engine assembly lube or clean engine oil.
17   Complete the installation by reversing the steps in the removal procedure.

## 27  Intake manifold — removal and installation

1   Remove the air cleaner, being sure to label the lines and hoses as to their proper locations.
2   Remove the PCV hose.
3   Disconnect the negative battery cable.
4   Drain the cooling system as described in Chapter 1.
5   Remove the carburetor as described in Chapter 4.
6   Remove the carburetor base gasket.
7   Disconnect the vacuum lines from the carburetor spacer.
8   Remove the EGR valve.
9   Remove the carburetor spacer.
10   Remove the carburetor spacer gasket.
11   Remove the throttle linkage and set it to one side for clearance.
12   Remove the heater hose from the intake manifold.
13   Remove the upper alternator bracket.
14   If equipped, remove the PULSAIR air valve bracket.
15   Remove the bolts that secure the intake manifold to the cylinder head and lift off the intake manifold.
16   Remove the manifold gasket.
17   If the intake manifold is to be replaced with another, transfer any remaining components still attached to the old manifold to the new one.
18   Before installing the manifold, clean the cylinder head and manifold gasket surfaces. All old gasket material and sealing compound must be removed prior to installation.
19   Apply a thin bead of RTV-type sealant to the intake manifold and cylinder head mating surfaces. Be certain that the sealant will not spread into the air or coolant passages when the manifold is installed.
20   Place a new intake manifold gasket on the manifold, place the manifold in position against the cylinder head and install the mounting bolts finger tight.
21   Tighten the manifold mounting bolts to the specified torque in the sequence shown in the accompanying illustration. Work up to the torque

**2B**

in three or four steps.

22  Install the remaining components in the reverse order of removal.

23  Fill the radiator with coolant, start the engine and check for leaks. Check the carburetor idle speed and adjust if necessary, as described in Chapter 1.

## 28  Exhaust manifold — removal and installation

1  If the vehicle is equipped with air conditioning, carefully examine the routing of the hoses and the mounting of the compressor. You may be able to remove the exhaust manifold without disconnecting the air conditioning system. If you are in doubt, take the vehicle to a dealer or other qualified automotive repair shop to have the system depressurized. **Caution:** *Do not, under any circumstances, disconnect any lines while the system is under pressure.*

2  Remove the air cleaner.

3  Remove the carburetor pre-heat tube.

4  Remove the engine oil dipstick tube.

5  Remove the exhaust sensor located on the exhaust manifold.

6  Remove the compressor mounting bracket.

7  Label the four spark plug wires as to their positions. Disconnect them and move them to the side for clearance.

8  Disconnect the exhaust pipe from the exhaust manifold. The exhaust pipe can be hung from a piece of wire attached to the frame.

9  Remove the exhaust manifold end bolts first, then remove the center bolts and the exhaust manifold.

10  Remove the exhaust manifold gasket.

11  Before installing the manifold, clean the mating surfaces on the cylinder head and manifold. All old gasket material should be removed.

12  Place a new exhaust manifold gasket into position on the cylinder head, then place the manifold into position and install the mounting bolts finger tight.

13  Tighten the manifold mounting bolts to the specified torque in the sequence shown in the accompanying illustration. Work up to the final torque in three or four steps.

14  Install the remaining components in the reverse order of removal, using new gaskets wherever one has been removed.

15  Start the engine and check for exhaust leaks between the manifold and cylinder head and between the manifold and exhaust pipe.

## 29  Cylinder head — removal

**Note:** *If the engine has been removed from the vehicle, disregard the following steps which do not apply.*

1  Remove the intake manifold as described in Section 27.

2  Remove the exhaust manifold as described in Section 28.

3  Remove the bolts that secure the alternator bracket to the cylinder head.

4  Disconnect the air conditioning compressor and swing it out of the way for clearance. *Do not disconnect any of the lines unless the system has been depressurized.*

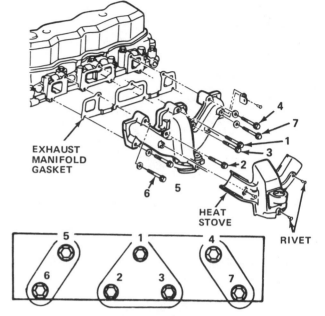

Fig. 2.16   Exhaust manifold installation and bolt tightening sequence (Sec 28)

5  Disconnect all electrical and vacuum lines from the cylinder head.

6  Remove the upper radiator hose.

7  Disconnect the spark plug wires and remove the spark plugs. Be sure to label the plug wires as to their correct locations.

8  Remove the rocker arm cover. To break the gasket seal, it may be necessary to strike the cover with your hand or a rubber mallet. Do not pry on the sealing surfaces.

9  In disassembling the valve train components, it is important that once removed, all of the components be kept separate so they can be installed in their original positions. A cardboard box or rack numbered according to engine cylinders, can be used for this.

10  Remove each of the rocker arm nuts or bolts (photo).

11  Lift the rocker arms off.

12  Remove the pushrods (photo).

13  Remove the thermostat housing from the cylinder head.

14  Remove all vacuum valves and switches from the cylinder head.

15  Remove the engine lifting brackets.

16  Remove the air conditioning compressor mounting bracket.

17  Loosen each of the cylinder head mounting bolts one turn at a time until they can be removed. Note the length and position of each bolt to aid in reinstallation.

18  Lift the head free of the engine. If the head is stuck to the engine block, do not attempt to pry it free, as this may damage the sealing surfaces. Instead, use a hammer and a block of wood to dislodge the head.

19  Remove the cylinder head gasket.

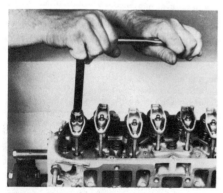

29.10  Removing the rocker arms from the pivots

29.12  Removing the pushrods

30.5  The cylinder head mounting bolts should be coated with sealant (arrows) prior to installation

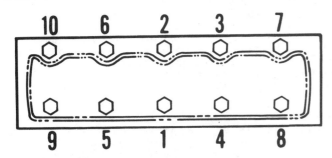

Fig. 2.17  Recommended tightening sequence for the cylinder head bolts (Sec 30)

## 30  Cylinder head — installation

1    If not already done, thoroughly clean the gasket surfaces on both the cylinder head and the engine block. Do not scratch or otherwise damage the sealing areas.
2    To get the proper torque readings, the threads of the head bolts must be clean. This also holds true for the threaded holes in the engine block. Run a tap through these holes to ensure that they are clean.
3    Place the gasket in place over the engine block dowel pins.
4    Carefully lower the cylinder head onto the engine, over the dowel pins and the gaskets. Be careful not to move the gasket while doing this.
5    Coat both the threads of the cylinder head attaching bolts and the point at which the head and stem meet with a sealing compound and install each finger tight. Do not tighten any of the bolts at this time (photo).
6    Tighten each of the bolts a little at a time in the sequence shown in the accompanying illustration. Continue tightening in this sequence until the proper torque reading is obtained. As a final check, work around the head in a logical front-to-rear sequence to make sure none of the bolts have been overlooked.
7    Install the exhaust manifold as described in Section 28.
8    Install each of the valve lifters (if removed) in its proper bore.
9    Place a small amount of engine assembly lube on each end of the pushrods and install each in its original position. Make sure the pushrods are seated properly in the lifter cavities.
10   Place each of the rocker arms and corresponding rocker balls onto its original stud or bolt. The rocker balls and valve stem ends of the rocker arms should receive a small amount of engine assembly lube.
11   Tighten the rocker arm nuts/bolts to the specified torque.
12   Install the rocker arm cover.
13   Install the intake manifold as described in Section 27.
14   Install the remaining engine components in the reverse order of removal.
15   Fill the radiator with coolant, start the engine and check for leaks. Adjust the ignition timing as required. Be sure to recheck the coolant level once the engine has warmed up to operating temperature and cooled back down again.

## 31  Crankshaft pulley hub and front oil seal — removal and installation

Note: If the engine has been removed from the vehicle, disregard the following steps which do not apply.

1    Remove the engine drivebolts. Refer to the appropriate Chapters for each accessory.
2    Remove the radiator to provide working clearance.
3    With the parking brake applied and the shifter in Park (automatic) or in gear (manual) to prevent the engine from turning over, remove the crank pulley bolt. There is considerable torque on this bolt and a breaker bar will probably be necessary.
4    Mark the position of the pulley in relation to the hub (photo). Remove the bolts that secure the crank pulley to the hub and lift off the pulley.
5    Using a hub puller, remove the hub from the crankshaft (photo).
6    Carefully pry out the oil seal from the front cover with a large screwdriver. Be sure not to distort the cover.
7    Install the new seal with the helical lip toward the rear of the engine. Drive the seal into place using a special front oil seal installing tool or an appropriate-size socket.
8    Apply a light coat of oil to the inside lip of the seal.
9    Position the pulley hub on the crankshaft and, using a slight twisting motion, slide it through the seal until it bottoms against the crankshaft gear. The crank pulley hub bolt can also be used to press the hub into position (photo).
10   Install the crank pulley onto the hub, aligning the marks made during removal.
11   Install the crank pulley hub bolt and tighten it to the specified torque.
12   Complete the installation by reversing the removal steps. Tighten the drivebelts to their proper tension.

**2B**

## 32  Timing gear cover — removal and installation

Note: If the engine has been removed from the vehicle, disregard the following steps which do not apply.

1    Remove the crank pulley hub as described in Section 31.
2    Remove the lower alternator bracket.
3    Remove the nuts that secure the front engine mount to the cradle.
4    Remove the fan shroud and, if equipped, the air conditioner compressor bracket.
5    Loosen the drivebelts.
6    Remove the bolts that secure the timing gear cover to the engine block and oil pan.
7    Pull the cover forward slightly and, using a sharp knife or other suitable cutting tool, cut the front oil pan seal flush with the cylinder block at both sides of the cover.
8    Remove the timing gear cover.
9    Remove the timing gear cover gasket.
10   Using a degreaser, clean all dirt and old gasket material from the sealing surfaces of the timing gear cover, engine block and oil pan.
11   Replace the front oil seal by carefully prying it out of the timing

31.4  Marking the position of the crankshaft pulley in relation to the hub

31.5  Using a hub puller to remove the hub from the crankshaft

31.9  Pushing the hub onto the crankshaft with the hub bolt

gear cover with a large screwdriver. Be sure not to distort the cover.
12  Install the new seal with the helical lip toward the inside of the cover. Drive the seal into place using a special front oil seal installing tool or an appropriate-size socket. A flat block of wood will also work (photo).
13  Prior to installing the cover, install a new front oil pan gasket. Cut the ends off of the gasket as shown in the accompanying figure and install it on the cover by pressing the rubber tips into the holes provided.
14  Apply a thin coat of RTV-type gasket sealant to the timing gear cover gasket and place it in position on the cover.
15  Apply a bead of RTV-type sealant to the joint between the oil pan and engine block.
16  Using the crank pulley hub as a centering tool, insert the hub into

the front cover seal and place the cover in position on the block with the hub on the crankshaft.
17  Install the oil pan-to-cover bolts and partially tighten them.
18  Install the bolts that secure the cover to the block and tighten all of the mounting bolts to the specified torque.
19  Remove the hub from the front cover seal.
20  Complete the installation by reversing the removal procedure.

### 33  Oil pump driveshaft — removal and installation

**Note:** *If the engine has been removed from the vehicle, disregard the*

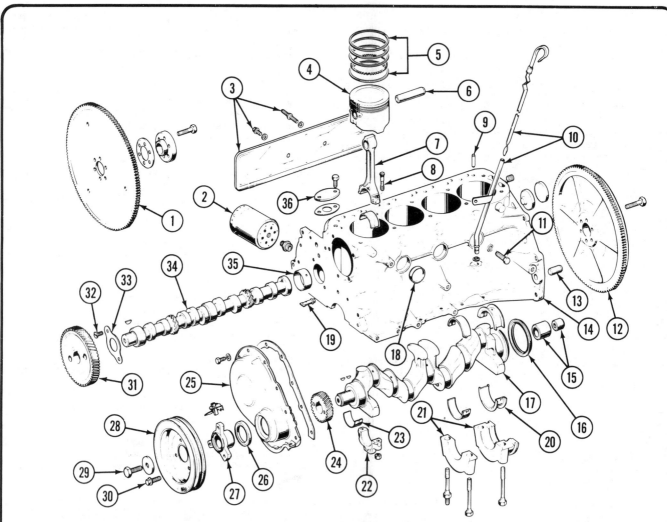

Fig. 2.18   Engine lower end components — exploded view

| | | | |
|---|---|---|---|
| 1  Driveplate and ring gear automatic transmission) | 11  Camshaft button | 19  Timing gear oiler | 28  Crankshaft pulley |
| 2  Oil filter | 12  Flywheel and ring gear (manual transmission) | 20  Main bearings | 29  Crankshaft pulley hub bolt |
| 3  Pushrod cover and bolts | 13  Dowel pin | 21  Main bearing caps | 30  Crankshaft pulley bolt |
| 4  Piston | 14  Engine block | 22  Connecting rod bearing cap | 31  Camshaft timing gear |
| 5  Piston rings | 15  Pilot and/or converter bushing | 23  Connecting rod bearing | 32  Camshaft thrust plate screw |
| 6  Piston pin | 16  Rear main oil seal | 24  Crankshaft gear | 33  Camshaft thrust plate |
| 7  Connecting rod | 17  Crankshaft | 25  Timing gear cover | 34  Camshaft |
| 8  Connecting rod bolt | 18  Block core soft (freeze) plug | 26  Timing gear cover oil seal | 35  Camshaft bearing |
| 9  Dowel pin | | 27  Crankshaft pulley hub | 36  Oil pump driveshaft retainer plate, gasket and bolt |
| 10  Dipstick and tube | | | |

*following steps which do not apply.*

1   Remove the air cleaner.
2   Remove the carburetor bowl vent line at the rocker arm cover.
3   Remove the upper alternator bracket.
4   Remove the alternator.
5   Remove the oil pump driveshaft retainer plate bolts.
6   Remove the bushing.
7   Remove the shaft and gear assembly.
8   Thoroughly clean the sealing surfaces on the cylinder block and retainer plate.
9   Inspect the gear teeth to see if they are chipped or broken. Replace the gear if necessary.
10  Install the oil pump driveshaft into the block and turn it until it engages with the camshaft drive gear in the oil pump body.
11  Apply a 1/16-inch (1.5 mm) diameter bead of RTV-type sealant to the retainer plate so that it completely seals around the oil pump driveshaft hole in the block (photo). Install the retainer plate mounting bolts and tighten them securely.
12  Complete the installation by reversing the removal procedure.

## 34   Oil pan — removal and installation

1   Due to clearance problems with the chasis crossmember, the oil pan can only be removed with the engine out of the vehicle.
2   Remove the oil pan retaining bolts and lift off the oil pan. It may be necessary to use a rubber mallet to break the seal.
3   Prior to installing the oil pan, clean any dirt or old gasket material from the sealing surfaces of the oil pan and engine block.
4   The oil pan gasket consists of four separate gasket pieces. Each must be carefully installed in its proper place to form a good junction with the other pieces it joins with.

   a) Install a rear oil pan gasket in the rear main bearing cap and apply a small quantity of RTV-type sealant in the depressions where the pan gasket engages in the block.
   b) Install the front oil pan gasket on the timing gear cover, pressing the tips into the holes provided in the cover (photo).
   c) Install the side gaskets on the oil pan, using grease to hold them in place.

**Fig. 2.19   The front oil pan gasket must be cut as shown to form a proper seal with the side gaskets (Sec 34)**

CUT THIS PORTION
FROM NEW SEAL

   d) Trim the ends off of the front gasket as indicated in the accompanying illustration to form a good joint with the side gaskets.
   e) Apply a bead of RTV-type sealant at the split lines between the front gasket and the side gaskets. The pan can now be installed.

5   Place the oil pan into position against the block (photo) and insert the rear and side mounting bolts. Tighten these bolts snugly before installing the front bolts in the timing cover. Tighten all of the bolts to the specified torque.

## 35   Oil pump — removal and installation

1   Remove the oil pan as described in Section 34.
2   Remove the two oil pump flange mounting bolts and the nut from the main bearing cap bolt.
3   Lift off the oil pump and screen as an assembly.
4   If the oil pump is to be overhauled, refer to Section 36.
5   To install the pump, align the shaft so it mates with the oil pump driveshaft tang.

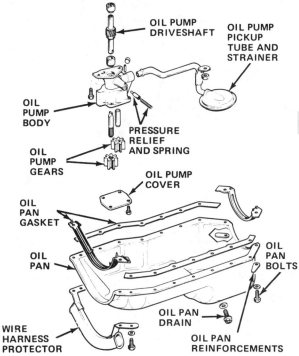

OIL PUMP DRIVESHAFT

OIL PUMP PICKUP TUBE AND STRAINER

OIL PUMP BODY

PRESSURE RELIEF AND SPRING

OIL PUMP GEARS

OIL PUMP COVER

OIL PAN GASKET

OIL PAN

OIL PAN BOLTS

OIL PAN DRAIN

WIRE HARNESS PROTECTOR

OIL PAN REINFORCEMENTS

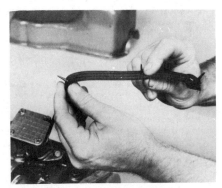

**Fig. 2.20   Oil pump and pan components — exploded view**

**2B**

32.12   Using a block of wood to install the front oil seal in the timing gear cover

33.11   Apply sealant to the retainer plate prior to installation

34.4   During installation the rubber tips on the front oil pan gasket should be pressed into the holes in the timing gear cover

34.5   Lower the oil pan carefully into position and do not disturb the gaskets

36.3   Removing the drive gear and shaft and the idler gear from the oil pump body

36.4A   Removing the pressure regulator valve retaining pin with needle-nose pliers

36.4B   Withdrawing the pressure regulator valve assembly

36.6   If the gears show signs of wear or damage they should be replaced with new ones

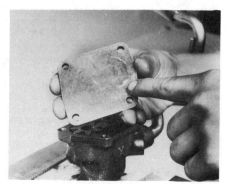

36.7   Inspect the pump cover for wear

6    Place the oil pump housing flange in position and install the mounting bolt(s). No gasket is needed between the pump flange and the block.
7    Install the oil pump screen bracket over the main bearing cap bolt and install the nut.
8    Tighten the pump mounting bolt(s) and screen support nut to the specified torque.
9    Install the oil pan.

### 36   Oil pump — disassembly, inspection and reassembly

1    In most cases it will be more practical and economical to replace a faulty oil pump with a new or rebuilt unit. If it is decided to overhaul the oil pump, check on availability of internal parts before beginning.
2    Remove the pump cover retaining screws and the pump cover. Index mark the gear teeth to permit reassembly in the same position.
3    Remove the idler gear, drive gear and shaft from the body (photo).
4    Remove the pressure regulator valve retaining pin (photo), the regulator valve and the related parts (photo).
5    The screen assembly is factory-fitted to the pump body and cannot be separated.
6    Wash all the parts in solvent and dry them thoroughly. Inspect the body for cracks, wear and damage. Inspect the gears (photo).
7    Check the drive gear for looseness in the pump body and the inside of the pump cover for wear that would permit oil leakage past the ends of the gears (photo). If either the gears or body are worn or damaged, the entire oil pump assembly must be replaced.
8    Inspect the pickup screen and pipe assembly for damage to the screen, pipe and relief grommet.
9    Install the pressure regulator valve and related parts.
10   Install the drive gear and shaft in the pump body, followed by the idler gear with the smooth side toward the pump cover opening. Lubricate the parts with engine oil.
11   Install the cover and tighten the screws to the specified torque.
12   Turn the driveshaft to ensure that the pump operates freely.

### 37   Flywheel and rear main oil seal — removal and installation

1    To gain access to the flywheel, either the engine or the transmission must be removed from the vehicle. If other engine work is needed, remove the engine as described in Section 22. If no other work necessitating the removal of the engine needs to be done, it would be easier to remove the transmsission as described in Chapter 7.
2    If equipped with a manual transmission, remove the clutch from the flywheel as described in Chapter 8.
3    The flywheel can be unbolted from the rear flange of the crankshaft. To prevent the flywheel from turning, a long screwdriver or similar tool can be run through the flywheel and positioned against the engine block (photo).
4    Once the bolts are removed, the flywheel can be lifted off.
5    Remove the flywheel spacer if so equipped.
6    If the rear main bearing seal must be replaced, pry it out of its bore.
7    Examine the flywheel ring gear for any broken or chipped teeth. If this condition exists, the flywheel must be replaced with a new one.
8    *On manual transmission flywheels*, inspect the clutch friction face for scoring. Light scoring may be corrected using emery cloth, but where there is deep scoring the flywheel must be replaced with a new one or clutch damage will soon occur.
9    *On automatic transmission flywheels*, examine the converter securing bolt holes for distortion. This condition, too, necessitates the replacement of the flywheel.
10   Before installing the flywheel, clean the mating surfaces of the flywheel and the crankshaft.
11   If the oil seal was removed, apply a light coat of engine oil to the inside lip of the new seal and install it in its bore.
12   To install the flywheel, use a new spacer (if equipped) and position it in place against the crankshaft and insert the mounting bolts, securing them only finger tight. It is a good idea to use a thread locking agent such as Loctite, or equivalent, on the bolt threads.
13   Again, while preventing the flywheel from turning, tighten the bolts

37.3 A long screwdriver can be used to prevent the flywheel from turning during bolt removal

38.13 Support the camshaft inside the block (arrow) during removal (withdraw the camshaft straight out, taking care not to gouge the bearing surfaces with the cam lobes)

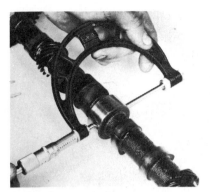

38.17 Measuring the cam bearing journal diameter with a micrometer

38.21 Lubricate the camshaft lobes and journals prior to installation of the shaft in the block (the dial indicator is used here to verify that the piston is at Top Dead Center)

38.22 The camshaft and crankshaft gears must be positioned with the timing marks (arrows) aligned

40.5 Installing the main bearings in the block

a little at a time until they are all at the specified torque.
14 Complete the remainder of the installation procedure by reversing the removal steps.

## 38 Camshaft and bearings — removal and installation

1 Remove the engine as described in Section 22 and mount it on a suitable stand.
2 Remove the rocker arm cover.
3 Loosen the rocker arm nuts/bolts and pivot the rocker arms clear of the pushrods.
4 Remove the pushrods.
5 Remove the pushrod cover.
6 Remove the valve lifters as described in Section 26.
7 Remove the distributor.
8 Remove the fuel pump.
9 Remove the oil pump driveshaft and gear assembly.
10 Remove the front pulley hub as described in Section 31.
11 Remove the timing gear cover as described in Section 32.
12 Remove the two camshaft thrust plate screws by working through the holes in the camshaft gear.
13 While supporting the camshaft with your fingers inserted through the fuel pump hole to prevent damaging the camshaft bearings, carefully and slowly pull the camshaft straight out from the block (photo).
14 If the gear must be removed from the camshaft, it must be pressed off. If you do not have access to a press, take it to your dealer or an automotive machine shop. The thrust plate must be positioned so that the Woodruff key in the shaft does not damage it when the shaft is pressed out.
15 Examine the bearing surfaces and the surfaces of the cam lobes. The oil pan may have to be removed to thoroughly inspect the bearings. Surface scratches, if they are very shallow, can be removed by rubbing with a fine emery cloth or oilstone. Any deep scoring will necessitate a new camshaft.

16 Mount the camshaft on V-blocks and use a dial gauge to measure lobe lift. Reject a camshaft which does not meet the specified limits.
17 Using a micrometer, measure the journal diameters (photo). Again, reject a camshaft which does not meet the specified limits.
18 If the camshaft bearings are worn, they must be replaced using the following procedure:

 a) Remove the oil pan if it is still in place.
 b) Remove the flywheel.
 c) Driving from the inside out, remove the expansion plug from the rear cam bearing.
 d) Using a camshaft bearing remover set, available from a dealer or auto parts store, drive out the front bearing toward the rear.
 e) Drive out the rear bearing toward the front.
 f) Using an extension on the bearing remover, drive out the center bearing toward the rear.
 g) Install the new bearings by reversing the removal procedure. Be sure all of the oil holes are aligned. **Note:** *The front bearing must be driven in until it is approximately 1/8-inch from the front of the cylinder block in order to uncover the oil hole to the timing gear oil nozzle.*
 h) After installing the new bearings, install a new camshaft rear expansion plug flush with the rear surface of the block.
 i) Reinstall the flywheel and oil pan.

19 If the camshaft gear has been removed from the camshaft, it must be pressed on prior to installation of the camshaft.

 a) Support the camshaft in an arbor press by using press plate adaptors behind the front journal.
 b) Place the gear spacer ring and the thrust plate over the end of the shaft.
 c) Install the Woodruff key in the shaft keyway.
 d) Install the camshaft gear and press it onto the shaft until it bottoms against the gear spacer ring.
 e) Use a feeler gauge to check the end clearance of the thrust plate. It should be 0.0015 to 0.0050-inch. If the clearance is

40.10   Place the Plastigage strip (arrow) on the journal, parallel to the journal axis

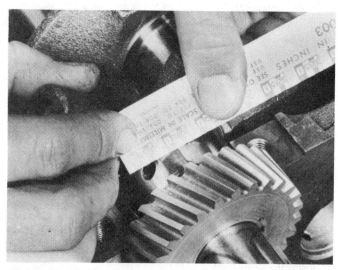

40.14   The oil clearance is obtained by comparing the crushed Plastigage to the scale printed on the container

less than 0.0015-inch, the spacer ring should be replaced. If the clearance is more than 0.0050-inch, the thrust plate should be replaced.

20   Prior to installing the camshaft, verify that the number one piston is at TDC. Coat each of the lobes and journals liberally with a moly-based grease or engine assembly lube.

21   Slide the camshaft into the engine block, again taking extra care not to damage the bearings (photo).

22   Position the camshaft and crankshaft gears so that the valve timing marks line up (photo). With the shafts in this position, the engine is in the number four (4) cylinder firing position.

23   Install the camshaft thrust plate mounting screws and tighten them to the specified torque.

## 39   Crankshaft — removal

1   Remove the engine from the vehicle as described in Section 22.
2   Remove the crankshaft pulley and hub assembly as described in Section 31.
3   Remove the oil pan.
4   Remove the oil pump assembly.
5   Remove the timing gear cover.
6   Remove the pistons and connecting rods from the crankshaft as described in Chapter 2A.
7   Remove the flywheel as described in Section 37.
8   Refer to Chapter 2A for the remainder of the crankshaft removal procedure.

## 40   Crankshaft — installation and main bearing oil clearance check

**Note:** *If a new or reground crankshaft is being installed, or if the original crankshaft has been reground, make sure the correct bearings are used.*

1   Crankshaft installation is generally one of the first steps in engine reassembly; it is assumed at this point that the engine block and crankshaft have been cleaned, inspected and repaired or reconditioned.
2   Position the engine with the bottom facing up.
3   Remove the main bearing cap bolts and lift out the caps. Lay them out in the proper order to help ensure correct installation.
4   If they are still in place, remove the old bearing inserts from the block and the main bearing caps. Wipe the main bearing surfaces of the block and caps with a clean, lint-free cloth (they must be kept spotlessly clean).
5   Clean the back side of the new main bearing inserts and lay one

bearing half in each main bearing saddle (in the block) (photo). Place the other bearing half from each bearing set in the corresponding main bearing cap. Make sure the tab on the bearing insert fits into the recess in the block or cap. Also, the oil holes in the block and cap must line up with the oil holes in the bearing insert. *Do not hammer the bearing into place and do not nick or gouge the bearing faces. No lubrication should be used at this time.*

6   The thrust bearings must be installed in the number five (rear) cap and saddle.

7   Clean the faces of the bearings in the block and the crankshaft main bearing journals with a clean, lint-free cloth. Check or clean the oil holes in the crankshaft, as any dirt here can only go one way — straight through the new bearings.

8   Once you are certain that the crankshaft is clean, carefully lay it in position (an assistant would be very helpful here) in the main bearings with the counterweights lying sideways.

9   Before the crankshaft can be permanently installed, the main bearing oil clearance must be checked.

10   Trim seven pieces of the appropriate type of Plastigage slightly shorter than the width of the main bearings and place one piece on each crankshaft main bearing journal, parallel with the journal axis (photo). Do not lay them across any oil holes.

11   Clean the faces of the bearings in the caps and install the caps in their respective positions (do not mix them up) with the arrows pointing toward the front of the engine. Do not disturb the Plastigage.

12   Starting with the center main and working out toward the ends, tighten the main bearing cap bolts, in three steps, to the specified torque. *Do not rotate the crankshaft at any time during this operation.*

13   Remove the bolts and carefully lift off the main bearing caps. Keep them in order. Do not disturb the Plastigage or rotate the crankshaft. If any of the main bearing caps are difficult to remove, tap gently from side-to-side with a soft-faced hammer to loosen them.

14   Compare the width of the crushed Plastigage on each journal to the scale printed on the Plastigage container to obtain the main bearing oil clearance (photo). Check the Specifications to make sure it is correct.

15   If the clearance is not correct, double-check to make sure that you have the right size bearing inserts. Also, recheck the crankshaft main bearing journal diameters and make sure that no dirt or oil was between the bearing inserts and the main bearing caps or the block when the clearance was measured.

16   Using a piece of hardwood or your fingernail, carefully scrape all traces of the Plastigage material off the main bearing journals and/or the bearing faces. Do not nick or scratch the bearing faces.

17   Carefully lift the crankshaft out of the engine. Clean the bearing faces in the block, then apply a thin layer of clean, high-quality moly-

based grease or engine assembly lube to each of the bearing faces. Be sure to coat the thrust bearing faces as well. Make sure the crankshaft journals are clean, then carefully lay it back in place in the block. Clean the faces of the bearings in the caps, then apply a thin layer of clean, high-quality moly-based grease or engine assembly lube to each of the bearing faces and install the caps in their respective positions with the arrows pointing toward the front of the engine. Install the bolts and tighten the bolts in caps one through four to the specified torque, starting with the center main and working out toward the ends. Work up to the final torque in three steps. Tighten the bolts in the number five (rear) cap to 10 ft-lb, then use a lead or brass hammer to tap the crankshaft to the rear, then the front, to center the thrust bearing. Tighten the rear cap bolts to the specified torque.

18  Rotate the crankshaft a number of times by hand and check for any obvious binding.

19  Next, check the crankshaft end play. This can be done with a feeler gauge or a dial indicator set (see Section 12 in Chapter 2A).

20  Lubricate the seal lip with moly-based grease or engine assembly lube, then center the seal over the rear end of the crankshaft with the seal lip facing the *front* of the engine. Using a soft-faced hammer, carefully drive the seal into the groove in the main bearing cap and block until it is seated. Make sure it is driven in squarely.

21  Install the Woodruff key in the front of the crankshaft, then slip the timing gear into place.

22  Refer to the appropriate Sections and install the piston/connecting rod assemblies, the camshaft, the oil pump, the oil pan, the flywheel, the timing gear cover and the pulley hub.

---

### 41  Engine — installation

1  Lower the engine carefully into the engine compartment and mate it to the transmission. *On manual transmissions,* make sure the transmission input shaft is correctly installed in the pilot bushing and clutch disc.

2  Connect the hoses to the power steering pump.

3  Connect the heater hoses to the heater core.

4  Connect the coolant temperature sending unit, oil pressure sending unit, choke, solenoid and mixture control solenoid wires.

5  Connect the carburetor and evaporative system vacuum hoses.

6  Connect the carburetor bowl vent hose.

7  Connect the alternator wiring harness.

8  Attach the throttle cable to the carburetor and secure it with the bracket.

9  Place the fan shroud in position over the fan and install the radiator and hoses. Attach the shroud to the radiator and fill the radiator with the specified coolant.

10  Raise the vehicle and support it securely.

11  *On automatic transmissions,* align the converter-to-driveplate marks made during removal, then install the attaching bolts and tighten them to the specified torque. Apply thread-locking compound to the bolt threads before installing them.

12  Install the transmission-to-torque converter housing attaching bolts and tighten them to the specified torque.

13  *On manual transmissions,* install the flywheel inspection plate and clutch hydraulic slave cylinder.

14  Install the engine mount nuts and tighten them securely.

15  Install the starter motor and bracket.

16  Connect the cable and solenoid wire to the starter.

17  Connect the distributor wires.

18  Connect the exhaust pipe to the manifold and install the oxygen sensor wire (if so equipped).

19  Connect the negative battery cable and body ground wire.

20  Install the air cleaner assembly.

21  Fill the engine to the correct level with the recommended oil.

22  Refer to Chapter 2A for the initial start-up and break-in procedures.

**2B**

# Chapter 2 Part C  In-line six-cylinder engine

*Refer to Chapter 13 for Specifications and information related to 1984 through 1986 models*

## Contents

Camshaft and bearings — inspection and replacement ...... 59
Camshaft and timing chain/sprockets — installation ........ 67
Camshaft — removal ................................. 51
Crankshaft — removal ...................... Chapter 2A
Crankshaft — inspection.................... Chapter 2A
Crankshaft — installation and main bearing oil clearance
  check .......................................... 64
Cylinder head and rocker gear — installation ............. 69
Cylinder head — cleaning and inspection ........ Chapter 2A
Cylinder head — disassembly ................. Chapter 2A
Cylinder head — reassembly .................. Chapter 2A
Cylinder head — removal ............................. 48
Engine — installation ............................... 71
Engine — removal.................................... 45
Engine block — cleaning............................. Chapter 2A
Engine block — inspection .................... Chapter 2A
Engine disassembly — general information ....... Chapter 2A
Engine mount flexible cushions — replacement .......... 44
Engine overhaul — general information .......... Chapter 2A
Engine rebuilding alternatives ................ Chapter 2A
Engine removal — methods and precautions ...... Chapter 2A
External components — installation.................... 70
External components — removal....................... 46
Flywheel and starter ring gear — inspection and servicing ... 61
Flywheel/driveplate — installation .................... 65
Flywheel/driveplate — removal ....................... 55

General information ............................... 42
Initial start-up and break-in after overhaul ........ Chapter 2A
Lubrication system — general information ............. 54
Main and connecting rod bearings — inspection ... Chapter 2A
Main and connecting rod bearings — selection ........... 63
Oil pan — removal .................................. 52
Oil seals — replacement ............................. 62
Oil pump and oil pan — installation .................... 66
Oil pump — disassembly, inspection and reassembly ....... 60
Oil pump — removal ................................. 53
Oversize and undersize component designation .......... 43
Piston/connecting rod assembly — installation and
  bearing oil   clearance check .................. Chapter 2A
Piston/connecting rod assembly — inspection ..... Chapter 2A
Piston/connecting rod assembly — removal ..... Chapter 2A
Piston rings — installation .................... Chapter 2A
Repair operations possible with the
  engine in the vehicle ..................... Chapter 2A
Rocker gear — inspection and overhaul .................. 56
Rocker gear — removal............................... 47
Timing chain and sprockets — inspection ............... 58
Timing cover, chain and sprockets — removal ............ 50
Valve lifters — installation............................ 68
Valve lifters — description and removal ................. 49
Valve lifters — inspection and overhaul ................ 57
Valves — servicing ........................... Chapter 2A

## Specifications

## General

| | |
|---|---|
| Displacement ................................. | 232 or 258 cu in |
| Bore and stroke | |
|   232 cu in engine............................ | 3.750 x 3.50 in |
|   258 cu in engine............................ | 3.750 x 3.895 in |
| Oil pressure | |
|   600 rpm................................... | 13 psi |
|   Above 1600 rpm ........................... | 37 to 75 psi |

## Engine block

| | |
|---|---|
| Cylinder bore | |
|   Diameter................................ | 3.7501 to 3.7533 in |
|   Taper limit | |
|     1972 through 1981 ...................... | 0.005 in |
|     1982 and 1983 ........................ | 0.001 in |
|   Out-of-round limit | |
|     1972 through 1981 ...................... | 0.003 in |
|     1982 and 1983 ........................ | 0.001 in |
| Deck warpage limit............................. | 0.006 in max. |

## Pistons and rings

Piston-to-cylinder bore clearance
    Standard . . . . . . . . . . . . . . . . . . . . . . . . . . . . . . .    0.0009 to 0.0017 in
    Preferred . . . . . . . . . . . . . . . . . . . . . . . . . . . . . .    0.0012 to 0.0013 in
Piston ring side clearance
    1972 through 1980
        Compression (standard) . . . . . . . . . . . . . . . . . . . .    0.0015 to 0.003 in
        Compression (preferred) . . . . . . . . . . . . . . . . . . . .    0.0015 in
        Oil control (standard) . . . . . . . . . . . . . . . . . . . . . .    0.001 to 0.008 in
        Oil control (preferred) . . . . . . . . . . . . . . . . . . . . .    0.003 in
    1981 through 1983
        Compression (standard) . . . . . . . . . . . . . . . . . . . .    0.0017 to 0.0032 in
        Compression (preferred) . . . . . . . . . . . . . . . . . . . .    0.0017 in
        Oil control (standard) . . . . . . . . . . . . . . . . . . . . . .    0.001 to 0.008 in
        Oil control (preferred) . . . . . . . . . . . . . . . . . . . . .    0.003 in
Piston ring end gap
    Compression (all) . . . . . . . . . . . . . . . . . . . . . . . .    0.010 to 0.020 in
    Oil control
        1972 and 1973 only . . . . . . . . . . . . . . . . . . . . . .    0.015 to 0.055 in
        All others . . . . . . . . . . . . . . . . . . . . . . . . . . . . .    0.010 to 0.025 in
Piston pin diameter . . . . . . . . . . . . . . . . . . . . . . . . .    0.9304 to 0.9309 in
Piston pin-to-piston clearance
    Standard . . . . . . . . . . . . . . . . . . . . . . . . . . . . . . .    0.0003 to 0.0005 in
    Preferred . . . . . . . . . . . . . . . . . . . . . . . . . . . . . .    0.0005 in

## Crankshaft

Main journal
    Diameter
        1972 through 1981 . . . . . . . . . . . . . . . . . . . . . . . .    2.4986 to 2.5001 in
        1982 and 1983 . . . . . . . . . . . . . . . . . . . . . . . . . .    2.4996 to 2.5001 in
    Taper limit . . . . . . . . . . . . . . . . . . . . . . . . . . . . .    0.0005 in
    Out-of-round limit . . . . . . . . . . . . . . . . . . . . . . . .    0.0005 in
Main bearing oil clearance
    1972 and 1973 . . . . . . . . . . . . . . . . . . . . . . .    0.001 to 0.002 in
    1974 through 1980
        Standard . . . . . . . . . . . . . . . . . . . . . . . . . . . .    0.001 to 0.003 in
        Preferred . . . . . . . . . . . . . . . . . . . . . . . . . . .    0.0025 in
    1981 through 1983
        Standard . . . . . . . . . . . . . . . . . . . . . . . . . . . .    0.001 to 0.0025 in
        Preferred . . . . . . . . . . . . . . . . . . . . . . . . . . .    0.002 in
Connecting rod journal
    Diameter . . . . . . . . . . . . . . . . . . . . . . . . . . . . . .    2.0934 to 2.0955 in
    Taper limit . . . . . . . . . . . . . . . . . . . . . . . . . . . . .    0.005 in
    Out-of-round limit . . . . . . . . . . . . . . . . . . . . . . . .    0.0005 in
Connecting rod bearing oil clearance
    1972 and 1973 . . . . . . . . . . . . . . . . . . . . . . .    0.001 to 0.002 in
    1974 and 1975
        Standard . . . . . . . . . . . . . . . . . . . . . . . . . . . .    0.001 to 0.003 in
        Preferred . . . . . . . . . . . . . . . . . . . . . . . . . . .    0.0025 in
    1976 through 1980
        Standard . . . . . . . . . . . . . . . . . . . . . . . . . . . .    0.001 to 0.0025 in
        Preferred . . . . . . . . . . . . . . . . . . . . . . . . . . .    0.0015 to 0.002 in
    1981 through 1983
        Standard . . . . . . . . . . . . . . . . . . . . . . . . . . . .    0.001 to 0.003 in
        Preferred . . . . . . . . . . . . . . . . . . . . . . . . . . .    0.0015 to 0.002 in
Connecting rod end play
    1972 . . . . . . . . . . . . . . . . . . . . . . . . . . . . . . . .    0.008 to 0.010 in
    1973 through 1980 . . . . . . . . . . . . . . . . . . . . . . .    0.005 to 0.014 in
    1981 through 1983 . . . . . . . . . . . . . . . . . . . . . . .    0.010 to 0.019 in
Crankshaft end play . . . . . . . . . . . . . . . . . . . . . . . .    0.0015 to 0.0065 in

## Camshaft

Bearing journal diameter
    Number 1 . . . . . . . . . . . . . . . . . . . . . . . . . . . . . .    2.029 to 2.030 in
    Number 2 . . . . . . . . . . . . . . . . . . . . . . . . . . . . . .    2.019 to 2.020 in
    Number 3 . . . . . . . . . . . . . . . . . . . . . . . . . . . . . .    2.009 to 2.010 in
    Number 4 . . . . . . . . . . . . . . . . . . . . . . . . . . . . . .    1.999 to 2.000 in
Bearing oil clearance . . . . . . . . . . . . . . . . . . . . . . . .    0.001 to 0.003 in
Lobe lift
    1972 through 1974 . . . . . . . . . . . . . . . . . . . . . . .    0.254 in
    1975 and 1976 . . . . . . . . . . . . . . . . . . . . . . . . . .    0.232 in
    1977 through 1979
        232/258 with 1 bbl. carb. . . . . . . . . . . . . . . . . . .    0.232 in
        258 with 2 bbl. carb. . . . . . . . . . . . . . . . . . . . .    0.248 in
    1980 . . . . . . . . . . . . . . . . . . . . . . . . . . . . . . . . .    0.248 in

**2C**

## Camshaft (continued)

| | |
|---|---|
| 1981 through 1983 . . . . . . . . . . . . . . . . . . . . . . . . . . . | 0.253 in |
| End play . . . . . . . . . . . . . . . . . . . . . . . . . . . . . . . . . . . | Zero (engine operating) |

## Cylinder head and valve train

| | |
|---|---|
| Head warpage limit . . . . . . . . . . . . . . . . . . . . . . . . . . | 0.006 in max. |
| Intake valve seat angle . . . . . . . . . . . . . . . . . . . . . . . . | 30° |
| Exhaust valve seat angle . . . . . . . . . . . . . . . . . . . . . . . | 44.5° |
| Intake valve seat width. . . . . . . . . . . . . . . . . . . . . . . . . | 0.040 to 0.060 |
| Exhaust valve seat width . . . . . . . . . . . . . . . . . . . . . . . | 0.040 to 0.060 |
| Valve seat runout limit . . . . . . . . . . . . . . . . . . . . . . . . . | 0.0025 in |
| Valve guide inside diameter . . . . . . . . . . . . . . . . . . . . . | 0.3735 to 0.3745 in |
| Intake valve face angle . . . . . . . . . . . . . . . . . . . . . . . . . | 29° |
| Exhaust valve face angle . . . . . . . . . . . . . . . . . . . . . . . | 44° |
| Valve margin width . . . . . . . . . . . . . . . . . . . . . . . . . . . . | 1/32 in min. |
| Valve stem diameter. . . . . . . . . . . . . . . . . . . . . . . . . . . | 0.3715 to 0.3725 in |
| Valve stem-to-guide clearance . . . . . . . . . . . . . . . . . . | 0.001 to 0.003 in |
| Valve spring free length | |
|   1972 and 1973 . . . . . . . . . . . . . . . . . . . . . . . . . . . | Not available |
|   1974 through 1976 | |
|     With rotators . . . . . . . . . . . . . . . . . . . . . . . . . . . | 2.00 in (approx.) |
|     Without rotators . . . . . . . . . . . . . . . . . . . . . . . . . | 2.234 in (approx). |
|   1977 | |
|     258 2 bbl. only . . . . . . . . . . . . . . . . . . . . . . . . . . | 1.987 in (approx.) |
|     All others . . . . . . . . . . . . . . . . . . . . . . . . . . . . . . | 2.234 in (approx.) |
|   1978 through 1983 . . . . . . . . . . . . . . . . . . . . . . . . | 1.99 in (approx.) |
| Lifter/tappet type . . . . . . . . . . . . . . . . . . . . . . . . . . . . | Hydraulic |
| Valve lash adjustment . . . . . . . . . . . . . . . . . . . . . . . . . | Zero |
| Lifter bore diameter | |
|   1972 and 1973 . . . . . . . . . . . . . . . . . . . . . . . . . . . | Not available |
|   1974 through 1980 . . . . . . . . . . . . . . . . . . . . . . . . | 0.905 to 0.906 in |
|   1981 through 1983 . . . . . . . . . . . . . . . . . . . . . . . . | 0.9055 to 0.9065 in |
| Lifter diameter | |
|   1972 and 1973 . . . . . . . . . . . . . . . . . . . . . . . . . . . | Not available |
|   1974 through 1983 . . . . . . . . . . . . . . . . . . . . . . . . | 0.904 to 0.9045 in |
| Lifter-to-bore clearance | |
|   1972 and 1973 . . . . . . . . . . . . . . . . . . . . . . . . . . . | Not available |
|   1974 through 1980 . . . . . . . . . . . . . . . . . . . . . . . . | 0.001 to 0.002 in |
|   1981 through 1983 . . . . . . . . . . . . . . . . . . . . . . . . | 0.001 to 0.0025 in |
| Pushrod diameter | |
|   1972, 1973 and 1975 . . . . . . . . . . . . . . . . . . . . . . | Not available |
|   1974 . . . . . . . . . . . . . . . . . . . . . . . . . . . . . . . . . . . | 0.294 to 0.303 in |
|   1976 through 1980 . . . . . . . . . . . . . . . . . . . . . . . . | 0.312 to 0.313 iin |
|   1981 through 1983 . . . . . . . . . . . . . . . . . . . . . . . . | 0.312 to 0.315 in |
| Pushrod length | |
|   1972, 1973 and 1975 . . . . . . . . . . . . . . . . . . . . . . | Not available |
|   1974 . . . . . . . . . . . . . . . . . . . . . . . . . . . . . . . . . . . | 9.656 to 9.666 in |
|   1976 . . . . . . . . . . . . . . . . . . . . . . . . . . . . . . . . . . . | 9.595 to 9.615 in |
|   1977 through 1983 . . . . . . . . . . . . . . . . . . . . . . . . | 9.640 to 9.660 in |

## Oil pump

| | |
|---|---|
| Gear-to-body clearance | |
|   1972 through 1980 . . . . . . . . . . . . . . . . . . . . . . . . | 0.0005 to 0.0025 in |
|   1981 through 1983 . . . . . . . . . . . . . . . . . . . . . . . . | 0.002 to 0.004 in |
| Gear end clearance | |
|   1972 through 1976 and 1981 through 1983. . . . . . . . . . | 0.002 to 0.006 in |
|   1977 through 1980 . . . . . . . . . . . . . . . . . . . . . . . . | 0.002 to 0.008 in |

## Oversize and undersize component code letter definition

### Code letter

| | | |
|---|---|---|
| B | All cylinder bores . . . . . . . . . . . . . . . . . . . . . . . . . | 0.010 in oversize |
| M | All crankshaft main bearing journals . . . . . . . . . . . | 0.010 in undersize |
| P | All connecting rod bearing journals . . . . . . . . . . . . | 0.010 in undersize |
| C | All camshaft bearing bores . . . . . . . . . . . . . . . . . . | 0.010 in oversize |

## Torque specifications

| | Ft-lbs |
|---|---|
| Camshaft sprocket bolts . . . . . . . . . . . . . . . . . . . . . . | 45 to 55 |
| Carburetor mounting nuts . . . . . . . . . . . . . . . . . . . . . | 12 to 15 |
| Connecting rod cap nuts | |
|   1972 through 1976 . . . . . . . . . . . . . . . . . . . . . . . . | 26 to 30 |
|   1977 through 1983 . . . . . . . . . . . . . . . . . . . . . . . . | 33 |
| Cylinder head bolts | |
|   1972 . . . . . . . . . . . . . . . . . . . . . . . . . . . . . . . . . . . | 80 to 85 |
|   1973 through 1980 . . . . . . . . . . . . . . . . . . . . . . . . | 105 |
|   1981 through 1983 . . . . . . . . . . . . . . . . . . . . . . . . | 85 |

| | |
|---|---|
| Crankshaft pulley-to-damper bolt...................... | 20 to 25 |
| Exhaust manifold bolts ............................. | 20 to 25 |
| Fan and hub assembly bolts ......................... | 15 to 25 |
| Driveplate-to-torque converter bolts ................. | 20 to 25 |
| Flywheel/driveplate-to-crankshaft bolts ............... | 100 to 110 |
| Intake manifold bolts .............................. | 20 to 25 |
| Main bearing cap bolts ............................. | 75 to 85 |
| Oil pump cover bolts | |
| 1972 ......................................... | 6 to 7.5 |
| 1973 through 1983 ............................. | 6 |
| Oil pump mounting bolts | |
| Short ......................................... | 8 to 12 |
| Long .......................................... | 15 to 18 |
| Oil pan bolts | |
| 1/4 x 20 ...................................... | 5 to 9 |
| 5/16 x 18...................................... | 10 to 13 |
| Bridged rocker pivot bolt | |
| 1973, 1975 and 1976 .......................... | 21 |
| 1977 through 1983 ............................. | 19 |
| Rocker arm shaft bolts | |
| 1972 ......................................... | 19 to 22 |
| 1974 ......................................... | 21 |
| Vibration damper bolt | |
| 1972 through 1976 ............................. | 50 to 60 |
| 1977 through 1983 ............................. | 80 |
| Water pump bolts................................. | 10 to 15 |

## 42  General information

The six-cylinder in-line engine is made of cast iron, with a removable cylinder head, intake and exhaust manifolds.

The valves are mounted in the cylinder head and are actuated by a camshaft located in the block via pushrods, rocker arms and hydraulic lifters. Depending on the year of production, the rocker arms are mounted in either of two ways. Some models use a bridged rocker arm pivot, which is attached to the cylinder head by cap screws. On other models the rocker arms operate on a common shaft.

The crankshaft is supported in the block by seven main bearings. The plain bearing inserts for the crankshaft and connecting rods are removable.

The distributor is driven by a gear on the camshaft, which in turn drives the positive displacement oil pump.

Along with the cylinder head and manifolds, the water pump, timing chain cover and bellhousing can be unbolted from the block.

## 43  Oversize and undersize component designation

1  Some engines are built with oversize or undersize cylinder bores, crankshaft main bearing journals, connecting rod journals or camshaft bearing bores.
2  A code designating the presence of oversize or undersize components is stamped on the cylinder block oil filter boss located between the distributor and the ignition coil.
3  Refer to the Specifications and compare the letter code with the information in the chart to determine which components are oversize or undersize.

## 44  Engine mount flexible cushions — replacement

1  Inspect the engine mount flexible cushions periodically to deter-

**2C**

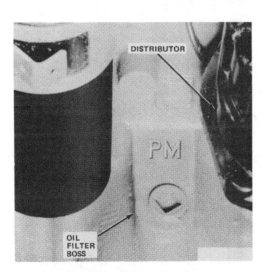

Fig. 2.21  Oversize/undersize
component code location (Sec 43)

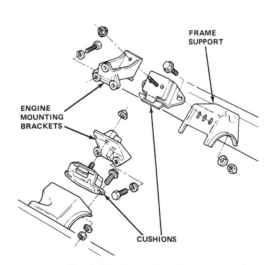

Fig. 2.22  Typical engine mount and
flexible cushion component layout (Sec 44)

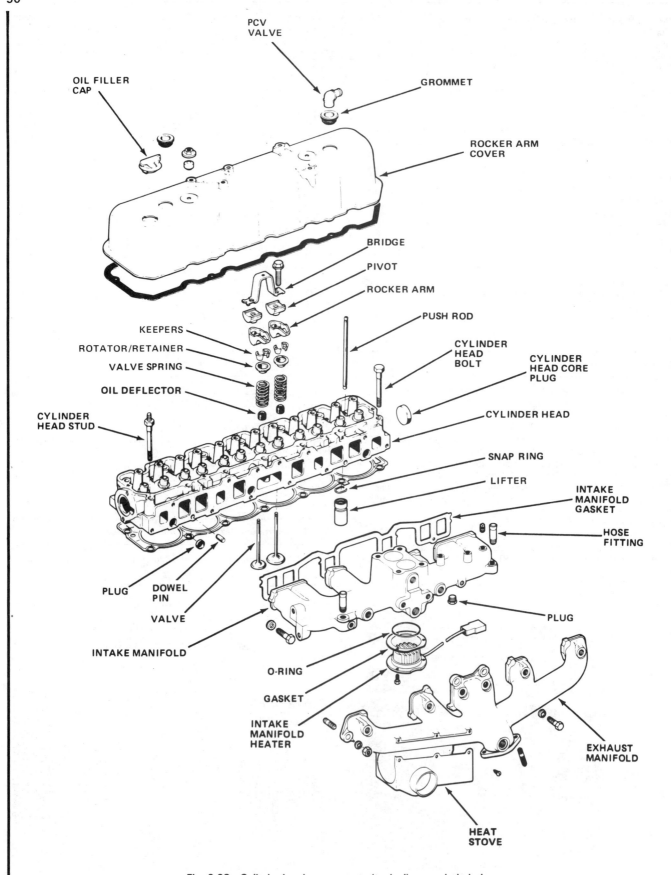

Fig. 2.23  Cylinder head components (typical) — exploded view

mine if they have become hard, split or separated from the metal backing.

2    If it is necessary to replace the cushions, it can be accomplished by supporting the weight of the engine or transmission in the area of the cushion.

## 45    Engine — removal

**Note:** *The following sequence of operations does not necessarily need to be performed in the order given. It is, rather, a checklist of everything that must be disconnected or removed before the engine can be lifted out of the vehicle. If your vehicle is equipped with an automatic transmission, the engine removal procedure will be slightly different from the procedure for a vehicle equipped with a manual transmission. It is very important that all linkages, electrical wiring, hoses and cables be removed or disconnected before attempting to lift the engine clear of the vehicle, so double-check everything thoroughly.*

**Caution:** *If the vehicle is equipped with air conditioning, have the lines disconnected by an automotive air conditioning mechanic. Do not attempt to do this at home, because serious injury or damage could result.*

1    Open the hood and tilt it all the way back to provide clearance.
2    Disconnect the negative cable from the battery. Drain the engine oil by referring to Chapter 1.
3    Remove the air cleaner assembly and disconnect the fuel line from the fuel pump.
4    Raise the vehicle and support it securely on jackstands.
5    Unbolt the exhaust pipe from the manifold and disconnect the oxygen sensor, if so equipped.
6    Remove the starter motor.
7    Disconnect the distributor and oil pressure sending unit wires.
8    *On manual transmission-equipped models,* disconnect the clutch and transmission linkage, then remove the flywheel inspection plate. Remove the bellhousing-to-engine bolts.
9    *On automatic transmission-equipped models,* mark the relative position of the torque converter-to-driveplate, then remove the attaching bolts. Remove the torque converter housing-to-engine bolts.
10    Lower the vehicle and support the transmission with a jack.
11    Tag or mark all of the vacuum hoses and disconnect them.
12    Disconnect the bowl vent hose and mixture control solenoid wire from the carburetor (not all vehicles).
13    Disconnect the wires from the alternator.
14    Disconnect the throttle linkage and the choke and solenoid wire from the carburetor (not all vehicles).
15    Disconnect the coolant temperature sending unit wire from the engine.
16    Drain the coolant into a suitable container and remove the lower radiator hose. Remove the heater hose.
17    Remove the fan shroud, upper radiator hose, engine fan, radiator

and shroud. If equipped with an automatic transmission, disconnect the cooler lines from the radiator before removing the radiator.
18    If so equipped, remove the power steering pump and drivebelt and position the pump out of the way. Do not disconnect the power steering hoses.
19    Remove the engine mount nuts.
20    Attach a suitable lifting device to the engine. Raise the engine and remove the front engine mounts from the engine, then move it carefully forward to disengage it from the transmission. It may be necessary to raise and lower the transmission with the jack to separate the engine from the transmission. Lift the engine from the engine compartment.

## 46    External components — removal

1    With the engine removed from the vehicle and separated from the transmission, the external components should be removed before disassembly of the engine begins.
2    From the right-hand side of the engine, remove the following components:

*The fuel pump*
*The engine mounting bracket*
*The oil filter cartridge (a chain wrench or special removal tool will be required to unscrew this)*
*The ignition coil*
*The distributor and spark plug wires*

3    From the left-hand side of the engine, remove the following components:

*The alternator and mounts*
*The engine mounting bracket*
*The EGR valve, back pressure sensor and coolant temperature switch (emissions control models)*
*The solenoid vacuum valve and connections (emissions control models)*
*The intake manifold and carburetor (after disconnecting the PCV valve-to-cylinder head cover hose)*
*The exhaust manifold and air cleaner hot air intake*

4    Unscrew and remove the vibration damper bolt.
5    Draw off the damper from the front of the crankshaft using a suitable puller, if necessary.
6    *On vehicles with a manual transmission,* unbolt and remove the clutch assembly from the flywheel as described in Chapter 7.
7    From the front face of the engine, remove the following components:

*The water pump*
*The thermostat housing cover and the thermostat*

## 47    Rocker gear — removal

1    Remove the rocker arm cover bolts and then lift off the cover and gasket.
2    *On all models except 1972 and 1974,* the rocker arms pivot on

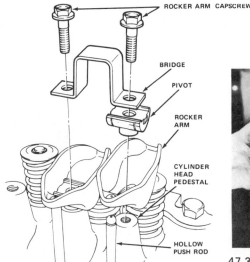

Fig. 2.24  Bridged rocker arm pivot components — exploded view (Sec 47)

ROCKER ARM CAPSCREW
BRIDGE
PIVOT
ROCKER ARM
CYLINDER HEAD PEDESTAL
HOLLOW PUSH ROD

47.3  Separating the bridge-type rocker arm assembly from the cylinder head

47.5  Remove the pushrods and mark them so they can be returned to their original locations

**2C**

a bridge assembly and the pushrods are hollow to serve as oil galleries supplying oil to the rocker assemblies.

3   Remove the rocker arm bridge assemblies by unscrewing the two cap bolts. Keep all components in their original order (photo).

4   *On 1972 and 1974 models,* unscrew and remove the rocker shaft mounting bolts and lift the shaft, complete with the rocker arms, from the cylinder head.

5   Remove the pushrods and keep them in their original order (photo).

## 48   Cylinder head — removal

1   If the cylinder head is being removed with the engine still in the vehicle, remember to:

   a) Drain the cooling system and disconnect the hoses.
   b) Remove the intake and exhaust manifolds.
   c) Remove the ignition coil and disconnect the spark plug wires.

2   Remove the rocker arm cover and rocker gear.

3   Disconnect the wire from the coolant temperature sending unit.

4   Working from the center out, unscrew each of the cylinder head bolts one turn at a time in a diagonal sequence.

5   Lift off the cylinder head and remove the gasket.

## 49   Valve lifters — description and removal

1   The lifters are hydraulic and consist of a body, plunger, spring, check valve, metering disc, cap and lock ring.

2   By means of charging and leak-down cycles and the contact of the lifters with the lobes of the camshaft, zero lash is maintained.

3   The lifters can be withdrawn (photo) after removing the cylinder head and pushrods as described elsewhere in this Chapter. **Note:** *Removal of the lifters will most likely require a special valve lifter removal tool (available at tool and auto parts stores).*

## 50   Timing cover, chain and sprockets — removal

1   If these components are being removed with the engine in the vehicle, remember to:

   a) Drain the cooling system.
   b) Remove the radiator.
   c) Remove the fan and pulley.
   d) Remove the vibration damper and pulley.

2   Unscrew and remove the cover mounting bolts and the bolts which retain the front of the oil pan to the timing cover.

3   Lift the timing cover to disengage the oil pan-to-cover sealing strip. Failure to observe this operation will cause damage to the oil pan gasket, which will then have to be replaced after removal of the oil pan.

4   Withdraw the timing cover and gasket and the oil slinger.

5   Unscrew and remove the camshaft retaining bolt and washer.

6   Withdraw the camshaft sprocket, crankshaft sprocket and timing chain as an assembly.

## 51   Camshaft — removal

1   If the camshaft is being removed with the engine in the vehicle, remember to:

   a) Remove the radiator and air-conditioner condenser.
   b) Remove the cylinder head, pushrods and lifters.
   c) Remove the timing chain and sprockets.
   d) Remove the distributor and fuel pump.
   e) Remove the radiator grille and front bumper.

2   Withdraw the camshaft from the front of the engine, taking great care not to damage the camshaft bearings with the lobes or eccentrics as they pass through.

## 52   Oil pan — removal

1   Raise the front of the vehicle and support it securely.

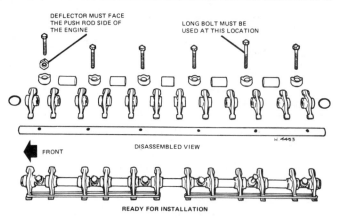

Fig. 2.25   Rocker shaft-type valve gear components — exploded view (Sec 47)

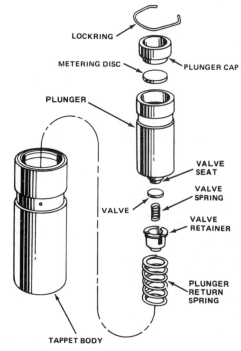

Fig. 2.26   Hydraulic valve lifter — exploded view (Sec 49)

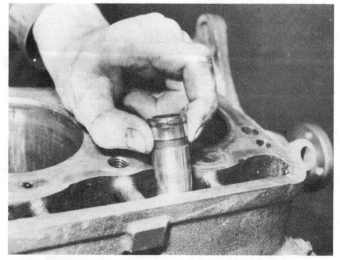

49.3   Removing a valve lifter

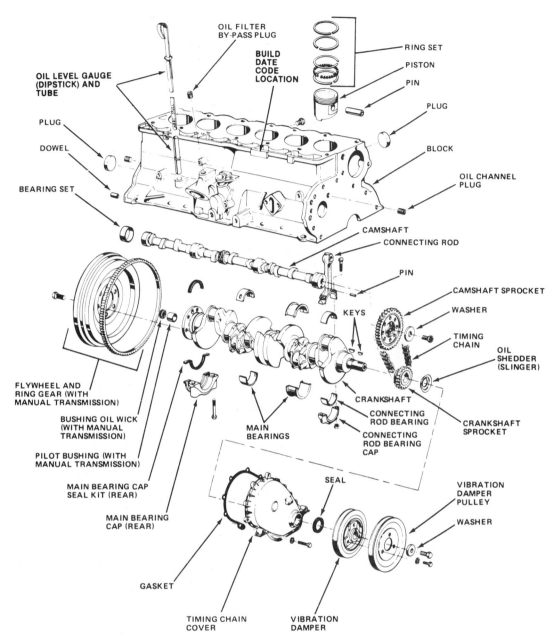

**Fig. 2.27  Engine block components — exploded view**

2   Support the engine with a suitable lifting device and disconnect the front engine mounts.

3   Disconnect the steering idler arm and loosen the sway bar link nuts to the end of their threads. Remove the sway bar clamp bolts and lower the sway bar.

4   Unbolt the front frame crossmember; pull it down and wedge it into position with wood blocks.

5   Remove the right-hand engine mount bracket from the engine.

6   Loosen the lower control arm strut rod bolts.

7   Drain the engine oil into a suitable container.

8   Remove the starter motor, if necessary, for clearance.

9   Remove the oil pan bolts and lower the pan from the engine.

### 53   Oil pump — removal

1   With the oil pan removed, the oil pump can be unbolted from the engine block.

2   Do not attempt to dismantle or alter the position of the oil pick-up tube. If the pressure relief valve has to be dismantled, then the pick-up tube will have to be moved and will necessitate replacing the tube assembly.

### 54   Lubrication system — general information

The oil pump is a gear type, driven by an extension of the distributor driveshaft, which in turn is driven by a gear on the camshaft.

The pressurized oil passes through the full-flow oil filter and then through galleries and passages to all moving components. Oil holes in the connecting rod bearing caps provide splash-type lubrication of the camshaft lobes, distributor drive gear, cylinder walls and piston pins.

The hydraulic valve lifters receive oil directly from the main oil gallery. An oil pressure switch is mounted on the right-hand side of the block.

## 55 Flywheel/driveplate — removal

1    Unscrew and remove the bolts which secure the flywheel (or driveplate) to the crankshaft rear flange.
2    If difficulty is experienced when loosening the bolts due to the rotation of the crankshaft, wedge a block of wood between the crankshaft web and the inside of the engine block. Alternatively, wedge the starter ring gear by inserting a cold chisel at the starter motor opening.
3    Lift the flywheel (or driveplate) from the crankshaft flange.
4    Unbolt and remove the engine endplate. Now is a good time to check the rear engine block core plug for security and evidence of leakage.

## 56 Rocker gear — inspection and overhaul

1    *On bridged rocker arm models,* this is simply a matter of examining the rocker arms and bridged pivot assemblies for wear and replacing parts as appropriate.
2    *On all other models,* examine the rocker arm faces for wear. If it is slight, it may be removed by gently rubbing on an oilstone. If the wear is deep or if the shaft if grooved or scored, dismantle the complete rocker assembly and replace parts as necessary.
3    Disassembly can be carried out after driving out the roll pin from one end of the shaft and removing the spring washer.
4    Reassemble as shown in the accompanying illustration. Make sure that the rocker shaft oil holes face toward the cylinder head.

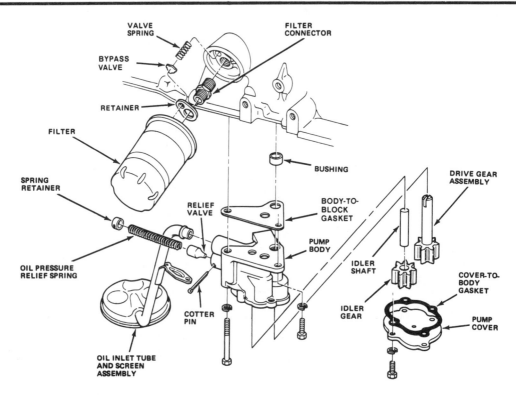

Fig. 2.28   Oil pump and filter components — exploded view (Sec 60)

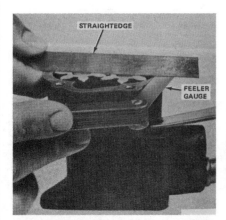

Fig. 2.29   Checking the oil pump gear end clearance with a straightedge and feeler gauge (Sec 60)

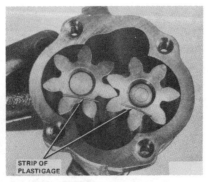

Fig. 2.30   Checking the oil pump gear end clearance with Plastigage (Sec 60)

Fig. 2.31   Checking the oil pump gear-to-body clearance with a feeler gauge (Sec 60)

5   Take the time to examine the pushrods for wear and distortion and replace any which require it.

## 57   Valve lifters — inspection and overhaul

1   The hydraulic lifters are described in Section 49.
2   Visually examine the lifter surfaces for wear or scoring. If the cam lobe contact face has worn concave, the lifter must be replaced. The camshaft will require changing as well. Never use a worn camshaft with new lifters or vice versa.
3   Checking the leak-down time for each lifter is a job for your dealer who has the necessary testing device. Any that take more than the specified time (20 to 110 seconds) must be replaced.

## 58   Timing chain and sprockets — inspection

1   Examine the teeth of the camshaft and crankshaft sprockets. If they are worn or chipped, replace the sprocket.
2   Wear in the chain can only be satisfactorily checked by comparing it with a new one but (when installed on the sprockets) if it can be deflected more than a *total* of 1/2-inch, then it should be replaced or the timing will be upset.

## 59   Camshaft and bearings — inspection and replacement

1   Examine the bearing surfaces and the surfaces of the cam lobes. Surface scratches, if shallow, can be removed by rubbing with fine emery cloth or an oilstone. Any deep scoring will necessitate a new camshaft.
2   The camshafts used in engines without EGR systems differ from those installed in engines with EGR systems and they are not interchangeable.
3   The camshaft runs in four plain insert-type bearings which have larger bores at the front to permit easier withdrawal of the camshaft.
4   Replacement of the bearings is definitely a job for an automotive machine shop, since special equipment is required.
5   Camshaft end play is automatically maintained at zero (while the engine is running) by the action of the helical cut distributor/oil pump drive gear which holds the camshaft sprocket thrust face against the cylinder block.

## 60   Oil pump — disassembly, inspection and reassembly

1   Remove the oil pump cover and gasket.
2   Place a straightedge across the gears and pump body and use a feeler gauge blade to measure the gear end clearance.
3   Alternatively, place a strip of Plastigage across the full width of each gear, install the cover and tighten the retaining screws evenly and securely. Remove the cover and measure the Plastigage with the scale on the envelope.

4   Compare the gear end clearance to the Specifications.
5   Check the gear-to-pump body inner wall clearance and compare this measurement to the Specifications.
6   If any of the measurements are out of the specified range, replace the oil pump assembly with a new one.
7   To remove the oil pressure relief valve, extract the cotter pin and withdraw the valve and spring. Installation is the reverse of removal and a new pick-up tube must be installed (photos).
8   Pack the interior of the pump with petroleum jelly to provide a self-priming action and use a new gasket when reassembling the pump.

## 61   Flywheel and starter ring gear — inspection and servicing

1   Examine the clutch contact surface of the flywheel (*manual transmission models*) for scoring, burn marks, deep ridges and cracks. If any of these conditions exist, or if the surface is highly polished, have the flywheel resurfaced and balanced at an automotive machine shop.
2   Check the starter ring gear for worn and chipped teeth. If damage is evident, the ring gear must be replaced with a new one (*manual transmission models*). On *automatic transmission models*, the driveplate must be replaced with a new one if the ring gear is damaged or worn.

## 62   Oil seals — replacement

1   The timing cover seal and the crankshaft rear oil seal should be replaced as part of the engine overhaul procedure.
2   Use a suitable diameter piece of tubing or a socket and a hammer to carefully drive the old seal out of the timing cover.
3   Apply a light coat of RTV-type sealant to the outer diameter of

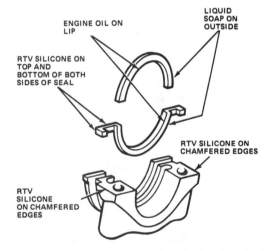

Fig. 2.32   Rear main oil seal installation details (Sec 62)

2C

60.7A   Insert the relief valve and spring

60.7B   Insert the spring retainer

60.7C   Push in on the retainer and install a new cotter pin

the new seal. Place the seal in position with the lip facing *in* and carefully drive it in until it bottoms in the recess.

4    Drive out the old rear main seal with a brass drift and a hammer until it protrudes sufficiently from the engine block to be gripped with pliers and removed. Remove the lower seal from the main bearing cap.

5    Clean the main bearing cap and engine block to remove any traces of gasket sealer.

6    Coat the lip of the seal with engine oil or grease and the upper contact surface with liquid soap. Insert the seal into the groove in the engine block with the lip facing *forward*.

7    Coat both sides of the lower seal ends with RTV-type sealant, taking care not to apply it to the seal surface. Coat the lip of the seal with engine oil or grease and the curved outer surface with liquid soap.

8    Install the lower seal in the main bearing cap with the lip facing *forward* and seat it securely.

9    When installing the main bearing cap, apply a coat of RTV-type sealant to the chamfered contact surfaces.

## 63    Main and connecting rod bearings — selection

1    The crankshaft and bearing inspection procedures are included in Chapter 2A. The condition and measured size of the crankshaft journals will determine the bearings to be installed when the engine is reassembled.

2    If a new or reground crankshaft is installed, the size of each journal should be indicated by a color-coded mark on the adjacent cheek or counterweight, toward the rear (flanged) end of the crankshaft. The bearing inserts are also color coded (on the edge of the insert). The accompanying charts (one for main bearings, one for rod bearings) should be consulted to determine the correct bearings to use. **Caution:**

*Always check the bearing oil clearance with Plastigage during final installation of the crankshaft and/or piston/connecting rod assemblies.*

3    If necessary to achieve the desired oil clearance, different size upper and lower bearing inserts may be used on the same journal but the size difference must never exceed 0.001-inch. **Caution:** *The odd size inserts must all be either in the caps or block (main bearings). In the case of connecting rod bearings, the odd size inserts must all be either in the caps or rods.*

4    If the original crankshaft is reground, the automotive machine shop that reconditions the journals should supply bearings that will produce the desired oil clearance.

## 64    Crankshaft — installation and main bearing oil clearance check

1    Crankshaft installation is generally one of the first steps in engine reassembly; it is assumed at this point that the engine block and crankshaft have been cleaned and inspected and repaired or reconditioned.

2    Position the engine with the bottom facing up.

3    Remove the main bearing cap bolts and lift out the caps. Lay them out in the proper order to help ensure that they are installed correctly.

4    If they are still in place, remove the old bearing inserts from the block and the main bearing caps. Wipe the main bearing surfaces of the block and caps with a clean, lint-free cloth (they must be kept spotlessly clean).

5    Clean the back sides of the new main bearing inserts and lay one bearing half in each main bearing saddle in the block. Lay the other bearing half from each bearing set in the corresponding main bearing cap. Make sure the tab on the bearing insert fits into the recess in the block or cap (photo). Also, the oil holes in the block and cap must line

| Crankshaft Connecting Rod Journal Color and Diameter in Inches (Journal Size) | Bearing Color Code | |
|---|---|---|
| | Upper Insert Size | Lower Insert Size |
| Yellow  —2.0955 to 2.0948 (Standard)<br>Orange  —2.0948 to 2.0941 (0.0007 Undersize)<br>Black  —2.0941 to 2.0934 (0.0014 Undersize)<br>Red  —2.0855 to 2.0848 (0.010 Undersize) | Yellow  — Standard<br>Yellow  — Standard<br>Black  — .001-Inch Undersize<br>Red  — .010-Inch Undersize | Yellow  — Standard<br>Black  — .001-inch Undersize<br>Black  — .001-inch Undersize<br>Red  — .010-inch Undersize |

Fig. 2.33   Connecting rod bearing selection chart (Sec 63)

| Crankshaft Main Bearing Journal Color Code and Diameter in Inches (Journal Size) | Bearing Color Code | |
|---|---|---|
| | Upper Insert Size | Lower Insert Size |
| Yellow  —2.5001 to 2.4996 (Standard)<br>Orange  —2.4996 to 2.4991 (0.0005 Undersize)<br>Black  —2.4991 to 2.4986 (0.001 Undersize)<br>Green  —2.4986 to 2.4981 (0.0015 Undersize)<br>Red  —2.4901 to 2.4896 (0.010 Undersize) | Yellow  — Standard<br>Yellow  — Standard<br>Black  — .001-inch Undersize<br>Black  — .001-inch Undersize<br>Red  — .010-inch Undersize | Yellow  — Standard<br>Black  — .001-inch Undersize<br>Black  — .001-inch Undersize<br>Green  — .002-inch Undersize<br>Red  — .010-inch Undersize |

Fig. 2.34   Main bearing selection chart (1972 through 1980 only) (Sec 63)

| Crankshaft Main Bearing Journal 1-6 Color Code and Diameter in Inches (Journal Size) | Bearing Color Code | |
|---|---|---|
| | Upper Insert Size | Lower Insert Size |
| Yellow  — 2.5001 to 2.4996 (Standard)<br>(63.5025 to 63.4898 mm) | Yellow  — Standard | Yellow  — Standard |
| Orange  — 2.4996 to 2.4991 (0.0005 Undersize)<br>(63.4898 to 63.4771 mm) | Yellow  — Standard | Black  — 0.001-inch Undersize (0.025 mm) |
| Black  — 2.4991 to 2.4986 (0.001 Undersize)<br>(63.4771 to 63.4644 mm) | Black  — 0.001-inch Undersize (0.025 mm) | Black  — 0.001-inch Undersize (0.025 mm) |
| Green  — 2.4986 to 2.4981 (0.0015 Undersize)<br>(63.4644 to 63.4517 mm) | Black  — 0.001-inch Undersize (0.025 mm) | Green  — 0.002-inch Undersize (0.051 mm) |
| Red  — 2.4901 to 2.4896 (0.010 Undersize)<br>(63.2485 to 63.2358 mm) | Red  — 0.010-inch Undersize (0.254 mm) | Red  — 0.010-inch Undersize (0.254 mm) |

Fig. 2.35   Main bearing selection chart (1981 — journals 1-6; 1982 and 1983 — journals 2-6) (Sec 63)

up with the oil holes in the bearing insert. *Do not hammer the bearing into place and do not nick or gouge the bearing faces. No lubrication should be used at this time.*

6  The flanged thrust bearing must be installed in the number three (3) cap and saddle (photo).

7  Clean the faces of the bearings in the block and the crankshaft main bearing journals with a clean, lint-free cloth. Check or clean the oil holes in the crankshaft, as any dirt here can only go one way —

straight through the new bearings. Install the rear seal (Section 62).

8  Once you are certain that the crankshaft is clean, carefully lay it in position (an assistant would be very helpful here) in the main bearings with the counterweights lying sideways (photo).

9  Before the crankshaft can be permanently installed, the main bearing oil clearance must be checked.

10  Trim seven pieces of the appropriate type of Plastigage (so they are slightly shorter than the width of the main bearings) and place one

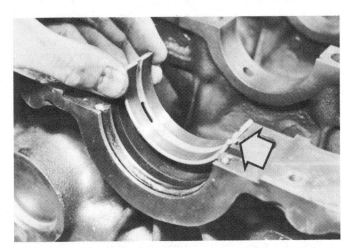

64.5  Make sure the tab (arrow) on the bearing insert fits into the recess in the block

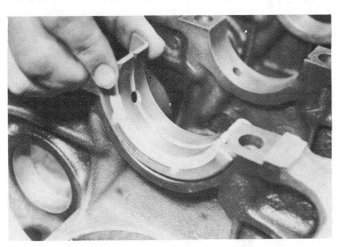

64.6  The thrust bearing must be installed in the number three cap and saddle.

**2C**

| Crankshaft Main Bearing Journal 7 Color Code and Diameter in Inches (Journal Size) | Bearing Color Code | |
|---|---|---|
| | Upper Insert Size | Lower Insert Size |
| Yellow  — 2.4995 to 2.4990 (Standard) (63.4873 to 63.4746 mm) | Yellow  — Standard | Yellow  — Standard |
| Orange  — 2.4990 to 2.4985 (0.0005 Undersize) (63.4746 to 63.4619 mm) | Yellow  — Standard | Black  — 0.001-inch Undersize (0.025 mm) |
| Black  — 2.4985 to 2.4980 (0.001 Undersize) (63.4619 to 63.4492 mm) | Black  — 0.001-inch Undersize (0.025 mm) | Black  — 0.001-inch Undersize (0.025 mm) |
| Green  — 2.4980 to 2.4975 (0.0015 Undersize) (63.4492 to 63.4365 mm) | Black  — 0.001-inch Undersize (0.025 mm) | Green  — 0.002-inch Undersize (0.051 mm) |
| Red  — 2.4895 to 2.4890 (0.010 Undersize) (63.2333 to 63.2206 mm) | Red  — 0.010-inch Undersize (0.254 mm) | Red  — 0.010-inch Undersize (0.254 mm) |

**Fig. 2.36  Main bearing selection chart (1981 through 1983 — journal 7) (Sec 63)**

| Crankshaft No. 1 Main Bearing Journal Color Code and Diameter In Inches (mm) | Cylinder Block No. 1 Main Bearing Bore Color Code and Size In Inches (mm) | Bearing Insert Color Code | |
|---|---|---|---|
| | | Upper Insert Size | Lower Insert Size |
| Yellow — 2.5001 to 2.4996 (Standard) (63.5025 to 63.4898mm) | Yellow — 2.6910 to 2.6915 (68.3514 to 68.3641mm) | Yellow — Standard | Yellow — Standard |
| | Black  — 2.6915 to 2.6920 (68.3641 to 68.3768mm) | Yellow — Standard | Black  — 0.001-inch Undersize (0.025mm) |
| Orange — 2.4996 to 2.4991 (0.0005 Undersize) (63.4898 to 63.4771mm) | Yellow — 2.6910 to 2.6915 (68.3514 to 68.3641mm) | Yellow — Standard | Black  — 0.001-inch Undersize (0.025mm) |
| | Black  — 2.6915 to 2.6920 (68.3641 to 68.3768mm) | Black — 0.001-inch Undersize (0.025mm) | Green — 0.002-inch Undersize (0.051mm) |
| Black — 2.4991 to 2.4986 (0.001 Undersize) (63.4771 to 63.4644mm) | Yellow — 2.6910 to 2.6915 (68.3514 to 68.3641mm) | Black  — 0.001-inch Undersize (0.025mm) | Black  — 0.001-inch Undersize (0.025mm) |
| | Black  — 2.6915 to 2.6920 (68.3641 to 68.3768mm) | Black  — 0.001-inch Undersize (0.025mm) | Green — 0.002-inch Undersize (0.051mm) |
| Green — 2.4986 to 2.4981 (0.0015 Undersize) (63.4644 to 63.4517mm) | Yellow — 2.6910 to 2.6915 (68.3514 to 68.3641mm) | Black  — 0.001-inch Undersize (0.025mm) | Green — 0.002-inch Undersize (0.051mm) |
| Red — 2.4901 to 2.4986 (0.010 Undersize) (63.2485 to 63.2358mm) | Yellow — 2.6910 to 2.6915 (68.3541 to 68.3641mm) | Red  — 0.010-inch Undersize (0.254mm) | Red  — 0.010-inch Undersize (0.254mm) |

**Fig 2.37  Main bearing selection chart (1982 and 1983 — journal 1) (Sec 63)**

piece on each crankshaft main bearing journal, parallel with the journal axis. Do not lay them across any oil holes.

11   Clean the faces of the bearings in the caps and install the caps in their respective positions (do not mix them up) with the arrows pointing toward the front of the engine. Do not disturb the Plastigage.

12   Starting with the center main and working out toward the ends, tighten the main bearing cap bolts, in three steps, to the specified torque. *Do not rotate the crankshaft at any time during this operation.*

13   Remove the bolts and carefully lift off the main bearing caps. Keep them in order. Do not disturb the Plastigage or rotate the crankshaft. If any of the main bearing caps are difficult to remove, tap gently from side-to-side with a soft-faced hammer to loosen them.

14   Compare the width of the crushed Plastigage on each journal to the scale printed on the Plastigage container to obtain the main bearing oil clearance. Check the Specifications to make sure it is correct.

15   If the clearance is not correct, double-check to make sure you have the right size bearing inserts. Also, recheck the crankshaft main bearing journal diameters and make sure that no dirt or oil was between the bearing inserts and the main bearing caps or the block when the clearance was measured.

16   Carefully scrape all traces of the Plastigage material off the main bearing journals and/or the bearing faces. Do not nick or scratch the bearing faces.

17   Carefully lift the crankshaft out of the engine. Clean the bearing faces in the block, then apply a thin, uniform layer of clean, high-quality moly-based grease (or engine assembly lube) to each of the bearing faces. Be sure to coat the thrust flange faces as well as the journal face of the thrust bearing in the number three (3) main. Make sure the crankshaft journals are clean, then lay it back in place in the block. Clean the faces of the bearings in the caps, then apply a thin, uniform layer of clean, moly-based grease to each of the bearing faces and install the caps in their respective positions with the arrows pointing toward the front of the engine. Install the bolts and tighten them to the specified torque, starting with the center main and working out toward the ends.

Work up to the final torque in three steps.

18   Rotate the crankshaft a number of times by hand and check for any obvious binding.

19   The final step is to check the crankshaft end play. This can be done with a feeler gauge or a dial indicator set. Refer to Chapter 2A, Section 12, for the procedure to follow.

## 65   Flywheel/driveplate — installation

1   Install the engine rear plate over the locating dowels.

2   Attach the flywheel (or driveplate) to the crankshaft rear flange and tighten the bolts to the specified torque. Apply a wrench to the vibration damper bolt to prevent the crankshaft from rotating as the flywheel bolts are tightened.

## 66   Oil pump and oil pan — installation

1   Locate a new oil pump gasket on the lower flange of the block (photo).

2   Install the oil pump/pick-up tube assembly and tighten the mounting bolts (photo).

3   Position a new oil pan gasket on the block and then bolt on the oil pan, tightening the bolts to the specified torque. Follow a crisscross pattern to avoid warping the pan. Make sure the drain plug is tight.

## 67   Camshaft and timing chain/sprockets — installation

1   Lubricate the camshaft and carefully insert the camshaft from the front of the engine.

66.1   Be sure to use a new gasket when installing the oil pump

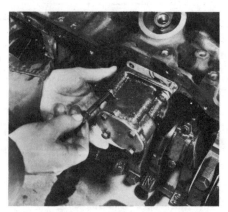

66.2   Installing the oil pump

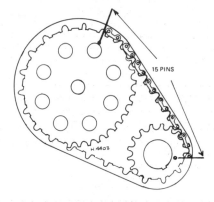

Fig. 2.38   Correct relationship of crankshaft and camshaft sprockets (Sec 67)

67.5   Remember to install the oil slinger (arrow) before attaching the timing chain cover to the block

67.6   Be careful not to damage the seal when installing the timing chain cover

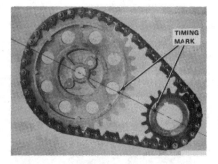

Fig. 2.39   With the camshaft sprocket timing mark at the 1 o'clock position, the timing marks must be 15 pins apart (Sec 67)

2   With the engine positioned with the cylinder head surface up, turn the crankshaft so that the keyway is vertical and at the top.
3   Engage the camshaft and crankshaft sprockets within the timing chain and install them as an assembly so that a line drawn through the sprocket timing marks will also pass through the centers of the sprockets. Obviously the camshaft will have to be rotated and a certain amount of repositioning of the camshaft sprocket within the loop of the chain will be required to achieve this.
4   Secure the camshaft sprocket and then check the timing. To do this, set the camshaft sprocket timing mark to the one o'clock position. There should be 15 chain pins between the sprocket timing marks (as shown in the accompanying illustration).
5   Attach the oil slinger to the front of the crankshaft sprocket (photo).
6   Install a new oil seal in the timing chain cover (Section 62), then attach the cover to the engine with a new gasket. Tighten the bolts finger tight at this time (photo).
7   Apply grease to the oil seal contact surfaces of the vibration damper and push it into position. If necessary, tap the timing cover from side to side (or up and down) to center it and enable the damper to be withdrawn and installed easily.
8   Now tighten the timing chain cover bolts securely.
9   Install the damper and tighten the mounting bolt to the specified torque. Use a block of wood inserted between the crankshaft and the engine block to prevent crankshaft rotation.
10  Locate a new gasket on the front face of the cylinder block (use RTV-type sealant on the gasket).
11  Install the water pump.

## 68   Valve lifters — installation

Note: The camshaft must be in place before the lifters are installed.

1   Apply engine assembly lube or moly grease to the lifters, then install them in their original bores.
2   If new lifters are being installed, a new camshaft must also be installed. If a new camshaft was installed, then use new lifters as well. Never install used lifters unless the original camshaft is used and the lifters can be installed in their original locations.

## 69   Cylinder head and rocker gear — installation

Note: The valve lifters must be in place before the head is installed.

1   If not already done, thoroughly clean the gasket surfaces on both the cylinder head and the engine block. Do not scratch or otherwise damage the sealing areas.
2   To get the proper torque readings, the threads of the head bolts must be clean. This also holds true for the threaded holes in the engine block. Run a tap through these holes to ensure that they are clean.
3   Apply a thin, even coat of AMC Perfect Seal gasket sealer (or equivalent) to both sides of the new head gasket. Caution: Do not apply the gasket sealer to the cylinder head or block and do not allow any sealer to enter the cylinder bores. Place the gasket in position over the engine block dowel pins. Make sure the side marked TOP is facing up.
4   Carefully lower the cylinder head onto the engine, over the dowel pins and the gasket. Be careful not to move the gasket while doing this.
5   Install the head bolts and tighten them finger tight.
6   Tighten each of the bolts, a little at a time, in the sequence shown in the accompanying illustration. Continue tightening in this sequence until the proper torque reading is obtained. As a final check, work around the head in a logical front-to-rear sequence to make sure none of the bolts have been overlooked.
7   Lubricate the pushrod ends with engine assembly lube or moly grease and install them. Make sure they are seated in the lifter cavities.
8   Lubricate the rocker arm contact surfaces, then install the rocker arms or shaft assembly and tighten the bolts to the specified torque. Be sure to lubricate the rocker arm pivots with engine assembly lube or moly grease.
9   Lay a new gasket in place, then install the rocker arm cover.

## 70   External components — installation

1   Install the thermostat (pin hole up) and cover using a new gasket.
2   On vehicles with a manual transmission, attach the clutch assembly to the flywheel as described in Chapter 8.
3   Install the intake and exhaust manifolds.
4   Install the EGR valve, the back pressure sensor, the coolant temperature switch and the solenoid vacuum valve and connections (all components of the emissions control system).
5   Install the engine mount brackets.
6   Install the alternator.
7   Attach the air cleaner hot air duct to the exhaust manifold.
8   Install the distributor as described in Chapter 5.
9   Install the ignition coil.
10  Install the spark plugs and wires.
11  Install the fuel pump.
12  Check that the oil filter cartridge threaded fitting is tight, grease the filter sealing ring and screw it on with hand pressure only.

## 71   Engine — installation

1   Lower the engine carefully into the engine compartment and at-

**2C**

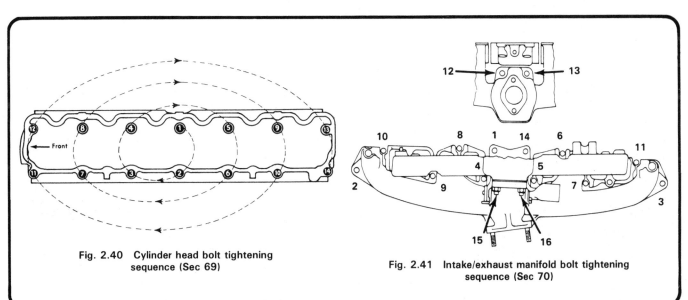

Fig. 2.40  Cylinder head bolt tightening
sequence (Sec 69)

Fig. 2.41  Intake/exhaust manifold bolt tightening
sequence (Sec 70)

tach it to the transmission. *On manual transmissions,* make sure the transmission input shaft is correctly installed in the pilot bushing and clutch disc.

2    Install the power steering pump and drivebelt.

3    Connect the heater hoses to the heater core.

4    Connect the coolant temperature sending unit, oil pressure sending unit, choke, solenoid and mixture control solenoid wires.

5    Connect the carburetor and evaporative system vacuum hoses.

6    Connect the carburetor bowl vent hose.

7    Connect the alternator wiring harness.

8    Attach the throttle linkage to the carburetor.

9    Place the fan shroud in position over the fan and install the radiator and hoses. Attach the shroud to the radiator and fill the radiator with the specified coolant. Attach the cooler lines to the radiator (automatic transmission only).

10   Raise the vehicle and support it securely.

11   *On automatic transmissions,* align the converter-to-driveplate marks made during removal, then install the attaching bolts and tighten

them to the specified torque. Apply thread-locking compound to the bolt threads before installing them.

12   Install the transmission-to-torque converter housing attaching bolts and tighten them securely.

13   *On manual transmissions,* install the flywheel inspection plate and hook up the clutch and transmission linkages.

14   Install the engine mount nuts and tighten them securely.

15   Install the starter motor.

16   Connect the battery cable and solenoid wire to the starter.

17   Connect the distributor wires.

18   Connect the exhaust pipe to the manifold and install the oxygen sensor wire (if so equipped).

19   Connect the negative battery cable to the battery.

20   Install the air cleaner assembly.

21   Fill the engine to the correct level with the recommended oil.

22   Refer to Chapter 2A for the initial start-up and break-in procedures.

23   Have the air conditioning lines hooked up and the system recharged by an air conditioning technician.

# Chapter 2 Part D  V8 engine

**Contents**

| | |
|---|---|
| Camshaft — installation | 89 |
| Camshaft — removal | 83 |
| Crankshaft — inspection | Chapter 2A |
| Crankshaft — installation and main bearing | |
| oil clearance check | 95 |
| Crankshaft — removal | 94 |
| Cylinder head — cleaning and inspection | Chapter 2A |
| Cylinder head — disassembly | Chapter 2A |
| Cylinder head — installation | 91 |
| Cylinder head — reassembly | Chapter 2A |
| Cylinder head — removal | 79 |
| Engine block — cleaning | Chapter 2A |
| Engine block — inspection | Chapter 2A |
| Engine disassembly — general information | Chapter 2A |
| Engine mounts — replacement | 74 |
| Engine overhaul — general information | Chapter 2A |
| Engine rebuilding alternatives | Chapter 2A |
| Engine removal — methods and precautions | Chapter 2A |
| Engine — disassembly and reassembly sequence | 76 |
| Engine — installation | 97 |
| Engine — removal | 75 |
| General information | 72 |
| Initial start-up and break-in after overhaul | Chapter 2A |
| Intake manifold — installation | 92 |
| Intake manifold — removal | 78 |
| Main and connecting rod bearings — inspection | Chapter 2A |
| Main and connecting rod bearings — selection | 96 |
| Oil pan — installation | 93 |
| Oil pan — removal | 77 |
| Oil pump — disassembly, inspection and reassembly | 85 |
| Oil pump — installation | 87 |
| Oil pump — removal | 84 |
| Oil seal replacement | 86 |
| Oversize and undersize component designation | 73 |
| Piston/connecting rod assembly — inspection | Chapter 2A |
| Piston/connecting rod assembly — installation and | |
| bearing oil clearance check | Chapter 2A |
| Piston/connecting rod assembly — removal | Chapter 2A |
| Piston rings — installation | Chapter 2A |
| Repair operations possible with the engine | |
| in the vehicle | Chapter 2A |
| Timing chain cover — installation | 90 |
| Timing chain cover — removal | 80 |
| Timing chain and sprockets — installation | 88 |
| Timing chain and sprockets — removal | 82 |
| Timing chain wear check | 81 |
| Valves — servicing | Chapter 2A |

---

**Specifications**

## General

| | |
|---|---|
| Displacement | 304 cu in |
| Cylinder numbering (viewed from radiator, front-to-rear) | |
| Left bank | 1-3-5-7 |
| Right bank | 2-4-6-8 |
| Firing order | 1-8-4-3-6-5-7-2 |
| Compression pressure | 140 psi |
| Maximum variation between cylinders | 20 psi |
| Oil pressure | |
| 600 rpm | 13 psi |
| 1600 rpm and above | 37 psi minimum, 75 psi max. |

## Cylinder bore

| | |
|---|---|
| Taper limit | 0.005 in |
| Out-of-round limit | 0.003 in |
| Deck warpage limit | 0.008 in |

## Pistons and rings

| | |
|---|---|
| Piston-to-cylinder bore clearance | |
|     Standard | 0.0010 to 0.0018 in |
|     Preferred | 0.0014 in |
| Piston ring side clearance | |
|     Top ring | |
|         Standard | 0.0015 to 0.0035 in |
|         Preferred | 0.0015 in |
|     2nd ring | |
|         Standard | 0.0015 to 0.003 in |
|         Preferred | 0.0015 in |
|     Oil ring | 0.0011 to 0.008 in |
| Piston ring end gap | |
|     Top and 2nd ring | |
|         Standard | 0.010 to 0.020 in |
|         Preferred | 0.010 to 0.012 in |
|     Oil ring | 0.010 to 0.025 in |
| Piston pin-to-rod clearance | Press fit |
| Piston pin-to-bore clearance | |
|     Standard | 0.0003 to 0.0005 in |
|     Preferred | 0.0005 in |

## Crankshaft and flywheel

| | |
|---|---|
| Main journal diameter | |
|     1, 2, 3 and 4 | 2.7474 to 2.7489 in |
|     Rear main (5) | 2.7464 to 2.7479 in |
| Main bearing oil clearance | |
|     1, 2, 3 and 4 | |
|         Standard | 0.001 to 0.003 in |
|         Preferred | 0.0017 to 0.0020 in |
|     Rear main (5) | |
|         Standard | 0.002 to 0.004 in |
|         Preferred | 0.0025 to 0.003 in |
| Connecting rod journal | |
|     Diameter | 2.0934 to 2.0955 in |
|     Taper limit | 0.0005 in |
|     Out-of-round limit | 0.0005 in |
| Connecting rod bearing oil clearance | |
|     Standard | 0.001 to 0.003 in |
|     Preferred | 0.0020 to 0.0025 in |
| Connecting rod end play | 0.006 to 0.0018 in |
| Crankshaft end play | 0.003 to 0.008 in |

## Camshaft

| | |
|---|---|
| Bearing journal diameter | |
|     1 | 2.1195 to 2.1205 in |
|     2 | 2.0895 to 2.0905 in |
|     3 | 2.0595 to 2.0605 in |
|     4 | 2.0295 to 2.0305 in |
|     5 | 1.9995 to 2.0005 in |
| Bearing oil clearance | |
|     Standard | 0.001 to 0.003 in |
|     Preferred | 0.0017 to 0.0020 in |
| Lobe lift | 0.266 in |
| End play | Zero |
| Timing chain total allowable deflection | 7/8 in |

## Cylinder heads and valve train

| | |
|---|---|
| Head warpage limit | 0.008 in max. |
| Valve seat angle | |
|     Intake | 30° |
|     Exhaust | 44.5° |
| Valve seat width | 0.040 to 0.060 in |
| Valve seat runout limit | 0.0025 in max. |
| Valve face angle | |
|     Intake | 29° |
|     Exhaust | 44° |
| Valve stem diameter | 0.3715 to 0.3725 in |
| Valve guide diameter | 0.3735 to 0.3745 in |
| Valve stem-to-guide clearance | 0.001 to 0.003 in |
| Valve margin width | 1/32 in minimum |
| Valve lifter type | Hydraulic |
| Lifter diameter | 0.9040 to 0.9045 in |
| Lifter bore diameter | 0.9055 to 0.9065 in |
| Lifter-to-bore clearance | 0.001 to 0.0025 in |

## Oil pump

| | |
|---|---|
| Gear end clearance . . . . . . . . . . . . . . . . . . . . . . . . . . . . . . . | 0.002 to 0.006 in |
| Gear-to-body clearance . . . . . . . . . . . . . . . . . . . . . . . . . . . . | 0.0005 to 0.0025 in |
| Oil pressure relief valve opening pressure . . . . . . . . . . . . . . | 75 psi |

## Oversize and undersize component code letter definition

Code letter

| | | |
|---|---|---|
| B | Cylinder bore . . . . . . . . . . . . . . . . . . . . . . . . . . . . . | 0.010 in oversize |
| M | Main bearings. . . . . . . . . . . . . . . . . . . . . . . . . . . . . . | 0.010 in undersize |
| F | Connecting rod bearings . . . . . . . . . . . . . . . . . . . . . | 0.010 in undersize |
| PM | Main and connecting rod bearings . . . . . . . . . . . . . . | 0.010 in undersize |
| C | Camshaft bearing bores . . . . . . . . . . . . . . . . . . . . . | 0.010 in oversize |

## Torque specifications

| | Ft-lbs | Nm |
|---|---|---|
| Camshaft gear screw . . . . . . . . . . . . . . . . . . . . . . . . . . . . . | 30 | 41 |
| Carburetor adapter . . . . . . . . . . . . . . . . . . . . . . . . . . . . . . . | 12 to 15 | 16 to 20 |
| Carburetor mounting nuts . . . . . . . . . . . . . . . . . . . . . . . . . . | 12 to 15 | 16 to 20 |
| Connecting rod nuts | | |
|    1972 through 1975 . . . . . . . . . . . . . . . . . . . . . . . . . | 28 | 38 |
|    1976 through 1983 . . . . . . . . . . . . . . . . . . . . . . . . . | 33 | 45 |
| Crankshaft pulley-to-damper bolts . . . . . . . . . . . . . . . . . . . | 17 to 28 | 24 to 38 |
| Cylinder head bolts. . . . . . . . . . . . . . . . . . . . . . . . . . . . . . . | 110 | 149 |
| Driveplate-to-torque converter bolts . . . . . . . . . . . . . . . . . | 22 | 30 |
| Exhaust manifold bolts | | |
|    3/8 in . . . . . . . . . . . . . . . . . . . . . . . . . . . . . . . . . . . | 25 | 34 |
|    5/16 in . . . . . . . . . . . . . . . . . . . . . . . . . . . . . . . . . . | 15 | 20 |
| Exhaust pipe-to-manifold bolts . . . . . . . . . . . . . . . . . . . . . | 15 to 25 | 20 to 34 |
| Fan and hub assembly . . . . . . . . . . . . . . . . . . . . . . . . . . . . | 12 to 25 | 16 to 34 |
| Flywheel or driveplate-to-crankshaft bolts . . . . . . . . . . . . . | 105 | 142 |
| Intake manifold . . . . . . . . . . . . . . . . . . . . . . . . . . . . . . . . . | 43 | 58 |
| Main bearing cap bolts . . . . . . . . . . . . . . . . . . . . . . . . . . . | 100 | 136 |
| Oil pan screws | | |
|    1/4 in . . . . . . . . . . . . . . . . . . . . . . . . . . . . . . . . . . . | 5 to 9 | 7 to 12 |
|    5/16 in . . . . . . . . . . . . . . . . . . . . . . . . . . . . . . . . . . | 9 to 13 | 12 to 18 |
| Oil pump cover. . . . . . . . . . . . . . . . . . . . . . . . . . . . . . . . . . | 4.5 | 6.0 |
| Oil relief valve cap . . . . . . . . . . . . . . . . . . . . . . . . . . . . . . . | 28 | 38 |
| Rocker arm bolt . . . . . . . . . . . . . . . . . . . . . . . . . . . . . . . . . | 16 to 26 | 22 to 35 |
| Spark plugs . . . . . . . . . . . . . . . . . . . . . . . . . . . . . . . . . . . . | 22 to 33 | 30 to 45 |
| Starter motor bolts . . . . . . . . . . . . . . . . . . . . . . . . . . . . . . | 13 to 25 | 18 to 34 |
| Thermostat housing bolts . . . . . . . . . . . . . . . . . . . . . . . . . | 10 to 18 | 14 to 24 |
| Timing chain cover-to-block bolts . . . . . . . . . . . . . . . . . . . | 18 to 33 | 24 to 45 |
| Vibration damper bolt* | | |
|    1972 through 1975 . . . . . . . . . . . . . . . . . . . . . . . . . | 55 | 76 |
|    1976 and 1978 . . . . . . . . . . . . . . . . . . . . . . . . . . . . . | 80 | 108 |
|    1977 and 1979 through 1983. . . . . . . . . . . . . . . . . . . | 90 | 122 |
| Water pump bolts. . . . . . . . . . . . . . . . . . . . . . . . . . . . . . . . | 4 to 5 | 5 to 6 |

***Note:** The vibration damper bolt on 1978 through 1983 models should be lubricated before installation.*

2D

### 72   General information

The 90 degree V8 engine is made of cast iron and features overhead valves. The camshaft is located in the V of the cylinder block and actuates the valves through hydraulic lifters, pushrods and rocker arms. The rocker arms are fastened to the cylinder head in pairs by bridged pivots.

The positive displacement, gear-type oil pump is incorporated into the timing case cover and is driven by the distributor shaft.

The crankshaft is supported by five two-piece insert-type main bearings.

### 73   Oversize and undersize component designation

1   Some engines may have oversize or undersize cylinder bores, crankshaft main bearing journals, connecting rod journals and/or camshaft bearing bores.

2   A code designating the presence of oversize or undersize components is stamped on the tag located on the right bank rocker arm cover. The oversize/undersize code is located adjacent to the engine build date code on the tag.

3   Refer to the Specifications Section and compare the letter code with the information in the chart to determine which components are oversize or undersize.

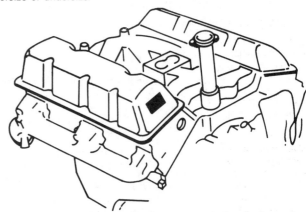

**Fig. 2.42   The engine build date and oversize/undersize codes are located on the right side rocker arm cover (Sec 73)**

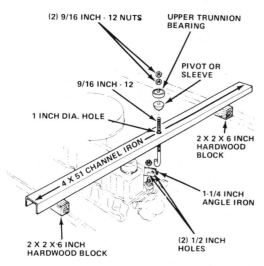

Fig. 2.43  Typical engine lifting/supporting fixture
which can be fabricated and used when replacing
engine mount cushions (Sec 74)

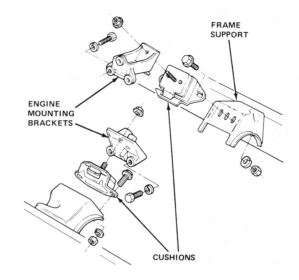

Fig. 2.44  Typical engine mount component
layout — exploded view (Sec 74)

## 74  Engine mounts — replacement

1   Rubber engine mounts support the engine at three points. These
mounts should be inspected periodically to make sure they haven't
become hard, split or separated from the metal backing.
2   The mount cushions can be replaced after supporting the
engine/transmission weight with a jack, hoist or holding fixture.

## 75  Engine — removal

**Note:** *The following sequence of operations does not necessarily need
to be performed in the order given. It is, rather, a checklist of everything
that must be disconnected or removed before the engine can be lifted
out of the vehicle. If your vehicle is equipped with an automatic
transmission, the engine removal procedure will be slightly different
from the procedure for vehicles equipped with a manual transmission.
It is very important that all linkages, electrical wiring, hoses and cables
be removed or disconnected before attempting to lift the engine clear
of the vehicle, so double-check everything thoroughly.*

1   Open the hood and tilt it completely back.
2   Remove the air cleaner assembly.
3   Drain the coolant into a suitable container, then remove the heater
hoses and radiator hoses.
4   *On automatic transmission equipped models,* disconnect and plug
the transmission fluid cooler lines.
5   Remove the radiator and engine cooling fan.
6   Disconnect and plug the power steering hoses and remove the
power steering pump assembly.
7   If the vehicle is equipped with air conditioning, have the system
discharged by a dealer service department or properly trained technician. **Caution:** *Do not attempt to disconnect the air conditioning system
components until the system has been safely discharged, as serious
injury could result.*
8   Remove the air conditioning compressor.
9   If equipped with cruise control, remove the servo bellows and
mounting bracket as an assembly.
10  Disconnect the negative battery cable from the battery.
11  Disconnect the fuel supply and return lines at the chassis
connections.
12  Disconnect the engine wiring harness and move it out of the way.
13  Disconnect the vacuum line from the power brake unit.
14  Disconnect the heater damper door vacuum line at the intake
manifold.
15  *On automatic transmission equipped models,* disconnect (but do

not remove) the filler tube at the right cylinder head.
16  Remove the nuts from the front engine mount support cushions.
17  Connect a suitable lifting device to the engine and raise it sufficiently to support the engine's weight.
18  Remove the left front engine support cushion and bracket.
19  *On four wheel drive models equipped with a manual transmission,*
remove the transfer case shift lever boot, floor mat and transmission
access cover.
20  *On automatic transmission equipped vehicles,* remove the upper
torque converter-to-engine bolts.
21  *On manual transmission equipped models,* remove the upper clutch
housing-to-engine bolts.
22  Unbolt and disconnect the exhaust pipes from the manifolds and
support bracket.
23  Remove the starter motor.
24  Support the transmission with a jack.
25  *On automotic transmission equipped models,* remove the inspection cover and mark the relative position of the converter and driveplate.
26  Remove the converter-to-driveplate bolts by rotating the crankshaft
pulley nut with a wrench to provide access to each bolt.
27  Remove any remaining bolts retaining the engine to the transmission. *On manual transmission equipped models,* remove the clutch housing lower cover for access to the remaining bolts.
28  Withdraw the engine forward and lift it up at an angle to remove
the engine from the vehicle.

## 76  Engine — disassembly and reassembly sequence

1   To completely disassemble the engine, remove the following items
in the order given:

*Oil pan*
*Intake manifold*
*Cylinder head/valve train components*
*Timing chain cover*
*Timing chain and sprockets*
*Camshaft*
*Piston/connecting rod assemblies*
*Crankshaft*
*Oil pump*

2   Engine reassembly is basically the reverse of disassembly. Install
the following components in the order given:

*Oil pump*
*Crankshaft*
*Piston/connecting rod assemblies*

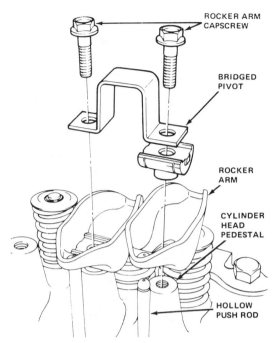

Fig. 2.45   Rocker arm assembly components — exploded view
(Sec 79)

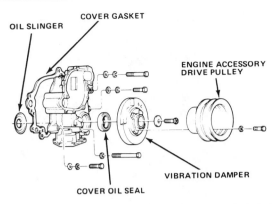

Fig. 2.46   Timing chain cover components — exploded view
(Sec 80)

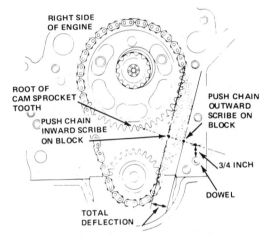

Fig. 2.47   Checking timing chain wear (deflection) (Sec 81)

2D

*Timing chain and sprockets*
*Camshaft*
*Timing chain cover*
*Cylinder head/valve train components*
*Intake manifold*
*Oil pan*

## 77   Oil pan — removal

1   Remove the bolts attaching the oil pan to the engine block.
2   Tap on the pan with a soft-faced hammer, to break the gasket seal,
and lift the oil pan off the engine.
3   Remove the oil pan neoprene seals.
4   Using a gasket scraper, remove all traces of gasket from the oil
pan and engine block gasket surfaces.
5   Clean the oil pan with solvent and dry it thoroughly. Check the
gasket sealing surfaces for distortion.

## 78   Intake manifold — removal

1   Remove the carburetor and linkage (Chapter 4).
2   Remove the retaining bolts and lift the manifold from the engine.
3   Remove the metal gasket and the end seals.

## 79   Cylinder head — removal

1   Remove the rocker arm covers. The covers are installed with a
formed-in-place RTV-type gasket and it may be necessary to tap them
sharply with a soft-faced hammer to break the seal.
2   Remove the intake manifold.
3   Remove the rocker arm assembly bolts/nuts.
4   Remove the rocker arm assemblies and pushrods, keeping them
in order so they can be reinstalled in their original locations.
5   Loosen the cylinder head bolts 1/4-turn at a time, working from the
inside out. Remove the bolts, then lift off the cylinder head and
gasket. It may be necessary to tap the head sharply with a soft-faced
hammer around its circumference to break the gasket seal.

## 80   Timing chain cover — removal

1   Remove the vibration damper bolt.
2   Using a suitable puller, remove the vibration damper.
3   Remove the timing cover mounting bolts. Since these bolts are
of varying lengths, mark the location of each one at the time of removal
so they can be reinstalled in the same locations.
4   Remove the cover by pulling it straight out, off the locating dowels.
5   Pry the oil seal out and clean the bore. Clean the gasket surfaces
of the timing cover and engine block.

## 81   Timing chain wear check

1   Remove the timing chain cover.
2   Rotate either the crankshaft or camshaft sprocket until there is
no slack in the right side of the chain.
3   To determine a reference point for deflection measurement, move
3/4 of an inch up from the dowel on the right side of the engine and
make a mark at this location. Place a straightedge across the timing
chain from a point at the lowest root of the camshaft sprocket to the
marked position. Grasp the chain at this point to use as a reference,
move the chain in toward the centerline of the engine and mark the
point of maximum deflection. Move the chain out to the point of maximum deflection and make another mark.
4   Measure the distance between the two marks to determine the
total deflection (as shown in the accompanying illustration).
5   If the deflection is beyond the maximum allowed in the
Specifications, replace the chain with a new one. If the chain is replaced,
new sprockets probably should be used as well.

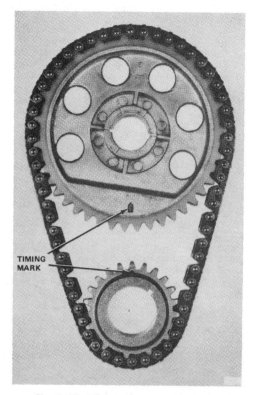

Fig. 2.48  The marks on the sprockets must be aligned before removing the chain and sprockets (Sec 82)

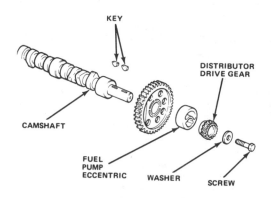

Fig. 2.49  Camshaft components — exploded view (Sec 83)

KEY

CAMSHAFT

FUEL PUMP ECCENTRIC

DISTRIBUTOR DRIVE GEAR

WASHER

SCREW

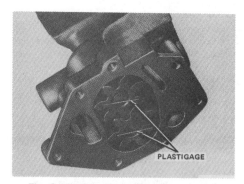

Fig. 2.51  Checking oil pump gear end clearance with Plastigage (Sec 85)

PLASTIGAGE

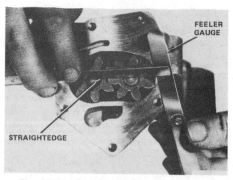

Fig. 2.52  Checking oil pump gear end clearance with a feeler gauge and straightedge (Sec 85)

FEELER GAUGE

STRAIGHTEDGE

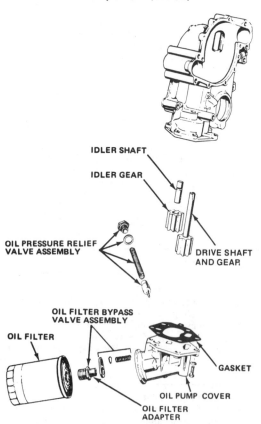

IDLER SHAFT

IDLER GEAR

OIL PRESSURE RELIEF VALVE ASSEMBLY

DRIVE SHAFT AND GEAR

OIL FILTER BYPASS VALVE ASSEMBLY

OIL FILTER

GASKET

OIL PUMP COVER

OIL FILTER ADAPTER

Fig. 2.50  Oil pump components — exploded view (Sec 85)

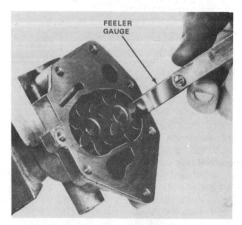

FEELER GAUGE

Fig. 2.53  Checking oil pump gear-to-body clearance (Sec 85)

## 82   Timing chain and sprockets — removal

1   Remove the vibration damper and pulley.
2   Remove the timing chain cover.
3   Remove the camshaft retaining screw and washer, distributor drive gear and fuel pump eccentric.
4   Rotate the crankshaft until the zero timing mark on the sprocket is aligned with, and closest to, the zero timing mark on the camshaft sprocket as shown in the accompanying illustration.
5   Remove the crankshaft and camshaft sprockets and the timing chain as an assembly.

## 83   Camshaft — removal

1   Remove the pushrods and valve lifters.
2   Remove the distributor.
3   Remove the vibration damper and timing chain cover.
4   Install the vibration damper screw and two washers and use a wrench to rotate the crankshaft until the timing mark is aligned with the centerline of the camshaft sprocket.
5   Remove the retaining screws from the camshaft and crankshaft.
6   Remove the fuel pump eccentric and distributor drive gear from the camshaft.
7   Remove the crankshaft and camshaft sprockets and timing chain as an assembly.
8   Remove the camshaft from the engine block, taking care not to damage the lobes or bearing surfaces.
9   Inspect the distributor drive gear and fuel pump eccentric for wear and damage. Inspect the camshaft bearing journals for excessive wear and evidence of seizure. If the journals are damaged, the bearings in the block are probably damaged as well. Both the camshaft and bearings will have to be replaced with new ones. Check the cam lobes for pitting, grooves, scoring or flaking. Inspect the valve lifter faces (that ride on the cam lobes) for concave wear. **Note:** *Never install used lifters on a new camshaft. If the original camshaft and lifters are installed, make sure the lifters are returned to the bores they were removed from. If they get mixed up, new lifters must be used.*

## 84   Oil pump — removal

1   The oil pump is an integral part of the timing chain cover with the cavity in the cover forming the body of the pump.
2   Remove the retaining bolts and lift the oil pump cover, the gasket and the oil filter as an assembly away from the timing chain cover.

## 85   Oil pump — disassembly, inspection and reassembly

1   Slide the drive gear assembly and idler gear from the pump body.
2   Unscrew the pressure relief valve cap and remove the valve and spring.
3   Check the operation of the relief valve by inserting the poppet valve and making sure it slides back and forth freely. If it does not, replace the pump cover and the valve with new components.
4   The distance between the end of the pump gear and the cover is the gear end clearance. This can be checked in either of two ways.

   a)   Place a strip of Plastigage across the full width of each gear, install the pump cover and tighten the bolts to the specified torque. Remove the cover and measure the Plastigage with the scale on the container to determine if the clearance is within the Specifications.
   b)   Place a straightedge across the gears and the pump body and select a feeler gauge which will fit freely but snugly between the straightedge and the body. Make sure the gears are pushed as far up into the body as possible.

5   If the clearance is excessive, check the gears for excessive wear. If the gear is obviously not badly worn and a thinner cover gasket will not bring the clearance within the specified limit, replace the gears and idler shaft.
6   To check the gear-to-body clearance, insert a feeler gauge be-
tween the gear tooth end and the pump body inner wall opposite the point of gear mesh as shown in the accompanying illustration. Select a gauge which fits snugly, yet can be inserted freely. Rotate the gears and measure the clearance of each tooth in turn.
7   If the gear-to-body clearance is greater than specified, replace the gears and idler shaft.
8   Slide the gear and idler shaft assembly into the pump body and insert the pressure relief valve and spring, secure it with the cap. **Note:** *The oil pump must be packed with petroleum jelly (not grease) prior to installation to ensure self-priming action.*

## 86   Oil seal replacement

### *Front timing chain cover seal*
1   The seal should be replaced with a new one whenever the timing chain cover is removed.
2   Remove the old seal and clean the cavity.
3   Apply a gasket sealant such as Permatex No. 2 or equivalent to the outer circumference of the seal.
4   Install the seal evenly in the timing case, using a large socket or block of wood and a hammer to seat it completely in the cavity.
5   Prior to installing the crankshaft vibration damper, apply a light coat of engine oil or grease to the seal-to-damper contact surface.

### *Rear main bearing oil seal*
6   Remove the rear main bearing and discard the old lower seal.
7   Clean all traces of sealer from the main bearing cap.
8   Gently drive out the upper seal, using a hammer and brass drift, until it protrudes sufficiently to be grasped with pliers and pulled out.
9   If the crankshaft is in place, wipe the contact surface area clean and apply a light coat of engine oil.
10   Coat the lip of the seal with engine oil or grease and the upper contact surface with liquid soap. Insert the seal into the groove in the engine block with the lip facing forward.
11   Coat both sides of the lower seal ends with RTV-type sealant, taking care not to apply it to the seal surface. Coat the lip of the seal with engine oil or grease and the curved outer surface with liquid soap as shown in the accompanying illustration.
12   Install the lower seal in the main bearing cap with the lip facing forward and seat it securely.
13   When installing the main bearing cap, apply a coat of RTV-type sealant to the chamfered contact surfaces.

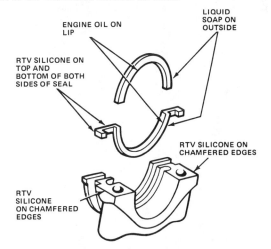

**Fig. 2.54   Rear main bearing oil seal installation details (Sec 86)**

## 87   Oil pump — installation

1   Pack the interior of the pump with petroleum jelly to provide a self-priming action. **Caution:** *Do not use grease for this purpose.*
2   Using a new gasket, place the pump and filter assembly in position and install the retaining bolts. Tighten them to the specified torque.

## 88   Timing chain and sprockets — installation

1   Assemble the timing chain, crankshaft and camshaft sprockets with the timing marks aligned as shown in the accompanying illustration.
2   Install the sprockets and chain onto the crankshaft and camshaft.
3   Install the fuel pump eccentric and distributor drive gear with the eccentric REAR stamping facing the camshaft sprocket.
4   Install the camshaft washer and screw. Tighten the screw to the specified torque.
5   Rotate the crankshaft until the camshaft sprocket timing mark is at the 3 o'clock position. Counting from the pin directly adjacent to the timing mark, there must be 20 pins between the camshaft sprocket mark and the crankshaft sprocket mark as shown in the accompanying illustration.
6   Install the crankshaft oil seal and timing chain cover.
7   Install the vibration damper and pulley.

## 89   Camshaft — installation

1   Lubricate the camshaft very thoroughly with engine assembly lube or moly-based grease.
2   Carefully insert the camshaft into the block, taking care not to contact the bearing surfaces with the cam lobes.
3   Install the timing chain and sprocket assembly.
4   Install the oil slinger on the crankshaft.
5   Install the fuel pump eccentric and drive gear on the camshaft, tightening the retaining screw to the specified torque.
6   Install the timing chain case using a new gasket and oil seal.
7   Install the vibration damper and pulley, tightening the retaining bolts to the specified torque.
8   Coat the hydraulic lifters with engine assembly lube or moly-based grease. Install each lifter into the bore from which it was originally removed.
9   Lubricate the ends of each pushrod with engine assembly lube

or moly-based grease and install them in their original locations.
10   Install the rocker arm assemblies.
11   Install the rocker arm covers.
12   Install the fuel pump.
13   Rotate the crankshaft until the number 1 piston is at top dead center (TDC) on the compression stroke. This can be determined by placing your finger over the number 1 cylinder spark plug hole and turning the crankshaft pulley bolt with a wrench in a clockwise direction until pressure is felt. The timing mark on the vibration damper should be aligned with the TDC index mark on the timing degree scale.
14   Insert the distributor so the rotor is aligned with the number 1 terminal of the cap when fully in place (Chapter 5). Install the distributor cap.

## 90   Timing chain cover — installation

1   Remove the lower locating dowel, taking care not to damage it.
2   Cut both sides of the oil pan gasket off flush with the engine block.
3   Apply RTV-type gasket sealant to both sides of the new timing cover gasket and attach the gasket to the cover.
4   Attach the new front oil pan seal to the bottom of the timing chain cover.
5   If a new oil pan gasket is used, use the old gaskets as a guide and trim them to correspond to the amount cut off in Step 2. Line up the tongues of the new gasket pieces with the oil pan seal and cement them into place on the cover with RTV-type gasket sealant. Apply gasket sealant to the cut-off edges of the original pan gasket, place the timing cover in position and install the bolts. Tighten the bolts slowly and evenly until the cover aligns with the upper dowel. Insert the lower dowel and carefully drive it into position. Install the lower bolts and then tighten all of the cover bolts to the specified torque.
6   If RTV-type sealant is used, apply a 1/8-inch bead to the timing cover flanges. Place the cover in position and install the bolts in their marked positions. Insert the lower locating dowel into the block and drive it into position. Install the remaining bolts and tighten them to the specified torque. Apply a bead of RTV-type sealant to the pan-to-

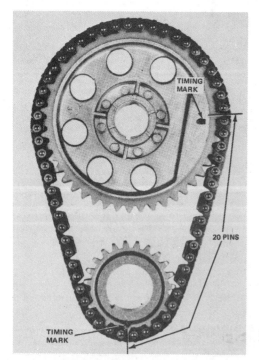

Fig. 2.55  For proper valve timing, there must be 20 pins between the sprocket timing marks (Sec 88)

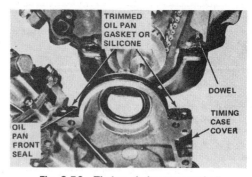

Fig. 2.56   Timing chain cover and oil pan seal installation details (Sec 90)

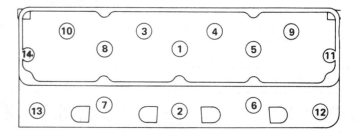

Fig. 2.57   Cylinder head bolt tightening sequence (Sec 91)

cover joint and press it into place with your finger. Apply a thread-locking compound to the oil pan bolts and install them.
7   Install the vibration damper and tighten the bolt to the specified torque.

### 91  Cylinder head — installation

1   Apply an even coat of non-hardening gasket sealant to both sides of the new cylinder head gasket.
2   Place the gasket in position on the engine block with the stamped TOP designation facing up.
3   Prior to installing the head bolts, clean the threads with a wire brush so the bolts will not bind when installed.
4   Place the cylinder head in position on the engine block.
5   Install the bolts finger tight, making sure they thread smoothly into the block with no binding.
6   Tighten the bolts evenly to the specified torque in the sequence shown in the accompanying illustration.
7   Install the intake manifold.
8   Install the pushrods and rocker arm assemblies in their original positions. Make sure the pushrod ends are lubricated with a dab of engine assembly lube or moly-based grease and that the bottom end of each rod is centered in the valve lifter plunger cup. Tighten the rocker arm bolts/nuts one turn at a time, alternately, to avoid bending or breaking the bridge (if so equipped).
9   Apply a 1/8-inch bead of RTV-type sealant to the gasket surface of the rocker arm cover.
10  Place the cover in position on the cylinder head, install the bolts and tighten them evenly and securely.

### 92  Intake manifold — installation

1   If a new intake manifold is to be installed, transfer the EGR valve and back pressure sensor, thermostat housing, coolant temperature sensor and CTO valve from the old unit.
2   Coat both sides of the manifold gasket with RTV-type sealant.
3   Place the gasket in position on the alignment locators at the rear of the cylinder heads. Hold the rear of the gasket in place and align it with the front locators.
4   Install the end seals and apply a coat of Permatex No. 2 sealant.
5   Lower the manifold into position and install the retaining bolts finger tight.
6   After making sure the bolts are properly started with no binding, tighten them to the specified torque in a crisscross pattern.

### 93  Oil pan — installation

1   Install the front oil seal in the timing chain cover. Coat the ends of the seal with RTV-type sealant.
2   Coat the rear oil pan seal curved surface and the end seal tabs with RTV-type sealant and install the seal in the rear main bearing cap. Make sure the seal is completely seated.
3   Cement the oil pan side gasket to the engine block sealing surfaces with gasket sealant. Apply a generous coat of RTV-type sealant to the gasket ends.
4   Install the oil pan and bolts and tighten the bolts to the specified torque in a crisscross pattern.

### 94  Crankshaft — removal

1   Before removing the crankshaft, you must remove the flywheel/driveplate, the rear oil seal housing, the cylinder heads, the oil pan, the timing chain cover and the timing chain and sprockets.
2   With the engine upside-down, remove the oil pick-up tube and screen assembly.
3   Remove the piston assemblies from the engine block as described in Chapter 2A.
4   Refer to Chapter 2A for the remaining crankshaft removal steps.

### 95  Crankshaft — installation and main bearing oil clearance check

1   Crankshaft installation is generally one of the first steps in engine reassembly; it is assumed at this point that the engine block and crankshaft have been cleaned, inspected and repaired or reconditioned.
2   Position the engine with the bottom facing up.
3   Remove the main bearing cap bolts and lift out the caps. Lay them out in the proper order to help ensure that they are installed correctly.
4   If they are still in place, remove the old bearing inserts from the block and the main bearing caps. Wipe the main bearing surfaces of the block and caps with a clean, lint-free cloth (they must be kept spotlessly clean).
5   Clean the back side of the new main bearing inserts and lay one bearing half in each main bearing saddle in the block. Lay the other bearing half from each bearing set in the corresponding main bearing cap. Make sure the tab on the bearing insert fits into the recess in the block or cap. Also, the oil holes in the block and cap must line up with the oil holes in the bearing insert. *Do not hammer the bearing into place and do not nick or gouge the bearing faces. No lubrication should be used at this time.*
6   The flanged thrust bearing must be installed in the number three (3) (center) cap and saddle.
7   Clean the faces of the bearings in the block and the crankshaft main bearing journals with a clean, lint-free cloth. Check or clean the oil holes in the crankshaft, as any dirt here can only go one way — straight through the new bearings.
8   Once you are certain that the crankshaft is clean, carefully lay it in position (an assistant would be very helpful here) in the main bearings with the counterweights lying sideways.
9   Before the crankshaft can be permanently installed, the main bearing oil clearance must be checked.
10  Cut five pieces of the appropriate type of Plastigage slightly shorter than the width of the main bearings. Place one piece on each crankshaft main bearing journal, parallel with the journal axis. Do not lay them across any oil lines.
11  Clean the faces of the bearings in the caps and make sure the caps are not mixed up. Install the caps in their respective positions with the arrows pointing toward the front of the engine. Do not disturb the Plastigage.
12  Starting with the center main and working out toward the ends, tighten the main bearing cap bolts, in three steps, to the specified torque. *Do not rotate the crankshaft at any time during this operation.*
13  Remove the bolts and carefully lift off the main bearing caps. Keep them in order. Do nut disturb the Plastigage or rotate the crankshaft. If any of the main bearing caps are difficult to remove, tap gently from side-to-side with a soft-faced hammer to loosen them.
14  Compare the width of the crushed Plastigage on each journal to the scale printed on the Plastigage container (photo) to obtain the main bearing oil clearance. Check the Specifications to make sure it is correct.
15  If the clearance is not correct, double-check to make sure that

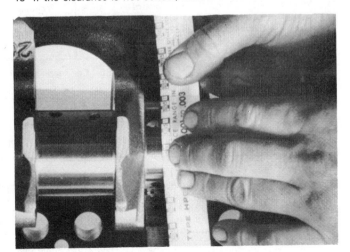

95.14  Comparing the width of the crushed Plastigage to the scale on the container

2D

you have the right size bearing inserts. Also, make sure that no dirt or oil was between the bearing inserts and the main bearing caps or the block when the clearance was measured.

16 Carefully scrape all traces of the Plastigage material off the main bearing journals and/or the bearing faces. Do not nick or scratch the bearing faces.

17 Carefully lift the crankshaft out of the engine. Clean the bearing faces in the block, then apply a thin, uniform layer of clean, high-quality moly-based grease (or engine assembly lube) to each of the bearing faces. Be sure to coat the thrust flange faces as well as the journal face of the thrust bearing in the number three (center) main. Make sure the crankshaft journals are clean, then carefully lay it back in place in the block. Clean the faces of the bearings in the caps, then apply a thin layer of clean, high-quality moly-based grease to each of the bearing faces and install the caps in their respective positions with the arrows pointing toward the front of the engine. Install the bolts and tighten them to the specified torque, starting with the center main and working out toward the ends. Work up to the final torque in three steps.

18 Rotate the crankshaft a number of times by hand and check for any obvious binding.

19 The final step is to check the crankshaft end play. This can be done with a feeler gauge or a dial indicator set. Refer to Chapter 2A, Section 12, for the procedure to follow.

## 96   Main and connecting rod bearings — selection

1   The crankshaft and bearing inspection procedures are included in Chapter 2A. The condition and measured size of the crankshaft journals will determine the bearings to be installed when the engine is reassembled.

2   If a new or reground crankshaft is installed, the size of each journal should be indicated by a color coded mark on the adjacent cheek or counterweight, toward the rear (flanged) end of the crankshaft. The bearing inserts are also color coded (on the edge of the insert). The accompanying charts (one for main bearings, one for rod bearings) should be consulted to determine the correct bearings to use. **Caution:** *Always check the bearing oil clearance with Plastigage during final installation of the crankshaft and/or piston/connecting rod assemblies.*

3   If necessary to achieve the desired oil clearance, different size upper and lower bearing inserts may be used on the same journal but the size difference must never exceed 0.001-inch. **Caution:** *The odd size inserts must all be either in the caps or block (main bearings). In the case of connecting rod bearings, the odd size inserts must all be either in the caps or rods.*

4   If the original crankshaft is reground, the automotive machine shop that reconditions the journals should supply bearings that will produce the desired oil clearance.

## 97   Engine — installation

1   Lower the engine slowly and carefully into the engine compartment. Align the transmission input shaft with the engine. On manual transmission models this will require aligning the splines of the input shaft and clutch plate.

2   Install the transmission housing retaining bolts and tighten them securely.

3   Remove the jack supporting the transmission.

4   *On automatic transmission equipped models,* align the marks made on the converter and driveplate and install the retaining bolts. Be sure to tighten them to the specified torque.

5   Install the automatic transmission inspection cover or the manual transmission lower cover.

6   Install the starter motor.

7   *On four wheel drive models,* attach the left front engine support cushion and bracket to the cylinder block and tighten the bolts securely.

8   Lower the engine weight fully onto the engine supports and remove the lifting device.

9   Install the front engine mount support cushion retaining nuts and tighten them securely.

10 Connect the exhaust pipes to the manifolds and bracket.

11 Connect the automatic transmission filler tube bracket to the cylinder head.

12 Install the cruise control vacuum servo bellows and bracket assembly.

13 Connect the electrical harness, throttle linkage and vacuum and fuel lines to the engine.

14 Install the air conditioner compressor.

15 Install the power steering pump and hoses. Refill the reservoir to the specified level.

16 Install the radiator, hoses and cooling fan. *On automatic transmission equipped models,* connect the transmission fluid cooler lines to the radiator.

17 Fill the radiator with the specified coolant. Add the correct amount of the specified type of oil to the engine.

18 Install the air cleaner assembly and connect the battery negative cable.

19 Refer to Chapter 2A for the initial start-up and recommended break-in procedures.

| Crankshaft Connecting Rod Journal Color and Diameter in Inches (Journal Size) | Bearing Color Code | |
|---|---|---|
| | Upper Insert Size | Lower Insert Size |
| Yellow  −2.0955 to 2.0948 (Standard)<br>Orange  −2.0948 to 2.0941 (0.0007 Undersize)<br>Black   −2.0941 to 2.0934 (0.0014 Undersize)<br>Red    −2.0855 to 2.0848 (0.010 Undersize) | Yellow  — Standard<br>Yellow  — Standard<br>Black   — .001-Inch Undersize<br>Red    — .010-Inch Undersize | Yellow  — Standard<br>Black   — .001-inch Undersize<br>Black   — .001-inch Undersize<br>Red    — .010-inch Undersize |

Fig. 2.58   Connecting rod bearing selection chart (Sec 96)

| Crankshaft Main Bearing Journal Color Code and Diameter in Inches (Journal Size) | Bearing Color Code | |
|---|---|---|
| | Upper Insert Size | Lower Insert Size |
| Yellow  −2.7489 to 2.7484 (Standard)<br>Orange  −2.7484 to 2.7479 (0.0005 Undersize)<br>Black   −2.7479 to 2.7474 (0.001 Undersize)<br>Green   −2.7474 to 2.7469 (0.0015 Undersize)<br>Red    −2.7389 to 2.7384 (0.010 Undersize) | Yellow  — Standard<br>Yellow  — Standard<br>Black   — .001-inch Undersize<br>Black   — .001-inch Undersize<br>Red    — .010-inch Undersize | Yellow  — Standard<br>Black   — .001-inch Undersize<br>Black   — .001-inch Undersize<br>Green   — .002-inch Undersize<br>Red    — .010-inch Undersize |

Fig. 2.59   Main bearing selection chart (Sec 96)

# Chapter 2 Part E   V6 engine

## Contents

| | |
|---|---|
| Camshaft — removal and installation . . . . . . . . . . . . . . . . . | 108 |
| Clutch and flywheel — removal and installation . . . . . . . . . | 109 |
| Crankshaft — inspection . . . . . . . . . . . . . . . . | Chapter 2A |
| Crankshaft — installation and main bearing oil clearance check . . . . . . . . . . . . . . . . . . . . . . . . . . . | 115 |
| Crankshaft — removal . . . . . . . . . . . . . . . . . . . . . . . | 112 |
| Cylinder head — cleaning and inspection . . . . . . . . | Chapter 2A |
| Cylinder head — disassembly . . . . . . . . . . . . . . | Chapter 2A |
| Cylinder head — reassembly . . . . . . . . . . . . . . . | Chapter 2A |
| Cylinder head — removal and installation . . . . . . . . . . . | 106 |
| Engine block — cleaning . . . . . . . . . . . . . . . . . | Chapter 2A |
| Engine block — inspection . . . . . . . . . . . . . . . . | Chapter 2A |
| Engine — disassembly and reassembly sequence . . . . . . . . | 101 |
| Engine disassembly — general information . . . . . . . | Chapter 2A |
| Engine external components — installation . . . . . . . . . . . | 116 |
| Engine external components — removal . . . . . . . . . . . . | 102 |
| Engine — installation . . . . . . . . . . . . . . . . . . . . . . . . | 117 |
| Engine overhaul — general information . . . . . . . . . | Chapter 2A |
| Engine rebuilding alternatives . . . . . . . . . . . . . . | Chapter 2A |
| Engine — removal . . . . . . . . . . . . . . . . . . . . . . . | 100 |
| Engine removal — methods and precautions . . . . . | Chapter 2A |
| General information . . . . . . . . . . . . . . . . . . . . . . . . . | 98 |
| Initial start-up and break-in after overhaul . . . . . . . | Chapter 2A |
| Main and connecting rod bearings — inspection . . . | Chapter 2A |
| Oil pan — removal and installation . . . . . . . . . . . . . . . | 110 |
| Oil pump — inspection and installation . . . . . . . . . . . . . | 113 |
| Oil pump intake pipe and screen — removal and installation . . . . . . . . . . . . . . . . . . . . . . . . . . . . . | 111 |
| Oil pump — removal . . . . . . . . . . . . . . . . . . . . . . . . | 103 |
| Piston/connecting rod assembly — inspection . . . . . | Chapter 2A |
| Piston/connecting rod assembly — installation and bearing oil clearance check . . . . . . . . . . . . . . . . | Chapter 2A |
| Piston/connecting rod assembly — removal . . . . . . . | Chapter 2A |
| Piston rings — installation . . . . . . . . . . . . . . . . . | Chapter 2A |
| Pushrods and valve lifters — removal, inspection and installation . . . . . . . . . . . . . . . . . . . . . . . . . . . . . | 107 |
| Rear main bearing oil seal — replacement . . . . . . . . . . . | 114 |
| Repair operations possible with the engine in the vehicle . . . . . . . . . . . . . . . . . . . . . . . . . . . . | Chapter 2A |
| Timing chain cover — removal and installation . . . . . . . . . | 104 |
| Timing chain and sprockets — removal and installation . . . . . . . . . . . . . . . . . . . . . . . . . . . . | 105 |
| Undersize/oversize component designation . . . . . . . . . . . | 99 |
| Valves — servicing . . . . . . . . . . . . . . . . . . . . . . | Chapter 2A |

**2E**

## Specifications

### General

| | |
|---|---|
| Type . . . . . . . . . . . . . . . . . . . . . . . . . . . . . . . . . . . . . . | 90° V6 |
| Displacement . . . . . . . . . . . . . . . . . . . . . . . . . . . . . . . . | 225 cu in |
| Bore and stroke . . . . . . . . . . . . . . . . . . . . . . . . . . . . . . | 3.750 x 3.400 in |
| Compression ratio | |
|   Federal . . . . . . . . . . . . . . . . . . . . . . . . . . . . . . . . . . | 9.0 : 1 |
|   California . . . . . . . . . . . . . . . . . . . . . . . . . . . . . . . . . | 7.4 : 1 |
| Normal oil pressure . . . . . . . . . . . . . . . . . . . . . . . . . . . . | 33 psi at 2400 rpm |
| Cylinder numbering (front-to-rear) | |
|   Right bank . . . . . . . . . . . . . . . . . . . . . . . . . . . . . . . . | 2-4-6 |
|   Left bank . . . . . . . . . . . . . . . . . . . . . . . . . . . . . . . . . | 1-3-5 |

### Engine block

| | |
|---|---|
| Cylinder bore | |
|   Taper limit . . . . . . . . . . . . . . . . . . . . . . . . . . . . . . . . | 0.005 in |
|   Out-of-round limit . . . . . . . . . . . . . . . . . . . . . . . . . . . | 0.003 in |
| Piston-to-cylinder bore clearance | |
|   Standard . . . . . . . . . . . . . . . . . . . . . . . . . . . . . . . . . | 0.001 in |
|   Service limit . . . . . . . . . . . . . . . . . . . . . . . . . . . . . . . | 0.0015 in |

## Pistons and rings

| | |
|---|---|
| Piston ring side clearance | |
| Standard | |
| Top ring | 0.002 in |
| 2nd ring | 0.003 in |
| Oil ring | 0.0015 in |
| Service limit | |
| Top ring | 0.0035 in |
| 2nd ring | 0.005 in |
| Oil ring | 0.0085 in |
| Piston ring end gap | |
| Standard | |
| Compression rings | 0.010 in |
| Oil ring | 0.015 in |
| Service limit | |
| Compression rings | 0.020 in |
| Oil ring | 0.035 in |
| Piston pin diameter | 0.9334 to 0.9397 in |
| Piston pin-to-piston clearance | |
| Standard | 0.004 in |
| Service limit | 0.0017 in |
| Piston pin-to-connecting rod clearance | 0.0007 to 0.0017 in |

## Cylinder heads

| | |
|---|---|
| Valve seat angle | 45º |
| Valve seat width | |
| Standard | 1/16 in |
| Service limit | 5/64 in |
| Valve stem diameter | |
| Intake | 0.3415 to 0.3427 |
| Exhaust | |
| Top | 0.3402 to 0.3412 |
| Bottom | 0.3397 to 0.3407 |
| Valve head diameter | |
| Intake | 1.625 in |
| Exhaust | 1.3750 in |
| Valve stem-to-guide clearance | |
| Intake | 0.0012 to 0.0032 in |
| Exhaust | |
| Top | 0.0015 to 0.0035 in |
| Bottom | 0.002 to 0.004 in |
| Valve margin width | 1/32 in minimum |
| Valve *stem* installed height | 1.925 in above cylinder head |
| Valve spring pressure (length at specified pressure) | 1.640 in at 59 to 64 lb/1.260 in at 168 lb |

## Crankshaft and flywheel

| | |
|---|---|
| Main journal | |
| Diameter | 2.4995 in |
| Taper limit | 0.002 to 0.0023 in |
| Out-of-round limit | 0.0015 in |
| Main bearing oil clearance | |
| Standard | 0.0005 in |
| Service limit | 0.0021 in |
| Connecting rod journal | |
| Diameter | 2.000 in |
| Taper limit | 0.003 in |
| Out-of-round limit | 0.0015 in |
| Connecting rod bearing oil clearance | |
| Standard | 0.020 in |
| Service limit | 0.0023 in |
| Connecting rod end play | 0.005 to 0.0012 in total for two rods |
| Crankshaft end play | 0.004 to 0.008 in |
| Flywheel clutch face runout limit | 0.0015 in |

## Camshaft and valve train

| | |
|---|---|
| Bearing journal diameter | |
| 1 | 1.755 to 1.756 in |
| 2 | 1.725 to 1.726 in |
| 3 | 1.695 to 1.696 in |
| 4 | 1.665 to 1.666 in |
| Bearing oil clearance | |
| Standard | 0.0015 in |
| Service limit | 0.0040 in |
| Lifter type | Hydraulic |

Lifter-to-bore clearance
   Standard . . . . . . . . . . . . . . . . . . . . . . . . . . . . . . . . . . . . . . . . .   0.0015 in
   Service limit . . . . . . . . . . . . . . . . . . . . . . . . . . . . . . . . . . . . . . .   0.0030 in
Rocker arm-to-shaft clearance . . . . . . . . . . . . . . . . . . . . . . . . .   0.0017 to 0.0032 in

## Oil pump gear end clearance . . . . . . . . . . . . . . .   0.0023 to 0.0058 in

## Oversize and undersize component code letter definition

**Code letter**

| | | |
|---|---|---|
| A | Main and connecting rod bearings . . . . . . . . . . . . . . | 0.010 in undersize |
| B | Pistons . . . . . . . . . . . . . . . . . . . . . . . . . . . . . . . . . . . . . . | 0.010 in oversize |
| AB | . . . . . . . . . . . . . . . . . . . . . . . . . . . . . . . . . . . . . . . . . . . . | Combination of A and B |
| R | . . . . . . . . . . . . . . . . . . . . . . . . . . . . . . . . . . . . . . . . . . . . | Short block |
| S | . . . . . . . . . . . . . . . . . . . . . . . . . . . . . . . . . . . . . . . . . . . . | Service engine |

## Torque specifications

| | Ft-lb | Nm |
|---|---|---|
| Main bearing cap bolts . . . . . . . . . . . . . . . . . . . . . . . . . . . . . | 80 to 110 | 129 to 162 |
| Connecting rod cap nuts . . . . . . . . . . . . . . . . . . . . . . . . . . . . | 30 to 40 | 41 to 54 |
| Cylinder head bolts . . . . . . . . . . . . . . . . . . . . . . . . . . . . . . . . | 65 to 85 | 88 to 109 |
| Fan pulley-to-vibration damper bolts . . . . . . . . . . . . . . . . . | 18 to 25 | 25 to 34 |
| Flywheel-to-crankshaft bolts . . . . . . . . . . . . . . . . . . . . . . . . | 50 to 65 | 68 to 88 |
| Vibration damper bolt . . . . . . . . . . . . . . . . . . . . . . . . . . . . . . | 140 | 190 |
| Oil pan bolts . . . . . . . . . . . . . . . . . . . . . . . . . . . . . . . . . . . . . | 10 to 16 | 14 to 22 |
| Oil pan drain plug . . . . . . . . . . . . . . . . . . . . . . . . . . . . . . . . . | 30 to 40 | 41 to 54 |
| Oil pump cover-to-timing chain cover . . . . . . . . . . . . . . . . . | 8 to 12 | 11 to 17 |
| Oil pump pressure relief valve . . . . . . . . . . . . . . . . . . . . . . . | 25 to 30 | 34 to 41 |
| Oil screen housing . . . . . . . . . . . . . . . . . . . . . . . . . . . . . . . . | 6 to 9 | 8 to 12 |
| Oil pan baffle . . . . . . . . . . . . . . . . . . . . . . . . . . . . . . . . . . . . | 9 to 13 | 12 to 17 |
| Oil gallery plugs . . . . . . . . . . . . . . . . . . . . . . . . . . . . . . . . . . | 20 to 30 | 27 to 41 |
| Oil filter . . . . . . . . . . . . . . . . . . . . . . . . . . . . . . . . . . . . . . . . | 10 to 15 | 14 to 20 |
| Timing chain cover bolts . . . . . . . . . . . . . . . . . . . . . . . . . . . | 25 to 33 | 34 to 45 |
| Water pump bolts . . . . . . . . . . . . . . . . . . . . . . . . . . . . . . . . . | 6 to 8 | 8 to 11 |
| Fan driven pulley bolt . . . . . . . . . . . . . . . . . . . . . . . . . . . . . | 17 to 23 | 23 to 32 |
| Thermostat housing bolts . . . . . . . . . . . . . . . . . . . . . . . . . . | 17 to 23 | 23 to 32 |
| Intake manifold bolts . . . . . . . . . . . . . . . . . . . . . . . . . . . . . . | 45 to 55 | 61 to 75 |
| Exhaust manifold bolts . . . . . . . . . . . . . . . . . . . . . . . . . . . . | 15 to 20 | 20 to 27 |
| Carburetor-to-intake manifold bolts . . . . . . . . . . . . . . . . . . | 10 to 15 | 14 to 20 |
| Fuel pump bolts . . . . . . . . . . . . . . . . . . . . . . . . . . . . . . . . . . | 17 to 23 | 23 to 32 |
| Engine mount-to-block bolts . . . . . . . . . . . . . . . . . . . . . . . . | 50 to 75 | 68 to 102 |
| Fuel pump eccentric and timing chain sprocket -to-camshaft bolt . . . . . . . . . . . . . . . . . . . . . . . . . . . . . . . . . | 40 to 55 | 54 to 75 |
| Rocker arm cover bolts . . . . . . . . . . . . . . . . . . . . . . . . . . . . | 3 to 5 | 4 to 7 |
| Rocker arm shaft bracket bolts . . . . . . . . . . . . . . . . . . . . . . | 25 to 35 | 34 to 48 |
| Alternator bracket-to-cylinder head bolts . . . . . . . . . . . . . . | 30 to 40 | 41 to 54 |
| Alternator pivot bolt . . . . . . . . . . . . . . . . . . . . . . . . . . . . . . . | 30 to 40 | 41 to 54 |
| Alternator bracket-to-timing chain cover bolt . . . . . . . . . . . | 18 to 25 | 24 to 34 |
| Starter motor bolts . . . . . . . . . . . . . . . . . . . . . . . . . . . . . . . . | 30 to 40 | 41 to 54 |
| Starter motor brace . . . . . . . . . . . . . . . . . . . . . . . . . . . . . . . | 9 to 13 | 12 to 17 |
| Distributor hold-down clamp bolt . . . . . . . . . . . . . . . . . . . . | 10 to 15 | 14 to 20 |
| Spark plugs . . . . . . . . . . . . . . . . . . . . . . . . . . . . . . . . . . . . . | 25 to 35 | 34 to 48 |
| Bellhousing-to-block bolts . . . . . . . . . . . . . . . . . . . . . . . . . . | 30 to 40 | 41 to 54 |
| Timing chain damper-to-block bolts . . . . . . . . . . . . . . . . . . | 6 to 9 | 8 to 12 |
| Movable timing chain damper bolt . . . . . . . . . . . . . . . . . . . . | 10 to 15 | 14 to 20 |

2E

## 98  General information

The 90 degree V6 engine used in these vehicles is made of cast iron and features overhead valves. The aluminum rocker arms are mounted on tubular steel shafts which are secured to the cylinder heads by brackets. A camshaft, mounted in the block and driven by a chain off the crankshaft, operates the valves through hydraulic lifters, pushrods and the rocker arms.

The crankshaft is supported by four main bearings. The number two bearing is flanged to control crankshaft end play. The crankshaft and connecting rod bearing shells are replaceable.

The full-skirt aluminum pistons are cam ground and tin plated and feature two compression and one oil control ring. The piston pin is press fit in the upper end of the connecting rod.

The oil pump is located at the front of the engine, under the timing chain cover, and draws oil from the crankcase-located pick-up and screen assembly through a drilled passage in the cylinder block.

## 99  Undersize/oversize component designation

1   Some engines have oversize or undersize main and connecting rod bearings and/or pistons.
2   A code letter denoting the presence of oversize or undersize components, as well as other important information, is stamped on the engine block front face, below the right rocker arm cover.
3   Refer to the Specifications and compare the code letters on the engine block with the chart to determine which components are undersize or oversize.

## 100  Engine — removal

**Note:** *The following sequence of operations does not necessarily need to be performed in the order given. It is, rather, a checklist of everything that must be disconnected or removed before the engine can be lifted* *out of the vehicle. It is very important that all linkages, electrical wiring, hoses and cables be removed or disconnected before attempting to lift the engine clear of the vehicle, so double-check everything thoroughly.*

1    Remove the hood and disconnect the battery cables (negative first, then positive).
2    Remove the air cleaner assembly.
3    Drain the coolant from the radiator and the engine into a suitable container.
4    Drain the engine oil into a suitable container.
5    Disconnect the alternator wiring harness from the regulator.
6    Disconnect the fuel evaporative purge valve at the PCV valve.
7    Remove the radiator hoses and support bars. Remove the radiator.
8    Unplug the engine wiring harnesses at the firewall.
9    If so equipped, remove the exhaust emissions control air pump, distribution manifold and anti-backfire valve.
10   Disconnect the cables and wires and remove the starter.
11   Disconnect and plug the fuel hoses at the right frame rail.
12   Disconnect the choke cable from the carburetor and remove the bracket.

13   Unbolt the exhaust pipes from the manifolds.
14   Support the transmission with a jack.
15   Remove the front engine-to-mount bolts.
16   Attach a lifting device to the engine and raise it sufficiently to remove the slack in the hoist chain or cable.
17   Remove the engine-to-bellhousing bolts.
18   Raise the engine slightly and slide it forward to release it from the transmission shaft and clutch assembly.
19   Raise the engine slowly and carefully to remove it from the vehicle.

## 101   Engine — disassembly and reassembly sequence

1    To completely disassemble the engine, remove the following items in the order given.

   *Engine external components*
   *Oil pump*
   *Timing chain cover*
   *Timing chain and sprockets*

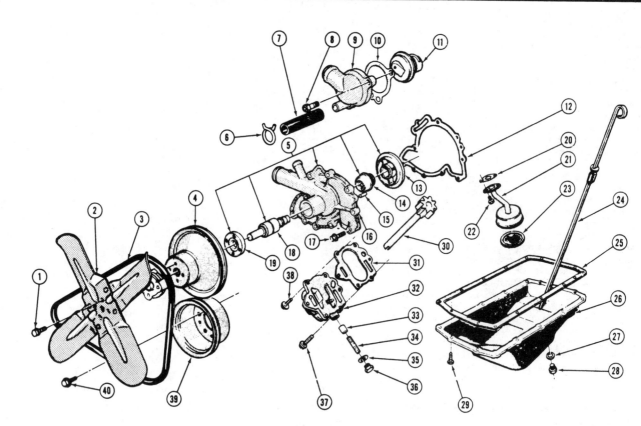

**Fig. 2.60  Engine external components**

|   |   |   |
|---|---|---|
| 1  Bolt and washer | 15  Dowel pin | 28  Drain plug |
| 2  Fan assembly | 16  Water pump cover | 29  Bolt and washer |
| 3  Drivebelt | 17  Bolt | 30  Oil pump shaft and gear |
| 4  Fan driven pulley | 18  Water pump shaft and bearing | 31  Oil pump cover gasket |
| 5  Water pump | 19  Fan hub | 32  Valve bypass and cover assembly |
| 6  Hose clamp | 20  Oil suction pipe gasket | 33  Oil pressure valve |
| 7  Thermostat bypass hose | 21  Oil suction housing, pipe and flange | 34  Valve bypass spring |
| 8  Bolt | 22  Bolt | 35  Oil pressure valve cap gasket |
| 9  Water outlet elbow | 23  Oil pump screen | 36  Oil pressure valve cap |
| 10  Gasket | 24  Dipstick | 37  Screw (1/4-20 x 1-3/8-in) |
| 11  Thermostat | 25  Oil pan gasket | 38  Screw (1/4-20 x 1-1/8-in) |
| 12  Water pump gasket | 26  Oil pan | 39  Fan drive pulley |
| 13  Water pump impeller and insert | 27  Drain plug gasket | 40  Bolt |
| 14  Water pump seal |   |   |

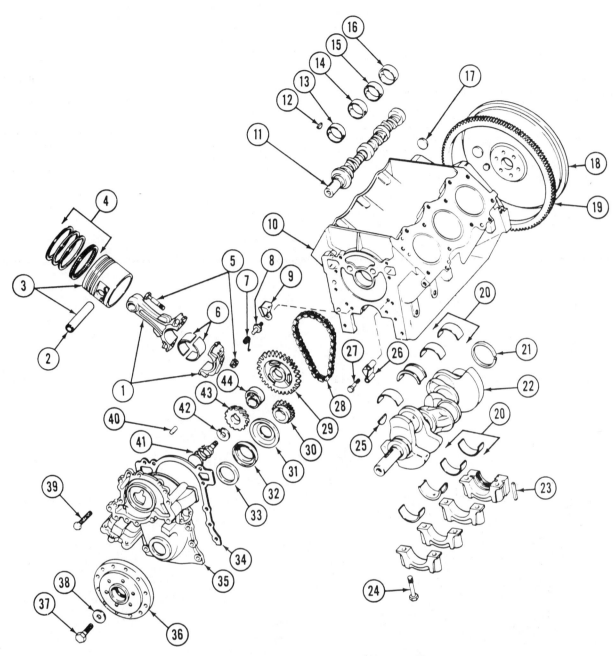

**Fig. 2.61  Exploded view of engine internal components**

| | | |
|---|---|---|
| 1  Connecting rod assembly | 16  Camshaft bearing (rear) | 30  Crankshaft sprocket |
| 2  Piston pin | 17  Rear camshaft plug | 31  Crankshaft oil slinger |
| 3  Piston and pin assembly | 18  Flywheel | 32  Crankshaft oil shedder |
| 4  Piston ring set | 19  Starter ring gear | 33  Front crankshaft seal packing |
| 5  Connecting rod bolt and nut | 20  Crankshaft bearing set | 34  Timing chain cover gasket |
| 6  Connecting rod bearing | 21  Rear main bearing oil seal | 35  Timing chain cover |
| 7  Damper spring | 22  Crankshaft | 36  Vibration damper |
| 8  Damper bolt | 23  Rear main bearing neoprene oil seal | 37  Bolt |
| 9  Timing chain damper | 24  Main bearing cap bolt | 38  Washer |
| 10  Engine block | 25  Woodruff key | 39  Bolt |
| 11  Camshaft | 26  Timing chain damper | 40  Dowel pin |
| 12  Woodruff key | 27  Damper bolt | 41  Camshaft thrust retainer and bolt |
| 13  Camshaft bearing (front) | 28  Timing chain | 42  Washer |
| 14  Camshaft bearing (number 2) | 29  Camshaft sprocket | 43  Distributor drive gear |
| 15  Camshaft bearing (number 3) | | 44  Fuel pump eccentric |

2E

*Cylinder heads*
*Pushrods and valve lifters*
*Camshaft*
*Clutch and flywheel*
*Oil pan*
*Oil pump intake pipe and screen*
*Piston/connecting rod assemblies*
*Crankshaft*

2    Engine assembly is basically the reverse of disassembly. Install the following components in the order given.

*Crankshaft*
*Piston rings*
*Piston/connecting rod assemblies*
*Oil pump intake pipe and screen*
*Oil pan*
*Clutch and flywheel*
*Camshaft*
*Pushrods and valve lifters*
*Cylinder heads*
*Timing chain and sprockets*
*Timing chain cover*
*Oil pump*
*Engine external components*

## 102   Engine external components — removal

1    Disconnect the vent hose, distributor vacuum hose and fuel line from the carburetor.
2    Disconnect the distributor wires from the ignition coil and the coolant temperature sending unit wire.
3    Remove the bolts and lift the intake manifold from the engine.
4    Unbolt and remove the exhaust manifolds.
5    Disconnect the vacuum hose and wiring harness from the distributor and remove the hold-down bolt. Carefully lift the distributor and bracket from the timing chain cover.
6    Remove the spark plugs, wires and brackets.
7    Disconnect the hose and unbolt and remove the fuel pump.
8    Remove the alternator, brackets and drivebelt.
9    Remove the fan assembly and water pump.
10   Unscrew and remove the oil filter.
11   Disconnect the oil pressure sending unit wire and unscrew the sending unit from the engine.
12   Remove the oil dipstick and tube.
13   Remove the attaching bolts and withdraw the crankshaft pulley.

14   Remove the bolt and washer retaining the vibration damper to the crankshaft. Tap around the circumference of the damper with a soft-faced hammer and withdraw it from the crankshaft (a puller may be required for this procedure).

## 103   Oil pump — removal

1    Remove the five retaining bolts and lift the oil pump and cover away from the timing chain cover.
2    Remove the oil pump gears.

## 104   Timing chain cover — removal and installation

1    Remove the retaining bolts and separate the timing chain cover and gasket from the engine.
2    Remove the old oil seal and shedder.
3    Remove all traces of old gasket material, taking care not to damage the sealing surface. Wash the cover thoroughly with solvent and dry it with compressed air or clean, lint-free cloths. Inspect the cover, particularly the gasket sealing surface, for damage, cracks and nicks.
4    Roll up a length of new packing material in the seal cavity, working from the back of the cover. Overlap the ends of the packing at the top. Drive a new oil shedder into place and stake it in position at three or four locations.
5    Rotate a large wood dowel or hammer handle around the opening to size the packing and shedder and produce a snug fit around the crankshaft vibration damper hub.
6    Make sure the contact surface of the engine block is clean and free of nicks and other damage and install the cover, using a new gasket. Install the retaining bolts and tighten them in a crisscross pattern to the specified torque.
7    If the oil pump has not been removed, the cover must be removed and the cavity packed with petroleum jelly as described in Section 113.

## 105   Timing chain and sprockets — removal and installation

1    Remove the pulley bolt and oil slinger from the crankshaft.
2    Remove the bolt and washer and slide the fuel pump eccentric and distributor gear off the camshaft.
3    Use two pry bars or large screwdrivers to pry alternately on the camshaft and crankshaft sprockets until the camshaft sprocket is loose.

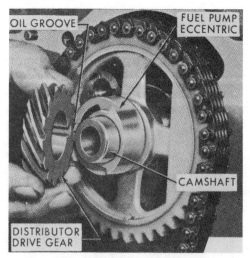

Fig. 2.62   Installing the distributor drive gear and fuel pump eccentric on the camshaft (Sec 105)

Fig. 2.63   Timing chain sprocket marks properly aligned (Sec 105)

Lift the sprocket and chain assembly from the engine.

4   Wash the sprockets, chain, eccentric and distributor gear thoroughly with solvent and inspect them for wear and damage.

5   Prior to installation, rotate the crankshaft so the number one (1) piston is at top dead center. Install the camshaft sprocket temporarily and turn the camshaft until the timing marks are aligned as shown in the accompanying illustration.

6   Remove the camshaft sprocket, attach the timing chain to the sprockets and install the entire assembly, making sure the timing marks are aligned. Have an assistant hold the spring-loaded chain dampers out of the way while sliding the assembly into place.

7   Install the oil slinger on the crankshaft *with the concave side toward* *the engine.*

8   Slide the fuel pump eccentric and Woodruff key onto the camshaft with the oil groove facing the *front*.

9   Install the distributor drive gear, washer and bolt. Tighten the bolt to the specified torque.

### 106   Cylinder head — removal and installation

1   Remove the rocker arm cover.

2   Loosen the rocker arm assembly bolts 1/4-turn at a time until they

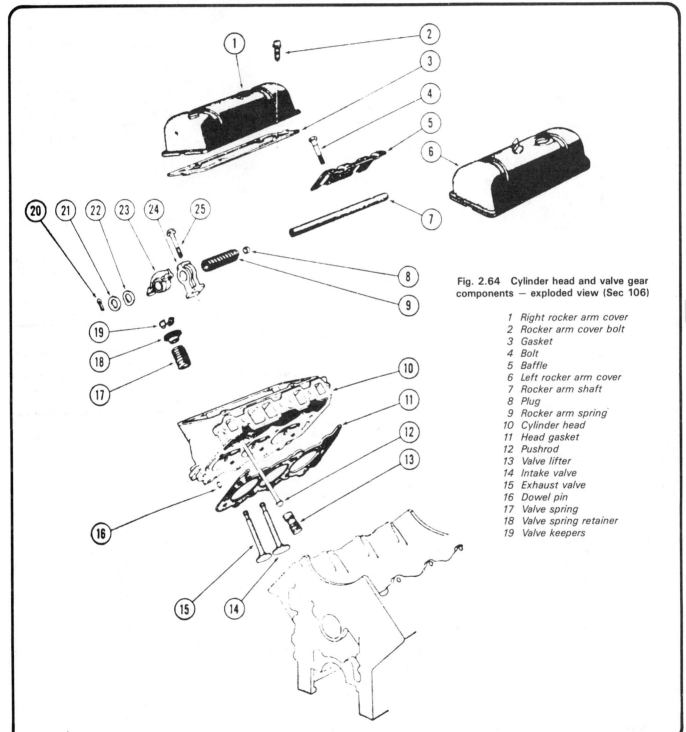

Fig. 2.64  Cylinder head and valve gear components — exploded view (Sec 106)

1   Right rocker arm cover
2   Rocker arm cover bolt
3   Gasket
4   Bolt
5   Baffle
6   Left rocker arm cover
7   Rocker arm shaft
8   Plug
9   Rocker arm spring
10  Cylinder head
11  Head gasket
12  Pushrod
13  Valve lifter
14  Intake valve
15  Exhaust valve
16  Dowel pin
17  Valve spring
18  Valve spring retainer
19  Valve keepers

2E

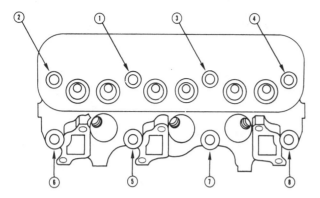

Fig. 2.65  Cylinder head bolt tightening sequence (Sec 106)

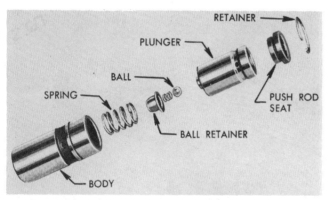

Fig. 2.67  Valve lifter components — exploded view (Sec 107)

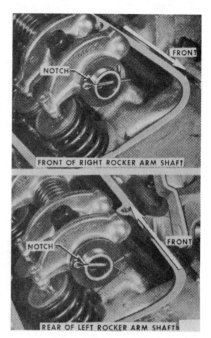

Fig. 2.66  Proper rocker arm shaft alignment (Sec 106)

are completely loose. Leave the bolts in place so the assembly can be lifted from the head. Remove the pushrods (Section 107).

3   Loosen the cylinder head bolts 1/4-turn at a time, in a crisscross pattern, then remove them.

4   Remove the cylinder head and gasket. It may be necessary to tap around the outer edge of the head with a soft-faced hammer to break the gasket seal. Repeat the procedure for the remaining cylinder head.

5   Prior to installation, clean the cylinder head bolts thoroughly and coat the threads with Perfect Seal sealing compound (or its equivalent). Make sure the gasket surfaces of the head(s) and block are clean.

6   Coat both sides of the new head gaskets with a suitable aerosol spray sealant, then position the gaskets on the block. The alignment dowels will hold them in position. Carefully lower the cylinder heads into position. Make sure they fit properly over the dowel pins.

7   Install the bolts and tighten them to the specified torque, one turn at a time, following the sequence shown in the accompanying illustration.

8   Install the pushrods (Section 107).

9   Place the rocker arm assemblies in position with the notches at the end of the shafts positioned as shown in the accompanying illustration. Tilt the rocker arm assembly toward the pushrod to securely seat the rod end in the arm seat. Install the retaining bolts.

10  Draw the rocker arm assembly down evenly by tightening the bolts a little at a time until the specified torque is reached.

11  Install the rocker arm covers and gaskets. Do not overtighten the bolts or oil leaks may result.

## 107  Pushrods and valve lifters — removal, inspection and installation

1   Remove the rocker arm covers and rocker arm assemblies (Section 106), then remove the pushrods one at a time and place them in a marked piece of cardboard to ensure reinstallation in their original locations.

2   Remove the cylinder head(s) (Section 106), then remove the lifters one at a time and place them in a marked container to ensure reinstalla-

tion in their original positions.

3   Clean the pushrods and lifters thoroughly with solvent and dry them with compressed air or clean, lint-free cloths.

4   Inspect the contact surfaces of the pushrods for wear, damage and roughness. To determine if the pushrod is bent, roll it on a flat surface such as a piece of glass. Replace any worn, damaged or bent pushrods with new ones.

5   Inspect the lifters for galling, pitting, wear on the contact surfaces and grooves or scoring along the sides. If there is excessive varnish on the lifter, disassemble it and submerge it in a suitable solvent for at least an hour to dissolve the deposits. Clean the varnish from the lifter(s) and reassemble them. Replace any excessively worn or damaged lifters with new ones.

6   Lubricate the lifter bores with clean engine oil and the cam contact faces with engine assembly lube or moly-based grease. Install the lifters in their original locations. **Note:** *If new lifters are being installed, a new camshaft must also be installed. If a new camshaft was installed, then use new lifters as well. Never install used lifters unless the original camshaft is used and the lifters can be installed in their original locations.*

7   Install the cylinder heads (Section 106).

8   Lubricate the ends of the pushrods with engine assembly lube or moly-based grease and install them in their original locations.

9   Install the rocker arm assemblies and rocker arm covers (Section 106).

## 108  Camshaft — removal and installation

1   Remove the timing chain and sprockets (Section 105), the cylinder heads (Section 106), and the pushrods and lifters (Section 107).

2   Carefully withdraw the camshaft from the engine block, taking care not to damage the bearing surfaces by striking them with the cam lobes.

3   Before installation, lubricate the cam lobes and bearing journals with engine assembly lube or moly-based grease.

4   Refer to the note in Section 107, Step 6.

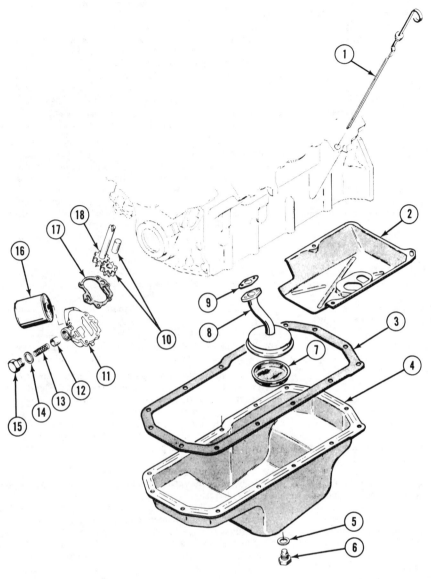

Fig. 2.68  Oil pump and oil pan
components — exploded view (Sec 110)

1  Dipstick
2  Oil pan baffle
3  Gasket
4  Oil pan
5  Drain plug gasket
6  Drain plug
7  Oil pump screen
8  Oil suction housing, pipe
    and flange
9  Oil suction pipe gasket
10  Oil pump idler gear
11  Valve bypass and cover
    assembly
12  Oil pressure valve
13  Spring
14  Gasket
15  Oil pressure relief valve
    cap
16  Oil filter
17  Oil pump cover gasket
18  Oil pump shaft and gear

2E

### 109  Clutch and flywheel — removal and installation

1    Mark the location of the clutch cover to ensure reinstallation in the
same position. Loosen the retaining bolts, one turn at a time, following a crisscross pattern, until all six bolts are loose. Remove the bolts
and the clutch cover assembly.
2    Remove the retaining bolts and separate the flywheel from the
crankshaft.
3    Inspect the clutch contact surface of the flywheel for cracks and
score marks and the starter ring gear for broken and damaged teeth.
A properly equipped shop can resurface the flywheel or replace the
starter ring gear if they are badly damaged.
4    To install, place the flywheel in position, install the retaining bolts
and tighten them in a crisscross pattern to the specified torque.
5    Check the flywheel runout to make sure it is within the
Specifications by mounting a dial indicator on the engine with the stem
on the clutch contact surface. Rotate the flywheel several revolutions
to determine the runout.
6    Attach the clutch cover to the flywheel, aligning it with the marks
made during removal, and install the bolts. Tighten the bolts a little
at a time, following a crisscross pattern, to the specified torque.

### 110  Oil pan — removal and installation

1    With the engine inverted, remove the bolts securing the oil pan to
the engine block.
2    Tap on the pan with a soft-faced hammer to break the gasket seal,
then lift the oil pan off the engine.
3    Using a gasket scraper, scrape off all traces of the old gasket from
the engine block, the timing chain cover and the oil pan. Be especially
careful not to nick or gouge the gasket sealing surface of the timing
chain cover (it is made of aluminum and is quite soft).
4    Clean the oil pan with solvent and dry it thoroughly. Check the
gasket sealing surfaces for distortion.
5    Before installing the oil pan, apply a thin coat of RTV-type gasket
sealer to the engine block gasket sealing surfaces. Lay a new oil pan
gasket in place and carefully apply a coat of gasket sealer to the oil
pan gasket surface.
6    Gently lay the oil pan in place (do not disturb the gasket) and install the bolts. Start with the bolts closest to the center of the pan and
tighten them to the specified torque following a crisscross pattern. Do
not overtighten them or leakage may occur.

## 111   Oil pump intake pipe and screen — removal and installation

1   Remove the two attaching bolts and lift the intake pipe and screen assembly away from the engine.
2   Pry the screen from the housing and wash the whole assembly thoroughly with solvent. Dry it with compressed air or clean, lint-free cloths. Install the screen.
3   To install the intake pipe, place the assembly in position with a new gasket and install the retaining bolts. Tighten the bolts to the specified torque.

## 112   Crankshaft — removal

1   Before removing the crankshaft, you must remove the flywheel, the cylinder heads, the oil pan, the oil pump intake pipe and screen, the timing chain cover and the timing chain and sprockets by referring to the appropriate Sections.
2   Remove the piston/connecting rod assemblies from the block as described in Chapter 2A. Be sure to mark each connecting rod and bearing cap so they will be properly mated during reassembly.
3   Refer to Chapter 2A for the remainder of the crankshaft removal procedure. **Note:** *It may be necessary to use a special tool (available at automotive parts stores or a dealer) for removal of the rear main cap because of the tight fit. As an alternative, a large wood dowel can be inserted into the bearing cap bolt hole and used as a lever to loosen the cap.*

## 113   Oil pump — inspection and installation

1   Wash the oil pump cover and gears thoroughly with solvent and dry them with compressed air or clean, lint-free cloths.
2   Inspect the gears for wear, scoring and damage. The gears should always be replaced in pairs.
3   Remove the oil pressure relief valve cap, spring and plunger. *Do not remove the oil filter bypass valve plunger and spring as they are staked in place.*
4   Wash the valve components thoroughly with solvent. Dry and inspect the relief valve plunger for wear and scoring. Check the spring to see if it is worn or collapsed. Insert the relief valve plunger into the bore and make sure it is an easy slip fit with no side-to-side movement. Replace the plunger and/or the cover if the side movement is excessive. Check the oil filter bypass to make sure it is flat with no nicks, cracks or warping. Replace any worn or damaged components with new ones.
5   Temporarily install the oil pump gears in the timing chain cover and use a feeler gauge and straightedge to check the gear end clearance.
6   Remove the gears and pack the oil pump cavity in the timing chain cover with petroleum jelly to provide a self-priming action when the engine is started. *Do not use grease.* Install the gears, making sure the

petroleum jelly is forced into every part of the cavity between the gear teeth.
7   Lubricate the pressure relief valve plunger and spring with clean engine oil. Install the assembly in the cover and tighten the valve cap to the specified torque.
8   Place the oil pump cover in position and install the retaining bolts. Tighten them to the specified torque following a crisscross pattern.

## 114   Rear main bearing oil seal — replacement

1   The braided fabric seals are pressed into the engine block and main bearing cap grooves. A neoprene stick-type seal is also used in the grooves in the sides of the rear main bearing cap. This seal is under-size when installed and swells when exposed to oil and heat.
2   Remove the old seals from the bearing cap and engine block.
3   Position the new braided seals in the grooves and use a wooden dowel or hammer handle to push them down until they project 1/16-inch above the cap and block surfaces. Cut off the ends of the seal flush with the bearing cap and block. Just prior to installation of the main bearing cap, lubricate the seal with clean engine oil.
4   After the rear main bearing cap is installed, the neoprene seals are inserted. Soak the seals in kerosene for approximately 1-1/2 minutes, insert them into the bearing cap grooves and soak the ends with kerosene. Use a hammer to peen the seal ends over to make a good seal at the upper parting line of the bearing cap and engine block.

## 115   Crankshaft — installation and main bearing oil clearance check

1   Crankshaft installation is generally one of the first steps in engine reassembly. It is assumed at this point that the engine block and crankshaft have been cleaned and inspected and repaired or reconditioned.
2   Position the engine with the bottom facing up.
3   Remove the main bearing cap bolts and lift out the caps. Lay them out in the proper order to help ensure that they are installed correctly.
4   If they are still in place, remove the old bearing inserts from the block and the main bearing caps. Wipe the main bearing surfaces of the block and caps with a clean, lint-free cloth (they must be kept spotlessly clean).
5   Clean the back sides of the new main bearing inserts and lay one bearing half in each main bearing saddle in the block and the other bearing half from each bearing set in the corresponding main bearing cap. Make sure the tab on the bearing insert fits into the recess in the block or cap. Also, the oil holes in the block and cap must line up with the oil holes in the bearing insert. **Caution:** *Upper bearing halves have an oil groove, while lower halves are plain. They must not be interchanged. Do not hammer the bearing into place and do not nick or gouge the bearing faces. No lubrication should be used at this time.*
6   The flanged thrust bearing must be installed in the number two

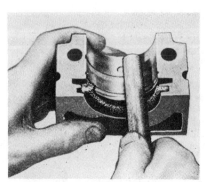

Fig. 2.69  Installing the rear main bearing oil seal (Sec 114)

Fig. 2.70  Intake manifold end seal installation (Sec 116)

Fig. 2.71  Intake manifold gasket installation (Sec 116)

cap and saddle. Install the upper oil seal in the block (Section 114).

7   Clean the faces of the bearings in the block and the crankshaft main bearing journals with a clean, lint-free cloth. Check or clean the oil holes in the crankshaft, as any dirt here can only go one way — straight through the new bearings.

8   Once you are certain that the crankshaft is clean, carefully lay it in position (an assistant would be very helpful here) in the main bearings with the counterweights lying sideways.

9   Before the crankshaft can be permanently installed, the main bearing oil clearance must be checked.

10   Trim four pieces of the appropriate type of Plastigage (slightly shorter than the width of the main bearings) and place one piece on each crankshaft main bearing journal, parallel with the journal axis. Do not lay them across any oil holes.

11   Clean the faces of the bearings in the caps and install the caps in their respective positions (do not mix them up) with the arrows pointing toward the front of the engine. Do not disturb the Plastigage.

12   Starting with the number one main and working out toward the ends, tighten the main bearing cap bolts, in three steps, to the specified torque. *Do not rotate the crankshaft at any time during this operation.*

13   Remove the bolts and carefully lift off the main bearing caps. Keep them in order. Do not disturb the Plastigage or rotate the crankshaft. If any of the main bearing caps are difficult to remove, tap gently from side-to-side with a soft-faced hammer to loosen them.

14   Compare the width of the crushed Plastigage on each journal to the scale printed on the Plastigage container to obtain the main bearing oil clearance. Check the Specifications to make sure it is correct.

15   If the clearance is not correct, double-check to make sure that you have the right size bearing inserts. Also, recheck the crankshaft main bearing journal diameters and make sure that no dirt or oil was between the bearing inserts and the main bearing caps or the block when the clearance was measured.

16   Carefully scrape all traces of the Plastigage material off the main bearing journals and/or the bearing faces. Do not nick or scratch the bearing faces.

17   Carefully lift the crankshaft out of the engine. Clean the bearing faces in the block, then apply a thin, uniform layer of clean, high-quality moly-based grease (or engine assembly lube) to each of the bearing faces. Be sure to coat the thrust flange faces as well as the journal face of the thrust bearing in the number two main. Make sure the crankshaft journals are clean, then carefully lay it back in place in the block. Clean the faces of the bearings in the caps, then apply a thin, uniform layer of clean, high-quality moly-based grease to each of the bearing faces and install the caps in their respective positions with the arrows pointing toward the front of the engine. Install the lower rear main oil seal (Section 114). Install the bolts and tighten them to the specified torque, but leave the number two (thrust) bearing cap bolts finger tight. Pry the crankshaft back and forth several times to align the thrust bearing surfaces, then tighten the number two bearing cap bolts. Work up to the final torque in three steps.

18   Rotate the crankshaft a number of times by hand and check for any obvious binding.

19   The final step is to check the crankshaft end play. This can be done with a feeler gauge or a dial indicator set. Refer to Chapter 2A, Section 12, for the procedure to follow.

### 116   Engine external components — installation

1   Lubricate the outer surface of the crankshaft vibration damper hub to prevent damage to the front oil seal and place the damper in position on the crankshaft. Install the bolt and washer and tighten the bolt to the specified torque.

2   Install the crankshaft pulley and the six retaining bolts. Tighten the bolts to the specified torque.

3   Install the oil dipstick and tube.

4   Install the oil pressure sending unit in the cylinder block.

5   Install the starter motor and bracket.

6   Lubricate the gasket with a film of engine oil and install the oil filter.

7   Install the cooling fan, hub drive pulley and water pump.

8   Install the fuel pump and tighten the retaining bolts to the specified torque.

9   Install the alternator and drivebelt.

10   Install the spark plugs, wires and brackets.

11   Install the distributor (Chapter 5).

12   Install the exhaust manifolds and tighten the retaining bolts to the specified torque.

13   Attach a new rubber intake manifold seal to the front and rear rails of the engine block with the pointed ends installed snugly against both the block and cylinder heads. Place the intake manifold in position and install the two cap bolts through the manifold and into the cylinder heads to act as guides. Raise the manifold slightly and place the two gaskets in position between the manifold and each cylinder head. The gasket must be installed with the three holes aligned with the manifold and cylinder head ports. Install the bolt in the open-sided hole on the right side of the manifold, followed by the two long bolts at the front. Install the remaining bolts and tighten them to the specified torque in the sequence shown in the accompanying illustration.

14   Connect the distributor, ignition coil and coolant temperature sending unit leads.

15   Attach the vent and distributor vacuum hoses and fuel line to the carburetor.

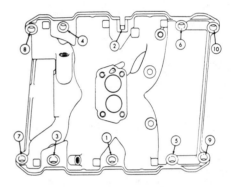

Fig. 2.72   Intake manifold bolt tightening sequence (Sec 116)

### 117   Engine — installation

1   Lower the engine carefully into the vehicle, align it with the bellhousing and engage the transmission shaft and clutch plate splines as the engine is moved to the rear. Install the engine block-to-bellhousing bolts and tighten them to the specified torque.

2   Install the front engine mount bolts.

3   Remove the lifting device and connect the exhaust pipes to the manifolds.

4   Connect the choke cable bracket to the carburetor.

5   Connect the fuel hoses and lines to the engine.

6   Connect the wiring harness on the firewall to the engine.

7   If equipped, install the exhaust emission air pump, the pump manifold and anti-backfire valve.

8   Install the radiator, support rods and hoses.

9   Install the air cleaner assembly.

10   Connect the battery cables (positive first, then negative) and install the hood.

11   Refer to Chapter 2A for the initial start-up and break-in procedures.

**2E**

# Chapter 2 Part F
# L- and F-head four-cylinder engines

## Contents

| | |
|---|---|
| Camshaft — installation . . . . . . . . . . . . . . . . . . . . . . . . . . . . 143 | Engine rebuilding alternatives . . . . . . . . . . . . . . . . . Chapter 2A |
| Camshaft — removal . . . . . . . . . . . . . . . . . . . . . . . . . . . . . . 135 | Engine — removal . . . . . . . . . . . . . . . . . . . . . . . . . . . . 120 |
| Clutch and flywheel — installation . . . . . . . . . . . . . . . . . 146 | Engine removal — methods and precautions . . . . . . Chapter 2A |
| Clutch and flywheel — removal . . . . . . . . . . . . . . . . . . . . 132 | Floating oil intake — removal, inspection and |
| Crankshaft — inspection . . . . . . . . . . . . . . Chapter 2A | installation . . . . . . . . . . . . . . . . . . . . . . . . . . . . . . . . . . 127 |
| Crankshaft — installation and main bearing oil | General information . . . . . . . . . . . . . . . . . . . . . . . . . . . . 118 |
| clearance check . . . . . . . . . . . . . . . . . . . . . . . . . . . . 145 | Initial start-up and break-in after overhaul . . . . . . . Chapter 2A |
| Crankshaft rear main oil seal — replacement . . . . . . . . . . 141 | Main and connecting rod bearings — inspection . . . Chapter 2A |
| Crankshaft — removal . . . . . . . . . . . . . . . . . . . . . . . . . . . 133 | Oil pan — removal and installation . . . . . . . . . . . . . . . . 126 |
| Cylinder head (F-head engine) — cleaning and | Oil pump — disassembly, inspection and reassembly . . . . . . 140 |
| inspection . . . . . . . . . . . . . . . . . . . . . . . . . . . Chapter 2A | Oil pump — installation . . . . . . . . . . . . . . . . . . . . . . . . . 152 |
| Cylinder head (F-head engine) — disassembly . . . . . Chapter 2A | Oil pump — removal . . . . . . . . . . . . . . . . . . . . . . . . . . . . 123 |
| Cylinder head (F-head engine) — installation . . . . . . . 150 | Oversize and undersize component designation . . . . . . . . 119 |
| Cylinder head (F-head engine) — reassembly . . . . . . Chapter 2A | Piston/connecting rod assembly — inspection . . . . . Chapter 2A |
| Cylinder head (F-head engine) — removal . . . . . . . . . . 125 | Piston/connecting rod assembly — installation and |
| Cylinder head (L-head engine) — cleaning and | bearing oil clearance check . . . . . . . . . . . . . . . Chapter 2A |
| inspection . . . . . . . . . . . . . . . . . . . . . . . . . . . . . . . . . . 139 | Piston/connecting rod assembly — removal . . . . . . . . . . 128 |
| Cylinder head (L-head engine) — installation . . . . . . . . . 151 | Piston rings — installation . . . . . . . . . . . . . . . . . . Chapter 2A |
| Cylinder head (L-head engine) — removal . . . . . . . . . . 124 | Repair operations possible with the engine |
| Engine block — cleaning. . . . . . . . . . . . . . . . . Chapter 2A | in the vehicle . . . . . . . . . . . . . . . . . . . . . . . . . . Chapter 2A |
| Engine block — inspection . . . . . . . . . . . . . . . . . Chapter 2A | Timing gear or chain cover — installation . . . . . . . . . . . . 149 |
| Engine block valve seats and guides — servicing. . . . . . . . 138 | Timing gear or chain cover — removal . . . . . . . . . . . . . . 129 |
| Engine disassembly — general information . . . . . . . Chapter 2A | Timing gears or chain and sprockets — installation . . . . . . . 148 |
| Engine — disassembly and reassembly sequence. . . . . . . . 121 | Timing gears or chain and sprockets — removal . . . . . . . . 130 |
| Engine external components — installation . . . . . . . . . . . 153 | Valves and springs (in block) — installation . . . . . . . . . . 144 |
| Engine external components — removal . . . . . . . . . . . . . 122 | Valves and springs (in block) — removal . . . . . . . . . . . . . 134 |
| Engine front plate — installation . . . . . . . . . . . . . . . . . . 147 | Valve lifters — inspection. . . . . . . . . . . . . . . . . . . . . . . . 137 |
| Engine front plate — removal . . . . . . . . . . . . . . . . . . . . 131 | Valve lifters — installation . . . . . . . . . . . . . . . . . . . . . . . 142 |
| Engine — installation . . . . . . . . . . . . . . . . . . . . . . . . . . 154 | Valve lifters — removal . . . . . . . . . . . . . . . . . . . . . . . . . 136 |
| Engine overhaul — general information . . . . . . . . . Chapter 2A | Valves — servicing. . . . . . . . . . . . . . . . . . . . . . . . . Chapter 2A |

## Specifications

## General

| | |
|---|---|
| Type . . . . . . . . . . . . . . . . . . . . . . . . . . . . . . . . . . . . . . . | In-line four-cylinder with F- or L-head valve configuration |
| Displacement . . . . . . . . . . . . . . . . . . . . . . . . . . . . . . . . . . | 134 cu in |
| Firing order . . . . . . . . . . . . . . . . . . . . . . . . . . . . . . . . . | 1-3-4-2 |
| Cylinder numbering (from front-to-back) . . . . . . . . . . . . . . | 1-2-3-4 |
| Bore and stroke . . . . . . . . . . . . . . . . . . . . . . . . . . . . . . | 3-1/8 x 4-3/8 in |
| Oil pressure | |
| L-head to S/N 44417 . . . . . . . . . . . . . . . . . . . . . . . . . | 50 psi at 30 mph |
| L-head S/N 44417 and on . . . . . . . . . . . . . . . . . . . . . . | 35 psi at 2000 rpm |
| F-head . . . . . . . . . . . . . . . . . . . . . . . . . . . . . . . . . . . . | 35 psi at 2000 rpm |

## Valve timing

| | |
|---|---|
| Intake valve | |
| Opens . . . . . . . . . . . . . . . . . . . . . . . . . . . . . . . . . . . . . | 9° BTC |
| Closes . . . . . . . . . . . . . . . . . . . . . . . . . . . . . . . . . . . . . | 50° ABC |
| Exhaust valve | |
| Opens . . . . . . . . . . . . . . . . . . . . . . . . . . . . . . . . . . . . . | 47° BBC |
| Closes . . . . . . . . . . . . . . . . . . . . . . . . . . . . . . . . . . . . . | 12° ATC |

## Engine block

| | |
|---|---|
| Cylinder bore diameter | 3.125 to 3.127 in |
| Taper limit | 0.005 in |
| Out-of-round limit | 0.005 in |
| Deck warpage limit | 0.010 in |

## Pistons and rings

| | |
|---|---|
| Piston diameter (near bottom of skirt) | 3.1225 to 3.1245 in |
| Piston to cylinder bore clearance | 0.003 in (see Chapter 2A) |
| Piston ring side clearance | |
| Top ring | 0.002 to 0.004 in |
| 2nd ring | 0.0015 to 0.0035 in |
| Oil ring | 0.001 to 0.0025 in |
| Piston ring end gap | |

| Cylinder bore oversize | Ring size | End gap |
|---|---|---|
| Standard to 0.009 in | Standard | 0.007 to 0.045 in |
| 0.010 to 0.019 in | 0.020 in | 0.007 to 0.017 in |
| 0.020 to 0.024 in | 0.020 in | 0.007 to 0.029 in |
| 0.025 to 0.029 in | 0.030 in | 0.007 to 0.017 in |
| 0.030 to 0.034 in | 0.030 in | 0.007 to 0.029 in |
| 0.035 to 0.039 in | 0.040 in | 0.007 to 0.017 in |
| 0.040 in | 0.040 in | 0.007 to 0.017 in |

| | |
|---|---|
| Piston pin diameter | 0.8119 to 0.8121 in |
| Piston pin-to-piston clearance | |
| Standard | 0.0001 in |
| Service limit | 0.0003 in |
| Connecting rod end play | 0.004 to 0.010 in |

## Crankshaft and flywheel

| | |
|---|---|
| Main journal | |
| Diameter | 2.3331 to 2.3341 in |
| Taper limit | 0.001 in |
| Out-of-round limit | 0.001 in |
| Main bearing oil clearance | |
| Standard | 0.0003 in |
| Service limit | 0.0029 in |
| Connecting rod journal | |
| Diameter | 1.9375 to 1.9383 in |
| Taper limit | 0.001 in |
| Out-of-round limit | 0.001 in |
| Connecting rod bearing oil clearance | |
| Standard | 0.001 in |
| Service limit | 0.0019 in |
| Crankshaft end play | 0.004 to 0.006 in |
| Flywheel clutch face runout limit | 0.005 in |

## Camshaft

| | |
|---|---|
| Bearing journal diameter | |
| 1 | 2.1860 to 2.1855 in |
| 2 | 2.1225 to 2.1215 in |
| 3 | 2.0600 to 2.0590 in |
| 4 | 1.6230 to 1.6225 in |
| Bearing oil clearance | |
| Standard | 0.001 in |
| Service limit | 0.0025 in |
| End play | 0.004 to 0.007 in |

## Cylinder head and valve train

| | |
|---|---|
| Head warpage limit | |
| L-head | 1/32 in |
| F-head | 0.010 in |
| Valve seat angle | 45º |
| Valve seat width | 3/32 to 1/8 in |
| Valve seat runout limit | 0.002 in |
| Valve face angle | 45º |
| Valve margin width | 1/32 in minimum |
| Valve stem diameter | |
| Intake | 0.3733 to 0.3738 in |
| Exhaust | 0.371 to 0.372 in |
| Valve stem-to-guide clearance | |
| Intake | 0.0007 to 0.0022 in |
| Exhaust | 0.0025 to 0.0045 in |
| Valve spring free length (intake and exhaust) | |
| L-head | 2.50 in |
| F-head | 1.97 in |

2F

## Cylinder head and valve train (continued)

Valve spring pressure (lbs at specified length)
Open
    Standard . . . . . . . . . . . . . . . . . . . . . . . . . . . . . . . . . . . . . . . . . . . . 120 at 1.750 in
    Service limit . . . . . . . . . . . . . . . . . . . . . . . . . . . . . . . . . . . . . . . . . . 110 at 1.750 in
Closed
    Standard . . . . . . . . . . . . . . . . . . . . . . . . . . . . . . . . . . . . . . . . . . . . 53 at 2.109 in
    Service limit . . . . . . . . . . . . . . . . . . . . . . . . . . . . . . . . . . . . . . . . . . 47 at 2.109 in
Lifter type . . . . . . . . . . . . . . . . . . . . . . . . . . . . . . . . . . . . . . . . . . . . . . . . . Mechanical
Lifter diameter . . . . . . . . . . . . . . . . . . . . . . . . . . . . . . . . . . . . . . . . . . . . . 0.6245 to 0.6240 in
Lifter-to-bore clearance . . . . . . . . . . . . . . . . . . . . . . . . . . . . . . . . . . . . 0.0005 to 0.002 in

## Oil pump

Early model L-head engine (to engine S/N 44417)
    Rotor end play . . . . . . . . . . . . . . . . . . . . . . . . . . . . . . . . . . . . . . . . . 0.002 to 0.005 in
    Pump shaft end play . . . . . . . . . . . . . . . . . . . . . . . . . . . . . . . . . . . . 0.002 to 0.004 in
Late model L-head engine (engine S/N 44417 and on) and all F-head engines
    Rotor lobe clearancce . . . . . . . . . . . . . . . . . . . . . . . . . . . . . . . . . . 0.010 in or less
    Rotor end play . . . . . . . . . . . . . . . . . . . . . . . . . . . . . . . . . . . . . . . . . 0.004 in
    Outer rotor-to-pump body clearance . . . . . . . . . . . . . . . . . . . 0.012 in or less
    Rotor thickness variance . . . . . . . . . . . . . . . . . . . . . . . . . . . . . . 0.001 in or less
    Driven gear-to-pump body running clearance
        L-head . . . . . . . . . . . . . . . . . . . . . . . . . . . . . . . . . . . . . . . . . . . 0.003 to 0.010 in
        F-head . . . . . . . . . . . . . . . . . . . . . . . . . . . . . . . . . . . . . . . . . . . 0.022 to 0.051 in
    Pump cover warpage limit . . . . . . . . . . . . . . . . . . . . . . . . . . . . . 0.001 in

## Oversize and undersize component code letter definition

Code letter
    A    Main and connecting rod bearings . . . . . . . . . . . . . . 0.010 in undersize
    B    Pistons . . . . . . . . . . . . . . . . . . . . . . . . . . . . . . . . . . . . . . . . 0.010 in oversize
    AB   . . . . . . . . . . . . . . . . . . . . . . . . . . . . . . . . . . . . . . . . . . . . . . Combination of A and B

## Torque specifications

| | Ft-lb | Nm |
|---|---|---|
| Camshaft thrust plate bolt . . . . . . . . . . . . . . . . . . . . . . | 26 | 35 |
| Camshaft gear or sprocket bolt . . . . . . . . . . . . . . . . . . | 30 to 40 | 41 to 55 |
| Main bearing cap bolts . . . . . . . . . . . . . . . . . . . . . . . . | 65 to 75 | 88 to 101 |
| Connecting rod cap nuts . . . . . . . . . . . . . . . . . . . . . . . | 35 to 45 | 48 to 61 |
| Cylinder head bolts . . . . . . . . . . . . . . . . . . . . . . . . . . . | 60 to 70 | 82 to 95 |
| Flywheel bolts . . . . . . . . . . . . . . . . . . . . . . . . . . . . . . . | 35 to 41 | 48 to 55 |
| Manifold assembly bolts . . . . . . . . . . . . . . . . . . . . . . . | 29 to 35 | 33 to 48 |
| Oil pan bolts . . . . . . . . . . . . . . . . . . . . . . . . . . . . . . . . | 9 to 14 | 12 to 19 |
| Piston pin lock screw . . . . . . . . . . . . . . . . . . . . . . . . . | 35 to 41 | 48 to 55 |
| Spark plugs . . . . . . . . . . . . . . . . . . . . . . . . . . . . . . . . . | 25 to 33 | 34 to 48 |
| Rocker arm cover nuts (F-head) . . . . . . . . . . . . . . . . . | 7 to 10 | 9.5 to 13.6 |
| Rocker arm assembly nuts (F-head) . . . . . . . . . . . . . . | 30 to 36 | 41 to 48 |
| Valve lifter cover bolts (all) . . . . . . . . . . . . . . . . . . . . | 7 to 10 | 9.5 to 13.6 |
| Water outlet bolts . . . . . . . . . . . . . . . . . . . . . . . . . . . | 20 to 25 | 27 to 34 |
| Water pump bolts . . . . . . . . . . . . . . . . . . . . . . . . . . . . | 12 to 17 | 16 to 23 |

---

### 118   General information

The F- and L-head engines used in these models are four-cylinder in-line designs of cast iron construction. The crankshaft is supported by three insert-type replaceable bearings.

Earlier models were L-head types with later models featuring an F-head design.

On the L-head (flathead) engine, the valves and valve gear are located completely within the engine block with only the combustion chamber located in the removable cast iron cylinder head. The intake valves of the F-head design are located in the cylinder head and are actuated by the camshaft through a conventional rocker arm and pushrod arrangement. The F-head exhaust valves are located in the engine block as on the earlier L-head.

Other than the cylinder head design, the F- and L-head engines are virtually identical in layout and construction.

---

### 119   Oversize and undersize component designation

1    Some engines have oversize or undersize main and connecting rod bearings and/or pistons.

2    A code letter denoting the presence of oversize or undersize com-

ponents is stamped on the engine block immediately following the serial number.

3    Refer to the Specifications and compare the letter code on the engine block with the chart to determine which components are undersize or oversize.

---

### 120   Engine — removal

**Note:** *The following sequence of operations does not necessarily need to be performed in the order given. It is, rather, a checklist of everything that must be disconnected or removed before the engine can be lifted out of the vehicle. It is very important that all linkages, electrical wiring, hoses and cables be removed or disconnected before attempting to lift the engine clear of the vehicle, so double-check everything thoroughly.*

1    Open the hood and tilt it completely back.

2    Drain the cooling system through the petcocks located at the bottom of the radiator and at the lower right side of the engine block.

3    Disconnect the positive cable from the battery.

4    Remove the radiator and heater hoses.

5    Remove the engine cooling fan assembly.

6    Remove the radiator brace (if so equipped) and the radiator.

7   Disconnect and plug the fuel hose at the fuel pump.
8   Remove the air cleaner assembly and disconnect the windshield wiper motor hose.
9   Disconnect the choke and throttle controls from the carburetor.
10  Disconnect the starter cables and remove the starter motor.
11  Disconnect the wires from the generator.
12  Remove the ignition coil primary wire.
13  Disconnect the wires from the oil pressure and coolant temperature sending units.
14  Unbolt the exhaust pipe from the manifold.
15  On the F-head engine, disconnect the spark plug wires, then remove the bracket and the rocker arm cover.
16  Remove the two nuts and bolts from the front engine mounts and remove the supports, which will lower the engine sufficiently to provide access to the top two bolts on the bellhousing.

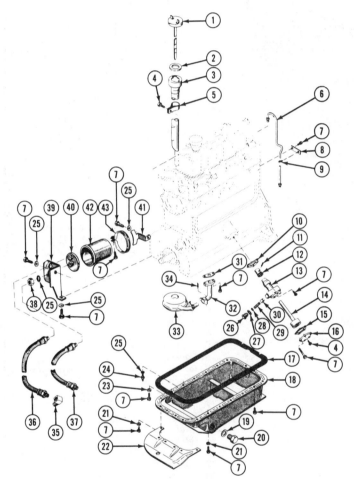

**Fig. 2.73  Oil pump and pan components — exploded view**

| | | |
|---|---|---|
| 1  Oil filler cap | 16  Oil pump cover | 31  Gasket |
| 2  Gasket | 17  Oil pan gasket | 32  Oil float support |
| 3  Oil filler tube | 18  Oil pan | 33  Float assembly |
| 4  Bolt | 19  Drain plug gasket | 34  Cotter pin |
| 5  Bracket | 20  Drain plug | 35  Elbow fitting |
| 6  Crankcase-to-cylinder head oil line | 21  Lock washer | 36  Oil filter inlet tube |
| 7  Screw | 22  Fan pulley shield | 37  Oil filter outlet tube |
| 8  Oil line bracket | 23  Spacer | |
| 9  Fastener | 24  Oil filter bracket stud | 38  Jam nut |
| 10  Gasket | 25  Lock washer | 39  Bracket |
| 11  Pin | 26  Retainer | 40  Oil filter base |
| 12  Oil pump driven gear | 27  Gasket | 41  Filter brace |
| 13  Oil pump | 28  Shim | 42  Oil filter assembly |
| 14  Shaft and rotors | 29  Spring | 43  Clamp |
| 15  Cover gasket | 30  Plunger | |

17  Attach a lifting device and raise the engine sufficiently to remove the slack in the hoist or cable.
18  Remove the flywheel bellhousing-to-engine bolts.
19  Carefully pull the engine forward until it is clear of the bellhousing and lift it from the vehicle.

### 121  Engine — disassembly and reassembly sequence

1   To completely disassemble the engine, remove the following items in the order given:

> Engine external components
> Oil pump
> Cylinder head
> Oil pan
> Floating oil pick-up
> Piston/connecting rod assemblies
> Timing gear cover
> Timing gears or sprockets and chain
> Engine front plate
> Clutch and flywheel
> Crankshaft
> Valves and springs (in block)
> Camshaft
> Valve lifters

2   Engine assembly is basically the reverse of disassembly. Install the following components in the order given:

> Valve lifters
> Camshaft
> Valves and springs (in block)
> Crankshaft
> Clutch and flywheel
> Engine front plate
> Timing gears or chain
> Timing gear cover
> Piston rings
> Piston/connecting rod assemblies
> Floating oil pick-up
> Oil pan
> Cylinder head
> Oil pump
> Engine external components

### 122  Engine external components — removal

1   Unbolt and remove the water pump.
2   *On L-head engines,* remove the crankcase ventilator tube (if so equipped). Remove the attaching nuts and pull the intake and exhaust manifolds from the engine. Remove the gaskets.
3   *On F-head engines,* remove the five retaining nuts and pull the exhaust manifold off the studs. Remove the gaskets.
4   Wrap a piece of wire around the oil filler tube and a suitable pry bar. Pull the tube from the crankcase by prying on the engine block with a bar while tapping the base of the tube to loosen it from the crankcase.
5   Unbolt and remove the water outlet and thermostat.
6   Remove the crankshaft pulley nut and use a puller to remove the pulley.
7   On crankcase ventilator-equipped models, remove the bolt and gasket which secure the valve to the block. Remove the crankcase vent body and valve cover plate.

### 123  Oil pump — removal

1   The oil pump is located on the left side of the engine and is driven off the camshaft by a spiral gear. The distributor is driven off the oil pump by a slot in the end of the shaft. The tongue in the distributor and slot in the pump shaft are machined off-center so the two shafts can mesh in only one position. Consequently, when removing the oil pump with the distributor installed, always remove the cap and mark the location of the distributor rotor so the pump can be reinstalled in

**2F**

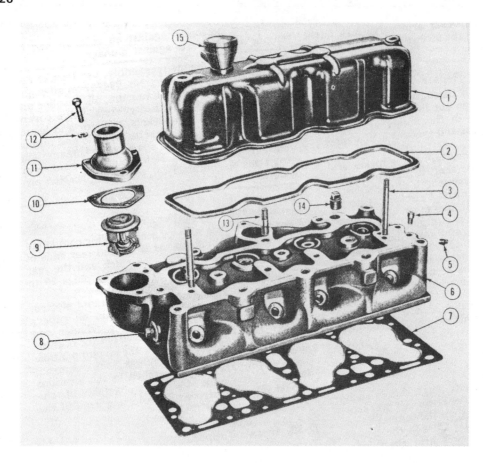

**Fig. 2.74  F-head engine cylinder head components — exploded view**

1   Rocker arm cover
2   Gasket
3   Cover stud
4   Connector
5   Pipe plug
6   Cylinder head
7   Gasket
8   Pipe plug
9   Thermostat
10  Gasket
11  Water outlet fitting
12  Screw and lock washer
13  Carburetor mounting stud
14  Pipe plug
15  Crankcase vent

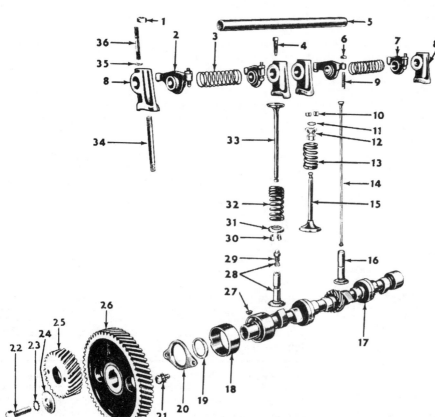

**Fig. 2.75  F-head valve gear components — exploded view**

1   Nut
2   Left rocker arm
3   Rocker arm shaft spring
4   Rocker shaft lock screw
5   Rocker shaft
6   Nut
7   Right rocker arm
8   Rocker arm shaft bracket
9   Intake valve lifter adjustment screw
10  Intake valve keepers
11  Oil seal
12  Intake valve spring retainer
13  Intake valve spring
14  Intake valve pushrod
15  Intake valve
16  Intake valve lifter
17  Camshaft
18  Camshaft front bearing
19  Camshaft thrust plate spacer
20  Camshaft thrust plate
21  Bolt and lock washer
22  Bolt
23  Lock washer
24  Camshaft gear washer
25  Crankshaft gear
26  Camshaft gear
27  Woodruff key
28  Exhaust valve lifter
29  Lifter adjusting screw
30  Exhaust valve keepers
31  Valve rotator assembly
32  Exhaust valve spring
33  Exhaust valve
34  Rocker shaft support stud
35  Washer
36  Rocker arm cover stud

the same position without disturbing the ignition timing.

2   If the engine is in the vehicle and is not going to be dismantled, position the number one (1) piston at top dead center on the compression stroke. If the distributor is already removed, sight through the installation hole and verify that the oil pump slot is in the near vertical position.

3   Remove the attaching bolts and carefully slide the oil pump and driveshaft out.

### 124   Cylinder head (L-head engine) removal

1   Remove the spark plugs, the cylinder head retaining nuts and the coolant temperature sending unit.

2   Remove the cylinder head and discard the gasket. It may be necessary to tap around the outer circumference of the head with a soft-faced hammer to break the gasket seal.

### 125   Cylinder head (F-head engine) — removal

1   Remove the rocker arm cover from the cylinder head.

2   Remove the rocker arm shaft support nuts and lift the assembly from the cylinder head. Remove the intake valve pushrods one at a time and tag them or place them in a marked rack to ensure reinstallation in their original positions.

3   Remove the bypass hose from the front of the cylinder head. Disconnect the oil line at the flare nut and remove the rocker arm studs.

4   Remove the cylinder head bolts, including the one located below the carburetor, inside the intake manifold.

5   Lift the cylinder head from the engine block. It may be necessary to tap lightly around the circumference of the head with a soft-faced hammer to break the gasket seal.

### 126   Oil pan — removal and installation

1   With the engine upside-down, remove the bolts securing the oil pan to the engine block.

2   Tap on the pan with a soft-faced hammer to break the gasket seal and lift the oil pan off the engine.

3   Using a gasket scraper, scrape off all traces of the old gasket from the engine block and the oil pan.

4   Clean the oil pan with solvent and dry it thoroughly. Check the gasket sealing surfaces for distortion.

5   Before installing the oil pan, apply a thin coat of RTV-type gasket sealer to the engine block gasket sealing surfaces. Lay a new oil pan gasket in place and carefully apply a coat of gasket sealer to the exposed side of the gasket.

6   Gently lay the oil pan in place (do not disturb the gasket) and install the bolts. Start with the bolts closest to the center of the pan and tighten them to the specified torque using a crisscross pattern. Do not overtighten them or leakage may occur.

### 127   Floating oil intake — removal, inspection and installation

1   Remove the two retaining bolts and lift off the oil intake assembly.

2   Clean the float, screen and tube thoroughly with solvent.

3   Inspect the float support flange and the engine block contact area to make sure they are flat and free of nicks, which could cause air leaks and fluctuating oil pressure.

4   Install the oil intake assembly and retaining bolts (use a new gasket).

### 128   Piston/connecting rod assembly — removal

1   Prior to removing the piston/connecting rod assemblies, remove the manifolds, the oil pump, the cylinder head, the oil pan and the floating oil pick-up by referring to the appropriate Sections.

2   Refer to Chapter 2A for the remaining steps in this procedure.

### 129   Timing gear or chain cover — removal

1   Remove the retaining nuts and bolts from the cover.

2   Remove the timing gear cover, the timing indicator and the gasket. You may have to tap the cover lightly with a soft-faced hammer to break the gasket seal.

3   Remove the oil slinger and the spacer from the crankshaft.

### 130   Timing gears or chain and sprockets — removal

1   Remove the attaching bolts and use a puller to remove the timing gears or sprockets and chain.

2   Remove the Woodruff keys from the camshaft and crankshaft.

### 131   Engine front plate — removal

Remove the retaining bolts and separate the engine front plate from the block. Discard the old gasket.

### 132   Clutch and flywheel — removal

1   Unbolt and remove the flywheel bellhousing.

2   Mark the relative position of the clutch and flywheel for reinstallation in their original positions.

3   Remove the four clutch retaining bolts which are diagonally opposed to one another. Loosen the two remaining bolts one turn at a time until the clutch spring pressure is relieved.

4   Remove the clutch assembly, taking care not to let the clutch plate fall.

5   Remove the retaining bolts and carefully pry the flywheel from the crankshaft.

6   Inspect the flywheel for scoring and wear on the friction face and warpage and damage to the starter ring gear.

### 133   Crankshaft — removal

1   Slide the thrust washer and end play adjusting shims from the end of the crankshaft.

2   Remove the two pieces of main bearing cap packing from between the sides of the bearing cap and the engine block.

3   Refer to Chapter 2A for the remaining steps in this procedure.

### 134   Valves and springs (in block) — removal

1   The intake and exhaust valves on the L-head engine and the exhaust valves on the F-head are located in the engine block.

2   After removing the valve spring cover, use clean, lint-free cloths to block off the three exhaust valve chamber holes so the valve keepers cannot accidentally fall in.

3   Use a valve spring compressor to compress the springs on the valves which are closed (seated against the valve seat).

4   Remove the valves, springs, retainers and keepers. Rotate the camshaft to close the remaining valves and repeat the operation. If a valve cannot be easily removed, remove the spring and clean the carbon deposits from the valve stem. Mark all of the valve components or keep them in a rack so they will be reinstalled in their original locations.

### 135   Camshaft — removal

1   Push the valve lifters all the way into the block so they will not contact the camshaft lobes. Use a clothespin (or equivalent) to hold the lifters up in the valve chamber.

2   If so equipped, remove the camshaft thrust plate, screws and spacer.

**2F**

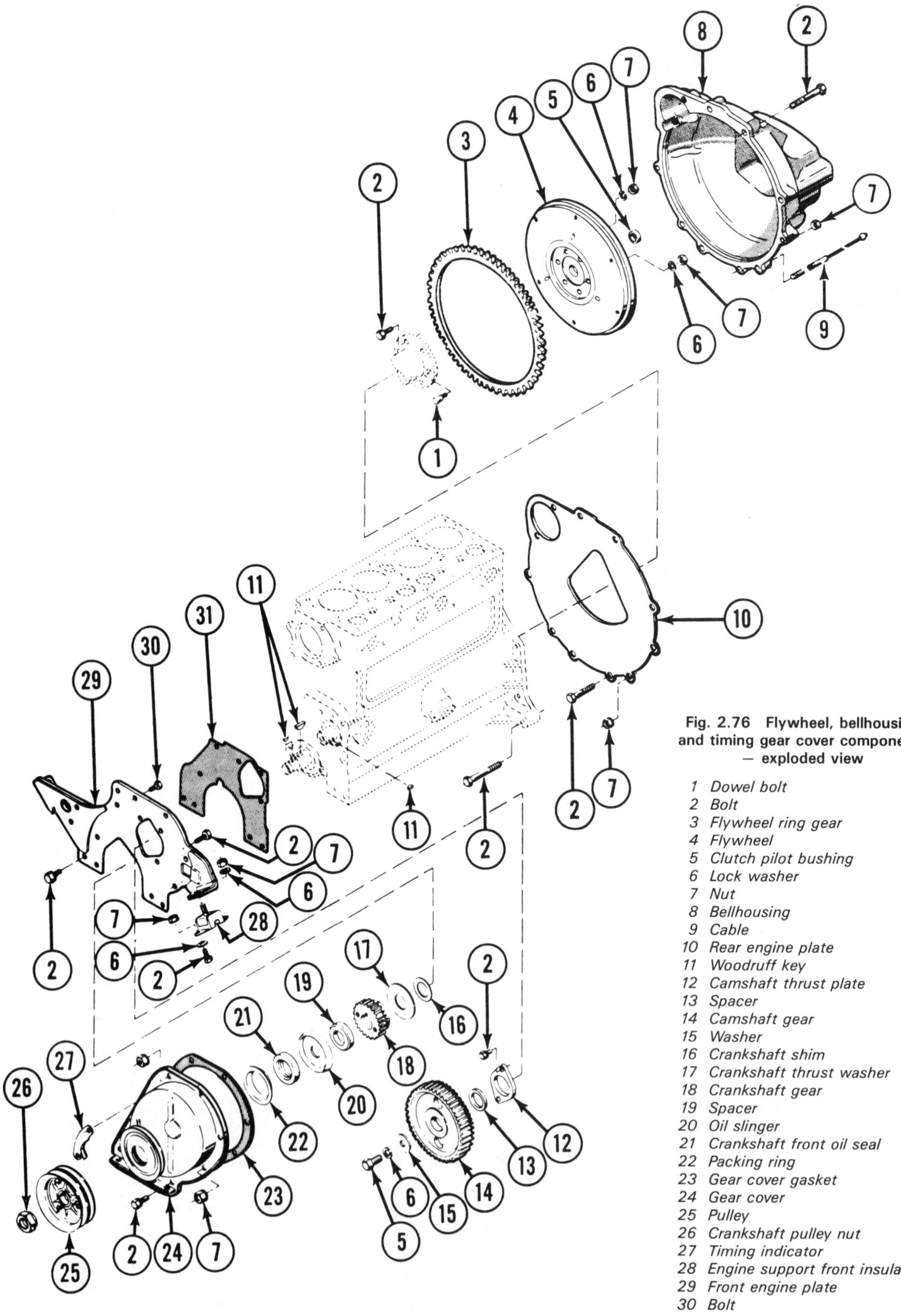

Fig. 2.76 Flywheel, bellhousing
and timing gear cover components
— exploded view

1 Dowel bolt
2 Bolt
3 Flywheel ring gear
4 Flywheel
5 Clutch pilot bushing
6 Lock washer
7 Nut
8 Bellhousing
9 Cable
10 Rear engine plate
11 Woodruff key
12 Camshaft thrust plate
13 Spacer
14 Camshaft gear
15 Washer
16 Crankshaft shim
17 Crankshaft thrust washer
18 Crankshaft gear
19 Spacer
20 Oil slinger
21 Crankshaft front oil seal
22 Packing ring
23 Gear cover gasket
24 Gear cover
25 Pulley
26 Crankshaft pulley nut
27 Timing indicator
28 Engine support front insulator
29 Front engine plate
30 Bolt
31 Front plate gasket

3  Pull the camshaft directly out of the engine block, taking care not to scrape the bearing surfaces with the cam lobes.

## 136  Valve lifters — removal

1  Remove the valve lifters from the bottom (crankcase side) of the engine block.
2  Mark the lifters or place them in a rack which is marked so they will be reinstalled in their original locations.

## 137  Valve lifters — inspection

1  Clean the lifters thoroughly with solvent and dry them with a clean, lint-free cloth or compressed air.
2  Inspect the contact surfaces of each lifter for wear, cracks and other damage. Make sure the adjustment screw can be turned only with a wrench as they are self-locking.
3  Measure each lifter diameter and its corresponding bore diameter to determine the lifter-to-bore clearance. If it is excessive, new lifters and block service will be required.

## 138  Engine block valve seats and guides — servicing

1  After cleaning and inspecting the engine block (Chapter 2A), the valve seats and guides must be inspected and repaired, if necessary.
2  Inspect the valve seats for cracks, pits, burned areas and ridges.
3  Measure the width of each seat and compare it to the Specifications.
4  Check the valve seat runout with a dial indicator to determine if it is out-of-round. If a dial indicator is not available, apply a light layer of pencil lead to the face of each valve and insert the valves, one at a time, into position. Press on each valve and rotate it one-quarter of a turn. Remove the valve and check to see if the pencil lead transferred evenly to the valve seat. If it did not, the seat is in need of service.
5  Measure the inside diameters of the valve guides (at both ends and the center of each guide) with a small hole gauge and a 0-to-1 inch micrometer. Record the measurements for future reference. These

measurements, along with the valve stem diameter measurements, will enable you to compute the valve stem-to-guide clearance. This clearance, when compared to the Specifications, will be one factor that will determine the extent of the valve service work required. The guides are measured at the ends and at the center to determine if they are worn in a bell-mouth pattern (more wear at the ends). If they are, guide reconditioning or replacement is an absolute must.
6  Carefully inspect each valve face for cracks, pits and burned spots. Check the valve stem and neck for cracks. Rotate the valve and check for any obvious indication that it is bent. Check the end of the stem for pits and excessive wear. The presence of any of the above conditions indicates a need for valve service by a professional.
7  Measure the width of the valve margin (on each valve) and compare it to the Specifications. Any valve with a margin narrower than specified will have to be replaced with a new one.
8  Measure the valve stem diameter. By subtracting the stem diameter from the valve guide diameter, the valve stem-to-guide clearance is obtained. Compare the results to the Specifications. If the stem-to-guide clearance is greater then specified, the guides will have to be reconditioned or replaced and new valves may have to be installed, depending on the condition of the old ones.
9  Check the ends of each valve spring for wear and pits. Measure the free length and compare it to the Specifications. Any springs that are shorter then specified have sagged and should not be reused. Stand the spring on a flat surface and check it for squareness.
10  Check the spring retainers and keepers for obvious wear and cracks. Any questionable parts should not be reused because extensive damage will occur in the event of failure during engine operation.

## 139  Cylinder head (L-head engine) — cleaning and inspection

1  Scrape off any traces of old gasket material and sealing compound from the head gasket sealing surface.
2  Remove any scale that may have built up around the coolant passages.
3  It is a good idea to run an appropriate size tap into each of the threaded holes to remove any corrosion or thread sealant that may be present. If compressed air is available, use it to clear the holes of debris produced by this operation.
4  Clean the cylinder head with solvent and dry it thoroughly. Com-

**2F**

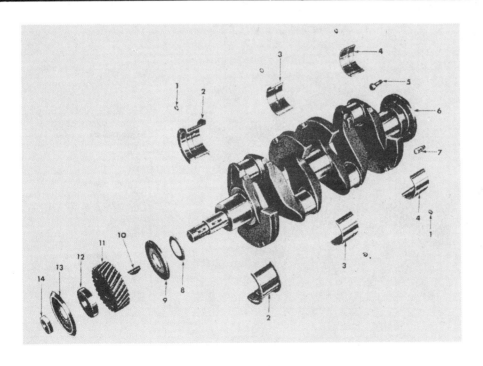

Fig. 2.77 Crankshaft components — exploded view

1  Bearing dowel
2  Front main bearing
3  Center main bearing
4  Rear main bearing
5  Flywheel
6  Crankshaft
7  Flywheel dowel bolt
8  Crankshaft shim
9  Thrust washer
10  Woodruff key
11  Crankshaft gear
12  Gear spacer
13  Oil slinger
14  Front oil seal

pressed air will speed the drying process and ensure that all holes and recessed areas are clean.

5    Inspect the head very carefully for cracks, evidence of coolant leakage and other damage. If cracks are found, a new cylinder head should be obtained.

6    Using a straightedge and a feeler gauge, check the head gasket surfaces for warpage. If the head is warped beyond the limits given in the Specifications, it can be resurfaced at an automotive machine shop.

### 140   Oil pump — disassembly, inspection and reassembly

1    Early models were equipped with an oil pump of slightly different design, which used gears to pump the oil. The later model pump employs an inner and outer rotor within the pump and features an oil pressure relief valve mounted on the pump body instead of in the cover as on the early model pump.

2    To disassemble either pump, file off the end of the driven gear retaining pin, drive it out with a hammer and small punch and remove the gear. Remove the pump cover and withdraw the gears or rotors and shaft.

3    To check the clearance of the rotors on late model pumps, match the rotors together with one lobe of the inner rotor pushed completely into the outer rotor notch. Insert a feeler gauge as shown in the accompanying illustration and measure the rotor lobe clearance. Replace the rotors if the clearance exceeds the Specifications.

4    Insert a feeler gauge between the outer rotor and the body of the pump to determine the clearance. If the clearance exceeds the Specifications, replace the pump body.

5    Inspect the pump cover of both model pumps for wear and scoring and check it with a straightedge and feeler gauge to make sure the flatness is within the Specifications.

6    Measure the thickness of the late model pump rotors and make sure both rotors are within the specified tolerance.

7    Install the pump cover without the gasket and verify that the pump shaft cannot be turned because of interference between the gears and the cover. Remove the cover, install the gasket and reinstall the cover and bolts. The shaft should now turn freely showing that the end play of the pump shaft is within the Specifications.

8    Install the driven gear on the pump shaft and check the running clearance between the gear and the pump body with a feeler gauge.

9    Reassemble the oil pump, remove the cover plug and fill it with engine oil to provide a self-priming action. Replace the plug.

### 141   Crankshaft rear main oil seal — replacement

1    On early L-head engines, wick packing is used to seal the rear crankshaft main bearing. On later L-head and all F-head engines, a steel-backed lip seal is used.

2    Install the wick packing into the machined groove in the block and main bearing cap. Use a round piece of wood or a steel rod to roll the packing securely into the groove, starting at one end and working

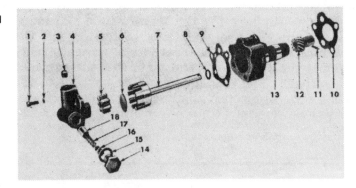

**Fig. 2.78   Early-type oil pump components — exploded view (Sec 140)**

1   Cover-to-body screw
2   Cover-to-body screw gasket
3   Cover plug
4   Cover
5   Gear
6   Rotor disc
7   Shaft assembly
8   Shaft gasket
9   Cover gasket
10  Oil pump-to-block gasket
11  Driven gear pin
12  Driven gear
13  Oil pump body
14  Oil relief spring retainer
15  Oil relief spring retainer gaskets
16  Relief spring shims
17  Relief plunger spring
18  Relief plunger

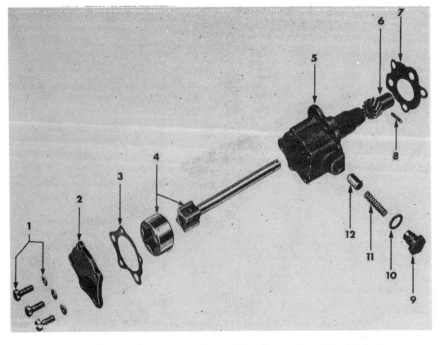

**Fig. 2.79   Late-type oil pump components — exploded view (Sec 140)**

1   Cover screw
2   Cover
3   Cover gasket
4   Shaft and rotors
5   Body assembly
6   Driven gear
7   Pump gasket
8   Gear retaining pin
9   Relief valve retainer
10  Relief valve retainer gasket
11  Relief valve spring
12  Relief valve plunger

toward the center. Start at the opposite end and then roll toward the center until the packing is firmly seated. Cut off the protruding ends of the packing flush with the cap.

3   Lubricate the lip-type seals with a light film of grease to ease installation and then slide the seals into place in the block and bearing cap.

4   Apply a light coat of gasket sealant to the sides and face of the bearing cap and install it.

5   Insert the two rear bearing cap packings into the holes between the bearing cap and the block. Do not cut these packings off as they are designed to protrude so that they will be crushed and form a tight seal when the oil pan is installed.

## 142   Valve lifters — installation

1   Lubricate each lifter with engine assembly lube or moly-based grease.

2   With the engine inverted, begin at the rear of the block and install the lifters in sequence. Hold them in position with clothespins.

## 143   Camshaft — installation

1   Lubricate the camshaft bearing and lobe surfaces and the camshaft bearings in the block with engine assembly lube or moly-based grease.

2   Carefully insert the camshaft into the engine, taking care not to damage the bearing surfaces. Do not allow the end of the camshaft to sharply strike the expansion plug at the back of the bore.

3   Install the camshaft thrust plate and slide the thrust plate spacer onto the end of the camshaft with the beveled inner edge facing the camshaft.

4   Install any shims which were removed. These are placed between the shoulder and spacer. Install the thrust plate attaching bolts and tighten them to the specified torque.

5   Check the end play of the camshaft with a dial indicator at the rear face of the camshaft gear and thrust plate. If there is too little end play, it can be corrected by removing the shims.

## 144   Valves and springs (in block) — installation

1   Oil the stems and insert the valves into the guides from which they were removed.

2   Install the valve springs and retainers on each valve.

3   Slide the top end of the spring onto the bottom end of the valve guide and use a large screwdriver to snap the spring and retainer over the lifter adjusting screw. The two closely wound coils of each spring should be seated against the block at the top.

4   Rotate the crankshaft to bring each lifter to its lowest point (in turn) and use a compressor tool to hold the valves down and install the keepers.

5   Remove any rags used to seal off the engine block openings.

6   The valves should be adjusted to the specified clearance as described in Chapter 1.

7   Install the valve lifter cover (use a new gasket).

Fig. 2.80   Measuring the late model oil pump rotor lobe clearance (Sec 140)

Fig. 2.81   Checking the late model oil pump outer rotor-to-pump body clearance (Sec 140)

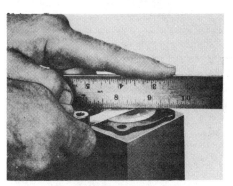

Fig. 2.82   Checking the oil pump cover flatness with a straightedge and feeler gauge (Sec 140)

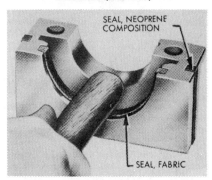

Fig. 2.83   Installing early-type rear main bearing seal packing with a wooden dowel (Sec 141)

2F

Fig. 2.84   Timing gear marks (arrows) properly aligned (Sec 148)

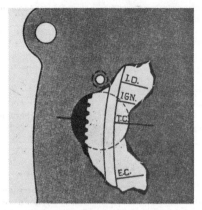

Fig. 2.85   The flywheel TC mark aligned with the cover hole (indicating that the number one and four pistons are at Top Dead Center) (Sec 148)

Fig. 2.86   Timing chain sprockets properly aligned (Sec 148)

### 145   Crankshaft — installation and main bearing oil clearance check

1   Crankshaft installation is generally one of the first steps in engine reassembly; it is assumed at this point that the engine block and crankshaft have been cleaned and inspected and repaired or reconditioned.
2   Position the engine with the bottom facing up.
3   Remove the main bearing cap bolts and lift out the caps. Lay them out in the proper order to help ensure that they are reinstalled correctly.
4   If they are still in place, remove the old bearing inserts from the block and the main bearing caps. Wipe the main bearing surfaces of the block and caps with a clean, lint-free cloth (they must be kept spotlessly clean).
5   Clean the back sides of the new main bearing inserts and lay one bearing half in each main bearing saddle in the block and the other bearing half from each bearing set in the corresponding main bearing cap. Make sure that the tab on the bearing insert fits into the recess in the block or cap. Also, the oil holes in the block and cap must line up with the oil holes in the bearing insert. *Do not hammer the bearing into place and do not nick or gouge the bearing faces. No lubrication should be used at this time.*
6   The flanged thrust bearing must be installed in the number one (front) cap and saddle. Note: *It is possible to incorrectly install the front main bearing. The bearing must be installed in the cap with the narrower of the two radial oil grooves toward the front edge of the cap. If this bearing is not properly installed, the oil grooves in the two halves of the bearing will not match at the parting line and premature failure of the bearing will result.* Install the upper and lower rear main oil seal sections as described in Section 141.
7   Clean the faces of the bearings in the block and the crankshaft main bearing journals with a clean, lint-free cloth. Check or clean the oil holes in the crankshaft; any dirt here can only go one way — straight through the new bearings.
8   Once you are certain that the crankshaft is clean, carefully lay it in position in the main bearings with the counterweights lying sideways. An assistant would be very helpful here.
9   Before the crankshaft can be permanently installed, the main bearing oil clearance must be checked.
10   Trim three pieces of the appropriate type of Plastigage (slightly shorter than the width of the main bearings) and place one piece on each crankshaft main bearing journal, parallel with the journal axis. Do not lay them across any oil holes.
11   Clean the faces of the bearings in the caps and install the caps in their respective positions (do not mix them up) with the arrows pointing toward the front of the engine. Do not disturb the Plastigage.
12   Starting with the center main and working out toward the ends, tighten the main bearing cap bolts, in three steps, to the specified torque. *Do not rotate the crankshaft at any time during this operation.*
13   Remove the bolts and carefully lift off the main bearing caps. Keep them in order. Do not disturb the Plastigage or rotate the crankshaft. If any of the main bearing caps are difficult to remove, tap gently from side-to-side with a soft-faced hammer to loosen them.

14   Compare the width of the crushed Plastigage on each journal to the scale printed on the Plastigage container to obtain the main bearing oil clearance. Check the Specifications to make sure it is correct.
15   If the clearance is not correct, double check to make sure that you have the right size bearing inserts. Also, recheck the crankshaft main bearing journal diameters and make sure that no dirt or oil was between the bearing inserts and the main bearing caps or the block when the clearance was measured.
16   Carefully scrape all traces of the Plastigage material off the main bearing journals and/or the bearing faces. Do not nick or scratch the bearing faces.
17   Carefully lift the crankshaft out of the engine. Clean the bearing faces in the block, then apply a thin, uniform layer of clean, high-quality moly-based grease (or engine assembly lube) to each of the bearing faces. Be sure to coat the thrust flange faces as well as the journal face of the thrust bearing in the number one (front) main. Make sure the crankshaft journals are clean, then carefully lay it back in place in the block. Clean the faces of the bearings in the caps, then apply a thin, uniform layer of clean, high-quality moly-based grease to each of the bearing faces and install the caps in their respective positions with the arrows pointing toward the front of the engine (refer to Section 141 and note the special instructions related to the rear main bearing cap). Install the bolts and tighten them to the specified torque, starting with the center main and working out toward the ends. Work up to the final torque in three steps.
18   Rotate the crankshaft a number of times by hand and check for any obvious binding.
19   The final step is to check the crankshaft end play. This can be done with a feeler gauge or a dial indicator set. Refer to Chapter 2A, Section 12, for the procedure to follow.

### 146   Clutch and flywheel — installation

1   Make sure the mating surfaces of the crankshaft and the flywheel are clean and free of nicks and damage which could affect alignment.
2   Place the flywheel in position on the alignment dowels, install the retaining bolts and tighten them to the specified torque in a crisscross pattern.
3   Attach a dial indicator to the engine plate with the stem resting on the flywheel clutch contact face. Rotate the crankshaft and check the runout. Compare it to the Specifications.
4   Use a clutch alignment tool to align the clutch plate, place the pressure plate assembly in position and install the retaining bolts. Tighten the bolts a little at a time in a crisscross pattern so as not to distort the pressure plate. Remove the alignment tool.
5   Place the bellhousing in position and install the retaining bolts. The long bolts that go through the lugs on the crankcase and the ones below are installed with the nuts on the bellhousing side. The other bolts are installed from the rear, except for the screw attaching the top of the starter motor.

### 147   Engine front plate — installation

1   Place the gasket in position on the engine plate.
2   Attach the plate to the engine with the gasket reaching all the way down to the bottom of the crankcase. Install the bolts and tighten them securely.

### 148   Timing gears or chain and sprockets — installation

1   On timing gear-equipped engines, install the crankshaft gear, followed by the camshaft gear. The timing marks on the gears must be aligned as shown in the accompanying illustration, which can be accomplished by turning the camshaft or crankshaft.
2   Once the marks on the gears are in alignment, remove the camshaft gear, install the Woodruff key and reinstall the gear, using the retaining bolt to draw it into position. *Do not attempt to drive the gear onto the camshaft, as it could damage the plug at the rear of the shaft.* Tighten the bolt to the specified torque.
3   Prior to installing the sprockets on timing chain-equipped engines, rotate the crankshaft until the number one and number four pistons are at top dead center. This can be verified by sighting through the inspection hole in the flywheel cover and making sure the TC mark on the flywheel is aligned with the cover.
4   Install the sprockets so the punch marks on the rims are directly opposite each other, turning the camshaft as necessary.
5   Remove the camshaft sprocket. Place the timing chain on the crankshaft sprocket and the camshaft sprocket in the chain and install the assembly. With the timing marks properly aligned, as shown in the illustration, install the camshaft sprocket bolts and tighten them to the specified torque.
6   Install the oil slinger and spacer on the crankshaft and (if removed) the timing gear oil jet in the tapped hole in the front of the engine block. The oil jet hole should be directed so the oil will go against the camshaft driven gear, just ahead of where it engages with the crankshaft gear. **Note:** *A new timing gear oil jet entered production with L-head engine S/N 3J-166871 (F-head engine S/N 4J-250095). The earlier jet has a 0.070-inch diameter aperture; the later jet has a 0.040-inch aperture. The later jet reduces oil pressure variation at the number one connecting rod bearing. It is recommended that the 0.040-inch jet be installed in engines with serial numbers lower than above whenever it has been necessary to replace a scored or burned number one connecting rod bearing.*

### 149   Timing gear or chain cover — installation

1   Apply a coat of RTV-type gasket sealant to the contact surface of the timing cover and place the gasket in position.
2   Carefully place the cover and timing pointer in position and install the attaching bolts. Tighten the bolts evenly and securely.

### 150   Cylinder head (F-head engine) — installation

1   Apply a thin coat of sealant to both sides of the cylinder head gasket and place the gasket in position on the engine block with the crimped edges down.

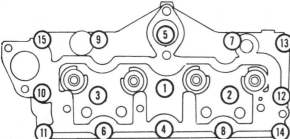

Fig. 2.87   *F-head engine* cylinder head bolt-tightening sequence (Sec 150)

2   Lower the cylinder head into position, install the bolts and tighten them to the specified torque in the sequence shown in the accompanying illustration.
3   Insert the ball ends of the pushrods securely into the intake valve lifters in the block.
4   Install the rocker arm assembly on the mounting studs, making sure the lifters, pushrods and rocker arms are in alignment.
5   Install the nuts on the rocker arm assembly studs and tighten them evenly to the specified torque.
6   Adjust the valve clearances (Chapter 1).
7   Coat both sides of the rocker arm cover gasket with RTV-type sealant and attach the gasket to the cover.
8   Place the rocker arm cover in position and install the retaining bolts. Tighten the bolts to the specified torque.

### 151   Cylinder head (L-head engine) — installation

1   Without using any gasket sealer, place the head gasket in position on the block.
2   Lower the cylinder head into position. Install the retaining bolts and tighten them to the specified torque, in three steps, following the sequence shown in the accompanying illustration.

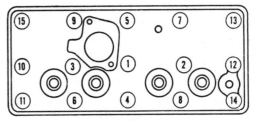

Fig. 2.88   Cylinder head bolt-tightening sequence for the *L-head engine* (Sec 151)

### 152   Oil pump — installation

1   Rotate the crankshaft and timing gear or sprockets so the timing marks are aligned.
2   Attach the gasket to the pump.
3   Begin inserting the oil pump shaft into the left side of the engine with the wider side of the shaft on top and the bolt holes aligned. Insert a long screwdriver into the distributor shaft opening on the opposite side of the block and turn the slot in the oil pump shaft until it is in the 9:30 o'clock position.
4   Remove the screwdriver and use a flashlight to make sure that the slot is in the proper position.
5   Insert the screwdriver and use it to guide the oil pump shaft gear into engagement with the camshaft gear as the pump is lowered into position.
6   Remove the screwdriver and make sure that the oil pump distributor tang slot is now in the 11 o'clock position. If it is not, repeat the operation.
7   Coat the threads of the attaching bolts with gasket sealant and install them.

### 153   Engine external components — installation

1   Install the crankcase ventilator valve assembly.
2   Install the distributor (Chapter 5).
3   Install the crankshaft pulley and nut.
4   Install the thermostat and water inlet (Chapter 3).
5   Install the water pump (Chapter 3).
6   Insert the oil filler tube into the block with the beveled end facing away from the crankshaft. Tap the tube into place with a hammer, using a piece of wood to protect the end.
7   *On F-head engines,* install the exhaust manifold, using a new gasket, and tighten the retaining nuts to the specified torque.
8   *On L-head engines,* install the manifolds, using new gaskets, and the crankcase ventilator tube.

**2F**

### 154   Engine — installation

1   Lower the engine into the vehicle and connect it to the transmission.
2   Install the front engine mounts and remove the lifting device.
3   Connect the exhaust pipe to the manifold.
4   Connect the spark plug, oil and coolant temperature sending unit, ignition coil and generator wires.
5   Install the starter motor and connect the wires.
6   Connect the choke and throttle controls to the carburetor.
7   Connect the windshield wiper motor hose and install the air cleaner assembly.
8   Connect the fuel hose to the fuel pump.
9   Install the cooling fan, the radiator and brace and the radiator and heater hoses.
10  Fill the cooling system and crankcase with the specified coolant and oil.
11  Connect the positive battery cable.

# Chapter 3   Cooling, heating and air conditioning systems

**Contents**

Air conditioning components — removal and
  installation . . . . . . . . . . . . . . . . . . . . . . . . . . .  10
Air conditioning system — check . . . . . . . . . . . . . . . . . . .  5
Antifreeze — general information . . . . . . . . . . . . . . . . . .  6
Coolant level check . . . . . . . . . . . . . . . . . . . . . . . .  Chapter 1
Coolant temperature sending unit — removal and
  installation . . . . . . . . . . . . . . . . . . . . . . . . . . .  9
Cooling system check . . . . . . . . . . . . . . . . . . . . . .  Chapter 1
Cooling system servicing (draining, flushing and
  refilling) . . . . . . . . . . . . . . . . . . . . . . . . . . .  Chapter 1

Drivebelt check and adjustment . . . . . . . . . . . . . . . .  Chapter 1
General information . . . . . . . . . . . . . . . . . . . . . . . . .  1
Heater system — general information . . . . . . . . . . . . . . .  8
Radiator — removal and installation . . . . . . . . . . . . . . .  2
Radiator — servicing . . . . . . . . . . . . . . . . . . . . . . . .  7
Thermostat — removal and installation . . . . . . . . . . . . . .  3
Underhood hoses — check and replacement . . . . . . .  Chapter 1
Water pump — removal and installation . . . . . . . . . . . . . .  4

**Specifications**

## Thermostat rating

| | |
|---|---|
| F- and L-head four-cylinder engines . . . . . . . . . . . . . . . . . . . | 190ºF |
| V6 engine . . . . . . . . . . . . . . . . . . . . . . . . . . . . . . . . . . | 190ºF |
| In-line six-cylinder engines | |
| 1971 and 1972 . . . . . . . . . . . . . . . . . . . . . . . . . . . . | 195ºF |
| 1973 . . . . . . . . . . . . . . . . . . . . . . . . . . . . . . . . . . | 205ºF |
| 1974 through 1983 . . . . . . . . . . . . . . . . . . . . . . . . . | 195ºF |
| V8 engine . . . . . . . . . . . . . . . . . . . . . . . . . . . . . . . . . | 195ºF |
| 151 cu in four-cylinder engine . . . . . . . . . . . . . . . . . . . . | 195ºF |

## Radiator cap pressure rating *(all models)* . . . . . .  15 psi

## Torque specifications

| | Ft-lb | Nm |
|---|---|---|
| Alternator adjusting bolt . . . . . . . . . . . . . . . . . . . . . . . . . | 15 to 20 | 20 to 27 |
| Generator adjusting bolt . . . . . . . . . . . . . . . . . . . . . . . . . | 20 to 25 | 27 to 34 |
| Fan-to-hub bolt . . . . . . . . . . . . . . . . . . . . . . . . . . . . . . | 15 to 20 | 20 to 27 |
| Thermostat housing bolts | | |
| F- and L-head four-cylinder engines . . . . . . . . . . . . . . . . . | 20 to 25 | 27 to 34 |
| V6 engine . . . . . . . . . . . . . . . . . . . . . . . . . . . . . . . . | 17 to 23 | 23 to 31 |
| In-line six-cylinder engines . . . . . . . . . . . . . . . . . . . . . | 10 to 18 | 14 to 25 |
| V8 engine . . . . . . . . . . . . . . . . . . . . . . . . . . . . . . . . | 10 to 18 | 14 to 25 |
| 151 cu in four-cylinder engine . . . . . . . . . . . . . . . . . . . | 22 | 30 |
| Water pump bolts | | |
| F- and L-head four-cylinder engines . . . . . . . . . . . . . . . . . | 12 to 17 | 17 to 29 |
| V6 engine . . . . . . . . . . . . . . . . . . . . . . . . . . . . . . . . | 6 to 8 | 8 to 11 |
| In-line six-cylinder engines . . . . . . . . . . . . . . . . . . . . . | 9 to 18 | 12 to 24 |
| V8 engine | | |
| Water pump-to-block . . . . . . . . . . . . . . . . . . . . . . . . | 18 to 33 | 24 to 44 |
| Water pump-to-timing cover . . . . . . . . . . . . . . . . . . . | 4 | 6 |
| 151 cu in four-cylinder engine . . . . . . . . . . . . . . . . . . . | 25 | 30 |

## 1   General information

The cooling system on all models consists of a radiator, belt-driven water pump, fan, thermostat and associated hoses.

Coolant is circulated through the radiator tubes and is cooled by air passing through the cooling fins. The coolant is circulated by a pump mounted on the front of the engine and turned by a crankshaft-driven drivebelt. The fan is bolted to the water pump pulley and draws air through the radiator at low speeds and when the vehicle is stopped.

A thermostat allows the engine to warm up quickly by remaining closed until the coolant in the radiator, heater, intake manifold and cylinder head is at operating temperature. The thermostat then opens, allowing full circulation of coolant throughout the cooling system.

Some models are equipped with a coolant expansion reservoir. As the radiator coolant expands, a pressure relief valve in the cap allows the coolant to flow through the overflow hose into the reservoir. When the system cools and contracts, there is a pressure drop and the coolant is drawn back into the radiator.

## 2   Radiator — removal and installation

**Caution:** *The engine must be completely cool when this procedure is performed.*

1    Remove the radiator cap and the drain cock and drain the coolant into a suitable container.

2    Disconnect the upper radiator hose and coolant overflow or recovery tube.

3    Remove the fan shroud (if so equipped).

4    Remove the upper radiator mounting screws or bolts.

5    *On automatic transmission-equipped models,* disconnect and plug the transmission fluid cooler lines at the radiator.

6    Disconnect the lower radiator hose, remove the lower mounting screws or bolts and lift the radiator carefully out of the vehicle. Refer to Section 7 for radiator servicing information.

7    To install, place the radiator in position and install the mounting screws or bolts.

8    Install the fan shroud (if so equipped).

**Fig. 3.1   Typical engine compartment cooling system component layout (V8 engine shown)**

| | | |
|---|---|---|
| 1  Fan | 4  Radiator cap | 7  Water pump |
| 2  Fan shroud | 5  Upper radiator hose | 8  Heater hose |
| 3  Overflow tube | 6  Water pump drivebelt | 9  Thermostat housing |

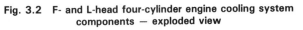

**Fig. 3.2   F- and L-head four-cylinder engine cooling system components — exploded view**

1  Radiator cap
2  Radiator
3  Fan retaining bolt
4  Hose clamp
5  Upper radiator hose
6  Fan
7  Fan spacer
8  Drivebelt
9  Double groove pulley
10  Single groove pulley
11  Water pump bearing and shaft
12  Pipe plug
13  Bearing retainer spring
14  Water pump body
15  Thermostat
16  Gasket
17  Water outlet housing
18  Gasket
19  Water pump impeller
20  Water pump seal
21  Seal washer
22  Lower radiator hose
23  Radiator drain cock

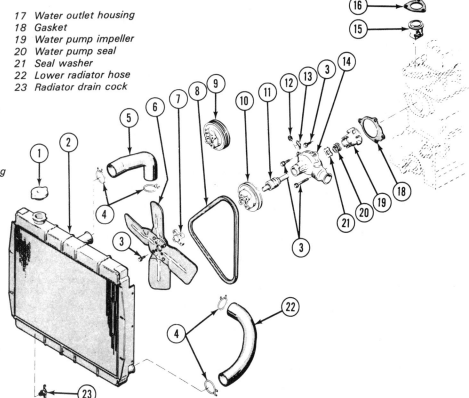

**3**

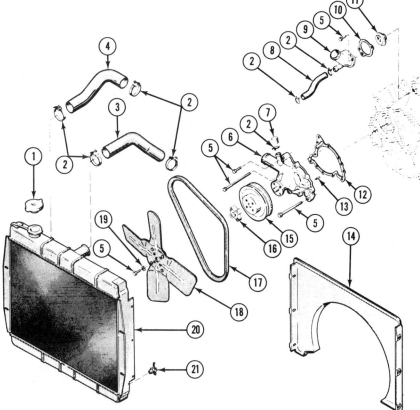

**Fig. 3.3   V6 engine cooling system components — exploded view**

1  Radiator cap
2  Hose clamp
3  Upper (inlet) radiator hose
4  Lower (outlet) radiator hose
5  Fan retaining bolt
6  Water pump assembly
7  Cap
8  Thermostat bypass hose
9  Water outlet housing
10  Water outlet housing gasket
11  Thermostat
12  Water pump gasket
13  Dowel pin
14  Radiator shroud
15  Fan pulley
16  Fan spacer
17  Drivebelt
18  Fan
19  Fan bolt lock washer
20  Radiator
21  Radiator drain cock

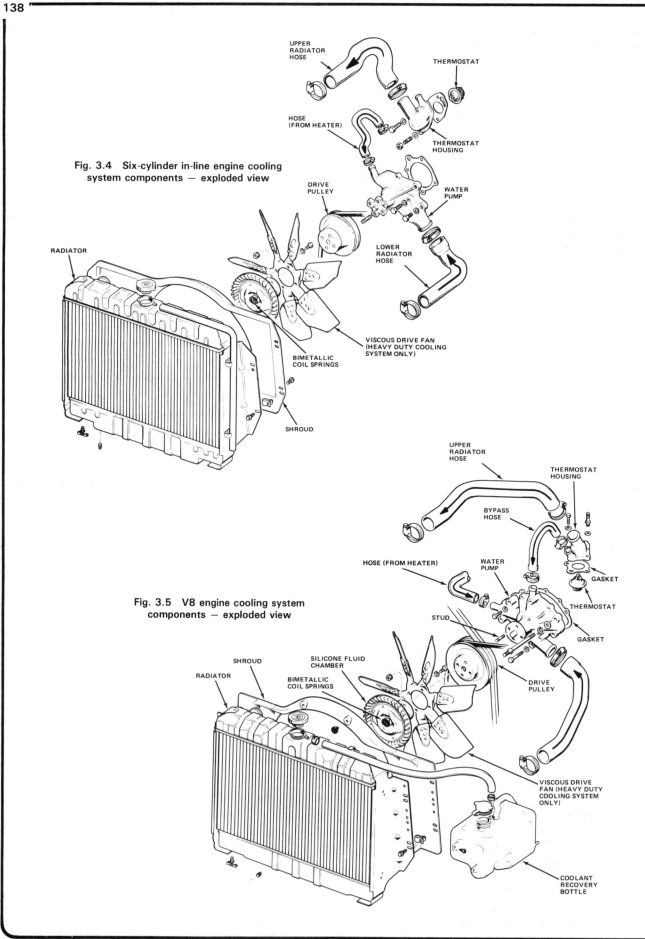

UPPER RADIATOR HOSE

THERMOSTAT

HOSE (FROM HEATER)

THERMOSTAT HOUSING

Fig. 3.4   Six-cylinder in-line engine cooling
system components — exploded view

DRIVE PULLEY

WATER PUMP

LOWER RADIATOR HOSE

RADIATOR

BIMETALLIC COIL SPRINGS

VISCOUS DRIVE FAN (HEAVY DUTY COOLING SYSTEM ONLY)

SHROUD

UPPER RADIATOR HOSE

THERMOSTAT HOUSING

BYPASS HOSE

HOSE (FROM HEATER)

WATER PUMP

GASKET

THERMOSTAT

STUD

GASKET

Fig. 3.5   V8 engine cooling system
components — exploded view

SILICONE FLUID CHAMBER

SHROUD

BIMETALLIC COIL SPRINGS

RADIATOR

DRIVE PULLEY

VISCOUS DRIVE FAN (HEAVY DUTY COOLING SYSTEM ONLY)

COOLANT RECOVERY BOTTLE

9   Install the drain cock and overflow or recovery hose.
10   Remove the plugs and reconnect the automatic transmission fluid cooler lines to the radiator.
11   Connect the hoses, fill the radiator with the specified coolant and install the cap.
12   Start the engine and allow it to reach normal operating temperature, then check carefully for leaks.
13   Allow the engine to cool completely, then check the coolant level (add more coolant if required).

## 3   Thermostat — removal and installation

**Caution:** *The engine must be completely cool when this procedure is performed.*

1   On all models, the thermostat is located under the water outlet housing (to which the upper radiator hose is attached) on the front of the engine. If the thermostat is functioning properly, the temperature gauge should rise to the normal operating temperature quickly and then stay there, only rising above the normal position occasionally when the engine gets unusually hot. If the engine does not rise to normal operating temperature quickly, or if it overheats, the thermostat should be removed and checked or replaced.
2   Remove the radiator cap, then drain coolant from the radiator until the level is below the level of the thermostat.
3   Remove the upper radiator hose from the water outlet or housing. On some models it will be necessary to remove the intake manifold or thermostat bypass hoses from the housing to facilitate removal of the housing.
4   Remove the retaining bolts, grasp the housing firmly and separate it from the engine.
5   Note the position of the thermostat so the new one can be installed in the same direction.
6   Lift the thermostat from the engine.
7   Use a gasket scraper to remove all traces of gasket material from the housing and the engine gasket mating surfaces.

8   Place the new thermostat in position (be sure to seat it securely in the recess or groove).
9   Apply RTV-type gasket sealant to both sides of a new gasket and place it in position on the housing.
10   Attach the housing to the engine and tighten the retaining bolts to the specified torque.
11   Reconnect the upper radiator hose to the thermostat housing. Reconnect any other hoses that were removed.
12   Fill the radiator to the specified level.
13   Start the engine, allow it to reach normal operating temperature and check for leaks.

## 4   Water pump — removal and installation

**Caution:** *The engine must be completely cool when this procedure is performed.*

1   Drain the radiator coolant into a suitable container. Disconnect the negative battery cable from the battery.
2   If so equipped, unbolt the fan shroud and separate it from the radiator.
3   Disconnect the hoses from the water pump.
4   Remove the drivebelt(s) and fan assembly.
5   Some models may require the removal of some air conditioning components to provide access to the water pump (Section 10).
6   Unbolt and remove the water pump. It may be necessary to grasp the pump securely and rock it back-and-forth to break the gasket seal.
7   Use a gasket scraper to clean all traces of gasket material from the water pump and engine surfaces.
8   **Note:** *Some later six-cylinder models use a serpentine drivebelt which drives the water pump in the reverse of normal rotation. Replacement water pumps and fans for these vehicles must be of the correct type and are marked REV or REVERSE.*
9   Apply a thin coat of RTV-type gasket sealer to the new gasket and install it on the water pump. Place the pump into position and secure it with the bolts. Make sure the accessory brackets are installed in their

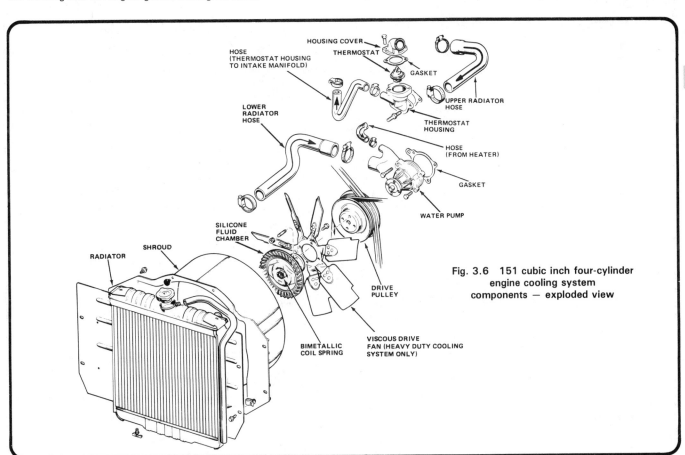

Fig. 3.6   151 cubic inch four-cylinder engine cooling system components — exploded view

original positions.
10  Tighten the water pump bolts to the specified torque.
11  Install the engine components in the reverse order of removal.
12  Adjust all drivebelts to the proper tension (Chapter 1).
13  Connect the negative battery cable and fill the radiator with the
specified coolant. Start the engine and allow it to idle until the upper
radiator hose gets hot. Check for leaks. With the engine hot (cap still
removed), fill the radiator with more coolant mixture until the level is
1/2-inch below the bottom of the filler neck. Install the radiator cap
and check the coolant level periodically during the next few miles of
driving, adding coolant as necessary.

## 5   Air conditioning system — check

   Maintenance consists of keeping the system charged with refrigerant,
the compressor drivebelt tensioned properly and making sure the condenser is free of leaves and debris. *Do not use a screen in front of the
condenser because it will restrict the air flow.* The receiver/drier features
a sight glass which provides a visual check of the refrigerant level. A
continuous stream of bubbles in the glass indicates the system is not
charged properly with refrigerant. Check the sight glass with the engine
running at a fast idle and with the air conditioning controls set for maximum cooling. Have an assistant cycle the fan blower switch from Off
to High. If a short burst of bubbles appears when the switch is turned
on and disappears when it is turned off, the system is properly charged.

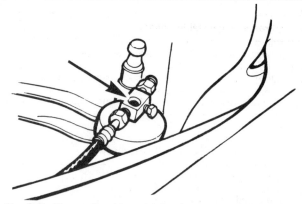

Fig. 3.7   The receiver/dryer (sight glass arrowed) is located
in the right front corner of the engine compartment (Sec 5)

If no bubbles are observed, the system is empty and must be taken
to a dealer or properly equipped shop for recharging.
   **Caution:** *Any work on the air conditioning system should be done
only after the system has been discharged by a dealer service department or properly equipped shop.* Some components, such as the compressor, can be unbolted and moved out of the way for access pur-
poses with the hoses still connected (Section 10).

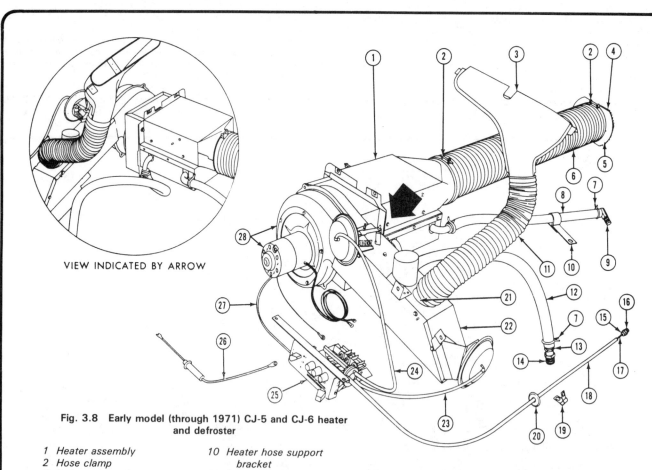

VIEW INDICATED BY ARROW

Fig. 3.8   Early model (through 1971) CJ-5 and CJ-6 heater
and defroster

|  |  |  |
|---|---|---|
| 1   Heater assembly | 10   Heater hose support bracket | 18   Heater control tube | 24   Heater control tube |
| 2   Hose clamp |  | 19   Clip | 25   Heater control assembly |
| 3   Defroster nozzle | 11   Defroster hose | 20   Grommet | 26   Fuse holder assembly |
| 4   Air duct screen | 12   Hot water hose | 21   Defroster bushing | 27   Control panel-to-heater |
| 5   Air duct and heater collar | 13   Heater nipple | 22   Heat distributor |       Bowden wire |
| 6   Air duct intake tube | 14   Reducing bushing |       assembly | 28   Blower and air inlet |
| 7   Hose clamp | 15   Inverted flared tube nut | 23   Heater control tube |       assembly |
| 8   Straight hot water hose | 16   Tube nut connector |  |  |
| 9   Heater tube elbow | 17   Heater control tube |  |  |

## 6 Antifreeze — general information

It is recommended that the cooling system be filled with a water/ethylene glycol based antifreeze solution which will give protection down to at least −20°F at all times. This provides protection against corrosion and increases the coolant boiling point. When handling antifreeze, do not spill it on the vehicle's paint, since it will cause damage if not removed immediately.

The cooling system should be drained, flushed and refilled at least every other year. The use of antifreeze solutions for periods of longer than two years is likely to cause damage and encourage the formation of rust and scale in the system.

Before adding antifreeze to the system, check all hose connections and the tightness of the cylinder head bolts, since antifreeze tends to search out and leak through even the most minute openings.

The exact mixture of antifreeze to water which you should use depends upon the relative weather conditions. The mixture should contain at least 50 percent antifreeze. The mixture should never contain more than 70 percent antifreeze.

## 7 Radiator — servicing

1   The radiator should be kept free of obstructions such as leaves, paper, insects, etc. which could affect cooling efficiency.
2   Periodically inspect the radiator for bent cooling fins, signs of coolant leakage and cracks around the upper and lower tanks. Carefully straighten any bent fins, using the blade of a screwdriver.
3   Check the filler neck sealing surface for dents, which could affect the sealing effectiveness of the radiator cap. Check the pressure rating of the cap and have it tested by a service station.
4   The radiator can be flushed as described in Chapter 1.

5   Any necessary radiator repairs should be performed by a reputable radiator repair shop.

## 8 Heater system — general information

These models are equipped with heater/defroster units which use a blower motor to circulate air through a duct system under the dash. Engine coolant directed by valves through the heater core provides heat for the system.

Air is drawn through the cowl intake into the heater core and duct system. A system of doors controls air mixture and movement within the ducts.

The various systems used are basically similar and component replacement can be accomplished with simple hand tools and the help of the accompanying illustrations. *Always disconnect the negative battery cable before beginning work.* Also, prior to removing the heater core, the cooling system should be cold to avoid the possibility of burns. Drain the coolant level to below the heater core.

## 9 Coolant temperature sending unit — removal and installation

**Caution:** *The engine must be completely cool when this procedure is performed.*

1   If the coolant temperature sending unit has been determined to be faulty, obtain a replacement.
2   Disconnect the wire from the unit.
3   Apply sealant to the threads of the replacement unit.
4   Use a wrench to remove the old unit and immediately install the new one. Because the unit threads into a coolant passage, there will be some coolant spillage. Check the level after the replacement has been installed.

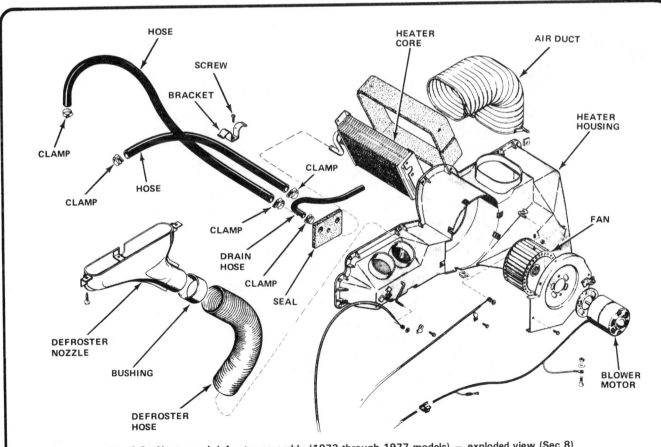

Fig. 3.9  Heater and defroster assembly (1973 through 1977 models) — exploded view (Sec 8)

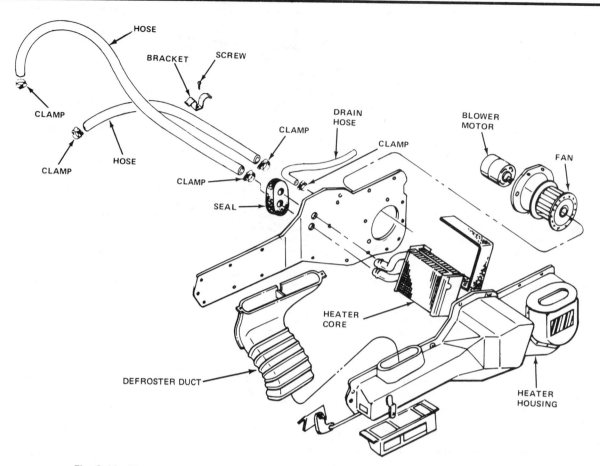

Fig. 3.10   Heater and defroster assembly (1978 through 1981 models) — exploded view (Sec 8)

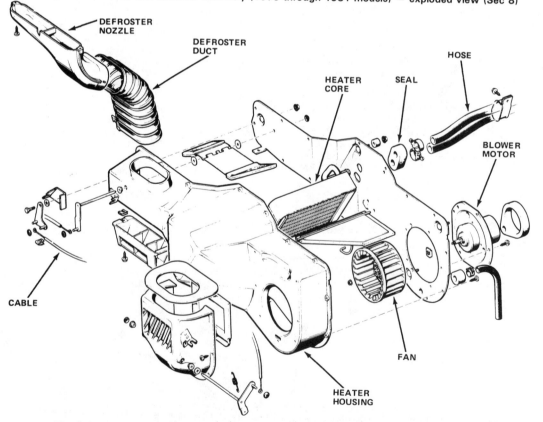

Fig. 3.11   1982 and 1983 model heater assembly components — exploded view (Sec 8)

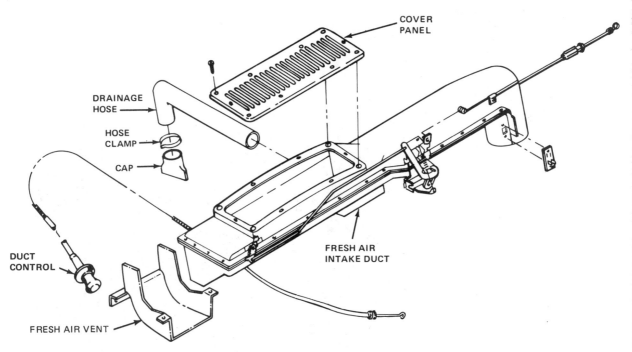

Fig. 3.12  Later model air intake assembly components — exploded view (Sec 8)

Fig. 3.13  F- and L-head engine coolant temperature
sending unit location (Sec 9)

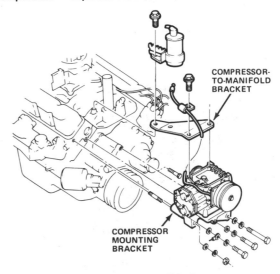

Fig. 3.14  V8 engine air conditioning compressor
installation (Sec 10)

**10  Air conditioning components — removal and installation**

**Caution:** *The air conditioning system is under high pressure and should be discharged by a dealer service department or air conditioning technician before any work is performed or hoses disconnected.*

1  Some components can be unbolted and moved out of the way to provide access with the hoses still connected. Do not stretch or pinch the hoses during these operations.

*Compressor*

2  Disconnect the negative battery cable from the battery.
3  Have the system discharged, disconnect the lines and plug the openings.
4  *On V8 models,* disconnect the compressor clutch wire and loosen and remove the drivebelts. On some models it will be necessary to remove the alternator and the coil. Unbolt the compressor and mounting bracket and remove them as an assembly.
5  *On six-cylinder models,* remove the compressor and alternator drivebelts. Remove the alternator adjusting bolt and upper mounting bolt and loosen the lower mounting bolt. Remove the idler assembly. Remove the retaining bolts and separate the compressor from the engine.
6  *On 1981 through 1983 six-cylinder models* using the serpentine drivebelt, remove the drivebelt and alternator. Unbolt and remove the compressor from the engine mounting bracket.
7  Installation on all models is the reverse of the removal procedure. Adjust the drivebelt tension and have the air conditioning system recharged. Connect the negative battery cable.

*Condenser and receiver/dryer assembly*

8  With the system discharged, drain the radiator, remove the fan shroud and radiator (Section 2) and disconnect the pressure line from the condenser. Make sure all disconnected lines and hoses are plugged.
9  Remove the retaining bolts and tilt the bottom of the condenser toward the engine.
10  From under the vehicle, disconnect the evaporator hose at the receiver/dryer.

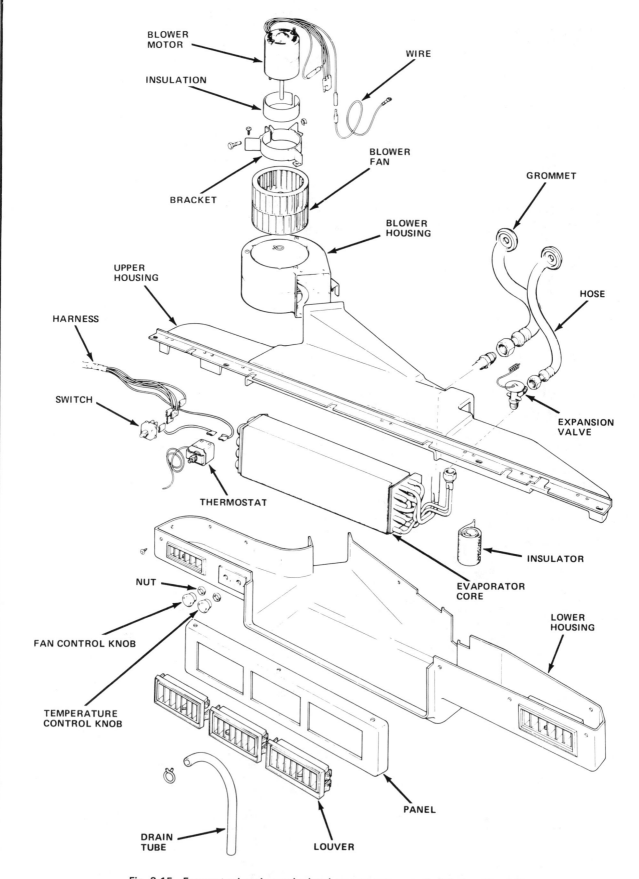

Fig. 3.15  Evaporator housing and related components — exploded view (Sec 10)

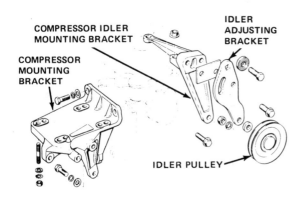

Fig. 3.16 Typical 49-state in-line six-cylinder air conditioning compressor installation (Sec 10)

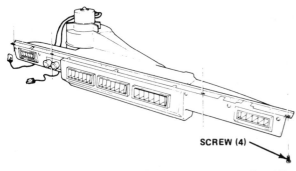

Fig. 3.17 Evaporator housing panel installation (Sec 10)

11 Remove the condenser and receiver/dryer assembly from the vehicle.
12 To install, place the condenser in position and connect the evaporator hose to the receiver/dryer. Install the retaining bolts and connect the pressure line to the condenser.
13 Install the radiator, fan and shroud.
14 Fill the radiator with the specified coolant and have the air conditioning system recharged.

### Receiver/dryer

15 Remove the condenser as described above and disconnect the evaporator and condenser lines at the receiver/dryer.
16 Remove the screws and separate the receiver/dryer from the condenser.
17 Installation is the reverse of removal.

### Evaporator housing assembly

18 With the system discharged, disconnect the inlet line from the compressor and the receiver/dryer-to-evaporator hose.
19 Remove the hose clamps and the dash grommet retaining screws, followed by the evaporator housing-to-instrument panel and mounting bracket screws.
20 Lower the housing from the instrument panel and pull the hoses through the opening.
21 The evaporator assembly components can now be removed. The blower motor can be replaced without discharging the air conditioning system.
22 To install, push the hoses up through the grommet opening and then push the grommet into place. Install the screws.
23 Raise the evaporator into position and install the retaining screws.
24 Install the hose clamps and the grommet retaining screws.
25 Connect the receiver/dryer-to-evaporator hose and inlet-to-compressor line.
26 Have the system recharged.

3

# Chapter 4   Fuel and exhaust systems

*Refer to Chapter 13 for Specifications and information related to 1984 through 1986 models*

## Contents

Air filter replacement . . . . . . . . . . . . . . . . . . . . . . .   Chapter 1
Autolite/Motorcraft 2100 and 2150 carburetors
  (V8 engine)—overhaul and adjustment . . . . . . . . . . . . . .   13
Carburetors — application . . . . . . . . . . . . . . . . . . . . . .   7
Carburetor choke check (late models only) . . . . . . .   Chapter 1
Carburetor mounting torque check . . . . . . . . . . . .   Chapter 1
Carburetor — removal and installation . . . . . . . . . . . . . . . .   9
Carburetor — servicing . . . . . . . . . . . . . . . . . . . . . . .   8
Carter BBD carburetor (in-line six-cylinder engine) — overhaul
  and adjustment . . . . . . . . . . . . . . . . . . . . . . . .   14
Carter YF carburetor (F- and L-head four-cylinder
  engines) — overhaul and adjustment . . . . . . . . . . . .   10
Carter YF carburetor (in-line six-cylinder engine) — overhaul
  and adjustment . . . . . . . . . . . . . . . . . . . . . . . .   11
Engine idle speed adjustment . . . . . . . . . . . . . . . .   Chapter 1
Exhaust heat valve check . . . . . . . . . . . . . . . . . .   Chapter 1
Exhaust system — check and component replacement . . . . .   18
Fuel filter replacement . . . . . . . . . . . . . . . . . . . . .   Chapter 1
Fuel lines and hoses — check and replacement . . . . . . . . . .   6
Fuel pump — check . . . . . . . . . . . . . . . . . . . . . . . . . .   4
Fuel pump — general information . . . . . . . . . . . . . . . . . . .   3
Fuel pump — removal and installation . . . . . . . . . . . . . . . .   5
Fuel system check . . . . . . . . . . . . . . . . . . . . . . .   Chapter 1
Fuel tank — removal and installation . . . . . . . . . . . . . . . .   16
Fuel tank — cleaning and repair . . . . . . . . . . . . . . . . . .   17
General information . . . . . . . . . . . . . . . . . . . . . . . . .   1
Oil bath-type air cleaner service . . . . . . . . . . . . .   Chapter 1
Rochester 2G carburetor (V6 engine) — overhaul and
  adjustment . . . . . . . . . . . . . . . . . . . . . . . . . .   12
Rochester 2SE and E2SE carburetors (151 cu in four-cylinder
  engine) — overhaul and adjustment . . . . . . . . . . . . . .   15
Throttle linkage — check and adjustment . . . . . . . . . . . . . .   2

## Specifications

### Carter YF Carburetor *(F- and L-head four-cylinder engines)*

L-head engine — float level
  CJ-2A, CJ-3A . . . . . . . . . . . . . . . . . . . . . . . . .   3/8 in
  CJ-3B, CJ-5, CJ-6 . . . . . . . . . . . . . . . . . . . . . . .   5/16 in
F-head engine (non-emission controlled)
  Float level
    Early (CJ-2B) . . . . . . . . . . . . . . . . . . . . . .   5/16 in
    Late (CJ-3B, CJ-5, CJ-6 . . . . . . . . . . . . . . . . .   17/64 in
  Dashpot setting . . . . . . . . . . . . . . . . . . . . . . . .   1/8 in
F-head engine (emission controlled)
  Float level . . . . . . . . . . . . . . . . . . . . . . . . . .   17/64 in
  Dashpot setting . . . . . . . . . . . . . . . . . . . . . . . .   1/8 in

### Rochester 2G carburetor

Non-emission controlled
  Float level . . . . . . . . . . . . . . . . . . . . . . . . . .   1-3/32 in
  Float drop . . . . . . . . . . . . . . . . . . . . . . . . . . .   1-7/8 in
  Accelerator pump rod adjustment . . . . . . . . . . . . . . . .   1-5/32 in
  Initial idle *speed* adjustment screw setting . . . . . . . . . .   3 turns in
  Initial idle *mixture* screw setting . . . . . . . . . . . . . .   2 turns out
  Dashpot setting . . . . . . . . . . . . . . . . . . . . . . . .   1/8 in
Emission controlled
  Float level . . . . . . . . . . . . . . . . . . . . . . . . . .   1-5/32 in
  Float drop . . . . . . . . . . . . . . . . . . . . . . . . . . .   1-7/8 in
  Accelerator pump rod adjustment . . . . . . . . . . . . . . . .   1-5/32 in
  Initial idle *speed* adjustment screw setting . . . . . . . . . .   3 turns in
  Initial idle *mixture* screw setting . . . . . . . . . . . . . .   2 turns out
  Dashpot setting . . . . . . . . . . . . . . . . . . . . . . . .   1/8 in

## Carter YF carburetor *(in-line six-cylinder engine)*

| | |
|---|---|
| Float level | |
|   1973 | 0.450 in |
|   1974 through 1978 | 0.476 in |
| Float drop | |
|   1973 | 1.25 in |
|   1974 through 1978 | 1.38 in |
| Initial choke plate-to-air horn clearance | 0.215 in |
| Fast idle cam setting | |
|   1973 | Index mark (choke closed) |
|   1974 through 1978 | 0.195 in |
| Choke unloader | 0.275 in |
| Automatic choke setting | |
|   Standard | 1 notch rich |
|   Altitude compensator equipped | 2 notches rich |
| Dashpot setting | 0.075 to 0.095 in |
| Fast idle speed | 1600 rpm |
| Idle drop | |
|   Automatic transmission | 25 rpm |
|   Manual transmission | 50 rpm |

## Autolite/Motorcraft 2100 and 2150 carburetors

| | |
|---|---|
| Dry float level | |
|   1973 | 3/8 in |
|   1974 and 1975 | 0.400 in |
|   1976 through 1979 | 0.555 in |
|   1980 and 1981 | 0.375 in |
| Wet float level | |
|   1973 | 3/4 in |
|   1974 and 1975 | 0.78 in |
|   1976 through 1981 | 0.93 in |
| Initial choke plate clearance | |
|   1973 through 1975 | 0.130 in |
|   1976 through 1978 | |
|     Manual transmission | 0.130 in |
|     Automatic transmission | 0.140 in |
|   1979 through 1981 | |
|     Manual transmission (49-states) | 0.125 in |
|     Automatic transmission (49-states) | 0.128 in |
|     California (all models) | 0.120 in |
| Fast idle cam setting | |
|   1973 through 1975 | 0.130 in |
|   1976 through 1978 | |
|     Manual transmission | 0.120 in |
|     Automatic transmission | 0.126 in |
|   1979 through 1981 | 0.113 in |
| Automatic choke setting | 1-1/2 to 2-1/2 notches rich |
| Dashpot | |
|   1973 and 1974 | 0.140 in |
|   1975 | 0.095 in |
|   1976 | 0.075 in |
|   1977 | 0.093 in |
| Choke unloader | 0.250 in |
| Bowl vent clearance | 0.120 in |
| Fast idle speed | 1400 to 1600 rpm |

## Carter BBD carburetor *(In-line six-cylinder engine)*

| | |
|---|---|
| Float level | 0.25 in |
| Vacuum piston gap | |
|   1977 and 1978 | 0.040 in |
|   1979 through 1983 | 0.035 in |
| Initial choke plate clearance | |
|   1977 and 1978 | 0.128 in |
|   1979 | |
|     Carburetor numbers 8185, 8187, 8195 | 0.140 in |
|     Carburetor numbers 8186, 8188 | 0.150 in |
|     Carburetor number 8229 | 0.128 in |
|   1980 | |
|     Carburetor numbers 8256, 8257, 8253 | 0.128 in |
|     Carburetor number 8254 | 0.120 in |
|     Carburetor number 8255 | 0.140 in |
|     Carburetor number 8277 | 0.116 in |

**4**

## Carter BBD carburetor *(In-line six-cylinder engine)* (continued)

| | |
|---|---|
| 1981 through 1983 | |
|   Carburetor numbers 8302, 8303, 8306, 8307, 8338 . . . | 0.140 in |
|   Carburetor number 8311 . . . . . . . . . . . . . . . . . . . . . . . | 0.120 in |
|   Carburetor number 8351 . . . . . . . . . . . . . . . . . . . . . . . | 0.130 in |
|   Carburetor number 8349 . . . . . . . . . . . . . . . . . . . . . . . | 0.128 in |
| Fast idle cam setting . . . . . . . . . . . . . . . . . . . . . . . . . . . . . | 0.095 in |
| Choke cover setting | |
| 1977 and 1978 . . . . . . . . . . . . . . . . . . . . . . . . . . . . . . | 2 notches rich |
| 1979 . . . . . . . . . . . . . . . . . . . . . . . . . . . . . . . . . . . . . . . | 1/2 to 1-1/2 notches rich |
| 1980 | |
|   Carburetor numbers 8253, 8254, 8255, 8256, 8257 . . . | 2 notches rich |
|   Carburetor number 8277 . . . . . . . . . . . . . . . . . . . . . . . | 1/2 to 1-1/2 notches rich |
| 1981 . . . . . . . . . . . . . . . . . . . . . . . . . . . . . . . . . . . . . . . | 1 notch rich |
| 1982 and 1983 | |
|   Carburetor numbers 8338, 8339, 8360, 8362, 8364, | |
|     8367 . . . . . . . . . . . . . . . . . . . . . . . . . . . . . . . . . . | 1 notch rich |
|   Carburetor number 8349 . . . . . . . . . . . . . . . . . . . . . . . | 2 notches rich |
|   Carburetor number 8351 . . . . . . . . . . . . . . . . . . . . . . . | − 1/2 to +1-1/2 notches rich |
| Choke unloader . . . . . . . . . . . . . . . . . . . . . . . . . . . . . . . | 0.280 in |
| Accelerator pump setting | |
| 1978 . . . . . . . . . . . . . . . . . . . . . . . . . . . . . . . . . . . . . . . | 0.440 in |
| 1979 and 1980 | |
|   Carburetor numbers 8185, 8187, 8195, 8253, 8255, | |
|     8256 . . . . . . . . . . . . . . . . . . . . . . . . . . . . . . . . . . | 0.470 in |
|   Carburetor numbers 8186, 8188, 8229, 8254, 8257, | |
|     8277 . . . . . . . . . . . . . . . . . . . . . . . . . . . . . . . . . . | 0.520 in |
| 1981 through 1983 . . . . . . . . . . . . . . . . . . . . . . . . . . . | 0.520 in |
| Fast idle speed setting | |
| 1977 and 1978 . . . . . . . . . . . . . . . . . . . . . . . . . . . . . . | 1700 rpm |
| 1979 | |
|   Carburetor numbers 8185, 8187, 8195 (automatic) . . . . | 1600 rpm |
|   Carburetor numbers 8186, 8188, 8195, 8229 (manual) . . | 1500 rpm |
| 1980 | |
|   Carburetor numbers 8253, 8255, 8256 (automatic) . . . . | 1850 rpm |
|   Carburetor numbers 8254, 8255, 8257, 8277 (manual) . . | 1700 rpm |
| 1981 through 1983 | |
|   Carburetor numbers 8302, 8338, 8349, 8360, 8362 | |
|     (automatic) . . . . . . . . . . . . . . . . . . . . . . . . . . . . . . | 1850 rpm |
|   Carburetor numbers 8303, 8311, 8339, 8349, 8351, | |
|     8364, 8367 (manual) . . . . . . . . . . . . . . . . . . . . . . . | 1700 rpm |

## Rochester 2SE carburetor

| | |
|---|---|
| Float level | |
| 1980 . . . . . . . . . . . . . . . . . . . . . . . . . . . . . . . . . . . . . . . | 0.216 in |
| 1981 | |
|   Carburetor number 17081790 . . . . . . . . . . . . . . . . . . . | 0.208 in |
|   Carburetor number 17081791 . . . . . . . . . . . . . . . . . . . | 0.256 in |
| 1982 . . . . . . . . . . . . . . . . . . . . . . . . . . . . . . . . . . . . . . . | 0.169 in |
| 1983 . . . . . . . . . . . . . . . . . . . . . . . . . . . . . . . . . . . . . . . | 0.216 in |
| Pump stem height | |
| 1980 . . . . . . . . . . . . . . . . . . . . . . . . . . . . . . . . . . . . . . . | 0.500 in |
| 1981 through 1983 . . . . . . . . . . . . . . . . . . . . . . . . . . . | 0.128 in |
| Fast idle cam adjustment | |
| 1980 . . . . . . . . . . . . . . . . . . . . . . . . . . . . . . . . . . . . . . . | 18° |
| 1981 . . . . . . . . . . . . . . . . . . . . . . . . . . . . . . . . . . . . . . . | 25° |
| 1982 and 1983 . . . . . . . . . . . . . . . . . . . . . . . . . . . . . . | 18° |
| Air valve link . . . . . . . . . . . . . . . . . . . . . . . . . . . . . . . . . | 2° |
| Primary vacuum break | |
| 1980 . . . . . . . . . . . . . . . . . . . . . . . . . . . . . . . . . . . . . . . | 20° |
| 1981 . . . . . . . . . . . . . . . . . . . . . . . . . . . . . . . . . . . . . . . | 19° |
| 1982 and 1983 . . . . . . . . . . . . . . . . . . . . . . . . . . . . . . | 21° |
| Unloader | |
| 1980 and 1981 . . . . . . . . . . . . . . . . . . . . . . . . . . . . . . | 32° |
| 1982 and 1983 . . . . . . . . . . . . . . . . . . . . . . . . . . . . . . | 34° |
| Secondary lockout | |
| 1980 . . . . . . . . . . . . . . . . . . . . . . . . . . . . . . . . . . . . . . . | 0.004 to 0.012 in |
| 1981 through 1983 | |
|   Carburetor number 17081791 . . . . . . . . . . . . . . . . . . . | 0.85 in |
|   Carburetor numbers 1708190, 17082380, 17082381 . . | 0.050 to 0.080 in |
| Choke coil lever plug gauge | |
|   Carburetor numbers 17080685, 17081791 . . . . . . . . . . | 0.85 in |
|   Carburetor numbers 17081790, 17082380, 17082381 . . . | 0.050 to 0.080 in |
| Fast idle speed | |
| 1980 . . . . . . . . . . . . . . . . . . . . . . . . . . . . . . . . . . . . . . . | 2400 rpm |

1981
    Carburetor number 17081790 . . . . . . . . . . . . . . . . . . . .    2400 rpm
    Carburetor number 17081791 . . . . . . . . . . . . . . . . . . . .    2600 rpm
1982 and 1983 . . . . . . . . . . . . . . . . . . . . . . . . . .    2400 rpm

## Rochester E2SE carburetor

Float level
    1980 and 1981 . . . . . . . . . . . . . . . . . . . . . . . . . .    7/32 in
    1982 . . . . . . . . . . . . . . . . . . . . . . . . . . . . . . .    0.169 in
    1983 . . . . . . . . . . . . . . . . . . . . . . . . . . . . . . .    0.138 in
Pump stem height
    1980 and 1981 . . . . . . . . . . . . . . . . . . . . . . . . . .    0.500 in
    1982 and 1983 . . . . . . . . . . . . . . . . . . . . . . . . . .    0.128 in
Fast idle cam adjustment . . . . . . . . . . . . . . . . . . . . . . .    18º
Air valve link . . . . . . . . . . . . . . . . . . . . . . . . . . . .    2º
Primary vacuum break
    1980 and 1981 . . . . . . . . . . . . . . . . . . . . . . . . . .    20º
    1982 and 1983 . . . . . . . . . . . . . . . . . . . . . . . . . .    19º
Unloader
    1980 and 1981 . . . . . . . . . . . . . . . . . . . . . . . . . .    32º
    1982 and 1983 . . . . . . . . . . . . . . . . . . . . . . . . . .    34º
Secondary lockout
    1980 and 1981 . . . . . . . . . . . . . . . . . . . . . . . . . .    0.004 to 0.012 in
    1982 and 1983 . . . . . . . . . . . . . . . . . . . . . . . . . .    0.050 to 0.080 in
Choke coil lever plug gauge
    1980 and 1981 . . . . . . . . . . . . . . . . . . . . . . . . . .    0.085 in
    1982 . . . . . . . . . . . . . . . . . . . . . . . . . . . . . . .    0.050 to 0.080 in
    1983 . . . . . . . . . . . . . . . . . . . . . . . . . . . . . . .    0.085 in
Fast idle speed setting
    1980 through 1982 . . . . . . . . . . . . . . . . . . . . . . . .    2400 rpm
    1983 . . . . . . . . . . . . . . . . . . . . . . . . . . . . . . .    2500 rpm

## Torque specifications

| | Ft-lb | Nm |
|---|---|---|
| Carburetor-to-intake manifold nuts | | |
|   F- and L-head four-cylinder | 10 to 16 | 14 to 22 |
|   V6 | 10 to 15 | 14 to 21 |
|   In-line six-cylinder | 12 to 19 | 16 to 25 |
|   V8 | 12 to 15 | 16 to 21 |
|   151 cu in four-cylinder | 10 to 16 | 14 to 22 |
| Fuel pump bolts | | |
|   F- and L-head four-cylinder | 13 to 17 | 18 to 23 |
|   V6 | 10 to 15 | 14 to 21 |
|   In-line six-cylinder | 13 to 19 | 17 to 25 |
|   V8 | 13 to 19 | 18 to 25 |
|   151 cu in four-cylinder | 12 to 18 | 16 to 24 |
| Exhaust pipe-to-manifold nuts | | |
|   F- and L-head four-cylinder | 29 to 35 | 39 to 47.5 |
|   V6 | 15 to 20 | 21 to 27 |
|   In-line six-cylinder | 18 to 28 | 24 to 38 |
|   V8 | 15 to 25 | 21 to 34 |
|   151 cu in four-cylinder | 34 to 40 | 47 to 54 |

4

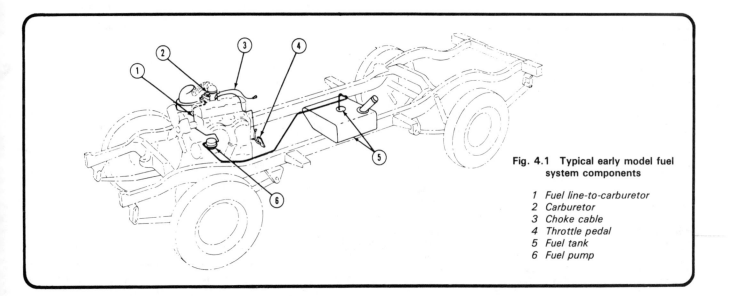

Fig. 4.1  Typical early model fuel
system components

1  Fuel line-to-carburetor
2  Carburetor
3  Choke cable
4  Throttle pedal
5  Fuel tank
6  Fuel pump

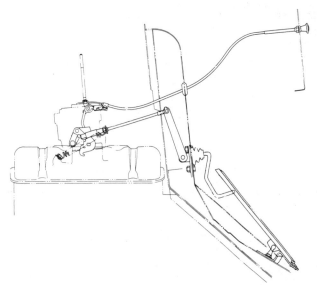

**Fig. 4.2   Typical early model throttle linkage component layout (Sec 2)**

## 1   General information

The fuel system consists of the fuel tank, a fuel pump which draws fuel to the carburetor, and associated hoses, lines and filters.

The exhaust system is composed of pipes, heat shields and mufflers for carrying exhaust gases from the engine to the rear of the vehicle. Later models incorporate catalytic converters into the system to reduce exhaust emissions. Catalytic converter-equipped vehicles must use unleaded fuel only.

## 2   Throttle linkage — check and adjustment

1   Periodically check the full length of the throttle linkage for wear, looseness and damage.
2   With the engine off, observe the linkage as an assistant pushes the throttle pedal down completely and releases it. Watch the action of the linkage to determine if there are any worn joints or bent links. Make sure the return springs are securely seated and not stretched. Replace any worn or damaged components with new ones.
3   Adjust the linkage if the throttle does not open completely.
4   Lubricate the linkage joints with a few drops of engine oil or spray lubricants such as graphite or silicone.

## 3   Fuel pump — general information

All models are equipped with mechanical fuel pumps which are actuated by an eccentric on the camshaft.

Later model pumps are sealed and must be replaced as a unit if a fault develops. Early model pumps can be disassembled, although it is always a good idea to replace a faulty unit with a new one.

The fuel sediment bowl or filter screen on early model fuel pumps should be removed and cleaned periodically.

Early model F- and L-head engines are equipped with fuel pumps which incorporate a vacuum pump to actuate the windshield wipers.

## 4   Fuel pump — check

**Caution:** *Gasoline is extremely flammable and extra precautions must be taken when working on any part of the fuel system. Do not smoke or allow open flames or bare light bulbs near the work area. Also, do not work in a garage if a natural gas-type appliance with a pilot light is present.*

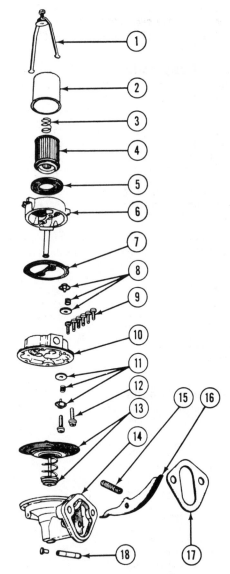

**Fig. 4.3   F-head four-cylinder engine fuel pump components — exploded view (Sec 3)**

| | |
|---|---|
| 1   Retainer | 10   Valve housing |
| 2   Bowl | 11   Valve assembly |
| 3   Spring | 12   Screws |
| 4   Filter | 13   Diaphragm and oil seal |
| 5   Gasket | 14   Pump body |
| 6   Pump body | 15   Cam lever spring |
| 7   Gasket | 16   Cam lever |
| 8   Valve assembly | 17   Gasket |
| 9   Screws | 18   Cam lever pin and plug |

1   Inspect the fuel pump for signs of leakage. If the pump itself is leaking, replace it with a new one (Section 5). If the inlet or outlet connections are leaking, tighten or replace them as necessary.
2   To check the fuel pump operation, disconnect the outlet hose and route it into a suitable container.
3   Disconnect and ground the ignition coil wire and turn the engine over with the starter while observing the fuel pump outlet hose. The pump should produce definite spurts of fuel. If it does not or if very little fuel is seen, replace the pump with a new one.

## 5   Fuel pump — removal and installation

**Caution:** *Gasoline is extremely flammable and extra precautions must*

*be taken when working on any part of the fuel system. Do not smoke
or allow open flames or bare light bulbs near the work area. Also, do
not work in a garage if a natural gas-type appliance with a pilot light
is present.*

1    Place clean rags or wadded-up newspapers under the fuel pump
to catch any gasoline which may be spilled during removal.
2    To remove the pump, detach the fuel inlet and outlet (as well as
all other) lines. Use two wrenches to prevent damage to the pump and
flare-type fittings.
3    Remove the mounting bolts, pump and gasket.
4    Remove all traces of gasket material from the pump and engine
mating surfaces.
5    Coat both sides of a new gasket with RTV-type gasket sealant and
place the gasket in position on the pump.
6    Place the pump in position, making sure the actuating lever seats
securely against the camshaft eccentric. Install the mounting bolts.
7    Connect the fuel and other hoses or lines to the fuel pump.
8    Start the engine and check carefully for leaks.

## 6   Fuel lines and hoses — check and replacement

**Caution:** *Gasoline is extremely flammable and extra precautions must
be taken when working on any part of the fuel system. Do not smoke
or allow open flames or bare light bulbs near the work area. Also, do
not work in a garage if a natural gas-type appliance with a pilot light
is present.*

1    All fuel lines, hoses and connections should be inspected periodically for damage, leaks and deterioration.
2    Check all rubber hoses for cracks, splits and signs of hardening.
Partially kink or squeeze the hoses to see if cracks appear. Grasp each
hose at the points of connection to make sure they aren't brittle or
hardened and move them back-and-forth to check for cracks.
3    Look for areas where oil or grease have accumulated, wipe the hose
clean and inspect for damage. Petroleum products break down the rubber and make it soft.
4    Measure the length of each hose to be replaced and cut off a short
(no more than 1/2-inch) piece from the end. With the length measurement information and sample pieces, go to an automotive parts store
to obtain replacement hose. The sample piece will make the selection
of the proper inside diameter hose easier. It is a good idea to obtain
replacement screw-type hose clamps to replace any original equipment
clamps which are bent or damaged.
5    Inspect the metal fuel lines to make sure they aren't bent, dented,
cracked or leaking. Check the flare nut connections for tightness, using two wrenches to avoid damage to the line and component. Be
careful not to overtighten them. Replacement fuel line and fittings are
also available at automotive parts stores. A tube-flaring tool will be
necessary for installing the fittings. Use only steel tubing for the fuel
lines, as copper or aluminum tubing does not have enough durability
to withstand normal operating conditions.
6    If only one section of a metal fuel line is damaged, it can be cut out
and replaced with a piece of rubber hose. The rubber hose should be
cut four inches longer than the section it is replacing so there will be
about two inches of overlap between the rubber and metal tubing at
either end of the section. Screw-type hose clamps should be used to
secure both ends of the repaired section.
7    If a section of metal line longer than six inches is being removed,
use a combination of metal tubing and rubber hose so the rubber hose
lengths will not be longer than ten inches. **Caution:** *Never use rubber
hose within four (4) inches of any part of the exhaust system.*

## 7   Carburetors — application

1    The models covered in this manual were equipped with a variety
of carburetors over their long production life.
2    The Carter YF carburetor was used on the F- and L-head four-
cylinder and some models of the in-line six-cylinder engine.
3    Later models of the six-cylinder engine were equipped with the
Carter BBD carburetor.
4    The V6 engine was equipped with the Rochester 2G carburetor.
5    V8 engines use the Autolite/Motorcraft 2100 and the very similar
2150 carburetor. The 2150 differs from the 2100 in that it incor-

porates an altitude compensation device.
6    The 151 cubic-inch four-cylinder engine is equipped with the
Rochester 2SE on 49-state models and the electronic E2SE version
in California.

## 8   Carburetor — servicing

**Caution:** *Gasoline is extremely flammable and extra precautions must
be taken when working on any part of the fuel system. Do not smoke
or allow open flames or bare light bulbs near the work area. Also, do
not work in a garage if a natural gas-type appliance with a pilot light
is present.*

1    A thorough road test and check of carburetor adjustments should
be done before any major carburetor service. Specifications for some
adjustments are listed on the vehicle Emissions Control Information
label found in the engine compartment.
2    Some performance complaints directed at the carburetor are actually a result of loose, misadjusted or malfunctioning engine or electrical components. Others develop when vacuum hoses leak, are disconnected or are incorrectly routed. The proper approach to analyzing carburetor problems should include a routine check of the following areas:
3    Inspect all vacuum hoses and actuators for leaks and proper installation (see Chapter 6, *Emissions control systems*).
4    Tighten the intake manifold nuts and carburetor mounting nuts
evenly and securely.
5    Perform a cylinder compression test (Chapter 1).
6    Clean or replace the spark plugs as necessary (Chapter 1).
7    Check the condition of the spark plug wires (Chapter 1).
8    Inspect the ignition primary wires and check the vacuum advance
operation. Replace any defective parts.
9    Check the ignition timing with the vacuum advance line disconnected and plugged.
10   Adjust the carburetor idle mixture as described in the appropriate
Section.
11   Check the fuel pump operation as described in Section 4.
12   Inspect the heat control valve in the air cleaner for proper operation (refer to Chapter 1).
13   Remove the carburetor air filter element and blow out any dirt with
compressed air. If the filter is extremely dirty, replace it with a new one.
14   Inspect the crankcase ventilation system (see Chapter 6).
15   Carburetor problems usually show up as flooding, hard starting,
stalling, severe backfiring, poor acceleration and lack of response to
idle mixture screw adjustments. A carburetor that is leaking fuel and/or
covered with wet-looking deposits definitely needs attention.
16   Diagnosing carburetor problems may require that the engine be
started and run with the air cleaner removed. While running the engine
without the air cleaner, it is possible that it could backfire. A backfiring situation is likely to occur if the carburetor is malfunctioning, but
removal of the air cleaner alone can lean the air/fuel mixture enough
to produce an engine backfire.
17   Once it is determined that the carburetor is indeed at fault, it should
be disassembled, cleaned and reassembled using new parts where
necessary. Before dismantling the carburetor, make sure you have a
carburetor rebuild kit, which will include all necessary gaskets and internal parts, carburetor cleaning solvent and some means of blowing
out all the internal passages of the carburetor. To do the job properly,
you will also need a clean place to work and plenty of time and patience.
18   It should be noted that it is often easier and more convenient to
replace the carburetor with a rebuilt unit instead of overhauling the
original carburetor. If a rebuilt carburetor is purchased, be sure to deal
with a reputable auto parts store.

## 9   Carburetor — removal and installation

**Caution:** *Gasoline is extremely flammable and extra precautions must
be taken when working on any part of the fuel system. Do not smoke
or allow open flames or bare light bulbs near the work area. Also, do
not work, in a garage if a natural gas-type appliance with a pilot light
is present.*

1    Remove the air cleaner assembly.
2    Mark or tag all hoses and lines connected to the carburetor to
simplify reinstallation.

**4**

3   Disconnect the throttle linkage, vacuum hoses, choke linkage and other hoses and wires from the carburetor.
4   Remove the retaining nuts and lift the carburetor from the manifold.
5   Carefully clean the gasket surfaces of the carburetor, spacer or gasket and intake manifold. Inspect them for nicks and damage which could affect carburetor-to-manifold sealing. Replace the gasket or spacer with a new one if it is bent, damaged or distorted.
6   Place the carburetor and spacer or gasket in position and install the retaining nuts. Tighten the nuts evenly and securely in a crisscross pattern.
7   Connect the throttle linkage, vacuum hoses, fuel lines and other hoses and wires to the carburetor.
8   Install the air cleaner assembly.

## 10  Carter YF carburetor (F- and L-head four-cylinder engines) — overhaul and adjustment

1   Remove the fast idle connector rod by prying the pin spring and clevis clip free.
2   Remove the air horn and bowl cover retaining screws and the choke tube clamp assembly.
3   Remove the air horn and gasket.
4   Remove the ball check valve retainer ring, turn the air horn assembly over and tap it lightly to dislodge the ball check valve and retainer.
5   Loosen the throttle shaft arm-to-shaft locking screw and remove the arm and pump connector link.
6   Remove the retaining screws and lift the diaphragm assembly from the carburetor body.
7   On early models, remove the pump intake strainer housing with the tip of a knife blade.
8   With the air horn inverted, remove the pin and float. Turn the air horn over and catch the needle pin and seat.
9   Remove the metering rod jet and low speed jet. Do not attempt to remove any of the pressed-in components such as the nozzle, pump jet or air bleed.
10  Remove the mounting screws and separate the flange assembly from the body.

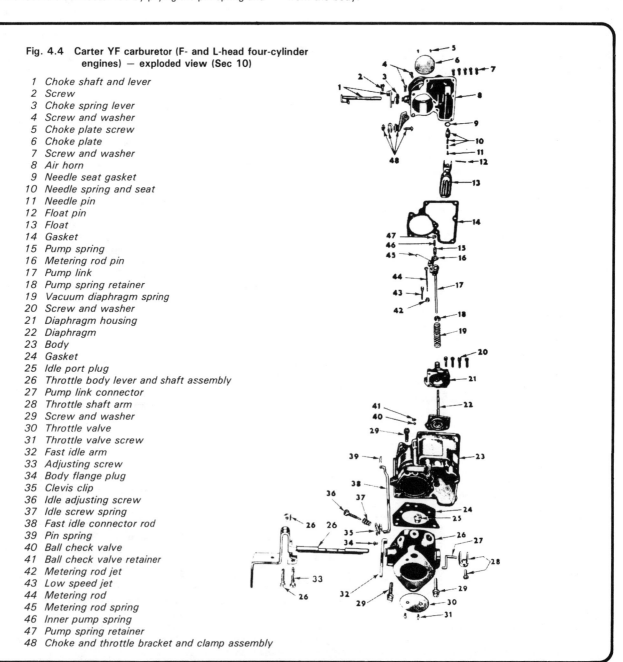

Fig. 4.4  Carter YF carburetor (F- and L-head four-cylinder engines) — exploded view (Sec 10)

1   Choke shaft and lever
2   Screw
3   Choke spring lever
4   Screw and washer
5   Choke plate screw
6   Choke plate
7   Screw and washer
8   Air horn
9   Needle seat gasket
10  Needle spring and seat
11  Needle pin
12  Float pin
13  Float
14  Gasket
15  Pump spring
16  Metering rod pin
17  Pump link
18  Pump spring retainer
19  Vacuum diaphragm spring
20  Screw and washer
21  Diaphragm housing
22  Diaphragm
23  Body
24  Gasket
25  Idle port plug
26  Throttle body lever and shaft assembly
27  Pump link connector
28  Throttle shaft arm
29  Screw and washer
30  Throttle valve
31  Throttle valve screw
32  Fast idle arm
33  Adjusting screw
34  Body flange plug
35  Clevis clip
36  Idle adjusting screw
37  Idle screw spring
38  Fast idle connector rod
39  Pin spring
40  Ball check valve
41  Ball check valve retainer
42  Metering rod jet
43  Low speed jet
44  Metering rod
45  Metering rod spring
46  Inner pump spring
47  Pump spring retainer
48  Choke and throttle bracket and clamp assembly

11 Remove the idle adjustment screw, spring, idle port rivet, throttle lever assembly, washer, fast idle arm, throttle plate and shaft assembly.
12 Pry out the seal retainer and remove the throttle shaft seal. Do not remove the vacuum passage orifice, which is pressed into place.
13 Remove the choke valve screws, unhook the choke spring and slide the shaft out of the housing.
14 The carburetor is now completely disassembled and should be cleaned and inspected for wear. After the carburetor components have been soaked in solvent to remove dirt, gum and carbon deposits, they should be rinsed in kerosene and dried, preferably with compressed air. Do not use a wire brush to clean the carburetor and clean all passages with compressed air rather than wire or drill bits, which could enlarge them. Inspect the throttle and choke shafts for grooves, wear and excessive looseness. Check the throttle and choke plates for nicks and smoothness of operation. Inspect the carburetor body and components for cracks. Check the floats for leaks by submerging them in water which has been heated to just below the boiling point. Leaks will be indicated by the appearance of bubbles. Check the float arm needle contact surface for grooves. If the grooves are light, polish the needle contact surface with crocus cloth or steel wool. Replace the floats if the shafts are badly worn. Inspect the gasket mating surfaces for burrs and nicks. Replace any distorted springs and all screws and bolts with stripped heads.
15 Install the throttle shaft seal and retainer in the flange casting.
16 Install the fast idle arm, washer and lever assembly on the throttle shaft. Slide the shaft into position and install the throttle valve.
17 Install the idle port rivet plug and the idle adjusting screw and spring.
18 Attach the flange assembly to the body casting, using a new gasket.
19 Install the low speed jet assembly.
20 On early models, install the pump intake strainer in the pump diaphragm housing and press it carefully into the recess. Replace the strainer with a new one if it is even slightly damaged.
21 Install the pump diaphragm assembly in the housing and then install the lower diaphragm spring and retainer.
22 Install the pump lifter link, metering rod arm, upper pump spring and retainer, followed by the metering rod jet.

23 Insert the screws into the housing while making sure the edges of the diaphragm are not wrinkled. Lower the assembly into place and tighten the screws evenly, following a crisscross pattern, until they are secure.
24 Install the throttle shaft seal, dust seal washer and shaft seal spring on the shaft.
25 Install the pump connector link in the throttle arm assembly and then install the shaft arm assembly on the throttle shaft. Guide the connector link into the pump lifter link hole. Make sure the linkage does not bind in any position. If there is binding, loosen the clamp screw in the throttle arm, adjust it slightly and retighten the screw.
26 Install the pump check disc, retainer and lock ring.
27 Install the metering rod and pin spring and connect the metering rod spring.
28 Make sure the flat on the metering rod arm is parallel to the flat on the pump lifter link. Seat the throttle and press down on the upper end of the diaphragm shaft until the diaphragm bottoms in the vacuum chamber. Push down on the metering rod to make sure it seats properly in the casting. If it does not seat properly or seats before the rod arm makes contact with the lifter link flat, adjust it by bending the lip on the metering rod arm.
29 Install the needle seat and gasket assembly, needle float and pin. The stop shoulder on the float pin must be facing away from the carburetor bore.
30 With the float bowl inverted, allow the weight of the float to rest on the needle and spring. Measure the distance between the float and carburetor body as shown in the accompanying illustration to deter-

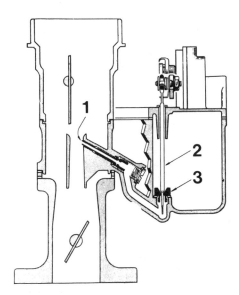

**Fig. 4.5 Early model YF carburetor (F- and L-head four-cylinder engines) (Sec 10)**

1 Main nozzle          3 Metering jet
2 Metering rod

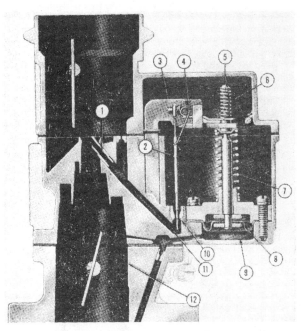

**Fig. 4.6 YF carburetor (F- and L-head four-cylinder engines) high-speed circuit and metering rod assembly (Sec 10)**

1 Nozzle                    7 Pump diaphragm spring
2 Metering rod              8 Diaphragm assembly
3 Pump lifter link          9 Chamber
4 Metering rod arm assembly 10 Metering rod jet
5 Diaphragm shaft           11 Carburetor casting
6 Upper pump spring         12 Carburetor bore

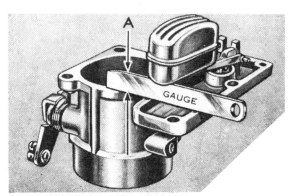

**Fig. 4.7 YF carburetor (F- and L-head four-cylinder engines) float level measurement (Sec 10)**

mine the float level. Compare this measurement to the Specifications and adjust as necessary by bending the float arm lip.

31  Install the air horn and choke tube assembly. Tighten the retaining screws in a crisscross pattern, starting with the center screws.

32  Slide the fast idle connector rod into position with the offset portion on the top and the pin on the outside. Install the fast idle connecting rod spring.

33  Install the carburetor.

34  With the engine at normal operating temperature adjust the idle speed.

35  Turn the mixture screw in or out, as required, until the smoothest idle is obtained (you may have to readjust the idle speed).

## 11   Carter YF carburetor (in-line six-cylinder engine) — overhaul and adjustment

1    Remove the carburetor as described in Section 9.

### Overhaul

2    On models equipped with a choke pulldown motor, remove the retaining screws, disconnect the choke pulldown link and remove the motor assembly, disengaging the link from the choke shaft lever.

3    Remove the choke retaining screws, housing retainers, spring housing assembly, gasket, baffle plate and fast idle link.

4    Remove the screws securing the air horn assembly to the carburetor and remove the air horn, gasket and solenoid bracket assembly.

5    With the air horn assembly upside down, remove the float pin, float and lever assembly. Turn the air horn assembly over and catch the needle pin, spring and needle and remove the needle seat and gasket.

6    Remove the air cleaner bracket. File the staked ends off the screws retaining the choke plate and remove the screws and plate. Remove the choke link lever and screw.

7    Turn the main body casting upside down and catch the accelerating pump check ball and weight and (if equipped) hot idle compensator.

8    Remove the mechanical bowl vent operating lever assembly from the throttle shaft.

9    Loosen the throttle shaft screw and remove the arm and pump connector link.

10   Remove the fast idle cam and shoulder screw.

11   Remove the accelerating pump diaphragm housing screws and lift the pump diaphragm assembly out as a unit.

12   Disengage the metering rod spring from the rod and remove the rod from the arm assembly. Sketch the location of any washers which may be used in shimming the springs so they can be reinstalled in the same location. Compress the upper pump spring and remove the spring retainer, spring and pump diaphragm assembly from the housing.

13   Use the proper size jet tool or screwdriver to remove the main metering rod jet and low speed jet.

14   On models with a temperature-compensated accelerator pump, remove the bleed valve plug from the main body with a punch. Loosen the bleed valve screw and remove the valve.

15   Remove the retaining screws and separate the throttle body from the main body of the carburetor.

16   File the staked throttle plate retaining screws and remove the screws and plate. Slide the throttle shaft and lever assembly out of the carburetor. Be sure to note the location of the ends of the spring on the throttle shaft to simplify reinstallation. Also be sure to note the position of the idle limiter cap tab to ensure proper reassembly. After removing the cap, count the number of turns required to lightly seat the needle and make a note of it for reference during reassembly.

17   The carburetor is now completely disassembled and should be cleaned and inspected for wear. After the carburetor components have been soaked in solvent to remove dirt, gum and carbon deposits, they should be rinsed in kerosene and dried, preferably with compressed air. Do not use a wire brush to clean the carburetor and clean all passages with compressed air rather than wire or drill bits, which could enlarge them. Inspect the throttle and choke shafts for grooves, wear and excessive looseness. Check the throttle and choke plates for nicks and smoothness of operation. Inspect the carburetor body and components for cracks. Check the floats for leaks by submerging them in water which has been heated to just below the boiling point. Leaks will be indicated by the appearance of bubbles. Check the float arm needle contact surface for grooves. If the grooves are light, polish the

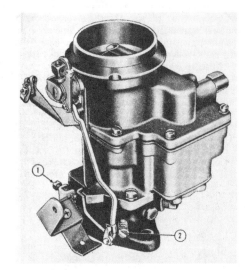

**Fig. 4.8   Early model F-head engine YF carburetor adjustment screw locations (Sec 10)**

*1  Idle speed screw*
*2  Fuel/air mixture screw*

needle contact surface with crocus cloth or steel wool. Replace the floats if the shafts are badly worn. Inspect the gasket mating surfaces for burrs and nicks. Replace any distorted springs and screws and bolts which have stripped threads.

18   To begin reassembly, install the throttle shaft and lever assembly in the throttle body flange. Make sure the bushings and springs are in the positions noted during disassembly. Position the throttle plate on the throttle shaft with the notch aligned with the slotted idle port. Install the throttle plate, using new screws. Tighten the screws so they are snug and then move the throttle plate around to make sure that it doesn't bind in the bore. Make sure that the idle speed screw is backed off when checking the throttle plate fit. Reposition the plate as necessary, tighten the screws and stake or peen them in place. Install the idle speed screw and turn it out the same number of turns recorded during removal.

19   Attach the main body to the throttle body flange and tighten the screws evenly and securely.

20   Install the low speed jet and main metering rod jet.

21   Install the pump diaphragm in the pump diaphragm housing. Place the pump diaphragm spring on the diaphragm shaft and housing assembly. Install the spring shim washers, spring retainer, pump lifter link metering rod arm and spring assembly and upper pump spring on the diaphragm shaft. Depress the spring and install the upper pump and spring retainer.

22   Assemble the metering rod on the metering rod arm so the rod hangs down. Place the looped end of the metering rod spring around the upper end of the rod. Align the diaphragm pump with the housing, making sure the holes are lined up. Install the mounting screws to maintain alignment.

23   Insert the screws into the housing while making sure the edges of the diaphragm are not wrinkled. Lower the assembly into place and tighten the screws evenly, following a crisscross pattern, until they are secure.

24   Place the pump bleed valve and washer in position and install the retaining screw. Install a new welch plug, using a 1/4-inch flat drift punch to seat it.

25   Install the fast idle cam and shoulder screw, throttle shaft arm and pump connector link and tighten the lock screw.

26   Install the E-clip, spacer, wave washer and bowl vent actuating lever and tighten the retaining screw. Install the hot idle compensator valve and accelerator pump check ball and weight.

27   Insert the choke shaft assembly through the choke housing. Slip the pulldown link lever into the air horn and tighten the retaining screw.

28   Place the choke plate in position on the choke shaft and install the retaining screws snugly, but not tight. Check the choke plate for bin-

155

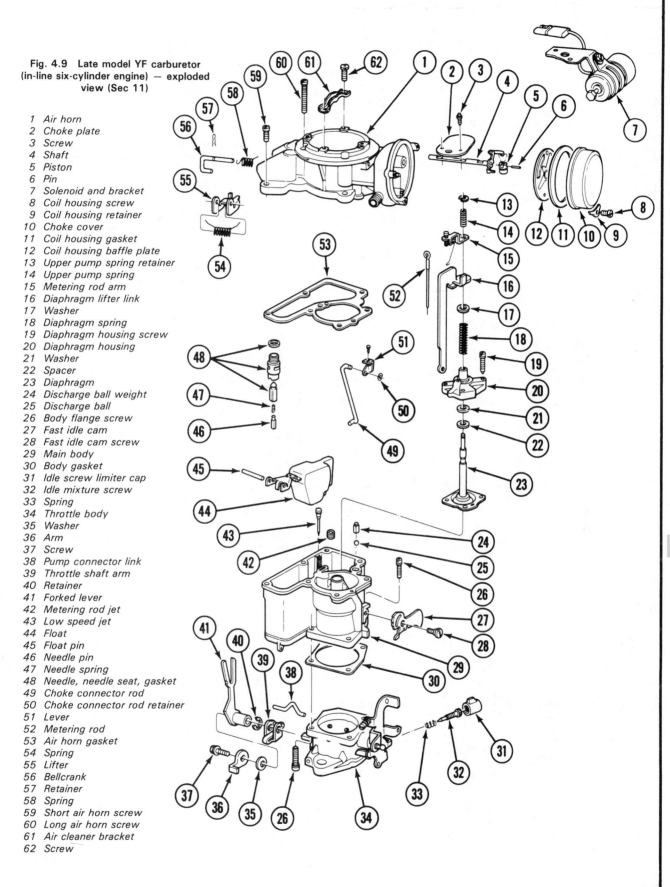

Fig. 4.9 Late model YF carburetor
(in-line six-cylinder engine) — exploded
view (Sec 11)

1 Air horn
2 Choke plate
3 Screw
4 Shaft
5 Piston
6 Pin
7 Solenoid and bracket
8 Coil housing screw
9 Coil housing retainer
10 Choke cover
11 Coil housing gasket
12 Coil housing baffle plate
13 Upper pump spring retainer
14 Upper pump spring
15 Metering rod arm
16 Diaphragm lifter link
17 Washer
18 Diaphragm spring
19 Diaphragm housing screw
20 Diaphragm housing
21 Washer
22 Spacer
23 Diaphragm
24 Discharge ball weight
25 Discharge ball
26 Body flange screw
27 Fast idle cam
28 Fast idle cam screw
29 Main body
30 Body gasket
31 Idle screw limiter cap
32 Idle mixture screw
33 Spring
34 Throttle body
35 Washer
36 Arm
37 Screw
38 Pump connector link
39 Throttle shaft arm
40 Retainer
41 Forked lever
42 Metering rod jet
43 Low speed jet
44 Float
45 Float pin
46 Needle pin
47 Needle spring
48 Needle, needle seat, gasket
49 Choke connector rod
50 Choke connector rod retainer
51 Lever
52 Metering rod
53 Air horn gasket
54 Spring
55 Lifter
56 Bellcrank
57 Retainer
58 Spring
59 Short air horn screw
60 Long air horn screw
61 Air cleaner bracket
62 Screw

4

ding, then tighten the screws and peen or stake them in place.

29  Install the needle seat and gasket in the air horn. Turn the air horn over and install the needle, pin spring, needle pin, float and lever assembly and float pin. Adjust the float level as described below.

30  Align the bowl vent flapper valve with the vent rod, making sure that the spring is properly installed on the vent rod shaft. Install the spring retainer.

31  Place a new air horn gasket in position and install the air horn, making sure that the mechanical fuel bowl vent engages the forked actuating lever. Install the solenoid bracket.

32  Install the choke coil housing (with the identification marks facing out), the gasket and baffle plate. The thermostatic spring must engage the choke lever tang and not be stopped by the baffle plate retaining tab (if so equipped). Set the choke housing to the index mark specified on the Emissions Control Information label and tighten the screws.

33  Install the air cleaner bracket and fast idle link.

34  Engage the choke pulldown link with the choke fast lever and the pulldown diaphragm rod. Place the diaphragm bracket on the air horn and install the attaching screws. Connect the pulldown vacuum hose to the diaphragm housing.

35  Adjust the carburetor to the specifications listed on the Emissions Control Information label.

## Float level adjustment

36  Invert the air horn and measure the clearance from the top of the float to the bottom of the air horn with a suitable gauge. The air horn should be held at eye level during this procedure and the float lever should be resting on the needle pin.

37  Bend the float arm as necessary to bring the float level within the specified range. Do not bend the tab at the end of the float arm as this prevents the float from striking the bottom of the fuel bowl when the bowl is empty.

## Float drop adjustment

38  With the carburetor air horn held upright and the float hanging free, measure the distance from the air horn gasket surface to the top of the end of the float. Compare this float drop measurement to the Specifications.

39  To adjust, bend the tab at the end of the float arm.

## Metering rod adjustment

40  With the air horn removed, back out the idle speed adjusting screw until the throttle plate is closed tightly in the bore.

41  Push down on the end of the pump diaphragm until it bottoms.

42  To adjust the metering rod, hold the diaphragm down and turn the

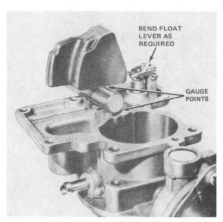

Fig. 4.10  YF carburetor (in-line six-cylinder engine) float level adjustment (Sec 11)

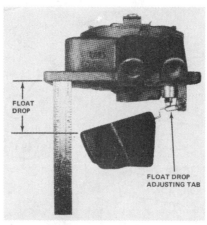

Fig. 4.11  YF carburetor (in-line six-cylinder engine) float drop measurement and adjustment (Sec 11)

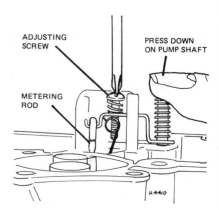

Fig. 4.12  Metering rod adjustment (YF carburetor) (Sec 11)

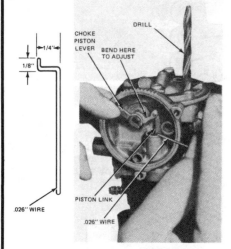

Fig. 4.13  Initial choke plate adjustment and gauge fabrication (YF carburetor) (Sec 11)

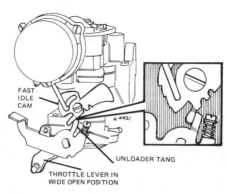

Fig. 4.14  YF carburetor choke unloader adjustment (Sec 11)

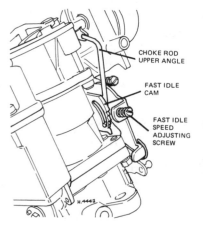

Fig. 4.15  Fast idle cam linkage adjustment (YF carburetor) (Sec 11)

adjustment screw until the metering rod just bottoms in the body casting as shown in the accompanying illustration. Turn the adjustment screw clockwise one additional turn for final adjustment.

### Initial choke plate-to-air horn clearance adjustment

43  Bend a 0.026-inch diameter wire at a 90° angle approximately 1/8-inch from the end to fabricate a wire gauge as shown in the accompanying illustration.
44  Open the throttle partially and close the choke plate to position the choke piston at the top of its bore.
45  Hold the choke plate closed, release the throttle and insert the wire gauge into the piston slot and against the outboard side of the piston bore. Push down on the piston with the gauge until the bent end enters the piston bore slot. Keep the gauge in place and push on the choke piston lever to move the piston up and lock the gauge in position.
46  Measure the choke plate lower edge-to-air horn wall clearance with a gauge or drill bit shank.
47  Use a needle-nose pliers to carefully bend the choke piston lever and adjust the clearance. Decrease the clearance by bending the lever toward the piston and increase it by bending the lever away from the piston.
48  Install the choke baffle plate, gasket cover and retaining screws. On 1973 through 1977 models, adjust the cover to the specified setting and tighten the retaining screws. On 1978 models, turn the cover counterclockwise toward the rich side and tighten one retaining screw. The final adjustment is made after the fast idle cam linkage is adjusted.

### Fast idle cam linkage adjustment

49  Place the fast idle screw on the second step of the fast idle cam and against the shoulder of the high step.
50  Check the clearance between the lower edge of the choke plate and the air horn wall using a gauge or drill bit shank. Compare this measurement to the Specifications.
51  To adjust, bend the choke plate connecting rod until the proper choke plate-to-air horn wall clearance is achieved.

### Choke unloader adjustment

52  Hold the throttle completely open while pushing the choke plate toward the closed position. Measure the clearance between the choke plate lower edge and the air horn wall with a drill bit shank. Compare this measurement to the Specifications.
53  To adjust, bend the unloader tang which contacts the fast idle cam.
54  After adjustment, operate the throttle to make sure the linkage does not bind.
55  There should be a 0.070-inch clearance between the unloader tang and carburetor body with the throttle completely open after adjustment.

### Bowl vent adjustment

56  Disconnect the emissions canister hose from the carburetor and attach a new piece of clean hose to the bowl vent.
57  Place the throttle on the high step of the fast idle cam and blow into the hose. There should be considerable resistance felt, indicating the vent is closed.
58  Move the fast idle cam until the throttle screw drops to the third step of the cam. Blow into the hose to verify that the bowl vent has opened and that pressure is relieved.
59  Repeat the test procedure to verify that the bowl vent is properly adjusted.
60  If no pressure is felt with the throttle on the high step of the cam, the vent is not closing. If the pressure is not released on the third step of the cam, the vent is not opening. Adjust by bending the forked end of the lever.

### Altitude compensator adjustment

61  Some models are equipped with an altitude compensation device which features a compensation circuit that prevents a too-rich mixture at altitudes above 4000 feet. The altitude compensator is adjusted manually.
62  When operating the vehicle above 4000 feet, use a screwdriver to turn the compensator plug counterclockwise approximately 2-1/2 turns to the outer (high-altitude) seat position.
63  Below 4000 feet, adjust the plug clockwise to the inner seat position.
64  The plug has two positions; all the way in (low altitude) or all the way out (above 4000 feet). Do not adjust the plug to any other position.

### Idle speed and fuel/air mixture adjustment

65  Prior to idle speed or mixture adjustment the following precautions must be taken and conditions exist:

> Parking brake securely set
> Transmission must be in Drive (automatic) or Neutral (manual)
> Engine at normal operating temperature
> Air cleaner installed
> Adjust idle speed before adjusting the fuel/air mixture
> The engine must not be idled for more than three minutes (if the adjustment takes more than three minutes, run the engine for one minute at 2000 rpm in Neutral)

66  Attach a tachometer to the engine, following the manufacturer's instructions.
67  Turn the idle speed adjustment screw to obtain the specified idle speed.
68  If the carburetor is equipped with a solenoid, turn the nut on the plunger to obtain the specified idle speed and tighten the locknut (if so equipped). Disconnect the solenoid wire and adjust the carburetor idle speed screw to achieve an idle of 500 rpm, then reconnect the wire.
69  On non-catalytic converter-equipped vehicles, the manufacturer recommends that mixture adjustments be made using special infrared analyzer equipment. Consequently, these models should be taken to your dealer or a properly equipped shop for mixture adjustment. The idle drop procedure, described below, is used on catalytic converter-equipped models.
70  Adjust the idle mixture screw to the full rich stop (counter-

**4**

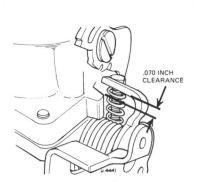

Fig. 4.16  Checking choke unloader-to-body clearance (Sec 11)

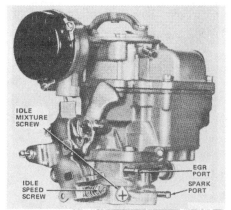

Fig. 4.17  YF carburetor adjustment screw locations (Sec 11)

Fig. 4.18  Dashpot adjustment (YF carburetor) (Sec 11)

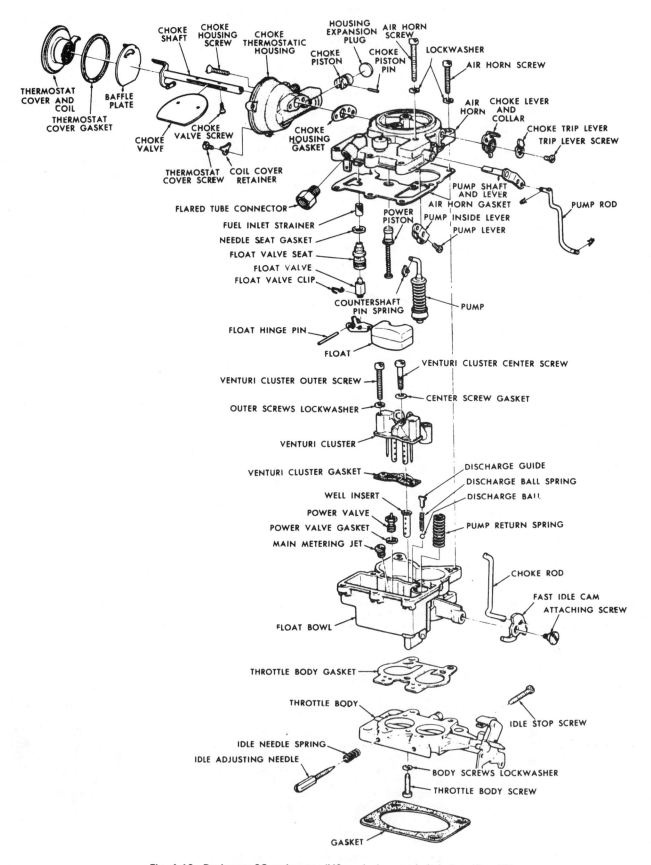

Fig. 4.19  Rochester 2G carburetor (V6 engine) — exploded view (Sec 12)

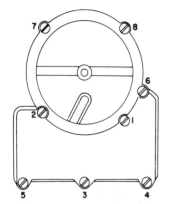

Fig. 4.20  2G carburetor air horn screw tightening sequence (Sec 12)

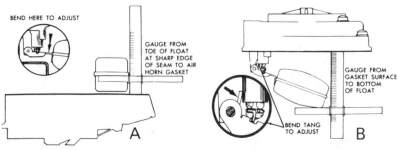

Fig. 4.21  Float adjustment (2G carburetor) (Sec 12)

A Float level          B Float drop

(counterclockwise), note the position of the screw head slots and remove the plastic limiter caps. This can be accomplished by threading a No. 10 sheet metal screw into the center of the cap.

71  Connect a tachometer and perform the idle speed adjustment procedure described above.

72  Beginning at the full rich position (Step 70), turn the mixture screw clockwise in the lean direction until there is an rpm drop. Turn the screw in a counterclockwise direction until the highest rpm previously attained is obtained. This is the lean best idle.

73  Turn the idle mixture screw until the specified idle drop is reached.

74  If the final reading varies more than 30 rpm up or down from the idle speed specification, repeat the idle speed adjustment.

75  Install a new idle mixture screw limiter cap with the ear of the cap against the full rich stop, taking care not to alter the mixture setting.

## Dashpot adjustment

76  Set the throttle at the curb idle position, depress the dashpot stem completely and measure the stem-to-throttle lever clearance. Compare this measurement to the Specifications.

77  To adjust, loosen the locknut and turn the dashpot until the specified clearance is obtained.

## Fast idle adjustment

78  The fast idle adjustment is made with the engine at normal operating temperature, the EGR valve and TCS solenoid disconnected and the fast idle screw contacting the second step and against the shoulder of the high step of the fast idle cam. Turn the fast idle adjustment screw to obtain the specified rpm setting.

## 12  Rochester 2G carburetor (V6 engine) — overhaul and adjustment

### Overhaul

1  Remove the fast idle cam retaining screw, then remove the cam from the end of the choke rod. The upper end of the rod cannot be removed until the air horn has been detached from the float bowl.

2  Remove the air horn attaching screws and lockwashers, then lift off the air horn.

3  Remove the float hinge pin and lift off the float. The float needle and pull clip (where applicable) can now be removed from the float arm.

4  Unscrew the float needle seat and remove the gasket.

5  Depress the power piston and release it to allow it to snap free.

6  Remove the pump plunger assembly and inner pump lever from the shaft by loosening the set screws on the inner lever.

7  If the pump assembly is to be overhauled, break off the flattened end of the pump plunger stem; the replacement pump uses a grooved pump plunger stem and retaining clip. After removing the inner pump lever and pump assembly, remove the outer lever and shaft assembly from the air horn. Remove the plastic washer from the pump plunger shaft.

8  Remove the gasket from the air horn.

9  Remove the fuel inlet baffle (next to the needle seat).

10  Taking care not to bend the choke shaft, remove the choke valve. The ends of the retaining screws may have to be filed away to permit

removal of the screws.

11  Remove the choke valve shaft. Remove the fast idle cam rod and lever from the shaft.

12  Remove the pump plunger return spring from the float bowl pump well, then invert the bowl and remove the aluminum ball.

13  Remove the main metering jets, power valve and gasket from inside the float bowl.

14  Remove the three screws which retain the venturi cluster; remove the cluster and gasket.

15  Use a needle-nose pliers to remove the pump discharge spring retainer, then remove the spring and check ball from the discharge passage.

16  Remove the three large throttle body-to-bowl attaching screws and lockwashers. Remove the throttle body and gasket.

17  Remove the thermostatic choke coil cover (three screws and retainers) and gasket from the choke housing. Do not remove the cap baffle from beneath the coil cover.

18  Remove the choke housing baffle plate.

19  From inside the choke housing, remove the two attaching screws; remove the housing and gasket.

20  Remove the screw from the end of the intermediate choke shaft, then remove the choke lever from the shaft. Remove the inner choke coil lever and shaft assembly from the choke housing, followed by the rubber dust seal.

21  Further disassembly is not recommended, particularly with regard to the throttle valves or shaft, since it may be impossible to reassemble the valves correctly in relation to the idle discharge orifices. If it is necessary to remove the idle mixture needles, break off the plastic limiter caps (if so equipped) then count the number of turns required to bottom the needles and install replacements in exactly the same position. New limiter caps should be installed after running adjustments have been made.

22  Clean all metal parts with solvent. Do not immerse rubber parts, plastic parts, diaphragm assemblies or pump plungers, because permanent damage will result. Do not probe the jets with wire; instead, blow through them with clean, dry, compressed air. Examine all parts for cracks, distortion, wear and other damage; replace as necessary. Discard all gaskets and the fuel inlet filter.

23  Assembly is essentially the reverse of the disassembly procedure, but the following points should be noted:

  a)  If new idle mixture screws were used, and the original setting was not noted, install the screws finger tight to seat them, then back off one (1) turn as a preliminary adjustment.

  b)  When installing the rubber dust seal in the choke housing cavity, the seal lip faces toward the carburetor after the housing is installed.

  c)  When installing the venturi cluster, make sure that a gasket is installed on the center screw.

  d)  Install the choke valve with the letters RP or the part number facing up.

  e)  Carry out float level and float drop checks as specified below.

  f)  Install and tighten the air horn screws as shown.

  g)  After reassembly, carry out the adjustments listed below.

### Float level measurement and adjustment

24  Hold the air horn assembly upside down and measure the distance from the air horn gasket surface to the top of the float toe. Compare this measurement to the Specifications and bend the float arm as necessary to adjust.

**4**

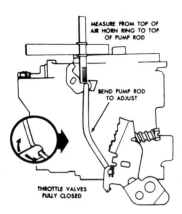

**Fig. 4.22   Accelerator pump adjustment (2G carburetor) (Sec 12)**

**Fig. 4.23   2G carburetor external components (Sec 12)**

1   Fuel inlet
2   Choke
3   Choke cable bracket
4   Idle speed adjusting screw
5   Idle fuel mixture screws

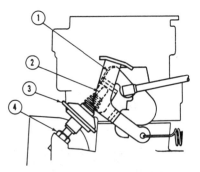

**Fig. 4.24   Dashpot adjustment (2G carburetor) (Sec 12)**

1   Throttle lever      3   Dashpot
2   Plunger             4   Locknut

### Float drop measurement and adjustment

25  Hold the air horn upright and measure the distance from the gasket surface to the bottom outer end of the float pontoon. Bend the float tang to bring the measurement within the specified range.

### Accelerator pump clearance measurement and adjustment

26  Unscrew the curb idle adjustment screw and completely close the throttle valves. Measure from the top of the air horn ring to the top of the pump rod. Bend the pump rod to adjust the clearance.

### Curb idle and mixture adjustment

27  Connect a tachometer to the engine. With the engine at normal temperature, the air cleaner installed, the ignition timing and dwell correctly set and all emissions devices in working order, turn the adjustment screw until the idle is as specified.
28  Adjust the idle mixture screws until a smooth idle is achieved. Readjust the idle speed as necessary.

### Dashpot adjustment

29  The dashpot should be adjusted with the engine at normal operating temperature and the idle speed and mixture correctly adjusted. With the engine at idle, loosen the dashpot locknut and turn the dashpot assembly until the plunger contacts the throttle lever. Turn the dashpot assembly 2-1/2 turns toward the throttle lever, depress the plunger and tighten the locknut. Check the adjustment by opening the throttle and allowing it to snap closed. There should be approximately a two-second delay before the throttle closes.

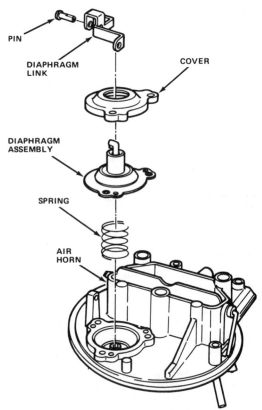

**Fig. 4.25   Choke modulator assembly components (2100/2150 carburetor) (Sec 13)**

---

## 13   Autolite/Motorcraft 2100 and 2150 carburetors V8 engine) — overhaul and adjustment

### Overhaul

1   Before disassembly, clean the exterior of the carburetor with solvent and wipe it off using a lint-free rag.
2   Remove the air cleaner anchor screw and automatic choke control rod retainer.
3   Remove the air horn attaching screws, lockwashers, carburetor identification tag, air horn and gasket.
4   Loosen the screw securing the choke control rod to the choke shaft lever. Remove the choke control rod and slide out the plastic dust seal.
5   Remove the choke plate screws after filing off the staked ends and remove the choke plate by sliding it out of the top of the air horn. Slide the choke shaft out of the air horn.
6   Remove the choke modulator assembly.
7   From the automatic choke, remove the fast idle cam retainer, thermostatic choke spring housing, clamp and retainer.
8   Remove the choke housing assembly, gasket and fast idle cam and

rod from the fast idle cam lever.
9   Use a screwdriver to pry the float shaft retainer out of the fuel inlet seat on the main body. Remove the float, float shaft and fuel inlet needle assembly.
10  Remove the retainer and float shaft from the float lever and remove the fuel filler bowl.
11  Remove the fuel inlet needle, seat filter screen and main jets.
12  Remove the booster venturi, metering rod assembly and gasket. Turn the main body upside down and let the accelerator pump, discharge weight and ball fall into your hand.
13  Disassemble the lift rod from the booster by removing the lift rod spring retaining clip and spring and separating the lift rod assembly from the booster. Do not remove the metering rod hanger from the lift rod.

**Fig. 4.26 Autolite/Motorcraft 2100/2150 carburetor components — exploded view (Sec 13)**

1  Compensator choke shaft
2  Retainer
3  Compensator choke valve
4  Choke valve screw
5  Compensator choke rod
6  Choke valve
7  Choke shaft
8  Air horn
9  Air horn retaining screw (4)
10  Air horn gasket
11  Float shaft retainer
12  Float and lever assembly
13  Float shaft
14  Needle retaining clip
15  Curb idle adjusting screw
16  Curb idle adjusting screw spring
17  Throttle shaft and lever assembly
18  Dashpot
19  Dashpot locknut
20  Dashpot bracket
21  Dashpot bracket retaining screw
22  Adjusting screw
23  Carriage
24  Electric solenoid
25  Mounting bracket
26  Throttle valve retaining screw
27  Throttle valve
28  Needle and seat assembly
29  Needle seat gasket
30  Main jet
31  Main body
32  Nylon valve
33  Pump return spring
34  Pump diaphragm
35  Pump lever pin
36  Pump cover
37  Pump rod
38  Pump rod retainer
39  Pump lever
40  Pump cover retaining screw
41  Fuel inlet fitting
42  Power valve gasket
43  Power valve
44  Power valve cover gasket
45  Power valve cover
46  Power valve cover retaining screw
47  Idle limiter cap
48  Idle mixture screw
49  Idle mixture screw spring
50  Retainer
51  Retainer
52  Fast idle lever retaining nut
53  Fast idle lever pin
54  Retainer
55  Thermostat choke shaft
56  Fast idle cam rod
57  Choke shield

58  Choke shield retaining screw
59  Piston passage plug
60  Heat passage plug
61  Choke cover retaining clamp
62  Choke cover retaining screw
63  Choke cover
64  Choke cover gasket
65  Thermostat lever retaining screw
66  Thermostat lever
67  Choke housing retaining screw
68  Choke housing
69  Choke shaft bushing
70  Fast idle cam lever adjusting screw
71  Choke diaphragm
72  Hose
73  Link
74  Screw
75  Fast idle speed adjusting screw
76  Fast idle lever

77  Fast idle cam
78  Choke housing gasket
79  Pump discharge check ball
80  Pump discharge weight
81  Booster venturi gasket
82  Booster venturi assembly
83  Air distribution plate
84  Pump discharge screw
85  Retainer
86  Choke rod
87  Gasket
88  Compensation chamber
89  Gasket
90  Screw
91  Aneroid
92  Screw
93  Choke lever retaining screw
94  Choke plate lever
95  Choke rod seal

4

14  Remove the roll pin from the accelerator pump cover, using a suitable punch. Retain the roll pin and remove the accelerator pump link and rod assembly, pump cover, diaphragm assembly and spring.
15  To remove the nylon valve from the accelerator pump assembly, grasp it firmly and pull it out. Examine the valve and, if the tip is broken off, be sure to remove it from the fuel bowl. Discard the valve.
16  Turn the main body upside down and remove the enrichment valve cover and gasket. Using an eight-point socket, remove the enrichment valve and gasket.
17  Remove the idle fuel mixture adjusting screws and springs. Remove the idle screw limiter caps.
18  Remove the fast idle adjusting lever assembly and then remove the idle screw and the spring from the lever.
19  Before removing the throttle plates, lightly scribe along the throttle shaft and mark each plate for reinstallation in the proper bore. File off the staked portion of the throttle plate screws before removing them. Remove any burrs from the shaft after plate removal so that the shaft can be withdrawn without damage to the throttle shaft bores. Be ready to catch the mechanical high-speed cam located between the throttle plates when the shaft is removed.

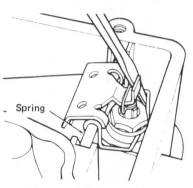

Fig. 4.27   Removing the 2100/2150 carburetor float shaft retainer with a screwdriver (Sec 13)

Fig. 4.28   2100/2150 carburetor float bowl component layout (Sec 13)

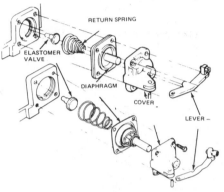

Fig. 4.29   Accelerator pump assembly components (2100/2150 carburetor) (Sec 13)

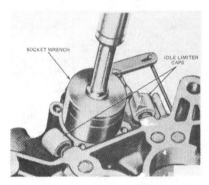

Fig. 4.30   A socket wrench is used to remove and install the enrichment valve assembly (2100/2150 carburetor) (Sec 13)

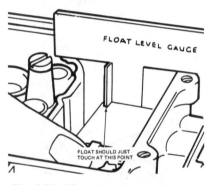

Fig. 4.31   Measuring the dry float level (2100/2150 carburetor) (Sec 13)

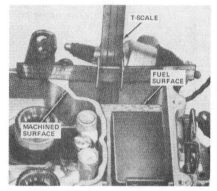

Fig. 4.32   Using a T-scale to measure the 2100/2150 carburetor wet float level (Sec 13)

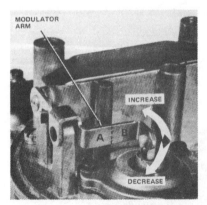

Fig. 4.33   *Early model* 2100/2150 initial choke plate clearance adjustment (Sec 13)

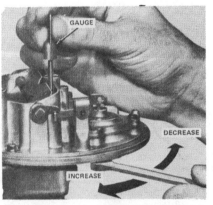

Fig. 4.34   *Later model* 2100/2150 initial choke plate clearance adjustment (Sec 13)

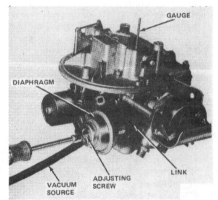

Fig. 4.35   Initial choke plate adjustment on altitude compensator-equipped 2150 carburetor (Sec 13)

20 If an altitude compensator is installed, remove the four screws at taching the assembly to the main body and remove the compensator assembly. Remove the three acrews holding the aneroid valve and separate the aneroid, gasket and valve.

21 Disassembly is no complete and all parts should be thoroughly cleaned in solvent. Remove any sediment from the fuel bowl and passages, taking care not to scratch any of the passages. Remove all traces of gaskets with a scraper.

22 Reassembly is basically the reverse of disassembly, but note the following:

   a) Check that all holes in new gaskets are properly punched and that they are free of foreign material.
   b) When installing a new nylon valve in the accelerator pump assembly, lubricate the tip before inserting it into the accelerator pump cavity hole. Reach into the fuel bowl with needle-nose pliers and pull the valve tip into the fuel bowl. Cut off the tip ahead of the retainer shoulder.
   c) Install the idle mixture adjusting screws by turning them with your fingers until they just contact the seat, then back them off two turns. Do not install the limiter caps at this time. The enrichment valve cover and gasket must be installed next as the limiter stops on the cover provide a positive stop for the limiter caps.
   d) After installing the throttle plates in the main body, hold the assembly up to the light. Little of no light should be seen between the throttle plates and bores. Tighten and stake the throttle plate screws at this time.
   e) When checking the float setting, make sure that the nylon valve in the accelerator pump does not interfere with the float.

## Dry float level measurement and adjustment

23 Press down on the float tab to raise the float to a position where the fuel inlet needle is lightly seated.

24 Use a scale of float level gauge to measure the distance between the fuel bowl machined surface and the flat surface of the float at the free end. Compare this measurement to the Specifications.

25 Bend the float tab to adjust, taking care to hold the fuel inlet needle off the seat to prevent damage to the Viton-tipped needle.

## Wet float level measurement and adjustment

**Caution:** *Because fuel vapors are present during this procedure, make sure all smoking materials are extinguished and that no open flames are present.*

26 With the vehicle parked on a level surface and the engine at normal operating temperature, remove the air cleaner assembly and anchor screw from the carburetor.

27 Remove the air horn retaining screws and the carburetor identification tag. Start the engine with the air horn and gasket in place and allow it to idle for one minute.

28 Turn off the engine and remove the air horn and gasket.

29 Use a scale to measure the distance from the carburetor machined top surface to the surface of the fuel. This measurement should be made at least 1/4-inch away from any vertical surface to ensure accuracy, because the surface of the fuel is actually slightly higher at the edges. Compare the measurement to the Specifications.

30 To adjust the fuel level, bend the float tab up where it contacts the fuel inlet level to raise the fuel level and down to lower it.

31 After adjustment, replace the air horn and gasket and run the engine for one minute before repeating the check and adjustment procedure.

32 Install the air horn (using a new gasket) and air cleaner assembly.

## Automatic choke adjustment

33 Loosen the choke cover screws and rotate the cover in the desired direction. The rich setting is to the right (clockwise) and the lean to the left (counterclockwise).

## Initial choke plate clearance measurement and adjustment

34 On standard models, rotate the choke cover 1/4-turn counterclockwise toward the rich setting side. On altitude compensator-equipped models, open the throttle and rotate the choke cover until the choke plate is closed. On all models, tighten one choke cover retaining screw.

35 On standard models, disconnect the choke heat inlet tube and align the fast idle speed adjusting screw with the index (second) step of the fast idle cam. On altitude compensator models, close the throttle with the fast idle speed screw on the top step of the cam and apply vacuum to the choke diaphragm to hold it against the set screw.

36 On standard models, start the engine (without moving the accelerator linkage) and turn the fast idle adjusting screw counterclockwise three (3) full turns.

37 On all models, measure the clearance between the choke plate lower edge and the air horn wall with a gauge or drill bit shank. Compare this measurement to the Specifications.

38 After setting the choke to the specified position, tighten the choke cover screws.

39 On early models, adjust by bending the modulator arm as shown in the accompanying illustration. On later models, the clearance is adjusted by turning the set screw located at the bottom of the modulator. On altitude compensator-equipped models, turn the adjustment screw on the back of the diaphragm to attain the specified clearance.

40 Shut off the engine and connect the choke heat tube. Reset the choke cover only after adjusting the fast idle cam linkage.

## Fast idle cam adjustment

41 Push down on the fast idle cam lever until the fast idle adjusting screw is in contact with the index (second) step and against the shoulder of the high step.

42 Measure the choke plate lower edge-to-air horn wall clearance and check it against the Specifications.

43 Turn the fast idle cam lever screw to adjust the linkage.

44 Adjust the automatic choke and tighten the retaining screws.

4

Fig. 4.36 Fast idle cam linkage adjustment (2100/2150 carburetor) (Sec 13)

Fig. 4.37 2100/2150 carburetor choke unloader adjustment (Sec 13)

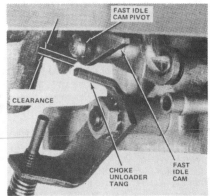

Fig. 4.38 Choke unloader fast idle cam clearance (2100/2150 carburetor) (Sec 13)

### Choke unloader adjustment

45   Hold the throttle completely open with pressure applied on the choke plate toward the closed position.

46   Measure the choke plate lower edge-to-air horn wall clearance and compare it to the Specifications.

47   Adjust the clearance by bending the choke unloader tang.

48   After adjustment, open the throttle until the unloader tang is directly below the fast idle cam pivot and check the clearance against the Specifications. Adjust as necessary and have an assistant push the throttle pedal down. Make sure the throttle linkage opens completely and, if it does not, adjust the throttle cable bracket or remove any excess padding from under the floor mat.

### Accelerator pump stroke adjustment

49   The accelerator pump overtravel lever has four adjustment holes and the pump lever has two. During normal operation, the pump rod should be in the third hole of the overtravel lever and the inboard hole of the pump lever.

50   In extremely hot weather the pump rod can be moved to the second hole of the overtravel lever and, in very cold weather, to the fourth hole to provide smoother acceleration.

51   Remove the operating rod from the retaining clip to move the rod to a different position on the overtravel lever. Move the clip to the desired position, insert the rod and snap the clip over the rod.

### Dashpot adjustment

52   With the throttle in the idle position, depress the dashpot stem and measure the stem-to-throttle clearance. Compare the measurement to the Specifications.

53   To adjust the clearance, loosen the locknut and turn the dashpot.

### Fast idle speed adjustment

54   Connect a tachometer to the engine and set the fast idle speed with the fast idle adjusting screw against the index mark (located on the second step) of the fast idle cam. The engine must be at normal operating temperature and the EGR and TCS solenoids disconnected. Turn the adjustment screw to obtain the specified setting.

### Idle speed adjustment

55   The idle speed must be adjusted with the engine at normal operating temperature, the air cleaner assembly installed and the transmission in Drive (automatic) or Neutral (manual). **Caution:** *Since the automatic transmission must be in Drive during adjustment, make sure the parking brake is firmly set.*

56   With a tachometer connected and the engine at idle, turn the adjustment screw to obtain the specified idle speed. If the carburetor is equipped with a solenoid, turn the hex screw on the solenoid to adjust the idle speed. Disconnect the solenoid wire and then adjust the idle speed screw to obtain an idle of 500 rpm. Reconnect the wire to the solenoid.

### Mixture adjustment

57   The manufacturer recommends that mixture adjustment on these models be accomplished with special infrared equipment. Consequently, the vehicle should be taken to a dealer or properly equipped shop for the adjustment.

---

**14   Carter BBD carburetor (in–line six–cylinder engine) – overhaul and adjustment**

### Overhaul

1   With the carburetor removed from the vehicle, clean away all external dirt.

2   Where applicable, remove the throttle position solenoid.

3   Where applicable, remove the vacuum throttle positioner.

4   Where applicable, remove the idle enrichment vacuum diaphragm, the vacuum nipple and diaphragm return spring (three screws).

5   Remove the retaining clip and take off the accelerator pump arm link.

6   Where applicable, remove the step–up piston cover plate and gasket.

7   Remove the screws and locks, then slide the accelerator pump arm lever out of the air horn. Lift out the vacuum piston and step–up rods.

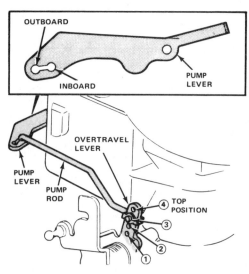

Fig. 4.39   Accelerator pump stroke adjustment (2100/2150 carburetor) (Sec 13)

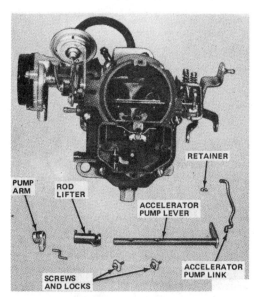

Fig. 4.40   BBD carburetor accelerator pump and lever assembly (Sec 14)

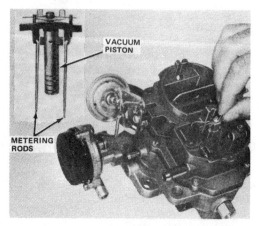

Fig. 4.41   Piston and metering rod assembly removal (BBD carburetor) (Sec 14)

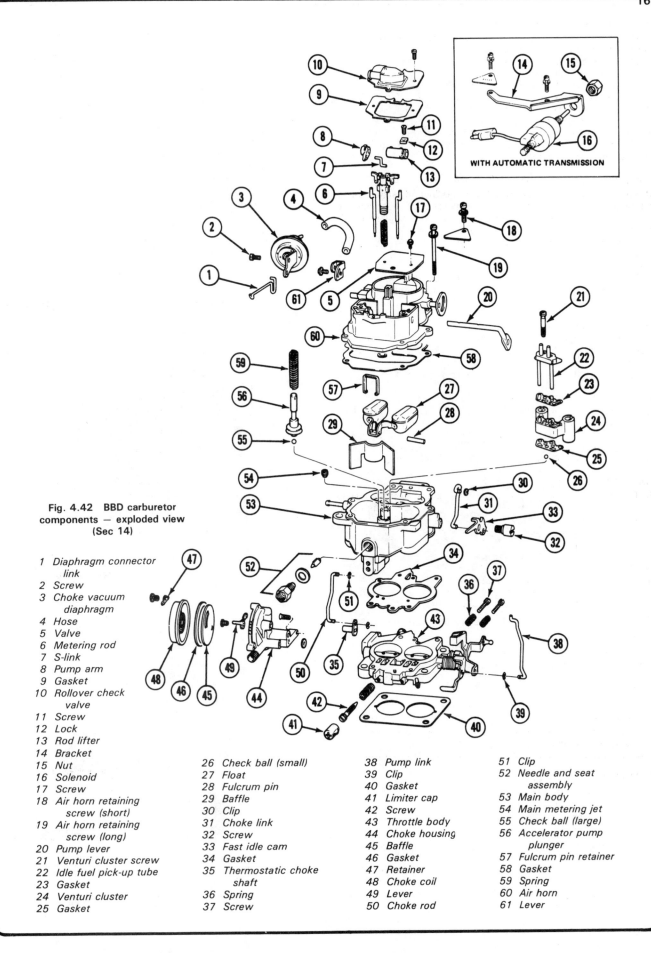

WITH AUTOMATIC TRANSMISSION

Fig. 4.42 BBD carburetor
components — exploded view
(Sec 14)

1   Diaphragm connector
    link
2   Screw
3   Choke vacuum
    diaphragm
4   Hose
5   Valve
6   Metering rod
7   S-link
8   Pump arm
9   Gasket
10  Rollover check
    valve
11  Screw
12  Lock
13  Rod lifter
14  Bracket
15  Nut
16  Solenoid
17  Screw
18  Air horn retaining
    screw (short)
19  Air horn retaining
    screw (long)
20  Pump lever
21  Venturi cluster screw
22  Idle fuel pick-up tube
23  Gasket
24  Venturi cluster
25  Gasket

26  Check ball (small)
27  Float
28  Fulcrum pin
29  Baffle
30  Clip
31  Choke link
32  Screw
33  Fast idle cam
34  Gasket
35  Thermostatic choke
    shaft
36  Spring
37  Screw

38  Pump link
39  Clip
40  Gasket
41  Limiter cap
42  Screw
43  Throttle body
44  Choke housing
45  Baffle
46  Gasket
47  Retainer
48  Choke coil
49  Lever
50  Choke rod

51  Clip
52  Needle and seat
    assembly
53  Main body
54  Main metering jet
55  Check ball (large)
56  Accelerator pump
    plunger
57  Fulcrum pin retainer
58  Gasket
59  Spring
60  Air horn
61  Lever

4

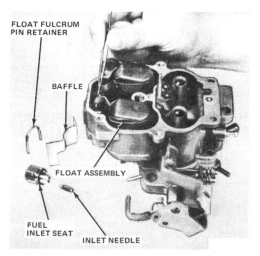

Fig. 4.43 Float assembly components (BBD carburetor) (Sec 14)

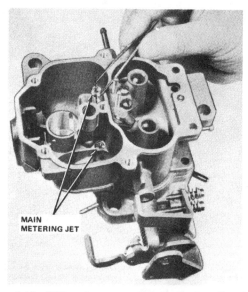

Fig. 4.44 BBD carburetor main metering jets (Sec 14)

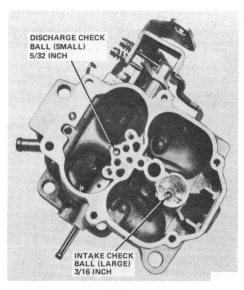

Fig. 4.45 Check ball locations (BBD carburetor) (Sec 14)

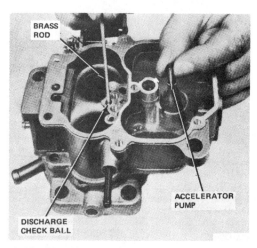

Fig. 4.46 Checking the BBD carburetor accelerator pump system (Sec 14)

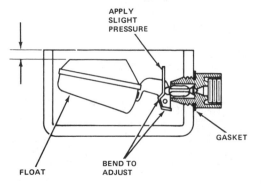

Fig. 4.47 BBD carburetor float level adjustment (Sec 14)

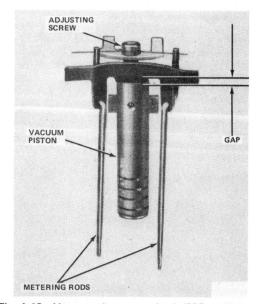

Fig. 4.48 Vacuum piston gap check (BBD carburetor) (Sec 14)

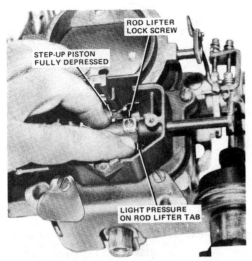

Fig. 4.49  Vacuum piston adjustment (BBD carburetor)
(Sec 14)

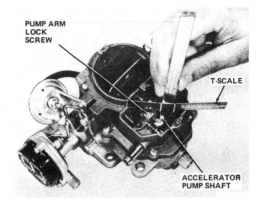

Fig. 4.50  Accelerator pump adjustment (BBD carburetor)
(Sec 14)

Fig. 4.51  Initial choke valve adjustment (BBD carburetor)
(Sec 14)

8  Remove the main body-to-choke vacuum hose.
9  Remove the choke diaphragm, linkage and bracket.
10  Remove the fast idle cam and linkage.
11  Remove the screws and take off the air horn.
12  Invert the air horn, compress the accelerator pump drive spring and remove the S-link so the pump can be removed.
13  Remove the fuel needle valve, seat and gasket.
14  Remove the retainer and baffle, then lift out the floats and fulcrum pin.
15  Remove the main metering jets.
16  Remove the venturi cluster and gaskets, but don't remove the orifice tubes or main vent tubes.
17  Invert the carburetor and drop out the pump discharge and intake check balls.
18  Note the positions of the limiter caps, then remove them and count the exact number of turns required to just bottom the idle mixture screws. Remove the screws and springs.
19  Remove the screws and separate the throttle body from the main body.
20  Don't dismantle the valve plates and shafts unless needed to replace worn parts.
21  Clean and inspect all components, and replace any that are worn.
22  Reassembly is the reverse of disassembly, using the new gaskets and components from the rebuild kit. After installing the accelerator pump discharge and intake check balls, fill the carburetor bowl about half-full with clean gasoline. Insert the pump piston into the cylinder and work it up-and-down to expel any air. Hold the discharge check ball down with a brass rod, raise and lower the accelerator pump piston and make sure no fuel is emitted from the intake or discharge passages. If there is leakage and the passages and ball seats are in good condition, replace the main body. During reassembly, measure the float setting as described below and reset the idle mixture screws to their original positions (Step 18).

## Float level adjustment
23  With the fuel inlet valve and floats installed in the carburetor, invert the body so the weight of the floats is on the valve.
24  Place a straightedge across the float bowl and measure the distance from the surface of the bowl edge to the crown of each float at its center. Check this measurement against the Specifications.
25  If adjustment is needed, bend the float lever. Always release the floats from the needle before adjusting to avoid damage to the synthetic rubber tip.

## Vacuum piston gap adjustment
26  Check the vacuum piston gap and compare it to the Specifications. Adjust as necessary by turning the adjusting screw at the top.

## Vacuum piston adjustment
27  With the vacuum piston and metering rod assembly correctly in-

stalled, back off the curb idle screw to close the throttles. Note the number of turns required.
28  Depress the piston completely while applying moderate pressure to the rod lifter tab and tighten the rod lifter screw.
29  Release the piston and rod lifter. Return the curb idle screw to the original position.

## Accelerator pump adjustment
30  Back off the curb idle adjusting screw to completely close the throttle plate and open the choke plate so the fast idle cam will allow the throttle plates to seat in the bores.
31  Back off the curb idle screw until it just contacts the stop, then back it off an additional two turns.
32  Measure the distance from the surface of the air horn to the top of the accelerator pump shaft and compare it to the Specifications.
33  To adjust, loosen the pump arm adjusting lock screw and rotate the sleeve to adjust the pump travel. Tighten the lock screw.

## Initial choke valve clearance adjustment
34  Loosen the cover screws and rotate the choke 1/4-turn in the rich direction. Tighten one screw.
35  Set the throttle plate sufficiently to place the fast idle screw on the high step of the cam.
36  Apply 19 inches of vacuum to the diaphragm to pull the plunger against the stop.
37  Measure the choke plate-to-air horn wall clearance and check it against the Specifications.
38  Bend the diaphragm connector link to adjust.

## Fast idle cam position adjustment
39  Perform the operations described in Steps 34 and 35.
40  Measure the choke plate-to-air horn wall clearance with a gauge or drill bit shank. There should be a slight drag when the drill or gauge is removed, if the adjustment is correct.
41  To adjust, bend the fast idle connector rod as necessary.

**4**

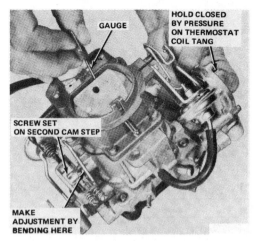

Fig. 4.52   Fast idle cam adjustment (BBD carburetor)
(Sec 14)

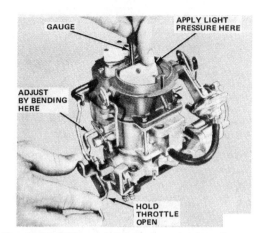

Fig. 4.53   BBD carburetor choke unloader adjustment
(Sec 14)

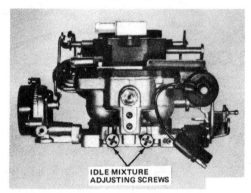

Fig. 4.54   BBD carburetor idle mixture adjusting screw
locations (Sec 14)

### Choke unloader adjustment

42  With the throttle held in the wide open position, apply light pressure to the choke plate and hold it in place.
43  Measure the choke plate-to-air horn wall clearance with a gauge or drill bit shank.
44  Adjust by bending the unloader tang, making sure that it operates smoothly after adjustment.

### Curb idle speed adjustment

45  The curb idle speed must be adjusted under the following conditions:

*Transmission in Neutral (manual) or Drive (automatic)*
*Parking brake securely set*
*Engine at normal operating temperature*
*Air cleaner installed*
*Tachometer properly attached*

46  Turn the adjustment screw to attain the specified idle speed.
47  If the carburetor is equipped with a solenoid, turn the nut on the solenoid to adjust the idle rpm, then tighten the locknut.
48  Disconnect the solenoid wire and adjust the carburetor idle screw to obtain a 500 rpm idle speed. Reconnect the solenoid wire.

### Mixture adjustment

49  The mixture adjustment preparations are the same as those for curb idle adjustment described in Step 45. Adjust the idle mixture screws to the full rich stop (counterclockwise), note the position of the screwhead slots and remove the plastic limiter caps. This can be accomplished by threading a no. 10 sheet metal screw into the center of the cap.
50  Adjust the idle speed. Use the procedures in Steps 47 and 48 for solenoid-equipped models.
51  Beginning at the full rich position (Step 49), turn the mixture screws clockwise in the lean direction until there is an rpm drop. Turn the screws in the counterclockwise direction until the highest rpm previously achieved is obtained. This is called the lean best idle.
52  Turn the idle mixture screws in small, even increments until the specified idle drop is reached.
53  If the final reading varies more than 30 rpm from the curb idle specification, repeat the idle speed adjustment, followed by the mixture lean best idle and idle drop adjustments (Steps 51 and 52).
54  Install new idle mixture screw limiter caps with the limiter cap ear against the full rich stop. Be careful not to change the mixture settings.

---

### 15   Rochester 2SE and E2SE carburetors (151 cu in four-cylinder engine) — overhaul and adjustment

### Overhaul

1   Mount the carburetor on a holding fixture to prevent damage to

15.1   A punch held in a vise can be used to support the carburetor if a stand is not available

the throttle valves. If no holding fixture is available, a suitable-size punch securely mounted in a vise is a good alternative (photo).
2   Remove the gasket from the air horn and the fuel inlet nut and filter assembly.
3   Remove the pump lever attaching screw, disconnect the pump rod from the lever and remove the lever (photo).
4   Disconnect the vacuum break diaphragm hose from the throttle body.

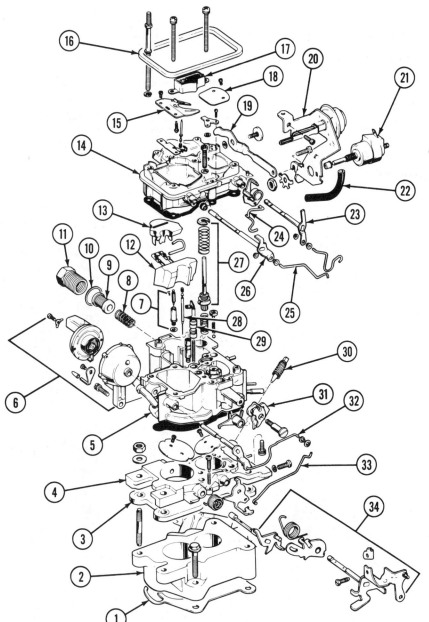

Fig. 4.55  Rochester 2SE carburetor
components — exploded view (Sec 15)

1  Gasket
2  Intake adapter
3  Insulator
4  Throttle body
5  Main body
6  Electric choke cover and coil
7  Needle seat assembly
8  Spring
9  Fuel filter
10  Gasket
11  Fuel inlet fitting
12  Float assembly
13  Filler block
14  Air horn
15  Air valve
16  Gasket
17  Vent screen
18  Choke plate
19  Pump lever
20  Vacuum break and bracket
21  Idle stop stolenoid
22  Vacuum hose
23  Vacuum break lever
24  Choke link
25  Air valve rod
26  Air valve lever
27  Accelerator pump
28  Metering rod
29  Power piston
30  Idle needle and spring
31  Fast idle cam
32  Intermediate choke rod
33  Pump rod
34  Throttle lever assembly

15.3  Removing the pump lever
attaching screw

15.5  Removing the idle speed
solenoid/vacuum break diaphragm
bracket

15.6  Lift off the idle speed
solenoid/vacuum break assembly and
disconnect the air valve rod from the
outside vacuum break plunger

5   Remove the screws that secure the idle speed solenoid/vacuum break diaphragm bracket (if so equipped) (photo).

6   Lift off the idle speed solenoid/vacuum break diaphragm assembly and disconnect the air valve rod from the outside vacuum break plunger (if so equipped) (photo).

7   Disconnect the vacuum break rod (if so equipped) from the inside vacuum break diaphragm plunger.

8   Pry off the clip that secures the intermediate choke rod lever and separate the rod from the lever (photo).

9   Remove the screws that secure the vent/screen assembly to the air horn and lift off the assembly.

10   Remove the retaining screws and lift the solenoid from the air horn (photo).

11   Remove the air horn retaining screws. If the carburetor is equipped with a hot idle compensator, it must be removed to gain access to the short air horn screw.

12   Rotate the fast idle cam up, lift off the air horn and disconnect the fast idle cam rod from the fast idle cam (photo).

13   Disengage the fast idle cam rod from the choke lever and save the bushing for later reassembly (photo).

14   If the pump plunger did not come out of the air horn during removal, remove the plunger from the pump well in the float bowl.

15   Compress the pump plunger spring and remove the spring retainer clip and spring from the piston.

16   Remove the air horn gasket from the float bowl.

17   Remove the pump return spring from the pump well.

18   Remove the plastic filler block that covers the float (photo).

19   Pull up on the retaining pin and remove the float valve and float assembly.

20   On E2SE carburetors, remove the float valve seat and gasket and the extended metering jet (photo).

21   On 2SE carburetors, refer to the accompanying illustration for the

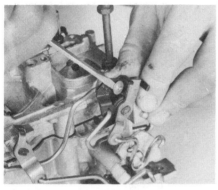

15.8   Use a screwdriver to pry off the clip securing the intermediate choke rod to the choke lever and separate the rod from the lever

15.10   After removing the retaining screws, use a slight twisting motion while lifting the solenoid out

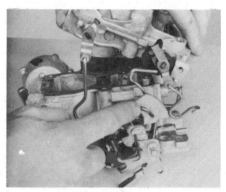

15.12   Removing the air horn

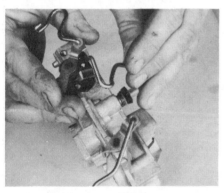

15.13   Removing the fast idle cam from the choke lever

15.18   Lifting out the filler block

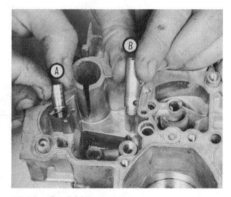

15.20   On E2SE carburetors, remove the float valve seat and gasket (A) and the extended metering jet (B) from the float bowl

15.22   When removing the discharge spring and check ball, do not pry on the white plastic retainer

15.23   Removing the choke housing-to-throttle body screws

15.28   Use a punch to break out the throttle body casting, then drive out the idle mixture needle cover plug

power piston removal operation.

22 Use needle-nose pliers to pull out the white plastic retainer and then remove the pump discharge spring and check ball (photo).

23 Remove the choke housing from the throttle body (photo).

24 Remove the four retaining screws and separate the throttle body from the float bowl.

25 Carefully file off the heads of the rivets securing the choke cover. Use a hammer and small punch to tap out the remainder of the rivet.

26 Remove the choke coil lever screw and lift out the lever.

27 Remove the intermediate shaft and lever assembly by sliding it out the lever side of the float bowl.

28 The plug covering the idle mixture needle should not be removed unless the needle needs replacing or normal cleaning procedures fail to clean the idle mixture passages. If removal is required, use a punch and hammer to drive the plug out (photo).

29 Clean the air horn, float bowl, throttle body and related components with clean solvent and blow them out with compressed air. A can of compressed air such as is available in camera stores can be used if an air compressor is not available. *Do not use a piece of wire for cleaning the jets and passages.*

30 The idle speed solenoid, mixture control solenoid, throttle position sensor, electric choke, pump plunger, diaphragm, plastic filler block and other electrical, rubber and plastic parts should *not* be immersed in carburetor cleaner because they will harden, swell or distort.

31 Make sure all fuel passages, jets and other metering parts are free of burrs and dirt.

32 Inspect the upper and lower surfaces of the air horn, float bowl and throttle body for damage. Be sure all material has been removed.

33 Inspect all lever holes and plastic bushings for excessive wear and out-of-round conditions and replace if necessary.

34 Inspect the float valve and seat for dirt, deep wear grooves and scoring and replace if necessary.

35 Inspect the float valve pull clip for proper installation and adjust if necessary.

36 Inspect the float, float arms and hinge pin for distortion or binding and correct or replace as necessary.

37 Inspect the rubber cup on the pump plunger for excessive wear or cracking.

38 Check the choke valve and linkage for excessive wear, binding or distortion and correct or replace as necessary.

39 Inspect the choke vacuum disphragm for leaks and replace if necessary.

40 Check the choke valve for freedom of movement.

41 Check the mixture control solenoid for binding or leaking in the following manner:

    a) Connect one end of a jumper wire to either end of the solenoid connector and the other end to the positive terminal of a battery.

    b) Connect another jumper wire between the other terminal of the solenoid connector and either the negative terminal of a battery or a ground.

    c) Remove the rubber seal and retainer from the end of the solenoid stem and attach a hand vacuum pump to it (photo).

    d) With the solenoid fully energized (lean position), apply at least 25 in-Hg of vacuum and time the leak-down rate from 20 in-Hg to 15 in-Hg. The leak-down rate should not exceed 5 in-Hg in five (5) seconds. If leakage exceeds that amount, replace the solenoid.

    e) To check if the solenoid is sticking in the down position, again pump about 25 in-Hg of vacuum into it, then disconnect the jumper lead to the battery and watch the pump gauge reading. It should fall to zero in less than one (1) second.

42 Prior to reassembling the carburetor, compare all old and new

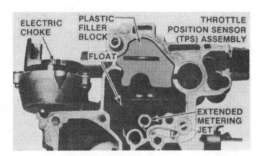

Fig. 4.56   Float bowl component layout (2SE/E2SE carburetor) (Sec 15)

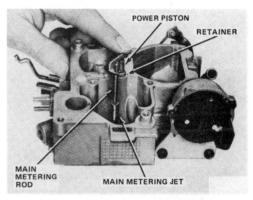

Fig. 4.57   Power piston removal (2SE/E2SE carburetor) (Sec 15)

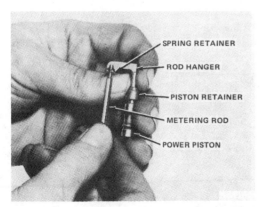

Fig. 4.58   Remove the metering rod from the 2SE carburetor power piston by compressing the spring on the top and aligning the groove with the slot in the holder (Sec 15)

Fig. 4.59   Removing the idle mixture screw (2SE/E2SE carburetor) (Sec 15)

gaskets back-to-back to be sure they match perfectly. Check especially that all the necessary holes are present and in the proper position in the new gaskets.

43 If the idle mixture needle and spring have been removed, reinstall by lightly seating the needle, then back it off three (3) turns. This will provide a preliminary idle mixture adjustment. Final idle mixture adjustment must be made after the carburetor is installed.

44 Install a new gasket on the bottom of the float bowl.

45 Mount the throttle body on the float bowl so that it is properly aligned over the locating dowels on the bowl and reinstall the attaching screws, tightening them evenly and securely. Be sure that the steps on the fast idle cam face toward the fast idle screw on the throttle lever when installed.

46 Inspect the linkage to make sure that the lockout tang properly engages in the slot of the secondary lockout lever and that the linkage moves freely without binding.

47 Attach the choke housing to the throttle body, making sure the locating lug on the rear of the housing sits in its recess in the float bowl.

48 Install the intermediate choke shaft and lever assembly into the float bowl by pushing it through from the throttle lever side.

49 Position the intermediate choke lever in the up position and install the thermostatic coil lever onto the end sticking into the choke housing. The coil lever is properly aligned when the coil pick-up tang is in the 12 o'clock position (photo). Install the attaching screw in the end of the intermediate shaft to secure the coil lever.

50 Three self-tapping screws supplied in the overhaul kit are used in place of the original pop rivets to secure the choke cover and coil assembly to the choke housing. Start the three screws into the housing, making sure that they start easily and are properly aligned (photo), then remove them again.

51 Place the fast idle screw on the highest step of the fast idle cam, then install the choke cover on the housing, aligning the notch in the cover with the raised casting projection on the housing cover flange. When installing the cover, be sure the coil pick-up tang engages the inside choke lever.

52 With the choke cover in place, install the three self-tapping screws and tighten them securely.

53 Install the pump discharge check ball and spring in the passage next to the float chamber, then place a new plastic retainer in the hole so that its end engages the spring and tap it lightly into place until the retainer top is flush with the bowl surface.

54 Install the main metering jet in the bottom of the float chamber.

55 Install the float valve seat assembly and gasket.

56 To make float level adjustments easier, bend the float arm up slightly at the notch shown in the photo before installing the float.

57 Attach the float valve to the float arm by sliding the lever under the pull clip. The correct installation of the pull clip is to hook the clip over the edge of the float on the float arm facing the float pontoon (photo). Install the float retaining pin in the float arm, then install the float assembly by aligning the valve in its seat and the float retaining pin in its locating channels in the float bowl.

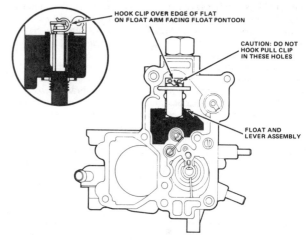

Fig. 4.60   Float needle pull clip installation (2SE/E2SE carburetor) (Sec 15)

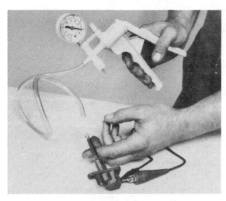

15.41   Testing the mixture control solenoid with a vacuum pump

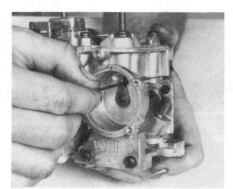

15.49   Installing the thermostatic coil lever with an Allen wrench

15.50   Reinstalling the choke cover using the self-tapping screws supplied with the overhaul kit

15.56   Prior to installation, bend the float arm slightly at the point indicated

15.57   During installation the float valve should be positioned on the arm as shown

15.58   Measuring the float adjustment

## Float level adjustment

58  Adjust the float level in the following manner. While holding the float retaining pin firmly in place, push down on the float arm at its outer end, against the top of the float valve, so the top of the float is the specified distance from the float bowl surface (photo). Bend the float arm as necessary to achieve the proper measurement by pushing down on the pontoon. See the Specifications for the proper float measurement for your vehicle. Visually check the float level after the adjustment.

59  On 2SE carbs, install the power piston spring in the piston bore. If the metering rod has been removed from the power piston assembly, reinstall the rod in the holder, making sure the spring is on top of the arm. Then install the assembly in the float bowl. Use care when installing the metering rod into the main metering jet so as not to damage the metering rod tip. Press down firmly on the power piston's plastic retainer until it is firmly seated in its recess and the top is flush with the top of the bowl casting. Light tapping may be required.

60  Install the plastic filler block over the float valve so that it is flush with the float bowl surface.

61  If the carburetor is equipped with a throttle position sensor, install the TPS return spring in the bottom of the well in the float bowl. Then install the TPS and connector assembly by aligning the groove in the electrical connector with the slot in the float bowl. When properly installed, the assembly should sit below the float bowl surface.

62  Install a new air horn gasket on the float bowl.

63  Install the pump return spring in the pump well (photo).

64  Reassemble the pump plunger assembly, lubricate the plunger cap with a thin coat of engine oil and install the pump plunger in the pump well (photo).

65  If used, remove the old plug plunger seal and retainer and the old seals and retainers in both locations and lightly stake both seal retainers in three places other than the original staking locations.

66  Install the fast idle cam rod in the lower hole of the choke lever.

67  If so equipped, apply a light coat of silicone grease or engine oil to the TPS plunger and push it through the seal in the air horn, so that about one-half of the plunger extends above the seal.

68  Prior to installing the air horn, apply a light coat of silicone grease or engine oil to the pump plunger stem to help it slip through the air horn seal.

69  Rotate the fast idle cam to the ''up'' position so it can be engaged with the lower end of the fast idle cam rod and, while holding down on the pump plunger assembly, carefully lower the air horn onto the float bowl, guiding the pump plunger stem through its seal.

70  Install the six air horn mounting screws and lock washers and two air cleaner bolts, tightening them in the proper sequence as shown in the accompanying illustration.

71  If so equipped, install a new seal in the the recess of the float bowl and the hot idle compensator valve.

72  Install a new rubber seal on the end of the mixture control solenoid stem until it is up against the boss on the stem (photo).

73  Using a 3/16-inch socket or other appropriate tool and a hammer (photo), drive the retainer over the mixture control solenoid stem just far enough to retain the rubber seal, while leaving a slight clearance between them for seal expansion.

74  Apply a light coat of engine oil on the rubber seal and, using a new gasket, install the mixture control solenoid in the air horn. Use a slight twisting motion while installing the solenoid to help the rubber seal slip into its recess.

75  Install the vent/screen assembly onto the air horn.

76  Install a plastic bushing in the hole in the choke lever with the small end facing out. Then with the intermediate choke lever at the 12 o'clock position, install the intermediate choke rod in the bushing. Install a new retaining clip on the end of the rod. An effective way of doing this is to use a broad screwdriver and a 3/16-inch regular socket as shown in the photo. Make sure the clip is not seated tightly against the bushing and that the linkage moves freely.

77  Engage the vacuum break rod with the inside vacuum break diaphragm plunger and the air valve rod with the outside plunger and mount the idle speed solenoid/vacuum break diaphragm assembly.

78  Engage the pump rod with the pump rod lever and mount the pump

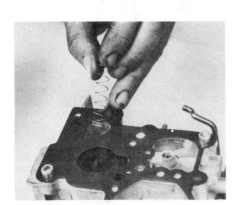

15.63  Inserting the pump return spring into the pump well

15.64  Inserting the pump plunger into the pump well

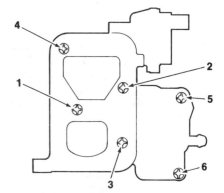

Fig. 4.61  Air horn screw tightening sequence (2SE/E2SE carburetor) (Sec 15)

4

15.72  Attaching a new rubber seal to the end of the mixture control solenoid stem

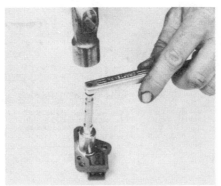

15.73  Tap the seal onto the mixture control solenoid stem using a hammer and socket

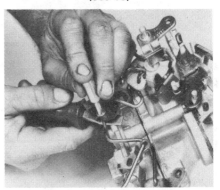

15.76  Using a small socket and screwdriver to install the retaining clip onto the intermediate choke rod to secure it to the choke lever

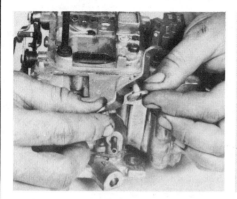

15.78 Inserting the pump rod mounting screw through the pump rod prior to installation

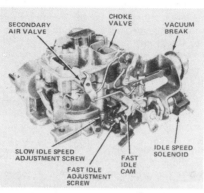

Fig. 4.62 2SE carburetor external component locations (Sec 15)

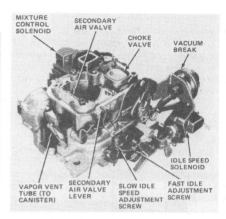

Fig. 4.63 E2SE carburetor adjustment locations (Sec 15)

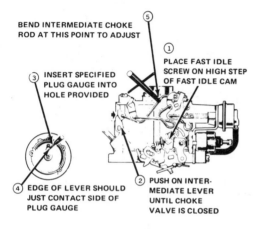

Fig. 4.64 Choke coil lever adjustment (2SE/E2SE carburetor) (Sec 15)

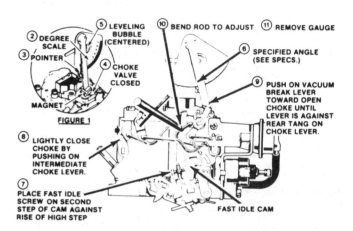

Fig. 4.65 Fast idle cam position adjustment (2SE/E2SE carburetor) (Sec 15)

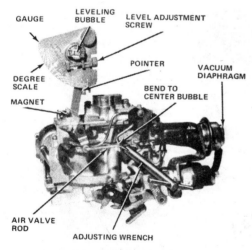

Fig. 4.66 Air valve rod adjustment (2SE/E2SE carburetor) (Sec 15)

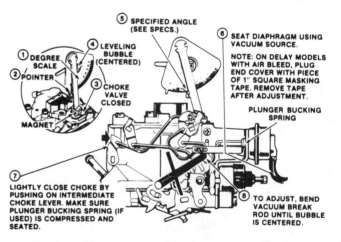

Fig.4.67 Primary vacuum break adjustment (2SE/E2SE carburetor) (Sec 15)

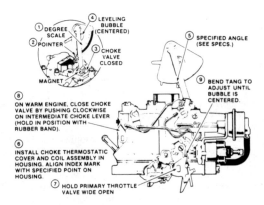

Fig.4.68   Choke unloader adjustment (2SE/E2SE carburetor) (Sec 15)

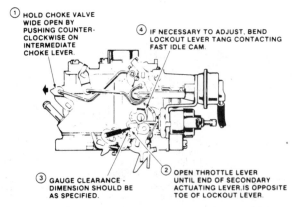

Fig. 4.69   Secondary lockout adjustment (2SE/E2SE carburetor) (Sec 15)

lever on the air horn with the washer between the lever and the air horn (photo).

79   Reconnect the vacuum break diaphragm hose to the fitting on the carburetor body.

80   Install the fuel filter so that the hole faces toward the inlet nut.

81   Place a new gasket on the inlet nut and install the nut. Be careful not to over tighten the nut since this could damage the gaskets and cause a fuel leak.

82   Install a new gasket on the top of the air horn.

*External linkage adjustments*

83   Refer to the accompanying illustrations (Fig. 4.62 through 4.69) and adjust the linkages as shown.

*Idle speed and mixture adjustment*

84   Prior to adjusting the idle speed or mixture, the following precautions must be taken and conditions exist:

*Parking brake securely set*
*Engine at normal operating temperature*
*Transmission in Drive (automatic) or Neutral (manual)*
*Tachometer connected to the ignition coil or pigtail wire connector*
*The air cleaner should be installed and all hoses connected or, if removed, the hoses should be plugged and the choke plate must be open*
*The air conditioner compressor wire must be unplugged and the deceleration vacuum hose disconnected and plugged*
*The ignition timing must be correctly adjusted*
*The engine must not be operated at idle for more than three (3) minutes*

85   Disconnect and plug the distributor vacuum hose and connect a timing light to the engine.

86   Adjust the ignition timing with the engine at or below the specified idle speed.

87   Connect the distributor vacuum hose and remove the timing light.

88   Disconnect the deceleration valve and purge hose from the vapor canister and plug the hoses. Remove the air cleaner if necessary for access.

89   On air conditioned models, adjust the idle speed screw to achieve the specified idle speed. Turn the air conditioning switch on, open the throttle momentarily and make sure the solenoid armature is fully extended. Adjust the solenoid idle screw to achieve the specified idle and turn the air conditioning switch off.

90   On non-air conditioned models, obtain the specified idle speed by adjusting the solenoid idle screw with the solenoid energized. Disconnect the solenoid wire connector and adjust the idle speed screw to obtain the specified idle speed. Reconnect the solenoid wire.

91   Disconnect and plug the EGR valve hose. With the fast idle speed screw on the top step of the fast idle speed cam, adjust the fast idle speed to the specified rpm.

92   Turn off the engine, remove the tachometer and reinstall any components or hoses removed during this procedure.

93   The fuel mixture adjustment on these models requires special tools and equipment and should be left to your dealer or a qualified shop.

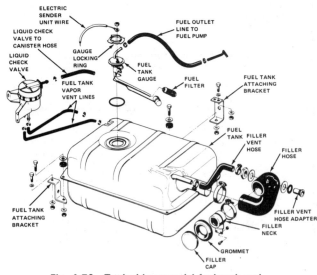

Fig. 4.70   Typical later model fuel tank and components — exploded view (Sec 16)

**4**

## 16   Fuel tank — removal and installation

**Caution:** *Gasoline is extremely flammable and extra precautions must be taken when working on any part of the fuel system. Do not smoke or allow open flames or bare light bulbs near the work area. Also, do not work in a garage if a natural gas-type appliance with a pilot light is present.*

1   The fuel tank on early models is located under the driver's seat and is retained by straps. On later models, it is located under the rear of the vehicle and is held in place by brackets and bolts.

2   Disconnect the negative battery cable from the battery.

3   Drain or siphon the fuel from the tank so it will be easier to handle.

4   On early models, remove the driver's seat.

5   On later models, raise the rear of the vehicle and support it securely.

6   On all models, mark the locations of all hoses attached to the tank, then remove them.

7   On early models, remove the strap retaining nuts and separate the tank from the vehicle.

8   On later models, support the tank with a jack, using a board to protect the tank on models which aren't equipped with a shield. Remove the retaining bolts and brackets and lower the tank from the vehicle.

9   To install the fuel tank on early models, place the tank in position, install the straps and connect the hoses. Install the driver's seat.

10   On later models, carefully raise the tank into position, install the brackets and tighten the bolts securely.

11   Connect the hoses and lower the vehicle.

12   Connect the negative battery cable.

## 17   Fuel tank — cleaning and repair

1   Drain and remove the fuel tank.
2   Remove the fuel tank gauge unit by removing the retaining screws.
3   Turn the tank over and empty out any remaining fuel.
4   If repair work must be done on the fuel tank *that does not involve any heat or flames*, the tank can be satisfactorily cleaned by running hot water into it and letting it overflow out the top for at least five (5) minutes. **This method, however, does not remove gasoline vapors.**
5   **If repair work involving heat or flame is necessary, have it done by an experienced professional.** The following, more thorough procedures should be used to remove all fuel and vapors from the tank.
6   Fill the tank completely with tap water, agitate vigorously and drain.
7   Add a gasoline emulsifying agent to the tank according to the manufacturer's instructions, refill with water, agitate approximately 10 minutes and drain.
8   Once again, flush with water to overflowing (for several minutes) and drain.
9   The tank is now ready for repair work.
10  Under no circumstances should repair work involving heat or flame be performed without first carrying out the above procedures.

## 18   Exhaust system — check and component replacement

Caution: *Inspection and repair of exhaust system components should* be done only after enough time has elapsed after driving the vehicle to allow the system components to cool completely. Also, when working under the vehicle, make sure it is securely supported on jackstands.

1   The exhaust system consists of the exhaust manifold, muffler, catalytic converter (if equipped), tailpipe and connecting pipes, brackets, hangers and clamps. The entire exhaust system is attached to the body or frame with mounting brackets and rubber hangers. If any one of the parts is improperly installed, excessive noise and vibration will be transmitted to the body.
2   Regular inspection of the exhaust system should be made to keep it safe and quiet. Look for any damaged or bent parts, open seams, holes, loose connections, excessive corrosion and other defects. Deteriorated exhaust system components should not be repaired; they should be replaced with new parts. Refer to Chapter 6 for catalytic converter removal and installation procedures.
3   If the components are extremely corroded or rusted together, it may be a good idea to have the work performed by a reputable muffler shop, since welding equipment will probably be required to remove the components.
4   Always work from the back to the front when removing exhaust system components. Penetrating oil applied to mounting bolts and nuts will make them much easier to remove. Always use new gaskets, hangers and clamps and apply anti-seize compound to mounting bolt threads when putting everything back together. Also, when replacing any exhaust system parts, be sure to allow enough clearance from all points on the underbody to avoid overheating the floor pan.

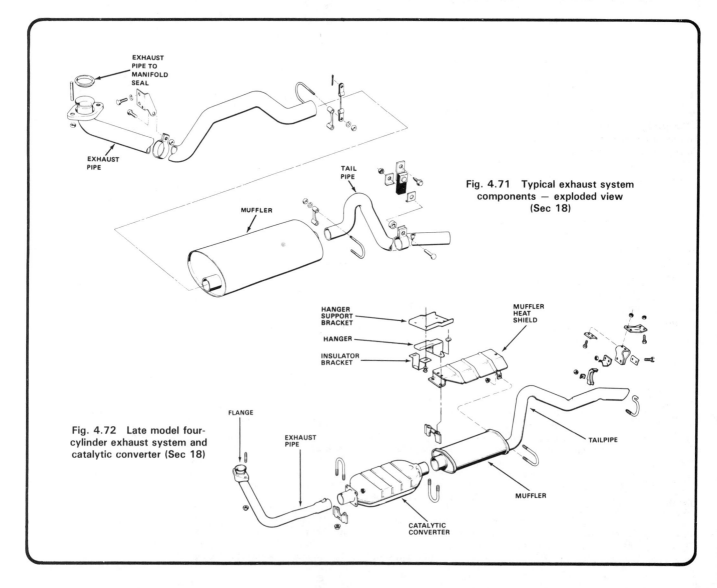

Fig. 4.71   Typical exhaust system components — exploded view (Sec 18)

Fig. 4.72   Late model four-cylinder exhaust system and catalytic converter (Sec 18)

# Chapter 5   Engine electrical systems

*Refer to Chapter 13 for information related to 1984 through 1986 models*

**Contents**

| | | | | |
|---|---|---|---|---|
| Alternator — brush replacement | 8 | Electronic ignition pick-up coil — removal and installation | 20 |
| Alternator — removal and installation | 7 | Electronic ignition system — check | 16 |
| Battery — check and maintenance | Chapter 1 | External voltage regulator — removal and installation | 6 |
| Battery — emergency jump starting | 3 | Generator — brush replacement | 10 |
| Battery — removal and installation | 2 | Generator — removal and installation | 9 |
| Battery cables — check and replacement | 4 | General information | 1 |
| Charging system — check | 5 | Ignition coil — removal and installation | 17 |
| Contact points and condenser — replacement and adjustment (1953 through 1974 models) | Chapter 1 | Ignition timing — check and adjustment | Chapter 1 |
| Conventional distributor — check | 21 | Spark plug replacement | Chapter 1 |
| Conventional ignition system — check | 15 | Spark plug wire, distributor cap and rotor — check and replacement | Chapter 1 |
| Distributor — removal and installation | 18 | Starter motor — brush replacement | 13 |
| Drivebelt check and adjustment | Chapter 1 | Starter motor — removal and installation | 12 |
| Electronic distributor — check | 22 | Starter solenoid — removal and installation | 14 |
| Electronic ignition module — removal and installation | 19 | Starting system — check | 11 |

**Specifications**

## Charging system

| | |
|---|---|
| Alternator and generator brush wear limit | 1/4 in |
| Generator brush spring tension | 40 oz. |
| Motorcraft alternator output voltage | |

| Temperature | Voltage range |
|---|---|
| 0 to 50 | 14.1 to 14.8 |
| 50 to 100 | 13.7 to 14.5 |
| 100 to 150 | 13.4 to 14.2 |
| 150 to 200 | 13.1 to 13.8 |

## Electronic ignition system

Coil resistance
  1974 through 1977

| | |
|---|---|
| Primary | 1 to 2 ohms |
| Secondary | 8000 to 17500 ohms |

  1978 through 1983 in-line six-cylinder and V8 engines
    Primary

| | |
|---|---|
| 75° | 1.13 to 1.23 ohms |
| 200° | 1.50 ohms |

    Secondary

| | |
|---|---|
| 75° | 7700 to 9300 ohms |
| 200° | 12000 ohms |

  1980 through 1983 four-cylinder engine

| | |
|---|---|
| Primary | Zero or near zero on the low scale |
| Secondary | Less than infinity on the high scale |
| Coil-to-ground | Infinity |

Cranking voltage test
  1974 through 1977

| | |
|---|---|
| Switch-on voltage | 12 to 13 volts |
| Cranking voltage | 9.6 volts |
| 1978 through 1983 six-cylinder and V8 engines | 6 volts |

Distributor ignition pickup coil resistance

| | |
|---|---|
| 1974 through 1977 | 1.6 to 2.4 ohms |
| 1978 through 1983 six-cylinder and V8 engines | 400 to 800 ohms |

  1980 through 1983 four-cylinder engine

| | |
|---|---|
| Pickup connector | 500 to 800 ohms |
| Connector-to-ground | Infinity |

## Conventional ignition system

Cranking voltage
  6-volt system .................................. 4.5 volts
  12-volt system ................................. 9 volts
Voltage drop test
  Battery cable-to-starter ......................... 0.2 or less
  Distributor primary terminal on the coil-to-the primary
    terminal on the distributor ..................... 0.05 or less
  Distributor coil terminal-to-distributor body ........... 0.05 or less

## Starting system

1953 through 1972 models — brush spring tension
  Autolite 6-volt .................................. 42 to 53 oz
  Autolite 12-volt ................................. 31 to 47 oz
  Delco 6-volt ................................... 24 oz
  Delco 12-volt
    MDM-6005, MDU-7004 ..................... 31 to 47 oz
    1107746 .................................. 35 oz
    1107391, 108366 and 1108375 ............. 32 to 40 oz
  Prestolite ..................................... 32 to 40 oz
1973 through 1983 models (six-cylinder and V8 only)
  Brush spring tension ............................ 40 oz
  Brush length .................................. 1/2 in
  Brush wear limit ............................... 1/4 in

## Torque Specifications

| | Ft-lb | Nm |
|---|---|---|
| Alternator bracket-to-engine ......................... | 23 to 30 | 31 to 41 |
| Alternator pivot bolt ............................... | 23 tto 30 | 31 to 41 |
| Starter motor-to-bellhousing ........................ | 15 to 20 | 21 to 28 |

### 1   General information

The engine electrical systems consist of the starting, charging and ignition systems.

The starting system is made up of the battery, starter relay switch, starter motor and solenoid and wiring. Some early models were not equipped with relays or solenoids for activating the starter drive and used Bendix spring or clutch devices to perform this function. Automatic transmission-equipped models feature a neutral start switch in the system to prevent starting except when the transmission is in Neutral or Park.

The charging system consists of the generator or alternator, voltage regulator, battery and associated wires and cables. On later models, the voltage regulator is an integral part of the alternator.

The ignition system consists of the distributor, coil, spark plugs, battery, associated wiring and, on V6 models, a ballast resistor on the coil. Later models use transistorized ignition components to perform some of the mechanical functions of the distributor (such as contact points and spark advance) for improved performance and emissions.

### 2   Battery — removal and installation

1   The battery is located in the engine compartment, usually to the right side of the engine. It is held in place by a hold-down frame and wing nuts or bolts and clamps at the base.

2   **Caution:** *Since the battery produces hydrogen gas, keep open flames and lighted cigarettes away from it at all times. Avoid spilling any of the electrolyte (battery fluid) on the vehicle or yourself. Always keep the battery in an upright position. Any spilled electrolyte should be flushed immediately with large quantities of water. Wear eye protection when working around the battery to prevent eye damage from splashed electrolyte. Always disconnect the negative (–) battery cable first, followed by the positive (+) cable.*

3   After the cables are disconnected from the battery, remove the clamp bolts or wing nuts and hold-down frame.

4   Carefully lift the battery from the tray and move it out of the engine compartment.

5   Prior to installation, make sure the negative cable is properly grounded with a clean and secure connection.

6   Place the battery in position in the tray and apply a thin coat of light grease or petroleum jelly to the base of the posts.

7   Connect the positive cable first, followed by the negative cable.

8   Install the retaining clamps and bolts or hold-down frame. Do not over tighten them or you may distort the battery.

### 3   Battery — emergency jump starting

Refer to the *Booster battery (jump) starting* procedure at the front of this manual.

### 4   Battery cables — check and replacement

1   Periodically inspect the entire length of each battery cable for damage, cracked or burned insulation and corrosion. Poor battery cable connections can cause starting problems and decreased engine performance.

2   Check the cable-to-terminal connections at the ends of the cables for cracks, loose wire strands and corrosion. The presence of white, fluffy deposits under the insulation at the cable terminal connection is a sign the cable is corroded and should be replaced. Check the terminals for distortion, missing mounting bolts or nuts and corrosion.

3   If only the positive cable is to be replaced, be sure to disconnect the negative cable from the battery first.

4   Disconnect and remove the cable(s) from the vehicle. Make sure the replacement cable(s) is the same length and diameter.

5   Clean the threads of the starter or ground connection with a wire brush to remove rust and corrosion. Apply a light coat of petroleum jelly to the threads to ease installation and prevent future corrosion. Inspect the connections frequently to make sure they are clean and tight.

6   Attach the cable(s) to the starter or ground connection and tighten the mounting nut(s) securely.

7   Before connecting the new cable(s) to the battery, make sure they reach the terminals without having to be stretched.

8   Connect the positive cable first, followed by the negative cable. Tighten the nuts and apply a thin coat of petroleum jelly to the terminal and cable connection.

### 5   Charging system — check

1   When a problem develops in the charging system, the first check should be for the obvious. Inspect all wires for damage, corrosion and

loose connections. Check the drivebelts to make sure they are in good condition and properly adjusted.

2  If the charging system is not working properly (indicated by the warning light staying on, ammeter showing discharge or a battery that is constantly discharged or overcharged), the alternator or generator output should be checked.

### Generator

3  Disconnect the armature (ARM) and battery (BAT) leads from the regulator and connect an ammeter between the two wires. Disconnect the field (FLD) lead from the regulator and, with the engine at idle, touch the lead to the regulator base. Increase the engine speed slowly and check the charging rate on the ammeter.

4  If the charging rate does not increase, there is a fault in the wiring harness or the generator is defective.

5  If an ammeter is not available, connect a 6 or 12-volt test light to the regulator terminal marked ''Armature.'' Start the engine and ground the other light lead. If the test light does not glow, the fault is either in the regulator or generator.

6  To localize the fault, disconnect the field and armature cables from the generator, connect a wire to the field terminal and ground the other end. Use a 60-watt, 110-volt test light to ground the armature terminal. The test light will glow at approximately 1500 rpm if the generator is operating properly, indicating a fault in the voltage regulator. The regulator should be replaced with a new one (Section 6) or checked and adjusted by an auto electric shop.

### Motorola alternator

7  Unplug the field connector and connect a jumper wire between the auxiliary and field terminals. Connect a voltmeter to the auxiliary terminal, start the engine and allow it to idle.

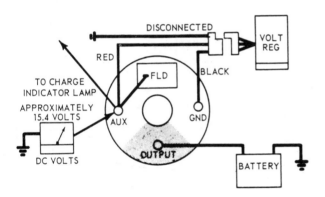

**Fig. 5.1  Motorola alternator output test details (Sec 5)**

8  If the output is more than 13 volts but less than 15 volts, the alternator is operating properly.

9  If the voltage rises to 15 or 16 volts, the regulator is faulty and should be replaced with a new one (Section 6).

10  If there is no current output, the alternator should be replaced with a new or rebuilt unit.

### Motorcraft alternator

11  Connect a voltmeter to the battery with the voltmeter positive lead on the positive post and the negative lead on the negative post.

12  Apply a load to the system by turning on the headlights and the heater or air conditioner blower motor.

13  Start the engine and slowly increase the speed to approximately 2000 rpm.

14  When the voltage stabilizes, compare the reading to the chart in the Specifications. If the reading is within the specified range, the alternator (and charging system) is operating properly. If the reading is high, the system is overcharging and if it is low, it is undercharging. Proceed with the appropriate checks to verify the conditions and locate the fault.

**Undercharging**

15  If the system is undercharging, turn off the engine and accessories and note the battery voltage at the terminals using a voltmeter.

16  Start the engine, turn on the electrical accessories and slowly increase the engine speed to approximately 2000 rpm.

17  Note the voltage reading and compare it to the one taken in Paragraph 15. If the reading has increased at least 0.5 volt, the charging system is operating properly. If the increase is less than 0.5 volt, the system is definitely undercharging.

18  If the test indicates undercharging, turn the ignition switch on and check for battery voltage at the voltage regulator S terminal. If there is no voltage, or if it is less than that of the battery, check the yellow wire for an open circuit and for a faulty connection at the regulator or the starter solenoid.

19  If no fault is found, disconnect the voltage regulator wires and connect one lead of an ohmmeter to the F terminal and the other to a good ground as shown in the accompanying illustration. The ohmmeter should indicate four (4) to 250 ohms. Less than four ohms indicates a short, while more than 250 ohms indicates an open, dirty brushes, or dirty slip rings. If the reading is not within the specifications, the alternator should be replaced or overhauled.

20  If the reading is within the specifications, connect the ohmmeter between the I and F terminals of the voltage regulator. No resistance should be indicated. If the reading is approximately ten (10) ohms, the regulator is damaged and should be replaced with a new one.

21  To further check the voltage regulator, connect a jumper wire between the A and F terminals of the plug as shown in the accompanying illustration, then repeat the tests in Steps 15 through 17. If undercharging is indicated, replace the voltage regulator.

22  If the output is within the specifications, disconnect the jumper wire, leaving the voltage regulator connector unplugged. Disconnect

**5**

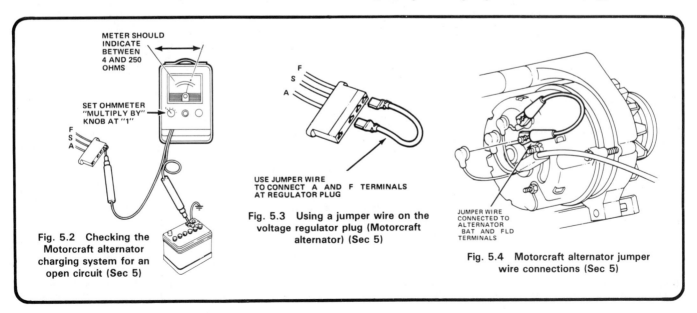

**Fig. 5.2  Checking the Motorcraft alternator charging system for an open circuit (Sec 5)**

**Fig. 5.3  Using a jumper wire on the voltage regulator plug (Motorcraft alternator) (Sec 5)**

**Fig. 5.4  Motorcraft alternator jumper wire connections (Sec 5)**

the wiring harness from the alternator field (FLD) terminal and connect a jumper wire between the battery (BAT) and FLD terminals as
shown in the accompanying illustrations.
23  Repeat the tests in Steps 15 through 17. If the output is within
the specifications, there is a fault in the wiring harness and it should
be replaced. If the output is low, there is a defect in the alternator and
it should be replaced or overhauled.

**Overcharging**
24  Connect a voltmeter positive lead to the battery positive post and
the negative lead to the negative post. With all electrical accessories
turned off, note the voltmeter reading.
25  Start the engine and slowly increase the speed to approximately
1500 rpm. The voltage should increase no more than two (2) volts over
the battery voltage noted in the previous Step. If it does increase more
than two (2) volts, the overcharging condition is verified.
26  Disconnect the voltage regulator connector and repeat the test.
If the voltage is within the specified range, the regulator is faulty and
must be replaced with a new one. If the voltage reading is still high,
the alternator wiring harness has a short and should be replaced.

### Delco alternator
27  These alternators feature an integral voltage regulator and most
testing of the charging system requires special equipment. However,
simple checks of undercharging and overcharging conditions can be
made with a voltmeter.

**Undercharging**
28  With the ignition switch on, check between the alternator No. 1,
No. 2 and battery (BAT) terminals and a good ground with a voltmeter.
A zero reading indicates an open circuit between the lead connection
and the battery. The vehicle should be taken to a repair shop for further testing because of the special equipment and techniques required.

**Overcharging**
29  Connect the voltmeter between the No. 2 terminal and a good
ground. If the reading is zero, the No. 2 circuit is open. If the
No. 2 circuit is not open and an obvious overcharge condition still exists, there is a fault in the alternator.

---

### 6  External voltage regulator — removal and installation

1  Unplug the connector, remove the attaching screws and lift the
voltage regulator from the engine compartment.
2  Place the new regulator in position, install the screws and plug in
the connector.

---

### 7  Alternator — removal and installation

1  Before removing the alternator, make sure the ignition switch is
off and the negative cable is disconnected from the battery.
2  Disconnect the electrical leads from the alternator.
3  Loosen the adjusting bolt and pivot bolt nut, then remove the
drivebelt from the pulley.
4  Remove the mounting bolts and lift the alternator from the engine
compartment.
5  To install the alternator, hold it in position, align the holes and install the bolts.
6  Place the drivebelt on the pulley, adjust the tension and tighten
the bolts.
7  Connect the electrical leads to the alternator.
8  Connect the negative cable to the battery.

---

### 8  Alternator — brush replacement

1  Worn or damaged brushes can reduce the alternator output. The
brushes generally do not require replacement until the vehicle has
reached very high mileage (generally over 75000 miles).

### Motorola alternator
2  On these models the entire brush assembly can be replaced with
the alternator in place in the vehicle. Before proceeding, disconnect
the negative battery cable from the battery.

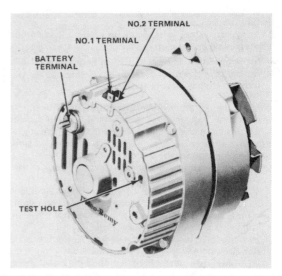

Fig. 5.5  Typical Delco alternator terminal locations (Sec 5)

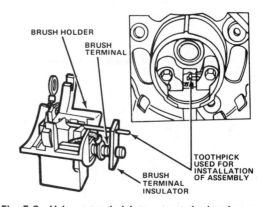

Fig. 5.6  Using a toothpick to retract the brushes on the
Motorcraft alternator (Sec 8)

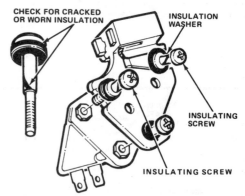

Fig. 5.7  Delco alternator brush holder inspection (Sec 8)

3  Disconnect the field lead from the alternator.
4  Remove the two self-tapping screws and the brush assembly cover.
5  Pull the brush assembly back carefully until it just clears the locating
pins, tip it away from the housing and remove it. Do not pull the
assembly straight back as the brushes can break off and fall into the
alternator.
6  Installation is the reverse of removal.

### Motorcraft alternator
7  Remove the alternator (Section 7) and scribe a line across the housing components to ensure correct reassembly. Remove the three housing through-bolts and the nuts and insulators from the rear housing.

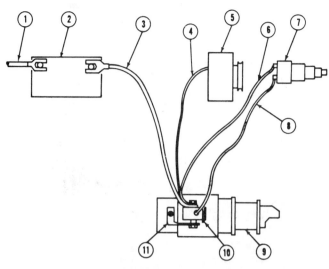

**Fig. 5.8   Early model starting system circuit components (Sec 11)**

| | | |
|---|---|---|
| 1 Ground cable | 5 Alternator | 8 Solenoid wire |
| 2 Battery | 6 Ignition switch | 9 Starter |
| 3 Positive cable | wire | 10 Solenoid |
| 4 Alternator wire | 7 Ignition switch | 11 Connector strap |

Carefully note the insulator locations.
8   Withdraw the rear housing section from the alternator.
9   Remove the brushes and springs from the brush holder assembly, which is located inside the rear housing.
10   Install the springs and new brushes in the holder assembly and hold them in place by inserting a toothpick through the rear housing as shown in the accompanying illustration. Make sure enough of the toothpick protrudes through the rear of the housing that it can be withdrawn later.
11   Attach the stator to the rear housing, rotor and front housing assembly, making sure the scribed marks line up.
12   Install the three housing through-bolts and rear end insulators and nuts, but do not tighten them.
13   Carefully extract the toothpick from the rear housing and tighten the through-bolts and rear housing nuts.
14   Install the alternator.

### Delco alternator

15   Remove the alternator.
16   Scribe marks on the alternator case components to make sure they are correctly aligned during reassembly.
17   Remove the four through-bolts retaining the rear housing.
18   Use a screwdriver to carefully pry between the stator assembly and front housing and separate the alternator components.
19   As the rotor and drive end assemblies are separated from the slip ring housing assembly, the brushes will spring out onto the rotor shaft and can become contaminated with grease. If the same brushes are reinstalled, they must be cleaned thoroughly.
20   Remove the brush holder assembly retaining screws and lift the assembly away. Note the order in which the parts are removed to simplify reassembly.
21   If the same brushes and holder assembly are to be reinstalled, inspect the brushes for wear and contamination and the brush springs for damage and corrosion. Check the insulating screws for cracked and worn insulation.
22   Install the springs and brushes in the brush holder. The brushes must slide in and out freely after installation, with no binding.
23   Retain the brushes in position in the holder by inserting a toothpick into the hole at the bottom of the frame.
24   Install the brush holder with the toothpick protruding through the hole in the alternator end frame.
25   Make sure the rotor shaft bearing surfaces are clean and position the housings with the scribe marks aligned. Install the through-bolts and nuts. Remove the toothpick from the holder assembly.

## 9   Generator — removal and installation

1   Disconnect the negative cable from the battery.
2   Disconnect the electrical leads from the generator, marking them to ensure reinstallation in their original locations.
3   Loosen the adjustment bolt, push the generator toward the engine and remove the drivebelt.
4   Remove the mounting bolts and lift the generator from the engine compartment.
5   To install the generator, place it in position and install the bolts finger tight. Place the drivebelt in the pulley groove and install the adjustment bolt.
6   Adjust the drivebelt tension and tighten the adjustment bolt securely, followed by the mounting bolt.
7   Connect the electrical leads to the generator.
8   Connect the negative cable to the battery.

## 10   Generator — brush replacement

1   The generator brushes should be replaced when they have worn to less than the specified length or if they have been damaged or contaminated with oil.
2   Remove the band on the rear of the generator (if so equipped).
3   Disengage the brushes from the holder arms and springs, remove the electrical lead retaining screws and separate the brushes from the generator.
4   The contact surface of the replacement brushes should already be radiused to conform to the commutator. If the brushes are not radiused, they must be contoured with sandpaper prior to installation so they will be in full contact with the commutator. To do this, wrap a piece of emery cloth around the commutator (rough side out, of course) and slip the brushes over it. Rotate the brushes or brush holder back and forth until the brushes match the contour of the commutator.
5   Connect the brush electrical leads and install the retaining screws.
6   Place the brushes in position and engage them in the holders. The brushes must move freely in the holders and be held against the commutator by the spring tension. Too high a spring pressure causes rapid brush and commutator wear and too little allows arcing and reduces generator output. Check the tension with a spring scale to make sure it is as specified.
7   Install the band.

## 11   Starting system — check

**Note:** *In order for the starting system to operate, the battery must be in a fully charged condition and the transmission must be in Neutral or Park. If the battery is not fully charged, or if the neutral start switch is faulty, recharge the battery or make any necessary repairs before trying to diagnose the starting system.*

1   If the starter does not turn, switch on the headlights and turn the key to Start or push down on the starting switch. If the headlights did not come on, or if they dim or go out when the starter is engaged (see note above), the battery and cable connections should be checked. If the headlights remain bright but the starter does not crank the engine, there is an open circuit somewhere in the system (some possible locations are the ignition switch and connections, the starter motor brushes, the solenoid or the starting switch on foot-operated early model starters). If the solenoid clicks once when the key is turned to Start, the battery and cable connections should be checked. It should be noted that a jammed starter drive, defective starter motor, engine mechanical problems and extremely low outside temperatures can affect starting system operation, but the previously mentioned possible problems are the most common.
2   The most likely cause of starting system problems (and one that is very easy to fix) is loose, corroded or defective battery cables and cable connections. Inspect the cables and check and clean the connections as described in Chapter 1.
3   Also, check the wiring and connections between the solenoid (if so equipped) and the ignition switch. Look for broken wires, burned insulation and loose or dirty connections.

**5**

4    On foot-operated starters, check the starting switch for proper operation. This is done by shorting across the terminals, taking care to make a good solid connection to prevent arcing. On early models, remove the starter motor and take off the outboard housing. Inspect the drive engagement mechanism to see if it is jammed, wipe it clean with a kerosene-dampened cloth and relubricate it with a thin film of light engine oil. The drive mechanism must be replaced with a new one if it is damaged.

5    If a voltmeter is available, it can be used very effectively to check voltage drops through the circuit wiring and connections. The first check should be a cranking voltage test (if the starter will operate at all). Hook the voltmeter positive (red) lead to the positive post of the battery and the negative (black) lead to the negative post. Crank the engine and note the voltmeter reading. If it is less than 4-1/2 volts on six (6) volt systems and nine (9) volts on a 12-volt system, the battery is not fully charged.

6    Next, attach the meter leads to the battery positive post and the solenoid or starter switch battery terminal. Turn the ignition switch on and note the voltmeter reading. It should be extremely low (approximately 0.2 volts or less). If not, there is excessive resistance (such as a dirty or loose connection) in that part of the circuit.

7    Repeat the test with the voltmeter leads attached to the negative post and the starter motor housing and the leads attached to the solenoid and starter switch battery and motor terminals. Remember, a high voltage reading means excessive resistance in that part of the circuit. Each wire and connector can be checked in this way.

8    If the voltage drop tests do not produce conclusive results and if you know the battery is good, then it is very likely that the starter motor is defective. It should be replaced with a new or rebuilt unit (refer to the appropriate Section in this Chapter for removal, installation and brush replacement procedures).

## 12  Starter motor — removal and installation

1    Disconnect the negative cable from the battery.

2    Disconnect the leads from the solenoid or starter switch, marking them as necessary to ensure reinstallation in their original positions. On some models it will be necessary to raise the front of the vehicle and support it securely on jackstands to gain access to the starter.

3    Unscrew and remove the starter motor mounting bolts and withdraw the motor from the engine bellhousing. On 151 cu in, four-cylinder engines, be sure to remove the spacer shims along with the starter motor and reinstall them in their original locations.

4    Installation is the reverse of removal.

## 13  Starter motor — brush replacement

1    The starter brushes should be replaced after the vehicle has reached very high mileage (approximately 75000 miles). Brushes which are worn, damaged or operating with low spring pressure will reduce the starter speed.

2    Remove the starter motor (Section 12).

### Early model Prestolite starter (F- and L-head four-cylinder and V6 engines)

3    Remove the band from the rear of the starter motor.

4    Remove the brushes from the holders and use a soldering iron to

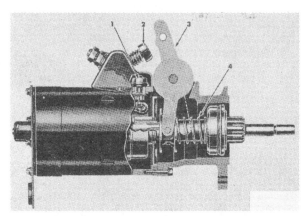

**Fig. 5.9  Foot-operated starter components (Sec 11)**

1  Contact plate nut        3  Actuation lever
2  Switch button           4  Bendix drive spring

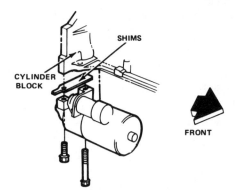

**Fig. 5.10   151 cu in four-cylinder engine starter motor and shim installation (Sec 12)**

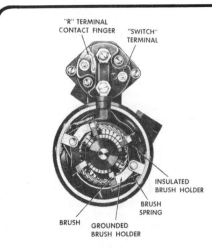

**Fig. 5.11   V6 engine Delco starter brush location (Sec 13)**

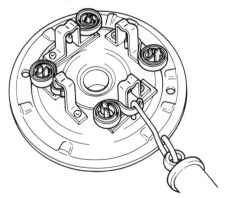

**Fig. 5.12   Checking the starter brush spring tension (in-line six-cylinder and V8 engines) (Sec 13)**

**Fig. 5.13   Typical remote-mounted, in-line, six-cylinder and V8 starter solenoid installation (Sec 14)**

unsolder the leads where they are attached to the field coil.
5 Open the loop in the field coil lead and insert the new brush pigtail all the way into the loop. Clinch the new brush lead tightly in the terminal and solder it in place.
6 Install the brushes in the holders and use a spring scale to make sure the brush spring tension is within the specified range. Hook the scale under the spring near the brush and pull on a line parallel with the side of the brush and note the reading just as the spring leaves the brush. Adjust the tension as necessary by twisting the spring at the holder with needle-nose pliers.

### Delco starter (V6 engine)
7 Disconnect the starter motor field coil connectors from the solenoid terminals. Unscrew and remove the through-bolts and remove the commutator end frame, the field frame assembly and the armature from the starter motor housing.
8 Pull the pivot pin out and remove the brush assemblies and spring. Remove the retaining screws and separate the brushes from the holders.
9 Installation is the reverse of removal.

### Prestolite starter
(in-line six-cylinder and V8 engines)
10 Remove the brush cover band and the starter motor drive yoke cover.
11 Withdraw the brushes from the holders, using a hooked piece of wire to retract the springs. Remove the retaining screws from the leads and lift the brushes from the starter. On some models it will be necessary to remove the through-bolts and disassemble the starter motor for access to the insulated brush leads if the brushes are sufficiently worn to require replacement. Cut off the brush leads as close as possible to the field coil connection.
12 With the brushes removed, check the brush spring tension with a spring scale to make sure it is within the specified limit. Adjust the tension by bending the spring with needle-nose pliers.
13 Solder the insulated brush leads to the field coil using rosin core solder.
14 Pull back the springs with the hooked piece of wire and install the brushes. Connect the electrical lead screws.
15 Reassemble the starter motor and install the brush cover band and drive yoke cover.

### Delco 5MT starter
(151 cu in, four-cylinder engine)
16 Disconnect the field winding connection from the solenoid terminal, then remove the starter motor through-bolts, followed by the end frame.
17 Remove the retaining screw and lift out the brush.
18 Inspect the brush holder for distortion and discoloration (indicating overheating, which could reduce the tension placed on the brushes). Replace the brush holder with a new one if it is defective.
19 Clean the brush assembly carefully and install the new brush. Check the movement of the brush in the holder to make sure there is no binding and that the brush contacts the commutator completely.
20 Install the retaining screw and reassemble the starter motor.

### 14 Starter solenoid — removal and installation

### Autolite and Prestolite starter motors
(F- and L-head four-cylinder and V6 engines)
1 Disconnect the negative battery cable from the battery.
2 Remove the nuts and washers securing the solenoid strap to the starter post and the ignition wire to the solenoid post.
3 Remove the mounting bolts and separate the solenoid from the starter motor.
4 Installation is the reverse of removal. Reconnect the negative battery cable.

### Delco starter motor (V6 engine)
5 Disconnect the negative battery cable and remove the two screws retaining the solenoid to the starter motor housing.
6 Lift the solenoid from the housing and disconnect the wires from the S terminal and battery terminal. Remove the solenoid.

7 Installation is the reverse of removal. Reconnect the negative battery cable.

### Prestolite starter motor
(in-line, six-cylinder and V8 engines)
8 The solenoid on these models is mounted separately from the starter motor and is located on the inner fender panel.
9 Disconnect the negative battery cable.
10 Disconnect the cables and wires from the solenoid.
11 Remove the mounting bolts and separate the solenoid from the fender.
12 Installation is the reverse of removal. Reconnect the negative battery cable.

### Delco 5MT starter motor (151 cu in, four-cylinder engine)
13 Disconnect the negative battery cable, followed by the solenoid field strap.
14 Remove the solenoid mounting bolts and motor terminal bolt. Grasp the solenoid and twist it to separate it from the starter motor.
15 Installation is the reverse of removal. Reconnect the negative battery cable.

### 15 Conventional ignition system — check

1 Check the ignition switch, wiring harness, spark plug wires and all ignition system connectors for damage, corrosion and loose connections. Inspect the distributor components (Section 21). Check and adjust the ignition timing as described in Chapter 1.
2 Measure the voltage at the coil terminals with a voltmeter while cranking the engine over with the starter. If the voltage is below that specified, there is a fault in the primary circuit or the coil. If there is no voltage at all, the coil should be replaced with a new one.
3 Remove the distributor cap and rotate the engine until the contact points are closed. Install the cap and turn the ignition on.
4 Connect one lead of the voltmeter to the primary terminal on the coil and the other lead to the distributor coil lead. If the voltage drop exceeds the Specifications, check for a corroded or loose connection.
5 Connect one voltmeter lead to the distributor coil wire terminal and the other to a good ground on the distributor body. If the voltage reading exceeds the Specifications, the points are misaligned or the point connections are loose.
6 Remove the distributor cap and open the points. The reading should rise to close to battery voltage. If the voltage is low, there is a short circuit in the distributor.
7 Disconnect the condenser lead, open the points and check the voltmeter reading. If the reading jumps to full battery voltage, there is a fault in the condenser and it should be replaced with a new one. If the voltage does not jump, replace the distributor with a new or rebuilt unit.
8 Connect the voltmeter to the battery negative post and a good ground on the distributor body. With the points closed there should be virtually no drop in voltage (very little deflection of the voltmeter needle). If there is a significant voltage drop, clean and tighten the battery cables.
9 Check for a similar voltage drop between the distributor body and a good ground on the engine block. If there is a voltage drop, remove the distributor and clean the mounting surfaces of the distributor body and block.

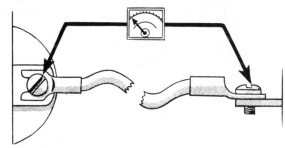

Fig. 5.14 When checking for voltage drop, make sure the voltmeter leads touch the circuit terminals rather than the cables to get an accurate reading (Sec 15)

## 16  Electronic ignition system — check

1    Check the ignition switch, wiring harness, sprark plug wires and all ignition system connectors for damage, corrosion and loose connections. Check the ignition timing as described in Chapter 1 and adjust as necessary. Inspect the distributor components for wear, damage and corrosion (Section 22).

### Ignition coil test

#### 1974 through 1977 models

2    With the engine at normal operating temperature and the ignition switch off, disconnect the coil positive and negative wire terminals.
3    Connect an ohmmeter (set on the low scale and calibrated to zero) to the positive and negative terminals and compare the reading to the Specifications (primary circuit resistance).
4    Connect the ohmmeter to the positive terminal and coil tower to check the secondary coil resistance. Compare the reading to the Specifications.
5    If the primary and secondary resistances are not as specified, the ignition coil should be replaced with a new one.

#### 1978 through 1983 V8 and in-line six-cylinder models

6    With the engine at normal operating temperature, grasp the connector at the top and remove it by pulling it directly away from the coil. Make sure the ignition switch is off.
7    Connect an ohmmeter (set at the low scale and calibrated to zero) to the positive and negative terminals of the coil and compare the readings to the Specifications (primary resistance).
8    To check the secondary resistance, connect the ohmmeter leads to the center tower and either the positive or negative terminal.
9    If either of the resistance checks is not within the specified range, replace the coil with a new one.

#### 1980 through 1983 four-cylinder models

10    With the ignition off, tag and disconnect the wires from the ignition coil.
11    Connect an ohmmeter (set at the high resistance scale) between the positive terminal and the grounded frame of the coil. The reading should be infinite resistance (no continuity).
12    Connect the ohmmeter between the positive and negative terminals using the low resistance scale of the ohmmeter to check the primary resistance.
13    To check the secondary resistance, connect the ohmmeter between

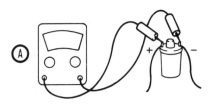

Fig. 5.15  Checking the coil primary (A) and secondary (B) resistance (Sec 16)

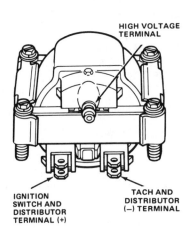

Fig. 5.16  1980 through 1983 four-cylinder engine ignition coil terminals (Sec 16)

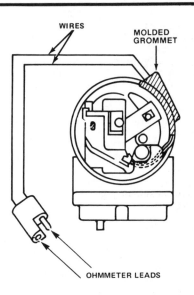

Fig. 5.17  Checking the pick-up assembly with an ohmmeter (Sec 16)

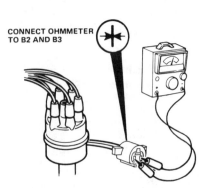

Fig. 5.18  Pick-up coil test lead connections (1978 through 1983 in-line six-cylinder and V8 models) (Sec 16)

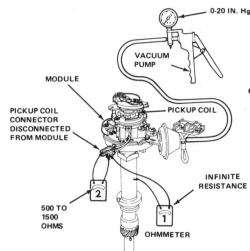

Fig. 5.19  1980 through 1983 four-cylinder distributor pick-up coil test (Sec 16)

1  Checking pick-up-to-ground resistance
2  Checking resistance at the connector

the negative terminal and the high voltage terminal, using the high resistance scale.

14 Compare all of the readings to the Specifications. Replace the ignition coil with a new one if any of the readings are out of the specified range.

### Cranking voltage test

15 The cranking voltage test checks whether the system is developing sufficient voltage to operate properly and requires a 0 to 16-volt voltmeter.

**1974 through 1977 models**

16 Connect the voltmeter positive lead to the coil positive terminal and the negative lead to the coil negative terminal.

17 Turn the ignition switch to the On position and record the voltage reading.

18 Crank the engine over and record the voltage reading.

19 If the voltage readings are lower than specified, check the battery, battery cables, ignition switch and the wiring between the battery and coil for damage, corrosion and loose connections.

**1978 through 1983 in-line six-cylinder and V8 models**

20 Connect the voltmeter positive lead to the ignition coil positive terminal and the voltmeter negative lead to a good engine ground.

21 Crank the engine over with the ignition switch and observe the voltmeter reading.

22 If the reading is below that specified, check the battery, battery cables, ignition switch and the wiring for damage, corrosion and loose connections.

**1980 through 1983 four-cylinder models**

23 The vehicle should be taken to a dealer or properly equipped shop for this test because of the special equipment and techniques required.

### Trigger wheel and pick-up coil test

**1974 through 1977 models**

24 With the ignition switch off, disconnect the pick-up connector and insert the ohmmeter leads as shown in the accompanying illustration. The ohmmeter should be set at the low scale.

25 Wiggle the wires to maintain contact and note the reading. The reading should remain constant despite the wire movement.

26 If the ohmmeter reading is not within the specified range, replace the pick-up assembly with a new one.

**1978 through 1983 in-line, six-cylinder and V8 models**

27 With the engine at normal operating temperature and the ignition off, disconnect the pick-up connector leading from the distributor.

28 With the ohmmeter set on the mid-range scale, insert the leads into the B2 and B3 terminals of the connector as shown in the accompanying illustration.

29 If the ohmmeter reading is not within the specified range, replace the pick-up coil assembly with a new one.

**1980 through 1983 four-cylinder models**

30 Remove the distributor cap and disconnect the pick-up coil from the module. Connect a vacuum pump or source to the advance control unit and apply 20 inches of vacuum.

31 With the ohmmeter set at mid-range, connect one lead to the connector and the other to a good ground such as the distributor body as shown in the accompanying illustration. The ohmmeter reading should not change when vacuum is applied to the advance control unit.

32 Connect both leads to the connector and check the resistance.

33 If either reading is not within the Specifications, replace the pick-up with a new one.

### Centrifugal advance check

34 With a timing light installed and the engine running at idle speed, disconnect the vacuum hose from the vacuum advance control unit on the distributor.

35 Observe the timing marks on the front of the engine and slowly accelerate the engine. The timing mark on the crankshaft pulley should appear to move smoothly in a direction away from the stationary mark on the timing tab. When the engine is slowed down, the mark should return to its original position.

36 If the above conditions are not met, the advance mechanism inside the distributor should be checked for broken governor springs and other problems.

### Vacuum advance check

37 With a timing light installed and the engine running at approximately 2500 rpm, remove the vacuum hose from the vacuum advance control unit on the distributor. When the hose is removed, the timing mark on the crankshaft pulley should appear to move closer to the stationary mark on the timing tag. When the hose is reconnected, the mark should move away again.

38 If reconnecting the vacuum hose produces an abrupt increase in advance, or none at all, the vacuum advance control unit is probably faulty.

---

### 17 Ignition coil — removal and installation

1 Disconnect all wires from the coil. On 1978 through 1983 six-cylinder and V8 models, this is accomplished by grasping the white plastic connector, squeezing it and pulling it away from the coil. On all models, remove the secondary coil wire by grasping the boot, twisting it one-half turn and pulling it out of the coil. It is a good idea to mark all wires and connections with tags so they will be reinstalled in their original positions. This is very important on later model electronic ignition systems, which can be damaged by incorrectly installed wiring.

**5**

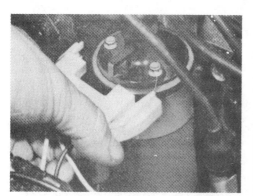

Fig. 5.20 The coil connector on 1978 through 1983 six-cylinder and V8 models is disconnected by grasping it and pulling it off (Sec 17)

Fig. 5.21 Always check the serial numbers and marking (arrow) to make sure the replacement coil is correct (Sec 17)

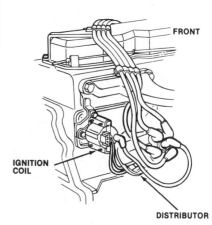

Fig. 5.22 The 1980 through 1983 four-cylinder engine coil is located on the engine block (Sec 17)

2    Remove the mounting screws or bolts and lift the coil from the engine compartment.

3    If a new coil is to be installed, great care must be taken to obtain the proper replacement unit. Problems associated with installation of the incorrect coil can range from hard starting to, on later models, damage to the ignition system.

4    Place the coil in position and install the mounting screws or bolts. The coil must be securely mounted.

5    Reconnect the wiring to the coil. After installation, check all wires to make sure they are correctly and securely installed before turning on the ignition.

## 18   Distributor — removal and installation

1    Disconnect the negative battery cable from the battery. Unplug or disconnect any wires from the distributor body and remove the distributor cap.

2    Disconnect the vacuum hose from the vacuum advance control unit on the distributor.

3    Pull the spark plug wires off the spark plugs. Pull only on the rubber boot, otherwise damage to the spark plug wire could result. It is a good idea to number each wire using a piece of tape.

4    Remove the spark plugs, then place your thumb over the number one spark plug·hole and turn the crankshaft in a *clockwise* direction until you can feel the compression pressure in the number one cylinder. Continue to slowly turn the crankshaft until the notch in the crankshaft pulley lines up with the O or TDC on the timing mark tab. At this point the number one piston is at TDC on the compression stroke. **Note:** *On in-line, six-cylinder engines it is crucial to make sure the number one*

*cylinder is on the compression stroke because the crankshaft pulley mark also aligns with the TDC mark when the number six cylinder is on the exhaust stroke.*

5    Scribe a line on the distributor body and make a corresponding mark on the engine block. Mark the position of the rotor in relationship to the distributor body.

6    Remove the bolt and clamp and carefully withdraw the distributor from the engine.

7    **Caution:** *Do not allow the engine to be cranked over until the distributor has been reinstalled.*

8    To install the distributor, line up the mating marks on the distributor and the engine. Slide the distributor into place. It may be necessary to move the distributor back-and-forth slightly to engage the gear. After the distributor is securely seated, the rotor must be pointing at the mark on the distributor.

9    Install the clamp and bolt finger tight.

10   Replace the spark plugs and install the plug wires.

11   Install the distributor cap and connect the wires and vacuum hose.

12   Connect the negative battery cable to the battery and check the ignition timing as described in Chapter 1. Don't forget to tighten the distributor clamp bolt when finished.

## 19   Electronic ignition module — removal and installation

### In-line, six-cylinder and V8 models

1    On these models the module is located on the firewall or inner fender panel.

2    Unplug the wires from the module.

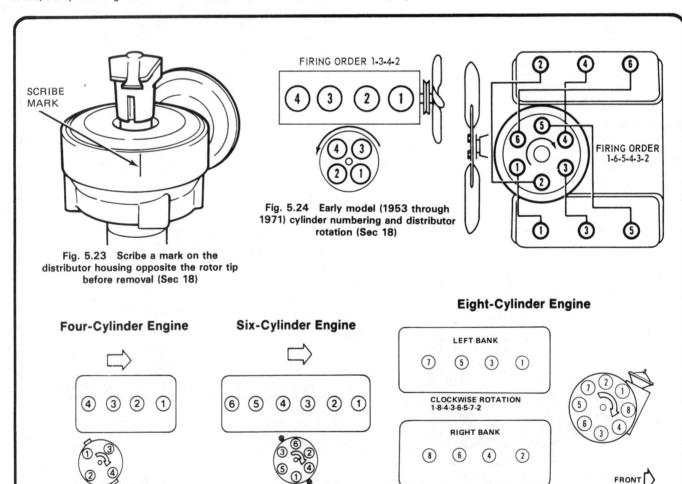

SCRIBE MARK

FIRING ORDER 1-3-4-2

Fig. 5.23   Scribe a mark on the distributor housing opposite the rotor tip before removal (Sec 18)

Fig. 5.24   Early model (1953 through 1971) cylinder numbering and distributor rotation (Sec 18)

FIRING ORDER 1-6-5-4-3-2

**Four-Cylinder Engine**

**Six-Cylinder Engine**

**Eight-Cylinder Engine**

LEFT BANK

CLOCKWISE ROTATION 1-8-4-3-6-5-7-2

RIGHT BANK

FRONT

Fig. 5.25   Later model (1971 through 1983) engine cylinder numbering and distributor rotation (Sec 18)

3   Remove the mounting screws and lift the module from the engine compartment.
4   Make sure the replacement module is exactly the same type as the original. Modules of similar appearance can have different electrical properties which could lead to damage of the ignition system.
5   Place the module in position and install the screws.
6   Apply dielectric silicone grease to the cavities and blades of the connectors to assure good electrical contact and plug them securely into the module.

## 151 cu in four-cylinder models

7   On these models the ignition module is part of the distributor assembly.
8   Remove the distributor cap.
9   Remove the two screws and lift the module out.
10  Noting the color of the wires to ensure installation in their original locations, unplug the pick-up coil wire connector and remove the module.
11  Installation is the reverse of removal. Do not remove the special

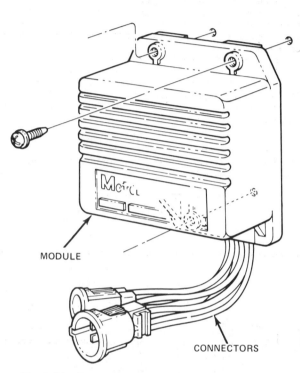

Fig. 5.26   Typical later model electronic ignition module installation (Sec 19)

MODULE

CONNECTORS

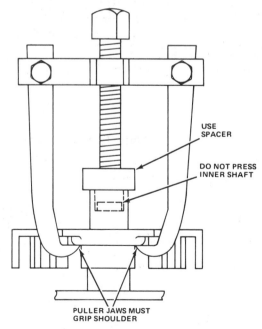

PULLER JAWS MUST GRIP SHOULDER

USE SPACER

DO NOT PRESS INNER SHAFT

Fig. 5.28   Using a small gear puller to remove the trigger wheel (Sec 20)

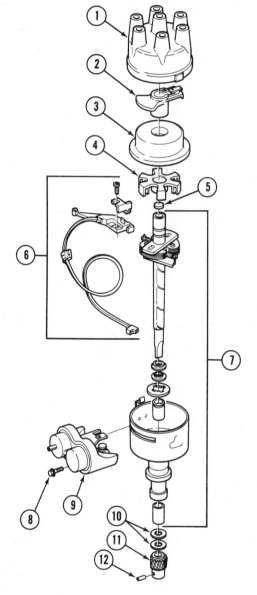

Fig. 5.27   1974 through 1977 electronic distributor component layout (six-cylinder and V8) (Sec 20 and 22)

1  Distributor cap
2  Rotor
3  Dust shield
4  Trigger wheel
5  Felt wick
6  Pick-up coil assembly
7  Distributor housing
8  Vacuum control screw
9  Vacuum advance control unit
10  Shim
11  Drive gear
12  Pin

5

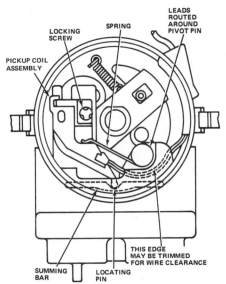

Fig. 5.29   1974 through 1977 electronic ignition pick-up coil installation details (Sec 20)

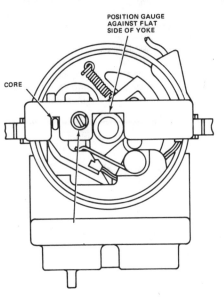

Fig. 5.30   Using a gauge to position the pick-up (Sec 20)

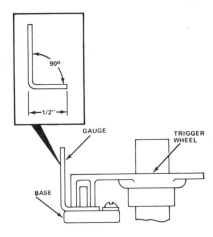

Fig. 5.31   Checking the trigger wheel-to-pick-up base clearance (1974 through 1977) (Sec 20)

dielectric silicone grease from the module or distributor base. If a replacement module is installed, it will have a package of the grease with it. Spread a layer of the grease on the metal face of the module and on the distributor surface before installation.

## 20   Electronic ignition pick-up coil — removal and installation

### 1974 through 1977 in-line six-cylinder and V8 models

1   Remove the distributor cap and lift off the rotor and dust cap.
2   Using a small gear puller, remove the trigger wheel. Make sure the jaws of the puller grip the inner shoulder of the trigger wheel securely and use a washer as a spacer on the top of the distributor shaft as shown in the accompanying illustration.
3   Loosen the ignition pick-up coil assembly screw approximately three (3) turns using a suitable driver bit tool or small needle-nose pliers.
4   Lift out the pick-up lead grommet and pull the leads out of the slot around the spring pivot pin. Lift the pick-up spring and release it, making sure it clears the lead as it is removed from the bracket.
5   To install the pick-up coil, place it on the bracket, making sure the locating pin fits properly into the summing bar. Place the spring into position and route the leads around the spring pivot pin. Install the lead grommet in the distributor and make sure the leads are positioned so they will not contact the trigger wheel.
6   It will be necessary to obtain or fabricate a gauge so the pick-up can be accurately positioned. Install the gauge and tighten the mounting screw. Position the pick-up and remove the gauge. Repeat the operation until the gauge can be removed and replaced without any side movement of the pick-up.
7   Tighten the mounting screw securely after the pick-up has been positioned and remove the gauge. Set the trigger wheel in position and make sure that the pick-up core is positioned in the center of the trigger wheel teeth so the teeth cannot touch it.
8   Use a deep socket to push the trigger wheel into place and tap it into position with a hammer. Bend a 0.050-inch wire (usually included with the new part) and check the trigger wheel-to-pick-up base clearance as shown in the accompanying illustration. The trigger wheel should just touch the gauge in the installed position.
9   Add five drops of light engine oil to the felt wick at the top of the yoke and install the dust shield, rotor and cap.

### 1978 through 1983 in-line, six-cylinder and V8 models

10   Remove the distributor cap and rotor.
11   Remove the trigger wheel. This can be done with a small gear puller

Fig. 5.32   1978 through 1983 six-cylinder and V8 distributor components (Sec 20 and 22)

(using a washer as a spacer on the top of the distributor shaft) or with two screwdrivers (used to lever the wheel off). Remove the pin from the wheel.
12   *On six-cylinder engines,* remove the pick-up coil retainer and washers from the base plate pivot pin.
13   *On V8 engines,* remove the snap-ring which retains the pick-up to the shaft. Remove the vacuum advance mechanism and move it out of the way.
14   Remove the harness tab ground screw and separate the pick-up assembly from the distributor.
15   To install the pick-up assembly, place it in position. *On six-cylinder engines,* insert the pick-up coil pin into the hole in the vacuum advance

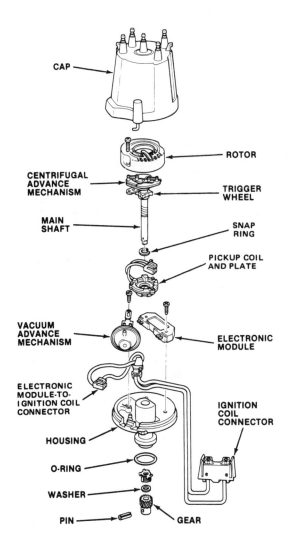

Fig. 5.33 1980 through 1983 four-cylinder distributor
component layout (Sec 20 and 22)

mechanism link. *On V8 engines,* attach the vacuum advance
mechanism lever and retainer to the pick-up coil pin.
16 *On six-cylinder engines,* install the washers and retainers on the
pivot pin so the pick-up coil is secured to the base plate. *On V8 engines,*
install the snap-ring.
17 Place the wiring harness in the distributor housing slot and install
the ground screw through the tab.
18 Position the trigger wheel on the distributor shaft with the long
portion of the teeth facing up. After aligning the trigger wheel with
the slot in the shaft, insert the retaining pin into the locating groove
and tap it into place with a small drift punch and hammer.
19 Install the rotor and cap.

### 151 cu in four-cylinder models

20 Remove the distributor.
21 Mark the relative location of the distributor gear on the shaft, drive
out the roll pin and remove the gear.
22 Remove the distributor shaft, complete with the rotor and advance
weights.
23 Remove the snap-ring on the top of the pick-up coil, disconnect
the wire from the module and remove the pick-up coil and plate
assembly. *The three screws should not be removed.*
24 Installation is the reverse of removal. Be sure to align the distributor
gear with the mark made during removal.

---

### 21 Conventional distributor — check

1 Remove the distributor cap and rotor.
2 Rotate the crankshaft until the point rubbing block is on one of
the high points of the cam. Grasp the distributor shaft firmly and move
it back-and-forth while observing the points. If there is enough play
in the shaft bushing to allow the points to open, the distributor is badly worn and should be replaced with a new or rebuilt unit.
3 As a further test, connect a dwell meter as described in Chapter I.
Start the engine and observe the dwell meter reading, then rev up the
engine. If the dwell varies more than two or three degrees as engine
speed increases, the distributor is worn and should be replaced with
a new or rebuilt unit.

---

### 22 Electronic distributor — check

1 Remove the distributor cap and rotor.
2 Grasp the distributor shaft firmly and move it back-and-forth. If
there is perceptible movement, the bushings are worn and the distributor
should be replaced with a new or rebuilt unit.

**5**

# Chapter 6 Emissions control systems

*Refer to Chapter 13 for information related to 1984 through 1986 models*

## Contents

Air Injection (AI) system .......................... 6
Catalytic converter ............................... 4
Evaporative Control System (ECS) ................. 3
Exhaust Gas Recirculation (EGR) system .............. 7
Feedback carburetor ............................. 9

General information ............................... 1
Positive Crankcase Ventilation (PCV) system ........... 2
Spark control system ............................. 5
Thermo-controlled Air Cleaner (TAC) ................. 8

## Specifications

### Torque specifications

| | Ft-lbs | Nm |
|---|---|---|
| Air injection pump mounting bolts | | |
|   F-head four-cylinder ..................... | 30 to 40 | 40 to 54 |
|   V6 ................................. | 30 to 40 | 40 to 54 |
|   In-line six-cylinder ................... | 20 | 27 |
|   V8 ................................. | 20 | 27 |
| Air injection pump adjusting bolt (all) ............. | 20 | 51 |
| Air injection manifold screws | | |
|   F-head four-cylinder ................... | 29 to 35 | 40 to 47 |
|   V6 ................................. | 25 to 30 | 34 to 40 |
|   In-line six-cylinder | | |
|     1972 through 1974 ............... | 15 | 20 |
|     1975 through 1983 ............... | 20 | 27 |
|   V8 ................................. | 38 | 52 |
| EGR valve | | |
|   In-line six-cylinder ................... | 13 | 17 |
|   V8 ................................. | 13 | 17 |
|   151 cu in four-cylinder ................ | 4 | 9 |
| Oxygen sensor | | |
|   In-line six-cylinder ................... | 31 | 42 |
|   151 cu in four cylinder ................ | 20 to 25 | 27 to 34 |

## 1 General information

To prevent pollution of the atmosphere, a number of emissions control systems are installed on these models. The combination of systems used depends on the year in which the vehicle was manufactured, the locale to which it was originally delivered and the engine type. The systems and engine combinations include:

*Positive Crankcase Ventilation (PCV) system — all engines except pre-1960 models*
*Fuel Evaporative Control System (ECS) — all engines except pre-1960 models*
*Exhaust Gas Recirculation (EGR) system — all engines except pre-1960 models*
*Air Injection (AI) system — all engines except early models*
*Spark control system — all later in-line six-cylinder, V8 and 151 cu in four-cylinder engines*
*Thermo-controlled Air Cleaner (TAC) — all later model engines*
*Catalytic converter — most engines after 1974*
*Feedback carburetor and oxygen sensor — 1980 through 1983 California models*

The Sections in this Chapter include general descriptions, checking procedures (where possible) and component replacement procedures (where applicable) for each of the systems listed above.

Before assuming that an emissions control system is malfunctioning, check the fuel and ignition systems carefully. In some cases, special tools and equipment, as well as specialized training, are required to accurately diagnose the causes of a rough-running or difficult-to-start engine. If checking and servicing become too difficult, or if a procedure is beyond the scope of the home mechanic, consult your dealer or a properly equipped shop. This does not necessarily mean, however, that the emissions control systems are all particularly difficult to maintain and repair. You can quickly and easily perform many checks and do most (if not all) of the regular maintenance at home with common tune-up and hand tools. **Note:** *The most frequent cause of emissions problems is simply a loose or broken vacuum hose or wiring connection. Therefore, always check the hose and wiring connections first.*

Pay close attention to the special precautions outlined in this Chapter (particularly those concerning the catalytic converter, feedback carburetor and oxygen sensor). It should be noted that the illustrations of the various systems may not exactly match the system installed on your particular vehicle (due to changes made by the manufacturer during production or from year-to-year).

## 2 Positive Crankcase Ventilation (PCV) system

### General description

1    This system is designed to reduce hydrocarbon (HC) emissions by routing blow-by gases (fuel/air mixture that escapes from the combustion chamber past the piston rings into the crankcase) from the crankcase to the intake manifold and combustion chamber where they are burned during engine operation.

2    The system is very simple and consists of rubber hoses and a small replaceable metering valve (PCV valve). Refer to Chapter 1 for illustrations of the PCV valve location.

### Checking and component replacement

3    Rough idling is the most common symptom of a defective PCV valve.

4    Remove the valve and inspect it for a build-up of oil sludge. Shake the valve to see if it rattles, which is an indication that it is not sludged up (photo). If there is a sludge build-up, clean the valve with solvent and blow out the hose with compressed air.

5    With the valve installed and the engine running, pinch off the hose and see if the idle speed drops about 50 rpm. If it does not, replace the valve with a new one.

6    Replacement of the PCV valve is described in Chapter 1.

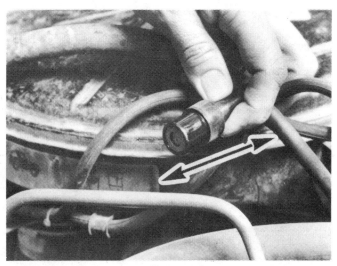

2.4   The PCV valve should rattle when shaken back-and-forth

## 3 Evaporative Control System (ECS)

### General description

1    This system is designed to trap and store fuel that evaporates from the carburetor and fuel tank which would normally enter the atmosphere and contribute to hydrocarbon (HC) emissions.

2    The system is quite simple and consists of a charcoal-filled canister and (depending on the model and year) a purge valve, a manifold vacuum purge line, a carburetor vacuum line, a liquid check valve in the fuel line and a relief valve in the fuel tank filler cap.

3    On the earlier versions of this system there are only two hose connections to the canister; one connected to the fuel tank vapor line and the other to the air cleaner. The fuel vapors are drawn from the canister to the air cleaner and into the engine by the vacuum developed by the air passing over the canister hose tube located in the snorkel. On later models, when the engine is off and a high-pressure condition begins to build in the fuel tank (caused by fuel evaporation), the charcoal in the canister absorbs the fuel vapor. On some models, the vapor from the carburetor also enters the canister. When the engine is started cold, the charcoal continues to absorb and store fuel vapors. As the engine warms up, the stored fuel vapors are routed to the intake manifold where they are inducted and burned during normal engine operation. As the engine vacuum increases, the secondary purge circuit opens so the vapors are purged at a higher rate. A liquid check valve incorporating a float and needle valve allows the free passage of vapors (but not liquid fuel) between the fuel tank and canister. The fuel tank filler cap features a calibrated two-way relief valve which allows outside air to enter the fuel tank and relieve the high vacuum.

### Checking

4    Checking the canister, replacing the filter pad and inspecting the lines and hoses are routine maintenance procedures. Refer to Chapter 1 for details.

5    If liquid fuel is found in the canister, replace the check valve with a new one.

6    To check the filler cap and relief valve, remove the cap and inspect

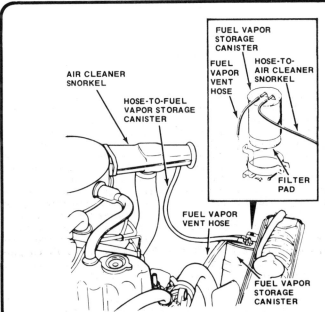

Fig. 6.1   Early model ECS system component location and layout (Sec 3)

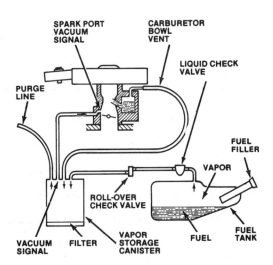

Fig. 6.2   Typical later model ECS system component layout (Sec 3)

6

the cap and filler neck for fuel stains, indicating fuel leakage.

7    Look for a damaged or deformed gasket and make sure the relief valve is not stuck. If the gasket and valve are not in good condition, replace the cap with a new one.

## Component replacement

8    Replacement and maintenance of the charcoal canister, filter pad and lines are covered in Chapter 1.

9    Replacement of the liquid check valve is very straight forward since it only involves disconnecting the hoses and clamps from the faulty part, unbolting it and installing the new one. Mark the hose connections before removal to avoid mixing them up.

## 4    Catalytic converter

### General description

1    The catalytic converter is designed to reduce hydrocarbon (HC) and carbon monoxide (CO) pollutants in the exhaust. The converter oxidizes these components and converts them to water and carbon dioxide.

2    The converter is located in the exhaust system and closely resembles a muffler. Two types of converters are used; a conventional oxidizing catalyst (COC) and a three-way catalyst (TWC). The COC converter controls the HC and CO pollutants when the exhaust gas is forced over the treated pellets and is sometimes called a two-way catalyst

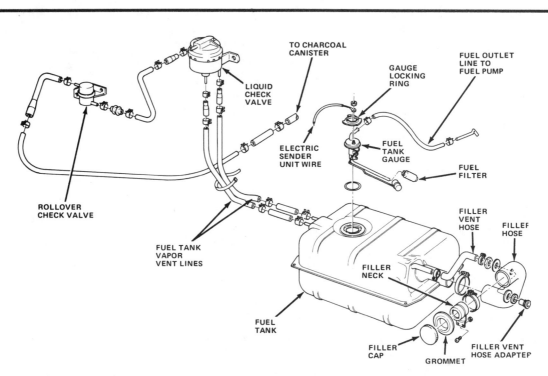

Fig. 6.3   ECS system fuel vapor control component layout (Sec 3)

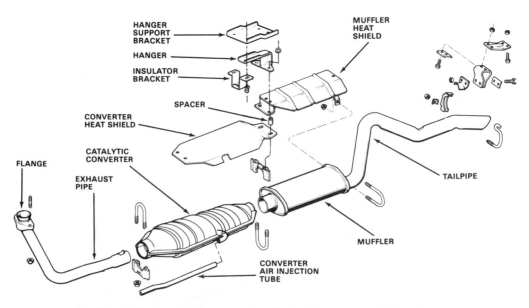

Fig. 6.4   Typical catalytic converter installation (three-way type) (Sec 4)

because it controls two of the three exhaust emissions. Three-way catalysts control HC and CO pollutants as well as oxides of nitrogen (NOx). The three-way catalyst consists of two converters in one shell with a mixing chamber between them. The front chamber honeycomb catalyst is treated with rhodium and platinum for controlling NOx, while the rear chamber is a two-way type. Air from the air injection system is injected into the mixing chamber to aid in the oxidation of pollutants.

3    **Caution:** *If large amounts of unburned gasoline enter the catalyst, it may overheat and cause a fire. Always observe the following precautions:*

*Use only unleaded gasoline*
*Avoid prolonged idling*
*Do not prolong engine compression checks*
*Do not fun the engine with a nearly empty fuel tank*
*Avoid coasting with the ignition turned off*
*Do not dispose of a used catalytic converter along with*
    *oily or gasoline soaked parts*

## Checking

4    The catalytic converter requires little if any maintenance and servicing at regular intervals. However, the system should be inspected whenever the vehicle is raised on a lift or if the exhaust system is checked or serviced.
5    Check all connections in the exhaust pipe assembly for looseness and damage. Also check all the clamps for damage, cracks and missing fasteners. Check the rubber hangers for cracks.
6    The converter itself should be checked for damage and dents (maximum 3/4-inch deep), which could affect its performance and/or be hazardous to your health. At the same time the converter is inspected, check the metal heat shield (if so equipped) for damage and loose fasteners.
7    Refer to the air injection system Section for information on components which work in conjunction with the air injection system and catalytic converter.

## Component replacement

8    Do not attempt to remove the catalytic converter until the complete exhaust system is cool. Raise the vehicle and support it securely on jackstands. Apply some penetrating oil to the clamp nuts and allow it to soak in. Disconnect the air injection tube from the converter fitting (if equipped).
9    Remove the nuts and clamps, then separate the converter from the exhaust pipes. Remove the old gaskets if they are stuck to the pipes.
10   Installation of the converter is the reverse of removal. Use new pipe gaskets and tighten the clamp bolts securely. Reconnect the air injection tube.

## 5   Spark control system

### General description

1    The spark control system is designed to reduce hydrocarbon (HC) and oxides of nitrogen (NOx) emissions by controlling ignition timing advance when the engine is cold or during certain driving conditions.
2    The spark control systems and devices used on these models may include:

*Transmission controlled spark (TCS) system*
*Coolant temperature override (CTO) switch*
*Vacuum advance control delay valve*
*Delay valve*
*Non-linear vacuum regulator (NLVR) system*

3    The TCS system is used on 1973 through 1978 models and controls NOx emissions by lowering the peak combustion temperature during the power stroke. This is accomplished by restricting the vacuum advance under certain conditions. System components include a solenoid vacuum valve located in or near the intake manifold, a solenoid control switch located in the transmission case (manual) or speedometer cable (automatic) and a coolant temperature override switch (CTO). The 1973 models are equipped with an ambient temperature switch instead of a CTO switch. It is located behind the left side of the radiator grille. This switch allows the system to operate at temperatures above 63°F. At low speeds on 1974 through 1978 models, with the engine temperature below normal operating temperature, full engine vacuum is supplied to the distributor advance mechanism. With the engine temperature above 160°F, the CTO blocks off the vacuum and the solenoid valve controls the ignition advance by releasing some or all of the vacuum to the atmosphere. At speeds over 38 mph (automatic)

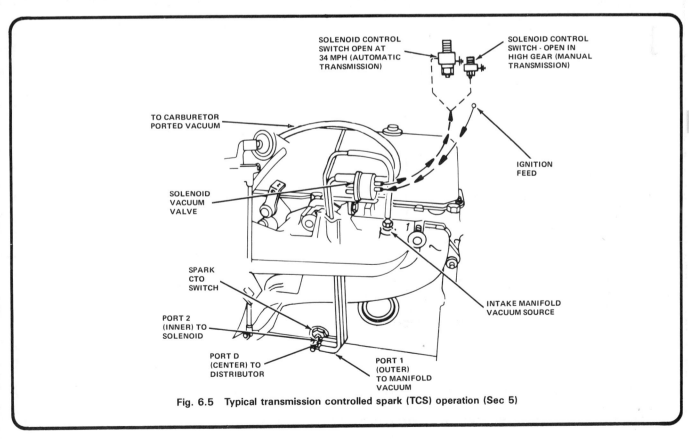

**Fig. 6.5   Typical transmission controlled spark (TCS) operation (Sec 5)**

or in high gear (manual), the solenoid is de-energized by the control switch and normal vacuum advance is used.

4    The CTO is used on most models in conjunction with a variety of emissions control devices. The CTO is threaded into a coolant passage and incorporates a thermal unit which reacts to coolant temperature by moving a check ball up or down, which opens or closes the switch ports. The opening or closing of these ports routes vacuum through the switch in accordance with the operation of the emissions system involved.

5    A delay valve is used in conjunction with the CTO to help control vacuum advance on 1980 through 1983 four-cylinder models. The valve reduces NOx emissions while improving driveability. When the coolant temperature is below 120°F and the vacuum increases because of sudden deceleration, the delay valve routes the air through a check valve to equalize the pressure. The CTO bypasses the delay valve when the temperature is above 120°F. Some models are equipped with a one-way reverse delay valve, which prevents sudden retarding of the ignition timing when the manifold vacuum drops due to sudden acceleration right after the engine is started.

6    The non-linear vacuum regulator (NLVR) valve system is used on 1979 through 1983 in-line, six-cylinder and V8 engines. The vacuum regulator is calibrated to provide a constant vacuum and maintain the ignition advance within limits under all driving conditions to reduce hydrocarbon emissions. The regulator has inlet ports for manifold and carburetor ported vacuum and an outlet port for the CTO valve switch. At low engine torque, the NLVR valve meters the proper amount of the high manifold vacuum present under these conditions. As the engine torque increases, the valve then uses the higher ported vacuum from the carburetor.

### Checking

7    The first check of the spark control system should always be a careful inspection of all the rubber hoses for cracks, kinks and proper installation.

**Transmission-controlled spark (TCS) system**

8    To test the TCS system, a vacuum gauge, test lamp and jumper wire are needed.

9    The TCS current supply is the first test of this system. With the

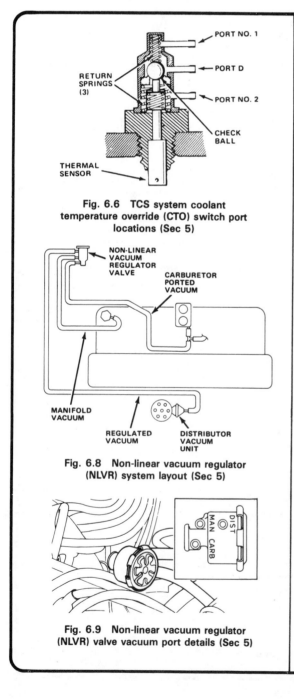

Fig. 6.6   TCS system coolant temperature override (CTO) switch port locations (Sec 5)

Fig. 6.8   Non-linear vacuum regulator (NLVR) system layout (Sec 5)

Fig. 6.9   Non-linear vacuum regulator (NLVR) valve vacuum port details (Sec 5)

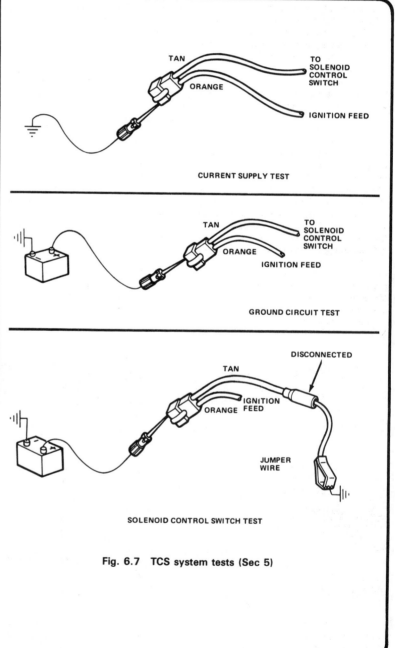

Fig. 6.7   TCS system tests (Sec 5)

ignition switch on, disconnect the wires from the solenoid vacuum valve and connect one lead of the test lamp to a good ground. Touch the other lead of the lamp to each connector terminal. The lamp should light at one of these terminals (on later models it will be the orange wire). If the lamp does not light, there is a fault in the ignition feed between the switch and the valve connector.

10   To check the ground circuit, shift the manual transmission into Neutral. On automatic transmission-equipped vehicles, raise the rear of the vehicle and support it securely on jackstands so the rear wheels are free to turn. Connect one lead of the test lamp to the battery positive terminal and touch the other lead to the solenoid vacuum valve ground wire terminal. This will be the terminal opposite the one which caused the test lamp to light in the previous test (on most models this will be the tan wire). On manual transmission models, shift into every gear but high and verify that the lamp remains lit. Shifting into high should cause the lamp to go out. On automatic transmission models, start the engine and shift into Drive. Watch the test lamp and accelerate the engine, noting the speed at which the lamp goes out, which indicates when the solenoid switch is opening. Decelerate the engine and note the speed at which the lamp lights, indicating the switch is closing. It should be between 28 and 38 mph. If the switch operates outside of this indicated range, replace it with a new one. If the lamp did not light at all during either of the tests, check the solenoid switch.

11   To check the solenoid switch, disconnect the wire from the switch at the transmission (manual) or speedometer cable (automatic). On later models the wire will be tan. Connect a jumper wire between the disconnected wire and a good ground. The test lamp should light when connected between the solenoid switch (tan) wire terminal and the battery positive terminal. If it does not, the switch is faulty and should be replaced with a new one. If the lamp does not light, the wire itself is faulty.

12   To test the solenoid vacuum valve, place the transmission in Neutral (manual) or Park (automatic), disconnect the vacuum advance line from the valve and connect a vacuum gauge. Start the engine, run it at between 1000 and 1500 rpm and verify that the gauge indicates no vacuum. With the engine still running, disconnect the wires from the valve. The gauge should now indicate vacuum. If it does not, the valve is faulty and should be replaced with a new one.

### Coolant temperature override (CTO) switch
13   The symptom of a faulty CTO switch is sluggish operation when the engine is cold (because vacuum is not reaching the distributor to actuate the advance mechanism). With the engine cold, tag and remove the vacuum hoses from the CTO switch. Connect a hose to the center port (D) and either use a vacuum pump or suck on the hose to create a vacuum while holding your finger over the top and bottom ports. Vacuum should be felt only at the *top* (No. 1) port. Reconnect the hoses, start the engine and run it until normal operating temperature is reached. Repeat the test and verify that the vacuum is felt only at the *bottom* (No. 2) port. If the CTO switch fails either of these tests, replace it with a new one.

5.18   When replacing a vacuum delay valve (arrow), note the installed direction (the dark side has a crosshatch pattern facing the component being controlled)

### Delay valves
14   A failed delay valve can cause poor throttle response. Since special equipment is needed to test a delay valve, the home mechanic should leave the checks to a dealer or properly equipped shop.

### Non-linear vacuum regulator (NLVR) valve
15   Remove the vacuum hose from the distributor port of the valve and connect a vacuum gauge. Start the engine and verify that the gauge reads approximately 7 in-Hg at idle. Further testing requires special equipment, so the home mechanic can either take the vehicle to a dealer or properly equipped shop or replace the valve with one that is known to be good.

## Component replacement
### TCS system
16   For all components, note the location of all wires or vacuum hoses before removal. Replacement of the components is a simple matter of removing the faulty one and replacing it with a new one. Make sure the hoses are correctly installed and tighten all mounting bolts and clamps securely.

### CTO switch
17   The CTO switch is threaded into a coolant passage, so removal should be done with the engine cold. The cooling system should be drained to below the level of the switch (see Chapter 1). Mark the hoses to simplify installation before disconnecting them. Apply thread sealant to the new switch before installing it and check for leaks when the job is done.

### Delay valves
18   Replacement of a delay valve is a simple matter of removing the vacuum hoses and installing a new valve. Be sure to note the direction the valve is facing before removing it. The valves are color coded and the darker side has a crosshatch pattern which faces toward the component being controlled (photo).

### NLVR valve
19   Tag the vacuum hoses before disconnecting them and replacing the valve. It is crucial that the hoses be connected to the correct ports.

---

## 6   Air Injection (AI) system

---

### General description
1   This system supplies air to the exhaust manifold to promote combustion of unburned hydrocarbons and carbon monoxide before they are allowed to exit the exhaust system. Some 1983 in-line, six-cylinder engines use a Pulse Air system which performs this function by using the positive and negative pulsations of the exhaust instead of an air pump to introduce the air.
2   The air injection system is composed of an air pump, diverter valve, check valve, air injection manifold, a CTO, on some six-cylinder models, and connecting hoses. The air pump is driven by a belt from the crankshaft and supplies compressed air to the exhaust manifold(s). The check valve prevents the reverse flow of exhaust gases into the system. The diverter valve directs the air from the pump into the manifold(s) or vents it into the atmosphere, depending on the engine operating conditions. Some later models with three-way catalytic converters use a dual air input system to inject air downstream into the converter mixing chamber.
3   The Pulse Air system consists of an air injection reed check valve, which opens and closes due to exhaust system pulsations, an air control valve, air switch solenoid, vacuum storage tank and micro computer unit (MCU), which switches the air upstream or downstream, and associated hoses. This system is part of the feedback carburetor system.

### Checking
4   Visually check the hoses, tubes and connections for cracks, loose fittings and separated parts.
5   Check the drivebelt tension and condition (refer to Chapter 1).

### Pulse Air system
6   Checking of this system is confined to the above inspections because of the special equipment necessary.

### Air pump
7   The air pump requires special tools for checking and servicing, so have the job done by your dealer or a properly equipped shop.

**6**

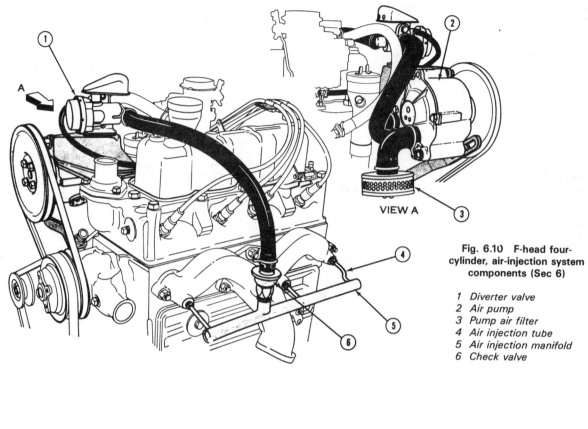

Fig. 6.10  F-head four-
cylinder, air-injection system
components (Sec 6)

1  Diverter valve
2  Air pump
3  Pump air filter
4  Air injection tube
5  Air injection manifold
6  Check valve

VIEW A

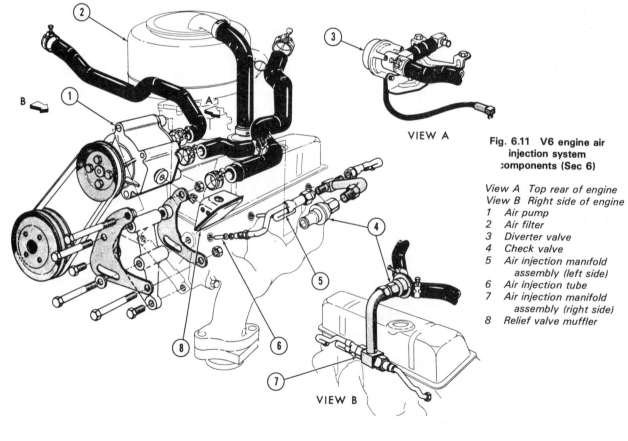

VIEW A

Fig. 6.11  V6 engine air
injection system
components (Sec 6)

View A  Top rear of engine
View B  Right side of engine
1  Air pump
2  Air filter
3  Diverter valve
4  Check valve
5  Air injection manifold
   assembly (left side)
6  Air injection tube
7  Air injection manifold
   assembly (right side)
8  Relief valve muffler

VIEW B

**Diverter valve**

8   With the engine idling, check the diverter valve vents to make sure little or no air is felt. Accelerate the engine to between 2000 and 3000 rpm and allow the throttle to snap shut. A burst of air should be felt at the vents. If there is no air, or if there is a backfire, check the vacuum line for restrictions and leaks. Accelerate the engine slowly and verify that at between 2500 and 3500 rpm, air is felt flowing from the valve vents.

**Check valve**

9   The air injection manifold tubes will be hot if the check valve has failed. With the engine idling, disconnect the hose at the check valve. If exhaust gas is escaping past the check valve, replace it with a new one.

**Air injection CTO**

10   With the engine idling and the coolant below normal operating temperature (approximately 160°F), disconnect the hose from the CTO at the air control valve. Place your finger over the end of the hose to verify that vacuum is present. Reconnect the hose and warm up the engine to normal operating temperature. Disconnect the hose and verify that vacuum is no longer present, indicating the valve is working properly. If the CTO fails these tests and the hoses are properly routed and not leaking, replace the valve with a new one.

**Dual air injection system**

11   This system operates in conjunction with the feedback carburetor and MCU and requires special equipment for testing. The diverter valve can be tested using the same procedures as for the conventional system.

## Component replacement

**Air pump**

12   The air pump must have all hoses and wires disconnected before it can be removed. Be sure to mark their locations to simplify installation. Loosen the pivot and adjusting bolts and then slip off the drivebelt. Remove the bolts and lift the pump from the bracket. When adjusting the drivebelt tension after installation, do not pry on the aluminum pump body itself as it could be distorted. Make sure the hoses are correctly installed before starting the engine.

**Check valve**

13   Disconnect the hose from the valve, then use a large wrench to remove the valve from the injection manifold (some penetrating oil may be required to loosen it). When installing the new check valve, apply anti-seize compound to the threads.

**Manifold**

14   The air injection manifold on in-line, six-cylinder engines can be

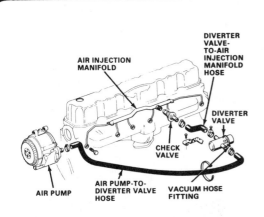

Fig. 6.12   Typical in-line six-cylinder engine air-injection component layout (Sec 6)

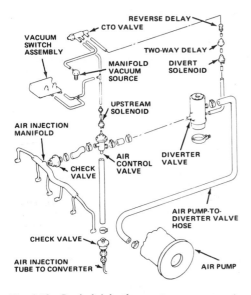

Fig. 6.13   Dual air-injection system components (Sec 6)

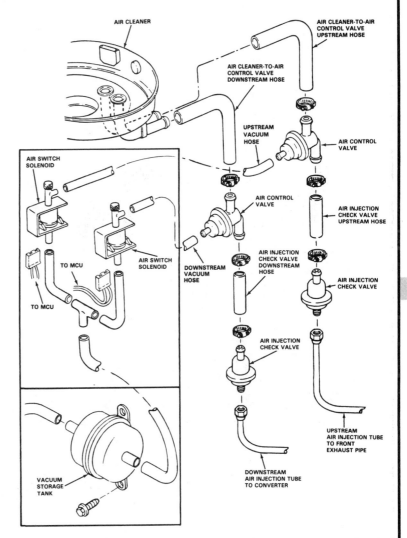

Fig. 6.14   The Pulse Air system used on 1983 six-cylinder engines (Sec 6)

6

removed only after the exhaust manifold is removed. Refer to Chapter 2 for further information. Use a flare nut wrench, if possible, on the air injection manifold fittings. It may be necessary to apply heat to the joint while rotating the injection tube with pliers to separate the connection. On V8 engines, the air injection manifold can be removed with the exhaust manifolds installed. Disconnect the air delivery hose and remove the injection manifold and tube assembly. Carbon build-up on the tubes may make removal difficult. After removing the assembly, separate the tubes and gaskets from the manifold.

### Air injection CTO

15   On models equipped with a CTO, the cooling system must be drained partially as the CTO is threaded into a coolant passage. To simplify installation, mark the hoses before disconnecting them. Apply thread sealant to the new valve before installing it and be sure to hook up the hoses securely and correctly.

### Diverter valve

16   The diverter valve is attached to a bracket or suspended in the hoses between the air pump and air injection manifolds. Mark the hoses to simplify installation. Remove the clamps and/or retaining bolts and lift the valve from the engine.

### Downstream air injection tube

17   The dual air injection system downstream tube should first be disconnected from the air supply hose at the check valve. Remove the check valve if it is going to be reused. Remove the retaining clamp and disengage the tube from the catalytic converter. It may be necessary to heat the joint to aid in removal. Installation is the reverse of removal.

---

## 7   Exhaust gas recirculation (EGR) system

---

### General description

1   This system recirculates a portion of the exhaust gases into the intake manifold in order to reduce the combustion temperatures and decrease the amount of nitrogen oxides produced.
2   The main component in the system is the EGR valve. It operates in conjunction with a vacuum amplifier (early models), a coolant temperature override (CTO) switch, delay valve (later models), thermal vacuum switch (TVS) (later models), vacuum dump valve (later models) and a back pressure sensor (later models).
3   At low engine temperatures, the CTO, TVS (if so equipped) and EGR are closed and the exhaust gas is not being recirculated. At high temperatures, the CTO opens and allows ported vacuum from the carburetor to actuate the EGR valve. The TVS is located in the air cleaner and, on models so equipped, it controls the vacuum to the EGR valve, opening at higher ambient temperatures to improve cold engine driveability. At low intake manifold vacuum levels, a vacuum dump valve is used to interrupt vacuum to the EGR valve on some models. Also, some later models have a delay valve in the vacuum line to apply the vacuum more gradually and avoid sudden activation of the EGR valve.
4   On four-cylinder 151 cu in engines, the EGR valve is located on a spacer plate beneath the carburetor; on V8 engines, at the rear of the intake manifold; on in-line six-cylinder engines, on the side of the intake manifold. Two types of EGR valves are used on these models: back pressure sensor-equipped (later 49-state and all California models) and non-back pressure type (1970 through 1975 49-state models). On non-back pressure type valves, the flow of exhaust gas is controlled by the vacuum signal overcoming the spring inside the EGR diaphragm, which opens it and allows exhaust gas recirculation. Back pressure sensor-equipped EGR valves use a combination of ported carburetor vacuum and back pressure from the exhaust manifold to control exhaust gas recirculation. The exhaust gas enters the sensor and controls the EGR valve opening if the back pressure is great enough. On early models the sensor is remote from the EGR valve and connected by a tube, while on later models it is integral with it.

### Checking

5   Check all vacuum lines and connections for damage and leaks.
### EGR valve
6   The most noticeable symptom when the EGR valve is stuck in the open position is poor cold engine driveability. With the engine idling and at normal operating temperature, check for proper opening of the valve by increasing engine speed to about 1500 rpm and then allowing the throttle to snap shut. Verify that there is definite movement of the valve diaphragm (photo). If there is no diaphragm movement,

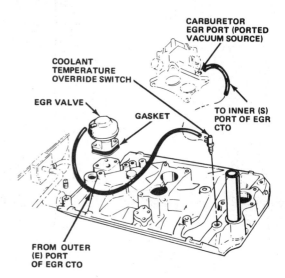

Fig. 6.15   Typical early (non-back pressure sensor) EGR system (Sec 7)

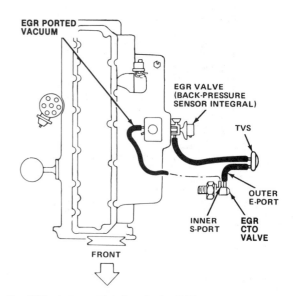

Fig. 6.16   Later model six-cylinder EGR system with back pressure sensor and TVS (Sec 7)

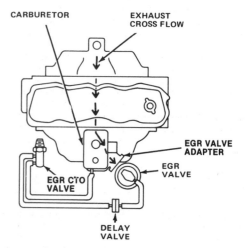

Fig. 6.17   Typical 151 cu in four-cylinder engine EGR system (Sec 7)

7.6   Checking the EGR valve by reaching underneath to feel for movement of the diaphragm

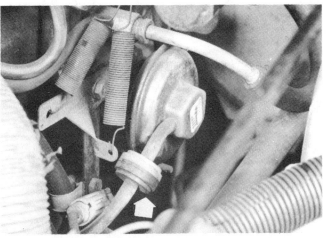

7.10   The black or red side of the delay valve (arrow) must always face the vacuum source and away from the EGR valve

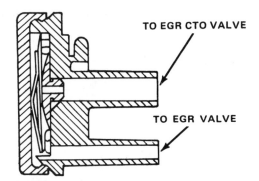

**Fig. 6.18   Thermal vacuum switch (TVS) port layout (Sec 7)**

TO EGR CTO VALVE

TO EGR VALVE

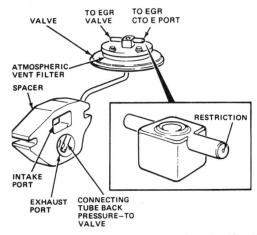

**Fig. 6.19   Non-integral back pressure EGR valve (Sec 7)**

VALVE | TO EGR VALVE | TO EGR CTO E PORT
ATMOSPHERIC VENT FILTER
SPACER
RESTRICTION
INTAKE PORT
EXHAUST PORT   CONNECTING TUBE BACK PRESSURE-TO VALVE

there may be a leak or break in a vacuum line. If the vacuum hoses and connections are all right, the EGR valve and/or back pressure sensor may be defective.

7   To check the EGR valve for proper operation, depress the valve diaphragm with the engine at an idle (normal operating temperature). There should be an immediate drop in engine speed, which indicates that the valve is allowing the flow of exhaust gas. If the idle is not changed by depressing the diaphragm, the gases are not reaching the combustion chamber (probably due to a plugged EGR passage in the intake manifold). If the engine idle is rough and does not change greatly when the disphragm is depressed, the EGR valve is not closing due to a fault in the hoses or the valve itself. If the hose routing and connections are all right, replace the valve with a new one.

8   At the specified intervals, the EGR valve should be removed, cleaned and inspected. Use a wire brush to clean the deposits of carbon from the metering pintle. Check and clean the exhaust gas passages in the valve using a small wire brush or drill bit. Coat the end of the drill with heavy grease and use pliers to rotate the bit in the passage. On nonback pressure-type valves, depress the diaphragm and place your finger securely over the vacuum inlet. Press on the diaphragm several times and verify that the pintle remains retracted. If it does not, the diaphragm is leaking and the valve should be replaced with a new one. On back pressure sensor-type EGR valves, apply vacuum to the inlet port with a hand pump to make sure it retracts the pintle and replace the valve if it does not.

**CTO**
9   With the engine cold, disconnect the vacuum hose leading from the CTO at the EGR valve. Connect a vacuum gauge to the hose or place your finger over the end and start the engine. Accelerate the engine to approximately 1500 rpm and verify that no vacuum is indicated. If there is vacuum, the CTO is faulty and should be replaced with a new one. Warm the engine up to normal operating temperature and repeat the test to make sure vacuum is now present. If it is not, replace the CTO with a new one.

**Delay valve**
10   The delay valve is located in the vacuum hose between the CTO and EGR valve. The only test for a suspected faulty valve is replacement with a unit known to be good. When inspecting it for faults, check for cracks and make sure the valve is installed facing in the proper direction. The black or red side always faces the vacuum source (photo).

**TVS**
11   With the air cleaner temperature below the TVS operating temperature (40° to 50°F/4.4° to 10°C), connect a vacuum pump to one fitting and a vacuum gauge to the other. Apply vacuum to the TVS and verify that no vacuum passes through it. Warm up the engine to normal operating temperature and repeat the vacuum check to make sure the TVS will now allow vacuum to pass through. If the TVS fails either test, replace it with a new one.

**Vacuum dump valve**
12   With the engine at normal operating temperature, disconnect the vacuum dump valve hose from the intake manifold (plug the manifold connection). Start the engine, accelerate it to about 2000 rpm and verify that vacuum exits from the exhaust ports at the bottom of the valve. Reconnect the hose to the intake manifold and repeat the test to make sure nó vacuum is coming from the valve exhaust ports. If the valve fails either test, replace it with a new one.

*Component replacement*
**EGR valve**
13   The EGR valve is easily removed after detaching the vacuum hose. Be sure to use a new gasket when installing the valve and check for leaks when the job is done.

**Non-integral back pressure valve**
14   The non-integral back pressure valve can be removed after mark-

**6**

ing and disconnecting the vacuum hoses. The EGR valve and back pressure valve are removed as an assembly. Clean the mating surfaces of the intake manifold before installation of the EGR and back pressure valve assembly. The CTO vacuum hose must be connected to the EGR valve fitting with the restriction as shown in the illustration.

### CTO

15  Because the CTO is threaded into a cooling system passage, the coolant must be drained to below the level of the valve before removal. Mark the hoses to simplify installation before removing them. Apply thread sealant to the new valve before installing it and make certain the hoses are hooked up properly.

### TVS

16  The TVS can be replaced after removing the air cleaner and element. Mark and disconnect the vacuum hoses. Remove the retaining clip and lift the TVS from the air cleaner housing. Installation is the reverse of removal. Be sure to install the vacuum hoses securely and correctly.

### Delay valve

17  The delay valve is replaced by disengaging it from the vacuum hose and installing a new one, making sure the hoses are secure. The valves are color coded and the black or red side must be facing toward the vacuum source.

### Vacuum dump valve

18  Replacement is a simple matter of disconnecting the vacuum hoses, removing the valve and installing a new one. Connect the vacuum hose leading from the EGR valve to port B, which is horizontal to the body valve, and the manifold vacuum hose to the vertical port A as shown in the accompanying illustration.

---

## 8  Thermo-controlled Air Cleaner (TAC)

### General description

1  This system is designed to improve driveability, prevent carburetor icing and reduce hydrocarbon emissions on later models because of the leaner fuel mixtures.

2  The system is made up of a heat shroud located on the exhaust manifold, a connecting hose and an air duct and valve assembly in the air cleaner snorkel. The air duct and valve assembly incorporates an air valve which is activated by a thermostat or vacuum motor. Later models have a delay valve in the vacuum motor hose to prevent the air valve trap door from closing when engine vacuum is low.

3  On thermostat-equipped systems, the air valve is held closed by spring pressure when the engine is cold and air is drawn from the shroud mounted on the exhaust manifold. As the engine warms up to operating temperature, the thermostat starts to open and air enters the air cleaner snorkle. When the thermostat is fully open, the air valve closes off the heated air from the manifold and allows air to enter only through the snorkel.

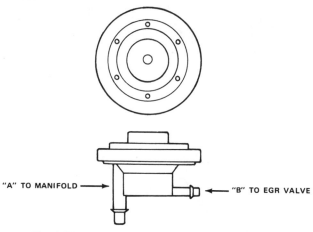

Fig. 6.20   EGR dump valve port layout (Sec 7)

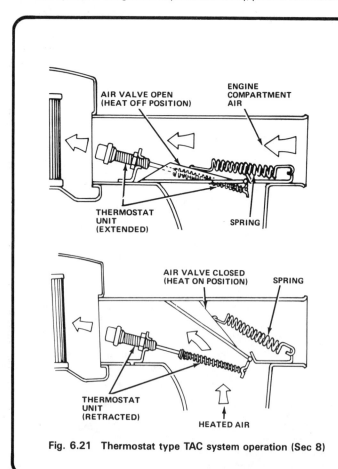

Fig. 6.21   Thermostat type TAC system operation (Sec 8)

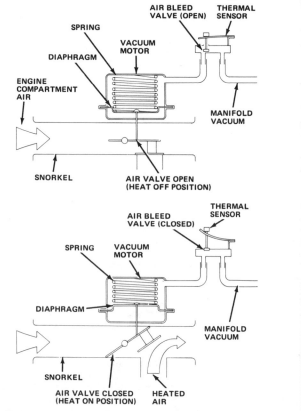

Fig. 6.22   Vacuum motor type TAC system operation (Sec 8)

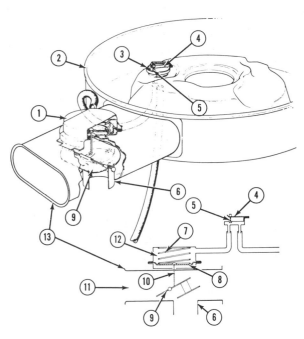

**Fig. 6.23  V6 engine TAC component layout (Sec 8)**

1  Vacuum motor
2  Air cleaner assembly
3  Thermal sensor
4  Sensor spring
5  Air bleed valve
6  Hot air duct
7  Diaphragm spring
8  Diaphragm
9  Air valve
10  Linkage
11  Air inlet
12  Vacuum chamber
13  Snorkel tube

4    On vacuum motor-type TAC systems, the manifold vacuum acting on the vacuum motor diaphgram holds the air valve closed when the engine is cold. With the valve closed, heated air from the exhaust manifold is directed into the engine. As the engine warms up, the thermal sensor in the air cleaner housing bleeds off manifold vacuum and spring pressure in the vacuum motor opens the air valve, allowing air to be drawn through the air cleaner snorkel. If the engine is accelerated hard, the manifold vacuum drops, causing the air valve to open and allows maximum air flow. Some later models use an air cleaner with a spring loaded trap door which is closed when the engine is off. When the engine is started, the resulting manifold vacuum operates the door, opening it. A vacuum delay valve keeps the door from closing abruptly when the vacuum drops or the engine is shut off.

### Checking

5    Refer to Chapter 1 for the general checking procedure. If the system is not operating properly, check the individual components as follows.
6    Check all vacuum hoses for cracks, kinks, proper routing and broken sections. Make sure the shroud and duct are in good condition as well.
7    Remove the flexible duct and manually operate the air control valve and (if equipped) the trap door. If the valve or trap door sticks or hangs up, replace it with a new unit.
8    On thermostat-equipped TAC systems, if the air valve does not open when the engine warms up to operating temperature, check the valve for binding and the spring for proper connection. If the valve is in good condition mechanically, the thermostat is defective and the air cleaner housing must be replaced with a new one.
9    On vacuum motor-equipped TAC systems, if the air valve does not open when the engine warms up, check for binding and vacuum leaks. If the mechanism is operating freely and there is no binding or vacuum leaks, remove the hose from the vacuum motor and connect a separate section of hose. Apply a vacuum with your mouth, a vacuum pump or manifold vacuum and see if the valve moves freely to the closed position, indicating it is working properly. If the valve moves to the open position, the thermal sensor is faulty and must be replaced with a new one. If the valve remains in the heat off position, replace the vacuum motor assembly. On some models this will require replacing the air cleaner housing.

**6**

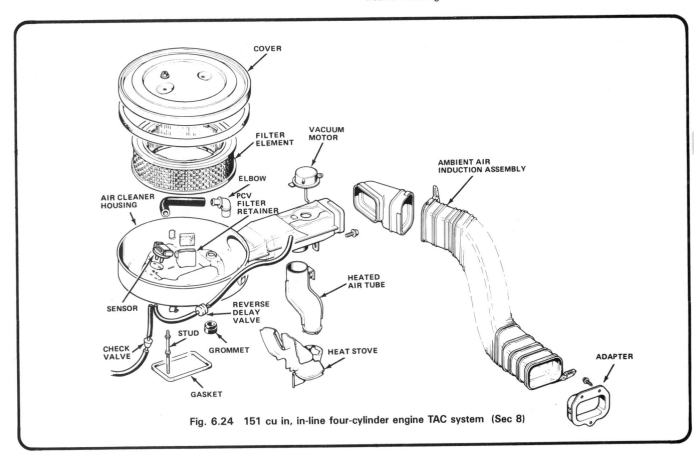

**Fig. 6.24  151 cu in, in-line four-cylinder engine TAC system  (Sec 8)**

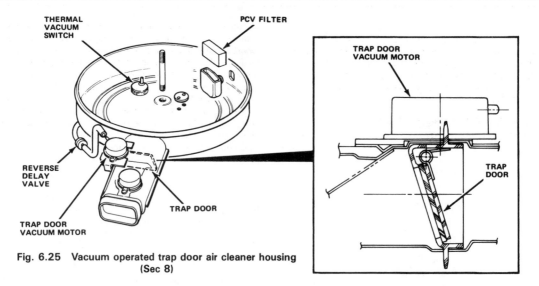

Fig. 6.25   Vacuum operated trap door air cleaner housing
(Sec 8)

10   On trap door-equipped models, remove the hose from the manifold and connect a vacuum pump. The trap door should open when vacuum is applied. If it does not, remove the hose from the motor and apply vacuum directly to it. If the door does not open, check for binding. If it does open, check the vacuum hose between the motor and the manifold for obstructions and leaks. If the hose appears to be in good condition, remove the delay valve, join the hoses and repeat the test. Replace the delay valve with a new one if the valve now opens. Replace the vacuum motor with a new one if the door swings freely, unaffected by vacuum.

## Component replacement

11   Replacement of the components is a simple matter of removing the faulty part and replacing it with a new one. Be sure to connect the hoses properly before checking the system operation.

## 9   Feedback carburetor

### General description

1   The feedback carburetor controls exhaust emissions while retaining driveability by maintaining a continuous interaction between the various emissions systems. The system is used on 1981 through 1983 in-line, six-cylinder and 151 cu in, four-cylinder engines.

2   The main components of the system are an exhaust gas oxygen sensor, an electronic control module (ECM) and a controlled air/fuel ratio carburetor.

3   The exhaust gas oxygen sensor is mounted in the exhaust pipe, upstream of the catalytic converter. It monitors the exhaust stream and sends information to the ECM concerning how much oxygen is present in the exhaust gases. The oxygen level is determined by how rich or lean the fuel mixture in the carburetor is.

4   The electronic control module (ECM) is essentially a small onboard computer located in the engine compartment on the left-hand inner fender panel on six-cylinder models and on the left-hand kick panel in the passenger compartment on four-cylinder models. The ECM monitors up to 15 engine/vehicle functions and controls as many as nine different operations. It is programmed with information specific to the model such as weight, final drive, etc., and can't be used on another vehicle. The ECM receives continuous information from the feedback system and processes it in accordance with its programming. It sends out electronic signals to the system components, modifying their performance.

5   The mixture control solenoid (four-cylinder engine) or air metering pins (six-cylinder engine) control the fuel flow in the carburetor, constantly adjusting the fuel/air mixture in accordance with the signals from the ECM.

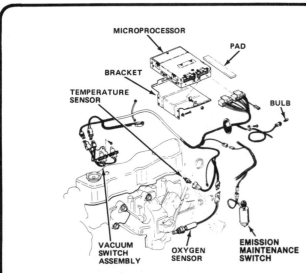

Fig. 6.26   151 cu in four-cylinder engine feedback carburetor emissions system component layout (Sec 9)

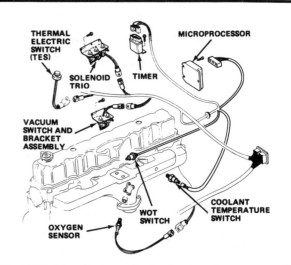

Fig. 6.27   Six-cylinder engine feedback system component layout (Sec 9)

*Checking*

6   Since this system requires special tools and techniques for maintenance and repair, any work on it should be left to your dealer or a qualified technician. Checking is confined to inspecting the system for broken and damaged components and vacuum leaks. The oxygen sensor should be checked or replaced at the specified intervals and the emissions maintenance switch reset.

*Component replacement (oxygen sensor)*

7   With the engine cold, unplug the wire connector and unscrew the sensor with a wrench. Four-cylinder engines require the use of a special tool (J-29533) for installation and removal. Clean the threads in the exhaust manifold, coat the threads of the sensor with anti-seize compound and install and tighten it to the specified torque. Install the wire connector, making sure the boot is not pushed closer than 1/2-inch from the sensor base. If equipped with an emissions system maintenance indicator light, the switch must be reset. The switch is located between the upper and lower speedometer cable on the left side of the dash in the engine compartment. Turn the reset screw *counterclockwise* 1/4-turn to the detent.

**6**

# Chapter 7 Part A  Manual transmission

**Contents**

External shift linkage — adjustment . . . . . . . . . . . . . . . . . . 5
General information . . . . . . . . . . . . . . . . . . . . . . . . . . . . . . 1
Oil level check . . . . . . . . . . . . . . . . . . . . . . . . . . Chapter 1
Planning major transmission work . . . . . . . . . . . . . . . . . . . . 6
Shift assembly — removal and installation . . . . . . . . . . . . . 4
SR4 four-speed transmission — disassembly, inspection
    and reassembly . . . . . . . . . . . . . . . . . . . . . . . . . . . . . . 12
Transmission (1953 through 1971 models) — removal
    and installation . . . . . . . . . . . . . . . . . . . . . . . . . . . . . . 2
Transmission (1972 through 1983 models) — removal
    and installation . . . . . . . . . . . . . . . . . . . . . . . . . . . . . . 3
Transmission oil change . . . . . . . . . . . . . . . . . . . Chapter 1
T4 four-speed transmission — disassembly,
    inspection and reassembly . . . . . . . . . . . . . . . . . . . . . . 13

T14A and T15A three-speed transmission — disassembly,
    inspection and reassembly . . . . . . . . . . . . . . . . . . . . . . 9
T5 five-speed transmission — disassembly,
    inspection and reassembly . . . . . . . . . . . . . . . . . . . . . . 14
T90C and T86AA three-speed transmission — disassembly,
    inspection and reassembly . . . . . . . . . . . . . . . . . . . . . . 7
T98A/T18A four-speed transmission — disassembly,
    inspection and reassembly . . . . . . . . . . . . . . . . . . . . . . 8
T150 three-speed transmission — disassembly,
    inspection and reassembly . . . . . . . . . . . . . . . . . . . . . . 10
T176 four-speed transmission — disassembly,
    inspection and reassembly . . . . . . . . . . . . . . . . . . . . . . 11

**Specifications**

## Column shift models

| | |
|---|---|
| Shifting clutch clearance . . . . . . . . . . . . . . . . . . . . . . . . . . . . . | 0.015 to 0.018 in |
| Shift dog-to-clutch slot clearance . . . . . . . . . . . . . . . . . . . . | 0.009 in |

## T90/T86AA three-speed transmission

| | |
|---|---|
| Interlock sleeve-to-shift lever clearance . . . . . . . . . . . . . . . | 0.001 to 0.007 in |
| Countershaft end play . . . . . . . . . . . . . . . . . . . . . . . . . . . . . | 0.012 to 0.018 in |

## T150 three-speed and T176 four-speed transmission

| | |
|---|---|
| Countershaft gear-to-case end play . . . . . . . . . . . . . . . . . . . | 0.004 to 0.018 in |
| Third-fourth synchronizer hub-to-snap-ring end play . . . . . . . . | 0.004 to 0.014 in |
| Reverse idler gear-to-case end play . . . . . . . . . . . . . . . . . . . | 0.004 to 0.018 in |
| Mainshaft snap-ring-to-second-third synchronizer hub . . . . . . | 0.004 to 0.014 in |
| Mainshaft gear train end play . . . . . . . . . . . . . . . . . . . . . . . . | 0.004 to 0.018 in |

## SR4 four-speed transmission

| | |
|---|---|
| Countershaft gear end play . . . . . . . . . . . . . . . . . . . . . . . . . | 0.004 to 0.018 in |
| Second gear end play . . . . . . . . . . . . . . . . . . . . . . . . . . . . . | 0.004 to 0.014 in |
| Output shaft end play . . . . . . . . . . . . . . . . . . . . . . . . . . . . . | 0.004 to 0.014 in |
| Blocking ring-to-cone seat clearance . . . . . . . . . . . . . . . . . . | 0.030 in |

## Torque specifications

### T90/T98A

| | Ft-lb | Nm |
|---|---|---|
| Fill and drain plugs | 10 to 20 | 14 to 27 |
| Front bearing cap bolt | 12 to 18 | 17 to 25 |
| Shift control housing bolts | 10 to 15 | 17 to 20 |
| Transfer case drive gear locknut | 145 to 155 | 197 to 210 |
| Transmission-to-transfer case bolts | 25 to 35 | 34 to 48 |

### T14A/T15A

| | Ft-lb | Nm |
|---|---|---|
| Backup light switch | 15 to 20 | 20 to 27 |
| Drain and fill plug | 10 to 20 | 14 to 27 |
| Front bearing cap bolts | 12 to 18 | 16 to 24 |
| Shift control housing-to-case bolts | 10 to 15 | 14 to 20 |
| Mainshaft rear bearing nut | 130 to 170 | 176 to 230 |
| Transfer case drive gear locknut | 145 to 155 | 197 to 210 |
| Transmission-to-transfer case bolts | 25 to 35 | 34 to 47 |
| TCS switch | 15 to 20 | 20 to 27 |

### T150

| | Ft-lb | Nm |
|---|---|---|
| Backup light switch | 15 to 20 | 20 to 27 |
| Drain and fill plugs | 10 to 20 | 14 to 27 |
| Front bearing cap bolts | 30 to 36 | 41 to 48 |
| Transfer case drive gear locknut | 145 to 155 | 197 to 210 |
| Transmission-to-transfer case bolts | 25 to 35 | 34 to 47 |
| TCS switch | 15 to 20 | 20 to 27 |

### T176

| | Ft-lb | Nm |
|---|---|---|
| Backup light switch | 10 to 20 | 14 to 27 |
| Drain and fill plugs | 10 to 20 | 14 to 27 |
| Front bearing cap bolts | 11 to 15 | 15 to 20 |
| Shift housing-to-transmission bolts | 11 to 15 | 15 to 20 |

### SR4

| | Ft-lb | Nm |
|---|---|---|
| Backup light switch | 8 to 12 | 11 to 16 |
| Adapter housing bolt | 18 to 27 | 24 to 37 |
| Detent plug | 8 to 12 | 24 to 37 |
| Fill plug | 15 to 25 | 20 to 34 |
| Front bearing cap bolt | 11 to 15 | 15 to 20 |
| Offset lever nut | 8 to 12 | 11 to 16 |
| Reverse lever pivot bolt | 15 to 25 | 20 to 34 |
| Shift control housing bolt | 7 to 12 | 9 to 16 |
| Transmission-to-clutch housing bolt | 45 to 65 | 61 to 65 |

### T4/T5

| | Ft-lb | Nm |
|---|---|---|
| Backup light switch | 12 to 18 | 16 to 24 |
| Adapter housing bolt | 11 to 15 | 15 to 20 |
| Fill plug | 15 to 25 | 20 to 34 |
| Front bearing cap bolt | 11 to 15 | 15 to 20 |
| Reverse lever pivot bolt | 15 to 25 | 20 to 34 |
| Shift control housing bolt | 15 to 25 | 10 to 34 |
| Transmission cover bolt | 5 to 9 | 7 to 12 |
| Transmission-to-clutch housing bolts | 45 to 65 | 61 to 88 |

**7A**

## 1  General information

These models were equipped with a variety of transmissions over their long production life.

The models from 1953 through 1971 were equipped with three and four-speed T90C, T86AA (V6) and T14A and T98/T18A four-speed transmissions. The 1972 through 1983 models used T14A, T15A, T150, T18A, T176, T4 and SR4 four-speed and T5 five-speed transmissions.

Early models (through some models of the CJ6A) were equipped with column shifters while all others had floor shifters.

## 2  Transmission (1953 through 1971 models) — removal and installation

1  The transmission and transfer case are removed and installed as a unit.

2  Drain the transmission and transfer case oil into a suitable container and replace the drain plugs.

3  Remove the inspection plate from the floor pan.

4  Remove the shift lever and housing from the transmission. On column shift models, remove the remote shift rods.

5  Remove the set screw from the transfer case shift lever pin, followed by the pin, shift levers and lever springs. On column shift models, remove the pivot pin cotter pin, attaching nut and shift lever.

6  On power take off-equipped models, remove the retaining screws and lift out the shift lever.

7  After marking their relative positions, remove the driveshafts from the transfer case. Disconnect the power take off driveshaft (if equipped) from the transfer case.

8  Disconnect the speedometer cable from the transfer case.

9  Disconnect the hand brake cable and the clutch release cable.

10  Place two jacks directly under the transmission and engine, using a block of wood to protect the oil pan.

11  Remove the nuts retaining the rear mount and transfer case rubber snubber to the crossmember.

12  Remove the crossmember and bolts.

13  Remove the transmission-to-bellhousing bolts and carefully pry the transmission to the right and disengage the clutch control lever tube ball joint.

14  Slowly lower the jacks and slide the transmission and transfer case assembly to the rear until the input shaft is clear of the bellhousing.

15  Lower the transmission and transfer case to the floor and remove them from the vehicle.

16  To separate the transmission from the transfer case, remove the transfer case rear cover and bolts. On power take off-equipped models, remove the shift unit.

17  Remove the transfer case drive gear and nut. If the drive gear cannot be removed, follow the procedure in Step 19.

18  Remove the attaching bolts and separate the transfer case from the transmission. If the transfer case drive gear is still in place, refer to the procedure in Step 19.

19  To keep the transmission mainshaft from pulling out of the case, loop a piece of wire around the shaft directly behind the second speed gear. Partially install one right-hand and one left-hand shift housing bolt, twist the wire and attach the ends to the bolts. Draw the wire up tightly to securely hold the mainshaft in place. Support the transfer case and use a large plastic hammer or a brass drift and a hammer to tap lightly on the end of the mainshaft and loosen the gear. Separate the transmission and transfer case.

20  Installation is the reverse of removal except for the following points:

   a)  When installing the front adapter plate, install the bearing retainer in the plate before positioning the plate against the bellhousing. When the adapter plate bolts have been securely tightened, it should be possible to remove the bearing retainer. If this is not possible, loosen the bolts and reposition the adapter plate until the bearing retainer can be removed.

   b)  Make sure the adapter plate bolt heads do not protrude beyond the face of the plate or prevent complete seating of the transfer case against it.

   c)  When the transfer case gear is installed on the transmission rear splined driveshaft, tighten the gear nut securely and insert the cotter pin. The cotter pin ends must be bent well into the nut slots to provide proper clearance for the power take off.

   d)  Be sure to refill the transmission and transfer case with the specified lubricant (Chapter 1).

## 3  Transmission (1972 through 1983 models) — removal and installation

1  The transmission and transfer case are removed and installed as an assembly.

2  Remove the floor shift lever knob, trim ring and boot, followed by the floor covering and the floorpan transmission access cover.

3  On T15 and T18A transmissions, remove the shift control assembly. On T176A, SR4, T4 and T5 transmissions, remove the shift lever and housing.

4  On models where the transfer case shifter will interfere with removal, remove the shift lever and bracket assembly.

5  Raise the vehicle and support it securely on jackstands.

6  Mark their relative positions to simplify installation and remove the front and rear driveshafts.

7  Support the engine by placing a jackstand under the clutch housing.

8  Remove the mounting nuts and bolts and detach the rear crossmember and support cushion.

9  Disconnect the speedometer cable and, depending on the model, the back up light switch, TCS, four-wheel drive indicator, parking brake cable and transfer case vent hose. On some V8 models, it will be necessary to disconnect the exhaust pipes from the manifolds.

10  Support the transmission/transfer case assembly with a jack.

11  Remove the transmission-to-bellhousing bolts and carefully move the transmission/transfer case assembly to the rear until the input shaft is clear of the bellhousing. Lower the assembly to the floor and remove it from the vehicle.

12  Remove the retaining bolts and separate the transmission from the transfer case.

13  Use needle-nose pliers to remove the pilot bushing lubricating wick (if equipped). Soak the wick in engine oil.

14  Clean the mating surfaces of the transmission and transfer case to remove old gasket material. Attach the transmission to the transfer case, using a new gasket.

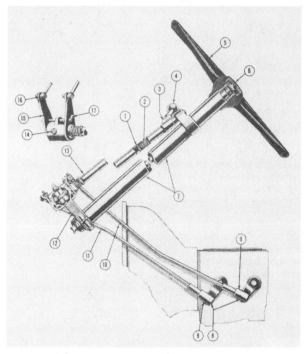

**Fig. 7.1  Column shift control components**

| 1 | Stop screw | 10 | Shift rod |
|---|---|---|---|
| 2 | Bias spring | 11 | Shift rod |
| 3 | Gearshift lever | 12 | Cross-shift bracket |
| 4 | Lever ball | 13 | Control shaft |
| 5 | Steering wheel | 14 | Lubrication fitting |
| 6 | Horn button | 15 | Lever and clutch |
| 7 | Column and bearing | 16 | Adjusting yoke |
| 8 | End nuts | 17 | Aligning rod |
| 9 | Shift rod ends | | |

15  Make sure the throwout bearing is in position in the fork and is centered over the pressure plate release lever. Install the lubricating wick (if equipped) in the pilot bushing.

16  Raise the transmission/transfer case unit into position with a jack and move it forward until the transmission is in place against the bellhousing and the input shaft is engaged in the pressure plate. Install the transmission mounting bolts and tighten them securely.

17  Install the crossmember and support cushion.

18  Remove the jack and jackstand supporting the engine.

19  Connect the exhaust pipes (V8 models).

20  Connect the speedometer cable and any wires which were removed from the transmission or transfer case.

21  Install the driveshafts, aligning the marks made during removal.

22  Lower the vehicle.

23  Install the transmission shift lever and housing or shift control assembly.

24  Install the transfer case shifter and bracket assembly (if removed).

25  Install the floor shift lever knob, trim ring and boot, followed by the access cover and floor cover.

## 4  Shift assembly — removal and installation

### T90 and T86AA remote control shift assembly

1  Disconnect and remove the shift rods from the transmission and clutch control, followed by the gearshift lever and fulcrum pin.

2  Remove the plates from the toe board located at the steering column. Remove the retaining screws and lift the remote control housing from the positioning pin on the steering column. Lower the assembly down and remove it through the floor pan.

3  Remove the lower clutch and shift lever, followed by the upper

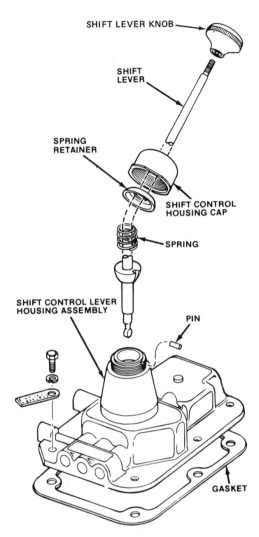

SHIFT LEVER KNOB

SHIFT
LEVER

SPRING
RETAINER

SHIFT CONTROL
HOUSING CAP

SPRING

SHIFT CONTROL LEVER
HOUSING ASSEMBLY

PIN

GASKET

**Fig. 7.2   Typical transmission shift control (T18A shown)**

clutch and shift lever, by turning them counterclockwise.
4    Before reassembly, check the clearance of the shift dog, where it engages in the clutch slot, with a feeler gauge. If the clearance is over 0.009-inch, replace the assembly.
5    Assemble the upper clutch lever assembly in the housing with the housing alignment hole facing toward the engine. Screw the upper lever housing in completely and then back it off one (1) full turn so the hole in the clutch lever is aligned with the hole in the housing.
6    Insert the lower clutch lever assembly into the housing and thread it in until the clutch faces make contact. Back the assembly out about one-half turn; this should align the hole in the lever with the one in the housing. Attach the unit to the steering column and adjust the rods (Section 5).
7    Check the assembly for proper shifting. If the shift dog catches on the edge of the clutch slot when the lever is moved up and down, disconnect the shift rod at the transmission and adjust the length.

### T90 and T86AA floor shift assembly
8    Remove the mounting bolts and separate the shift housing and gasket from the top of the transmission. Installation is the reverse of removal. Be sure to use a new gasket.

### T14A and T15A floor shift assembly
9    With the transmission in Neutral, remove the mounting bolts and separate the shift control lever housing assembly from the transmission.
10    Using a new gasket, carefully lower the shift lever assembly into position, making sure to securely seat the shifter forks in the synchronizer sleeves.

### T18A and T150 floor shift assembly
11    To remove the shift lever assembly, unscrew the shift control housing cap and remove the retainer and spring. Remove the locating pin and separate the shift lever from the transmission. Installation is the reverse of removal.
12    To remove the shift control housing assembly complete with the lever, remove the mounting bolts and separate the housing and gasket from the transmission. Installation is the reverse of removal.

### SR4, T4 and T5 floor shift assembly
13    Remove the shift lever housing mounting bolts and separate the assembly from the transmission. Installation is the reverse of removal.

### T176 floor shift assembly
14    Press down on the shift lever retainer, turn it counterclockwise and remove the lever, boot, spring and seat assembly.
15    To install the lever, place the assembly in position, press down on the retainer and turn it clockwise until it is securely seated.

## 5    External shift linkage — adjustment

1    Only early models with column shift levers can be adjusted.
2    Disconnect the shift rods from the remote control levers and check for binding of the remote control shaft on the steering column. Lubricate and adjust as necessary.
3    If the shifting action is not smooth and positive, place the transmission in Neutral and disconnect the shift rods at the transmission by removing the clevis pin.
4    Insert a short piece of 1/4-inch diameter rod through the gearshift levers and the housing, as shown in the accompanying illustration, by removing the clevis pins.
5    The shift rod yokes can now be adjusted at the transmission end until the clevis pins can be easily installed without moving the shift levers.
6    If shifting is difficult from first to second or the transmission sticks in first gear, shorten the low and reverse rod by rotating it one (1) turn at a time and checking the shift operation until the condition is corrected. Three (3) turns of the rod should be sufficient to make the adjustment.
7    If adjustment does not cure the shifting problem, check the shift mechanism for wear. Remove the grease fitting and insert a narrow feeler gauge into the opening to check the clearance between the shifting clutch faces. If the clearances are beyond those shown in the Specifications, the assembly must be removed and adjusted. Check the clearance of the shift dog (where it engages the clutch slots) with a feeler gauge. If the shift dog-to-clutch slot (clutch groove-to-cross pin) clearance is not as specified, the assembly must be replaced with a new one.

## 6    Planning major transmission work

1    Before beginning transmission disassembly, read through the entire procedure to familiarize yourself with the scope and requirements of the job.
2    One of the biggest problems a beginner will face when dismantling an assembly as complex as a transmission is trying to remember exactly where each part came from. To help alleviate this problem, it may be helpful to draw your own simple diagrams or take instant photos during the disassembly procedure. Laying each part out in the order in which it was removed and tagging parts will also be helpful.
3    Try to anticipate which parts may have to be replaced and have them available before beginning. Regardless of broken or badly worn components, there are certain items which must be replaced as a matter of course when the transmission is reassembled. These include gaskets, snap-rings, oil seals and sometimes bearings. You will also need some multi-purpose grease and RTV-type gasket sealer to properly reassemble the transmission.
4    Cleanliness is extremely important when working on a precision piece of equipment such as a transmission. The work area should be kept as clean and free of dirt and dust as possible. Also, adequate space should be available to lay out the various parts as they are removed.

**7A**

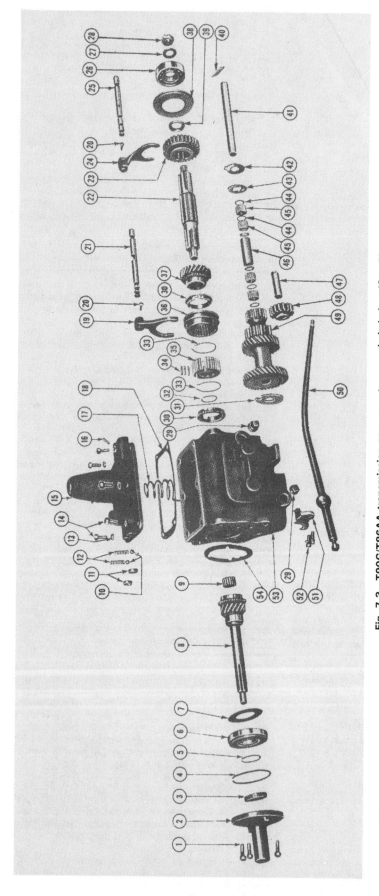

**Fig. 7.3  T90C/T86AA transmission components — exploded view (Sec 7)**

1  Bearing retainer bolt
2  Bearing retainer
3  Bearing retainer oil seal
4  Bearing snap-ring
5  Main drive gear snap-ring
6  Main drive gear bearing
7  Front bearing washer
8  Main drive gear
9  Pilot roller bearing
10  Poppet ball
11  Shift rail cap
12  Poppet spring
13  Lock washer
14  Shift housing bolt
15  Control housing
16  Interlock plunger

17  Shift lever spring
18  Shift tower gasket
19  High and intermediate
      shift fork
20  Shift fork pin
21  High and intermediate
      shift rail
22  Mainshaft
23  Sliding gear
24  Low and reverse
      shift fork
25  Low and reverse
      shift rail
26  Rear bearing
27  Mainshaft washer
28  Mainshaft nut

29  Filler plug
30  Blocking ring
31  Front countershaft
      thrust washer
32  Clutch hub snap-ring
33  Synchronizer spring
34  Synchronizer plate
35  Clutch hub
36  Clutch sleeve
37  Second speed gear
38  Rear bearing adapter
39  Bearing spacer
40  Lock plate
41  Countershaft
42  Rear countershaft
      thrust washer

43  Rear countershaft
      thrust washer
44  Countershaft bearing
      washer
45  Countershaft bearing
46  Countershaft bearing
      spacer
47  Reverse gear shaft
48  Reverse idler gear
49  Countershaft gear set
50  Shift lever
51  Oil collector
52  Oil collector screw
53  Transmission case
54  Bearing retainer gasket

## 7   T90C and T86AA three-speed transmission — disassembly, inspection and reassembly

### Disassembly

1   Remove the shift housing or cover plate and gasket.
2   The shift housing on floor shift models can be disassembled after removal, taking care not to lose the poppet balls and springs when the shift rails and forks are removed. On column shift models the main drive gear must be removed before the shift forks can be removed.
3   Remove the main drive gear bearing retainer (three screws) and gasket.
4   On early models, remove the socket head screws from the front of the case. The screws support the oil collector inside the case used on some early models.
5   Loosen the countershaft lock plate by tapping on the front end of the shaft. Remove the lock plate from the slots in the countershaft and reverse idler shaft.
6   Use a hammer and a brass drift to carefully drive the countershaft toward the rear of the case and remove it. The countershaft gear set will drop into the transmission case, which could dislodge the needle bearing rollers.
7   Remove the mainshaft rear bearing adapter, followed by the mainshaft assembly. The mainshaft assembly and gears are most easily removed through the rear bearing adapter opening. Be careful not to lose the pilot roller bearing when the shafts are separated.
8   On early models equipped with oil collectors, drive the main drive gear into the case sufficiently to provide clearance and remove the collector.
9   Remove the main drive gear from the case.
10   Remove the countershaft gear set and three thrust washers. Remove the washers, needle bearing rollers and spacer from the assembly.
11   Use a hammer and a brass drift to drive the reverse idler shaft and gear into the case, then remove them.

### Inspection

12   On early models with column shifts, it is important to inspect the poppet and interlock assembly which floats between the shift lever assemblies. If it is too long, the assembly will make shifting impossible; if it is too short, it will not act as an interlock to prevent the shifting of two gears at one time.
13   With the intermediate and high control arm in the second gear position, measure the clearance between the ends of the interlock sleeve and each shift lever notched surface. Check the clearances against those in the Specifications. If the clearances are beyond the specified limit, the transmission should be taken to a dealer or properly equipped shop to have the interlock sleeves replaced with new ones.
14   Inspect the notched surfaces of the shifting lever for roughness and nicks. Use a fine file to smooth out the surface as necessary and replace any badly damaged lever with a new one.
15   Wash the inside and outside of the transmission case thoroughly using solvent and a stiff brush.
16   Inspect the case for cracks and check the front and rear mating surfaces for nicks and burrs. Minor imperfections can be removed with a fine file. Inspect the bearing bores for scoring, cracks and nicks. If the bores are badly damaged or worn or if cracks are found in the case, replace the case with a new one.
17   Wash the gears thoroughly with solvent and inspect the teeth and bronze blocking rings for chips, wear and cracks. Inspect the bearings and bushings for wear and damage. Check the first and reverse sliding gear for smooth movement on the mainshaft. Make sure the clutch sleeve slides freely on the hub. Inspect the bearing retainer oil seal for damage. Replace any worn or damaged components with new ones.
18   Prior to reassembly, make sure the new gaskets match the transmission case and particularly that drilled oil passages have corresponding openings in the gaskets.

### Reassembly

19   Reassembly of the transmission is the reverse of disassembly, with attention paid to the following points:

   a)   Install the reverse idler gear into the case, followed by the shaft. Make sure the slot at the end of the shaft is properly aligned to allow installation of the lock plate.

   b)   Use heavy grease to retain the main drive gear bushings in place during installation.

   c)   After installing the mainshaft, turn the transmission case over and allow the gears to mesh to allow installation of the countershaft. Check the countershaft end play. The end play clearance is adjusted by installing the appropriate rear thrust washer.

   d)   Attach the large bronze thrust washer to the front of the case with the lip of the washer in the slot. Use heavy grease to retain the washer. Attach the steel thrust washer to the rear of the case and insert the countershaft sufficiently to hold the washer in place. Align the countershaft slot with the reverse idler gear shaft slot so the lock plate can be installed. Position the bronze washer against the rear end of the gear, place the countershaft in the running position and tap it into place with a hammer and brass drift.

## 8   T98A/T18A four-speed transmission — disassembly, inspection and reassembly

### Disassembly

1   Remove the shift control housing from the transmission case.
2   Before removing the two blocking rings and the direct-to-third clutch sleeve, mark them with a punch or fast-drying paint so they can be assembled in their original positions. Be sure to also mark the blocking ring and low-and-second speed gear.
3   Slide the low-and-second speed gear toward the rear of the transmission case and disengage the reverse shifting arm and shoe from the reverse idler gear. Remove the arm from the pivot.
4   Move the low-and-second speed gear into the Neutral position and remove the bearing retainer and gasket, followed by the snap-rings retaining the main drive gear and the outer race of the ball bearing.
5   Use a puller to remove the main drive gear ball bearing and then remove the oil slinger.
6   Remove the snap-ring retaining the mainshaft ball bearing outer race and remove the bearing with a puller. To gain sufficient clearance for the puller plates, it may be necessary to carefully tap the mainshaft to the rear.
7   Slide the direct-and-third clutch sleeve to the rear or third gear position. Separate the mainshaft assembly from the drive gear, taking care not to lose the pilot bearing rollers.
8   Remove the mainshaft by lifting it out of the top of the transmission case.
9   Remove the main drive gear from the case and then remove the bearing rollers from the gear.
10   Prior to disassembly of the mainshaft, mark the relationship of the synchronizer hubs and the splines.
11   Remove the snap-ring retaining the direct and third synchronizer, followed by the front blocking ring from the front of the shaft.
12   Slide the direct-and-third synchronizer and gear assemblies off the mainshaft.
13   Remove the snap-ring from the rear of the mainshaft and slide the second synchronizer assembly and the blocking ring off.
14   Remove the snap-rings and slide the thrust washer, bearing rollers, second-speed gear and spacer off the mainshaft.
15   To disassemble the synchronizer assemblies, wrap a cloth around the second-speed synchronizer assembly and push the clutch hub out of the low-and-second-speed gear in the opposite direction of the shift fork groove. After removing the cloth, lift the springs, balls and plates from the hub.
16   Remove the lockplate retaining the countershaft and reverse idler gear shaft and use a pry bar in the slot of the shaft to loosen it. Slip the shaft out of the housing and gear and lift the reverse idler gear assembly from the case.
17   If the countershaft is to be removed, use a brass drift to drive the shaft to the rear. Fabricate or obtain a dummy shaft made of steel rod measuring 1-1/8 inch in diameter and ten inches in length. Use a file to remove any sharp edges. With the countershaft even with the inside of the case, use the dummy shaft to force it the rest of the way out. The dummy shaft must be kept in contact with the countershaft at all times to prevent the bearing rollers and thrust washers from falling out.
18   With the dummy shaft in place, position the transmission case on its side and roll the countershaft gear cluster carefully out.

**7A**

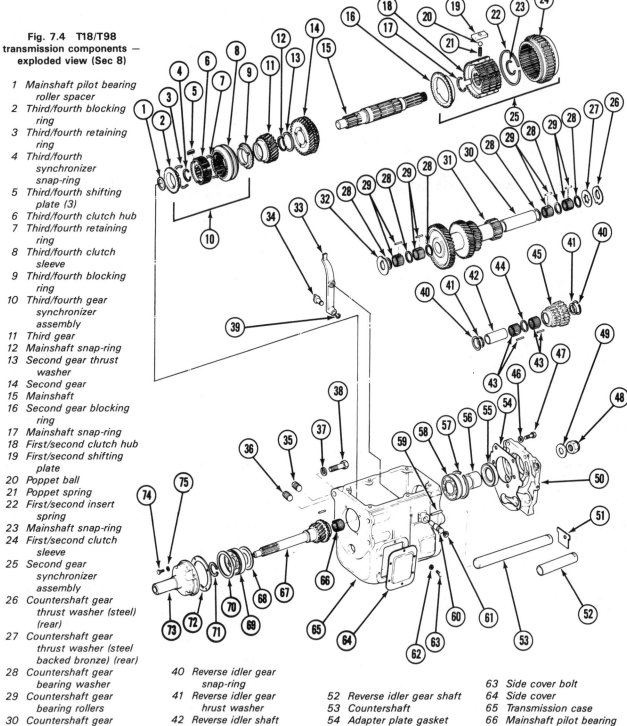

**Fig. 7.4 T18/T98 transmission components — exploded view (Sec 8)**

1 Mainshaft pilot bearing roller spacer
2 Third/fourth blocking ring
3 Third/fourth retaining ring
4 Third/fourth synchronizer snap-ring
5 Third/fourth shifting plate (3)
6 Third/fourth clutch hub
7 Third/fourth retaining ring
8 Third/fourth clutch sleeve
9 Third/fourth blocking ring
10 Third/fourth gear synchronizer assembly
11 Third gear
12 Mainshaft snap-ring
13 Second gear thrust washer
14 Second gear
15 Mainshaft
16 Second gear blocking ring
17 Mainshaft snap-ring
18 First/second clutch hub
19 First/second shifting plate
20 Poppet ball
21 Poppet spring
22 First/second insert spring
23 Mainshaft snap-ring
24 First/second clutch sleeve
25 Second gear synchronizer assembly
26 Countershaft gear thrust washer (steel) (rear)
27 Countershaft gear thrust washer (steel backed bronze) (rear)
28 Countershaft gear bearing washer
29 Countershaft gear bearing rollers
30 Countershaft gear bearing spacer
31 Countershaft gear
32 Countershaft gear thrust washer (front)
33 Reverse shifting arm
34 Reverse shifting arm shoe
35 Filler plug
36 Drain plug
37 Lock washer
38 Bolt (transmission-to-clutch housing)
39 C-washer

40 Reverse idler gear snap-ring
41 Reverse idler gear hrust washer
42 Reverse idler shaft sleeve
43 Reverse idler gear bearing rollers
44 Reverse idler gear bearing washer
45 Reverse idler gear
46 Lock washer
47 Adapter plate bolts
48 Drive gear locknut
49 Washer
50 Adapter plate
51 Countershaft/reverse idler shaft lockplate

52 Reverse idler gear shaft
53 Countershaft
54 Adapter plate gasket
55 Adapter plate seal
56 Speedometer gear spacer
57 Rear bearing locating snap-ring
58 Rear bearing
59 Reverse shifting arm pivot pin
60 Reverse shifting arm pivot
61 Reverse shifting arm pivot O-ring
62 Washer

63 Side cover bolt
64 Side cover
65 Transmission case
66 Mainshaft pilot bearing rollers
67 Clutch shaft
68 Front bearing retainer washer
69 Front bearing
70 Front bearing locating snap-ring
71 Front bearing lock ring
72 Front bearing cap gasket
73 Front bearing cap
74 Front bearing cap bolts
75 Lock washer

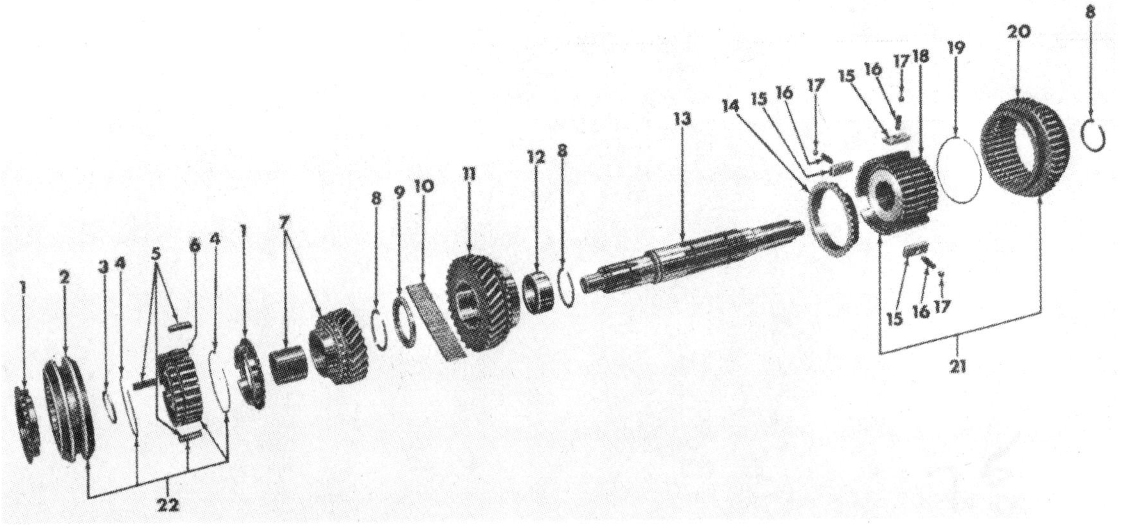

Fig. 7.5  T98 mainshaft component layout (Sec 8)

| | | | |
|---|---|---|---|
| 1 Blocking ring | 7 Third speed gear | 13 Mainshaft | 19 Retaining ring |
| 2 Direct and third clutch | assembly | 14 Blocking ring | 20 Low and second speed |
| sleeve | 8 Snap-ring | 15 Shifting plate | gear |
| 3 Snap-ring | 9 Thrust washer | 16 Poppet spring | 21 Second speed synchronizer |
| 4 Spring | 10 Bearing rollers | 17 Ball | assembly |
| 5 Shifting plate | 11 Second speed gear | 18 Low and second speed | 22 Direct and third synchronizer |
| 6 Direct and third clutch | 12 Spacer | clutch hub | assembly |
| hub | | | |

19  Remove the dummy shaft, thrust washers, bearing rollers and spacers.

20  To disassemble the reverse idler gear assembly, remove the snap-ring, then tap out the washers, bearing rollers, center spacer sleeve and remaining snap-ring.

21  To disassemble the shift control housing assembly, remove the lock wire and screws from the gearshift forks and rod ends. Remove the expansion plugs from the lever base.

22  Remove the center gearshift rod first by driving it out of the rear of the gearshift base with a punch and hammer. When withdrawing the rod, remove the interlock pin from the crossover hole in the rod. Before removing the rod, place your finger over the hole to prevent loss of the ball and spring. Remove the rod.

23  Remove the gearshift rod lock balls and spring and use a piece of wire to push the interlock plungers out of the pockets in the gearshift base center section.

24  To remove the reverse lock-out plunger from the reverse gearshift rod end, remove the cotter pin while holding your finger over the hole to prevent loss of the spring. Shake the spring and ball out and compress the spring and plunger sufficiently to expose the C-washer groove and remove the washer.

## Inspection

25  Clean the transmission case inside and out with solvent and a stiff brush.

26  Inspect the case for cracks and check the front and rear mating surfaces for nicks and burrs. Minor imperfections can be removed with a file. Inspect the bearing bores for scoring, cracks and nicks. If the bores are badly damaged or worn, or if cracks are found in the case, replace it with a new one.

27  Wash the gears and shafts with solvent. Inspect the gear teeth for chips, cracks and wear. Check the shafts for scoring, wear and nicks. Replace any worn or damaged components with new ones.

## Reassembly

28  Assemble the countershaft components with the dummy shaft. The bronze front thrust washer and the steel-backed bronze rear thrust washer should be coated with heavy grease before installation. Install the washers with the lugs engaged in the notches in the end of the gear cluster.

29  Place the assembly in the case and install the countershaft from the rear, keeping contact with the dummy shaft so the bearing rollers don't drop out. Tap the shaft lightly into position without seating it until the reverse idler gear assembly and shaft have been installed.

30  Install the reverse idler gear shaft in the case until the lock plate slot is adjacent to the countershaft slot. Insert the lock plate into the slots with the plate ends square with the slots. Install the lock plate screw and washer and alternately tap the shafts into position. With the lock plate and shafts in the correct position, tighten the screw.

31  To begin reassembly of the second-speed synchronizer assembly,

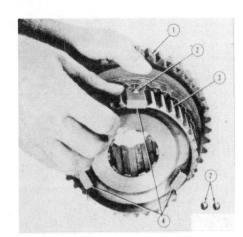

Fig. 7.6  Assembling the second-speed synchronizer (T18/T98) (Sec 8)

1 Low and second-speed gear
2 Ball
3 Low and second-speed clutch hub
4 Shifter plates

7A

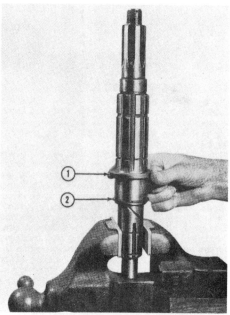

Fig. 7.7 Mainshaft snap-ring (2) and
thrust washer (1) installation (T98 only)
(Sec 8)

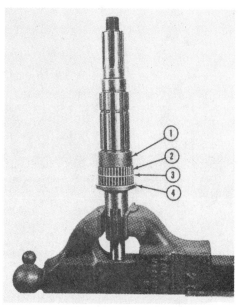

Fig. 7.8 Second-speed gear assembly
installation on the main gear shaft
(T98 only) (Sec 8)

1 Spacer        3 Rubber band
2 Roller bearings  4 Thrust washer

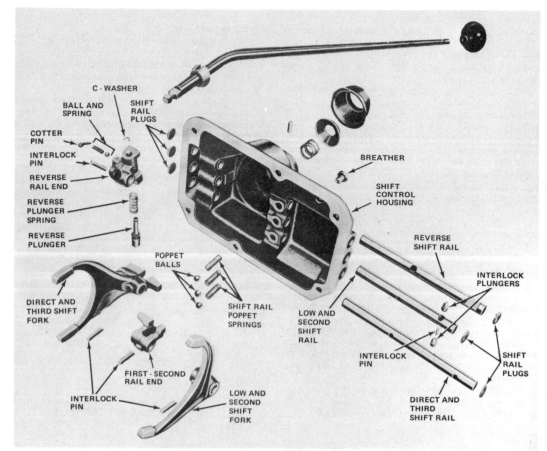

Fig. 7.9 T18/98 four-speed shift mechanism components (Sec 8)

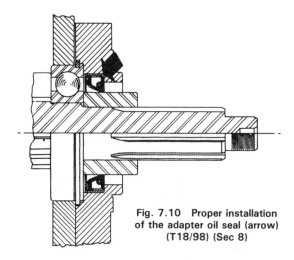

Fig. 7.10  Proper installation
of the adapter oil seal (arrow)
(T18/98) (Sec 8)

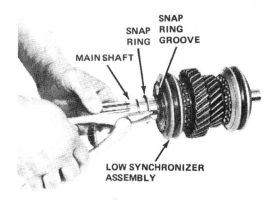

Fig. 7.11  Removal or installation of the first gear synchronizer
hub snap-ring (T14A/T15A) (Sec 9)

install the clutch hub into the low-and-second-speed gear, followed by the retaining ring.

32  Slide the hub out of the gear in the opposite direction of the shift fork groove until the holes in the hub are clear of the gear. Install the shifter plates and the springs.

33  Push the hub back into the gear until the springs touch the gear internal teeth and then push one of the shifter plates toward the gear center while installing the ball to hold it in position as shown in the accompanying illustration. Install the remaining two balls, following the same procedure. Use care when rotating the assembly so the hub won't slip out of the gear.

34  After the balls are installed, push the hub into the gear until the balls snap into the Neutral position.

35  Install the two springs in the high and intermediate clutch hub so that the spring tension is opposed.

36  Place the right (lipped) end of one spring in a slot of the hub and place the spring in position in the hub. Turn the hub around and, starting at the same slot, repeat the installation with the other spring. Install the three synchronizer shifting plates in the hub slots with the smooth side out. With the plates held in position, slip the second-and-direct-speed clutch sleeve over the hub so the long beveled edge is toward the long part of the clutch hub. Attach the two blocking rings to both sides of the hub and install the complete assembly on the mainshaft with the beveled edge of the clutch sleeve toward the front edge of the shaft.

37  The T18 second-speed gear-to-mainshaft is a slide fit, while the T98 uses roller bearings and requires the following procedure for assembly. Place the mainshaft securely in a vise, using wood blocks to protect the shaft surface, threaded end up.

38  Attach the snap-ring and thrust washer to the forward end of the second-speed position on the mainshaft as shown in the accompanying illustration. The recessed side of the thrust washer should cover the snap-ring.

39  Place a rubber band around the second-speed bearing surface and install the 34 bearing rollers, using the rubber band to retain them. With the rollers in place, install the spacer on the shaft as shown in the illustration.

40  Install the second-speed gear with the tapered shoulder up and slide it onto the bearing rollers far enough to hold them in place and remove the rubber band. Slide the gear completely over the bearings and install the rear snap-ring and the blocking ring on the tapered shoulder of the gear.

41  Install the second-speed synchronizer assembly on the mainshaft, aligning the marks made at the time of disassembly, and install the snap-ring.

42  With the tapered shoulder to the front, install the third-speed gear assembly on the shaft and slide the direct-and-third synchronizer onto the mainshaft. Make sure the alignment marks made during disassembly are lined up and install the snap-ring.

43  With the roller bearings in place in the front of the case, install the mainshaft assembly through the top of the case, taking care not to dislodge the bearings.

44  Install the main drive gear bearing retainer temporarily to provide

support, install the snap-ring on the mainshaft bearing and press the bearing into the case until the snap-ring seats.

45  Remove the bearing retainer and install the oil slinger onto the drive gear. Install the snap-ring on the main drive gear bearing and press the bearing and shaft into the case. Install the thickest snap-ring that will fit into the main drive gear groove.

46  Slide the drive gear bearing retainer on, hold it securely in place against the transmission and measure the distance between the retainer and the case with a feeler gauge. Install a gasket which is 0.003 to 0.005-inch thicker than the space between the retainer and case.

47  The remainder of transmission assembly is the reversal of disassembly, paying attention to the following points:

   a)  After reassembling the shift housing, be sure to use safety wire on all the shift fork and rod and lock screws.

   b)  Install new expansion plugs in the base of the shift housing.

   c)  Inspect the transmission breather for damage and obstructions and replace it if necessary.

   d)  The transmission adapter plate oil seal must be correctly positioned with the lip of the seal toward the transfer case as shown in the illustration.

## 9  T14A and T15A three-speed transmission — disassembly, inspection and reassembly

### Disassembly

1  Remove the transfer case gear locknut, followed by the drive gear, adapter and spacer. The second/third synchronizer sleeve must be moved forward and the first/reverse sleeve to the rear before the nut can be removed.

2  Use a center punch to make alignment marks in the front bearing cap and transmission case, then remove the cap and gasket.

3  Remove the front and rear bearing snap-rings, then use a puller to remove the bearings from the transmission case.

4  Remove the clutch shaft from the transmission case.

5  Move the second/third sychronizer sleeve into the second gear position and remove the mainshaft and gear train assembly.

6  Remove the lock plate retaining the idler shaft and countershaft and tap the shafts toward the rear to make removal easier.

7  Insert an arbor tool from the front of the transfer case and remove the countershaft.

8  Remove the countershaft gear thrust washers from the transmission case and the arbor tool, spacer washers, bearing rollers and center spacer from the countershaft gear.

9  Remove the reverse idler gear shaft, using a puller, followed by the gear, thrust washers and roller bearings as an assembly.

10  Remove the second/third synchronizer and snap-ring assembly.

11  Remove the second gear and blocking ring, followed by the reverse gear.

12  Remove the snap-ring retaining the first gear clutch hub and remove the first gear synchronizer assembly as shown in the accompanying illustration, then remove the first gear and blocking ring.

**7A**

13  Remove the synchronizer springs from the second/third synchronizer assembly and mark the sleeve and hub for ease of reassembly. Remove the sleeve and shifting plates from the hub.

### Inspection

14  Wash all of the transmission components with solvent. Use compressed air, if available, to dry all parts except the bearings. The needle and clutch shaft roller bearings can be cleaned by wrapping them in a clean cloth and submerging them in the solvent. Air dry the bearings only. Inspect the transmission case for cracks, stripped bolt hole threads, nicks, burrs and rough surfaces in the shaft bores and on the contact surfaces. Inspect all gears for broken, chipped and worn teeth. Check the blocking rings for wear and broken or worn teeth. Inspect the bearings, bores and shafts for wear, damage and galling. Check the thrust washers for wear and distortion and the snap-rings for distortion and lack of tension. Replace any damaged or worn components. When replacing a gear, the gear with which it meshes must also be replaced. Also, if a synchronizer requires replacement, check the shift fork which operates it to make sure it has the letter A stamped

on it. The letter is just under the shaft hole on the side opposite the pin. If the fork does not have the letter, it must be replaced with one which does.

### Reassembly

15  Prior to installation, lubricate the components using the specified transmission lubricant (Chapter 1).
16  Install the reverse idler gear, roller bearings and thrust washer, using AMC tool J-25202 (T14A) or J-25203 (T15A) as shown in the accompanying illustration.
17  Install the reverse idler shaft, which will force the tool out, and make sure the slotted end of the shaft is aligned correctly with the lock plate.
18  Install the center spacer and AMC arbor tool J-25199 (T14A) or J-25201 (T15A) into the countershaft gear bore.
19  Install the bearing washer at each end of the center spacer and slide the washers over the arbor tool until seated against the spacer.
20  Install the 22 roller bearings at each end of the countershaft gear, followed by the bearing washer over the bearings.
21  Coat the countershaft gear thrust washer with petroleum jelly (not

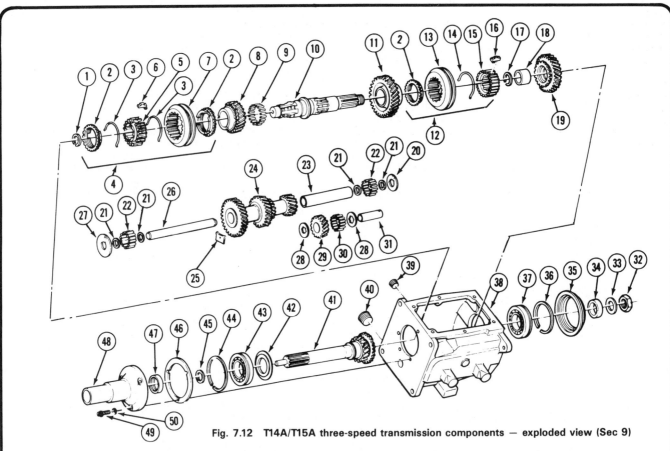

**Fig. 7.12   T14A/T15A three-speed transmission components — exploded view (Sec 9)**

| | | | |
|---|---|---|---|
| 1 Second/third synchronizer snap-ring | 13 First/reverse clutch sleeve | 24 Countershaft gear | 36 Rear bearing lock ring |
| 2 Blocking rings | 14 Synchronizer spring | 25 Countershaft/reverse idler shaft lockplate | 37 Rear bearing |
| 3 Synchronizer springs | 15 First gear clutch hub | 26 Countershaft | 38 Transmission case |
| 4 Second/third synchronizer assembly | 16 First gear shifting plate | 27 Countershaft gear thrust washer (front) | 39 Fill plug |
| 5 Second/third clutch hub | 17 First gear snap-ring | 28 Reverse idler gear thrust washer | 40 Drain plug |
| 6 Second/third shifting plate | 18 Reverse gear bushing (included with reverse gear) | 29 Reverse idler gear | 41 Clutch shaft |
| 7 Second/third clutch sleeve | 19 Reverse gear | 30 Reverse idler gear bushing rollers | 42 Front bearing retainer |
| 8 Second gear | 20 Countershaft gear thrust washer (rear) | 31 Reverse idler gear shaft | 43 Front bearing |
| 9 Mainshaft pilot bearing rollers | 21 Countershaft gear bearing washer | 32 Mainshaft locknut | 44 Front bearing lock ring |
| 10 Mainshaft | 22 Countershaft gear bearing rollers | 33 Mainshaft washer | 45 Front bearing snap-ring |
| 11 First gear | 23 Countershaft gear bearing spacer | 34 Mainshaft bearing spacer | 46 Front bearing cap gasket |
| 12 First gear synchronizer assembly | | 35 Rear bearing adapter | 47 Front bearing cap oil seal |
| | | | 48 Front bearing cap |
| | | | 49 Front bearing cap bolt |
| | | | 50 Lock washer |

chassis grease) and install it at the front of the case. Coat the small countershaft gear thrust washer with petroleum jelly and install it on the gear hub with the lip facing the groove in the case.

22  Position the countershaft gear assembly in the case, align the gear bores with the case bores and install the countershaft from the rear of the case. Make sure the lock plate slot in the shaft aligns correctly with the slot in the reverse idler gear shaft. This will force the arbor tool out.

23  Install the first gear and blocking ring onto the mainshaft.

24  Assemble the first gear synchronizer assembly and align the sleeve and hub using the marks made during disassembly. Install the sleeve shifting plates, insert the spring and then install the assembly onto the mainshaft.

25  Install the first gear clutch hub snap-ring. These are a select fit to eliminate end play, so be sure to use the snap-ring which is of the proper thickness. Use the thickest snap-ring which will fit in the groove.

26  Install the second gear and the blocking ring onto the mainshaft.

27  Assemble the second/third synchronizer assembly and align the sleeve and hub using the marks made during disassembly. Install the shifting plates and then insert the springs with the open ends opposite one another.

28  Install the second/third synchronizer assembly onto the mainshaft, followed by the snap-ring and blocking ring. Again, the snap-ring is a select fit to control end play, so make sure the correct one is used.

29  Install the reverse gear onto the mainshaft and then install the shaft and gear assembly in the transmission case.

30  Install the mainshaft pilot bearing rollers in the clutch shaft bore, using petroleum jelly (not chassis grease) to retain them in place. Position the clutch shaft in the case with the cutaway portion of the gear facing down as shown in the accompanying illustration. Take care not to displace the bearing rollers and guide the clutch onto the mainshaft. Install the front bearing retainer on the clutch shaft.

31  Installing the front and rear bearings involves the use of special tools. If they are not available, the transmission should be taken to a properly equipped shop. If the tools are available, use the following procedures.

32  Install the thrust yoke tool by inserting the tool yokes into the second gear groove and between the clutch shaft teeth and blocking ring and install the front and rear blocking rings. The front bearing can then be installed as shown in the accompanying illustration.

33  Install the rear bearing as shown in the accompanying illustration and then install the front and rear bearing retaining snap-rings. The rear snap-ring is the thicker of the two.

34  Inspect the front bearing cap oil seal and replace it with a new one if it is damaged, worn, loose or distorted.

35  Install the front bearing cap and new gasket with the oil drain slot aligned with the hole in the transmission case. Install the bolts and tighten them to the specified torque.

36  Shift both synchronizers into gear to prevent the mainshaft from turning and install the rear bearing adapter, spacer, transfer case gear, flat washer and driver gear retaining nut. Tighten the nut to the specified torque.

37  Shift the synchronizers into Neutral as shown in the accompanying illustration and check the operation of the gears in all positions. *The gears must be in the Neutral position before installing the case cover and gasket.*

38  This completes the reassembly of the transmission. To disassemble the shift control housing, remove the TCS switch and backup light switch (if so equipped). Remove the shift rail plugs from the rear of the housing by driving them sideways into the bore and then prying them out.

39  Move the first/reverse shift rail to the first gear position and remove the roll pin from the first/reverse shift fork and rail.

40  Slide the first/reverse fork to the rear, exposing the roll pin hole in the rail and insert a tapered punch into the hole. Rotate the first/reverse rail toward the second and third rail, aligning the groove at the rear of the first/reverse rail with the interlock plunger. Slide the first/reverse rail forward as far as it will go and remove the interlock

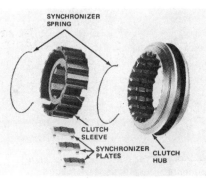

Fig. 7.13  Second/third synchronizer assembly components (T14A/T15A) (Sec 9)

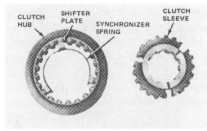

Fig. 7.14  First gear synchronizer assembly (T14A/T15A) (Sec 9)

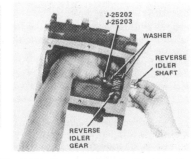

Fig. 7.15  Reverse idler shaft installation (T14A/T15A) (Sec 9)

Fig. 7.16  The main drive gear with the roller bearings installed (T14A/T15A) (Sec 9)

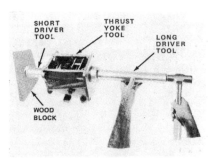

Fig. 7.17  Installing the T14A/T15A main drive gear bushing (Sec 9)

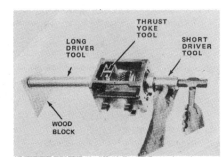

Fig. 7.18  Installing the mainshaft bearing (T14A/T15A) (Sec 9)

7A

plunger. Cover the poppet ball holes with a cloth during removal to prevent the loss of the ball and spring.

41  Remove the first/reverse rail by rotating it away from the second/third rail while pushing toward the rear of the housing.

42  Withdraw the first/second rail from the rear of the housing and then remove the roll pin from the second/third shift fork and rail. Again, cover the poppet ball holes with a cloth to avoid loss of the ball and spring.

43  Remove the second/third shift rail, followed by the shift lever retainer spring and the lever.

44  To reassemble, install the shift lever and retainer spring with the cone against the lever ball and the spring snapped in behind the shoulders in the cover.

45  Slide the second/third shift rail into the housing to the poppet boss and insert the poppet ball and spring. Compress the ball and spring, slide the rail to a point just past the boss and rotate the rail to position the shift lever slot toward the center of the housing.

46  Install the second/high fork, flanged side toward the front of the housing, and install the roll pin.

47  Hold the first/second shift fork in position with the flange side toward the rear of the housing and slide the first/second shift rail into the housing, through the fork, to the poppet boss. Insert the poppet ball and spring and compress the spring.

48  Push the shift rail as far forward as it will go and install the interlock plunger. Make sure the second/third shift rail is in the Neutral position and that the interlock plunger contacts the rail.

49  Rotate the first/reverse shift rail until the notch in the interlock end of the rod is facing away from the housing and then move the rail backward until the end contacts the interlock plunger.

50  Rotate the rail until the notch aligns with the interlock plunger and move the rail as far back as it will go. Align the roll pin holes and install the roll pin.

51  Install the shift rail sealing plugs and attach the switches to the housing.

## 10  T150 three-speed transmission — disassembly, inspection and reassembly

### Disassembly

1  Separate the transmission from the transfer case.

2  Move the second/third clutch sleeve forward and the first/reverse sleeve to the rear.

3  Remove the transmission fill plug and drain the lubricant into a suitable container.

4  Working through the fill plug hole, use a 3/16-inch diameter punch to drive out the countershaft roll pin as shown in the accompanying illustration.

5  Use an arbor tool to remove the countershaft and access plug as shown in the accompanying illustration.

6  Remove the countershaft from the rear of the transmission case and allow the countershaft gear to remain in the case.

7  Remove the large lock ring from the front bearing.

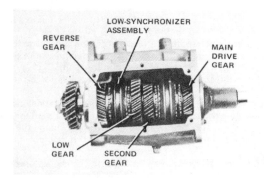

Fig. 7.19  T14A/T15A three-speed transmission with the mainshaft in the neutral position (Sec 9)

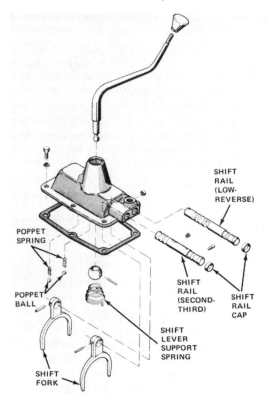

Fig. 7.20  T14A/T15A shift control housing components — exploded view (Sec 9)

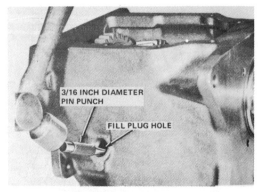

Fig. 7.21  Removing the countershaft roll pin (T150) (Sec 10)

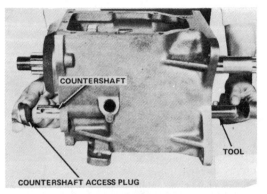

Fig. 7.22  Countershaft and access plug removal (T150) (Sec 10)

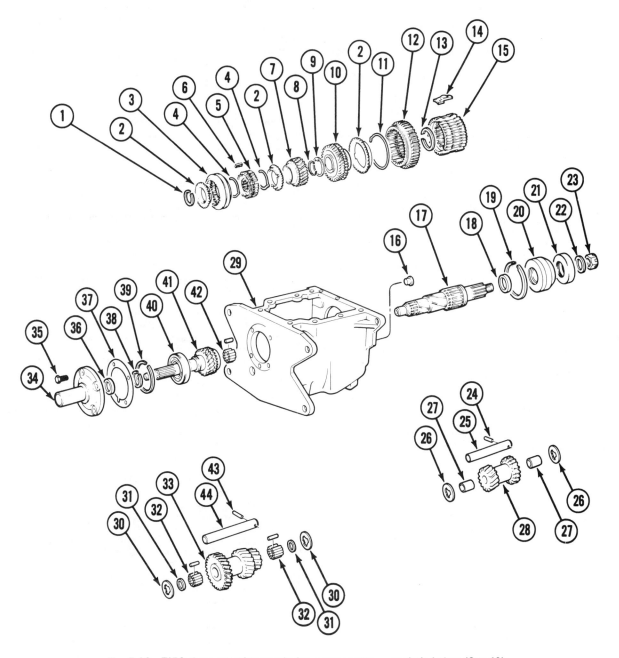

Fig. 7.23  T150 three-speed transmission components -- exploded view (Sec 10)

1  Mainshaft retaining snap-ring
2  Synchronizer blocking rings
3  Second/third synchronizer
   sleeve
4  Second/third synchronizer
   insert spring
5  Second/third hub
6  Second/third synchronizer
   insert
7  Second gear
8  First gear retaining snap-ring
9  First gear tabbed thrust washer
10  First gear
11  First/reverse synchronizer
   insert spring
12  First/reverse sleeve and gear
13  First/reverse hub retaining
   snap-ring

14  First/reverse synchronizer
   insert
15  First/reverse hub
16  Countershaft access plug
17  Mainshaft
18  Mainshaft spacer
19  Rear bearing adapter lock ring
20  Rear bearing and adapter
   assembly
21  Mainshaft rear oil seal
22  Flat washer
23  Locknut
24  Roll pin
25  Reverse idler gear shaft
26  Thrust washer
27  Bushing (part of idler gear)
28  Reverse idler gear

29  Transmission case
30  Thrust washer
31  Bearing retainer
32  Countershaft needle bearings
33  Countershaft gear
34  Front bearing cap
35  Bolt
36  Front bearing cap oil seal
37  Gasket
38  Front bearing retainer snap-ring
39  Front bearing lock ring
40  Front bearing
41  Clutch shaft
42  Mainshaft pilot roller bearings
43  Roll pin
44  Countershaft

**7A**

8   Remove the clutch shaft, front bearing and second/third synchronizer blocking ring assembly. If it is necessary to dismantle this assembly, take the clutch shaft to an automotive machine shop to have the bearing removed.

9   Use a brass drift and a hammer to drive out the rear bearing and adapter as shown in the illustration.

10   Remove the mainshaft assembly by tilting the spline end down and lifting the forward end up and out of the transmission case.

11   Remove the countershaft gear and arbor tool, followed by the thrust washers, countershaft roll pin and any mainshaft bearing rollers which may have fallen into the case.

12   Remove the reverse idler gear shaft and insert a brass drift through the clutch shaft bore. Tap on the shaft until the end with the roll pin clears the counterbore in the rear of the case and then remove the shaft, followed by the reverse idler gear and thrust washers.

13   To disassemble the mainshaft, remove the snap-ring from the front of the shaft, followed by the second/third synchronizer assembly and second gear. Mark the hub and sleeve to simplify reassembly. Also note the insert springs and inserts.

14   Remove the insert springs from the second/third synchronizer, remove the three inserts and separate the sleeve from the synchronizer hub.

15   Remove the first gear, blocking ring, tabbed thrust washer and snap-ring.

16   Note the positions of the inserts and spring, remove the snap-ring and remove the sleeve and gear, spring and inserts from the hub. Remove the spacer from the rear of the mainshaft.

17   Remove the hub from the output shaft. A press will be required for this and if one is not available, take the shaft to an automotive machine shop. *Do not attempt to hammer the hub off the shaft because it will be damaged.*

18   To disassemble the clutch shaft, remove the snap-ring and any remaining roller bearings and remove the front bearing with a press.

19   To disassemble the rear bearing adapter, place the adapter securely in a vise, using wood blocks to protect the surface. Using a pointed tool, remove the rear bearing snap-ring from the adapter.

20   Remove the adapter from the vise and press the bearing out of the adapter with a press. Removed the adapter lock ring.

21   Wash all of the components with solvent. If compressed air is available, dry everything except the bearings. The bearings should be air dried on a clean, lint-free cloth.

### Inspection

22   Inspect the transmission case for cracks in the bores, sides, bosses and bolt holes, and for stripped threads, nicks, burrs and rough surfaces in the shaft bores and on the gasket surfaces.

23   Inspect the gear and synchronizer assemblies for broken, chipped or worn teeth, damaged splines on the synchro hubs or sleeves, broken teeth or excessive wear of the blocking rings, bent or broken inserts and damaged needle bearings or bearing bores in the countershaft gear. Check the countershaft, clutch and idler shafts for nicked, broken or worn splines. Inspect the snap-rings for distortion or lack of tension. Inspect the reverse idler gear for worn bushings and the front and rear bearings for roughness, galling or damage. Replace any damaged or worn components with new ones.

### Reassembly

24   Prior to reassembly, lubricate the reverse idler gear shaft bore and bushings with transmission lubricant.

25   Coat the transmission case idler gear thrust washer surfaces with petroleum jelly (not chassis grease) and install the thrust washers. Engage the thrust washer locating tabs securely in the case slots.

26   Install the reverse idler gear and align the idler gear bore, thrust washers and transmission case bores. Insert the idler gear shaft from the rear of the case. Be sure to align and seat the roll pin in the shaft in the counterbore in the rear of the case.

27   Insert a feeler gauge between the thrust washer and the gear to check the end play and compare this measurement to the Specifications. If the end play is not as specified, remove the idler gear and replace the thrust washers with new ones.

28   Coat the countershaft needle bearings and bearing bores with petroleum jelly. Insert an arbor tool such as AMC tool J-25232 into the gear bore and install the needle bearings and retainer in each end of the gear.

29   Coat the countershaft gear thrust washer surfaces with petroleum jelly and position the thrust washers in the case, making sure to engage the tabs securely.

30   Insert the countershaft far enough into the rear case bore to hold the rear thrust washer in place. This will keep the thrust washer in place when the countershaft gear is installed.

31   Install the countershaft gear, but do not install the roll pin. Align the gear bore, thrust washers and case bores, then install the countershaft but do not remove the arbor tool completely.

32   Insert a feeler gauge between the washer and countershaft gear to measure the end play. Compare the end play measurement to the Specifications. If it is excessive, remove the gear and replace the thrust washers. After the correct end play has been obtained, install the arbor tool completely into the countershaft gear but leave the gear at the bottom of the case to provide clearance for mainshaft and clutch shaft installation. Leave the countershaft in the rear case bore so the thrust washer will be held in place.

33   Coat the mainshaft splines and machined surfaces with transmission lubricant. Carefully start the first/reverse synchronizer hub onto the output shaft splines by hand with the slotted end facing the front of the shaft. An arbor press must be used to press the hub onto the shaft, followed by installation of the snap-ring.

34   Coat the splines of the first/reverse hub with transmission lubricant and install the first/reverse sleeve and gear halfway onto the hub

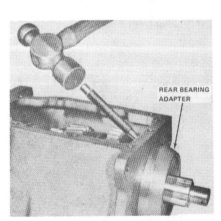

Fig. 7.24   Remove the rear bearing and adapter with a punch and hammer (T150) (Sec 10)

Fig. 7.25   Align the roll pin with the counterbore when installing the countershaft (T150 and T176) (Sec 10)

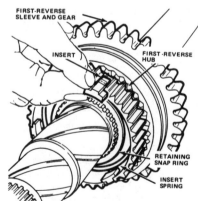

Fig. 7.26   First/reverse synchronizer hub insert installation (T150) (Sec 10)

with the gear end facing the rear of the shaft. Align the sleeve and hub marks made during disassembly.

35  Install the insert spring in the first/reverse hub, making sure the spring is bottomed in the hub and that it covers all three insert slots. Position the three T-shaped inserts in the hubs with the small ends in the hub slots and the large ends inside the hub as shown in the illustration.

36  Push the inserts completely into the hub to seat them on the insert spring and then slide the first/reverse sleeve and gear over the inserts until the inserts engage in the sleeve. Lubricate the bore and blocking ring surface of first gear with transmission lubricant and place the first gear blocking ring on the tapered surface of the gear.

37  Install the first gear on the output shaft, rotate it until the blocking ring notches engage the inserts in the first/reverse hub, install the tabbed thrust washer with the sharp edge facing out and install the snap-ring on the mainshaft as shown in the illustration.

38  Lubricate the second gear bore and blocking ring surface with transmission lubricant and place the blocking ring onto the tapered surface of the gear.

39  Install the second gear onto the output shaft with the tapered surface facing the front of the mainshaft.

40  Install one insert spring into the second/third hub, making sure it covers all three insert slots. Line up the marks made during disassembly to align the second/third sleeve with the hub and start the sleeve onto the hub.

41  Place the three inserts into the hub slots and on top of the insert spring, then push the sleeve completely onto the hub and engage the inserts in the sleeve. Install the remaining insert spring in exactly the same position as the first spring. The ends of both springs must cover the corresponding slots in the hub and the insert lip must fit over the spring as shown in the illustration.

42  Install the second/third synchronizer assembly onto the mainshaft and then rotate the second gear until the notches in the blocking ring engage the insert in the second/third synchronizer assembly.

43  Install the mainshaft snap-ring and measure the end play between the snap-ring and the second/third synchronizer hub with a feeler gauge as shown in the illustration. If the end play exceeds the specified limit, replace the thrust washer and all the snap-rings on the output shaft assembly. Install the spacer onto the rear of the mainshaft.

44  Install the mainshaft assembly in the case, making sure the first/reverse sleeve and gear is in the Neutral (centered) position on the hub so the gear end of the sleeve will clear the top of the case when the output shaft is installed.

45  Install the rear bearing into the bearing adapter. An arbor press must be used for this operation. Install the rear bearing retaining ring and the bearing adapter lock ring.

46  Support the mainshaft assembly and install the rear bearing and adapter in the case, using a soft-faced hammer to seat the adapter.

47  Press the front bearing onto the clutch shaft, install the snap-ring on the shaft and the lock ring in the front bearing groove.

48  Coat the clutch shaft bearing bore with petroleum jelly (not chassis grease) and install the 15 roller bearings.

49  Use transmission lubricant to coat the blocking ring surface of the clutch shaft and position the blocking ring on the shaft.

50  Support the mainshaft assembly and insert the clutch shaft through the front bearing bore in the case. Seat the mainshaft pilot in the clutch shaft roller bearings and tap the bearings into position using a soft-faced hammer.

51  Apply a thin coat of gasket sealer to the front bearing cap gasket and place the gasket in position, making sure the notch aligns with the oil return hole in the transmission case.

52  Pry out the old front bearing cap oil seal with a screwdriver. Install the new seal using a large socket.

53  Install the front bearing cap and bolts, tightening them to the specified torque. Make sure the case and cap alignment marks are lined up.

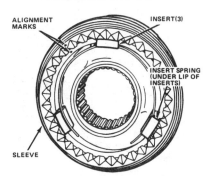

Fig. 7.27  Proper installation of the first/reverse hub snap-ring and insert spring (T150) (Sec 10)

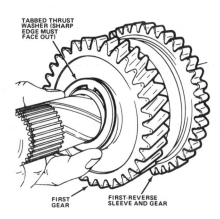

Fig. 7.28  Installing the first gear thrust washer (T150 and T176) (Sec 10)

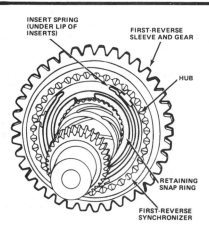

Fig. 7.29  Second/third synchronizer assembly installation details (T150 and T176) (Sec 10)

Fig. 7.30  Measuring the mainshaft gear train end play (T150 and T176) (Sec 10)

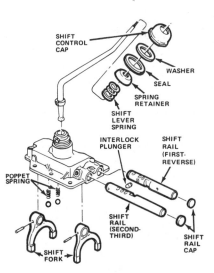

Fig. 7.31  Transmission shift lever mechanism components — exploded view (T150) (Sec 10)

**7A**

54  Fabricate a loop of wire about 20 inches long and pass it under the countershaft gear assembly. Raise the assembly with the wire and align the bore in the countershaft gear with the front thrust washer and countershaft. Start the countershaft into the gear using a soft-faced hammer and align the roll pin holes in the countershaft and the case.

55  Install the countershaft access plug in the rear of the case, using a soft-faced hammer to seat it.
56  Install the countershaft roll pin in the case, using a 1/2-inch diameter punch to seat the pin. Install the transmission filler plug.
57  Check the operation of the synchronizer sleeves by shifting into all gear positions. If it appears that the clutch shaft and mainshaft are

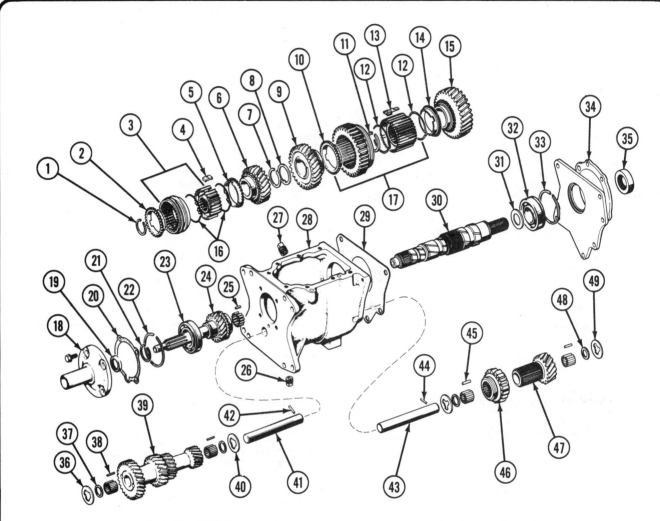

Fig. 7.32  T176 four-speed transmission components — exploded view (Sec 11)

| | |
|---|---|
| 1 Third/fourth gear snap-ring | 15 First gear |
| 2 Fourth gear synchronizer ring | 16 Third/fourth synchronizer spring |
| 3 Third/fourth gear clutch assembly | 17 First/second gear clutch assembly |
| 4 Third/fourth gear plate | 18 Front bearing cap |
| 5 Third gear synchronizer ring | 19 Oil seal |
| 6 Third speed gear | 20 Gasket |
| 7 Second gear snap-ring | 21 Snap-ring |
| 8 Second speed thrust washer | 22 Lock ring |
| 9 Second speed gear | 23 Front ball bearing |
| 10 Second gear synchronizer ring | 24 Clutch shaft |
| 11 Mainshaft snap-ring | 25 Roller bearing |
| 12 First/second synchronizer spring | 26 Drain plug |
| 13 Low/second plate | 27 Fill plug |
| 14 First gear synchronizer ring | 28 Case |
| | 29 Gasket |
| | 30 Spline shaft |
| | 31 First gear thrust washer |
| | 32 Rear ball bearing |

33 Snap-ring
34 Adapter plate
35 Adapter seal
36 Front countershaft gear thrust washer
37 Roller washer
38 Rear roller bearing
39 Countershaft gear
40 Rear countershaft thrust washer
41 Countershaft
42 Pin
43 Idler gear shaft
44 Pin
45 Idler gear roller bearing
46 Reverse idler sliding gear
47 Reverse idler gear
48 Idler gear washer
49 Idler gear thrust washer

binding, check for sticking of the blocking rings on the first and second speed gear tapers.

58  Install the mainshaft rear seal into the bearing adapter using a large size socket.

59  Shift both synchronizers into gear so the gears won't turn, install the transfer case drive gear and locknut and tighten the nut to the specified torque. Shift the transmission into Neutral before installing it.

60  To disassemble the shift control housing, remove the backup light and TCS switches (if so equipped), unthread the shift control housing cap and remove the cap, gasket, spring retainer and lever assembly. Turn the housing over and mount it in a vise by clamping the shift lever tower, using blocks of wood to protect the surface.

61  Move the second/third shift rail to the rear of the housing and rotate the shift fork toward the first/reverse rail until the roll pin is accessible. Drive the roll pin out of the fork and rail with a punch and hammer. Remove the shift fork and roll pin.

62  Use a hammer and brass drift to remove the second/third shift rail, taking care to catch the rail plug as the rail drives it out of the housing. Don't lose the poppet ball as the rail is removed. Cover the poppet ball holes in the housing with tape before removing the shift rail and mark the location of the rail for ease of installation.

63  Rotate the first/reverse shift fork away from the housing notch to expose the roll pin. Drive the roll pin out with a punch and hammer and remove the fork. Because the roll pin hole is offset, mark the shift fork position to simplify installation.

64  Use a hammer and brass drift to remove the first/reverse shift rail, catching the plug as it is driven out. Do not lose the poppet ball. Cover the shift tower and poppet ball holes with cloth or tape before removing the shift rail and mark its location. Remove the poppet balls, springs, and interlock housing plunger from the housing.

65  To assemble, install the poppet springs and detent plug in the housing and insert the first/reverse shift rail into the housing. Install the shift fork onto the shift rail and the poppet ball on top of the spring in the first/reverse shift rail bore.

66  Push the poppet ball and spring down into the housing bore, using a punch or wooden dowel, and install the first/reverse shift rail.

67  Line up the roll pin holes in the first/reverse shift rail and shift fork, install the roll pin and move the rail to the center or Neutral position.

68  Insert the second/third shift rail into the housing. Install the poppet ball on top of the spring in the second/third shift rail bore.

69  Push the poppet ball and spring down into the housing with a wooden dowel or punch and install the second/third shift rail.

70  Line up the roll pin holes in the second/third shift rail and the shift fork and install the roll pin. Move the shift rail into the center (Neutral) detent.

71  Install the shift rail plugs in the housing. Remove the shift control housing from the vise.

72  As an assembly, install the shift lever, lever spring, spring retainer, gasket and shift control housing, tightening the cap securely.

73  Install the backup light and TCS switches.

---

## 11  T176 four-speed transmission — disassembly, inspection and reassembly

### Disassembly

1  Separate the transmission from the transfer case.

2  Unbolt and remove the shift control housing.

3  Two of the housing attachment bolts are dowel-type alignment bolts and it is important to note their location during removal so they can be installed in the same place during reassembly.

4  Drain the lubricant into a suitable container.

5  Remove the countershaft using an arbor tool such as AMC tool J-28342 or equivalent. Tap the countershaft out of the rear of the case.

6  Remove the locating and snap-rings from the rear bearing and remove the bearing with a puller.

7  Mark the relative position of the front bearing cap on the transmission case for ease of installation and remove the bearing cap and gasket.

8  Use a screwdriver to pry the oil seal out of the front bearing cap.

9  Remove the snap-ring from the front bearing and remove the clutch shaft and front bearing. This operation requires the use of a special puller (AMC tool J-25152 with adapter J-29344).

10  Remove the third/fourth blocking ring from the clutch shaft or the synchronizer hub.

11  Remove the front bearing from the clutch shaft, using a puller.

12  Remove the mainshaft pilot roller bearings from the clutch shaft.

13  Remove the mainshaft and gear train assembly and move the third/fourth synchronizer sleeve to the rear, into the third gear position. Tilt the rear end of the shaft down and lift the front end up and out of the case.

14  Remove the countershaft gear and arbor tool.

15  Remove the countershaft gear thrust washers as well as any pilot bearing rollers which may have fallen into the case.

16  Remove the reverse idler gear assembly and tap the idler gear shaft out of the rear of the case. Remove the gear assembly thrust washers.

17  Remove the needle bearings and bearing retainers from the reverse idler gear assembly. Remove the sliding gear from the idler gear, noting its position for reference during reassembly.

18  Remove the arbor tool and needle bearings and retainers from the countershaft gear.

19  Remove the third/fourth synchronizer and snap-ring from the mainshaft. Slide the hub out of the sleeve and remove the insert springs, inserts and blocking ring. Note the position of the insert spring position for reference during installation.

20  Remove the third gear from the mainshaft.

21  Remove the second gear, blocking ring and snap-ring from the mainshaft.

22  Remove the tabbed thrust washer from the mainshaft.

23  Remove the first/second synchronizer hub snap-ring. Remove the hub and reverse gear and sleeve assembly, marking them for reference during reassembly. Remove the insert springs from the hub, followed by the three inserts. Remove the sleeve and gear from the hub.

24  Remove the first gear thrust washer from the rear of the shaft and (if still installed), the first gear and blocking ring.

### Inspection

25  Wash all of the components thoroughly with solvent. If compressed air is available, dry all components except the bearings. The bearings should be air dried on a clean, lint-free cloth.

26  Inspect the transmission case for cracks in the bores, sides, bosses and bolt holes. Check the shaft bores, bolt holes and gasket surfaces for stripped threads, nicks, burrs and rough surfaces.

27  Inspect the gear and synchronizer assemblies for broken, chipped or worn teeth, damaged splines on the synchro hubs or sleeves, broken teeth or excessive wear of the blocking rings, bent or broken inserts and damage to the needle bearings or bearing bores. Check the countershaft, clutch and idler shafts for nicked, broken or worn splines. Inspect the snap-rings for distortion and lack of tension.

### Reassembly

28  Coat the reverse idler gear shaft bore and sliding gear with transmission lubricant. Install the sliding gear onto the reverse idler gear.

29  Install the arbor tool in the reverse idler gear and install the needle bearings and the bearing retainer on one end.

30  Coat the reverse idler gear thrust washers with petroleum jelly (not chassis grease) and install them in the case. These washers have flats which must be installed facing the mainshaft. The thrust washer locating tabs must engage the locating slots in the case.

31  Install the reverse idler gear assembly. Line up the gear bore, thrust washers and case bores and install the reverse idler gear shaft from the rear of the case. Be sure to seat the roll pin in the shaft, align the roll pin with the notch in the case and push the shaft into the rear of the case.

32  Measure the end play of the reverse idler gear by inserting a feeler gauge between the thrust washer and the gear. Compare the measurement to the Specifications. If the end play exceeds the specified limit, remove the idler gear and replace the thrust washers with new ones.

33  Coat the countershaft, gear bore, needle bearings and gear with petroleum jelly. Place the thrust washers in position in the case, making sure to engage the locating tabs in the case.

34  Insert the countershaft into the rear case bore far enough to retain the rear thrust washer in place.

35  Install the countershaft gear, line up the gear bore, thrust washers and bores in the case and install the countershaft part way. Make sure the arbor tool enters the front shaft bore in the case and is not removed completely.

36  Insert a feeler gauge between the washer and countershaft gear to measure the end play. Compare this measurement to the Specifications. If the end play is beyond the limit, remove the gear and replace the thrust washers with new ones. After the correct end play has been obtained, reinstall the arbor tool and allow the gear to remain in the

**7A**

bottom of the case. Make sure the countershaft remains in the rear case bore to hold the thrust washer in place.

37  Lubricate the mainshaft, synchronizer assemblies and gear bores with transmission lubricant.

38  Assemble the first/second synchronizer hub, reverse gear and sleeve. Install the gear and sleeve on the hub and place the assembly flat on a workbench. Drop the inserts into the hub slots and install the insert spring. Place the looped end of the spring in one insert, compress the spring ends and insert the spring ends under the lips of the two remaining inserts. Make sure the spring is under the lip of each insert. Turn the assembly over and install the remaining insert. This spring must be installed so the open end is 180º opposite the first spring.

39  Install the assembled first/second synchronizer hub and reverse gear sleeve and snap-ring on the mainshaft.

40  Install the first gear and blocking ring onto the rear of the mainshaft, followed by the thrust washer.

41  Install a new tabbed thrust washer on the mainshaft, making sure the tab is seated in the mainshaft tab.

42  Install the second gear and blocking ring onto the mainshaft and secure it with a new snap-ring.

43  Install the third gear and blocking ring on the mainshaft.

44  Assemble the third/fourth synchronizer and install the sleeve on the synchronizer hub, using the alignment marks made during disassembly. Place the hub and sleeve assembly flat on a workbench, drop the inserts into the hub slots and install the insert spring. Position the looped end of the spring in one insert, compress the spring ends and insert the spring ends under the remaining two insert lips. After turning the assembly over, install the remaining spring as described above, but with the open end 180º opposite the first spring.

45  Install the third/fourth synchronizer assembly on the mainshaft, followed by a new snap-ring.

46  Measure the end play between the synchronizer hub and snap-ring with a feeler gauge. Compare this measurement to the Specifications. If the end play is greater than that shown in the Specifications, replace the thrust washers and snap-ring with new ones.

47  Install the mainshaft geartrain assembly in the transmission case, making sure the synchronizers are in the Neutral position so the sleeves will clear the top of the case when the assembly is installed.

48  Install the snap-ring on the front bearing and partly install the front bearing on the clutch shaft. The bearing should not be completely installed at this time or the shaft will not clear the countershaft gear.

49  Coat the clutch shaft bearing bore and the mainshaft pilot bearing rollers with petroleum jelly (not chassis grease) and install the rollers in the bore.

50  Use transmission lubricant to coat the blocking ring surface of the clutch shaft and place the blocking ring in position on the shaft.

51  Support the mainshaft assembly and carefully insert the clutch shaft into the case through the front bearing bore. Seat the mainshaft pilot hub in the clutch shaft roller bearings and use a soft-faced hammer to tap the front bearing and the clutch shaft into the case.

52  Install the front bearing cap and bolts finger tight.

53  Position the rear bearing on the mainshaft but do not install the locating ring. Start the bearing onto the shaft with AMC tool J-29345 or equivalent (such as a piece of rod). Remove the tool and use a soft-faced hammer to complete the installation. With the bearing seated on the shaft, install the retaining snap-ring.

54  Remove the front bearing cap and seat the front bearing on the clutch shaft. Install the retaining snap-ring.

55  Apply a thin coat of gasket sealer to the front bearing cap gasket and place it in position on the case with the notch aligned with the oil return hole.

56  Pry the front bearing oil seal out with a screwdriver. Install a new oil seal using AMC tool J-25233 or the proper diameter socket.

57  Install the front bearing cap and bolts, tightening them to the specified torque.

58  Install the locating ring on the rear bearing, reseating the bearing if necessary with a soft-faced hammer.

59  Turn the transmission case on end, at the edge of a workbench, with the clutch shaft pointing down. Make sure the countershaft bore is accessible and have an assistant hold the case in position. Carefully align the countershaft gear bores with the thrust washers and case bores and tap the shaft into place, taking care not to let the arbor tool drop onto the floor as the shaft is installed.

60  Check the operation of the synchronizer sleeves by shifting into all the gear positions. Check the blocking rings for sticking on the

tapered portion of the gears if the clutch shaft and mainshaft appear to bind in Neutral. Free any sticking blocking rings with a screwdriver.

61  Fill the transmission with the specified lubricant and tighten the filler plug securely.

62  Install the shift control housing and a new gasket, tightening the bolts to the specified torque.

---

## 12  SR4 four-speed transmission — disassembly, inspection and reassembly

### Disassembly

1  Separate the transmission from the transfer case.

2  Place a drain pan under the transmission and adapter housing.

3  Remove the drain bolt (the bottom adapter housing mounting bolt) and drain the transmission lubricant.

4  Remove the flanged nut which attaches the shift rail to the offset lever. Remove the offset lever.

5  Remove the rest of the extension housing mounting bolts. Remove the housing.

6  Remove the transmission shift control housing and gasket. Note the locations of the two alignment (dowel) bolts. Discard the transmission cover gasket.

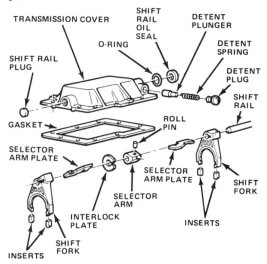

Fig. 7.33  SR4 transmission cover assembly components — exploded view (Sec 12)

7  Remove the C-clip that attaches the reverse lever to the reverse lever pivot bolt.

8  Remove the reverse lever pivot bolt. Remove the reverse lever and reverse lever fork as an assembly.

9  Punch or scribe some alignment marks in the front bearing cap and transmission case.

10  Remove the bearing cap and gasket. Discard the gasket.

11  Remove the speedometer gear snap-ring from the rear of the output shaft. Remove the speedometer gear and drive ball.

12  Remove the retaining snap-rings and the locating snap-rings from the front and rear bearings.

13  Remove the front bearing from the clutch shaft using AMC bearing remover J-8157-01, puller bolts J-26636, puller assembly J-25152 or equivalent.

14  Remove the clutch shaft from the transmission case.

15  Using the same bearing removal tool, remove the rear bearing from the output shaft.

16  Remove the output shaft with the geartrain intact. Do not let the first/second or third/fourth synchronizer sleeves separate from the hubs during shaft removal.

17  Push the reverse idler gear shaft out of the back of the transmission case. Remove the shaft and reverse idler gear.

18  Remove the countershaft from the back of the transmission case using AMC countershaft tool J-26624 or a suitable length of pipe of the proper diameter.

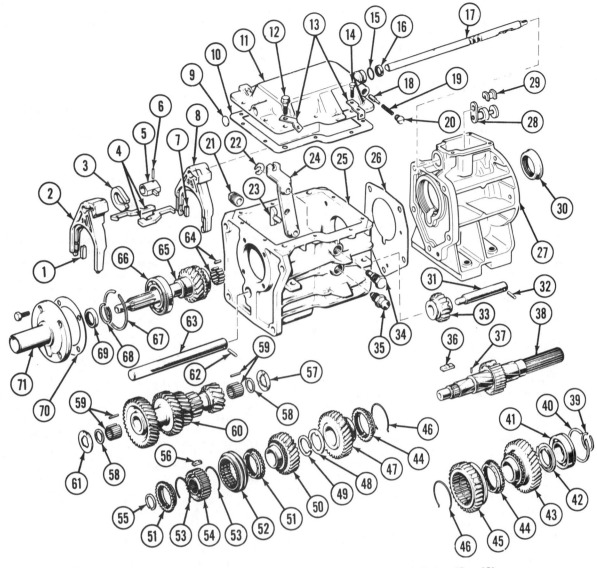

Fig. 7.34  SR4 four-speed transmission components — exploded view (Sec 12)

1  Third/fourth shift insert
2  Third/fourth shift fork
3  Selector interlock plate
4  Selector arm plate
5  Selector arm
6  Selector arm roll pin
7  First/second shift fork insert
8  First/second shift fork
9  Shift rail plug
10  Transmission cover gasket
11  Transmission cover
12  Transmission cover dowel bolt
13  Clip
14  Transmission cover bolt
15  Shift rail O-ring seal
16  Shift rail oil seal
17  Shift rail
18  Detent plunger
19  Detent spring
20  Detent plug
21  Fill plug

22  Reverse lever pivot bolt C-clip
23  Reverse lever fork
24  Reverse lever
25  Transmission case
26  Gasket
27  Adapter housing
28  Offset lever
29  Offset lever insert
30  Extension housing oil seal
31  Reverse idler shaft
32  Reverse idler shaft roll pin
33  Reverse idler gear
34  Reverse lever pivot bolt
35  Backup light switch
36  First/second synchronizer insert (3)
37  First gear roll pin
38  Rear bearing retaining snap-ring
39  Rear bearing retaining snap-ring
40  Rear bearing locating snap-ring

41  Rear bearing
42  First gear thrust washer
43  First gear
44  First/second synchronizer blocking ring (2)
45  First/reverse sleeve and gear
46  First/second synchronizer insert spring (2)
47  Second gear
48  Second gear thrust washer (tabbed)
49  Second gear snap-ring
50  Third gear
51  Third/fourth synchronizer blocking ring (2)
52  Third/fourth synchronizer sleeve
53  Third/fourth synchronizer insert spring
54  Third/fourth synchronizer hub
55  Output shaft snap-ring

56  Third/fourth synchronizer insert
57  Countershaft gear rear thrust washer (metal)
58  Countershaft needle bearing retainer
59  Countershaft needle bearing
60  Countershaft gear
61  Countershaft gear front thrust washer (plastic)
62  Countershaft roll pin
63  Countershaft
64  Clutch shaft roller bearings
65  Clutch shaft
66  Front bearing
67  Front bearing locating snap-ring
68  Front bearing retaining snap-ring
69  Front bearing cap oil seal
70  Front bearing cap gasket
71  Front bearing cap

7A

19   Remove the countershaft gear and loading tool as an assembly. Remove the countershaft gear thrust washers and any clutch shaft pilot bushings that fell into the transmission during disassembly. **Note:** *The front countershaft gear thrust washer is plastic. The rear washer is metal.*

20   Remove the countershaft loading tool from the countershaft gear. Remove the needle bearing retainers and needle bearings.

21   Before dismantling the output shaft geartrain, scribe alignment marks on the third/fourth synchronizer hub and sleeve for assembly reference.

22   Remove the snap-ring from the front of the output shaft. Remove the third/fourth synchronizer assembly.

23   Remove the blocking rings from the third/fourth synchronizer assembly. Remove the insert springs and inserts. Separate the synchronizer sleeve from the hub.

24   Remove third gear from the output shaft.

25   Remove the second gear retaining snap-ring and thrust washer. Remove second gear and the blocking ring.

26   Using a pair of side cutters, remove the first gear roll pin from the output shaft.

27   Remove first gear and the first gear blocking ring.

28   Scribe alignment marks on the first/second synchronizer sleeve and the output shaft for assembly reference.

29   Remove the insert spring and the inserts from the output shaft. **Note:** *The first/second/reverse hub is assembled and machined with the output shaft and is not removable.*

30   Remove the detent plug, spring and plunger. Place the selector arm plates and the shift rail in the Neutral (centered) position.

31   Rotate the shift rail counterclockwise until the selector arm disengages and the selector arm roll pin is accessible.

32   Remove the shift rail until the selector arm contacts the first/second shift fork.

33   Using a 3/16-inch pin punch, remove the roll pin and remove the shift rail.

34   Remove the shift forks, selector arm plates, selector arm and interlock plate.

35   Pry out the shift rail oil seal and O-ring with a screwdriver.

36   Using a hammer and punch, remove the shift rail plug.

37   Remove the nylon inserts and selector arm plates from the shift forks. Note their positions for assembly reference.

*Inspection*

38   Wash the transmission components thoroughly with solvent. Inspect the transmission case for cracks in the bores, sides, bosses and bolt holes and for stripped threads in the bolt holes. Check the geartrain and shift mechanism for broken, chipped or worn gear teeth, bent or broken inserts, weak or broken insert springs, damaged roller or needle bearings and bearing bores in the countershaft and hub, clutch shaft or reverse idler gear shaft. Check the snap-rings for distortion and lack of tension. Inspect the front and rear bearings for galling, damage and roughness. Inspect the shift mechanism for worn, damaged or bent inserts, forks, rails, arms, plates, interlocks and levers.

*Reassembly*

39   Install the nylon inserts and selector arm plates in the shift forks.

40   Apply sealer to the shift rail plug and install it.

41   Coat the shift rail and rail bores with petroleum jelly and insert the shift rail into the cover until the rail is flush with the inside edge of the cover.

42   Install the first/second shift fork (the larger of the two forks) in the cover and push the shift rail through the fork.

43   Position the selector arm and the C-shaped interlock plate in the cover. Insert the shift rail through the arm.

44   Position the third/fourth shift fork with the selector arm plate under the first/second plate.

45   Push the shift rail through the transmission cover bore.

46   Rotate the shift rail until the forward arm plate faces away from, but is parallel to, the cover.

47   Align the roll pin holes and install the roll pin. Be sure the pin is flush with the selector arm surface.

48   Install the detent plunger, spring and plug.

49   Install the shift rail O-ring.

50   Install the shift rail oil seal by first placing an oil seal protector tool such as AMC J-26628-2 over the threaded end of the shift rail.

51   Lubricate the lip of the oil seal and slide it over the protector and onto the shift rail.

52   Seat the oil seal in the transmission cover using an oil seal installer tool such as AMC J-26628-1.

53   Coat the output shaft and gear bores with transmission lubricant.

54   Install the first/second synchronizer sleeve on the output shaft using the reference marks for alignment.

55   Install the three synchronizer inserts and two insert springs in the first/second synchronizer sleeve. The insert spring tangs engage in the same synchronizer insert, but the open ends of the springs face away from each other.

56   Assemble first gear and the blocking ring and install them on the output shaft. Be sure the synchronizer inserts engage the blocking ring notches.

57   Install the first gear roll pin and then install the second gear and blocking ring on the output shaft. Be sure to engage the blocking ring notches.

58   Install the second gear thrust washer and snap-ring. The sharp edge of the washer faces out. Also, be sure to engage the washer tab in the output shaft notch.

59   Using a feeler gauge, measure second gear end play between the gear and thrust washer. End play should be 0.004 to 0.014-inch (0.1016 to 0.3556 mm). If end play exceeds the limit, replace the thrust washer, snap-ring and, if necessary, the synchronizer hub. **Note:** *If any output shaft gear is replaced, the countershaft gear must also be replaced.*

60   Assemble third gear and the blocking ring and install them on the output shaft.

61   Install the third/fourth synchronizer sleeve on the output shaft using the reference marks for alignment.

62   Install three synchronizer inserts and two insert springs in the third/fourth synchronizer sleeve. Install the insert springs as described in Step 55.

63   Install the third/fourth synchronizer assembly with the machined groove in the synchronizer hub facing forward and install the snap-ring.

64   Measure the third/fourth synchronizer end play. End play should be 0.004 to 0.014-inch (0.106 to 0.3556 mm). If end play exceeds the limit, replace the snap-ring and inspect the synchronizer hub for excessive wear on the thrust faces.

65   Coat the countershaft gear washers with petroleum jelly and position them in the transmission case. Install the plastic washer in the front of the case.

66   Insert the countershaft loading tool in the countershaft gear, install the 50 needle bearings in the front and rear of the gear and install the needle bearing retainers. Coat the bearings with petroleum jelly during installation.

67   Install the countershaft gear from the rear of the case. Be careful not to displace the thrust washers.

68   Install the reverse idler gear from the rear of the case. The shift lever groove faces the front of the case.

69   Install the output shaft and gear train. Be careful not to displace the synchronizer assemblies.

70   Install the fourth gear blocking ring in the third/fourth sychronizer sleeve.

71   Coat the pilot roller bearing bore of the clutch shaft with petroleum jelly and install 15 roller bearings. Install the clutch shaft and engage it with the third/fourth synchronizer sleeve and the blocking ring.

72   Using a bearing installation tool such as AMC J-22697, install the front bearing. Position the output shaft first gear against the rear of the case, align the bearing and install it completely onto the clutch shaft and into the case. **Note:** *The front bearing does not have an identifying notch in the race. The rear bearing has a notch.*

73   Install the front bearing retaining and locating snap-rings.

74   Using an oil seal installation tool such as AMC J-26625, install the front bearing cap oil seal.

75   Install the front bearing cap gasket and front bearing cap. Be sure to align the groove in the cap and the cutout in the gasket with the oil hole in the case. Coat the bearing cap bolts with non-hardening gasket sealer and install the bolts. Tighten the bolts to 13 ft-lbs (17.6 Nm).

76   Install the first gear thrust washer on the output shaft, facing the oil groove toward first gear.

77   Install the rear bearing using a bearing installation tool such as AMC J-25234.

78   Install the retaining and locating snap-rings on the rear bearing.

79   Install the speedometer gear drive ball, gear and snap-ring.

80   Apply non-hardening gasket sealer to the threads of the reverse

lever pivot bolt. Install the reverse lever and pivot bolt in the case and install the spring clip. Tighten the pivot bolt to 20 ft-lbs (27.1 Nm). Be sure the reverse lever fork is engaged in the reverse idler gear.

81  Use a punch or screwdriver to remove the adapter housing oil seal, Install the new seal so that the metal face of the seal is flush with or slightly below the edge of the seal bore.

82  Rotate the clutch shaft and observe the blocking rings. If they tend to stick on the gear cones, gently pry them off the cones with a screwdriver.

83  Place the reverse lever in the Neutral position and install the cover gasket and cover on the case. Install the cover bolts and tighten each one alternately until the final torque of 10 ft-lbs (13.5 Nm) is achieved. Be sure the two dowel bolts are in their proper locations.

84  Carefully install the adapter housing and gasket.

85  Fill the transmission with the specified lubricant and tighten the filler plug to 23 ft-lbs (31.1 Nm).

86  Attach the transmission to the transfer case.

---

## 13  T4 four-speed transmission — disassembly, inspection and reassembly

### Disassembly

1  Using a pin punch and hammer, remove the roll pin which attaches the offset lever to the shift rail.

2  Unbolt and remove the adapter housing from the transmission case.

3  Remove the detent ball and spring from the offset lever, followed by the roll pin from the adapter housing or offset lever.

4  Remove the countershaft rear thrust bearing and race.

5  Remove the transmission cover and shift fork assembly.

6  Remove the C-clip which retains the reverse lever to the reverse lever pivot bolt.

7  Remove the reverse lever pivot bolt, reverse lever and reverse lever fork as an assembly.

8  Punch alignment marks on the front bearing cap and the transmission case and remove the front bearing cap.

9  Remove the front bearing race and end play shims. Pry out the oil seal with a screwdriver.

10  Rotate the clutch shaft until the gear flat faces the countershaft and remove the clutch shaft.

11  Remove the thrust bearing and the roller bearings.

12  Remove the output shaft bearing race by tapping the front of the shaft with a soft-faced hammer.

13  Lift out the shaft assembly.

14  Remove the countershaft rear bearing using a brass drift and an arbor press.

15  Move the countershaft to the rear and lift the shaft out of the case. Remove the countershaft front washer from the case.

16  Remove the countershaft rear bearing spacer.

17  Remove the reverse idler shaft roll pin and remove the reverse idler shaft and gear.

18  Remove the countershaft rear bearing using an arbor press.

19  Remove the clutch shaft from the front bearing using a bearing removal tool such as AMC J-29721 and J-22912.

20  Remove the extension housing rear seal using a flat drift and a hammer.

21  Remove the backup light switch from the case.

22  To disassemble the output shaft gear train, first remove the thrust bearing washer from the front of the output shaft.

23  Remove the third/fourth synchronizer blocking ring, sleeve and hub as an assembly after scribing alignment marks on the sleeve and hub.

24  Remove the third/fourth synchronizer springs and inserts. Separate the synchronizer from the sleeve.

25  Remove the third gear from the shaft.

26  Remove the second gear snap-ring and thrust washer and remove second gear.

27  Remove the output shaft bearing using AMC puller J-29721 and AMC adapters 293-39 or a similar bearing puller set.

28  Remove the first gear thrust washer, roll pin (using diagonal pliers), first gear and the blocking ring.

29  Scribe alignment marks on the first/second gear synchronizer sleeve and the output shaft and remove the insert spring and inserts from the first/reverse sliding gear. Remove the gear from the output shaft. **Note:** *The first/second/reverse hub is part of the output shaft and is not*

*removable.*

30  Place the selector arm plates and shift rail in the Neutral (centered) position.

31  Rotate the shift rail counterclockwise until the selector arm disengages from the selector arm plates and the selector arm roll pin is accessible.

32  Pull back on the shift rail until the selector arm contacts the first/second shift fork.

33  Remove the roll pin using a 3/16-inch pin punch and remove the shift rail.

34  Remove the shift forks, selector arm plates, selector arm and interlock plate.

35  Pry out the shift rail oil seal and O-ring using a screwdriver.

36  Remove the shift rail plug using a hammer and punch.

37  Remove the nylon inserts and selector arm plates from the shift forks, noting their positions for assembly reference.

### Inspection

38  Refer to Section 12, Step 38 for transmission inspection procedures.

### Reassembly

39  Install the nylon inserts and selector arm plates in the shift forks.

40  Coat the edges of the shift rail plug with sealer and install the plug.

41  Coat the shift rail and shift rail bores with petroleum jelly and insert the rail in the cover until the end is flush with the inside edge of the cover.

42  Position the first/second shift fork in the cover and push the shift rail through the fork. **Note:** *The first/second shift fork is the larger of the two shift forks.*

43  Position the selector arm and interlock plate and insert the shift rail. The widest part of the plate faces away from the cover and the roll pin faces down and toward the rear of the cover.

44  Position the third/fourth shift fork with the selector arm plate under the first/second shift fork selector arm plate.

45  Insert the shift rail through the third/fourth shift fork and into the shift rail bore in the cover.

46  Rotate the shift rail until the selector arm plate at the forward end faces away from, but parallel to, the cover.

47  Align the roll pin holes and install the roll pin. Be sure it is installed flush with the selector arm surface.

48  Install the O-ring in the shift rail oil seal groove.

49  Install the shift rail oil seal by first placing an oil seal protector tool such as AMC J-26628-2 over the threaded end of the shift rail.

---

## 14  T5 five-speed transmission — disassembly, inspection and reassembly

### Disassembly

1  Remove the transmission filler plug and remove the lubricant using a siphon pump.

2  Remove the offset lever roll pin using a pin punch and hammer.

3  Remove the extension housing-to-transmission case bolts. Remove the housing and offset lever as an assembly.

4  Remove the detent ball, spring and roll pin from the offset lever.

5  Remove the plastic funnel, thrust bearing race and thrust bearing from the end of the countershaft or the inside of the extension housing.

6  Remove the transmission cover mounting bolts and remove the cover. Note the location of the dowel-type alignment bolts for assembly reference.

7  Remove the roll pin from the fifth gear shift fork using a hammer and punch. **Note:** *To prevent damage to the reverse shift rail, place a wood block under the fifth gear shift fork during roll pin removal.*

8  Remove the fifth gear synchronizer snap-ring and shift fork. Remove the fifth gear synchronizer assembly and detach fifth gear from the rear of the countershaft.

9  Remove the insert retainer, insert springs and inserts from the fifth gear synchronizer sleeve. Mark the position of the sleeve and hub for assembly reference.

10  Remove the snap-ring and separate the fifth speed driven gear from the rear of the output shaft using a tool such as AMC puller assembly No. J-25215.

11  Punch alignment marks on the front bearing cap and the transmis-

**7A**

sion case for assembly reference.

12 Remove the bearing cap mounting bolts and detach the bearing cap.

13 Remove the bearing race and end play shims from the cap. Pry out the bearing cap oil seal with a screwdriver.

14 Rotate the clutch shaft until the gear flat faces the countershaft and remove the clutch shaft from the transmission case. Remove the clutch shaft needle bearings, thrust bearing and race.

15 Remove the output shaft rear bearing race and lift the shaft assembly out of the case.

16 Unhook the overcenter link spring from the rear of the case. A homemade spring removal tool made of welding rod or wire would be helpful here.

17 Remove the reverse lever C-clip.

18 Rotate the reverse shift rail until it disengages from the reverse lever and remove the rail from the rear of the case.

19 Remove the reverse lever pivot pin, disengage the reverse lever from the idler gear and remove the reverse lever and fork assembly from the transmission case.

20 Remove the rear countershaft snap-ring and spacer.

21 Using an arbor press and a brass drift inserted through the clutch shaft opening in the front of the case, carefully press the countershaft assembly to the rear to remove the countershaft bearing.

22 Move the countershaft assembly to the rear and lift it out of the transmission case.

23 Remove the countershaft rear bearing spacer.

24 Remove the idler shaft roll pin.

25 Remove the idler shaft and gear from the transmission case.

26 Using an arbor press, remove the countershaft front bearing from the case.

27 Remove the clutch shaft front bearing using a bearing removal tool such as AMC No. J-29721 and J-22912-01.

28 Remove the rear extension housing seal using a flat drift and a hammer.

29 Remove the thrust bearing washer from the output shaft.

30 Remove the third/fourth synchronizer assembly and blocking ring. Mark the sleeve and hub for assembly reference.

31 Remove the third/fourth synchronizer insert springs and inserts and remove the sleeve from the hub.

32 Remove third gear from the output shaft.

33 Remove the second gear snap-ring, tabbed thrust washer and second gear from the shaft.

34 Remove the output shaft bearing using a puller such as AMC No. J-29721 and adapter No. 293-39.

35 Remove the first gear thrust washer, roll pin (using diagonal cutters), first gear and blocking ring.

36 Scribe alignment marks on the first/second gear synchronizer sleeve and the output shaft hub for assembly reference.

37 Remove the insert spring and inserts from the first/reverse sliding gear and remove the gear from the output shaft hub. **Note:** *The first/second/reverse hub is part of the output shaft and is not removable.*

38 Place the selector arm plates and shift rail in the Neutral (centered) position.

39 Rotate the shift rail counterclockwise until the selector arm disengages from the selector arm plates and the selector arm roll pin is accessible.

40 Pull back on the shift rail until the selector arm contacts the first/second shift fork.

41 Remove the roll pin using a 3/16-inch pin punch and remove the shift rail.

42 Remove the shift forks, selector arm plates, selector arm and interlock plate.

43 Pry out the shift rail oil seal and O-ring using a screwdriver.

44 Remove the shift rail plug using a hammer and punch.

45 Remove the nylon inserts and selector arm plates from the shift forks, noting their position for assembly reference.

## Inspection

46 See Section 12, Step 38 for information on inspecting the transmission components.

## Reassembly

47 Install the nylon inserts and selector arm plates in the shift forks.

48 Coat the edges of the shift rail plug with sealer and install the plug.

49 Coat the shift rail and shift rail bores with petroleum jelly and insert the rail into the cover until the end is flush with the inside edge of the cover.

50 Position the first/second shift fork in the cover annd push the shift rail through the fork. **Note:** *The first/second shift fork is the larger of the two shift forks.*

51 Position the selector arm and interlock plate and insert the shift rail. The widest part of the plate faces away from the cover and the roll pin faces down and toward the rear of the cover.

52 Position the third/fourth shift fork with the selector arm plate under the first/second shift fork selector arm plate.

53 Insert the shift rail through the third/fourth shift fork and into the shift rail bore in the cover.

54 Rotate the shift rail until the selector arm plate at the forward end faces away from, but parallel to, the cover.

55 Align the roll pin holes and install the roll pin. Be sure it is installed flush with the selector arm surface.

56 Install the O-ring in the shift rail oil seal groove.

57 Install the shift rail seal by first placing an oil seal protector tool such as AMC No. J-26628-2 over the threaded end of the shift rail.

58 Lubricate the lip of the oil seal and slide it over the protector and onto the shift rail.

59 Seat the oil seal in the transmission cover using an oil seal installer tool such as AMC No. J-26628-1.

60 Coat the output shaft and gear bores with transmission lubricant.

61 Install the first/second synchronizer sleeve on the output shaft using the reference marks for alignment.

62 Install three synchronizer inserts and two insert springs in the first/second synchronizer sleeve. The insert spring tangs engage in the same synchronizer insert but the open ends of the springs face away from each other.

63 Install the blocking ring and second gear on the output shaft.

64 Install the thrust washer and second gear snap-ring. Be sure the washer tab is seated in the output shaft notch.

65 Install the blocking ring and first gear on the output shaft.

66 Install the first gear roll pin.

67 Install the rear bearing on the output shaft using a bearing installer such as AMC tool No. J-2995 and an arbor press.

68 Install the first gear thrust washer.

69 Install third gear, the third and fourth gear synchronizer hub inserts and the sleeve on the output shaft. The hub offset faces forward.

70 Install the thrust bearing washer on the output shaft.

71 Coat the countershaft front bearing outer cage with Loctite 601 (or the equivalent) and install the countershaft front bearing flush with the case using an arbor press.

72 Coat the countershaft thrust washer with petroleum jelly. Install the washer with the tab corresponding to the depression in the case.

73 Stand the case on end and install the countershaft in the front bearing bore.

74 Install the ountershaft rear bearing spacer.

75 Coat the rear bearing with petroleum jelly and install it with a bearing installer such as AMC No. J-29895 and a sleeve tool such as AMC No. J-33032. The installed bearing should extend 0.125-inch beyond the case surface.

76 Position the reverse idler gear and install the idler shaft from the rear of the case. Install the roll pin.

77 Install the output shaft.

78 Install the front clutch shaft bearing on the clutch shaft using a bearing installer such as AMC tool No. J-2995 and an arbor press.

79 Coat 15 roller bearings with petroleum jelly and install them in the clutch shaft.

80 Install the clutch bearing and race in the clutch shaft.

81 Install the rear output shaft bearing race cap.

82 Install the fourth gear blocking ring.

83 Install the clutch shaft, engaging it in the third/fourth synchronizer sleeve and blocking ring.

84 Install the front bearing cap oil seal using an oil seal installation tool such as AMC No. J-26625.

85 Install the front bearing race in the front bearing cap but do not yet install the preload shims.

86 Temporarily install the front bearing cap.

87 Install the reverse lever, pivot bolt and C-clip. Coat the pivot bolt threads with non-hardening gasket sealer. Be sure the reverse lever fork engages the idler gear.

88 Install the fifth speed driven gear and snap-ring.

89 Install fifth gear on the countershaft.

90 Insert the reverse rail from the rear of the case and rotate it until

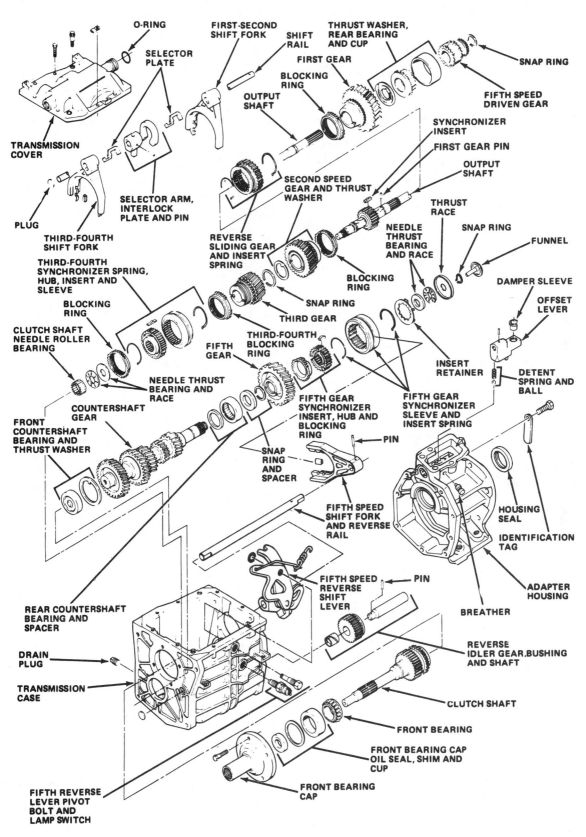

Fig. 7.35  T5 five-speed transmission components — exploded view (Sec 14)

it engages in the fifth speed reverse lever.

91  Install the reverse lever overcenter link spring.

92  Using reference marks for alignment, assemble the fifth gear synchronizer sleeve, insert springs and insert retainer.

93  Install the plastic inserts on each side of the fifth speed shift fork.

94  Place the fifth gear synchronizer assembly on the fifth speed shift fork and slide them onto the countershaft and reverse rail.

95  Place a wood block under the rail and fork assembly and install the roll pin.

96  Install the thrust race against the fifth speed synchronizer hub and install the snap-ring.

97  Coat the thrust race and bearing with petroleum jelly and install the bearing against the thrust race.

98  Install the lipped thrust race over the thrust bearing and install the plastic funnel in the end of the countershaft gear.

99  Temporarily install the extension housing.

100  Turn the transmission case on end and mount a dial indicator on the extension housing with the indicator stylus on the end of the output shaft.

101  Rotate the output shaft and zero the dial indicator.

102  Pull up on the output shaft until the end play is removed. Read the dial indicator and use the dimension to determine the thickness of the bearing preload shim.

103  Select a shim pack measuring 0.001 to 0.005-inch (0.003 to 0.013 mm) thicker than the end play.

104  Set the transmission down on its side and remove the bearing cap and race.

105  Add the necessary shims to the bearing cap and install the clutch shaft bearing race in the cap.

106  Apply some non-hardening gasket sealer to the case mating surface of the front bearing cap. Install the cap using the alignment marks and tighten the attaching bolts to 13 ft-lbs (18 Nm).

107  Recheck the end play. There must be no end play.

108  Remove the extension housing.

109  Move the shift forks and synchronizer rings to the Neutral position.

110  Apply non-hardening gasket sealer to the cover mating surfaces of the transmission case. Lower the cover assembly while aligning the shift forks and synchronizer sleeves. Center the cover to engage the reverse lever and install the two dowel bolts.

111  Install the remaining cover bolts and tighten them to 10 ft-lbs (14 Nm). Apply non-hardening gasket sealer to the extension housing mating surface of the transmission case and install the extension housing to a position where the shift rail just enters the shift cover opening.

112  Install the offset lever and spring with the detent ball in the neutral guide plate detent.

113  Install the extension housing bolts and tighten them to 23 ft-lbs (31 Nm).

114  Install the roll pin and the damper sleeve in the offset lever.

115  Coat the backup light switch with non-hardening gasket sealer and install the switch in the case.

# Chapter 7 Part B Automatic transmission

## Contents

Automatic transmission — diagnosis . . . . . . . . . . . . . . . . . . 16
Automatic transmission fluid change . . . . . . . . . . . Chapter 1
Automatic transmission — removal and installation . . . . . . . 21
Fluid level check . . . . . . . . . . . . . . . . . . . . . . . . Chapter 1
General information . . . . . . . . . . . . . . . . . . . . . . . . . . . 15

Neutral safety switch — check, adjustment
  and replacement . . . . . . . . . . . . . . . . . . . . . . . . . . . . . . . . . 19
Throttle linkage — adjustment . . . . . . . . . . . . . . . . . . . . . 18
Transmission band — adjustment . . . . . . . . . . . . . . . . . . . 20
Transmission shift linkage — adjustment . . . . . . . . . . . . . . 17

---

## Specifications

### Torque specifications

| | Ft-lb | Nm |
|---|---|---|
| Converter inspection cover bolts . . . . . . . . . . . . . . . . . . . . . | 8 | 11 |
| Converter-to-driveplate bolts . . . . . . . . . . . . . . . . . . . . . . . | 33 | 45 |
| Cooler line fitting . . . . . . . . . . . . . . . . . . . . . . . . . . . . . . . | 15 | 20 |
| Front band adjustment screw | | |
|   With adapter tool . . . . . . . . . . . . . . . . . . . . . . . . . . . . | 3 | 4 |
|   Without adapter tool . . . . . . . . . . . . . . . . . . . . . . . . . . | 6 | 8 |
| Front band adjustment screw locknut . . . . . . . . . . . . . . . | 35 | 47 |
| Gearshift rod trunnion locknut . . . . . . . . . . . . . . . . . . . | 9 | 12 |
| Rear band adjustment screw . . . . . . . . . . . . . . . . . . . . . | 4 | 5 |
| Rear band adjustment screw locknut . . . . . . . . . . . . . . . . | 35 | 47 |
| Neutral safety switch . . . . . . . . . . . . . . . . . . . . . . . . . . . | 24 | 33 |
| Oil pan bolts . . . . . . . . . . . . . . . . . . . . . . . . . . . . . . . . . | 12 | 17 |
| Manual lever-to-shaft nut . . . . . . . . . . . . . . . . . . . . . . . . | 8 | 11 |
| Shift lever-to-manual shaft . . . . . . . . . . . . . . . . . . . . . . . | 20 | 27 |
| Linkage swivel clamp nut . . . . . . . . . . . . . . . . . . . . . . . . | 4 | 5 |
| Transmission-to-engine bolts . . . . . . . . . . . . . . . . . . . . . | 35 | 47 |
| Transmission-to-transfer case bolts . . . . . . . . . . . . . . . . . | 20 | 27 |

**7B**

---

### 15  General information

Beginning with the 1976 model year, these vehicles were optionally equipped with a three-speed automatic transmission. Power from the engine passes through a hydraulic torque converter to the transmission. On later models the torque converter incorporates a lock-up device providing a positive connection between the engine and transmission at certain speeds. Fluid from the transmission is circulated through an oil cooler located in the lower tank of the radiator.

Due to the complexity of the automatic transmission and the special tools required, an overhaul should not be undertaken by the home mechanic. Consequently, the procedures in this Chapter are limited to general diagnosis, routine maintenance and adjustment and transmission removal and installation.

If the transmission requires major repair work, it should be done by an AMC dealer or a reputable automotive or transmission repair shop specializing in this type of work. You can, however, remove and install the transmission yourself and save the expense, even if the repair work is done by a transmission specialist. **Caution:** *If it becomes necessary to tow a disabled vehicle, refer to the towing instructions at the front of this manual to avoid severe transmission damage caused by lack of lubrication.*

## 16  Automatic transmission — diagnosis

Automatic transmission malfunctions may be caused by four general conditions: poor engine performance, improper adjustments, hydraulic malfunctions and mechanical malfunctions. Diagnosis of these problems should always begin with a check of the easily repaired items: fluid level and condition, shift linkage adjustment and throttle linkage adjustment. Next, perform a road test to determine if the problem has been corrected or if more diagnosis is necessary. If the problem persists after the preliminary tests and corrections are completed, additional diagnosis should be done by an AMC dealer service department or a reputable automotive or transmission repair shop.

## 17  Transmission shift linkage — adjustment

### 1976 through 1979 models

1   Place the gearshift lever in Neutral, raise the vehicle and support it securely on jackstands.
2   Loosen the gearshift rod trunnion locknut enough to permit movement of the rod in the trunnion.
3   Place the outer range selector lever in the Neutral position and then tighten the trunnion locknut to the specified torque.
4   Lower the vehicle and check the operation of the gearshift lever in all positions. The vehicle should start only with the gearshift in the Park and Neutral positions and the lever should engage properly in all detent positions. Readjust the linkage, if necessary, to obtain the proper operation.

### 1980 through 1983 models

5   Raise the vehicle and support it securely on jackstands.
6   Loosen the shift rod trunnion jam nuts, remove the lockpin and disengage the trunnion and shift rod at the bellcrank.
7   Place the gearshift lever in Park and lock the steering column.
8   Move the manual lever on the transmission all the way to the rear into the Park (last) detent.
9   Check to make sure the park lock is engaged by turning the driveshaft. The driveshaft will not turn when the park lock is properly engaged.
10  Adjust the shift rod trunnion as necessary to obtain a free pin fit in the bellcrank arm and then tighten the trunnion jam nuts. Hold the shift rod so that it doesn't turn as the jam nuts are tightened. When properly adjusted there is no lash in the gearshift linkage. Lash is eliminated by pulling down on the shift rod and pressing up on the outer bellcrank.
11  Check adjustment of the linkage by making sure the engine starts only when the gearshift is in Park or Neutral. If the engine does not start or starts in any gear other than Park or Neutral, the Neutral safety switch (Section 19) is defective or the adjustment is incorrect.
12  Check the steering lock to make sure it operates smoothly and then lower the vehicle.

## 18  Throttle linkage — adjustment

1   The throttle linkage on 1979 through 1983 models can be adjusted to correct harsh, delayed or erratic shifting and lack of kickdown.

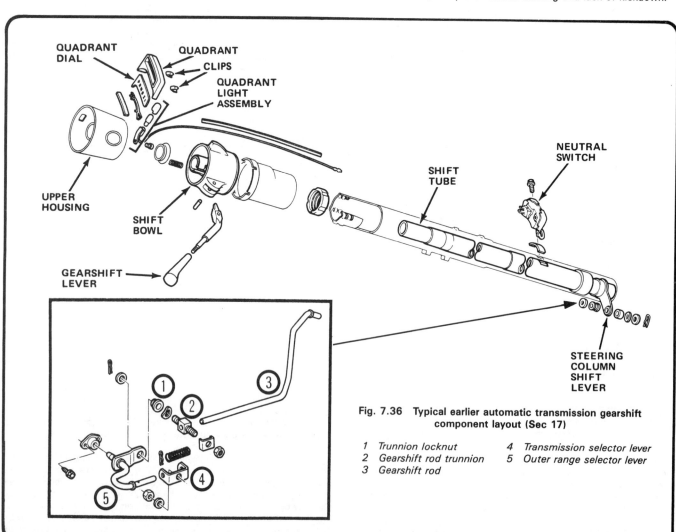

Fig. 7.36   Typical earlier automatic transmission gearshift component layout (Sec 17)

1   Trunnion locknut
2   Gearshift rod trunnion
3   Gearshift rod
4   Transmission selector lever
5   Outer range selector lever

## Four-cylinder engine

2    Remove the air cleaner assembly, then remove the spark plug wire separator from the throttle bracket and secure it out of the way.

3    From under the vehicle, hold the throttle control lever all the way to the rear, against the stop, and secure it with a spring.

4    In the engine compartment, block the throttle open and set the carburetor linkage completely off the fast idle cam. On air conditioning equipped models, turn the ignition switch on to energize the throttle stop solenoid.

5    Release the T-shaped cable adjuster clamp and lift the clamp up with a small screwdriver as shown in the illustration.

6    To remove the cable load on the throttle cable bellcrank, grasp the outer cable sheath and move the cable and sheath forward. Adjust the cable until there is no lash between the plastic cable and bellcrank ball. When this is achieved, lock the cable by pressing the T-shaped cable adjuster clamp until it snaps into place.

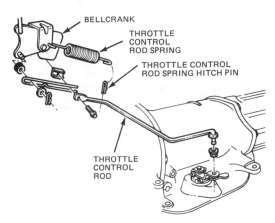

Fig. 7.37  Four-cylinder engine throttle cable adjustment
details (Sec 18)

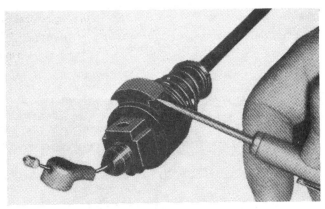

Fig. 7.38  Typical later six-cylinder throttle linkage
component layout (Sec 18)

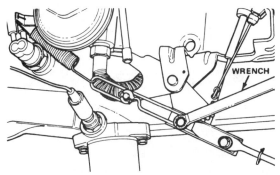

Fig. 7.39  1982 and later model automatic transmission
throttle linkage adjustment (Sec 18)

7    Turn the ignition off, install the spark plug wires and separator, connect the throttle stop solenoid on air conditioned models, install the air cleaner and remove the spring from the throttle control lever. Test drive the vehicle and check for proper shifting operation, readjusting as necessary.

## Six-cylinder engine

8    Remove the throttle control rod spring. On 1982 and later models, use the spring to hold the adjusting link against the nylon washer, in the forward position.

9    Block the choke open and set the throttle off the fast idle cam. On models equipped with a throttle-operated solenoid valve, turn the ignition switch on, to energize the solenoid, and open the throttle halfway to lock it. Return the throttle to the idle position.

10    Raise the vehicle and support it securely with jackstands.

11    Loosen the retaining bolts on the throttle control adjusting link.

12    Use a spare spring to hold the transmission throttle lever all the way forward, against the stop. Hook the spring to the torque converter boss or the linkage bellcrank.

13    On earlier models, pull on the end of the link until the lash is eliminated and then tighten the retaining bolt securely. On 1982 and later models, push on the end of the link to eliminate any lash, pull the clamp to the rear so the bolt bottoms in the rear of the rod slot. Tighten the forward clamp bolt. Pull the throttle control rod to the rear until the rod bolt bottoms in the front rod slot and tighten the rear retaining bolt.

14    Install the throttle control rod, remove the spring from the transmission lever and lower the vehicle.

## V8 engine

15    Remove the throttle control rod spring, raise the vehicle and support it securely on jackstands.

16    Secure the transmission throttle valve control lever forward against its stop, using the throttle control rod spring.

17    Block the choke open and set the throttle off of the fast idle cam. On throttle-operated, solenoid valve-equipped carburetors, turn the ignition switch on to energize the solenoid, then open the throttle halfway to lock it. Return the throttle to the idle position.

18    Loosen the throttle control rod adjustment link retaining bolt, remove the spring clip and move the nylon washer to the rear of the link.

19    Push on the end of the link until all lash has been eliminated, tighten the bolt and reinstall the nylon washer and clip.

20    Remove the spring from the linkage and reinstall it on the throttle control rod.

21    Lower the vehicle.

### 19    Neutral safety switch — check, adjustment and replacement

## 1976 through 1979 models

1    With the parking brake applied, check and adjust the shift linkage if necessary (Section 17).

2    Remove the switch from the base of the steering column.

3    Place the gearshift in the Park position and lock the steering column.

4    Move the actuating lever for the neutral switch until it aligns with the P stamped on the back of the switch.

5    Insert a 3/32-inch drill bit into the hole located below the N stamped on the back of the switch and move the lever until it stops against the drill.

6    Place the switch in position on the steering column, install the retaining screws and remove the drill bit.

7    Check the switch for proper operation. The engine should start with the gearshift in the Neutral and Park positions only and the back-up light should glow in Reverse.

## 1980 through 1983 models

8    The neutral and back-up light switches are combined into one unit. The switch has three terminals with the neutral switch being the center one. A ground for the starter solenoid circuit is provided through the gearshift lever in only the Neutral and Park positions.

9    Remove the wiring connector and test the switch terminal for continuity. Continuity should exist between the center terminal and transmission case only when the gearshift is in Neutral and Park. If the switch appears to be faulty, check the shift linkage (Section 17) before

**7B**

replacing the switch.
10  Prior to replacing the switch, place a container under it to catch the transmission fluid.
11  Remove the switch and allow the fluid to drain into the container.
12  Place the gearshift lever in Park and Neutral and check the lever finger position and lever and shaft alignment with the switch opening.
13  Install the switch and seal, tightening the bolts to the specified torque.
14  Test the switch for continuity and plug in the connector.
15  Check the transmission fluid level (Chapter 1), adding the specified fluid as necessary.

## 20   Transmission band — adjustment

1    The transmission bands should be adjusted at the specified intervals or when the automatic upshifts or downshifts become consistently harsh and/or erratic. *Adjustment is possible only on 1980 and later models.*
2    Raise the vehicle and support it on jackstands.

### Front band

3    The front band adjustment screw is located on the left side of the transmission, just above the throttle control levers.
4    Loosen the adjustment screw locknut and back it off five (5) turns. Check the adjusting screw to make sure it turns freely in the case, lubricating it if necessary.
5    Using a torque wrench and AMC adapter J-24065 and a 5/16-inch socket, tighten the adjustment screw to the specified torque. If the adapter tool is not used, the alternate torque must be used.
6    Back the screw off two (2) full turns.
7    Tighten the adjustment screw locknut to the specified torque while holding the screw so that it does not rotate.

### Rear band

8    The rear band adjustment screw is accessible after removing the oil pan. Consequently, it is convenient to make this adjustment at the time of the transmission fluid and filter change (Chapter 1).
9    Remove the oil pan.
10  Remove the adjustment screw locknut.
11  Tighten the adjusting screw to the specified torque with a torque wrench and 1/4-inch socket.
12  Back the adjustment screw off four (4) full turns.
13  Hold the screw so that it will nut turn, install the locknut and tighten it to the specified torque.
14  Install the oil pan and lower the vehicle.

## 21   Automatic transmission — removal and installation

1    Remove the fan shroud bolts (if equipped) and disconnect the transmission fill tube from the upper bracket.
2    Raise the vehicle and support it on jackstands.
3    Remove the torque converter inspection cover, starter motor and fill tube.
4    Mark the driveshafts and axle yokes to simplify installation. Disconnect the driveshafts at the transfer case yokes and secure them out of the way with wire.
5    On V8 engines, unbolt the exhaust pipes from the manifolds.
6    Disconnect the gearshift and throttle linkage, neutral safety switch wire and speedometer cable.
7    Mark the relationship of the converter and driveplate for reference during reassembly.
8    Remove the converter-to-driveplate bolts, rotating the crankshaft and driveplate to gain access to each of them.
9    Support the transmission/transfer case assembly with a jack. It is a good idea to attach the assembly to the jack with a chain.
10  Remove the rear crossmember, lower the transmission slightly and disconnect the fluid cooler lines.
11  Remove the transmission-to-engine mounting bolts and move the transmission and converter far enough to the rear to clear the crankshaft.
12  Hold the converter in place and lower the transmission with the jack until the converter housing clears the engine.

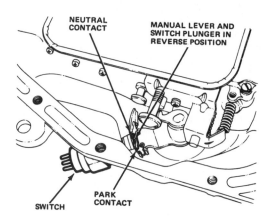

Fig. 7.40   Later model neutral/back-up light switch (oil pan removed for clarity) (Sec 19)

Fig. 7.41   Front transmission band adjustment using a torque wrench and adapter tool (Sec 20)

Fig. 7.42   Rear transmission band adjustment (Sec 20)

13  Remove the transfer case from the transmission.

14  To install, connect the transfer case to the transmission. Make sure the converter is securely engaged in the hub slots.

15  Raise the transmission/transfer case assembly into position and align the driveplate and converter marks made during removal. Move the engine as necessary to align the converter housing pilot holes with the dowels in the engine and install the two lower mounting bolts. Tighten the bolts enough to draw the transmission up to the engine.

16  Install the driveplate-to-converter bolts and tighten them to the specified torque.

17  Install the remaining transmission-to-engine mounting bolts and tighten them to the specified torque.

18  Connect the cooler lines and install the rear support cushion on the transmission.

19  Raise the transmission into position, install the crossmember and remove the jack.

20  Install the speedometer cable and the converter inspection cover.

21  Connect the exhaust pipes to the manifolds and install the starter motor.

22  Connect the gearshift and throttle linkage and the neutral safety switch wires.

23  Connect the driveshafts, using the alignment marks made during removal.

24  Lower the vehicle and adjust the shift linkage (Section 17).

# Chapter 7 Part C   Transfer case

**Contents**

General information . . . . . . . . . . . . . . . . . . . . . . . . . . 22
Model 18 transfer case — disassembly, inspection and
  reassembly . . . . . . . . . . . . . . . . . . . . . . . . . . . . . . 27
Model 20 transfer case — disassembly, inspection and
  reassembly . . . . . . . . . . . . . . . . . . . . . . . . . . . . . . 28
Model 300 transfer case — disassembly, inspection and
  reassembly . . . . . . . . . . . . . . . . . . . . . . . . . . . . . . 29

Oil level check . . . . . . . . . . . . . . . . . . . . . . . . . . . . Chapter 1
Oil seal replacement . . . . . . . . . . . . . . . . . . . . . . . . . 26
Quadra-Trac — disassembly, inspection and reassembly . . . . . 30
Quadra-Trac — stick-slip condition diagnosis and correction . . 24
Shift linkage — lubrication, check and adjustment . . . . . . . . 25
Transfer case (all models) — removal and installation . . . . . . . 23
Transfer case lubricant change . . . . . . . . . . . . . . . . Chapter 1

**Specifications**

## Model 18

| | |
|---|---|
| Mainshaft end play . . . . . . . . . . . . . . . . . . . . . . . . . . | 0.004 to 0.008 in |
| End play adjustment shims . . . . . . . . . . . . . . . . . . . . . | 0.003, 0.010, 0.031 in |

## Model 20

| | |
|---|---|
| Rear bearing cap end play | |
|   1966 through 1978 . . . . . . . . . . . . . . . . . . . . . | 0.001 to 0.003 in |
|   1979 . . . . . . . . . . . . . . . . . . . . . . . . . . . . | 0.002 to 0.005 in |
| Front output shaft end play | |
|   1966 through 1978 . . . . . . . . . . . . . . . . . . . . . | 0.001 to 0.003 in |
|   1979 . . . . . . . . . . . . . . . . . . . . . . . . . . . . | 0.002 to 0.005 in |

## Model 300

| | |
|---|---|
| Input gear-to-snap-ring clearance . . . . . . . . . . . . . . . . . | 0.003 in |
| Rear output shaft end play . . . . . . . . . . . . . . . . . . . . . | 0.001 to 0.005 in |
| Front output shaft end play . . . . . . . . . . . . . . . . . . . . . | 0.001 to 0.005 in |

## Torque specifications

| *Model 18* | Ft-lbs | Nm |
|---|---|---|
| Transfer case-to-transmission bolts . . . . . . . . . . . . . . . | 28 to 32 | 38 to 43 |

| *Model 20* | | |
|---|---|---|
| Transfer case-to-transmission bolts . . . . . . . . . . . . . . . | 28 to 32 | 38 to 43 |
| Front and rear output shaft yoke nuts | | |
|   1966 through 1978 . . . . . . . . . . . . . . . . . . . . | 225 to 250 | 306 to 340 |
|   1979 . . . . . . . . . . . . . . . . . . . . . . . . . . . | 90 to 150 | 122 to 203 |
| Front output shaft rear bearing cover-to-case bolts . . . . . . . | 28 to 32 | 38 to 43 |
| Intermediate shaft lockplate bolt . . . . . . . . . . . . . . . . . | 12 to 15 | 17 to 20 |
| Lower cover-to-case bolts . . . . . . . . . . . . . . . . . . . . . | 12 to 15 | 17 to 20 |
| Rear bearing cap assembly-to-case bolts . . . . . . . . . . . . . | 28 to 32 | 38 to 43 |
| Shift fork set screws . . . . . . . . . . . . . . . . . . . . . . . . | 12 to 15 | $7 to 20 |
| Shift rod housing-to-case bolts . . . . . . . . . . . . . . . . . . | 28 to 30 | 28 to 41 |

| *Model 300* | | |
|---|---|---|
| Bottom cover bolts . . . . . . . . . . . . . . . . . . . . . . . . . | 10 to 20 | 14 to 27 |
| Cover plate bolts . . . . . . . . . . . . . . . . . . . . . . . . . . | 25 to 40 | 34 to 54 |
| Front and rear output yoke nuts . . . . . . . . . . . . . . . . . . | 120 to 150 | 163 to 203 |
| Input shaft support bolts . . . . . . . . . . . . . . . . . . . . . . | 7 to 10 | 9 to 14 |
| Lockplate bolt . . . . . . . . . . . . . . . . . . . . . . . . . . . . | 20 to 25 | 27 to 34 |
| Front and rear bearing cap bolts . . . . . . . . . . . . . . . . . . | 35 | 47 |
| Shift fork set screws . . . . . . . . . . . . . . . . . . . . . . . . | 12 to 18 | 16 to 24 |

## Quadra-Trac

| Transfer case | | |
|---|---|---|
| Breather | 6 to 10 | 8 to 14 |
| Differential end cap bolts | 24 to 30 | 33 to 41 |
| Drain and fill plugs | 15 to 25 | 20 to 34 |
| Output shaft nut | 90 to 150 | 122 to 203 |
| Power takeoff cover-to-transfer case bolt | | |
|   3/8 in bolts | 15 to 25 | 20 to 30 |
|   5/16 in bolts | 10 to 20 | 14 to 27 |
| Speedometer adapter | 20 to 30 | 27 to 41 |
| Front cover-to-rear cover bolts | 15 to 25 | 20 to 34 |
| Transfer case-to-transmission bolts | 30 to 50 | 41 to 68 |
| **Reduction unit** | | |
| Fill plug | 15 to 25 | 20 to 34 |
| Power takeoff cover-to-case bolts | 15 to 25 | 20 to 34 |
| Reduction unit-to-transfer case bolts | | |
|   3/8 in bolt | 15 to 25 | 20 to 34 |
|   5/16 in bolt | 8 to 10 | 11 to 14 |
| Shift lever-to-shaft nut | 15 to 25 | 20 to 34 |

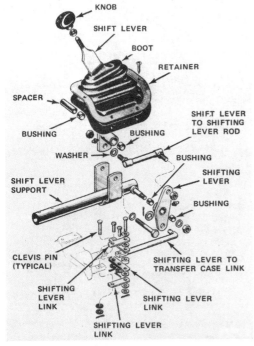

**Fig. 7.43 Model 20 transfer case shift mechanism components (Sec 23 and 25)**

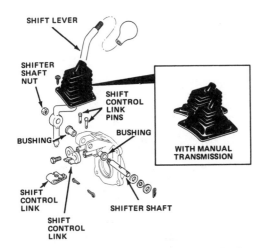

**Fig. 7.44 Model 300 transfer case shift mechanism components (Sec 23 and 25)**

## 22 General information

The transfer case is basically a transmission which passes the power from the engine and transmission to the front and rear driveshafts and axles. Over the long production life of these vehicles, four models of transfer cases were used: Spicer Models 18, 20 and 300 and the Warner Quadra-Trac. The Spicer transfer cases provide drive in two-wheel or four-wheel drive while the Quadra-Trac provides full time four-wheel drive by means of an integral limited slip differential. An optional low range reduction unit provides the Quadra-Trac transfer case with maximum braking and torque at low speeds.

## 23 Transfer case (all models) — removal and installation

1   Raise the vehicle and support it on jackstands.
2   Drain the transfer case lubricant into a suitable container.
3   Disconnect any components which are attached to the transfer case (such as the speedometer cable, parking brake cable, exhaust pipe brackets, vacuum hoses and, on some models, the shift levers).
4   Mark the relative positions of the driveshaft flanges and transfer case yokes to simplify reinstallation. Disconnect the driveshafts from the transfer case and fasten them out of the way with wire.
5   On later models, support the clutch housing and remove the rear crossmember.
6   Support the transfer case with a jack and remove the transfer case-to-transmission bolts.
7   Separate the transfer case from the transmission. On earlier model 18 and 20 transfer cases, brace the end of the transmission shaft so that it cannot move. Pull the transfer case to the rear to loosen the gear and then withdraw the case from the transmission. Make sure the transmission mainshaft bearing stays in the transmission.
8   To install the case, raise it into position and align the input gear splines with the transmission output shaft. Rotate the transfer case output shaft yoke to line up the splines, if necessary.
9   Make sure the holes are aligned, install the transfer case-to-transmission attaching bolts and tighten them to the specified torque.
10  Install the driveshafts, using the alignment marks made during removal.
11  Install any components which were disconnected from the transfer case during removal.
12  Fill the transfer case with the specified lubricant.
13  Lower the vehicle.

## 24 Quadra-Trac stick-slip condition diagnosis and correction

1   The stick-slip condition occurs when the clutch is released suddenly when driving at low speeds. The symptoms are a constant, pulsating, grunting or rasping noise issuing from the transfer case. The stick-slip condition is usually evident when turning the vehicle.
2   The stick-slip condition is caused by improper lubricant in the

**7C**

transfer case or mismatched tire types or sizes. The condition will also occur if the vehicle has not been driven for a week or more, but in this instance it is normal.

3    To correct the condition, drain the transfer case and fill it with the specified lubricant (Chapter 1) and make sure all four tires are of the same type and size and equally inflated.

## 25  Shift linkage — lubrication, check and adjustment

1    Check the shift linkage periodically for looseness and binding. Inspect the mechanism for worn, bent and damaged components. Clean, lubricate and adjust (if possible) the linkage and shift mechanism. Use penetrating oil when lubricating linkage components.

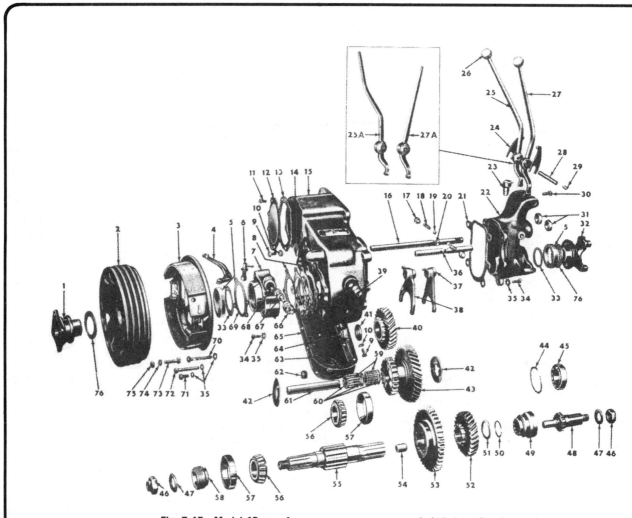

Fig. 7.45   Model 18 transfer case components — exploded view (Sec 27)

| | | | |
|---|---|---|---|
| 1 Companion flange | 21 Gasket | 37 Shift fork | 57 Bearing cup |
| 2 Brake drum | 22 Front cap | 38 Shift fork | 58 Speedometer gear |
| 3 Emergency brake | 23 Breather | 39 Filler pipe plug | 59 Needle bearings |
| 4 Operating lever | 24 Shift lever spring | 40 Mainshaft gear | 60 Bearing spacers |
| 5 Oil seal | 25 Shift lever | 41 Plain washer | 61 Intermediate shaft |
| 6 Lever stud | 25A Shift lever (used with | 42 Thrust washer | 62 Drain plug |
| 7 Rear cap | 4-speed transmission) | 43 Intermediate gear | 63 Gasket |
| 8 Shims | 26 Shift lever knob | 44 Snap-ring | 64 Nut |
| 9 Screw | 27 Shift lever | 45 Bearing | 65 Bottom cover |
| 10 Lock washer | 27A Shift lever (used with | 46 Nut | 66 Sleeve |
| 11 Bolt | 4-speed transmission) | 47 Washer | 67 Speedometer gear |
| 12 Rear cover | 28 Pivot pin | 48 Output clutch shaft | 68 Bushing |
| 13 Gasket | 29 Lubrication fitting | 49 Output clutch gear | 69 Gasket |
| 14 Lockplate | 30 Set screw | 50 Snap-ring | 70 Bolt |
| 15 Transfer case | 31 Oil seal | 51 Thrust washer | 71 Bolt |
| 16 Shift rod | 32 Front yoke | 52 Output shaft gear | 72 Bolt |
| 17 Poppet plug | 33 Gasket | 53 Sliding gear | 73 Bolt |
| 18 Poppet spring | 34 Bolt | 54 Bushing | 74 Lock washer |
| 19 Poppet ball | 35 Lock washer | 55 Output shaft | 75 Nut |
| 20 Interlock | 36 Shift rod | 56 Cone and rollers | 76 Output shaft seal |

## Model 18

2   The linkage on early models can be adjusted after loosening the locknut. Turn the adjuster in or out until there is 1/2-inch clearance between the floorpan and the shift lever bend with the lever in the four-wheel-drive Low position.

## Model 20

3   The linkage cannot be adjusted but capscrews retaining the shift lever support tube to the transfer case should be checked to make sure they are tightened securely.

## Model 300

4   The linkage is not adjustable but the shifter shaft nut should be checked to make sure it is tightened securely.

## Quadra-Trac

5   The shift mechanism for the Quadra-Trac transfer case is internal and not adjustable. The Emergency Drive control located in the glovebox directs engine vacuum to the control diaphragm on the transfer case. The vacuum hoses must be inspected periodically. Check for secure connections, cracks and leaks.

### 26   Oil seal replacement

1   The seals for the front and rear output shafts, as well as the shift rods, can be replaced with the transfer case in place in the vehicle.
2   Raise the vehicle and support it securely on jackstands.

## Output shaft oil seals

3   Mark the relationship of the driveshaft flange and output shaft yoke to ensure reinstallation in the original position.
4   Disconnect the driveshaft and fasten it out of the way with wire. On some models it will be necessary to support the transmission with a jack or jackstand and then remove the chassis crossmember to provide access.
5   Remove the output shaft nut and washer, using a holding tool such as AMC No. C-3281 or its equivalent.
6   Remove the driveshaft yoke using a puller such as AMC No. W-172 or its equivalent.
7   Remove the felt seal, oil seal and gasket using a puller such as AMC No. W-172 or its equivalent.
8   Install the new seal with AMC driver W-143 or its equivalent, followed by the gasket and felt seal.
9   Install the driveshaft yoke, washers and nut. Tighten the nut to the specified torque.
10   Install the driveshaft, tightening the nuts to the specified torque. Install the crossmember (if removed).

## Shift rod oil seals

11   If the left side shift rod oil seal on 1977 and later model 20 and 300 transfer cases must be replaced, place the shift lever in the 4L position.
12   Disconnect the shift lever linkage at the rods.
13   Use a puller such as AMC tool J-25175 or equivalent to remove the oil seal.
14   Install the replacement seal with AMC driver J-25167 or equivalent.
15   Connect the shift lever linkage.
16   Lower the vehicle.

### 27   Model 18 transfer case — disassembly, inspection and reassembly

## Disassembly

1   Remove the transfer case drive gear.
2   Remove the output shaft nuts, followed by the rear output shaft flange and brake drum (if equipped) and the front output shaft yoke.
3   Remove the bottom cover and the lockplate screw, lock washer and lockplate.
4   Drive out the intermediate shaft toward the rear of the case with a hammer and brass drift, taking care not to lose the thrust washers.
5   Through the bottom of the case, remove the intermediate gear, thrust washers, needle bearings and spacers.
6   Remove the poppet plugs, springs and balls on both sides of the

front bearing cap. Shift the front wheel shift lever to the forward or engaged position.
7   Unbolt and remove the front bearing cap complete with the clutch shaft, bearing, clutch gear, fork and shift rod. Take care not to lose the interlock between the shift rods.
8   On models so equipped, remove the parking brake backing plate and speedometer gear assembly.
9   With a soft-faced hammer, tap on the front end of the output shaft to drive the rear bearing cup from the case.
10   Use a wedge tool to pry the front bearing cone and roller assembly from its seat on the shaft.
11   Place a bearing cup removing ring on the output shaft between the front bearing and the gear. Use a soft-faced hammer to tap on the rear end of the output shaft and remove the bearing cup from the case.
12   Release the snap-ring, slide it forward on the shaft and drive the shaft through the case. The snap-ring, gears and thrust washer will remain in the case as the shaft is removed and can be removed from the bottom. Tap lightly on the end of the shaft (resting on a wooden block) to remove the rear bearing cone and roller assembly.
13   Remove the sliding gear shift fork set screw and the shift rod.
14   Remove the output shaft oil seal and shift rod seals as described in Section 26.
15   Remove the shifting fork and shifting rod set screw and remove the clutch gear and shifting fork as an assembly.
16   Remove the output clutch shaft by pressing it carefully through the bearing, followed by the bearing retainer snap-ring and the bearing.
17   Remove the output shaft oil seal as described in Section 26.
18   Remove the brake drum and companion flange retaining bolts and separate the drum from the flange.
19   Remove the oil seal as described in Section 26.
20   Remove the speedometer driven gear.
21   Remove the cap and brake backing plate from the transmission case, taking care not to lose the bearing adjusting shims.
22   Remove the speedometer gear.

## Inspection

23   Wash the transfer case and components thoroughly with solvent and dry them with compressed air if possible.
24   Inspect all the bearings, thrust washers, shafts, gears and the case for excessive wear, pitting, scoring, cracks and damage. Replace any worn or damaged components with new ones.

## Reassembly

25   Reassembly is basically the reverse of disassembly with attention paid to the procedures in the following steps.
26   Use a thimble and driver-type tool when installing the snap-ring on the output shaft.
27   To prevent damage to the assemblies, use a piece of tubing when installing the cone and roller assemblies on the output shaft.
28   Early model transfer cases used 1-1/8 inch caged needle bearings on the intermediate shaft. When installing the intermediate gear in these cases, insert the gear and support the front thrust washers with a pilot pin tool. Position the gears and the rear thrust washer and insert the shaft from the rear of the case.
29   On later model cases, a 1-1/4 inch diameter intermediate shaft was used and the bearings were of the individual roller and spacer type. A dummy shaft which is slightly smaller in diameter and shorter in width than the intermediate shaft is necessary for installation. Load the bearing rollers and spacers in the gear using the dummy shaft. Support the front thrust washer with your fingers, position the gears and rear thrust washer and insert the shaft from the rear of the case, driving out the dummy shaft.
30   If the speedometer driven gear bushing is replaced, use a bushing installing tool.
31   Check the end movement of the mainshaft when the rear bearing cap is installed. This determines the adjustment of the tapered roller bearings. The shaft end play must be within the specified range for the bearing to be properly adjusted. Selective shims are used for adjustment and the rear cap oil seal must not be installed until this is done. Install the oil seal as described in Section 26.
32   When the end yokes are installed on the output shafts, make sure the felt seals are installed in the oil seal guards.
33   When installing the shift rail oil seals in the front bearing cap, protect them with a thimble tool when passing over the notches (Section 26).

**7C**

## 28  Model 20 transfer case — disassembly, inspection and reassembly

### Disassembly

1   Remove the shift lever assembly, bottom cover and rear bearing cap.
2   Remove the intermediate shaft lockplate and drive the shaft out the rear of the case with a soft-faced hammer and an arbor tool such as AMC No. J-25142.

3   Remove the front output shaft nut, washer, shaft yoke and oil seal (Section 26).
4   Remove the cover plate, taking care not to damage the gaskets and shims.
5   Remove the front output shaft rear bearing, move the rear output shaft shift rod to the rear and remove the set screw, poppet ball and spring plugs.
6   Insert a punch through the pin hole in the rear output shaft shift

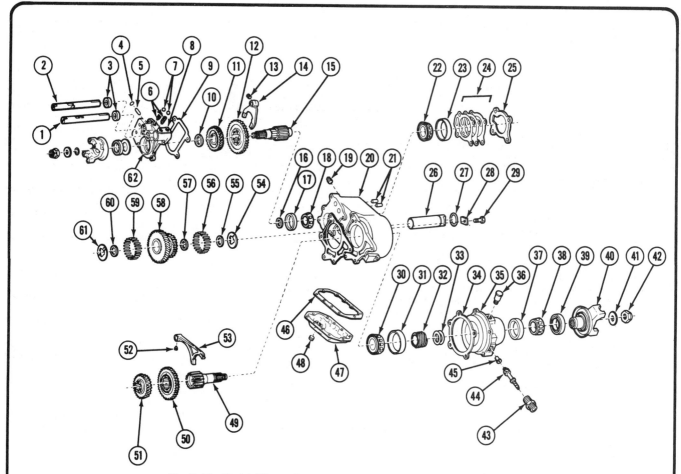

Fig. 7.46  Model 20 transfer case components — exploded view (Sec 28)

1  Shift rod – rear output shaft shift fork
2  Shift rod – front output shaft shift fork
3  Shift rod oil seal
4  Interlock plug
5  Interlock
6  Poppet ball spring
7  Poppet ball
8  Front bearing cap
9  Front bearing cap gasket
10  Front output shaft thrust washer
11  Front output shaft gear
12  Front output shaft sliding gear
13  Set screw
14  Front output shaft shift fork
15  Front output shaft
16  Front output shaft spacer

17  Front output shaft front bearing cup
18  Front output shaft front bearing
19  Filler plug
20  Transfer case
21  Thimble cover
22  Front output shaft rear bearing
23  Front output shaft rear bearing cup
24  Front output shaft rear bearing cup shims
25  Cover plate
26  Intermediate shaft
27  Intermediate shaft O-ring
28  Lockplate
29  Lockplate bolt
30  Rear output shaft front bearing
31  Rear output shaft front bearing cup

32  Speedometer drive gear
33  Rear output shaft bearing shim
34  Rear bearing cap gasket
35  Rear bearing cap
36  Breather
37  Rear output shaft rear bearing cup
38  Rear output shaft rear bearing
39  Rear bearing cap oil seal
40  Rear yoke
41  Rear yoke washer
42  Rear yoke nut
43  Speedometer sleeve
44  Speedometer driven gear
45  Speedometer bushing
46  Bottom cover gasket
47  Bottom cover
48  Drain plug
49  Rear output shaft

50  Rear output shaft sliding gear
51  Mainshaft gear
52  Set screw
53  Rear output shaft shift fork
54  Intermediate gear thrust washer
55  Intermediate gear bearing spacer
56  Intermediate gear shaft needle bearings
57  Intermediate gear bearing spacer
58  Intermediate gear
59  Intermediate gear shaft needle bearings
60  Intermediate gear bearing spacer
61  Intermediate gear thrust washer
62  Front bearing cap

rod, rotate the rod 1/4-inch *counterclockwise* and pull the rod from the case. Do not lose the poppet ball and spring.

7  Remove the front bearing cap retaining bolts and slide the cap off of the case and shift rod.

8  Remove the rear output shaft sliding gear and the shift rod.

9  Place the transfer case on wood blocks and drive the front output shaft out the rear of the case with a hammer and brass drift.

10  Remove the gears, spacer and bearing from the transfer case.

11  Remove the front output shaft shift fork set screw and pull the shift rod out of the fork.

12  Remove the shift rod thimbles with a socket.

13  Remove the arbor tool, thrust washers, spacers and roller bearing from the intermediate gear.

14  Use a brass drift and hammer to remove the front output shaft bearing cup.

15  Remove the shift rod seals (Section 26).

16  Remove the front output shaft rear bearing, using the sliding gear as a support. Mount the gear securely in a vise, using wood blocks to protect the surface. The shaft lever groove must be facing down. Insert the shaft through the gear splines and drive the shaft out of the bearing with a brass drift and hammer.

17  Remove the speedometer driven gear sleeve and gear from the cap.

18  Mount the bearing cap securely in a vise, using wood blocks, and remove the output shaft nut, yoke and oil seal (Section 26).

19  Remove the cap from the vise and, using the rear face of the cap as a support, drive the output shaft from the cap with a hammer and brass drift.

20  Lift the tapered bearing and drive bearing cup out of the bearing cap rear bore.

21  Drive the front bearing cup from the front bore and remove the speedometer drive gear and shims from the shaft. Keep the shims together to ease reassembly.

22  Remove the front bearing from the shaft and, if necessary, remove the speedometer driven gear from the bearing cap.

## Inspection

23  Wash the transfer case and components thoroughly with solvent and dry them with compressed air. Remove all gasket material from the mating surfaces.

24  Inspect the bearings, thrust washers, shafts, gears and the transfer case and bearing caps for cracks, excessive wear, pitting or scoring. Replace any unserviceable components with new ones.

## Reassembly

25  Install the front output shaft front bearing cup in the case with the cup flush with the exterior surface.

26  Install the shift rail thimbles.

27  Install the front bearing cap.

28  Support the front output shaft rear bearing on a 1/2-inch socket and install the shaft in the bearing with a brass drift and hammer.

29  Install the front output shaft shift rail poppet ball and spring, compress them and install the shaft rod part way into the case.

30  Install the front output shaft shift fork and position it so the set screw offset faces the front of the case.

31  Insert the front output shaft shift rod through the shift fork, align the set screw holes in the fork and rod and install the set screw, tightening it to the specified torque.

32  Install the front output shaft front bearing, spacer, sliding gear and output shaft gear with the shift fork groove in the sliding gear facing to the rear.

33  Insert the front output shaft through the gears, spacer and bearing.

34  Support the case on wood blocks and drive the front output shaft into the housing with a brass drift and hammer, making sure the bearing seats against the shoulder of the shaft.

35  Use a wood block and hammer to install the front output shaft rear bearing cup.

36  Install the speedometer driven gear bushing (if removed) in the rear bearing cap.

37  Install the front bearing cup in the rear bearing cap bore, followed by the front bearing on the shaft and install the rear bearing cup in the bore.

38  Install the speedometer drive gear and shims on the shaft.

39  Place the output shaft in the bearing cap and position the end of the shaft on a flat, firm surface. Place the rear cone and roller on the shaft. Drive the bearing onto the shaft and seat it against the shims.

40  Install the yoke seal, yoke, washer and nut (Section 26) and tighten the nut to the specified torque.

41  Clamp a dial indicator to the rear bearing cap and check the bearing cap end play by prying the rear output shaft back-and-forth. Compare this measurement to the Specifications.

42  The end play can be adjusted by installing shims adjacent to the speedometer drive gear.

43  Place the speedometer driven gear in the bearing cap and install the sleeve.

44  Attach the rear bearing assembly and shims to the transfer case, tightening the bolts to the specified torque.

45  Check the front output shaft end play by seating the rear bearing cup against the cover plate by striking the end of the front output shaft with a lead hammer. Mount a dial indicator on the front bearing cap and place the indicator stylus against the end of the output shaft. Pry the shaft to the rear and zero the indicator. Pry the shaft forward, observe the reading and compare it to the Specifications.

46  The end play is adjusted by adding or removing shims between the cover plate and the case. Repeat the end play measurement and adjustment procedure until the measurement is within the Specifications.

47  Install the rear output shaft shift rail poppet ball and spring in the shift rod housing, compress the ball and spring and install the shift shaft rail part way into the case. The front output shaft shift rail must be in Neutral with the interlock seated in the housing bore before installation.

48  Install the rear output shaft shift fork and sliding gear with the fork groove in the gear facing to the rear.

49  Align the set screw holes in the fork and rail and install the set screw, tightening it to the specified torque.

50  Assemble the intermediate gear rollers and spacers, using a suitable arbor tool.

51  Install the intermediate gear thrust washers in the case. The front washer can be held in place with petroleum jelly and the rear can be held in position by starting the shaft into the case.

52  Install the O-ring on the intermediate shaft and insert the intermediate gear into the case.

53  Insert the intermediate shaft into the case bore and tap the shaft into the gear, forcing the arbor tool out of the front.

54  Insert the intermediate shaft lockplate, transfer case identification tag, lock washer and lockplate bolt, tightening the bolt to the specified torque.

55  Install the rear bearing cap and gasket and slide the rear output shaft through the gear. Tighten the bearing cap bolts to the specified torque.

56  Install the front driveshaft seal and yoke (Section 26).

57  Install the bottom cover and gasket, tightening the bolts to the specified torque.

58  Install the shift rod seals (Section 26).

---

## 29  Model 300 transfer case — disassembly, inspection and reassembly

---

## Disassembly

1  Remove the shift lever assembly and the bottom cover bolts. Remove the bottom cover by inserting a putty knife between the cover and the case and working around the circumference to break the seal.

2  Remove the front and rear driveshaft yokes (Section 26) and discard the locknuts.

3  Remove the input shaft support attaching bolts and remove the support, rear output shaft gear and input shaft assembly. It may be necessary to use a putty knife to break the seal around the support.

4  Remove the rear output shaft clutch sleeve from the transfer case.

5  Remove and discard the snap-ring which retains the rear output shaft gear to the input shaft and remove the gear.

6  Remove and discard the input shaft bearing retaining snap-ring and remove the shaft and bearing from the support. Tap on the end of the shaft with a soft-faced hammer to aid in removal.

7  Use an arbor press to remove the input shaft bearing and end play shims from the shaft.

8  Remove and discard the input shaft seal, followed by the intermediate shaft lockplate and bolt.

9  Use a brass drift and hammer to tap the intermediate shaft out of the case. Discard the O-ring.

10  Remove the intermediate gear assembly thrust washers, needle

**7C**

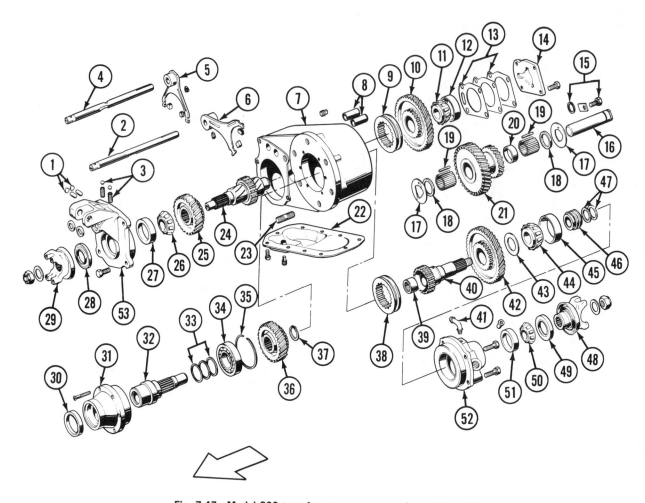

Fig. 7.47  Model 300 transfer case component layout (Sec 29)

1  Interlocks and plugs
2  Rear output shaft fork
    shift rod
3  Poppet balls and springs
4  Front output shaft fork
    shift rod
5  Front output shaft shift fork
6  Rear output shaft shift fork
7  Transfer case
8  Thimble covers
9  Front output shaft clutch
    sleeve
10 Front output shaft clutch
    gear
11 Front output shaft rear
    bearing
12 Front output shaft bearing
    race
13 Front output shaft end play
    shims
14 Cover plate
15 Lockplate, bolt and washer

16 Intermediate gear shaft
17 Thrust washer
18 Bearing spacer
19 Intermediate gear shaft
    needle bearings
20 Bearing spacer (thick)
21 Intermediate gear
22 Bottom cover
23 Transfer case-to-transmission
    stud
24 Front output shaft
25 Front output shaft gear
26 Front output shaft front
    bearing
27 Front output shaft front
    bearing race
28 Oil seal
29 Front yoke
30 Seal
31 Input shaft support

32 Input shaft
33 Shims
34 Input shaft bearing
35 Input shaft bearing snap-ring
36 Rear output shaft gear
37 Snap-ring
38 Rear output shaft clutch sleeve
39 Input shaft rear (pilot) bearing
40 Rear output shaft
41 Vent
42 Rear output shaft clutch gear
43 Thrust washer
44 Rear output shaft front bearing
45 Rear output shaft bearing race
46 Speedometer drive gear
47 End play shims
48 Rear yoke
49 Rear output shaft oil seal
50 Rear output shaft rear bearing
51 Bearing race
52 Rear bearing cap
53 Front bearing cap

bearings and bearing spacers.

11  Remove the rear bearing cap bolts and use a soft-faced hammer to tap on the cap to loosen it so it can be removed.

12  Remove the speedometer drive gear and end play shims from the rear output shaft.

13  Discard the rear output shaft oil seal and remove the bearings and races from the cap.

14  Remove the front and rear output shaft shift fork set screws.

15  Remove the shift rods by inserting a punch through the clevis pin holes in the rods and rotating them while pulling them from the case.

16  Remove the shift forks.

17  Remove the front cap retaining bolts and use a putty knife inserted between the cap and case to break the seal. Remove the cap.

18  Remove the front output shaft and shift rod seals (Section 26) and discard them.

19  Remove the front bearing race from the cap, using a suitable tool.

20  Remove the cover plate assembly, making sure to keep the end play shims together to simplify reassembly.

21  Move the front output shaft toward the front of the case and remove the rear bearing race from the case.

22  Remove the rear output shaft front bearing and support the case on wood blocks. Brace the clutch gear on a firm surface such as a workbench and tap the shaft out of the bearing with a soft-faced hammer. If the shaft does not come out easily it will be necessary to use an arbor press.

23  Remove the rear output shaft front bearing, thrust washer, clutch gear and output shaft from the case.

24  Remove the front output shaft using an arbor press.

25  Remove the front output shaft, clutch gear and sleeve and shaft rear bearing.

26  Remove the front output shaft front bearing using an arbor press and remove the front output shaft gear from the shaft.

27  Remove the input shaft rear needle bearing from the rear output shaft, using a tool such as AMC No. J-29369-1. Remove the shift rod thimbles with a socket.

## Inspection

28  Wash the transfer case and components thoroughly with solvent. Remove all traces of sealant material from the case and bearing cap mating surfaces. If compressed air is available, dry all components except the bearings, which must be dried with clean, lint-free cloths.

29  Inspect the components and case for excessive wear and damage. Inspect the gears for cracks, chips and broken or excessively worn teeth. Check the bearings for wear, pitting, scoring, flat spots and brinneling. Inspect the shafts for damaged splines, threads and bearing surfaces. Check the shift rods and bores for wear and damage. Replace any damaged or worn components with new ones.

## Reassembly

30  Install the shift rod thimbles, using thread locking compound.

31  Install the front output shaft gear on the output shaft, making sure the gear clutch teeth face the shaft gear teeth.

32  Press the front bearing onto the front output shaft with an arbor press, making sure the bearing seats against the gear.

33  Install the front output shaft in the case, followed by the clutch sleeve and gear on the shaft.

34  Install the front output shaft rear bearing using an arbor press.

35  Install the input shaft rear needle bearing in the rear output shaft using AMC tool J-29179 or its equivalent.

36  Place the rear output shaft clutch gear in the case and insert the shaft into the gear.

37  Press the thrust washer and front bearing onto the rear output shaft using an arbor press and tool.

38  Press the shims and bearing onto the input shaft with an arbor press and tool.

39  Install a new input shaft oil seal in the input shaft using AMC tool J-29184 or its equivalent.

40  Install the input shaft and bearing in the support, using a new snap-ring.

41  Install the rear output shaft gear on the input gear with a new snap-ring.

42  Use a feeler gauge to measure the clearance between the input gear and the retaining snap-ring. Check this measurement against the specifications. If the clearance is beyond the specified range, disassemble the input shaft and add shims between the input shaft and the shaft bearing.

43  Install the clutch sleeve onto the rear output shaft.

44  Apply sealant to the mating surface of the input shaft support and install the assembled support, shaft and gear in the case. Use two of the bolts to align the support on the case and tap it securely into position with a soft-faced hammer. Install the bolts and tighten them to the specified torque.

45  Install the rear bearing cap race with AMC tool J-9276-3 or its equivalent.

46  Install the rear bearing cap rear bearing race with AMC tool J-29182 or its equivalent.

47  Position the rear output shaft rear bearing in the bearing cap and install the driveshaft yoke seal (Section 26).

48  Install the speedometer gear and end play shims on the rear output shaft.

49  Apply sealant to the rear bearing cap mating surfaces and align it on the case with two mounting bolts. Tap the cap into position and install the bolts, tightening them to the specified torque.

50  Install the rear output shaft yoke and tighten the locknut to the specified torque (Section 26).

51  Clamp a dial indicator to the bearing cap. Pry the shaft back-and-forth to check the end play. If the end play is not within the specified range remove or add shims between the speedometer drive gear and output shaft rear bearing.

52  Install the front output shaft end play shims, the cover plate and the bolts, tightening the bolts to the specified torque. Apply thread locking compound to the threads before installing the bolts.

53  Install the front output shaft front bearing race using AMC tools J-8092 and J29181.

54  Install the front output shaft yoke oil seal and shift rod oil seals (Section 26).

55  Apply sealant to the mating surface of the front bearing cap, align it using two of the mounting bolts and tap the cap into position with a soft-faced hammer. Install the bolts and tighten them to the specified torque.

56  Tap on the end of the front output shaft with a soft-faced hammer to seat the rear bearing cup against the cover plate. Mount a dial indicator on the front bearing cap and place the stylus against the output shaft. Pry back-and-forth on the shaft to determine the end play. If the end play is not as specified, add or remove shims between the cover plate and the case.

57  Install the front shaft yoke (Section 26) and tighten the new locknut to the specified torque.

58  Insert the front and rear output shaft shift forks into the case.

59  Install the front output shaft shift rod poppet ball and spring in the front bearing cap, compress the ball and spring and install the front output shaft shift rod part way into the case.

60  Insert the front output shaft shift rod through the shift fork, align the set screw hole, install the set screw and tighten it to the specified torque.

61  Install the rear output shaft shift rod poppet ball and spring in the front bearing cap, compress the ball and spring and install the rear output shaft shift rail part way into the case. Make sure the front output shaft shift rod is in Neutral and the interlocks are seated in the cap bore.

62  Insert the rear output shaft shift rod through the shift fork, align the set screw hole, install the set screw and tighten it to the specified torque.

63  Install the needle bearing and spacers in the intermediate gear, using AMC tool J-25142 or its equivalent.

64  Install the intermediate gear thrust washers in the case with the tangs aligned in the grooves. Petroleum jelly can be used to hold the washers in place.

65  Install the new O-ring on the intermediate shaft and place the shaft in position in the case. Install the shaft in the case bore by tapping it into place until the arbor tool is forced out.

66  Install the shaft lockplate and bolt, tightening the bolt to the specified torque.

67  Install the bottom cover after applying sealant to the mating surface. Install the cover bolts and tighten them to the specified torque.

**7C**

## 30  Quadra-Trac — disassembly, inspection and reassembly

## Disassembly

**Reduction unit**

1  Remove the power takeoff cover and position an 11/16-inch deep

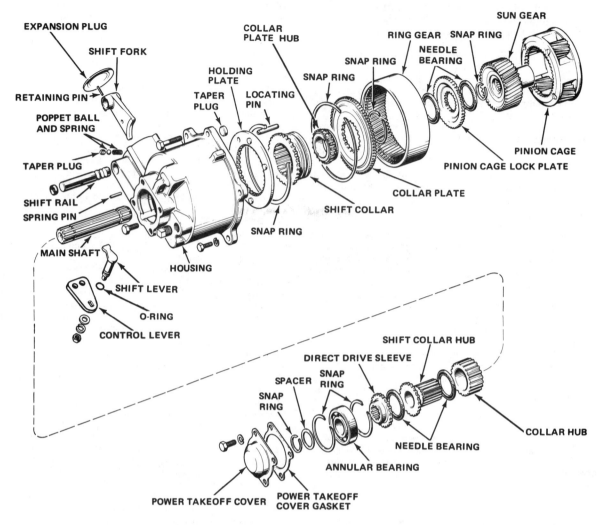

**Fig. 7.48  Quadra-Trac reduction unit components — exploded view (Sec 30)**

socket securely in a vise, allowing two inches of the socket to protrude. Mount the reduction unit on the socket with the socket entering the bore of the sun gear.

2    Move the reduction unit control lever to the rear, into the High Range position, remove the mainshaft retaining snap-ring and lift the reduction unit housing off the gear train.

3    Remove the direct drive sleeve and needle bearing, shift collar hub and needle bearing, reduction collar hub, ring gear and needle bearing as an assembly.

4    Remove the pinion cage lockplate and the needle bearings.

5    Remove the sun gear and mainshaft from the pinion cage but do not disassemble them.

6    Move the control level to the center or Neutral position and disengage the shift collar from the shift fork.

7    Move the control lever to the rear, to the High position and align the outer teeth on the shift collar with the inner teeth on the holding plate.

8    Move the shift fork and collar forward to the Low Range position. Remove the shift collar.

9    Remove the annular bearing and snap-ring.

10   Remove the shift fork locating pin by grasping it with pliers and using a pulling and rotating motion.

11   Remove the large expansion plug and shift rail taper plugs. Remove the control lever and then use a 3/16-inch punch to drive out the shift fork retaining pin.

12   Slide the shift rail forward and out of the fork and then remove the fork and shift rail poppet ball.

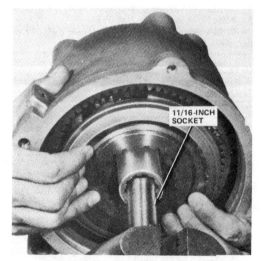

**Fig. 7.49  Mounting the Quadra-Trac reduction unit on an 11/16-inch socket set in a vise (Sec 30)**

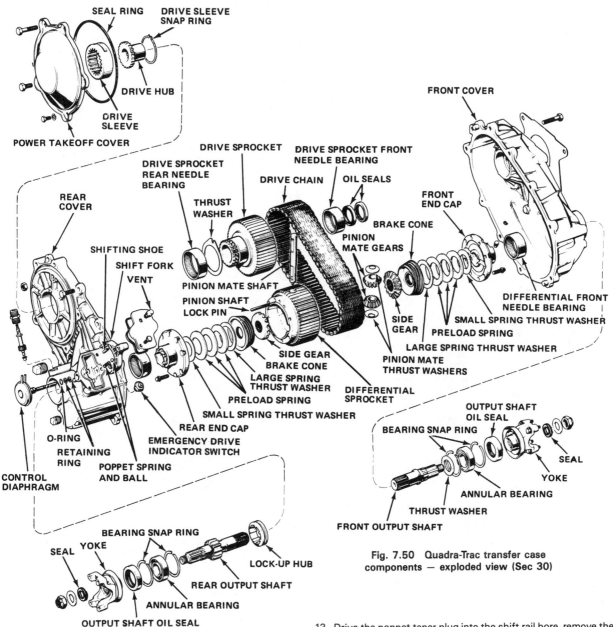

Fig. 7.50  Quadra-Trac transfer case
components — exploded view (Sec 30)

Fig. 7.51  Using a wood block to
position the Quadra-Trac transfer case
rear cover and drive chain for
disassembly (Sec 30)

13  Drive the poppet taper plug into the shift rail bore, remove the plug and the poppet spring and then remove the shift lever assembly and retaining pin.

14  Remove the reduction holding plate and snap-ring.

**Transfer case**

15  Remove the front and rear output shaft yoke retaining nuts, washers and seals (Section 26).

16  On models not equipped with a reduction unit, remove the power takeoff cover and seal ring.

17  Remove the retaining bolts and separate the front and rear transfer case covers.

18  Place the rear cover assembly on a workbench with the drive sprocket supported by a block of wood measuring 2 inches by 4 inches by 6 inches.

19  On non-reduction unit models, remove the drive hub and sleeve by expanding the snap-ring which is accessible through the slot in the outside edge of the sleeve.

20  On reduction unit-equipped models, remove the pinion cage from the drive sprocket rear splines.

21  Remove the case cover from the drive sprocket and differential assembly.

22  Remove the chain after sliding the drive sprocket toward the differential unit.

7C

23  The differential should be serviced as an assembly by your dealer or a qualified repair shop with the specialized tools necessary to work on these units.

## Inspection

24  Wash all components thoroughly with solvent. Except for the bearings, dry the components with compressed air, if available. Air dry the bearings or use lint-free cloths.
25  Inspect the reduction unit housing and transfer case covers for cracks and other damage. Remove all gasket material from the mating surfaces.
26  Inspect the shafts, gears, sprockets and end caps for cracks, excessive wear, pitting, galling and scoring. Check the drive chain for looseness and damage. Replace any unserviceable components with new ones.

## Reassembly

### Reduction unit

27  Install the holding plate in the case with the locating pins facing the interior and indexed in the case and the shift fork locating pin holes aligned.

Fig. 7.52  Installing the Quadra-Trac reduction unit holding plate (Sec 30)

28  Install the snap-ring with the tabs facing forward. Make sure the snap-ring seats securely in the groove and that it clears the shift fork.
29  Insert the shift fork locating pin, making sure it goes completely through the holding plate and seats in the housing.
30  Insert the shift lever, without the O-ring, into the housing with the lever end of the fork facing to the rear.
31  Install the O-ring in the shift lever shaft groove.
32  Move the shift lever in far enough to allow installation of the shaft tapered pin, install the pin and then insert the shift rail into the shift fork and rail bore, grooved end first.
33  Rotate the shift rail so the flat on the side is adjacent to the poppet spring and slide the rail in far enough to allow the fork to mesh with the lever and rail.
34  Push the rail through the shift fork until the end of the rail is flush with the edge of the poppet bore.
35  Place the poppet ball on the end of the spring and compress the ball and spring using the shift fork retaining pin as a tool.
36  Slide the shift rail over the poppet ball as far as the retaining pin will allow, remove the pin and move the shift rail to the first detent position.
37  Rotate the shift rail until the flat on the side faces the shift lever and the retaining pin bores in the rail and fork are aligned.
38  Slide the shift fork onto the shift rail, align the pin holes and install the retaining pin until it is flush with the fork surface.
39  Install the shift rail taper plugs, the poppet bore taper plug and the shift rail cover expansion plug.
40  Install the shift fork locating pin and then install the control lever on the shift lever.
41  To install the shift collar, position the shift fork in the Neutral (center) position and place the shift collar outer teeth in mesh with the holding plate inner teeth. The shift fork collar groove must be positioned just forward of the shift fork. Move the shift fork to the rear detent position and then move the shift collar to the rear and away from the fork

until the groove in the collar aligns with the fork. Engage the shift fork in the collar groove by moving the collar toward the fork.
42  Install the needle bearing and collar hub on the shift collar hub.
43  Install the ring collar, plate hub and retaining snap-rings.
44  Install the ring gear assembly on top of the collar hub with the ring gear open end facing up.
45  Install the needle bearing, pinion cage lockplate and another needle bearing onto that part of the shift collar hub which extends through the ring.
46  Slide the assembled parts toward the edge of the workbench far enough to expose the bore in the shift collar hub.
47  Support the assembly with one hand while inserting the mainshaft into the shift collar hub bore with the other, making sure the mainshaft and sun gear are completely seated.
48  Install the mainshaft and sun gear through the open end of the ring gear and hold the parts firmly together. Raise the assembly and mount it on the socket in the vise used for disassembly.
49  Install the needle bearing and direct drive sleeve on the mainshaft.
50  Align the splines on the assembled parts and install the housing, making sure that it is seated against the direct drive sleeve.
51  Install the rear spacer and snap-ring, making sure the snap-ring seats completely in the groove. The snap-ring is a select fit and the thickest snap-ring which will provide a 0.004 to 0.009-inch spacer clearance should be used.
52  Install the power takeoff cover and gasket, tightening the bolts to the specified torque.
53  Remove the reduction unit from the socket and install the pinion cage.

### Transfer case

54  Lubricate the bearing and thrust washer surfaces with clean transfer case lubricant.
55  Position the differential and drive sprocket in the proper relationship on the workbench using a wood block.

Fig. 7.53  Positioning the differential and drive sprocket for chain installation (Quadra-Trac transfer case) (Sec 30)

56  With the differential approximately two inches away from the drive sprocket, install the drive chain. Make sure the chain is properly engaged in the differential and drive sprocket teeth and remove any slack.
57  Insert the rear output shaft into the differential and move the lockup hub to the rear in the case cover.
58  Lubricate the drive sprocket thrust washer with transfer case lubricant and install it on the rear cover.
59  Install the rear cover on the drive sprocket and differential. If necessary, rotate the output shaft to align it with the lockup hub. Be careful not to displace the drive sprocket thrust washer during installation.
60  Assemble the drive hub, sleeve and snap-ring.
61  On non-reduction unit-equipped models, install the drive sleeve and hub on the drive sprocket, making sure the snap-ring seats securely.
62  On reduction unit-equipped models, make sure the oil baffle is in position and install the pinion case and snap-ring.
63  Apply a 1/16-inch bead of RTV-type sealant to the mating surfaces of the front and rear covers and install the front output shaft and thrust washer in the cover.
64  Align and install the front cover on the rear cover, install the attaching bolts and tighten them alternately and evenly to the specified torque.
65  Rotate the drive sleeve to make sure the drive sprocket turns freely, indicating the thrust washer was not displaced during assembly.
66  Install the power takeoff cover and seal ring.
67  Install the speedometer gear on the rear output shaft.
68  Install the front and rear output shaft seals and yokes (Section 26).

# Chapter 8   Driveline

**Contents**

Chassis lubrication . . . . . . . . . . . . . . . . . . . . . . . . . .   Chapter 1
Clutch pedal free play check . . . . . . . . . . . . . . . .   Chapter 1
Clutch pedal free play adjustment . . . . . . . . . . . . . . . . . .   3
Clutch — removal, inspection and installation . . . . . . . . . . .   2
Differential lubricant change . . . . . . . . . . . . . . . . . .   Chapter 1
Differential oil level check . . . . . . . . . . . . . . . . . . . .   Chapter 1
Driveshafts and universal joints — check . . . . . . . . . . . . . .   4
Driveshaft — removal and installation . . . . . . . . . . . . . . .   5
Front axle assembly — removal and installation . . . . . . . . . .   9
Front axleshaft oil seal — replacement . . . . . . . . . . . . . . .   8

Front axleshaft — removal and installation . . . . . . . . . . . . .   7
Full-floating axle bearings — lubrication
    and adjustment . . . . . . . . . . . . . . . . . . . . . . . . .   Chapter 11
General information . . . . . . . . . . . . . . . . . . . . . . . . . . .   1
Pinion oil seal — replacement . . . . . . . . . . . . . . . . . . . . .   13
Rear axle assembly — removal and installation . . . . . . . . . .   14
Rear axle seals — replacement . . . . . . . . . . . . . . . . . . . .   11
Rear axleshaft — removal and installation . . . . . . . . . . . . .   10
Rear hub — removal and installation . . . . . . . . . . . . . . . .   12
Universal joints — disassembly, overhaul and reassembly . . . .   6

---

**Specifications**

---

## Clutch

Driven plate lining wear limit . . . . . . . . . . . . . . . . . . . . . . .   1/16 in

## Torque specifications

### Front axle

|  | Ft-lb | Nm |
|---|---|---|
| Pinion nut |  |  |
|   Initial . . . . . . . . . . . . . . . . . . . . . . . . . . . . . . . . . . . | 210 | 271 |
|   In-service recheck . . . . . . . . . . . . . . . . . . . . . . . . . . | 200 to 220 | 285 to 298 |
| U-bolt . . . . . . . . . . . . . . . . . . . . . . . . . . . . . . . . . . . . . . . | 45 to 65 | 61 to 81 |
| Shackle nut . . . . . . . . . . . . . . . . . . . . . . . . . . . . . . . . . . . | 25 to 40 | 34 to 54 |
| Universal joint U-bolt nut . . . . . . . . . . . . . . . . . . . . . . . . . | 15 to 20 | 20 to 27 |
| Universal joint flange bolt . . . . . . . . . . . . . . . . . . . . . . . . | 25 to 45 | 34 to 61 |
| Drum brake backing plate . . . . . . . . . . . . . . . . . . . . . . . . | 25 to 35 | 34 to 47 |
| Disc brake caliper support key retaining screw . . . . . . . . . . | 15 to 18 | 20 to 24 |
| Shock absorber nut . . . . . . . . . . . . . . . . . . . . . . . . . . . . . | 35 to 50 | 47 to 68 |
| Wheel nut . . . . . . . . . . . . . . . . . . . . . . . . . . . . . . . . . . . . | 65 to 90 | 88 to 122 |

### Rear axle

|  | Ft-lb | Nm |
|---|---|---|
| Pinion bolt (all except tapered axleshaft) |  |  |
|   Initial . . . . . . . . . . . . . . . . . . . . . . . . . . . . . . . . . . . | 210 | 271 |
|   In-service recheck . . . . . . . . . . . . . . . . . . . . . . . . . . | 200 to 220 | 258 to 298 |
| U-bolt . . . . . . . . . . . . . . . . . . . . . . . . . . . . . . . . . . . . . . . | 45 to 65 | 61 to 81 |
| Shackle nut . . . . . . . . . . . . . . . . . . . . . . . . . . . . . . . . . . . | 25 to 40 | 34 to 54 |
| Universal joint U-bolt nut . . . . . . . . . . . . . . . . . . . . . . . . . | 15 to 20 | 20 to 27 |
| Universal joint flange bolts . . . . . . . . . . . . . . . . . . . . . . . . | 25 to 45 | 34 to 47 |
| Brake backing plate . . . . . . . . . . . . . . . . . . . . . . . . . . . . . | 25 to 40 | 34 to 54 |
| Axleshaft nut |  |  |
|   AMC/Jeep . . . . . . . . . . . . . . . . . . . . . . . . . . . . . . . . . | 250 | 339 |
|   Dana/Spicer . . . . . . . . . . . . . . . . . . . . . . . . . . . . . . . | 150 | 203 |
| Shock absorber nut . . . . . . . . . . . . . . . . . . . . . . . . . . . . . | 35 to 50 | 47 to 68 |
| Wheel nut . . . . . . . . . . . . . . . . . . . . . . . . . . . . . . . . . . . . | 65 to 90 | 88 to 122 |

## Clutch

Clutch housing-to-engine bolts

| | | |
|---|---|---|
| F- and L-head four-cylinder . . . . . . . . . . . . . . . . . . . . . . . . | 40 | 54 |
| V6 . . . . . . . . . . . . . . . . . . . . . . . . . . . . . . . . . . . . . | 45 to 60 | 61 to 81 |
| In-line six-cylinder | | |
|    Top . . . . . . . . . . . . . . . . . . . . . . . . . . . . . . . . . . | 35 | 47 |
|    Bottom . . . . . . . . . . . . . . . . . . . . . . . . . . . . . . . . | 45 | 61 |
| V8 . . . . . . . . . . . . . . . . . . . . . . . . . . . . . . . . . . . . . | 30 | 41 |
| 151 cu in four-cylinder . . . . . . . . . . . . . . . . . . . . . . . . | 46 to 62 | 62 to 84 |

Clutch cover-to-flywheel bolts

| | | |
|---|---|---|
| F- and L-head four-cylinder . . . . . . . . . . . . . . . . . . . . . . . . | 30 to 40 | 41 to 54 |
| V6 . . . . . . . . . . . . . . . . . . . . . . . . . . . . . . . . . . . . . | 30 to 40 | 41 to 54 |
| In-line six-cylinder . . . . . . . . . . . . . . . . . . . . . . . . . . . | 35 to 45 | 47 to 61 |
| V8 . . . . . . . . . . . . . . . . . . . . . . . . . . . . . . . . . . . . . | 35 to 45 | 47 to 61 |
| 151 cu in four-cylinder . . . . . . . . . . . . . . . . . . . . . . . . | 20 to 26 | 27 to 35 |

## 1  General information

Power from the engine is passed through the clutch, into the transmission and transfer case and then to the axles through the driveshafts.

The clutch disc is held in place against the flywheel by the pressure plate springs. During disengagement for gear shifting, the clutch pedal is depressed and operates the linkage to pull on the throwout lever so the throwout bearing pushes on the pressure plate springs, disengaging the clutch.

The driveshafts are one-piece construction with a universal joint at each end to allow for vertical movement of the axles. Each driveshaft is also equipped with a splined slip joint at one end to compensate for variations in length during operation.

## 2  Clutch — removal, inspection and installation

1   Raise the vehicle and support it securely on jackstands.
2   Remove the transmission and transfer case (Chapter 7).
3   Remove the starter motor, throwout bearing and clutch housing.
4   Mark the relationship of the clutch cover and flywheel for reference during reinstallation.
5   Loosen the clutch cover bolts one turn at a time, following a crisscross pattern, so the spring tension will be released gradually.
6   Remove the clutch cover and bolts, taking care that the driven plate does not fall. Note the direction which the driven plate faces, to simplify reassembly.
7   Inspect the flywheel and pressure plate contact surfaces for score

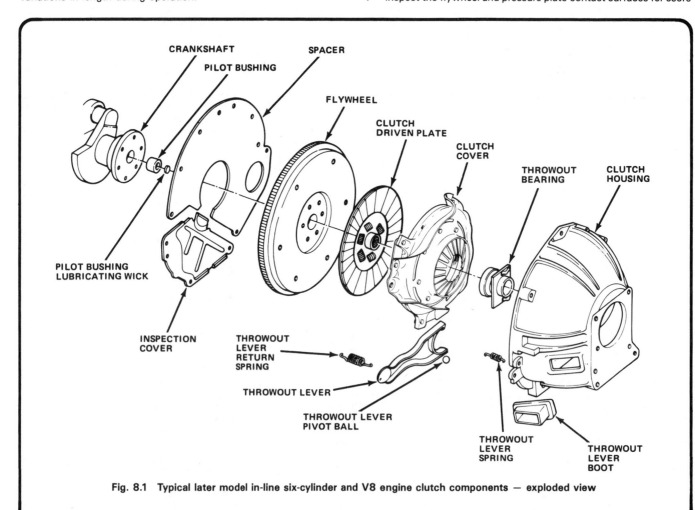

Fig. 8.1  Typical later model in-line six-cylinder and V8 engine clutch components — exploded view

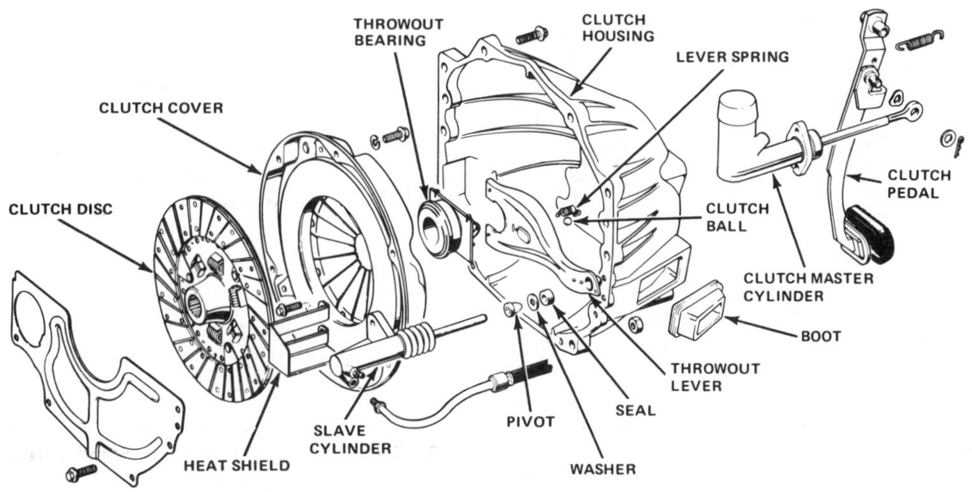

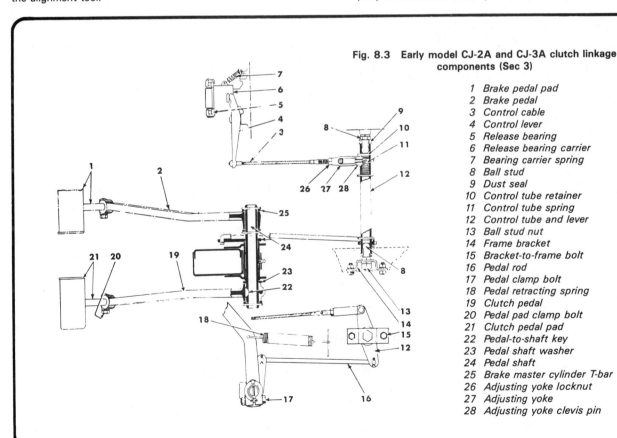

Fig. 8.2   151 cu in four-cylinder engine clutch assembly components — exploded view

marks, cracks and damage. If necessary, have these surfaces machined smooth or replace the components with new ones. Check the clutch plate lining thickness and compare it to the Specifications.

8   If equipped, remove the pilot bushing lubricating wick and soak it in engine oil.

9   Lightly lubricate the throwout lever pivot points with moly-based grease.

10  On models so equipped, install the pilot bushing lubricating wick.

11  Insert a clutch alignment tool or equivalent (such as the proper size screwdriver handle) through the clutch driven plate hub and use it to center the plate on the flywheel.

12  With the driven plate centered, place the clutch cover in position and install the mounting bolts finger tight. Tighten the bolts a little at a time, following a crisscross pattern, to the specified torque and remove the alignment tool.

13  Install the clutch housing and tighten the bolts to the specified torque.

14  Install the starter motor.

15  Attach the throwout bearing to the lever. Unless the vehicle has very low mileage, it is a good practice to install a new throwout bearing whenever the clutch is replaced.

16  Install the transmission and transfer case and lower the vehicle.

### 3  Clutch pedal free play adjustment

1   The clutch pedal free play should be checked (Chapter 1) and adjusted at the specified interval, when the clutch doesn't engage properly or when new clutch parts have been installed.

Fig. 8.3   Early model CJ-2A and CJ-3A clutch linkage
components (Sec 3)

1   Brake pedal pad
2   Brake pedal
3   Control cable
4   Control lever
5   Release bearing
6   Release bearing carrier
7   Bearing carrier spring
8   Ball stud
9   Dust seal
10  Control tube retainer
11  Control tube spring
12  Control tube and lever
13  Ball stud nut
14  Frame bracket
15  Bracket-to-frame bolt
16  Pedal rod
17  Pedal clamp bolt
18  Pedal retracting spring
19  Clutch pedal
20  Pedal pad clamp bolt
21  Clutch pedal pad
22  Pedal-to-shaft key
23  Pedal shaft washer
24  Pedal shaft
25  Brake master cylinder T-bar
26  Adjusting yoke locknut
27  Adjusting yoke
28  Adjusting yoke clevis pin

8

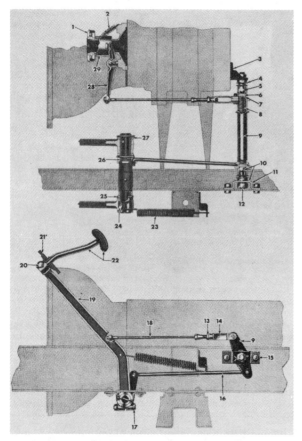

Fig. 8.4  Early model CJ-3B, CJ-5 and CJ-6 cross-shaft
tube and lever type clutch linkage (Sec 3)

| | |
|---|---|
| 1  Clutch release bearing | 16  Pedal release rod |
| 2  Carrier spring | 17  Pedal clamp bolt |
| 3  Ball stud | 18  Control cable |
| 4  Dust seal | 19  Clutch pedal |
| 5  Pad | 20  Screw and lock washer |
| 6  Retainer | 21  Draft pad |
| 7  Clevis yoke pin | 22  Pedal pad and shank |
| 8  Control tube spring | 23  Retracting spring |
| 9  Control lever and tube | 24  Pedal-to-shaft key |
| 10  Ball stud and bracket | 25  Washer |
| 11  Frame bracket | 26  Pedal shaft |
| 12  Ball stud nut | 27  Master cylinder tie bar |
| 13  Yoke locknut | 28  Control lever |
| 14  Adjusting yoke | 29  Bearing carrier |
| 15  Bolt | |

## 1953 through 1971 models

2   Three types of clutch linkages were used on these models. Early
model CJ-2A and CJ-3A vehicles used a combination cross tube and
cable mechanism, while early model CJ-3B, CJ-5 and CJ-6 vehicles
have a cross-shaft tube and lever-type linkage. V6 models were equipped with a cable-type clutch linkage.
3   To adjust the CJ-2A and CJ-3A linkage, loosen the clutch control
lever cable adjusting locknut and use a wrench to unscrew the cable
until the specified free play is achieved (Chapter 1). Tighten the locknut.
4   To adjust the cross-shaft tube and lever-type clutch linkage, loosen
the jam nut on the cable clevis and lengthen or shorten the clutch fork
cable to obtain the specified measurement. After adjustment, tighten
the jam nut securely.
5   On the cable-type clutch linkage, loosen the cable locknut and adjust the ball adjusting nut with the pedal in the up (clutch engaged) position until the slack is gone from the cable. Back the ball
adjusting nut off 2-1/2 turns to obtain the specified free play. Tighten
the locknut after completing the adjustment.

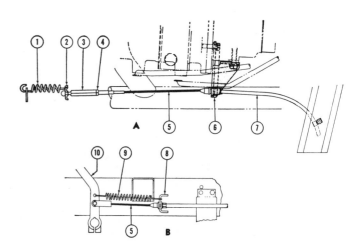

Fig. 8.5  Cable-type linkage layout and adjustment details (Sec 3)

| | |
|---|---|
| A  Top view, cable-to-clutch fork | B  Side view, cable-to-clutch pedal |
| 1  Clutch fork retracting spring | 6  Clutch cable support bracket |
| 2  Clutch fork | 7  Clutch cable housing |
| 3  Ball adjusting nut | 8  Anchor bracket-to-frame side rail |
| 4  Locknut | 9  Clutch pedal retracting spring |
| 5  Clutch cable | 10  Clutch pedal assembly |

## 1972 through 1975 models

6   Adjust the bellcrank outer support bracket to provide about
1/8-inch of bellcrank end play and lift the clutch pedal up against the
stop.
7   Adjust the lower ball pivot assembly on the clutch pedal-to-bell-
crank pushrod as necessary to position the bellcrank inner level parallel to the front face of the clutch housing. Adjust the clutch fork
release rod to obtain the specified free play.

## 1976 and later models

8   Loosen the release rod adjuster jam nut and have an assistant
hold the clutch pedal up against the stop. Turn the release rod adjuster in or out to obtain the specified free play. After adjustment, be sure
to tighten the adjuster jam nut securely.

## 4   Driveshafts and universal joints — check

1   The driveshafts should be checked periodically, usually at the time
of chassis lubrication, when the vehicle is raised.
2   Inspect the length of each driveshaft for damage, dents, under
coating material and mud and loose mounting nuts or bolts. Clean off
any foreign material, as it could cause vibration.
3   Check the splines of the slip yoke to make sure the driveshafts move
in and out smoothly, with no binding or looseness. A worn or damaged slip yoke will cause vibration when driving in the 40 to 60 mph range.
4   Wear in the needle roller bearings is characterized by vibration or
a clunking sound when accelerating. To check the needle roller bearings, try to turn the driveshaft with one hand while holding the flange
or coupling with the other. Any movement between the driveshaft and
the couplings is an indication of excessive wear.

## 5   Driveshaft — removal and installation

1   Raise the vehicle and support it securely on jackstands.
2   Mark the relationship between the driveshaft and the companion
flanges (photo).

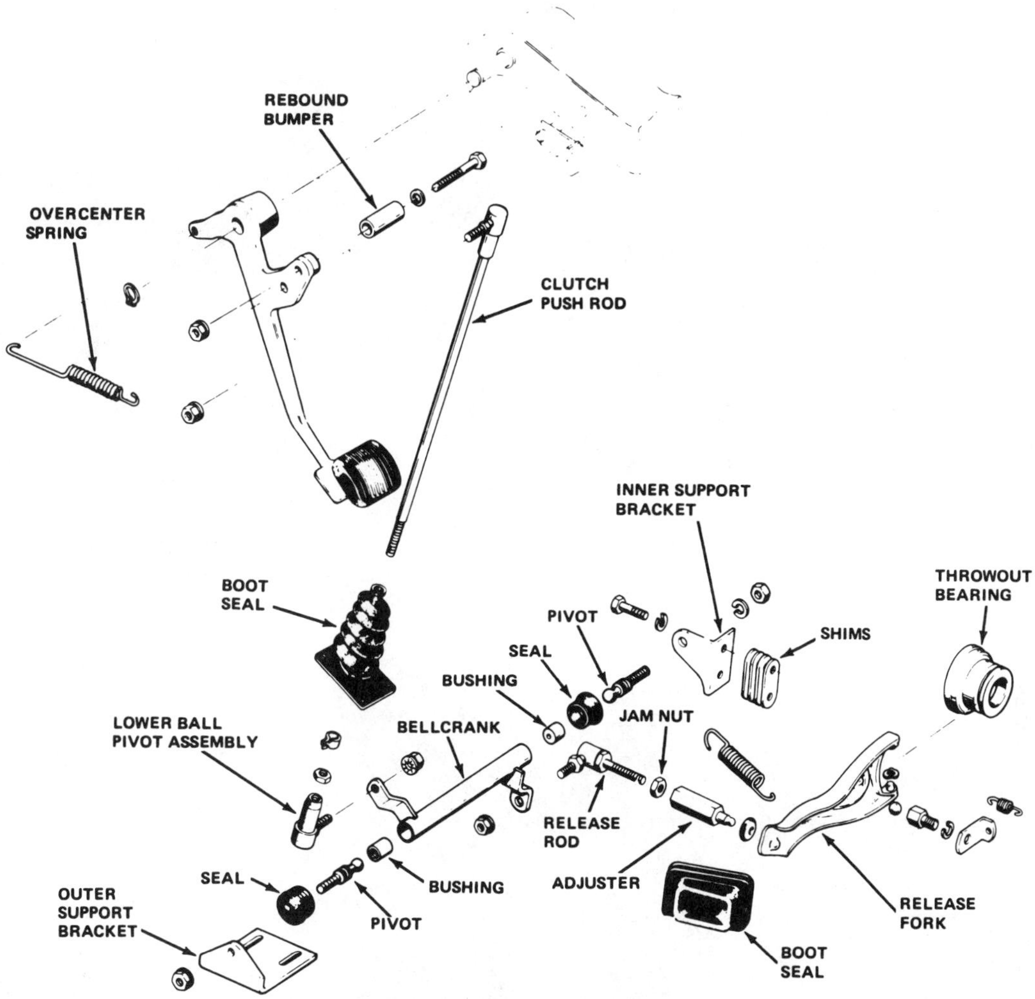

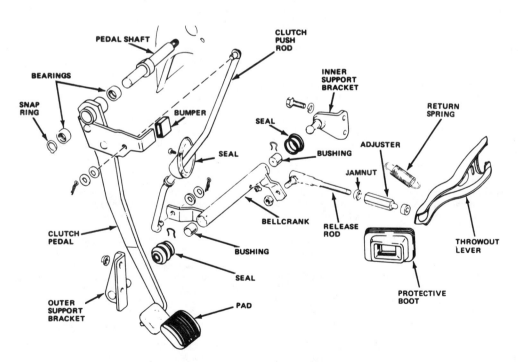

REBOUND BUMPER

OVERCENTER SPRING

CLUTCH PUSH ROD

BOOT SEAL

INNER SUPPORT BRACKET

THROWOUT BEARING

PIVOT

SEAL

BUSHING

JAM NUT

SHIMS

LOWER BALL PIVOT ASSEMBLY

BELLCRANK

RELEASE ROD

OUTER SUPPORT BRACKET

SEAL

PIVOT

BUSHING

ADJUSTER

BOOT SEAL

RELEASE FORK

Fig. 8.6   1972 through 1975 model clutch linkage component layout (Sec 3)

PEDAL SHAFT

CLUTCH PUSH ROD

BEARINGS

INNER SUPPORT BRACKET

RETURN SPRING

SNAP RING

BUMPER

SEAL

SEAL

BUSHING

ADJUSTER

JAMNUT

CLUTCH PEDAL

BELLCRANK

RELEASE ROD

THROWOUT LEVER

BUSHING

OUTER SUPPORT BRACKET

SEAL

PAD

PROTECTIVE BOOT

8

Fig. 8.7   1976 and later clutch linkage component layout (Sec 3)

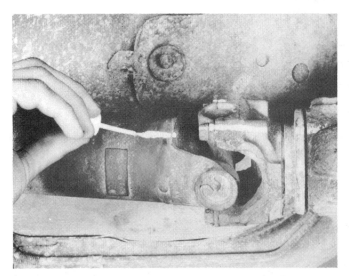

5.2   Marking the driveshaft and pinion flange to simplify
installation

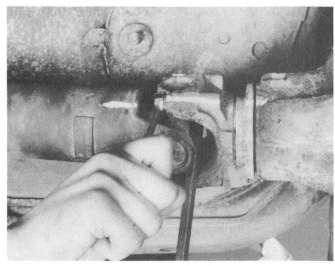

5.3   Removing a U-bolt nut, using a large screwdriver to
lock the driveshaft

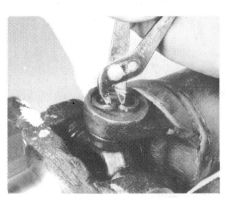

6.1   Using small pliers to remove the
U-joint snap-rings

6.3   Pressing the bearing caps out of
the U-joint with sockets and a vise

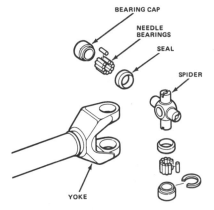

Fig. 8.8   Typical universal joint
components — exploded view (Sec 6)

3    Disconnect the universal joints by removing the nuts from the
U-bolts or strap retaining bolts (photo).
4    Lower the driveshaft and remove it from the vehicle.
5    Installation is the reverse of removal. Be sure to align the marks
made during removal and tighten the retaining bolts and nuts to the
specified torque.

## 6   Universal joints — disassembly, overhaul and reassembly

1    Carefully clean away all dirt from the ends of the bearings so the
snap-rings can be removed. If the snap-rings are very tight, tap the end
of the bearing cap (inside the snap-ring) to relieve the pressure (photo).
2    To remove the bearings from the yokes, you will need two sockets.
One should be large enough to fit into the yoke where the snap-rings
were installed and the other should have an inside diameter just large
enough for the bearing caps to fit into when they are forced out of
the yoke.
3    Mount the universal joint in a vise with the large socket on one
side of the yoke and the small socket on the other side, pushing against
the bearing cap. Carefully tighten the vise until the bearing is pushed
out of the yoke and into the large socket (photo). If it cannot be pushed all the way out, remove the universal joint from the vise and use
a pliers to finish removing the bearing.
4    Reverse the sockets and push out the bearing on the other side
of the yoke. This time, the small socket will be pushing against the cross-
shaped universal joint spider end.
5    Before pressing out the two remaining bearings, mark the spider

so it can be installed in the same relative position during reassembly.
6    The remaining universal joint can be disassembled following the
same procedure. Be sure to mark all components for each universal
joint so that they can be kept together and reassembled in the proper
position.
7    Clean the driveshaft and universal joint components with solvent
and dry them thoroughly.
8    Inspect the driveshaft for cracks and damage. Have the driveshaft
runout checked with a dial indicator. Replace the driveshaft with a new
one if any defects are found.
9    Check the spider journals for scoring, needle roller impressions,
rust and pitting. Replace it if any of the above conditions exist.
10   Check the sleeve yoke splines for wear and damage.
11   When reassembling the universal joint(s), replace all needle bearings, caps and dust seals with new ones. Many repair kits also contain
new spiders.
12   Before reassembly, pack each grease cavity in the spider ends
with a small amount of grease. Attach the dust seals to the spider with
the seal cavities facing in.
13   Apply a thin coat of grease to the dust seal lips and install the bearings and spider in the yoke using the vise and sockets that were used
to remove the old bearings. Work slowly and be very careful not to
damage the bearing caps as they are being pressed into the yokes.
14   Using the vise, press one of the bearing caps into the yoke about
1/4-inch.
15   Install the needle bearings in the cap (use grease to hold them in
place).
16   Insert the spider into the partially installed bearing cap, taking care
not to displace the needle bearing rollers.

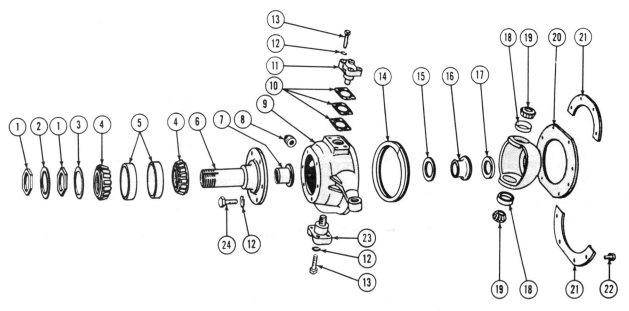

Fig. 8.9  Typical early model front axle steering knuckle components — exploded view (Sec 7)

| | | | |
|---|---|---|---|
| 1  Bearing adjusting nut | 7  Bushing | 13  Bolt | 19  Bearing cone and rollers |
| 2  Lock washer | 8  Filler plug | 14  Oil seal and backing ring | 20  Oil seal |
| 3  Lock washer | 9  Left knuckle and arm | 15  Thrust washer | 21  Retainer |
| 4  Bearing cone and rollers | 10  Shims | 16  Axle pilot | 22  Bolt |
| 5  Bearing cup | 11  Upper bearing cap | 17  Oil seal | 23  Lower bearing cap |
| 6  Spindle | 12  Lock washer | 18  Bearing cup | 24  Bolt |

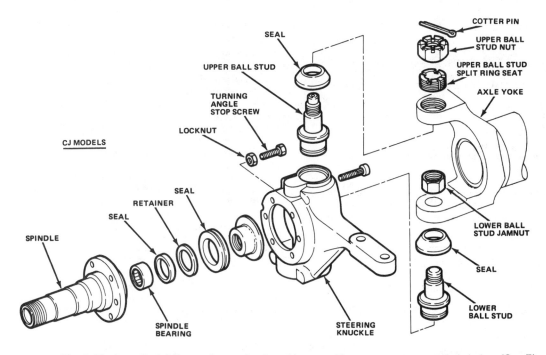

Fig. 8.10  Late model front axle steering knuckle assembly components — exploded view (Sec 7)

17  Stick the needle bearings into the opposite cap, then, while holding the spider in correct alignment, press both caps into place in the jaws of the vise.

18  Install the *new* snap-rings and repeat the installation procedure for the remaining two caps.

19  In extreme cases of wear or neglect, it is possible that the bearing cap housings in the yoke will have worn so much that the caps are a loose fit in the yokes. In such cases, replace the complete driveshaft assembly with a new one.

**7  Front axleshaft — removal and installation**

*Removal*

1  Raise the vehicle, support it securely on jackstands and remove the front wheels.

**1953 through 1979 models**

2  *On disc brake-equipped models,* remove the caliper.

8

3    Remove the hub cap, followed by the drive flange snap-ring.
4    *On disc braked equipped models,* remove the rotor hub bolts, cover and gasket.
5    *On drum brake equipped models,* remove the axle flange bolts and use AMC puller tool J-25133 (or equivalent) to remove the axle flange.
6    Straighten the lip of the lock washer and remove the locknut using AMC tool J-25103 (or equivalent). Remove the lock washer, the inner adjusting nut and the bearing lock washer.
7    *On drum brake equipped models,* remove the wheel hub and drum assembly complete with bearings, taking care not to damage the oil seal. If necessary, back off the brake adjuster sufficiently to allow removal of the drum. Remove the backing plate and brake line.
8    *On disc brake equipped models,* remove the outer bearing and brake rotor, followed by the adapter splash shield.
9    *On all models,* remove the spindle, grasp the axleshaft assembly and carefully withdraw it from the axle housing.

**1980 through 1983 models**
10    Remove the disc brake caliper.
11    Remove the bolts attaching the front hub to the axle and remove the hub body and gasket.
12    Remove the axleshaft retaining ring.
13    Straighten the lip of the lock washer and remove the outer locknut, lock washer, inner locknut and tabbed washer. Use AMC tool J-25103 (or equivalent) to remove the locknuts.
14    Remove the outer bearing, disc brake rotor, caliper adjuster and splash shield.
15    Remove the axle spindle.
16    Grasp the axleshaft securely and carefully withdraw it from the axle housing.

### Installation
**1953 through 1979 models**
17    Insert the axleshaft and universal joint assembly carefully into the axle housing, taking care not to damage the oil seal. Align the axleshaft and differential splines and push the shaft into place.
18    Install the spindle and inner bearing.
19    *On drum brake-equipped models,* install the brake support plate.
20    *On disc brake-equipped models,* install the splash shield and adapter.
21    Lubricate the outer wheel bearing (Chapter 11) and install it in the brake drum or rotor.
22    Install the brake drum or rotor, washer and adjusting nut and adjust the bearing (Chapter 11). Install the outer lock washer and nut, tighten the nut to the specified torque and bend the lip of the lock washer over the nut.
23    Install the drive flange, gasket, flange or brake rotor attaching bolts and snap-ring.
24    Install the caliper, rotor hub cover and bolts.
25    Install the hub cap.

**1980 through 1983 models**
26    Install the axleshaft and universal joint assembly into the axle housing with the shaft splines in place in the differential side gear.
27    Install the axle spindle, followed by the splash shield and disc brake caliper adapter.
28    Lubricate and install the outer bearing in the disc brake rotor and install the rotor on the spindle.
29    Install the tabbed washer and inner locknut, seat the bearings (Chapter 11) and install the lock washer and outer locknut. Tighten the locknut to the specified torque and bend the lip of the lock washer over the nut.
30    Lower the vehicle.

---

## 8    Front axleshaft oil seal — replacement

---

1    Raise the front of the vehicle and support it securely on jackstands.
2    Remove the front axleshaft (Section 7).

### 1953 through 1972 models
3    Remove the old steering knuckle seal which is held in place with eight screws. On early models the seal consists of two halves, while on later models the seal is made up of a split oil seal, backing ring assembly, oil seal felt and two retainer plate halves.
4    Inspect the spherical surface of the axleshaft for scoring, nicks and scratches which could damage the seal. Remove any minor im-

Fig. 8.11   Late model front axleshaft seal replacement (Sec 8)

perfections with fine sandpaper or emery cloth.
5    Before installation of the oil seal felt, make a diagonal cut across the top side so it can be slipped over the axleshaft.
6    Install the new seal and components and make sure the backing ring is toward the wheel. Install the axleshaft and lower the vehicle.

### 1973 through 1983 models
7    On these models the seal is located at the axleshaft stone shield. Slide the old seal off the axleshaft and discard it.
8    Remove the bronze thrust washer and inspect it for wear and damage. Replace the washer with a new one if it is noticeably nicked, scored or worn.
9    Carefully clean the grease and dirt from the thrust face area of the axleshaft.
10    Install the bronze washer with the chamfered side facing the seal.
11    Install the seal with the lip toward the spindle as shown in the accompanying illustration.
12    Pack the area around the axleshaft thrust face and then fill the seal area of the spindle with wheel bearing grease.
13    Install the axleshaft and lower the vehicle.

---

## 9    Front axle assembly — removal and installation

---

1    Raise the front of the vehicle and support it securely under the frame with jackstands.
2    Remove the front wheels.
3    Mark the relative positions of the universal joint and axle mating flange, disconnect the driveshaft and fasten it out of the way with a piece of wire.
4    Disconnect the steering linkage from the front axle.
5    Disconnect the shock absorbers at the axle housing.
6    Disconnect the breather tube (if equipped) from the axle housing.
7    Remove the disc brake calipers or drum brake backing plates and fasten them out of the way with wire.
8    Remove the axle U-bolt nuts and tie plate.
9    Place a jack under the axle housing and raise it sufficiently to release the spring tension.
10    Loosen but do not remove the upper spring shackle bolts.
11    Remove the lower spring shackle bolts and nuts and lower the spring to the floor.
12    Roll the jack and axle assembly carefully out from under the vehicle.
13    To install the axle, roll the jack and axle assembly into place under the vehicle.
14    Raise the springs into position and install the lower shackle bolts.
15    Rotate the axle assembly into position while lowering it onto the springs.
16    Install the U-bolts, tie plates and nuts.
17    Tighten the upper and lower shackle bolts and nuts.
18    Install the brake calipers or backing plates.
19    Connect the axle breather tube.
20    Connect the shock absorbers, steering linkage and driveshaft to the axle.
21    Install the wheels and lower the vehicle. With the vehicle weight resting on the suspension, check the U-bolt nuts and spring shackle nuts and bolts for proper torque.
22    Bleed and adjust the brakes as necessasry (Chapter 9).
23    Check the axle lubricant level (Chapter 1) and have the front end alignment checked by a properly equipped shop.

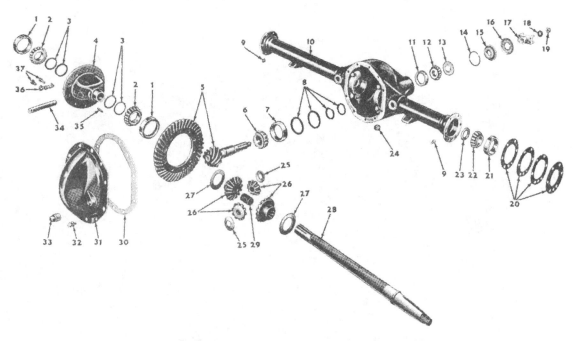

Fig. 8.12  Spicer/Dana semi-floating tapered axleshaft axle assembly component
layout — exploded view (Sec 10 through 14)

| | | | |
|---|---|---|---|
| 1 Bearing cup | 10 Housing | 19 Pinion nut | 29 Spacer |
| 2 Cone and rollers | 11 Outer bearing cup | 20 Shims | 30 Gasket |
| 3 Shims | 12 Outer bearing cone and rollers | 21 Cup | 31 Housing cover |
| 4 Differential case | 13 Oil slinger | 22 Cone and rollers | 32 Screw and lock washer |
| 5 Gear and pinion | 14 Gasket | 23 Oil seal | 33 Filler plug |
| 6 Inner bearing cone and rollers | 15 Oil seal | 24 Drain plug | 34 Lock pin |
| 7 Inner bearing cup | 16 Dust shield | 25 Thrust washer | 35 Pinion shaft |
| 8 Shims | 17 End yoke | 26 Differential gears | 36 Lock strap |
| 9 Fitting | 18 Washer | 27 Thrust washer | 37 Screw |
| | | 28 Axleshaft | |

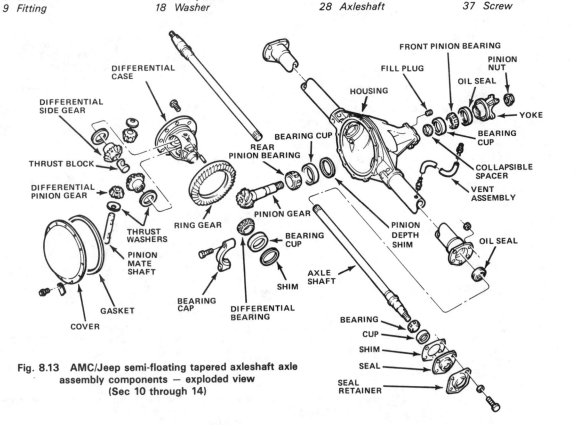

Fig. 8.13  AMC/Jeep semi-floating tapered axleshaft axle
assembly components — exploded view
(Sec 10 through 14)

8

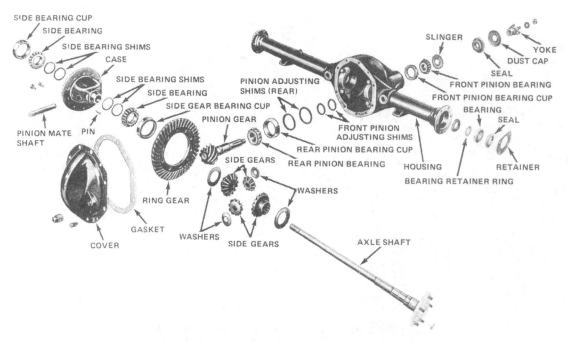

Fig. 8.14  Dana flanged axleshaft semi-floating rear axle assembly
components — exploded view (Sec 10 through 14)

## 10  Rear axleshaft — removal and installation

1   Most of these vehicles were equipped with semi-floating rear axles, although early models of the CJ-2 (through serial number 15453) used full-floating type axles. Two types of semi-floating axleshafts were used: tapered and flanged. Early models used Spicer/Dana tapered axles, while later models (after 1976) were equipped with axles manufactured by AMC/Jeep. Vehicles using flanged axleshafts were equipped with Dana 44 rear axles.

### Full-floating axles
2   It is not necessary to raise the vehicle when removing a full-floating axleshaft. Remove the screws which retain the axle flange to the hub and then screw two of these screws into the threaded holes in the flange to loosen the shaft. Withdraw the axleshaft from the housing.
3   To remove a broken axleshaft, first remove the outer piece and then loop a piece of stiff wire around the broken piece. Use the wire to pull the broken section of axleshaft from the housing. As an alternative, remove the other axle and use a rod or piece of pipe to push the broken section of axle out of the housing.

### Spicer/Dana tapered axles
4   Raise the rear of the vehicle, support it securely on jackstands and remove the wheel.
5   Remove the axleshaft cotter pin, nut and washer.
6   Back the brake adjuster off sufficiently to allow the drum to be removed.
7   Remove the hub (Section 12).
8   Remove the screws retaining the brake dust protector, grease and bearing retainers, brake and shim to the axle housing.
9   Disconnect and plug the brake line.
10  Remove the dust and oil shields.
11  Use a slide hammer puller to remove the axleshaft, bearing cone, roller and cup as shown in the accompanying illustration.
12  Inspect the oil seal to see if it is twisted, damaged or leaking. Replace it if necessary (Section 10).
13  A special puller is required to remove the bearing from the axle so this job should be left to a dealer or repair shop.
14  Installation of the axleshaft is the reverse of removal, taking care to install the original shims and tighten the axle nut to the specified torque.

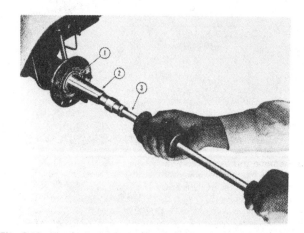

Fig. 8.15  Removing a tapered axleshaft with a slide hammer

1  Cone and roller        3  Slide hammer
2  Axleshaft

### AMC/Jeep tapered axles
15  Remove the axleshaft dust cap, nut and washer.
16  Raise the vehicle, support it securely and remove the wheel.
17  Remove the rear axle hub (Section 12).
18  Disconnect and plug the brake hose at the wheel cylinder and remove the brake support plate assembly, oil seal and shims from the axleshaft.
19  Use a puller to remove the axleshaft and bearing from the housing as shown in the accompanying illustration.
20  An arbor press is required to remove the bearing from the axle so this job should be left to a dealer or repair shop.
21  Install a new oil seal (Section 11).
22  Insert the axleshaft carefully into the housing, aligning the shaft splines with the differential gears.
23  Install the bearing cup.
24  Apply a coat of sealant to the axle tube flange to prevent the entry of dust and water into the housing.
25  Install the original shims, oil seal assembly, brake backing plate and

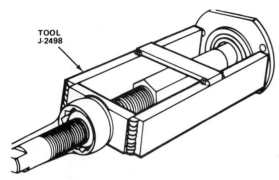

**Fig. 8.16  Removing the AMC/Jeep tapered axleshaft and bearing assembly with a special puller (Sec 10 through 13)**

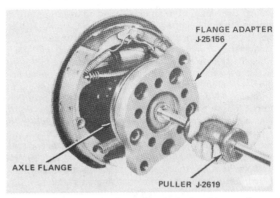

**Fig. 8.17  Removing a flanged axleshaft with a puller and adapter (Sec 10 through 13)**

**Fig. 8.18  Removing the hub using a puller (Spicer/Dana tapered axleshaft) (Sec 12)**

mounting bolts. Tighten the bolts to the specified torque.
26  Install the hub, brake drum and axle nut.
27  Install the wheel and hub cap and lower the vehicle.

### Dana 44 flanged axles
28  Raise the vehicle, support is securely on jackstands and remove the rear wheels.
29  Remove the brake drum.
30  Use a sharp tool to pierce the center of the axleshaft cup plug and pry the plug out.
31  Remove the nuts retaining the backing plate and retainer to the axle tube flange, working through the access hole in the shaft flange.
32  Remove the axleshaft using a puller and flange adapter such as AMC tools J-2619 and J-25156 (or equivalent) as shown in the accompanying illustration.
33  Remove the old bearing cup and oil seal from the axle housing tube.
34  Carefully insert the axleshaft into the housing making sure not to contact the oil seal. Apply a thin coat of wheel bearing grease to the outside circumference of the bearing cup prior to installation in the housing bearing bore.
35  Use a soft-faced hammer to tap the axleshaft flange and seat the bearing in the bearing bore.
36  Install the axleshaft retainer and brake backing plate on the axle housing and install a new cup plug in the axleshaft flange hole.
37  Install the brake drum and wheel and lower the vehicle.

---

### 11  Rear axle seals — replacement

1  Raise the rear of the vehicle, support it securely on jackstands and remove the rear wheels.

### Full-floating axles
2  The seals on these axles are located at the differential and replacement requires disassembly of the axle assembly. Consequently, seal

replacement on these models is beyond the scope of the home mechanic and the job should be left to a dealer or repair shop.

### Spicer/Dana tapered axles
3  Remove the hub (Section 12) and axleshaft (Section 10).
4  Carefully pry the old seal from the axle housing, noting the direction in which it is installed. Clean the seal seat in the axle housing with a clean, lint-free cloth.
5  Insert the new oil seal into the housing, making sure that it faces in the same direction as the original. Use a large socket to seat the seal in the housing, tapping it into place with a hammer.
6  Install the axleshaft and hub.

### AMC/Jeep tapered axles
7  Remove the hub (Section 12) and axleshaft (Section 10).
8  Carefully pry the old seal from the axle housing and wipe the seal cavity with a clean, lint-free cloth.
9  Coat the outer circumference of the seal with light oil and insert it into the housing. Use a large socket and hammer to carefully tap the seal squarely into place until it is seated completely.
10  Lightly coat the seal retainer with non-hardening sealant and install the axleshaft and hub.

### Dana 44 flanged axles
11  Remove the axleshaft (Section 10).
12  Remove the old oil seal from the axle housing using a slide hammer puller such as AMC tool C-637.
13  Wipe the seal bore out with a clean, lint-free cloth.
14  Install the new seal squarely in the housing using AMC tool W-186 or a large socket. Make sure it is completely seated.
15  Install the axleshaft.

---

### 12  Rear hub — removal and installation

1  Raise the rear of the vehicle, support it securely on jackstands and remove the rear wheels.

### Full-floating axles
2  Remove the axleshaft (Section 10).
3  Bend the lip of the lock washer away from the locknut and remove the locknut, washer and bearing adjusting nut and washer. Grasp the hub and rock it back and forth to dislodge the outer bearing. Remove the bearing and withdraw the hub from the axle.
4  Installation is the reverse of removal. Be sure to adjust the bearings (Chapter 11).

### Spicer/Dana tapered axles
5  Remove the axleshaft nut and use a puller to remove the hub as shown in the accompanying illustration.
6  Place the hub and drum on the tapered portion of the axleshaft and insert the key into the keyway. Install the axleshaft nut and tighten it to the specified torque.

### AMC/Jeep tapered axles
7  Remove the axleshaft dust cap, cotter key, nut and washer.

**8**

8    Remove the brake drum and mounting screws.
9    Remove the hub using a puller such as AMC tool J-25109-01 (or equivalent) as shown in the accompanying illustration.
10   To install the original hub, align the key in the hub with the keyway in the axleshaft, slide the hub onto the axleshaft as far as it will go and install the washer and nut. Tighten the nut to the specified torque after the vehicle has been lowered onto the wheels. If the cotter key hole is not aligned, tighten the nut sufficiently to allow insertion of the key. Do not loosen the nut to align the cotter key hole.
11   To install a replacement hub, align the key in the hub with the axleshaft keyway and slide the hub onto the shaft. Install two well oiled washers, the axleshaft nut, the brake drum and screws and the wheel.
12   Lower the vehicle and tighten the axleshaft nut until the specified distance from the end of the axleshaft to the hub outer face (1-5/16-inch) is obtained as shown in the accompanying illustration.
13   Remove the axleshaft nut and one washer. Install the nut and tighten it to the specified torque. To align the cotter key hole so the key can be inserted, tighten (never loosen) the nut.

## 13   Pinion oil seal — replacement

1    Raise the vehicle and support it securely on jackstands.
2    On models equipped with semi-floating rear axles with tapered axleshafts, remove the wheels and brake drums.
3    Mark the relative positions of the driveshaft and axle pinion yoke to simplify installation, then disconnect the driveshaft.
4    On semi-floating rear axles with flanged axleshafts, attach an in-lb torque wrench and socket to the pinion nut, rotate the pinion through

several revolutions and record the torque required to turn the nut.
5    On all models, remove the pinion nut using a yoke holding tool such as AMC tool J-8614-01 as shown in the accompanying illustration.
6    Mark the relative positions of the yoke and pinion for alignment reference during reinstallation.
7    Remove the yoke using a puller such as AMC tool J-8614-2 as shown in the accompanying illustration.
8    Inspect the yoke seal surface. If it is damaged, burred or scored, replace the yoke with a new one.
9    Use AMC tool J-9233 to draw the pinion seal out of the housing.
10   Coat the lip of the new seal with axle lubricant prior to installation. Insert the seal into position and tap it squarely into the housing with a hammer and a large socket or an installation tool such as AMC tool J-22661.
11   Install the yoke using the alignment marks made during removal.
12   On semi-floating axles with tapered axleshafts, install a new pinion nut and tighten it only sufficiently to remove the pinion bearing end play. Attach the in-lb torque wrench and rotate the pinion several times to determine an accurate reading of the torque required to initially turn it. Compare this reading with the one taken in Step 4 and add five (5) in-lb to determine the proper preload torque. If the reading is less than this, tighten the nut slightly and recheck the torque. Repeat this procedure and gradually tighten the nut until the proper torque is reached. **Caution:** *Do not over tighten the nut, as it will collapse the pinion spacer sleeve. The differential will then have to be disassembled and a new spacer installed.*
13   On all other axles, install the pinion nut and tighten it to the specified torque.
14   Connect the driveshaft, install the brake drums and wheels (if removed) and lower the vehicle.

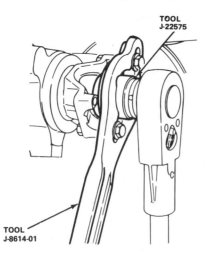

Fig. 8.19   Removing the AMC/Jeep tapered axleshaft hub using a puller (Sec 12)

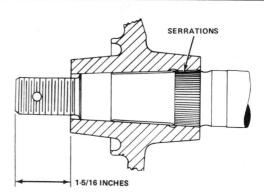

Fig. 8.20   The AMC/Jeep rear axle replacement hub must be installed with the specified distance between the axle end and hub face (Sec 12)

Fig. 8.21   Removing the axle pinion nut (Sec 13)

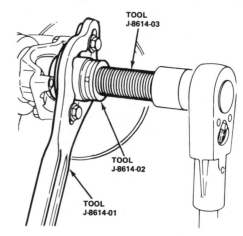

Fig. 8.22   Removing the axle pinion flange (Sec 13)

## 14  Rear axle assembly — removal and installation

1   Raise the rear of the vehicle, support it on jackstands and remove the rear wheels.
2   Disconnect the driveshaft from the axle and fasten it out of the way.
3   Disconnect the shock absorbers from the axle.
4   Disconnect and plug the brake hose at the T-fitting.
5   Disconnect the parking brake cable (if equipped).
6   Support the axle with a jack.
7   Remove the U-bolts and nuts.

8   Disconnect the rear shackles, slide the axle to the rear and remove it from the vehicle.
9   To install the axle, raise it into position, align the springs with the axel spring pads and install the U-bolts. Position the spring on the shackles and install the bolts finger tight.
10  Attach the brake line to the T-fitting and connect the parking brake cables.
11  Connect the driveshaft and shock absorbers to the axle.
12  Bleed and adjust the brakes (Chapter 9).
13  Install the wheels and lower the vehicle. Tighten the spring bolts to the specified torque.

# Chapter 9   Brakes

## Contents

Brake caliper — removal and installation . . . . . . . . . . . . . . . . 8
Brake caliper (1977 through 1979 models) — overhaul . . . . . . 9
Brake caliper (1980 through 1983 models) — overhaul . . . . . . 10
Brake check . . . . . . . . . . . . . . . . . . . . . . . . . . . . Chapter 1
Brake disc — inspection, removal and installation . . . . . . . . . 7
Brake drum — removal, inspection and installation . . . . . . . . 11
Brake system bleeding procedure . . . . . . . . . . . . . . . . . . . 3
Brake vacuum booster — check . . . . . . . . . . . . . . . . . . . . . 4
Brake vacuum booster — removal and installation . . . . . . . . . 5
Disc brake pads — replacement . . . . . . . . . . . . . . . . . . . . . 6
Drum brake shoes — removal, installation and adjustment . . . 12

Dual piston master cylinder — overhaul . . . . . . . . . . . . . . . . 18
Fluid level check . . . . . . . . . . . . . . . . . . . . . . . . . . . Chapter 1
General information . . . . . . . . . . . . . . . . . . . . . . . . . . . . . . 1
Hoses and brake lines — inspection and replacement . . . . . . . 2
Master cylinder — removal and installation . . . . . . . . . . . . . 16
Parking brake — adjustment . . . . . . . . . . . . . . . . . . . . . . . 14
Single piston master cylinder — overhaul . . . . . . . . . . . . . . . 17
Transfer case mounted drum-type parking
  brake — shoe replacement . . . . . . . . . . . . . . . . . . . . . . . 15
Wheel cylinder — removal, overhaul and installation . . . . . . . 13

## Specifications

### Disc brakes
Brake disc minimum thickness
  1977 and 1978 . . . . . . . . . . . . . . . . . . . . . . . . . . . . . .   1.120 in (28.5 mm)
  1979 through 1983 . . . . . . . . . . . . . . . . . . . . . . . . . . .   0.815 in (20.7 mm)
Brake disc thickness variation limit . . . . . . . . . . . . . . . . . .   0.001 in (0.02 mm)
Brake disc runout limit . . . . . . . . . . . . . . . . . . . . . . . . . .   0.005 in (0.12 mm)

### Torque specifications

|  | Ft-lb | Nm |
|---|---|---|
| Brake booster-to-dash . . . . . . . . . . . . . . . . . . . . . . . | 18 to 25 | 24 to 34 |
| Master cylinder-to-booster . . . . . . . . . . . . . . . . . . . . | 20 to 30 | 27 to 41 |
| Brake pedal pushrod nut . . . . . . . . . . . . . . . . . . . . . . | 25 to 40 | 34 to 54 |

### *Front disc brakes*

|  | | |
|---|---|---|
| Brake line-to-caliper fitting bolt . . . . . . . . . . . . . . . . . | 20 to 30 | 27 to 41 |
| Caliper support key retaining screw . . . . . . . . . . . . . . . | 15 to 18 | 20 to 24 |
| Caliper anchor bracket-to-steering knuckle . . . . . . . . . . | 100 | 136 |
| Brake support plate mounting nuts and bolts . . . . . . . . . | 30 to 35 | 41 to 47 |
| Bleeder screw . . . . . . . . . . . . . . . . . . . . . . . . . . . . . | 4 to 5 | 5 to 6 |

### *Front drum brakes*

|  | | |
|---|---|---|
| Backing plate bolts . . . . . . . . . . . . . . . . . . . . . . . . . . | 35 to 55 | 47 to 74 |
| Brake line-to-wheel cylinder fitting nut . . . . . . . . . . . . . | 10 to 15 | 14 to 23 |
| Bleeder screw . . . . . . . . . . . . . . . . . . . . . . . . . . . . . | 4 to 5 | 5 to 6 |
| Rear backing plate bolts/nuts . . . . . . . . . . . . . . . . . . . | 35 to 55 | 47 to 74 |

## 1   General information

These vehicles are equipped with four-wheel hydraulic brakes. Later models have separate systems for the front and rear brakes. The parking brake is connected mechanically to a drum-type brake located on the driveshaft at the rear of the transfer case on early models and to the rear-wheel brakes on later models.

Models manufactured through 1976 had drum brakes on all four wheels while later models had disc brakes at the front and drum brakes

at the rear. Later model drum brakes are self-adjusting. A vacuum operated brake booster was available on later models.

On 1974 and later models, a combination valve is used. The combination valve serves as a front junction block for the brake hydraulic system and contains a brake pressure differential warning section and a brake proportioning section. A failure in either brake system will cause the piston to move and contact a switch pin, completing an electrical circuit and providing power to the warning light on the dash. The proportioner section provides balanced front-to-rear pressure during hard braking, reducing the rear line pressure so the wheels don't lock up.

## 2 Hoses and brake lines — inspection and replacement

1    The brake hydraulic system has a series of flexible rubber hoses connecting the wheel cylinders or the calipers and the rear axle fitting to metal lines running the length of the frame. If an inspection (Chapter 1) reveals a problem with either a rubber hose or a metal line, the component must be replaced immediately for continued safe use of the vehicle.

2    Before replacing a line or hose, determine the cause of failure and remedy it or the hose or line will fail again. Often components such as exhaust pipes have come loose and are rubbing the line, causing the break or tear.

3    Replacement steel and flexible brake lines are commonly available from dealer parts departments and auto parts stores. **Caution:** *Do not, under any circumstances, use anything other than genuine steel or approved flexible brake hoses as replacement items.*

4    When removing a brake line or flare-nut hose fitting, always use the proper flare-nut wrenches when loosening and tightening the connections.

5    At the junction where a brake line meets a bracket supporting it and its connection, remove the spring clip with pliers or a vise grip after loosening the connection.

6    Steel brake lines are usually retained along their span with clips. Always remove these clips completely before removing any brake line that they are supporting. Always replace these clips when replacing a metal brake line, as they provide support and keep the lines from vibrating, which will fatigue and eventually break the line.

7    Once a line has been replaced, the hydraulic system must be bled to rid the system of any air bubbles. Refer to Section 3.

## 3 Brake system bleeding procedure

1    If the brake system has air in it, operation of the brake pedal will be spongy and imprecise. Also, on later models with combination valves (*1974 and later*) the warning light on the dash will go on if there is air in the valve. Air can enter the brake system whenever any part of the system is dismantled or if the fluid level in the master cylinder reservoir runs low. Air can also leak into the system through a hole too small to allow fluid to leak out. In this case, it indicates that a general overhaul of the brake system is required. **Note:** *Inspect all brake line flexible hoses, steel lines and connections. See Chapter 1 for visual inspections before bleeding the system. By doing this, you will save a lot of time and prevent fluid loss.*

2    On models equipped with a combination valve, it will be necessary to bypass the valve. *On 1974 through 1976 models with four-wheel drum brakes,* this is accomplished by removing the brake warning switch wire, switch terminal, plunger and spring from the combination valve. *On models with front disc brakes,* hold the metering valve section of the combination valve with AMC tool J-26869 (or equivalent) as shown in the accompanying illustration.

3    To bleed the brakes, you will need an assistant to pump the brake pedal, a supply of new brake fluid, an empty plastic container, a clear plastic or vinyl tube which will fit over the bleeder screw nipple and a wrench for the bleeder screw.

4    There are five locations at which the brake system is bled: the master cylinder, each front brake wheel cylinder and each rear brake wheel cylinder.

5    Check the fluid level at the master cylinder reservoir. Add fluid, if necessary, to bring the level up to the Full mark. Use only the recommended brake fluid, and do not mix different types. Never use fluid from a container that has been standing uncapped. You will have to check the fluid level in the master cylinder reservoir often during the bleeding procedure. If the level drops too far, air will enter the system through the master cylinder.

6    Raise the vehicle and set it securely on jackstands (refer to the *Jacking and towing* procedures at the front of this manual).

7    Remove the bleeder screw cap from the wheel cylinder or caliper assembly that is being bled. If more than one wheel must be bled, start with the one farthest from the master cylinder.

8    Attach one end of the clear plastic or vinyl tube to the bleeder screw nipple and place the other end (submerged in a small amount of clean brake fluid) in the container.

9    Loosen the bleeder screw slightly, then tighten it to the point where it is snug yet easily loosened.

10    Have an assistant pump the brake pedal several times and hold it in the fully depressed position.

11    With pressure on the brake pedal, open the bleeder screw approximately one-half turn. As the brake fluid is flowing through the tube and into the container, tighten the bleeder screw. Again, pump the brake pedal, hold it in the fully depressed position and loosen the bleeder screw momentarily. Do not allow the brake pedal to be released with the bleeder screw in the open position.

12    Repeat the procedure until no air bubbles are visible in the brake fluid flowing through the tube. Be sure to check the brake fluid level in the master cylinder reservoir while performing the bleeding operation.

13    Tighten the bleeder screw, remove the plastic or vinyl tube and install the bleeder screw cap.

14    Follow the same procedure to bleed the other wheel cylinder or caliper assemblies.

15    To bleed the master cylinder, have an assistant pump and hold the brake pedal. Momentarily loosen the brake line fittings, one at a time, where they attach to the master cylinder. Any air in the master cylinder will escape when the fittings are loosened. Brake fluid will damage painted surfaces, so use paper towels or rags to cover and protect the areas around the master cylinder.

16    Install the brake warning switch wire, terminal, plunger and spring or remove the metering tool on combination valve-equipped vehicles.

17    Check the brake fluid level in the master cylinder to make sure it is adequate, then test drive the vehicle and check for proper brake operation.

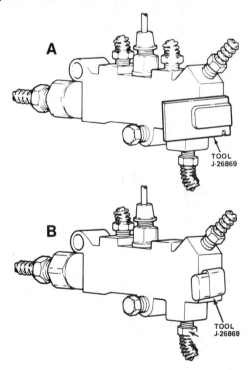

**Fig. 9.1   Combination valve metering valve tool installation (Sec 3)**

*A   1977 and 1978 models*
*B   1979 through 1983 models*

## 4 Brake vacuum booster — check

1    The most common symptom of a fault in the brake vacuum booster is lack of vacuum assist when the brakes are applied, so that excessive pedal effort is required.

2    To check the brake booster, turn the engine off and place the transmission in Neutral (manual transmission) or Park (automatic transmission). Apply the brakes several times to deplete the vacuum from the system and then, with light pressure, hold the pedal all the way down. Start the engine and verify that the pedal tends to fall away

9

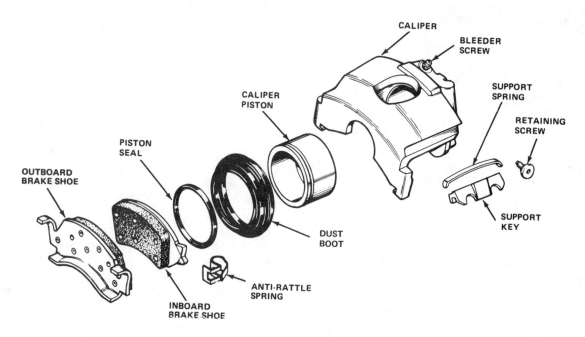

Fig. 9.2   1977 through 1981 disc brake caliper components — exploded view (Sec 6 through 10)

under foot pressure and require less pressure for brake application, indicating that the booster is working properly.
3    If the vacuum booster presure is not felt, the system is not functioning. Inspect the vacuum hose for damage and leaks.
4    If the vacuum booster operates properly but the brake pedal returns slowly or the brakes grab or drag, check the pedal mechanism and booster unit bellcrank and pivot pins. Lubricate the pedal pivot points and remove, clean, lubricate and install the bellcrank pivot pins.
5    If replacing the vacuum hose and cleaning and lubrication of the pedal mechanism and bellcrank pivot pins does not correct the problem, the booster is defective and must be replaced with a new one (Section 5).

## 5   Brake vacuum booster — removal and installation

1    Disconnect the booster pushrod at the brake pedal and discard the nut and bolt.
2    Disconnect the vacuum hose from the booster.
3    Remove the nuts and washers retaining the master cylinder to the booster and move the master cylinder out of the way.
4    Remove the mounting nuts and bolts and lift the vacuum booster and bellcrank assembly from the engine compartment.
5    To install the booster, place the booster and bellcrank assembly in position on the engine compartment dash panel, install the mounting nuts and bolts and tighten them to the specified torque.
6    Connect the vacuum hose.
7    Attach the master cylinder to the booster and tighten the nuts to the specified torque.
8    Align the pushrod with the brake pedal, install a new bolt and nut and tighten them to the specified torque.

## 6   Disc brake pads — replacement

1    Refer to Chapter 1 for a general inspection of the disc brake pads.
2    Before replacing the brake pads, siphon off and discard two-thirds of the fluid in the brake master cylinder reservoir.
3    Remove the front hub caps and loosen the wheel nuts. Raise the front of the vehicle, support it on jackstands and remove the wheels. Perform the disc brake pad replacement on one brake assembly at a time, using the assembled brake for reference if necessary.
4    Use a C-clamp or large screwdriver to bottom the piston in its bore

(photo).
5    *On 1977 through 1981 models,* remove the caliper support key screw with a 1/4-inch Allen wrench, use a hammer and punch to drive the key out and lift the caliper up and out of the anchor plate (photos).
6    *On 1982 and 1983 models,* remove the two seven (7) millimeter hex head mounting pins located on the back of the caliper and then lift the caliper off the anchor plate and rotor.
7    Fasten the caliper out of the way, taking care not to stretch or damage the brake hose.
8    *On 1977 through 1981 models,* remove the inboard brake pad from the anchor plate, noting the location of the anti-rattle spring to simplify installation. Remove the outboard pad from the caliper.
9    *On 1982 and 1983 models,* remove the outboard pad while holding the anti-rattle clip, followed by the inboard pad and anti-rattle clip as shown in the accompanying illustrations.
10   On all models, carefully clean the sliding surfaces of the caliper and anchor plate with a stiff brush or fine sandpaper to remove dirt and rust. **Note:** *Make an effort not to inhale any dust raised by this operation, as it may contain asbestos, which is harmful to your health.* Apply a thin coat of moly-based or high-temperature grease to the caliper and anchor plate sliding surfaces (photo).
11   *On 1977 through 1981 models,* install the anti-rattle spring on the rear flange of the inboard pad so the looped end is facing away from the brake disc. Install the pad and spring in the anchor plate, taking care not to dislodge the spring. Install the outboard pad in the anchor plate. Place the caliper in position over the anchor plate and brake disc, being careful not to tear or damage the piston boot. Align the caliper and anchor plate, insert the support key and spring and install the retaining screw, tightening it to the specified torque.
12   *On 1982 and 1983 models,* install the anti-rattle clip on the trailing edge of the anchor plate with the split end facing *away* from the disc. Hold the clip in the plate while installing the inboard pad. Install the outboard pad in the plate while holding the anti-rattle clip in place. Install the caliper over the anchor plate and brake disc, taking care not to damage the piston boot. Align the caliper and anchor plate, then install the mounting pins and tighten them to the specified torque.
13   On all models, fill the master cylinder reservoir to within 1/4-inch of the rim and depress the brake pedal several times to seat the new pads.
14   Install the wheels, lower the vehicle and check the master cylinder fluid level.
15   Before driving the vehicle but with the engine running, check for a firm brake pedal (if equipped with a vacuum booster) and bleed the brakes (Section 3) if necessary.

6.4  Using a screwdriver to push the piston back into its bore

6.5A  Removing the 1977 through 1981 caliper key retaining bolt with an Allen wrench

6.5B  Drive the caliper key out with a hammer and punch

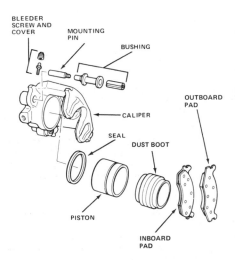

Fig. 9.3  1982 and 1983 disc brake caliper components — exploded view (Sec 6)

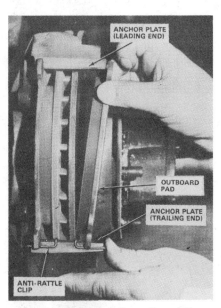

Fig. 9.4  Removing the outboard disc brake pad (1982 and 1983 models) (Sec 6)

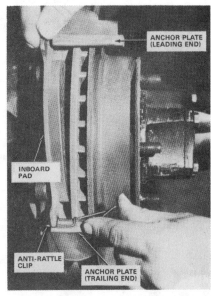

Fig. 9.5  1982 and 1983 model inboard brake pad removal (Sec 6)

6.10  Use your finger to lubricate the caliper and anchor plate sliding surfaces (arrows) with moly-based, high-temperature brake grease

## 7  Brake disc — inspection, removal and installation

### Inspection

1  Raise the front of the vehicle, support it securely on jackstands and remove the front wheels.
2  Remove the caliper and brake pads as described in Section 6.
3  Inspect the surface of the brake disc for severe score marks, cracks, chipped areas, excessive wear and alternate shiny/dark colored areas indicating hard spots. Moderate damage can be remedied by having the disc resurfaced on a brake lathe.
4  Check the thickness of the disc at the center of the lining contact area with a micrometer. The disc must be replaced with a new one if the measurement is less than shown in the Specifications.
5  Mount a dial indicator on a support stand or the spindle and place the stylus in contact with the center of the pad contact area on the disc. Zero the indicator, rotate the disc through one revolution and note the indicator reading. Compare this reading with the runout limit in the Specifications. If the runout is excessive, the rotor should either be resurfaced on a brake lathe or replaced with a new one.

### Removal

6  To remove the disc *on 1977 through 1979 models,* remove the hub cap and hub cover assembly. Remove the drive flange snap-ring and flange. Straighten the lip of the outer locknut retaining washer and

9

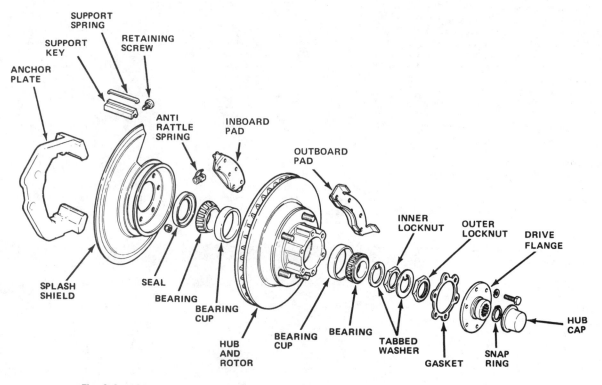

Fig. 9.6   1977 through 1979 disc brake and hub components — exploded view (Sec 7)

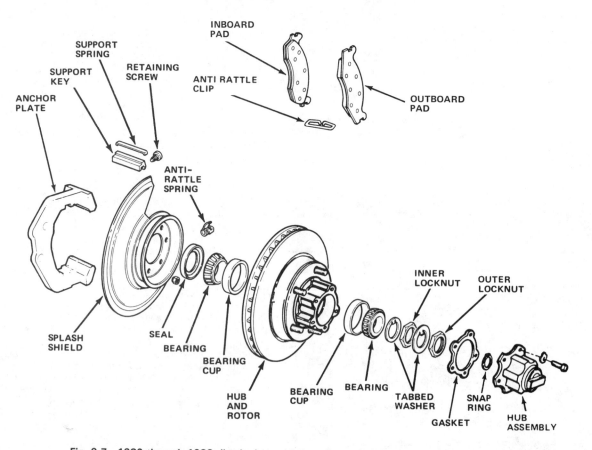

Fig. 9.7   1980 through 1983 disc brake and hub components — exploded view (Sec 7)

remove the outer locknut and washer and inner locknut and retaining washer. Grasp the brake disc and hub assembly firmly and withdraw it from the spindle. Remove the bearings from the hub.

7   *On 1980 through 1983 models,* remove the hub cap assembly from the hub. Remove the snap-ring retaining the hub to the axleshaft and straighten the lip on the outer locknut retaining washer. Remove the outer locknut and retaining washer, followed by the inner locknut and retaining washer, grasp the hub and disc assembly firmly and withdraw it from the spindle. Remove the bearings from the hub.

8   With the disc removed, it can be taken to a properly equipped brake shop to be resurfaced. Be sure to check the thickness of the disc after machining to verify that it is still within the specified limit.

## Installation

9   Lubricate the bearings and install them in the hub as described in Chapter 11.

10  Install the hub and disc assembly on the spindle.

11  *On 1977 through 1979 models,* install the inner retaining washer and locknut. Tighten the locknut to 50 ft-lbs and then back the nut off 1/3-turn. Install the washer and outer locknut, tighten it to 50 ft-lbs and then bend the washer lip over the nut. Install the drive flange and snap-ring, followed by the gasket hub cover, retaining bolts and hub cap.

12  *On 1980 through 1983 models,* install the tabbed inner washer and locknut and install the wheel with the nuts finger tight. Tighten the inner locknut to 50 ft-lbs while rotating the wheel to seat the bearings evenly. Back off the locknut 1/6-turn (approximately 45° to 65°). Install the outer tabbed washer and locknut, tighten the locknut to 50 ft-lbs and bend the lip of the washer over the nut. Install the snap-ring, new gasket, hub cover assembly and retaining bolts. Remove the wheel.

13  *On all models,* install the pads and calipers as described in Section 6.

14  Install the wheels and lower the vehicle.

---

### 8   Brake caliper — removal and installation

1   Siphon off and discard two-thirds of the fluid in the brake master cylinder reservoir.

2   Remove the front hub caps and loosen the wheel nuts. Raise the front of the vehicle, support it securely on jackstands and remove the wheels.

3   Bottom the caliper piston in its bore as described in Section 6, Step 4.

4   Thoroughly clean the area around the brake fitting.

5   Disconnect and plug the brake line (discarding the gaskets).

6   Remove the caliper as described in Section 6, Step 5 or 6, depending on the year of the vehicle.

7   Install the caliper as described in Section 6, Steps 10 through 12. Connect the brake line to the caliper fitting (using new gaskets).

8   Fill the master cylinder reservoir to within 1/4-inch of the top and bleed the brakes (Section 3).

9   Install the wheels, lower the vehicle and check the master cylinder fluid level.

10  Before driving the vehicle, check for a firm brake pedal (with the engine running on vacuum booster-equipped models).

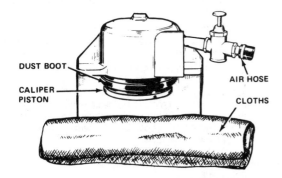

**Fig. 9.8   Using air pressure to remove the piston from the caliper (Sec 9)**

DUST BOOT

CALIPER PISTON

AIR HOSE

CLOTHS

---

### 9   Brake caliper (1977 through 1979 models) — overhaul

1   Drain any remaining fluid from the caliper into a container and place the caliper on a clean work surface.

2   Pad the inside of the caliper with rags to protect the piston. If compressed air is available, insert an air nozzle in the caliper fluid inlet port and slowly apply just enough air pressure to ease the piston out of the bore as shown in the accompanying illustration. **Caution:** *Do not place your fingers in front of the piston to catch it because excessive air pressure could eject it with enough force to cause injury.* As an alternative method, strike the caliper sharply on a wood block to dislodge the piston from the bore.

3   Remove the dust boot from the piston and discard it.

4   Remove the seal from the piston bore, using a wood or plastic tool to avoid damaging the bore surface. Discard the seal.

5   Remove the bleeder screw from the caliper.

6   Remove any rust or corrosion from the caliper exterior with a wire brush. Clean the caliper and piston with new brake fluid (*never use petroleum-based solvents to clean brake parts*). Inspect the piston for wear, damage and pitted areas. Inspect the caliper for damage, wear, nicks, pitted areas and corrosion in the bore. Check the support spring and anti-rattle springs for distortion and lack of tension. Replace any damaged or worn components with new ones.

7   Lubricate the piston and bore with clean brake fluid.

8   Install the seal in the groove in the bore by working it into position using your fingers only.

9   Install the bleeder screw in the caliper.

10  With the piston bore lubricated with clean brake fluid, position the dust boot on the bore. Do not lubricate the dust boot. Reach through the top of the boot and work the large lip into the groove at the upper edge of the bore. The boot must be securely seated in the groove.

11  Lubricate the piston and the small lip of the dust boot with clean brake fluid and position the piston over the lip.

12  Hold the piston in position over the boot lip and direct low pressure air (about 15 psi) into the fluid inlet port. Turn the compressor valve off and then back on to about 7 psi.

13  As the air pressure expands the seal, carefully work the piston into the boot until the boot seats in the piston groove. After the boot lip is seated in the piston groove, release the air pressure. The piston can now be pushed to the bottom of the bore using a hammer handle.

---

### 10   Brake caliper (1980 through 1983 models) — overhaul

1   Drain any remaining fluid into a container and place the caliper on a clean working surface.

2   Remove the piston from the caliper as described in Section 9, Step 2.

3   Remove the piston boot from the bore using a screwdriver to pry it out (take care not to scratch the bore). Discard the boot.

4   Remove the piston seal with a plastic or wooden tool and discard it.

5   Remove the bleeder screw from the caliper.

6   Remove the plastic sleeves and rubber bushings from the caliper mounting ears and discard them.

7   Wash the components thoroughly with clean brake fluid. Check the mounting pins for damaged threads and corrosion. Inspect the piston bore for heavy scratches, corrosion, nicks, cracks, wear and damage. Minor imperfections can be removed with crocus cloth. Inspect the piston for heavy scratches, score marks, corrosion and wear. Replace any worn or damaged components with new ones.

8   Lubricate the piston bore and the new seal with clean brake fluid.

9   Install the piston seal in the bore groove by working it into place with your fingers.

10  Lubricate the piston with clean brake fluid.

11  Install the replacement dust boot on the piston and slide the metal retainer portion over the open end of the piston. Pull the boot to the rear until the lip seats in the piston groove as shown in the accompanying illustration.

12  Push the metal retainer portion of the boot forward until it is flush with the open end of the piston and the fold can be snapped into place as shown in the accompanying illustration.

13  Insert the piston carefully into the bore, taking care not to displace the piston seal.

14  Use a wooden hammer handle to push the piston to the bottom

**9**

Fig. 9.9   Installing the caliper piston dust boot on the piston (1980 through 1983 models) (Sec 10)

Fig. 9.10   Positioning the caliper piston dust boot (1980 through 1983 models) (Sec 10)

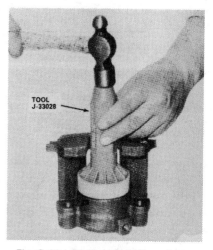

Fig. 9.11   Seating the caliper piston dust boot in the counterbore with an installing tool (1980 through 1983 models) (Sec 10)

of the bore.

15  Use a dust boot installer tool such as AMC No. J-33028 (available at your dealer) or equivalent (available at auto parts stores) to seat the metal retainer portion of the dust boot in the counterbore at the upper end of the piston bore.

16  Install the bleeder screw and tighten it securely (but not to the specified torque until after the caliper has been installed and the brakes bled).

17  Install the replacement plastic sleeves and rubber bushings in the mounting ears on the caliper.

### 11  Brake drum — removal, inspection and installation

#### Removal (front)

1  Raise the front of the vehicle, support it securely on jackstands and remove the hub cap.

2  Remove the drive flange snap-ring and axle flange bolts.

3  Remove the axle flange using a puller such as AMC tool J-25133 or its equivalent.

4  Bend back the lock washer lip and remove the outer nut, lock washer, adjusting nut and bearing lock washer. Back off the brake adjustment, if necessary, and withdraw the brake drum and hub assembly from the spindle.

#### Removal (rear)

5  Raise the rear of the vehicle, support it on jackstands and remove the wheels.

**Full-floating axle**

6  Remove the axleshaft and nut (Chapter 8).

7  Bend the lip of the lock washer back and remove the locknut and lock washer. Remove the bearing adjusting nut and washer, grasp the hub/brake drum assembly and move it from side-to-side until the outer bearing is free of the hub. Withdraw the hub/brake drum assembly from the axle, taking care not to drop the bearings.

**Semi-floating flanged axle**

8  Remove the brake drum locknuts and remove the drum.

**Semi-floating tapered axle**

9  Remove the hub/brake drum assembly as described in Chapter 8.

#### Inspection

10  Wipe the brake drum out with a clean cloth. **Note:** *Make an effort not to inhale this dust because it contains asbestos, which is harmful to your health.*

11  Wash the drum thoroughly with soap and water and dry it with a clean, lint-free cloth. If the drum is contaminated with grease or oil, clean the surface with alcohol.

12  Inspect the drum for cracks, deep scoring, distortion and hard spots which appear as a series of shiny or dark-colored areas on the shoe contact surface. Replace the drum with a new one if any of these conditions are present.

13  If the drum is out-of-round or lightly scored, have it turned by a properly equipped shop.

#### Installation (front)

14  Lubricate the wheel bearings (Chapter 11) and install the hub/drum assembly on the spindle.

15  Install the wheel washer and adjusting nut and tighten the nut while rotating the hub until drag is felt on the bearings. Back the nut off approximately 1/6-turn. Install the lock washer and nut and bend the lip of the washer over the nut.

16  Install the drive flange and bolts, followed by the snap-ring and hub cap.

#### Installation (rear)

**Full-floating axle**

17  Lubricate the wheel bearings (Chapter 11) and install the washer and nut. Install the wheel and spin it while tightening the nut until the bearings start to bind. Back the nut off approximately 1/6-turn until the wheel turns freely. Install the lock washer and nut, bending the lock washer lip over the nut. Remove the wheel and install the axleshaft.

**Semi-floating flanged axle**

18  Install the brake drum and locknuts.

**Semi-floating tapered axle**

19  Install the hub/drum assembly (Chapter 8).

#### Installation (all models)

20  On all models, install the wheels, adjust the brakes and lower the vehicle. *On later models with self-adjusting brakes,* it will not be necessary to adjust the brakes before lowering the vehicle. On these models, drive the vehicle in forward and reverse while making 10 or 15 brake applications to bring the pedal up to the proper level.

### 12  Drum brake shoes — removal, installation and adjustment

1  Raise the vehicle, support it securely on jackstands and remove the wheels.

2  Remove the brake drums (Section 11).

3  It is recommended that the old shoes be replaced with new or re-lined ones instead of new linings being installed on the original shoes. Also, it is recommended that shoes for both wheels on a particular axle be replaced at the same time.

#### Removal

**Non self-adjusting brakes**

4  Turn the adjustment eccentrics to the lowest side of the cam and remove the brake shoe return springs. Remove the hold-down spring

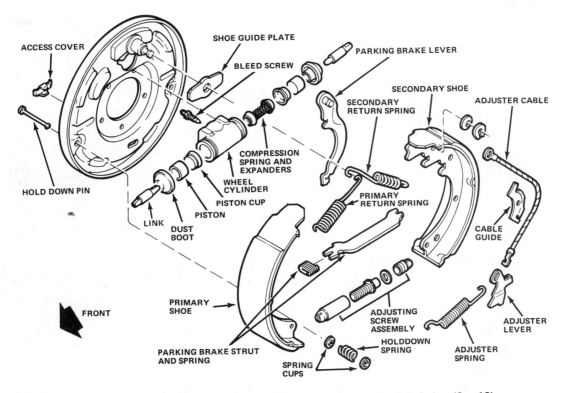

ACCESS COVER

SHOE GUIDE PLATE

BLEED SCREW

PARKING BRAKE LEVER

SECONDARY SHOE

SECONDARY RETURN SPRING

ADJUSTER CABLE

COMPRESSION SPRING AND EXPANDERS

WHEEL CYLINDER

PISTON CUP

PISTON

HOLD DOWN PIN

LINK

DUST BOOT

PRIMARY RETURN SPRING

CABLE GUIDE

PRIMARY SHOE

FRONT

PARKING BRAKE STRUT AND SPRING

ADJUSTING SCREW ASSEMBLY

HOLDDOWN SPRING

SPRING CUPS

ADJUSTER SPRING

ADJUSTER LEVER

Fig. 9.12  Typical late model drum brake components — exploded view (Sec 12)

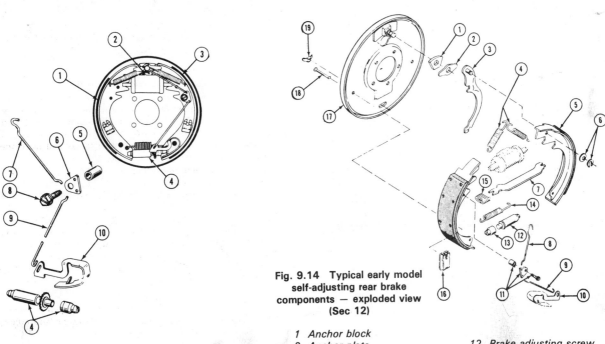

Fig. 9.13  Typical early model self-adjusting front wheel drum brake components — exploded view (Sec 12)

1  Primary shoe
2  Wheel cylinder
3  Secondary shoe
4  Adjusting screw assembly
5  Sleeve
6  Lever plate
7  Upper linkage rod
8  Screw
9  Lower linkage rod
10  Adjuster lever

Fig. 9.14  Typical early model self-adjusting rear brake components — exploded view (Sec 12)

1  Anchor block
2  Anchor plate
3  Parking brake lever and pin
4  Shoe return spring
5  Brake shoe
6  C-washer
7  Parking brake strut
8  Anchor end link
9  Actuator link
10  Lever shoe adjusting spring
11  Lever and sleeve screw
12  Brake adjusting screw (left-hand thread)
13  Brake adjusting screw (right-hand thread)
14  Adjusting screw spring
15  Strut spring
16  Hold-down spring
17  Backing plate
18  Hold-down pin
19  Adjusting hole plug

9

12.8A  Insert a screwdriver into the hold-down spring used on some later model brake shoes to disengage it

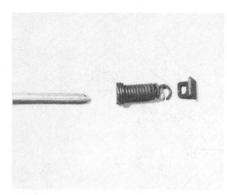

12.8B  The hold-down spring used on some later model self-adjusting drum brake shoes

12.9A  Removing the rear brake parking brake strut

12.9B  Disengage the parking brake cable (arrow) from the shoe lever as the rear brake shoe is removed

12.18  The adjuster screw must be installed in the fully retracted position

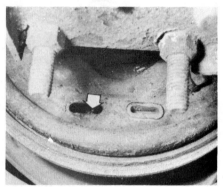

12.24  With the plug removed from the backing plate, the adjuster star wheel (arrow) is accessible

cup (using a brake tool or pliers) and separate the shoes from the backing plate.

**Self-adjusting brakes**

5    Grip the automatic adjuster lever with a pliers and remove the pivot hook from the hole in the secondary shoe.

6    Detach the shoe return springs.

7    Remove the adjuster cable, guide, lever and spring.

8    Remove the shoe hold-down springs. On some later models, this is accomplished by inserting a screwdriver and twisting the springs from their anchor plates (photos).

9    Remove the brake shoes, adjuster screw assembly and, in the case of the rear brakes, the parking brake strut (photo). Detach the parking brake cable from the lever as the shoe assembly is removed (photo).

**All models**

10    Place a wide rubber band or piece of wire around the wheel cylinders to retain them while the shoes are removed.

11    While all the brake parts are removed, carefully brush away any accumulations of dirt and dust from the backing plate and wheel cylinder. **Note:** *Make sure that no grease comes in contact with the brake shoes at any time. If it does, clean them thoroughly with denatured alcohol.*

12    Prior to installation, apply a small amount of high-temperature brake grease to the backing plate surfaces which come in contact with the sides of the brake shoes. **Note:** *Make sure that no grease comes in contact with the brake shoes at any time. If it does, clean them thoroughly with denatured alcohol.*

13    Apply a small amount of high-temperature grease to the contact points of the brake shoes, parking brake and adjuster levers, struts and springs.

## Installation

**Non self-adjusting brakes**

14    Install the brake shoes on the backing plate and remove the rubber band or wire from the wheel cylinder.

15    Install the adjuster eccentrics and brake shoe retaining springs.

**Self-adjusting brakes**

16    Place the brake shoes in position on the backing plate, remove the rubber band or wire from the wheel cylinder and install the hold-down springs.

17    Install the primary shoe return spring and then place the adjuster cable eyelet on the anchor pin, position the cable guide and install the secondary return spring.

18    Install the adjuster screw, after making sure that (on the rear brakes) the parking brake strut is correctly positioned and attached. Make sure the adjuster screw is threaded all the way into the sleeve to the minimum adjustment (photo).

19    Place the small hooked end of the adjuster spring in the large hole in the primary shoe and then place the large hooked end of the spring in the adjuster lever.

20    Engage the hooked end of the adjuster cable in the adjuster lever and locate the adjuster cable over the guide.

21    Pry the adjuster lever until the pivot hook engages in the large hole at the bottom of the secondary shoe.

**All models**

22    Make sure the shoes are correctly centered and install the brake drum (Section 11).

## Adjustment

**Non self-adjusting brakes**

23    Refer to Chapter 1 for the adjustment procedure for non self-adjusting brakes.

**Self-adjusting brakes**

24    Remove the access plug from the backing plate, insert a brake adjusting tool and, after depressing the adjusting lever, rotate the star wheel until the brake shoes are locked against the drum and the wheel won't turn (photo).

25    Back off the star wheel until the drum rotates freely and install the access plug.

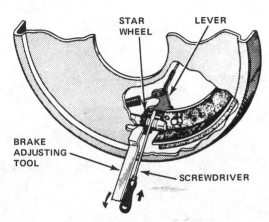

Fig. 9.15  Moving the brake adjuster star wheel with a tool inserted through the hole in the backing plate while unseating the adjuster lever with a screwdriver (Sec 12)

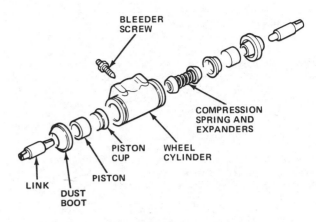

Fig. 9.16  Exploded view of a typical wheel cylinder (Sec 13)

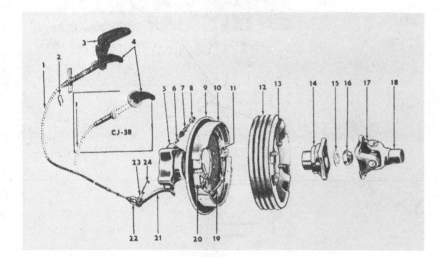

Fig. 9.17  Early model transfer case mounted drum-type parking brake (Sec 14)

| | |
|---|---|
| 1  Cable and conduit | 15  Washer |
| 2  Hand brake clip | 16  Nut |
| 3  Hand brake bracket | 17  Driveshaft flange |
| 4  Hand brake handle | yoke |
| assembly | 18  Rear driveshaft |
| 5  Rear cap | 19  Adjusting end |
| 6  Drive gear bushing | spring |
| 7  Driven gear | 20  Adjusting screw |
| 8  Driven gear sleeve | bracket |
| 9  Backing plate | 21  Operating lever |
| 10  Brake shoe | 22  Clevis |
| 11  Lever end return | 23  Retracting spring |
| spring | clip |
| 12  Brake drum | 24  Retracting spring |
| 13  Bolt | link |
| 14  Rear companion | |
| flange | |

**All models**

26  Install the wheels and lower the vehicle.

27  *On self-adjusting brake-equipped models,* drive the vehicle in forward and reverse while applying the brakes 10 or 15 times to complete adjustment.

---

**13  Wheel cylinder — removal, overhaul and installation**

1  If the wheel cylinder is leaking fluid around the piston, it should be removed and overhauled to restore braking performance. Before disassembling it, read through this entire procedure and make sure you have the correct rebuild kit. Also, you will need some new, clean brake fluid of the recommended type and some clean rags. Note: *Disassembly, overhaul and reassembly of the wheel cylinder must be done in a spotlessly clean work area to avoid contamination and possible failure of the brake hydraulic system components. If such a work area is not available, have it rebuilt by a dealer service department or a service station.*

2  Refer to Section 12 for the brake shoe removal procedure.

3  Although it is possible to overhaul a wheel cylinder while it is still attached to the backing plate, it is recommended that it be removed. To do this, disconnect the brake line from the cylinder and either plug the line or seal the master cylinder reservoir with a sheet of thin plastic to prevent loss of fluid and to keep contaminants from entering the brake system.

4  Remove the two small bolts on the back side of the backing plate which hold the cylinder to the plate. Remove the cylinder.

5  Next, carefully remove the rubber dust boot with your fingers.

6  You can now remove all the remaining parts within the cylinder housing; both pistons, the cups and the compression spring and expanders. An easy way to remove these parts is by tapping the cylinder on a piece of wood.

7  Examine the mating surfaces of the pistons and the cylinder walls. If there is scoring, evidence of metal-to-metal contact or bright wear areas, replace the complete cylinder assembly with a new one.

8  If the metal components are in good condition, discard the rubber boots and the cylinder cups and replace them with the new parts from the rebuild kit.

9  Thoroughly clean all the parts with new brake fluid. When cleaning the brake cylinder walls, wrap a clean white cloth around a stick and soak it in new brake fluid. Insert the stick, first in one side of the cylinder and then the other, and rotate it several times. Do not use a push-pull movement.

10  If the bleeder screw is stripped or damaged, replace it with a new one. If it is in good condition, use compressed air and blow out any foreign material that might block it and hinder the flow of brake fluid when bleeding the system.

11  You can now prepare the parts for reassembly. If your rebuild kit comes with a package of special grease, coat the piston cups, pistons and inside walls of the cylinder with it. If not, then coat these same parts with new, clean brake fluid.

12  Insert the spring first. Then, from either end of the cylinder, insert the piston cups, followed by the pistons. **Note:** *Make sure these parts are inserted correctly.*

13  Install the boots on the brake cylinder, then attach the cylinder to the backing plate and hook up the line.

14  Refer to Section 12 for the brake shoe installation procedure.

9

## 14  Parking brake — adjustment

1    Two types of parking brakes are used on these models. Early models used a drum brake located at the rear of the transfer case which locked the driveshaft and rear wheels when applied. On later models, the rear brake shoes are actuated by a system of levers and cables when the parking brake lever or foot pedal is applied.

2    Before adjusting either type of parking brake, first inspect the cables, connections and mechanism for damage, binding and corrosion. Replace any damaged components with new ones.

### Transfer case mounted drum-type parking brake

3    Make sure the brake handle is completely released and rotate the drum until one pair of the three sets of holes is over the adjusting screw star wheels in the brake.

4    Use the edge of the holes as a fulcrum for an adjusting tool or screwdriver and rotate each star wheel by moving the tool away from the center of the driveshaft until the shoes are locked against the drum.

5    Back the star wheels off seven (7) notches to achieve the proper running clearance. The operating lever-to-backing plate clearance should be 3/32-inch as shown in the accompanying illustration.

### Cable-operated rear brake shoe parking brake

6    Block the front wheels securely. Raise the rear of the vehicle and support it on jackstands.

7    Make sure the parking brake is released and loosen the parking brake cable equalizer locknut.

8    Tighten the equalizer nut until there is a slight drag when the rear wheels are turned.

9    Loosen the nut sufficiently to allow the rear wheels to turn freely and tighten the locknut.

10   Lower the vehicle.

Fig. 9.18   Early model drum-type parking brake adjustment (Sec 14)

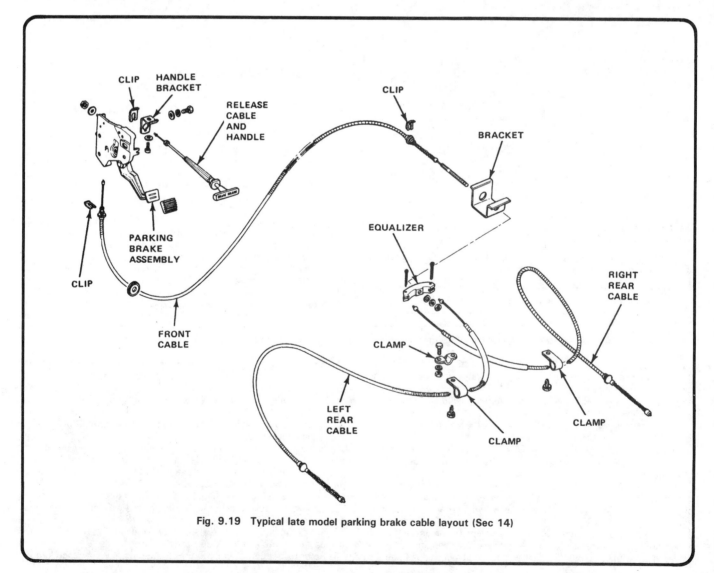

Fig. 9.19   Typical late model parking brake cable layout (Sec 14)

## 15 Transfer case mounted drum-type parking brake — shoe replacement

1 Raise the rear of the vehicle and support it securely on jackstands.
2 Remove the four mounting nuts and lower the driveshaft out of the way.
3 Remove the retracting spring clevis pin and spring pin, followed by the locknut, nut and washer from the transfer case output shaft. Use a puller to remove the universal joint companion flange and brake drum.
4 Remove the retracting springs and separate the brake shoes from the backing plate.
5 Carefully brush away any accumulations of dirt and dust from the backing plate and adjusting screw mechanism. **Note:** *Make an effort not to inhale this dust; it contains asbestos, which is harmful to your health.*
6 Before installing new shoes, back off the adjusting star wheels to the fully off position and lubricate the contact surfaces of the backing plate, brake shoes and adjuster mechanism with a small amount of high-temperature grease.
7 Install the brake shoes and return springs. The yellow spring fits next to the notched adjusting wheel screw and the black spring next to the cam.
8 Install the brake drum and universal joint flange and adjust the brake (Section 14).
9 Install the driveshaft and lower the vehicle.

## 16 Master cylinder — removal and installation

1 Place rags or newspapers under the master cylinder to catch and soak up any brake fluid that might spill during removal. **Note:** *Be careful not to spill any fluid on the painted surfaces of the vehicle as it will damage the paint. Wipe up any spilled fluid immediately.*
2 *On vehicles without a vacuum booster system,* disconnect the brake pushrod from the brake pedal.
3 Disconnect and plug the brake lines at the master cylinder.
4 Unbolt the master cylinder and lift it from the engine compartment.
5 Check for fluid leakage around the flange area at the base of the piston. If there is evidence of leakage, the master cylinder should be overhauled (Section 17 or 18) or replaced with a new or rebuilt unit.
6 Prior to installation, the master cylinder should be bled. Connect two lengths of tubing and actuate the piston(s) until the unit is primed with clean fluid and all air is bled out as shown in the accompanying illustration. If the master cylinder is not bled before installation, it can be done later when the brakes are bled (Section 3). It is recommended, however, that the unit be primed first.

7 Install the master cylinder and, on non-vacuum booster-equipped models, connect the pushrod to the brake pedal.
8 Connect the brake lines to the master cylinder.
9 Bleed the brake system (Section 3).

## 17 Single piston master cylinder — overhaul

1 Early models were equipped with single brake systems, which required only a single piston in the master cylinder.
2 Before the master cylinder is removed (Section 16), obtain the proper rebuild kit and read through the following procedure to make sure you have the correct kit. You will also need some new brake fluid of the recommended type and some clean rags. **Note:** *Disassembly, overhaul and reassembly of the master cylinder must be done in a spotlessly clean work area to avoid contamination and possible failure of the brake hydraulic system components. If such a work area is not available, have it rebuilt by a dealer service department or a properly equipped shop.*
3 Drain the fluid from the reservoir into a container and wash the master cylinder with denatured alcohol or clean brake fluid.
4 Dismantle the master cylinder by referring to the accompanying illustration. Wash the components with denatured alcohol or clean brake fluid.
5 Inspect the cylinder bore for heavy scoring, scratches and corrosion. Make sure the passages between the reservoir and piston bore are open and free of foreign material. Clean them with a wire if necessary. Light scratches or roughness in the bore can be removed by honing but a new unit should be obtained if the scoring or damage is extensive. The rebuild kit should contain a new piston, primary cup, valve and valve seat.
6 Install the valve seat in the end of the piston bore with the flat surface facing the valve.
7 Install the valve assembly, followed by the return spring and primary cup with the flat side of the cup toward the piston.
8 Install the piston, stop plate and lock wire retainer spring.
9 Install the fitting connection, using a new gasket.
10 Fill the reservoir half full of new, clean brake fluid and bleed the master cylinder as described in Section 16.

## 18 Dual piston master cylinder — overhaul

1 If the cylinder is leaking fluid around the piston, it should be removed and overhauled to restore braking performance. Before disassembling it, read through this procedure and make sure you have the correct rebuild kit. When you purchase the rebuild kit from your dealer, be sure

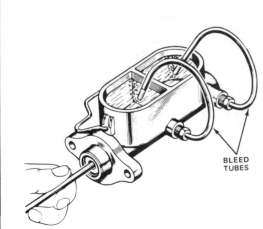

Fig. 9.20 Bleeding air from the master cylinder (Sec 16)

BLEED TUBES

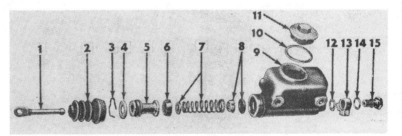

Fig. 9.21 Typical single piston master cylinder — exploded view (Sec 17)

| | |
|---|---|
| 1 Pushrod | 8 Piston valve seat |
| 2 Boot | 9 Reservoir |
| 3 Piston stop lock wire | 10 Filler cap gasket |
| 4 Stop plate | 11 Filler cap |
| 5 Piston | 12 Outlet fitting gasket |
| 6 Master cylinder cup | 13 Outlet fitting |
| 7 Return spring | 14 Outlet fitting bolt gasket |

9

to get two spare brake line fitting nuts also. You will need them to install the new tube seats. Also, you will need some new, clean brake fluid of the recommended type and some clean rags. **Note:** *Disassembly, overhaul and reassembly of the master cylinder must be done in a spotlessly clean work area to avoid contamination and possible failure of the brake hydraulic system components. If such a work area is not available, have it rebuilt by a dealer service department or a properly equipped shop.*

2    *On models built through 1975,* unscrew and remove the primary piston stop bolt located on the bottom of the master cylinder.

3    *On models with manual brakes,* slide the pushrod boot back and remove the retainer clip or snap-ring, pushrod and boot.

4    Press the primary spring in, using the pushrod or tool. Remove the snap-ring from the groove in the piston.

5    Remove and discard the primary piston assembly. A complete piston assembly is supplied with the rebuild kit.

6    Remove the secondary piston assembly by applying air pressure through the compensator port in the front reservoir.

7    On some models the residual check valves must be removed. To gain access to the check valves, the outlet tube seats must be removed with the self-tapping screws supplied in the rebuild kit. Thread the self-tapping screws into the tube seats and place two screwdriver tips under the screw head. Carefully pry the screw up and remove the tube seat.

8    Wash all metal parts with clean brake fluid or brake cleaning solvent. Use air pressure to remove dirt and cleaning solvent from the recesses and internal passages.

9    *On 1976 and later models* there are no check valves and the tube

seats rarely need replacement. If the seats are cracked, scored, loose or cocked in the fluid outlet port, they should be replaced. It might be preferable to buy a rebuilt master cylinder. Read through the entire procedure below before attempting to replace the tube seats on later model master cylinders.

   a)  Enlarge the holes in the tube seats using a 13/64-inch drill bit.
   b)  Place a flat washer on each tube seat and thread a 1/4-20 x 3/4-inch screw into the seat.
   c)  Tighten the screw until the tube seat is loose and remove the seat, screw and washer.
   d)  Remove all chips using compressed air and alcohol or brake cleaning solvent.
   e)  Install the tube fitting seats using the spare brake line fitting nuts to press the seats into place. Do not allow the seats to become cocked during installation and be sure the seats are completely bottomed.
   f)  Remove the brake line fitting nuts, remove all chips or burrs and rinse the master cylinder with alcohol or brake cleaning solvent. Blow out all passages using filtered compressed air.

10  Inspect the master cylinder bore for severe scoring, corrosion, pitting and damage. Replace the master cylinder with a new one if the imperfections in the bore cannot be removed by honing.

11  Before reassembly, dip each component in clean brake fluid.

12  *On models built through 1975,* install the piston washer, rear seal, protector and return spring on the secondary piston. Install the O-ring and front seal on the secondary piston. Be sure the flat faces of both seals face each other.

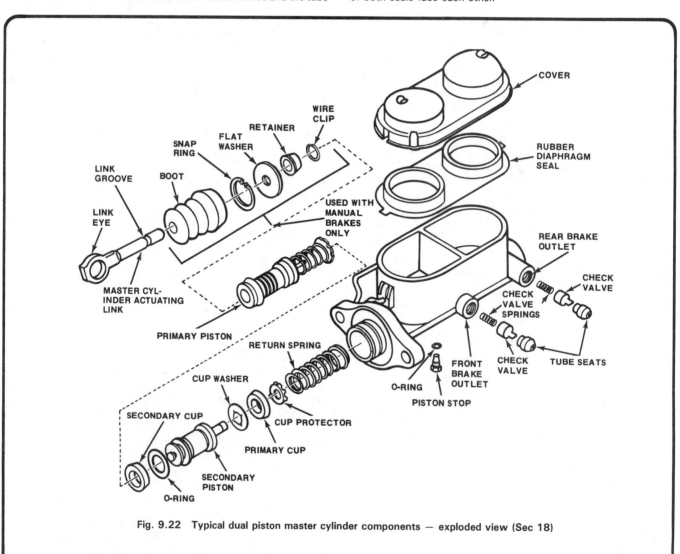

Fig. 9.22  Typical dual piston master cylinder components — exploded view (Sec 18)

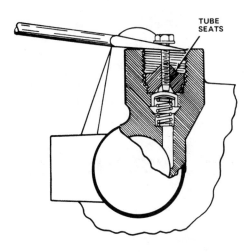

TUBE
SEATS

Fig. 9.23  Tube seat removal (Sec 18)

13  *On 1976 through 1983 models,* install the piston cups on the secondary piston. The cup installed in the groove at the end of the piston should have its lip facing *away* from the piston and the next cup lip should face *toward* the piston. Install the seal protector, piston seal, spring retainer and spring on the secondary piston. The piston seal lip should face the *interior* of the cylinder bore when the assembly is installed.

14  Lubricate the piston bore and piston assemblies with clean brake fluid.

15  Install the secondary piston assembly, spring end first, in the piston bore. Press the primary piston in using the pushrod or a tool. Secure the pistons in the bore with the snap-ring.

16  On models so equipped, install the piston stop, using a new O-ring.

17  On check valve-equipped models, place the new check valves over the check valve springs and install them in the fluid outlet holes, spring end first.

18  Install the tube seats (if removed) and press them into place with the brake line fitting nuts.

19  *On vehicles without power brakes,* install the pushrod and boot assembly.

20  Before the master cylinder is installed on the vehicle, the unit should be bled. Refer to Section 16 for the master cylinder bleeding procedure.

9

# Chapter 10   Chassis electrical system

## Contents

Battery check and maintenance . . . . . . . . . . . . . . .   Chapter 1
Bulb replacement . . . . . . . . . . . . . . . . . . . . . . . . . . . . .   5
Directional switch — check and replacement . . . . . . . . . . .   12
Electrical troubleshooting — general information . . . . . . . . .   2
Fuses and fusible links — general information . . . . . . . . . . .   3
General information . . . . . . . . . . . . . . . . . . . . . . . . . . . .   1
Headlight dimmer switch — check, removal and
   installation . . . . . . . . . . . . . . . . . . . . . . . . . . . . . . .   8
Headlight switch — removal and installation . . . . . . . . . . . .   7

Headlight replacement . . . . . . . . . . . . . . . . . . . . . . . . . . .   4
Horn — check and replacement . . . . . . . . . . . . . . . . . . . .   13
Ignition switch — removal and installation . . . . . . . . . . . . .   6
Instrument cluster — removal and installation . . . . . . . . . . .   14
Neutral safety switch — check, adjustment and
   replacement . . . . . . . . . . . . . . . . . . . . . . . . . . .   Chapter 7B
Speedometer — removal and installation . . . . . . . . . . . . . .   10
Speedometer cable — check, removal and installation . . . . . .   11
Windshield wiper motor — removal and installation . . . . . . . .   9

## Specifications

## Bulb application

| | Bulb type |
|---|---|
| **F- and L-head four-cylinder engine (6-volt system)** | |
| Headlight . . . . . . . . . . . . . . . . . . . . . . . . . . . . . . . . . | 5040-S or 6006 |
| Parking light . . . . . . . . . . . . . . . . . . . . . . . . . . . . . . . | 63 |
| Park and directional signal light . . . . . . . . . . . . . . . . . . . | 1158 |
| Stop, tail and directional signal light . . . . . . . . . . . . . . . . | 1158 |
| Instrument cluster lights . . . . . . . . . . . . . . . . . . . . . . . . | 51 |
| Instrument light . . . . . . . . . . . . . . . . . . . . . . . . . . . . . . | 55 |
| Flasher and directional signal lights . . . . . . . . . . . . . . . . . | P229D |
| **F-head four-cylinder and V6 engines (12-volt system)** | |
| Headlight . . . . . . . . . . . . . . . . . . . . . . . . . . . . . . . . . | 6012 |
| Parking and directional signal lights . . . . . . . . . . . . . . . . . | 1157NA |
| License plate light . . . . . . . . . . . . . . . . . . . . . . . . . . . . | 1155 |
| Side marker light . . . . . . . . . . . . . . . . . . . . . . . . . . . . . | 194 |
| Instrument cluster light . . . . . . . . . . . . . . . . . . . . . . . . . | 57 |
| Backup light indicator . . . . . . . . . . . . . . . . . . . . . . . . . . | 1156 |
| Hazard flasher light . . . . . . . . . . . . . . . . . . . . . . . . . . . | 57 |
| Brake warning light . . . . . . . . . . . . . . . . . . . . . . . . . . . | 57 |
| **All others (1972 and 1973)** | |
| Headlight . . . . . . . . . . . . . . . . . . . . . . . . . . . . . . . . . | 6012 |
| Parking and directional signal lights . . . . . . . . . . . . . . . . . | 1157NA |
| Side marker lights . . . . . . . . . . . . . . . . . . . . . . . . . . . . | 194 |
| Backup light . . . . . . . . . . . . . . . . . . . . . . . . . . . . . . . . | 1156 |
| License plate light . . . . . . . . . . . . . . . . . . . . . . . . . . . . | 1155 |
| Stop, tail and directional signal light . . . . . . . . . . . . . . . . | 1157 |
| Brake failure light . . . . . . . . . . . . . . . . . . . . . . . . . . . . | 57 |
| Charge, directional signal and high beam lights . . . . . . . . . | 53 |
| Directional signal flasher . . . . . . . . . . . . . . . . . . . . . . . . | Type 144 |
| Glove box light . . . . . . . . . . . . . . . . . . . . . . . . . . . . . . | 170 |
| Hazard warning, heater controls, instrument cluster and oil | |
|    pressure gauge lights . . . . . . . . . . . . . . . . . . . . . . . . | 57 |
| **All others (1974 through 1983)** | |
| Headlight . . . . . . . . . . . . . . . . . . . . . . . . . . . . . . . . . | 6014 |
| Parking and directional signal lights . . . . . . . . . . . . . . . . . | 1157 |
| Side marker lights . . . . . . . . . . . . . . . . . . . . . . . . . . . . | 194 |
| Backup light . . . . . . . . . . . . . . . . . . . . . . . . . . . . . . . . | 1156 |
| Stop, tail and directional signal light . . . . . . . . . . . . . . . . | 1157 |
| Instrument cluster lights . . . . . . . . . . . . . . . . . . . . . . . . | 53 |
| Indicator lights . . . . . . . . . . . . . . . . . . . . . . . . . . . . . . | 53 |
| Clock light . . . . . . . . . . . . . . . . . . . . . . . . . . . . . . . . . | 1892 |
| Automatic transmission column light . . . . . . . . . . . . . . . . | 1892 |
| Tachometer light . . . . . . . . . . . . . . . . . . . . . . . . . . . . . | 1895 |
| Radio light . . . . . . . . . . . . . . . . . . . . . . . . . . . . . . . . . | 1893 |

# Fuse application

| | Amperage |
|---|---|
| **F- and L-head four-cylinder engine (6-volt system)** | |
| Heater | 14 |
| Directional signal | 14 |
| **F- and L-head four-cylinder and V6 engines** | |
| Heater | 9 |
| Backup light | 14 |
| Windshield wiper | 14 |
| Directional signal | 9 |
| 4-way flasher | 14 |
| Brake warning light | 9 |
| **All others (1972 through 1974)** | |
| Directional signal | 9 |
| Backup lights | 9 |
| Brake warning light | 9 |
| Cigar lighter | 14 |
| Air-conditioner | 25 |
| Heater | 15 |
| 4-way flasher | 14 |
| Headlight circuit breaker | 25 |
| Control panel circuit breaker | 25 |
| **All others (1975 through 1977)** | |
| Directional signal | 10 |
| Backup lights | |
| 1975 | 9 |
| 1976 and 1977 | 15 |
| Brake warning light | |
| 1975 | 9 |
| 1976 and 1977 | 3 |
| Cigar lighter | 15 |
| Air-conditioner | 25 |
| Heater | 25 |
| Headlight circuit breaker | 24 |
| Instrument cluster | 3 |
| Windshield washer/wiper | 10 |
| Tail and stop lights | 20 |
| Radio | 10 (5 amp in-line) |
| Panel lights | 3 |
| **All others (1978 through 1983)** | Refer to fuse panel |

## 1  General information

This Chapter covers the repair and service procedures for the various electrical components not associated with the engine, as well as general information concerning troubleshooting the electrical circuits. Information about the battery, generator or alternator, distributor and starter motor can be found in Chapter 5.

The electrical system is a 6-volt (early models) or 12-volt, negative ground type with power supplied by a generator (early models) or alternator.

It should be noted that whenever portions of the electrical system are worked on, the negative battery cable should be disconnected to prevent electrical shorts and/or fires.

## 2  Electrical troubleshooting — general information

A typical electrical circuit consists of an electrical component, any switches, relays, motors, etc. related to that component and the wiring and connectors that connect the component to both the battery and the chassis. To aid in locating a problem in any electrical circuit, wiring diagrams for each model are included at the end of this Chapter.

Before tackling any troublesome electrical circuit, first study the appropriate diagrams to get a complete understanding of what makes up that individual circuit. Trouble spots, for instance, can often be narrowed down by noting if other components related to that circuit are operating properly or not. If several components or circuits fail at one time, chances are the problem lies in the fuse or ground connection, as several circuits often are routed through the same fuse and ground connections.

Electrical problems often stem from simple causes, such as loose or corroded connections, a blown fuse or melted fusible link. Prior to any electrical troubleshooting, always visually check the condition of the fuse, wires and connections in the problem circuit.

If testing instruments are going to be utilized, use the diagrams to plan ahead of time where you will make the necessary connections in order to accurately pinpoint the trouble spot.

The basic tools needed for electrical troubleshooting include a circuit tester or voltmeter (a 12-volt bulb with a set of test leads can also be used), a continuity tester (which includes a bulb, battery and set of test leads) and a jumper wire, preferably with a circuit breaker incorporated, which can be used to bypass electrical components.

Voltage checks should be performed if a circuit is not functioning properly. Connect one lead of a circuit tester to either the negative battery terminal or a known good ground. Connect the other lead to a connector in the circuit being tested, preferably nearest to the battery or fuse. If the bulb of the tester goes on, voltage is reaching that point (which means the part of the circuit between that connector and the battery is problem free). Continue checking along the entire circuit in the same fashion. When you reach a point where no voltage is present, the problem lies between there and the last good test point. Most of the time the problem is due to a loose connection. *Keep in mind that some circuits receive voltage only when the ignition key is in the Accessory or Run position.*

A method of finding shorts in a circuit is to remove the fuse and connect a test light or voltmeter in its place to the fuse terminals. There should be no load in the circuit. Move the wiring harness from side-to-side while watching the test light. If the bulb goes on, there is a short to ground somewhere in that area, probably where insulation has rubbed off of a wire. The same test can be performed on other components of the circuit, including the switch.

A ground check should be done to see if a component is grounded properly. Disconnect the battery and connect one lead of a self-powered test light such as a continuity tester to a known good ground. Connect the other lead to the wire or ground connection being tested. If the bulb goes on, the ground is good. If the bulb does not go on, the

**10**

ground is not good.

A continuity check is performed to see if a circuit, section of circuit or individual component is passing electricity through it properly. Disconnect the battery and connect one lead of a self-powered test light such as a continuity tester to one end of the circuit. If the bulb goes on, there is continuity, which means the circuit is passing electricity through it properly. Switches can be checked in the same way.

Remember that all electrical circuits are composed basically of electricity running from the battery, through the wires, switches, relays, etc. to the electrical component (light bulb, motor, etc.). From there it is run to the body (ground) where it is passed back to the battery. Any electrical problem is basically an interruption in the flow of electricity to and from the battery.

## 3   Fuses and fusible links — general information

The electrical circuits of the vehicle are protected by a combination of fuses and fusible links.

The fuse panel is located under the dash in the main electrical harness. Later models also incorporate circuit breakers for certain circuits and components.

Each of the fuses is designed to protect a specific circuit as identified on the fuse panel. If an electrical component has failed, your first check shold be the fuse. A fuse which has ''blown'' can be readily identified by inspecting the metal element inside the housing. If the element is broken, the fuse is inoperable and should be replaced with a new one. Circuit breakers reset automatically when the circuit is turned off. Fuses can be replaced by pulling out the old one and pushing in the new one.

It is important that the correct fuse be installed. The different electrical circuits need varying amounts of protection, indicated by the amperage rating on the fuse. A fuse with too low a rating will blow prematurely, while a fuse with too high a rating may not blow soon enough to avoid serious damage to other components or the wiring. *Never bypass the fuse with metal or foil. Serious damage to the electrical system could result.*

If the replacement fuse immediately fails, do not replace it with another until the cause of the problem is isolated and corrected. In most cases it will be a short circuit in the wiring caused by a broken or deteriorated wire.

In addition to fuses, the electrical system incorporates fusible links for overload protection. These links are used in circuits which are not ordinarily fused. The fusible links are located in the engine compartment and are replaced by unsoldering the ends and then soldering a replacement in place. The link must be wrapped with electrical tape.

If an electrical failure occurs in one of the circuits protected by a fusible link, check the link first. If the link is melted, replace it with a new one, but only after checking and correcting the electrical fault that caused the failure.

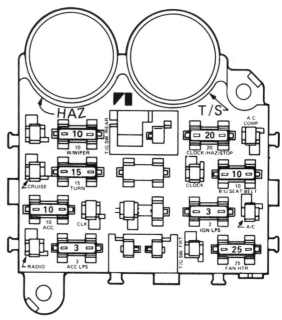

Fig. 10.1   Typical late model fuse panel (Sec 3)

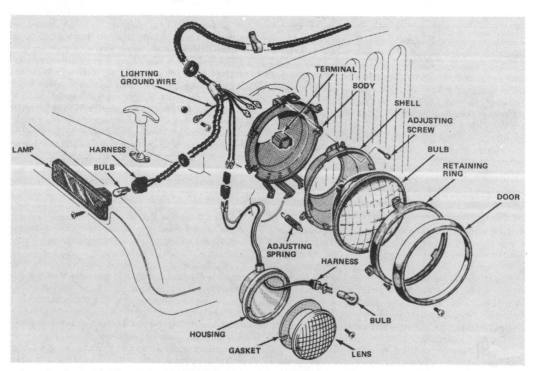

Fig. 10.2   Typical later model headlight and parking/directional light components — exploded view (Sec 4)

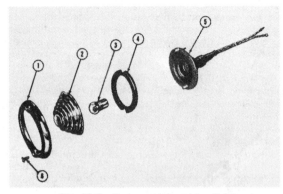

**Fig. 10.3  Early model parking light components — exploded view (Sec 5)**

| | | |
|---|---|---|
| 1 Bezel | 3 Bulb | 5 Housing |
| 2 Lens | 4 Gasket | 6 Screw |

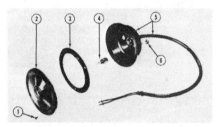

**Fig. 10.4  Early model tail, stop and directional light components (Sec 5)**

| | |
|---|---|
| 1 Screw | 4 Bulb |
| 2 Lens | 5 Housing and wire assembly |
| 3 Gasket | 6 Nut and washer |

### 4  Headlight replacement

1  Remove the headlight door attaching screw.
2  Pull the headlight door out slightly at the bottom, push up to disengage the upper retaining tab and lift the door off.
3  Loosen the headlight retaining ring screws, rotate the ring to disengage it and lift it away.
4  Pull the headlight out of the shell, unplug the connector and remove the headlight.
5  Plug the connector securely into the new headlight.
6  Place the headlight in the shell and install the retaining ring and door.

### 5  Bulb replacement

#### Parking/directional signal light
1  Remove the retaining screws, bezel, lens and gasket. Remove the bulb from the housing.
2  Install the new bulb, followed by the gasket, lens and bezel.

#### Side marker light
3  Remove the retaining screws and lift off the side marker light lens.
4  Grasp the bulb firmly and pull it from the socket.
5  Insert the new bulb and install the lens and screws.

#### Tail, stop, license and backup light
6  Remove the taillight lens, screws and gasket.
7  On later models, the backup light bulb is located in the taillight housing and the stop light bulb on the left side also illuminates the license plate.
8  On early models, the backup light is contained in a separate housing. Remove the snap-ring, lens and gasket to gain access to the bulb.
9  Replacement is the reverse of removal.

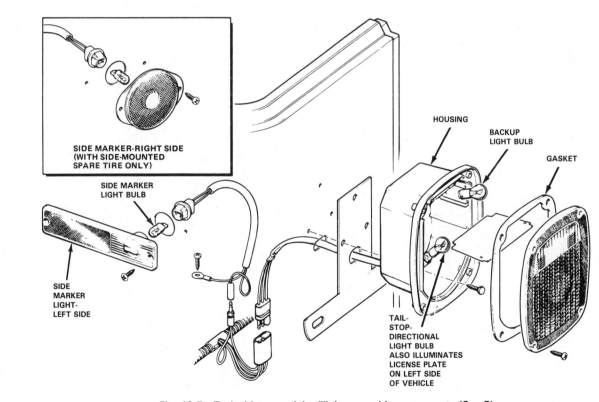

**Fig. 10.5  Typical later model taillight assembly components (Sec 5)**

**10**

## 6  Ignition switch — removal and installation

### 1953 through 1975 models

1    The ignition switch on these models is located in the instrument panel adjacent to the steering column.

2    The switch is held in place by a threaded bezel nut and, on later models, a tension spring. To remove the switch, press the body of the switch toward the instrument panel until the bezel can be turned counterclockwise and released from the notch pins.

3    Remove the bezel and pull the switch body back to release the spring tension.

4    Lower the switch from the dash and unplug it from the wiring harness.

5    To remove the cylinder from the switch, turn the switch to the On position and insert a piece of heavy wire through the cylinder release hole. Depress the spring loaded brass retainer ring until it clears the retaining ridge, allowing the cylinder to be withdrawn.

6    To install the cylinder, align the tang with the slot in the case, depress the retainer and insert the cylinder until the retainer snaps into place.

7    To install the switch, place the main compression spring on the switch body and then install the body in the instrument panel from the rear.

8    Insert the ignition key in the Off position and turn the switch body until the key is straight up and down.

9    Remove the key and push on the switch body so the notched bezel can be easily installed with the notches aligned with the notch pins.

10   Rotate the bezel clockwise to lock it in position with the word ''Starter'' at the top.

### 1976 through 1983 models

11   The ignition switch on these models is located on the lower section of the steering column and is connected to the key lock assembly by a remote lock rod. Two types of ignition switches are used: one for standard steering columns and another for tilt columns.

**Removal**

12   To remove either type of switch, place the key in the Off/Lock position and remove the two switch mounting screws. Disconnect the switch from the remote rod, unplug the harness connector and remove the switch from the column.

**Installation (standard column)**

13   Position the switch as shown in the accompanying illustration, with the actuator rod disconnected.

14   Move the slider to the extreme left, or Accessory position, position the actuator rod in the slider hole and attach the switch to the steering column taking care not to move the slider out of the detent. The right side of the switch must be toward the steering wheel.

15   Hold the key in the Accessory position and then push the switch down the column slightly to remove the slack from the actuator rod.

16   Tighten the mounting screws securely and install the white connector, followed by the black connector.

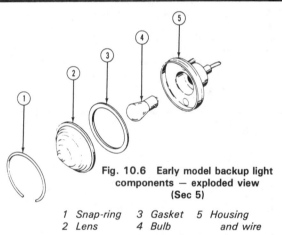

Fig. 10.6  Early model backup light components — exploded view (Sec 5)

1  Snap-ring    3  Gasket    5  Housing
2  Lens         4  Bulb          and wire

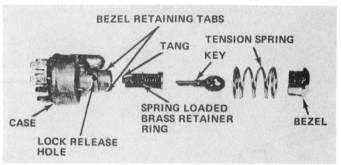

Fig. 10.7  Typical dash mounted ignition switch (Sec 6)

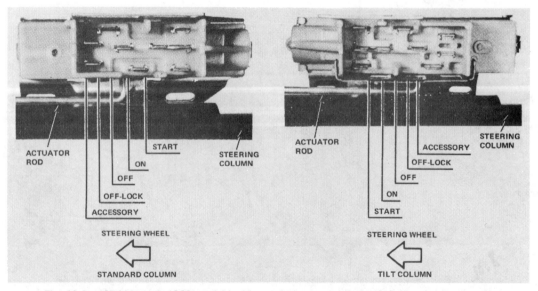

Fig. 10.8  1976 through 1983 model ignition switch actuator rod installation details (Sec 6)

**Installation (tilt column)**

17  With the actuator rod disconnected, place the switch in position as shown in the accompanying illustration.

18  Move the slider to the extreme right or Accessory position, the right side of the switch must face down, away from the steering column.

19  Position the actuator rod in the slider hole and attach the switch to the steering column with the screws finger tight.

20  Push the switch down lightly to remove the play from the actuator rod while holding the key in the Accessory position and taking care not to move the slider out of the detent.

21  Tighten the screws securely and plug in the white connector, followed by the black connector.

---

### 7  Headlight switch — removal and installation

1  Disconnect the negative battery cable from the battery.

2  Pull the light switch knob out to the On position.

3  Remove the switch knob. On some models the knob is retained by a setscrew or locknut while on others the entire knob and stem assembly can be withdrawn from the switch after pressing the release button on the switch.

4  Remove the switch retaining nut and bezel.

5  Lower the switch from the dash panel, disconnect it from the wiring harness and remove it.

6  To install the switch, connect the wiring harness, place the switch in position in the dash and install the nut and bezel. Install the control knob.

7  Connect the battery cable.

---

### 8  Headlight dimmer switch — check, removal and installation

1  The switch operation can be checked with a test light. Connect one test light lead to the switch input terminal and probe each output terminal with the other lead as the switch is operated. The current flow should alternate from one output terminal to the other as the switch is operated. Replace a faulty switch with a new one as follows:

2  Disconnect the negative battery cable from the battery.

3  In the engine compartment, disconnect the wiring harness, remove the retaining screws and separate the dimmer switch from the floorboard.

4  To install the switch, place it in position, install the retaining screws and connect the wiring harness.

5  Connect the battery cable to the battery.

---

### 9  Windshield wiper motor — removal and installation

*1953 through 1970 models*

1  Disconnect the vacuum hose, remove the mounting screws and lift the motor away. Installation is the reverse of removal.

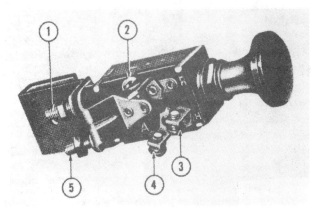

Fig. 10.9  Early model headlight switch terminals (Sec 7)

  1  Battery          4  Parking lights
  2  Rear lights      5  Auxiliary
  3  Headlights

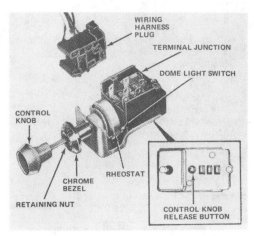

Fig. 10.10  Late model headlight switch (Sec 7)

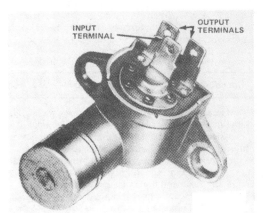

Fig. 10.11  Headlight dimmer switch terminals (Sec 8)

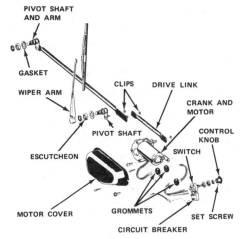

Fig. 10.12  Windshield wiper motor component layout
(1970 through 1976 models) (Sec 9)

**10**

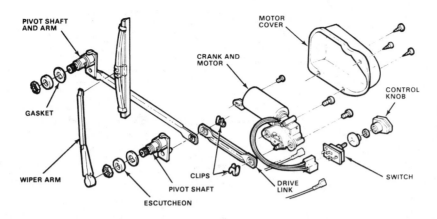

Fig. 10.13  1977 through 1983 model windshield wiper components (Sec 9)

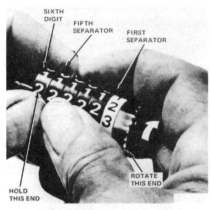

Fig. 10.14  To set the odometer, hold the 5th separator while rotating the last 5 numbers until the 6th number is obtained (repeat the procedure until the proper number alignment is achieved) (Sec 10)

Fig. 10.15  Removing the steering column lock plate (Sec 12)

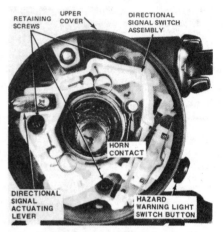

Fig. 10.16  Directional signal assembly installation details (Sec 12)

### 1971 through 1975 models

2    Remove the dash crash pad (if equipped).
3    Remove the plastic hole plug from the extreme left side of the bottom of the windshield frame air duct.
4    Disconnect the drive link from the motor crank.
5    Mark their locations and disconnect the wires from the switch.
6    Remove the cover and motor
7    Prior to installation, apply a bead of waterproof sealant around the contact surface of the motor cover. Install the motor, followed by the cover.
8    Connect the wires to the switch and the drive link to the motor crank.
9    Install the plastic hole plug and (if equipped) the crash pad.

### 1976 through 1983 models

10    Remove the crash pad (if equipped) and wiper motor cover.
11    Remove the hold-down knobs and fold the windshield down.
12    Remove the left access hole cover and disconnect the drive link from the left wiper pivot.
13    Unplug the wiring harness from the switch.
14    Remove the mounting screws and lift the motor from the vehicle.
15    Place the wiper motor in position, install the screws and connect the wiring harness to the switch.
16    Install the access hole cover and raise the windshield.
17    Install the crash pad (if equipped) and motor cover.

### 10    Speedometer — removal and installation

1    Remove the instrument cluster (Section 14).

2    Carefully uncrimp the bezel outer lip and remove the outer bezel, glass and retaining bezel.
3    Remove the mounting screws and separate the speedometer from the housing.
4    If the speedometer is being replaced with a new one, push down on the odometer retaining clip and twist it to disengage it and remove the odometer. Set the odometer to the proper mileage and install it, using needle-nose pliers. Be careful not to force the clip against the dial face.
5    Install the speedometer in the housing. Check the inside of the glass to make sure it is clean and free of fingerprints and install it along with the bezels. Carefully crimp the outer bezel in place in four places.
6    Install the instrument cluster.

### 11    Speedometer cable — check, removal and installation

1    A damaged or kinked speedometer cable is indicated if the speedometer is noisy or the needle action is jerky. A lack of lubrication can also cause these symptoms and can be corrected by disconnecting the cable at the speedometer head and squirting powdered graphite lubricant into the cable end and head contact surfaces.
2    To remove the speedometer, disconnect the cable at the speedometer head and transmission, remove the grommet and pull the cable into the engine compartment.
3    To check the cable, place it in an inverted "U" shape on a flat surface and cross the ends. Hold one end of the cable core lightly while turning the other end. The turning action should be smooth; if the core jerks or jumps, the cable should be replaced with a new one.
4    Installation is the reverse of removal. Be sure to lubricate the cable and speedometer head with graphite.

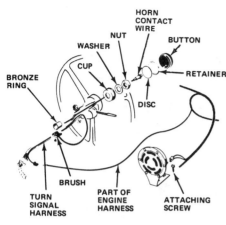

Fig. 10.17 Typical non-relay equipped
horn system layout (Sec 13)

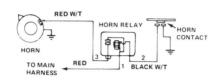

Fig. 10.18 1976 through 1983 relay
equipped horn system terminals
(Sec 13)

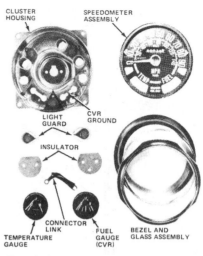

Fig. 10.19 Instrument cluster assembly
components (Sec 13)

## 12 Directional switch — check and replacement

1 Burned out bulbs and loose connections are the most common causes of problems in the directional signal system. If the flashing rate is about twice the normal rate, a shorted out bulb is indicated. If there is no signal at any bulb, check the fuse. If the fuse is good, install a new flasher unit (located in the fuse panel on most models). If the bulbs, fuse, flasher and wiring check out correctly, replace the directional switch.
2 Disconnect the negative battery cable from the battery.
3 *On models built through 1975,* the directional switch is clamped to the left side of the steering column by two Allen head screws. Replacement is accomplished by unplugging the electrical connector, removing the screws and lifting the switch away from the steering column. Installation is the reverse of removal.
4 *On 1976 through 1983 models,* the switch is located in the steering column. Remove the horn button by pulling straight out. Remove the screws, bushing, receiver, spring and steering wheel and nut (Chapter 11).
5 Lift the lock plate cover and use a compressor tool (AMC J-23653) to depress the lock plate as shown in the illustration.
6 Pry the round wire snap-ring from the steering shaft groove and remove the tool, snap-ring, lock plate, directional signal canceling cam, upper bearing preload spring and thrust washer from the steering shaft.
7 Depress the hazard warning light switch on the right side of the column and turn it in a counterclockwise dirrection to remove it.
8 Remove the directional switch wire harness connector block from the mounting bracket on the right side of the column. *On models equipped with an automatic transmission,* insert a stiff wire such as a paper clip into the lock tab retaining the shift quadrant light wire in the connector block.
9 Remove the screws and separate the directional switch and wiring harness from the column.
10 To install the switch, guide the wiring harness into position and align the switch assembly with the actuating lever pivot seated in the upper housing pivot boss and install the screws.
11 Install the switch lever and actuate the switch to make sure the assembly is properly installed.
12 Place the thrust washer, spring and directional signal canceling cam in place on the upper end of the steering shaft.
13 Align the lock plate splines with the steering shaft splines and place the lock plate in position so the directional signal canceling cam shaft protrudes through the dogleg opening in the lockplate.
14 Install the snap-ring, lock plate cover and steering wheel.
15 Install the steering wheel washer and nut, followed by the spring with the raised side up.
16 Install the receiver and bushing, making sure the receiver moves freely after the bushing screws are tightened.
17 Align the notch on the receiver with the nib on the horn button and push the button in until it snaps into place.

## 13 Horn — check and replacement

1 All models are equipped with a horn system consisting of a single horn mounted on the left inner fender well. Battery power activates the horn when the horn button is depressed, completing the circuit.
2 If the horn does not sound, use a test light or voltmeter to check the red (battery feed) wire.
3 A lack of voltage indicates a short circuit or, on later models (after 1975), a burned out fusible link.
4 Inspect the wiring between the horn, relay (on models after 1976) and battery for loose connections, corroded terminals and frayed wires. The horn assembly is attached to the fender well with cadmium plated (corrosion resistant) screws. Make sure they have not been replaced with non-plated screws which may not ground the horn properly.
5 On relay equipped systems (1976 through 1983), ground the number 2 terminal of the relay with a jumper wire. If the horn sounds, the relay and horn are operating properly. If the horn does not sound, ground the number 2 terminal and connect a jumper wire between the number 1 and number 3 terminals. If the horn sounds, the relay is faulty. The relay is encased in plastic and is located in the wiring harness under the left side of the instrument panel. If the relay is good, connect a jumper wire from the horn base to a good ground and repeat the tests. If the horn does not operate, it is faulty and must be replaced with a new one.
6 On non-relay equipped models, if battery power is reaching the horn, ground the black wire with the yellow tracer. If the horn does not sound, the horn assembly is faulty and should be replaced with a new one. If the horn operates, there is a fault in the steering column wiring.
7 To check the steering column wiring on all models, disconnect the negative battery cable, remove the horn button and inspect the horn contact and spring for damage and corrosion.
8 To replace the horn, disconnect the wiring harness plug, remove the screws and lift the assembly from the inner fender well. Installation is the reverse of removal.

## 14 Instrument cluster — removal and installation

1 Disconnect the negative battery cable from the battery.
2 Disconnect the speedometer cable (Section 11).
3 Remove the cluster mounting screws or nuts and lower the cluster assembly. On some models it will be necessary to remove two screws and lower the heater control bracket.
4 Mark their locations and remove the wires and the light bulbs.
5 Separate the cluster from the dash.
6 To install the cluster, connect the bulbs and wires, place the cluster assembly in position and install the mounting screws or nuts. Connect the speedometer cable.
7 Connect the negative battery cable.

**10**

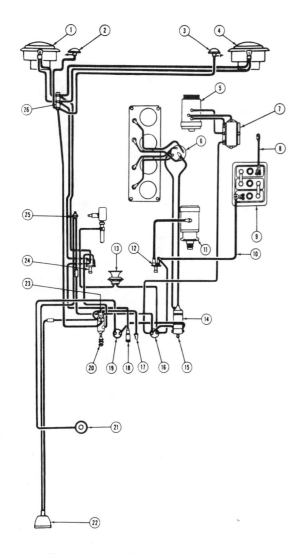

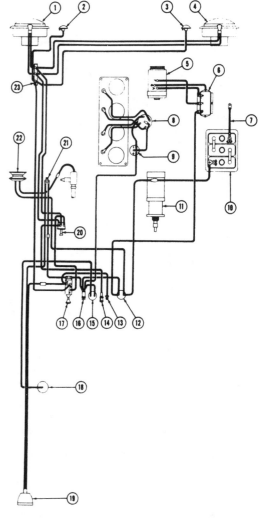

**Fig. 10.20    CJ-2A wiring diagram**

**Fig. 10.21    Early model CJ-3B wiring diagram**

| | | | |
|---|---|---|---|
| 1 | Left headlight | 14 | Ignition coil |
| 2 | Left parking light | 15 | Ignition switch |
| 3 | Right parking light | 16 | Ammeter |
| 4 | Right headlight | 17 | Dash light |
| 5 | Generator | 18 | Tell-tale light |
| 6 | Distributor | 19 | Fuel gauge |
| 7 | Voltage regulator | 20 | Light switch |
| 8 | Negative ground cable | 21 | Fuel gauge sending unit |
| 9 | Battery | 22 | Tail and stop light |
| 10 | Positive cable | 23 | Light switch circuit breaker |
| 11 | Starting motor | 24 | Dimmer switch |
| 12 | Starting switch | 25 | Stop light switch |
| 13 | Horn | 26 | Junction block |

| | | | |
|---|---|---|---|
| 1 | Left headlight | 13 | Dash light |
| 2 | Left parking light | 14 | Indicator light |
| 3 | Right parking light | 15 | Fuel gauge |
| 4 | Right headlight | 16 | Ignition switch |
| 5 | Generator | 17 | Light switch |
| 6 | Voltage regulator | 18 | Fuel gauge sending unit |
| 7 | Negative ground cable | 19 | Tail and stop light |
| 8 | Distributor | 20 | Dimmer switch |
| 9 | Ignition coil | 21 | Stop light switch |
| 10 | Battery | 22 | Horn |
| 11 | Starter motor | 23 | Junction block |
| 12 | Ammeter | | |

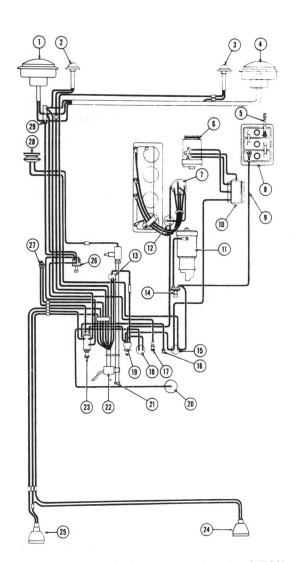

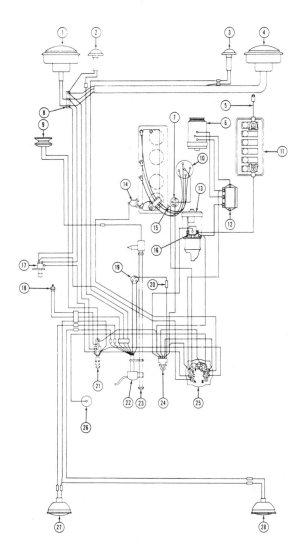

Fig. 10.22  Later model CJ-3B (up to serial number 35522)
wiring diagram

| 1 Left headlight | 17 Indicator light |
|---|---|
| 2 Left parking light | 18 Fuel gauge |
| 3 Right parking light | 19 Ignition switch |
| 4 Right headlight | 20 Fuel gauge sending unit |
| 5 Negative ground cable | 21 Horn button |
| 6 Generator | 22 Directional signal switch |
| 7 Distributor | 23 Light switch |
| 8 Battery | 24 Right tail and stop light |
| 9 Positive cable | 25 Left tail and stop light |
| 10 Voltage regulator | 26 Dimmer switch |
| 11 Starter motor | 27 Stop light switch |
| 12 Ignition coil | 28 Horn |
| 13 Signal flasher | 29 Junction block |
| 14 Starter switch | |
| 15 Ammeter | |
| 16 Dash light | |

Fig. 10.23  Later model CJ-3B (after serial number 35522)
wiring diagram

| 1 Left headlight | 20 Fuse |
|---|---|
| 2 Left parking and signal light | 21 Light switch |
| 3 Right parking and signal light | 22 Directional signal switch |
| 4 Right headlight | 23 Horn button |
| 5 Battery ground strap | 24 Ignition and starter switch |
| 6 Generator | 25 Instrument cluster |
| 7 Ignition coil | A Upper beam indicator |
| 8 Junction block | B Turn signal indicator |
| 9 Horn | C Instrument lights |
| 10 Distributor | D Oil pressure indicator |
| 11 Battery | E Charging indicator |
| 12 Voltage regulator | F Temperature gauge |
| 13 Starter motor | G Fuel gauge |
| 14 Oil pressure sending unit | H Instrument voltage regulator |
| 15 Coolant temperature sending unit | 26 Fuel gauge tank unit |
| 16 Solenoid switch | 27 Left tail and stop light |
| 17 Foot dimmer switch | 28 Right tail and stop light |
| 18 Stop light switch | |
| 19 Directional signal flasher | |

10

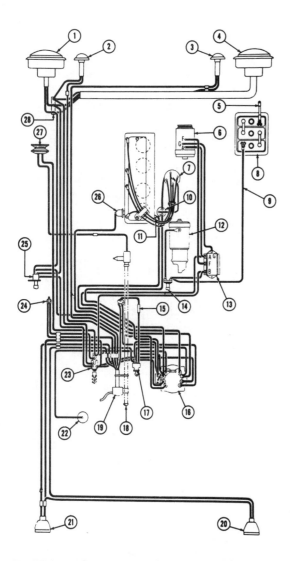

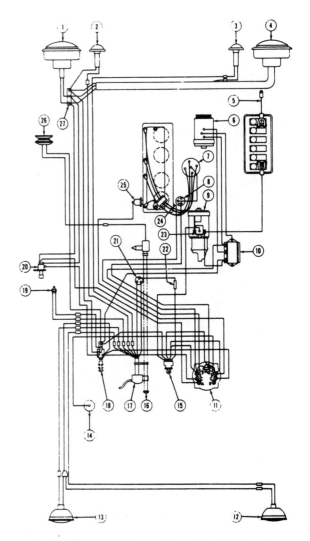

Fig. 10.24   CJ-5 (before serial number 49248) and CJ-6
(before serial number 12577) (with F-head four-cylinder
engine) wiring diagram

1   Left headlight
2   Left parking light
3   Right parking light
4   Right headlight
5   Negative ground cable
6   Generator
7   Distributor
8   Battery
9   Positive cable
10  Ignition coil
11  Coolant temperature
    sending unit
12  Starter motor
13  Voltage regulator
14  Starter switch
15  Fuse
16  Instrument cluster
17  Ignition switch
18  Horn button
19  Directional signal
    switch
20  Right tail and stop
    light
21  Left tail and stop
    light
22  Fuel gauge sending
    unit
23  Light switch
24  Stop light switch
25  Dimmer switch
26  Oil pressure sending
    unit
27  Horn
28  Junction block

Fig. 10.25   CJ-5 (after serial number 49248) and CJ-6
(after serial number 12577) (with F-head four-cylinder
engine) wiring diagram

1   Left headlight
2   Left parking and
    directional light
3   Right parking and
    directional light
4   Right headlight
5   Battery ground cable
6   Generator
7   Distributor
8   Ignition coil
9   Starting motor
10  Voltage regulator
11  Instrument cluster
A   Upper beam indicator
B   Turn signal indicator
C   Instrument lights
D   Oil pressure indicator
E   Charging indicator
F   Temperature gauge
G   Fuel gauge
H   Instrument voltage
    regulator
12  Right tail and stop
    light
13  Left tail and stop light
14  Fuel gauge tank unit
15  Ignition and starter
    switch
16  Horn button
17  Directional signal
    switch
18  Light switch
19  Stop light switch
20  Foot dimmer switch
21  Directional signal
    flasher
22  Fuse
23  Solenoid switch
24  Temperature sending
    unit
25  Oil pressure signal
    switch
26  Horn
27  Junction block

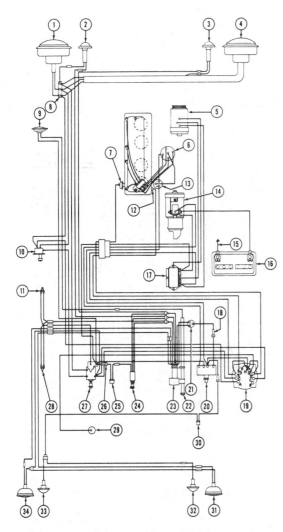

**Fig. 10.26  CJ-5 and CJ-6 (with later model F-head four-cylinder engine) wiring diagram**

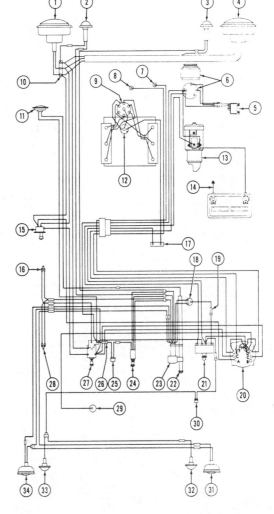

**Fig. 10.27  Early model with V6 engine wiring diagram**

| | | |
|---|---|---|
| 1 | Left headlight | |
| 2 | Left parking and signal light | |
| 3 | Right parking and signal light | |
| 4 | Right headlight | |
| 5 | Generator | |
| 6 | Ignition distributor | |
| 7 | Oil pressure sending unit | |
| 8 | Junction block | |
| 9 | Horn | |
| 10 | Foot dimmer switch | |
| 11 | Stop light switch — front | |
| 12 | Coolant temperature sending unit | |
| 13 | Ignition coil | |
| 14 | Starter motor | |
| 15 | Battery ground cable | |
| 16 | Battery | |
| 17 | Voltage regulator | |
| 18 | Fuse | |
| 19 | Instrument cluster | |
| A | Hi-beam indicator | |
| B | Auxiliary | |
| C | Instrument lights | |
| D | Oil pressure indicator | |
| E | Charging indicator | |
| F | Temperature indicator | |
| G | Fuel gauge | |
| H | Instrument voltage regulator | |
| 20 | Ignition and starter switch | |
| 21 | Flasher (directional signal) | |
| 22 | Horn button | |
| 23 | Directional signal switch | |
| 24 | 4-way flasher switch | |
| 25 | Flasher (4-way) | |
| 26 | Fuse | |
| 27 | Main light switch | |
| 28 | Stop light switch — rear | |
| 29 | Fuel gauge tank unit | |
| 30 | Back-up light switch | |
| 31 | Right tail and stop light | |
| 32 | Right back-up light | |
| 33 | Left back-up light | |
| 34 | Left tail and stop light | |

| | | |
|---|---|---|
| 1 | Left headlight | |
| 2 | Left parking and signal light | |
| 3 | Right parking and signal light | |
| 4 | Right headlight | |
| 5 | Voltage regulator | |
| 6 | Alternator | |
| 7 | Oil pressure sender | |
| 8 | Coolant temperature sender | |
| 9 | Ignition distributor | |
| 10 | Junction block | |
| 11 | Horn | |
| 12 | Ignition coil | |
| 13 | Starter motor | |
| 14 | Battery ground cable | |
| 15 | Foot dimmer switch | |
| 16 | Stop light switch — front | |
| 17 | Ballast resistor | |
| 18 | Flasher (directional signal) | |
| 19 | Fuse | |
| 20 | Instrument cluster | |
| A | Hi-beam indicator | |
| B | Auxiliary | |
| C | Instrument lights | |
| D | Oil pressure indicator | |
| E | Charging indicator | |
| F | Temperature indicator | |
| G | Fuel gauge | |
| H | Instrument voltage regulator | |
| 21 | Ignition and starter switch | |
| 22 | Horn button | |
| 23 | Directional signal switch | |
| 24 | 4-way flasher switch | |
| 25 | Flasher (4-way) | |
| 26 | Fuse | |
| 27 | Main light switch | |
| 28 | Stop light switch — rear | |
| 29 | Fuel gauge tank unit | |
| 30 | Back-up light switch | |
| 31 | Right tail and stop light | |
| 32 | Right back-up light | |
| 33 | Left back-up light | |
| 34 | Left tail and stop light | |

**10**

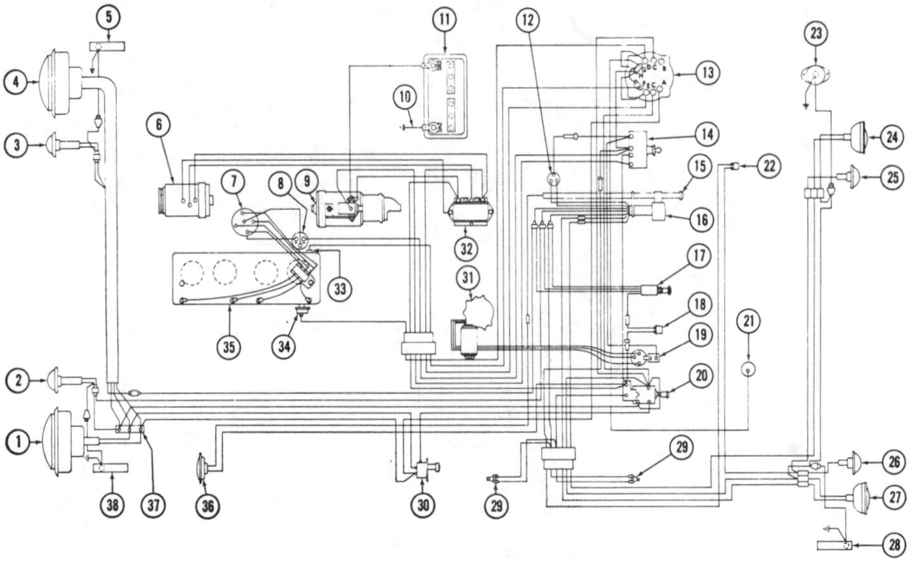

**Fig. 10.28  Typical later model with F-head four-cylinder engine wiring diagram**

1  Left headlight
2  Left parking and signal light
3  Right parking and signal light
4  Right headlight
5  Marker light — amber
6  Generator
7  Distributor
8  Ignition coil
9  Starter motor
10  Battery ground cable
11  12-volt battery
12  Flasher (directional signal)
13  Instrument cluster
A  Hi-beam indicator
B  Auxiliary
C  Instrument lights
D  Oil pressure indicator
E  Charging indicator
F  Temperature indicator
G  Fuel gauge indicator
H  Instrument voltage indicator
14  Ignition and starter switch
15  Horn button
16  Directional signal switch
17  4-way flasher switch
18  Flasher (4-way)
19  Windshield wiper motor switch
20  Main light switch
21  Fuel gauge tank unit
22  Back-up light switch
23  Marker light — red
24  Right tail and stop light
25  Right back-up light
26  Left back-up light
27  Right tail and stop light
28  Marker light — red
29  Stop light switch
30  Foot dimmer switch
31  Windshield wiper motor assembly
32  Voltage regulator
33  Coolant temperature sending unit
34  Oil pressure sending unit
35  Spark plugs and cables
36  Horn
37  Junction block
38  Marker light — amber

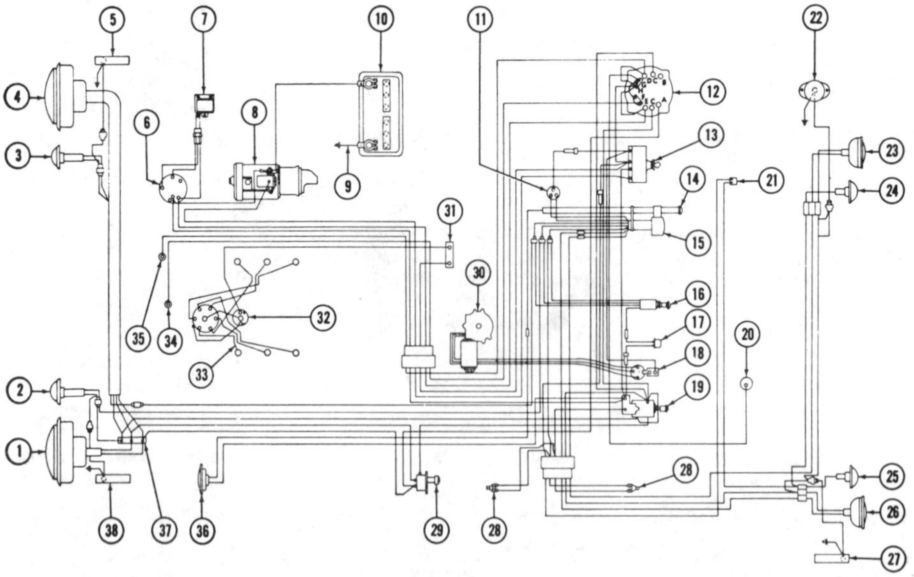

**Fig. 10.29  Later model with V6 engine wiring diagram**

1  Left headlight
2  Left parking and signal light
3  Right parking and signal light
4  Right headlight
5  Marker light — amber
6  Alternator
7  Voltage regulator
8  Starter motor
9  Battery ground cable
10  12-volt battery
11  Flasher (directional signal)
12  Instrument cluster
A  Hi-beam indicator
B  Auxiliary
C  Instrument lights
D  Oil pressure indicator
E  Charging indicator
F  Temperature indicator
G  Fuel gauge indicator
H  Instrument voltage regulator
13  Ignition and starter switch
14  Horn button
15  Directional signal switch
16  4-way flasher switch
17  Flasher (4-way)
18  Windshield wiper motor switch
19  Main light switch
20  Fuel gauge tank unit
21  Back-up light switch
22  Marker light — amber
23  Right tail and stop light
24  Right back-up light
25  Left back-up light
26  Left tail and stop light
27  Marker light — red
28  Stop light signal
29  Foot dimmer switch
30  Windshield wiper motor assembly
31  Ballast resistor
32  Ignition coil
33  Spark plugs and cables
34  Coolant temperature sending unit
35  Oil pressure sending unit
36  Horn
37  Junction block
38  Marker light — amber

| NO. | GA. | COLOR | INSTRUMENT AND CONTROL HARNESS |
|---|---|---|---|
| A-1 | 18 | BLUE-YELLOW TR. | CONN.-(TEMPERATURE SENDER) TO TEMPERATURE GAGE INDICATOR |
| A-2 | 18 | WHITE | FOOT DIMMER SWITCH (HI-BEAM) TO INSTR. CLUSTER (HI-BEAM IND.) |
| A-3 | 14 | RED-WHITE TR. | FOOT DIMMER SWITCH (HI-BEAM) TO HEADLAMP CONN. (HI-BEAM) |
| A-4 | 14 | GREEN | IGN. SWITCH (IGN. TERM.) TO INSTR. CLUSTER VOLT REGULATOR |
| A-5 | 18 | BLACK-WHITE TR. | CONN. SIG. LAMP FRONT RIGHT TO HAZARD WARNING SW. TO DIRECT SIGNAL SW. TO CLUSTER LAMP RIGHT TURN |
| A-6 | 18 | GRAY | CONN. (ALTERNATOR-AUX. TERM.) TO INSTR. CHARGE IND. TO INSTR. VOLT REG. |
| A-7 | 18 | PURPLE | CONN. (OIL PRESS. SENDER) TO OIL PRESS. IND. TO INSTR. VOLT REG. |
| A-8 | 18 | YELLOW-BLACK TR. | CONN. SIG. LAMP FRONT LEFT TO HAZARD WARNING SW. TO DIRECT SIGNAL SW. TO CLUSTER LAMP LEFT TURN |
| A-9 | 16 | BLACK | (GROUND.) FLASH MTG. TO LIGHT SW., WIPER & HAZARD LIGHTS |
| A-10 | 18 | WHITE | CONN. (FRAME HARN.-GAS GA. TANK UNIT) TO INSTR. GAS GA. INDICATOR |
| A-11 | 18 | RED-BLUE | LIGHT SWITCH "I" TERM. TO INSTR. CLUSTER LIGHTS TO HEATER LAMP |
| A-11A | 18 | RED BLUE TR. | LT. SWITCH (TERM. I) TO LAMPS LIGHTS, WIPER HAZARD TO INSTR. CLUSTER LAMP |
| A-12 | 10 | RED | SPLICE TO CONN. (START SOLENOID-BATT. TERM.) |
| A-13 | 14 | GREEN | IGNITION SWITCH (IGN. TERM.) TO CONN. COIL (+) TERM. |
| A-14 | 16 | LT. BLUE | IGNITION SWITCH (START TERM.) TO CONN. (START MOTOR SOLENOID-START. TERM.) |
| A-15 | 14 | GREEN | FOOT DIMMER SWITCH "B" TERM. TO LIGHT SWITCH "H" TERM. |
| A-17 | 16 | BROWN | LIGHT SWITCH-BATT. (B-2) TO CONN. (STOP LITE SW.) |
| A-18 | 16 | YELLOW | LIGHT SWITCH "R" TERM. TO CONN. (FRAME HARNESS-TAIL LIGHTS) |
| A-19 | 16 | LT. BLUE | LIGHT SWITCH "R" TERM. TO CONN. (PARK. TERM.) |
| A-23 | 16 | LT. BLUE | CONN. FRAME HARN. REAR LEFT TO HAZARD WARN. SW. TO DIRECT. SIG. SW. (LEFT TURN) |
| A-24 | | ORANGE | CONN.-FRAME HARN. REAR RIGHT TO HAZARD WARN. SW. TO DIRECT. SIG. SW. (RIGHT TURN) |
| A-12A | 12 | RED | SPLICE TO CONN. (IGN. SWITCH-BATT.) CIGAR LIGHTER |
| A-12B | 14 | RED | SPLICE TO CONN. (LIGHT SW.) B-1 |
| A-25 | 16 | BLACK | FOOT DIMMER SW. (LO-BEAM) TO HEADLAMP CONN. (LO-BEAM) |
| A-27 | 18 | BLACK YELLOW TR. | HORN TERM. TO CONN. (HORN BUTTON) |
| A-28 | 18 | WHITE-RED TR. | LIGHT SW (B-1) FUSED TO CONN. (HAZARD FLASHER) FEED |
| A-29 | 18 | RED | CONN. (IGN. SWITCH-ACC. TERM.) TO CONN. (DIRECT. SIGNAL FLASHER) FUSED |
| A-30 | 18 | YELLOW | W/S WIPER SWITCH TO W/S WASHER MOTOR |
| A-33 | 14 | RED-WH. TR | W/S WIPER SW. "B" TO IGN. (ACC. TERM.) |
| A-34 | 18 | GREEN WH. TR | CONN. (BACK-UP LIGHT SW.) TO CONN. (FRAME HARN.-BACK-UP LTS.) |
| A-36 | 16 | ORANGE | T.C. SWITCH TO IGN. OF SIG. SW. (IGN. TERM.) |
| A-37 | 16 | ORANGE | T.C. SW. TO T.C. VACUUM SOLENOID |
| A-39 | 16 | PINK | HAZARD FLASHER TO HAZARD SWITCH |
| A-45 | 14 | RED-WH. TR. | CONN. (HORN TERM.) TO SPLICE |
| A-52 | 18 | GREEN-WH. TR. | IGN. SWITCH (IGN. TERM.) FUSED TO CONN. (BACK-UP LIGHT SW.) |
| A-65 | 16 | BROWN | CONN. (TURN SIGNAL SWITCH) TO CONN. (STOP LITE SW.) |
| A-74 | 18 | WHITE | CONN. (TURN SIG. SWITCH-FLASHER TERM.) TO CONN. (FLASHER) |

| NO. | GA. | COLOR | HARNESS ASSY.-HEAD., PARK. & SIGNAL LAMPS |
|---|---|---|---|
| B-3 | 14 | RED-WHITE TR. | CONN. (HI-BEAM) TO CONN. (HEADLAMP -HI-BEAM-LT.) TO CONN. (HEADLAMP) (HI-BEAM-RT.) |
| B-5 | 18 | BLACK-YEL. TR. | CONN. (TURN SIGNAL SW.-RT. TURN) TO CONN. (DIR. SIGNAL LAMP RIGHT TURN |
| B-8 | 18 | YELLOW BL. TR. | CONN. (TURN SIGNAL SW.-LT. TURN) TO CONN. (DIR. SIGNAL LAMP LEFT TURN) |
| B-19 | 16 | LT. BLUE | CONN. (PARK. TERM.) TO CONN. (PARK LAMP-LT) TO CONN. (PARK. LAMP RIGHT) |
| B-25 | 16 | TAN | CONN. (LO-BEAM) TO CONN. (HEADLAMP-LO-BEAM-LT.) TO CONN. (HEADLAMP) (LO-BEAM-RT) |
| B-27 | 18 | BLACK-YEL. TR. | CONN. (STEER. COLUMN-HORN BUTTON) TO HORN TERM. |
| B-36 | 16 | ORANGE | CONN. (IGN. SWITCH-IGN. TERM.) TO CONN. (TEMP. OVERRIDE SW.) |
| B-37 | 16 | ORANGE | CONN. (VACUUM SOLENOID SW. TO CONN. (TEMP. OVERRIDE SW.) |
| B-45 | 14 | RED-WHITE TR. | CONN. (LIGHT SW.-BATT. TERM. TO HORN TERM.) |
| B-70 | 70 | BLACK | HEADLAMP GROUND TO GROUND MTG. (2 CABLES) |

| NO. | GA. | COLOR | HARNESS ASSY.-ENGINE (V-8) |
|---|---|---|---|
| C-1 | 18 | BLUE-YEL. TR. | CONN. (TEMP. INDICATOR TO TEMP. SENDER) |
| C-6 | 18 | GRAY | CONN. (CLUSTER "H" TERM.) TO ALTERNATOR (AUX. TERM.) TO ALTERNATOR REGULATOR (AUX. TERM.) |
| C-7 | 18 | PURPLE | CONN. (OIL PRESSURE INDICATOR) TO OIL PRESSURE SENDER |
| C-12 | 10 | RED | START. SOLENOID ("B" TERM) TO CONN. (CIRCUIT BREAKER FEED) |
| C-14 | 16 | LT. BLUE | CONN. (IGN. SW. START TERM.) TO SOLENOID (START. TERM.) |
| C-35 | 16 | BLACK | CONN. (TRANSMISSION SOLENOID) (T.C.S.) TO VACUUM SW. |
| C-37 | 16 | ORANGE | CONN. (SENSOR SW.) (T.C.S.) TO VACUUM SW. |
| C-38 | 20 | PINK | CONN. (IGN SW.-IGN. TERM.) TO COIL (+) TERM.-RESISTANCE WIRE 1.35 $\Omega$ MAX. |
| C-40 | 16 | YELLOW | START. SOLENOID (IGN.) TO ALTERNATOR REGULATOR (IGNITION) |
| C-42 | 14 | GREEN | COIL (+) TERM. TO STARTING SOLENOID (IGNITION) |
| C-43 | 14 | BLACK | ALTERNATOR REGULATOR (GROUND TERM.) TO ALTERNATOR (GRD.) |
| C-44 | 18 | GREEN-WH. TR. | ALTERNATOR REGULATOR (FIELD TERM.) TO ALTERNATOR (FIELD TERM.) |
| C-55 | 10 | YELLOW | STARTING SOLENOID ("B" TERM.) TO ALTERNATOR (OUTPUT TERM.) |

| NO. | GA. | COLOR | HARNESS ASSY.-ENGINE (6 CYL.) |
|---|---|---|---|
| D-1 | 18 | BLUE-YEL. TR. | CONN. (TEMP. INDICATOR) TO TEMPERATURE SENDER |
| D-6 | 18 | GRAY | CONN. (CLUSTER "H" TERM.) TO ALTERNATOR (AUX. TERM.) TO ALTERNATOR REG. (FIELD TERM.) |
| D-7 | 18 | PURPLE | CONN. (OIL PRESSURE INDICATOR) TO OIL PRESSURE SENDER |
| D-12 | 10 | RED | START. SOLENOID ("B" TERM.) TO CONN. (CIRCUIT BREAKER FEED) |
| D-14 | 16 | LT. BLUE | CONN. (IGNITION SW.-START. TERM.) TO SOLENOID (START. TERM.) |
| D-38 | 20 | PINK | CONN. (IGNITION SW.-IGN. TERM.) TO COIL (+) TERM. RESISTANCE WIRE 1.80 $\Omega$ |
| D-40 | 16 | YELLOW | START. SOLENOID (IGN.) TO ALTERNATOR REGULATOR (IGN.) |
| D-42 | 14 | GREEN | COIL (+) TERM. TO START. SOLENOID (IGN.) |
| D-43 | 16 | BLACK | ALTERNATOR REGULATOR (GRD. TERM.) TO ALTERNATOR (GRD. TERM.) |
| D-44 | 18 | GREEN WH. TR. | ALTERNATOR REGULATOR (FIELD TERM.) TO ALTERNATOR (FIELD TERM.) |
| D-55 | 10 | YELLOW | START. SOLENOID ("B" TERM.) TO ALTERNATOR (OUTPUT TERM.) |

| NO. | GA. | COLOR | CHASSIS WIRING HARNESS |
|---|---|---|---|
| E-10 | 18 | WHITE | CONN. (GAS GAGE-INSTR. UNJT) TO CONN. (GAS GAGE-TANK UNIT) |
| E-18 | 16 | YELLOW | CONN. (LIGHT SW.-"R" TERM.) TO CONN. (LT. TAIL LAMP & LT. MARKER LAMP) TO CONN. (RT. MARKER LAMP & RT. TAIL LAMP) |
| E-23 | 16 | LIGHT BLUE | CONN. (TURN SIGNAL SW.) TO CONN. (LEFT STOP & SIGNAL LT.) |
| E-24 | 16 | ORANGE | CONN. (TURN SIGNAL SW.) TO CONN. (RT. STOP & SIGNAL LIGHT) |
| E-34 | 18 | GREEN WH. TR. | CONN. (BACK UP LT. SW.) TO CONN. (BACK UP LIGHT (LT. & RT.) |

**1972 and 1973 model wiring diagram key**

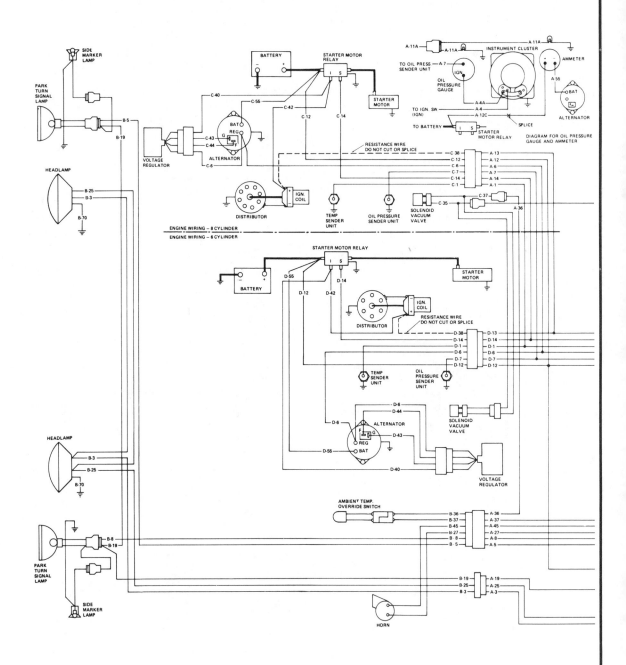

Fig. 10.30  1972 and 1973 model wiring diagram

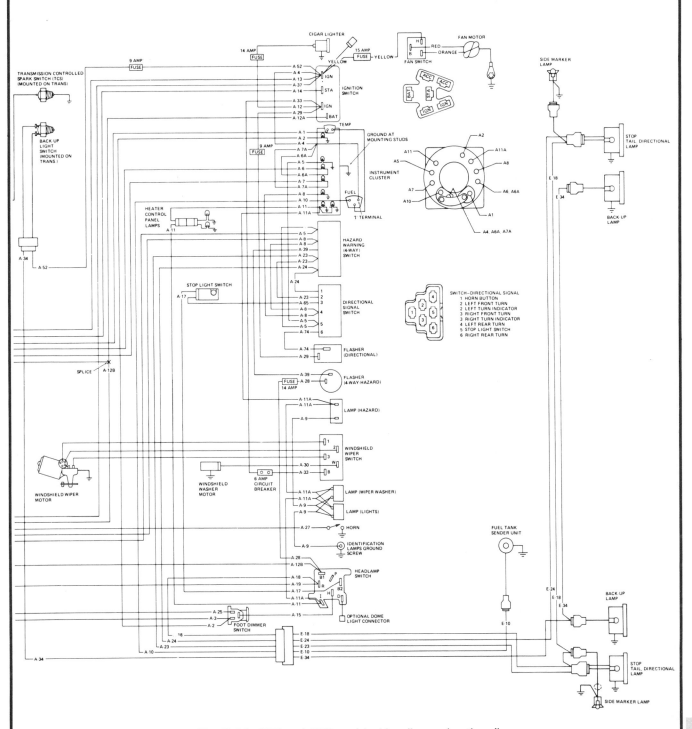

Fig. 10.31  1972 and 1973 model wiring diagram (continued)

10

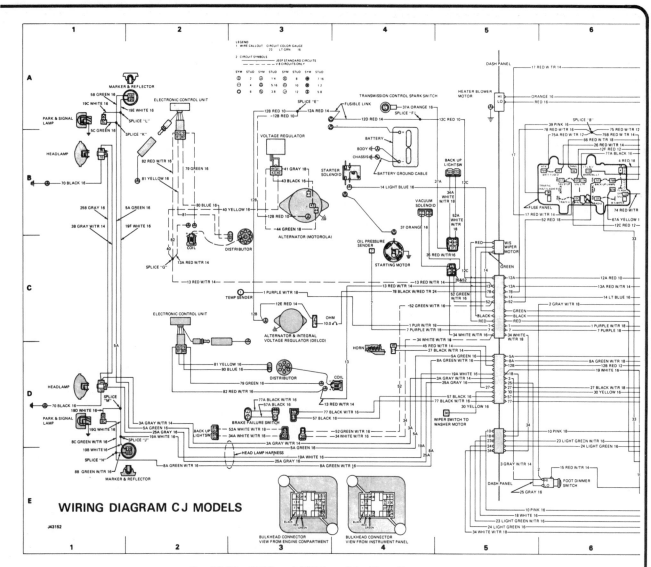

Fig. 10.32  1974 and 1975 model wiring diagram

| NOMENCLATURE | LOCATION | | NOMENCLATURE | LOCATION |
|---|---|---|---|---|
| Air & Defroster Light | C-8 | | Electronic Ignition Pack, V-8 | A-2 |
| Alternator, V-8 (Motorola) | B-3 | | Fuel Gauge | C-8 |
| Alternator/Regulator (Delco), 6 Cylinder | C-3 | | Fuel Sender | D-10 |
| Backup Lamp, Left Rear | D-11 | | Fuel Sender Connector | E-10 |
| Backup Lamp, Right Rear | B-11 | | Fuse Panel | B-6 |
| Backup Lamp Switch, 6 Cylinder | B-5 | | Fusible Link, Ignition Circuit | A-4 |
| Backup Lamp Switch, V-8 | D-2 | | Hazard Light | D-8 |
| Battery | B-4 | | Hazard Switch | B-9 |
| Battery Ground Cable | B-4 | | Headlamp, Left | D-1 |
| Brake Failure Switch | D-3 | | Headlamp, Right | B-1 |
| Brake Warning Light Connector | D-8 | | Headlamp Ground, Left | D-1 |
| Brake Warning Light | D-8 | | Headlamp Ground, Right | B-1 |
| Brake Warning Light Ground | D-8 | | Heater Blower Motor | A-5 |
| Cigar Lighter | A-8 | | Heater Blower Switch | B-8 |
| Coil, 6 Cylinder | D-4 | | High Beam Indicator | C-8 |
| Coil, V-8 | C-2 | | Horn | D-4 |
| Constant Voltage Regulator | C-8 | | Horn Button | B-8 |
| Dimmer Switch | E-6 | | Ignition Switch | A-8 & A-9 |
| Directional Signal Switch | B-9 & B-10 | | Instrument Cluster | C-8 |
| Distributor, 6 Cylinder | D-3 | | Instrument Panel Lights Ground | D-8 |
| Distributor, V-8 | C-3 | | Light Switch | E-8 & E-9 |
| Electronic Ignition Pack, 6 Cylinder | C-2 | | Light Switch Light | E-8 |

1974 and 1975 model wiring diagram key

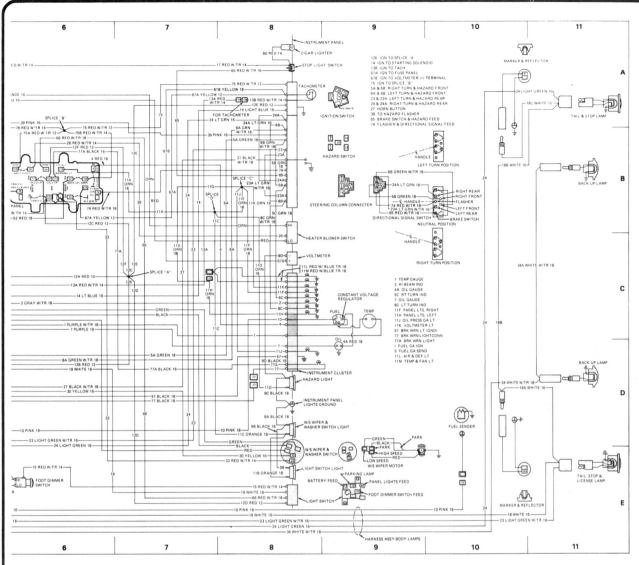

**Fig. 10.33  1974 and 1975 model wiring diagram (continued)**

| NOMENCLATURE | LOCATION |  | |
|---|---|---|---|
| Marker & Reflector, Left Front | E-2 | Splice "M" | D-1 |
| Marker & Reflector, Left Rear | E-10 | Starter Solenoid | B-4 |
| Marker & Reflector, Right Front | A-2 | Starting Motor | C-4 |
| Marker & Reflector, Right Rear | A-10 | Steering Column Connector | B-9 |
| Oil Gauge | C-8 | Stoplamp Switch | A-8 |
| Oil Pressure Gauge Light | C-8 | Tachometer Connector | A-8 |
| Oil Pressure Sender | C-4 | Tail, Stop & License Lamp, Left Rear | E-11 |
| Panel Lights, Left | C-8 | Tail & Stop Lamp, Right Rear | A-11 |
| Panel Lights, Right | C-8 | Temperature & Fan Light | C-8 |
| Park & Signal Lamp, Left Front | D-1 | Temperature Gauge | C-8 |
| Park & Signal Lamp, Right Front | A-1 | Temperature Sender | C-3 |
| Splice "A" | C-7 | Transmission Control Switch | A-4 |
| Splice "B" | B-6 | Turn Indicator & Hazard, Left | C-8 |
| Splice "C" | B-8 | Turn Indicator & Hazard, Right | C-8 |
| Splice "D" | B-7 | Vacuum Solenoid | B-4 |
| Splice "E" | A-3 | Voltage Regulator, V-8 | B-3 |
| Splice "F" | A-4 | Voltmeter | C-8 |
| Splice "G" | C-2 | Voltmeter Light | C-8 |
| Splice "H" | E-1 | Windshield Washer Motor Lead | D-5 |
| Splice "J" | D-1 | Windshield Wiper Motor | C-5 & E-9 |
| Splice "K" | A-1 | Windshield Wiper & Washer Switch | E-8 |
| Splice "L" | A-1 | Windshield Wiper & Washer Switch Lights | D-8 |

**1974 and 1975 model wiring diagram key (continued)**

**10**

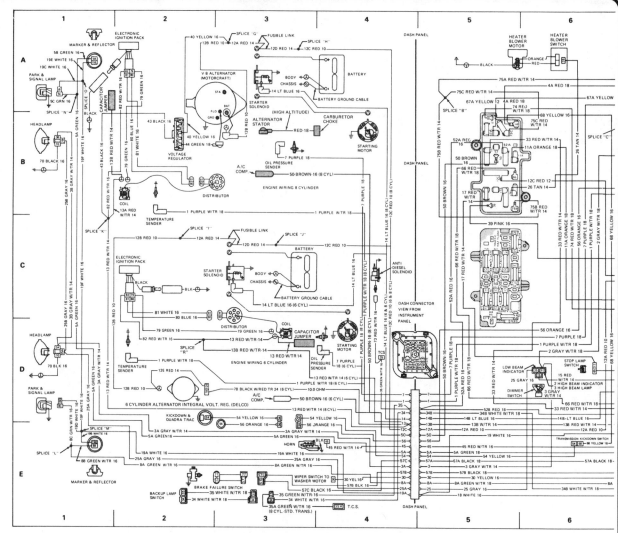

Fig. 10.34  1976 and 1977 model wiring diagram

| NOMENCLATURE | LOCATION |
|---|---|
| Alternator, V-8 (Motorcraft) | A-2 |
| Alternator/Regulator (Delco), 6 Cylinder | D-2 |
| Anti-Diesel Solenoid | C-4 |
| Backup Lamp, Left Rear | D-11 |
| Backup Lamp, Right Rear | C-11 |
| Backup Lamp Switch, Man. Trans. | E-2 |
| Backup Lamp Switch, Auto. Trans. | D-9 |
| Battery, 6 Cylinder | C-3 |
| Battery, V-8 | A-4 |
| Brake Failure Switch | E-3 |
| Brake Warning Light | C-9 |
| Cigar Lighter | D-9 |
| Coil, 6 Cylinder | D-3 |
| Coil, V-8 | B-2 |
| Dimmer Switch | D-6 |
| Directional Signal Switch | D-8 |
| Distributor, 6 Cylinder | D-3 |
| Distributor, V-8 | B-2 |
| Electronic Ignition Pack, 6 Cylinder | C-2 |
| Electronic Ignition Pack, V-8 | A-2 |
| Fuel Gauge | B-10 |
| Fuel Sender | D-10 |

| | LOCATION |
|---|---|
| Fuel Sender Connector | E-10 |
| Frame Harness Connector | E-9 |
| Fuse Panel | C-5 & C-6 |
| Fusible Link, Ignition Circuit, 6 Cylinder | C-3 |
| Fusible Link, Ignition Circuit, V-8 | A-3 |
| Headlamp, Left | D-1 |
| Headlamp, Right | B-1 |
| Headlamp Ground, Left | D-1 |
| Headlamp Ground, Right | B-1 |
| Heater Blower Motor | A-5 |
| Heater Blower Switch | A-6 |
| Heater Control Lights | A-7 & A-8 |
| High Beam Indicator | B-9 |
| Horn | E-3 |
| Horn Relay | C-7 |
| Ignition Switch | C-8 |
| Instrument Cluster | B-10 |
| Instrument Cluster Lights | B-9 |
| Instrument Panel Lights Ground | C-9 |
| Kickdown and Quadra-Trac Switch Connector | E-2 & E-3 |
| Light Switch | E-8 |
| Light Switch Light | E-9 |
| Marker & Reflector, Left Front | E-1 |

1976 and 1977 model wiring diagram key

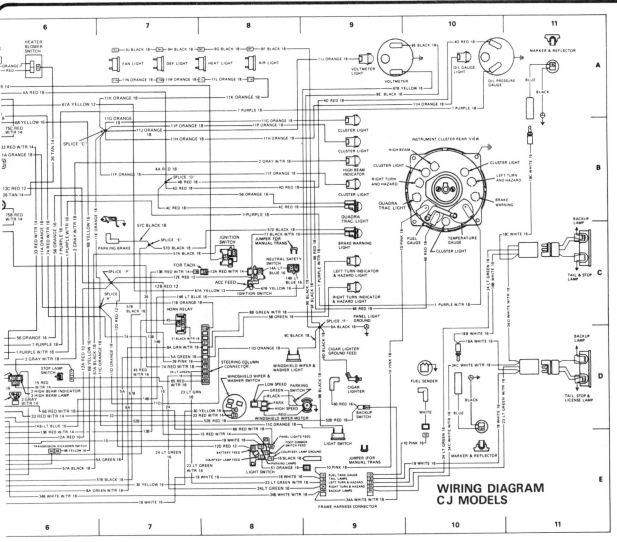

Fig. 10.35   1976 and 1977 model wiring diagram (continued)

| NOMENCLATURE | LOCATION | | |
|---|---|---|---|
| Marker & Reflector, Left Rear | E-10 | Splice "M" | E-1 |
| Marker & Reflector, Right Front | A-1 | Splice "N" | A-1 |
| Marker & Reflector, Right Rear | A-11 | Splice "O" | A-1 |
| Oil Pressure Gauge | A-10 | Splice "P" | C-7 |
| Oil Pressure Gauge Light | A-10 | Splice "R" | D-3 |
| Oil Pressure Sender, 6 Cylinder | D-4 | Starter Solenoid | A-3 & C-3 |
| Oil Pressure Sender, V-8 | B-3 | Starting Motor | B-4 & D-4 |
| Park & Signal Lamp, Left Front | D-1 | Steering Column Connector | D-8 |
| Park & Signal Lamp, Right Front | A-1 | Stoplamp Switch | D-6 |
| Resistance Wire, 6 Cylinder | D-3 | Tail, Stop & License Lamp, Left Rear | D-11 |
| Splice "A" | C-6 | Tail & Stop Lamp, Right Rear | C-11 |
| Splice "B" | C-6 | TCS System Connector | D-4 |
| Splice "C" | B-7 | Temperature Gauge | B-10 |
| Splice "D" | B-7 | Temperature Sender, 6 Cylinder | D-2 |
| Splice "E" | C-7 | Temperature Sender, V-8 | B-2 |
| Splice "F" | C-9 | Turn Indicator & Hazard, Left | C-9 |
| Splice "G" | A-3 | Turn Indicator & Hazard, Right | C-9 |
| Splice "H" | A-3 | Voltage Regulator Connector, V-8 | B-2 |
| Splice "I" | C-2 | Voltmeter | A-9 |
| Splice "J" | C-3 | Voltmeter Light | A-9 |
| Splice "K" | C-1 | Windshield Wiper Motor | D-8 |
| Splice "L" | E-1 | Windshield Wiper & Washer Switch | D-8 |
| | | Windshield Wiper & Washer Switch Light | D-8 |

1976 and 1977 model wiring diagram key (continued)

10

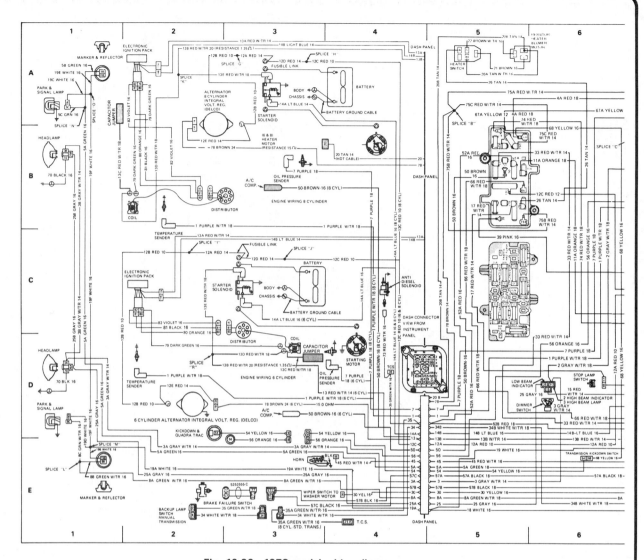

**Fig. 10.36  1978 model wiring diagram**

| NOMENCLATURE | LOCATION |
|---|---|
| Alternator/Regulator (Delco), V-8 | A-2 |
| Alternator/Regulator (Delco), 6 Cylinder | D-2 |
| Backup Lamp, Left Rear | D-11 |
| Backup Lamp, Right Rear | C-11 |
| Backup Lamp Switch, Man. Trans. | E-2 |
| Backup Lamp Switch, Auto. Trans. | D-9 |
| Battery, 6 Cylinder | C-3 |
| Battery, V-8 | A-4 |
| Brake Failure Switch | E-3 |
| Brake Warning Light | C-9 |
| Cigar Lighter | D-9 |
| Coil, 6 Cylinder | D-3 |
| Coil, V-8 | B-2 |
| Dimmer Switch | D-6 |
| Directional Signal Switch | D-8 |
| Distributor, 6 Cylinder | D-3 |
| Distributor, V-8 | B-2 |
| Electronic Ignition Pack, 6 Cylinder | C-2 |
| Electronic Ignition Pack, V-8 | A-2 |
| Fuel Gauge | B-10 |
| Fuel Sender | D-10 |
| Fuel Sender Connector | E-10 |

| | LOCATION |
|---|---|
| Frame Harness Connector | E-9 |
| Fuse Panel | C-5 & C-6 |
| Fusible Link, Ignition Circuit, 6 Cylinder | C-3 |
| Fusible Link, Ignition Circuit, V-8 | A-3 |
| Headlamp, Left | D-1 |
| Headlamp, Right | B-1 |
| Headlamp Ground, Left | D-1 |
| Headlamp Ground, Right | B-1 |
| Heater Blower Motor | A-5 |
| Heater Blower Switch | A-6 |
| Heater Resistor | A-6 |
| Heater Control Lights | A-7 & A-8 |
| High Beam Indicator | B-9 |
| Horn | E-3 |
| Horn Relay | C-7 |
| Ignition Switch | C-8 |
| Instrument Cluster | B-10 |
| Instrument Cluster Lights | B-9 |
| Instrument Panel Lights Ground | C-9 |
| Kickdown and Quadra-Trac Switch Connector | E-2 & E-3 |
| Light Switch | E-8 |
| Light Switch Light | E-9 |
| Marker & Reflector, Left Front | E-1 |

**1978 model wiring diagram key**

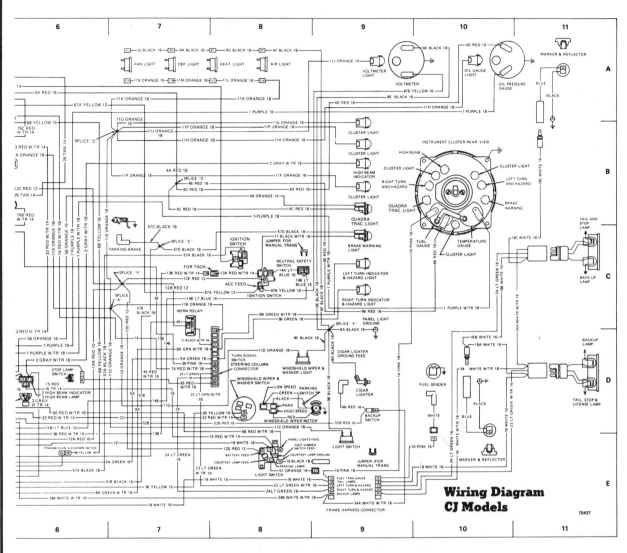

**Fig. 10.37  1978 Model wiring diagram (continued)**

| NOMENCLATURE | LOCATION |
|---|---|
| Marker & Reflector, Left Rear | E-10 |
| Marker & Reflector, Right Front | A-1 |
| Marker & Reflector, Right Rear | A-11 |
| Oil Pressure Gauge | A-10 |
| Oil Pressure Gauge Light | A-10 |
| Oil Pressure Sender, 6 Cylinder | D-4 |
| Oil Pressure Sender, V-8 | B-3 |
| Park & Signal Lamp, Left Front | D-1 |
| Park & Signal Lamp, Right Front | A-1 |
| Resistance Wire-Alternator, 6 Cylinder | D-3 |
| Resistance Wire-Alternator, 8 Cylinder | B-2 |
| Resistance Wire-Coil, 6 Cylinder | D-3 |
| Resistance Wire-Coil, 8 Cylinder | A-2 |
| Splice "A" | C-6 |
| Splice "B" | A-5 |
| Splice "C" | B-7 |
| Splice "D" | B-7 |
| Splice "E" | C-7 |
| Splice "F" | C-9 |
| Splice "G" | A-3 |
| Splice "H" | A-3 |
| Splice "I" | C-2 |
| Splice "J" | C-3 |

| | LOCATION |
|---|---|
| Splice "K" | A-2 |
| Splice "L" | E-1 |
| Splice "M" | E-1 |
| Splice "N" | A-1 |
| Splice "O" | A-1 |
| Splice "P" | C-7 |
| Splice "R" | D-3 |
| Starter Solenoid | A-3 & C-3 |
| Starting Motor | B-4 & D-4 |
| Steering Column Connector | D-8 |
| Stoplamp Switch | D-6 |
| Tail, Stop & License Lamp, Left Rear | D-11 |
| Tail & Stop Lamp, Right Rear | C-11 |
| TCS System Connector | D-4 |
| Temperature Gauge | B-10 |
| Temperature Sender, 6 Cylinder | D-2 |
| Temperature Sender, V-8 | B-2 |
| Turn Indicator & Hazard, Left | C-9 |
| Turn Indicator & Hazard, Right Voltmeter | C-9 A-9 |
| Voltmeter Light | A-9 |
| Windshield Wiper Motor | D-8 |
| Windshield Wiper & Washer Switch | D-8 |
| Windshield Wiper & Washer Switch Light | D-8 |

**10**

**1978 model wiring diagram key (continued)**

294

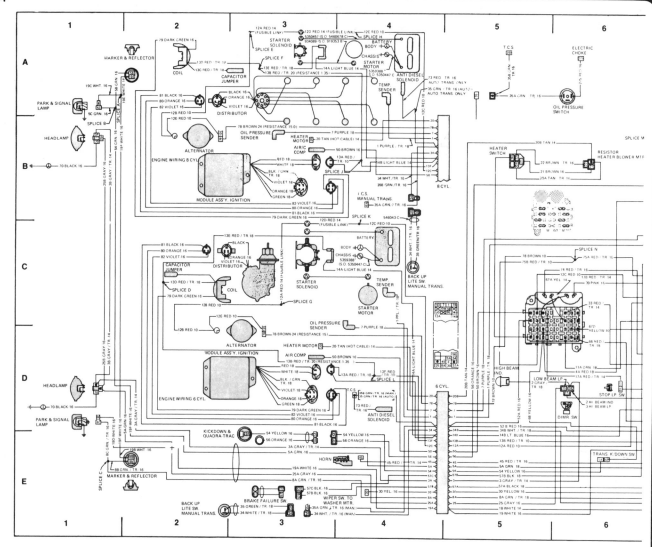

Fig. 10.38  1979 model wiring diagram

| NOMENCLATURE | LOCATION |
|---|---|
| Accessory Feed | C-8 |
| Air Conditioner Compressor, 8-Cylinder | B-3 |
| Alternator, 8-Cylinder | B-2 |
| Alternator, 6-Cylinder | D-3 |
| Anti-Diesel Solenoid, 8-Cylinder | A-4 |
| Anti-Diesel Solenoid, 6-Cylinder | D-4 |
| Back-up Lamp, Right Side | C-11 |
| Back-up Lamp, Left Side | D-11 |
| Back-up Light Switch Manual Transmission | C-4 |
| Back-up Light Switch Manual Transmission | E-2 |
| Battery, 8-Cylinder | A-4 |
| Battery, 6-Cylinder | C-4 |
| Body, 8-Cylinder | A-4 |
| Body, 6-Cylinder | C-4 |
| Brake Failure Switch | E-3 |
| Brake Warning Lamp | C-7 |
| Capacitor Jumper, 8-Cylinder | A-3 |
| Capacitor Jumper, 6-Cylinder | C-2 |
| Chassis, 8-Cylinder | A-4 |
| Chassis, 6-Cylinder | C-4 |
| Cigar Lighter Feed | D-9 |
| Coil, 8-Cylinder | A-2 |

| | |
|---|---|
| Coil, 6-Cylinder | C-2 |
| Dimmer Switch | D-6 |
| Distributor, 8-Cylinder | A-2 |
| Distributor, 6-Cylinder | C-3 |
| Electric Choke | A-6 |
| Fuel Gauge | B-8 |
| Fuel Sender | D-9 |
| Ground Air Lamp Feed | A-7 |
| Ground Defogger Lamp Feed | A-7 |
| Ground Fan Lamp Feed | A-8 |
| Ground Temperature Lamp Feed | A-7 |
| Headlamp, Right Side | B-1 |
| Headlamp, Left Side | D-1 |
| Heater Motor, 8-Cylinder | B-3 |
| Heater Motor, 6-Cylinder | D-3 |
| Heater Switch | B-5 |
| High Beam Indicator | D-5 |
| Horn | E-4 |
| Horn Relay | D-7 |
| Ignition Switch | C-8 |
| Kickdown & Quadra-Trac, 6-Cylinder | E-3 |
| Left Turn Indicator & Hazard Lamp | D-8 |
| Low Beam L.P. | D-6 |

1979 model wiring diagram key

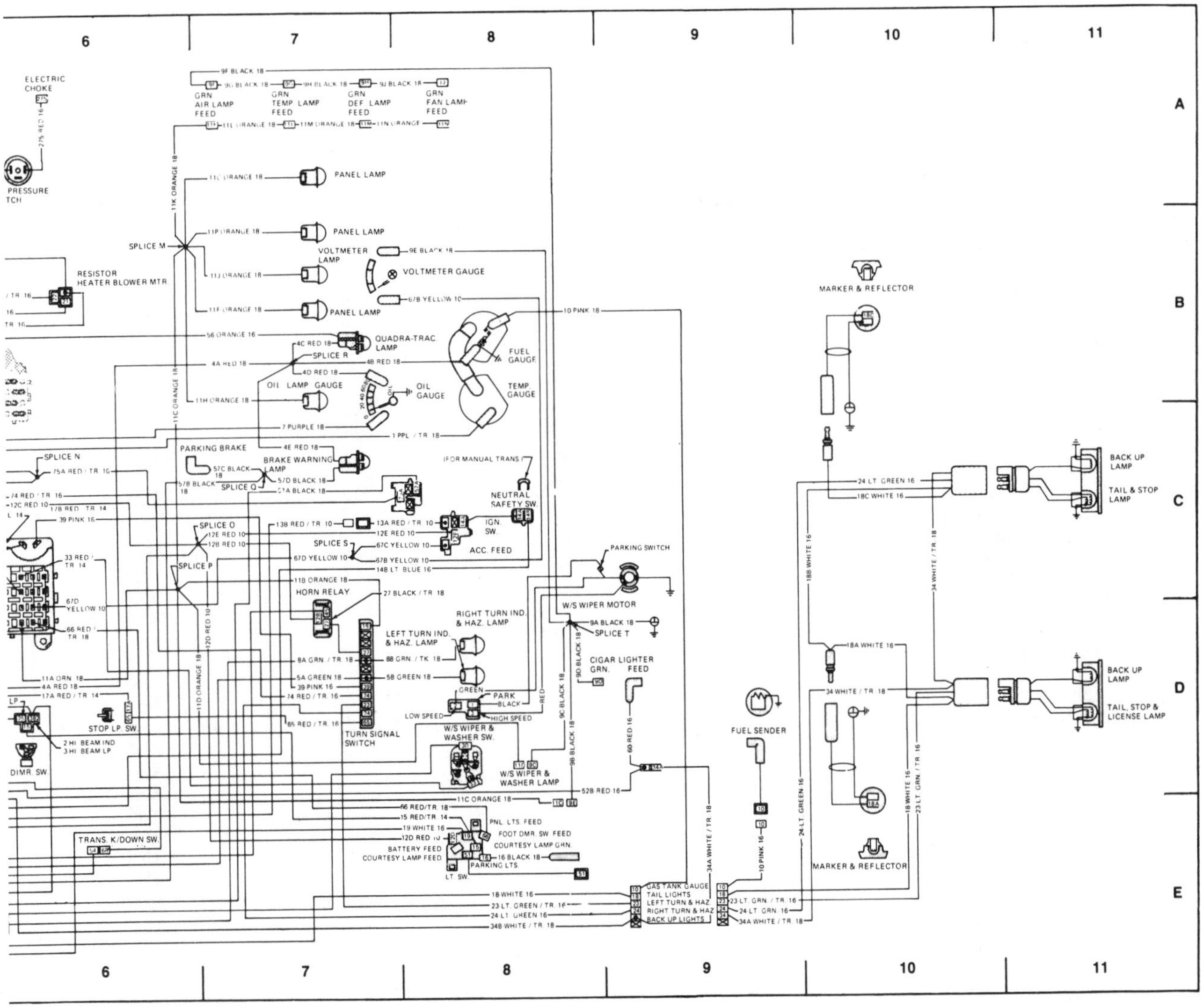

Fig. 10.39  1979 model wiring diagram (continued)

| NOMENCLATURE | LOCATION |
|---|---|
| Marker & Reflector, Right Side | A-2 |
| Marker & Reflector, Left Side | E-2 |
| Marker & Reflector, Right Side | B-10 |
| Marker & Reflector, Left Side | E-10 |
| Module Assembly Ignition, 8-Cylinder | B-2 |
| Module Assembly Ignition, 6-Cylinder | D-3 |
| Neutral Safety Switch | C-8 |
| Oil Lamp Gauge | B-7 |
| Oil Pressure Sender, 8-Cylinder | B-3 |
| Oil Pressure Sender, 6-Cylinder | C-4 |
| Oil Pressure Switch | A-6 |
| Panel Lamp | A-7 |
| Panel Lamp | B-7 |
| Park & Signal Lamp, Right Side | A-1 |
| Park & Signal Lamp, Left Side | D-1 |
| Parking Brake | C-7 |
| Quadra-Trac Lamp | B-7 |
| Resistor Heater Blower Motor | B-6 |
| Splice, 8-Cylinder | B-4 |
| Splice, 6-Cylinder | A-1 |
| Splice, 6-Cylinder | C-4 |
| Splice, 6-Cylinder | A-1 |
| Splice, 6-Cylinder | C-2 |
| Splice, 6-Cylinder | C-3 |
| Splice | B-6 |
| Splice | C-6 |
| Splice | C-6 |
| Splice | C-7 |
| Splice | C-7 |
| Starting Motor, 8-Cylinder | A-4 |
| Starting Motor, 6-Cylinder | C-4 |
| Starter Solenoid, 8-Cylinder | A-3 |
| Starter Solenoid, 6-Cylinder | C-3 |
| Stop Lamp Switch | D-6 |
| Tail & Stop Lamp, Right Side | C-11 |
| Tail & Stop Lamp, Left Side | D-11 |
| T.C.S. Manual Transmission | B-4 |
| Temperature Gauge | C-8 |
| Temperature Sender, 8-Cylinder | A-4 |
| Temperature Sender, 6-Cylinder | C-4 |
| Transmission Kickdown Switch | E-6 |
| Turn Signal Switch | D-7 |
| Voltmeter Gauge | B-7 |
| Windshield Wiper & Washer Lamp | D-8 |
| Windshield Wiper Motor | C-9 |
| Windshield Wiper & Washer Switch | D-8 |

1979 model wiring diagram key (continued)

10

| NOMENCLATURE | LOCATION |
|---|---|
| Accessory Feed | C-7 |
| Air Conditioner Compressor, 8-Cylinder | B-3 |
| Alternator, 8-Cylinder | B-2 |
| Alternator, 6-Cylinder | D-3 |
| Back-up Lamp, Right Side | C-11 |
| Back-up Lamp, Left Side | D-11 |
| Back-up Light Switch Manual Transmission | C-9, D-9 |
| Back-up Light Switch Automatic Transmission | D-9 |
| Battery, 8-Cylinder | A-4 |
| Battery, 6-Cylinder | C-4 |
| Body Ground, 8-Cylinder | A-4 |
| Body Ground, 6-Cylinder | C-4 |
| Brake Failure Switch | E-3 |
| Brake Warning Lamp | C-6 |
| Capacitor Jumper, 8-Cylinder | A-3 |
| Capacitor Jumper, 6-Cylinder | C-2 |
| Chassis Ground, 8-Cylinder | A-4 |
| Chassis Ground, 6-Cylinder | C-4 |
| Cigar Lighter Feed | D-7 |
| Coil, 8-Cylinder | A-2 |
| Coil, 6-Cylinder | C-3 |
| Dimmer Switch | D-5 |
| Distributor, 8-Cylinder | A-3 |
| Distributor, 6-Cylinder | C-3 |
| Electric Choke | B-5, E-1 |
| Fuel Gauge | B-7 |
| Fuel Sender | D-10 |
| Ground Air Lamp Feed | A-6 |
| Ground Defogger Lamp Feed | A-6 |
| Ground Fan Lamp Feed | A-7 |
| Ground Temperature Lamp Feed | A-6 |
| Headlamp, Right Side | B-1 |
| Headlamp, Left Side | D-1 |
| Heater Motor, 8-Cylinder | B-3 |
| Heater Motor, 6-Cylinder | D-3 |
| Heater Switch | B-5 |
| High Beam Indicator | D-5 |
| Horn | E-3 |
| Horn Relay | C-6 |
| Ignition Switch | C-7 |
| Left Turn Indicator & Hazard Lamp | E-7 |
| Low Beam L.P. | D-5 |
| Marker & Reflector, Right Side — Front | A-2 |
| Marker & Reflector, Left Side — Front | E-2 |
| Marker & Reflector, Right Side — Rear | B-10 |
| Marker & Reflector, Left Side — Rear | E-10 |
| Module Assembly Ignition, 8-Cylinder | B-3 |
| Module Assembly Ignition, 6-Cylinder | D-3 |

| NOMENCLATURE | LOCATION |
|---|---|
| Neutral Safety Switch | D-9 |
| Oil Lamp Gauge | B-6 |
| Oil Pressure Sender, 8-Cylinder | B-3 |
| Oil Pressure Sender, 6-Cylinder | D-3 |
| Panel Lamp | B-6 |
| Park & Signal Lamp, Right Side | A-1 |
| Park & Signal Lamp, Left Side | D-1 |
| Parking Brake | C-6 |
| Four Wheel Drive Indicator | C-9, D-9 |
| Resistor, Heater Blower Motor | B-5 |
| Splice A | A-2 |
| Splice B | B-2 |
| Splice C | C-2 |
| Splice D | E-2 |
| Splice E | E-2 |
| Splice F | E-2 |
| Splice G | A-3 |
| Splice H | A-3 |
| Splice I | A-3 |
| Splice J | B-3 |
| Splice K | C-3 |
| Splice L | C-3 |
| Splice M | D-4 |
| Splice N | B-5 |
| Splice O | B-5 |
| Splice P | C-5 |
| Splice Q | B-6 |
| Splice R | B-6 |
| Splice S | C-6 |
| Splice T | C-6 |
| Splice U | C-6 |
| Splice V | C-6 |
| Splice W | C-6 |
| Splice X | D-7 |
| Splice Y | E-8 |
| Starting Motor, 8-Cylinder | A-3 |
| Starting Motor, 6-Cylinder | C-4 |
| Starter Solenoid, 8-Cylinder | A-3 |
| Starter Solenoid, 6-Cylinder | C-3 |
| Stop Lamp Switch | D-5 |
| Tail & Stop Lamp, Right Side | C-11 |
| Tail & Stop Lamp, Left Side | D-11 |
| Temperature Gauge | B-7 |
| Temperature Sender, 8-Cylinder | A-4 |
| Temperature Sender, 6-Cylinder | C-4 |
| Turn Signal Switch | D-6 |
| Voltmeter Gauge | B-7 |
| Windshield Wiper & Washer Lamp | D-7 |
| Windshield Wiper Motor | C-9 |
| Windshield Wiper & Washer Switch | D-7 |

1980 through 1983 model wiring diagram key

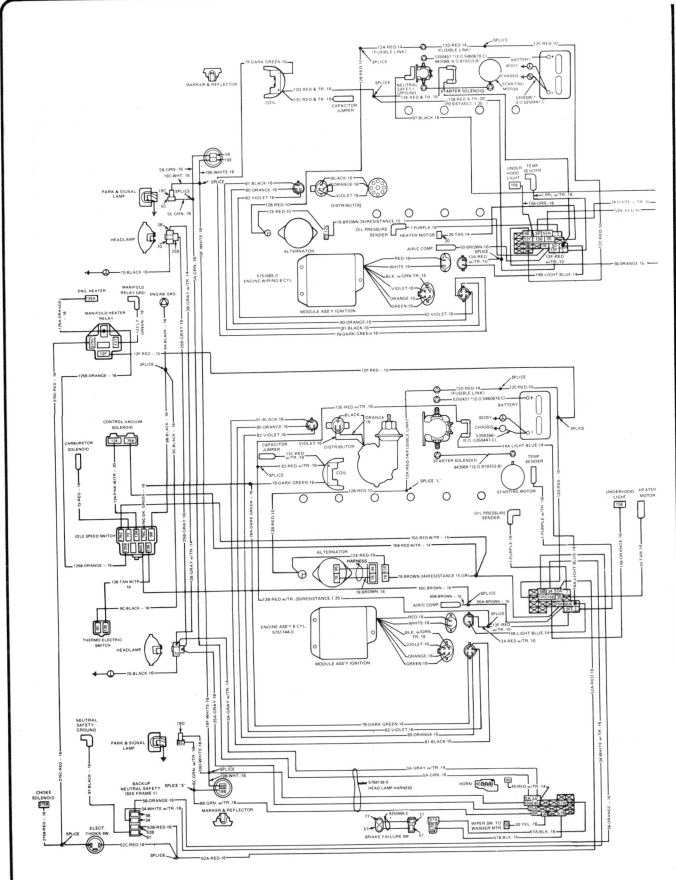

Fig. 10.40  1980 through 1983 model wiring diagram

10

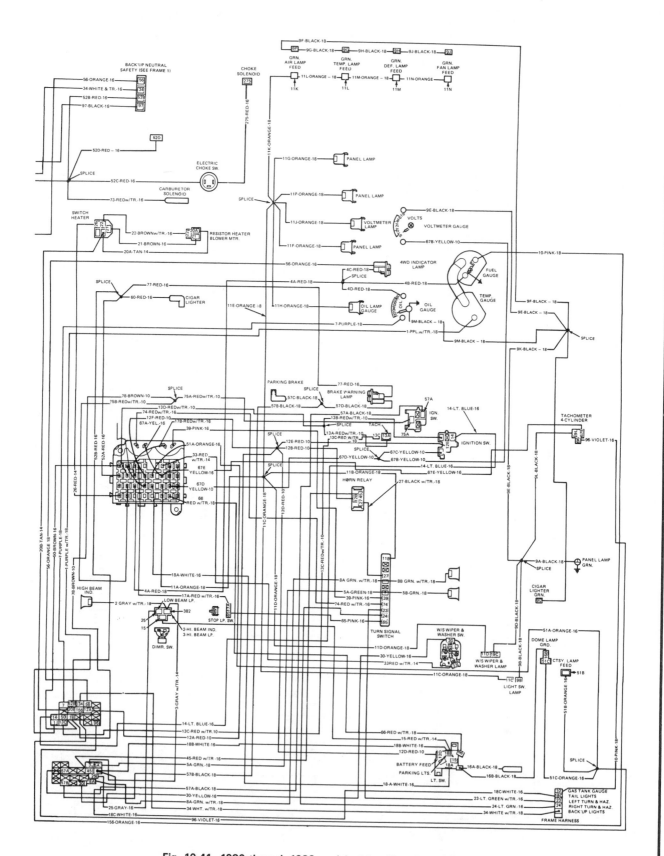

Fig. 10.41 1980 through 1983 model wiring diagram (continued)

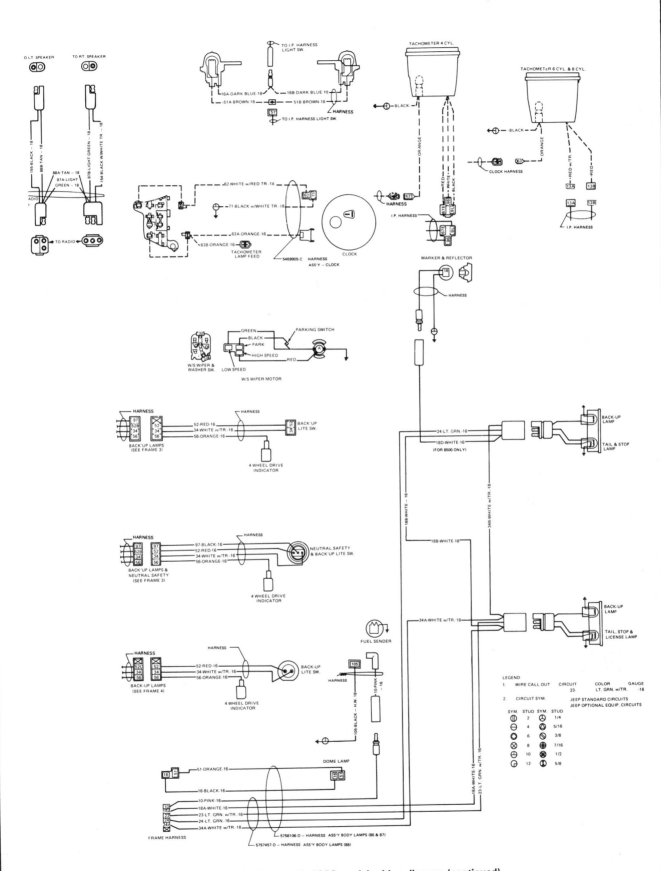

Fig. 10.42  1980 through 1983 model wiring diagram (continued)

# Chapter 11 Suspension and steering systems

**Contents**

Chassis lubrication . . . . . . . . . . . . . . . . . . . . . . . . Chapter 1
Drag link — removal and installation . . . . . . . . . . . . . . . . . . 11
Drivebelt check and adjustment . . . . . . . . . . . . . Chapter 1
Front hub — removal and installation . . . . . . . . . . . . . 5
Front spring — removal and installation . . . . . . . . . . . . . 4
Front stabilizer bar — removal and installation . . . . . . . . 2
General information . . . . . . . . . . . . . . . . . . . . . . . . . 1
Power steering fluid level check . . . . . . . . . . . . . Chapter 1
Power steering pump — removal and installation . . . . . . . . . 17
Power steering system — bleeding procedure . . . . . . . . . . . 18
Rear spring — removal and installation . . . . . . . . . . . . . . 6
Shock absorber — removal and installation . . . . . . . . . . . 3
Spring bushing — check and replacement . . . . . . . . . . . . . 7

Steering bellcrank — removal and installation . . . . . . . . . . . 14
Steering connecting rod — removal and installation . . . . . . . 12
Steering damper — removal and installation . . . . . . . . . . . . 15
Steering gear — removal and installation . . . . . . . . . . . . . 16
Steering knuckle — removal and installation . . . . . . . . . . . . 8
Steering wheel — removal and installation . . . . . . . . . . . . 19
Suspension and steering check . . . . . . . . . . . . . Chapter 1
Tie rod — removal and installation . . . . . . . . . . . . . . . . . 13
Wheel alignment — general information . . . . . . . . . . . . . . 20
Wheel bearing check . . . . . . . . . . . . . . . . . . . . Chapter 1
Wheel bearings — adjustment . . . . . . . . . . . . . . . . . . . . 9
Wheel bearings — inspection and lubrication . . . . . . . . . . . 10

**Specifications**

## Torque specifications

| | Ft-lb | Nm |
|---|---|---|
| Bellcrank shaft locknut . . . . . . . . . . . . . . . . . . . . . . . . . . . . . . | 70 to 90 | 95 to 122 |
| Bellcrank 7/16-inch locknut . . . . . . . . . . . . . . . . . . . . . . . . . . | 50 to 70 | 68 to 95 |
| Bellcrank support bracket . . . . . . . . . . . . . . . . . . . . . . . . . . . | 30 to 45 | 41 to 61 |
| Bellcrank-to-tie-rod end . . . . . . . . . . . . . . . . . . . . . . . . . . . | 38 to 45 | 41 to 61 |
| Drag link ball adjusting nut . . . . . . . . . . . . . . . . . . . . . . . . . | 20 | 27 |
| Drag link-to-bellcrank arm . . . . . . . . . . . . . . . . . . . . . . . . . | 20 | 27 |
| Pitman arm nut . . . . . . . . . . . . . . . . . . . . . . . . . . . . . . . . . | 185 | 251 |
| Power steering pump | | |
|     Adjusting nuts and bolts . . . . . . . . . . . . . . . . . . . . . . . . . . | 30 to 40 | 41 to 54 |
|     Mounting bracket bolts . . . . . . . . . . . . . . . . . . . . . . . . . | 30 to 40 | 41 to 54 |
| Steering knuckle upper ball-stud split ring seat . . . . . . . . . . | 50 | 68 |
| Upper ball-stud nut . . . . . . . . . . . . . . . . . . . . . . . . . . . . . . . | 100 | 136 |
| Lower ball-stud jam nut . . . . . . . . . . . . . . . . . . . . . . . . . . . | 85 | 115 |
| Steering connecting rod . . . . . . . . . . . . . . . . . . . . . . . . . . . | 60 | 81 |
| Steering tie-rod end nut . . . . . . . . . . . . . . . . . . . . . . . . . . . | 60 | 81 |
| Steering gear-to-frame bolts | | |
|   1949 to 1971 models | | |
|     7/16-inch bolts . . . . . . . . . . . . . . . . . . . . . . . . . . . . . | 45 to 55 | 61 to 75 |
|     3/8-inch bolts . . . . . . . . . . . . . . . . . . . . . . . . . . . . . | 30 to 40 | 41 to 54 |
|   1972 through 1983 models | | |
|     Steering gear-to-bracket bolt (hex head) . . . . . . . . . . . . | 70 | 95 |
|     Steering gear-to-bracket bolt (Torx head) . . . . . . . . . . . | 55 | 75 |
|     Steering gear-to-frame bolt . . . . . . . . . . . . . . . . . . . . | 55 | 75 |
| Steering shaft coupling bolt . . . . . . . . . . . . . . . . . . . . . . . . | 45 | 61 |
| Steering arm-to-tie-rod . . . . . . . . . . . . . . . . . . . . . . . . . . . | 50 | 68 |
| Steering arm nut . . . . . . . . . . . . . . . . . . . . . . . . . . . . . . . | 150 | 203 |
| Steering wheel nut . . . . . . . . . . . . . . . . . . . . . . . . . . . . . . | 20 to 30 | 27 to 41 |
| Wheel bearing outer locknut . . . . . . . . . . . . . . . . . . . . . . . | 50 | 68 |
| Wheel lug nuts . . . . . . . . . . . . . . . . . . . . . . . . . . . . . . . . | 65 to 80 | 88 to 108 |

## 1  General information

The front and rear suspension on all models consists of semi-elliptic springs with tubular shock absorbers. The axles are attached to the springs with U-bolts and tie plates which incorporate the lower shock absorber mounts. The springs are mounted parallel to the frame rails with the forward end of the front springs and the rear end of the rear springs attached with pivoting shackles. Later models are equipped with a front stabilizer bar.

Steering is a recirculating ball type with power assist available on later models. Later models also feature an energy-absorbing steering column and optional tilt steering wheel. Some later models incorporate a shock absorber-like damper in the steering linkage to reduce steering wheel kickback while driving on rough terrain.

## 2  Front stabilizer bar — removal and installation

1   Remove the connecting links from the spring tie plates and stabilizer bar.
2   Raise the front of the vehicle and support it securely on jackstands.

3   Remove the clamp nuts and separate the stabilizer bar from the vehicle.
4   Inspect the stabilizer bar for damage, distortion and corrosion. Check the cushions for cracks and damage and the clamps and nuts for damage, corrosion and stripped threads. Replace unserviceable components with new ones.
5   Place the stabilizer bar in position and install the clamp and bracket assembly with the nuts finger tight.
6   Lower the vehicle and install the connecting links with the nuts finger tight.
7   Tighten the stabilizer bar clamp nuts to the specified torque, followed by the connecting link nuts.

## 3  Shock absorber — removal and installation

1   Raise the vehicle, support it securely on jackstands and remove the wheels.
2   Raise the axle with a jack just enough to relieve the weight from the spring.
3   Remove the upper and lower mounting nuts and washers and remove the shock absorber and bushings.

Fig. 11.1  Typical front suspension component layout

| | | |
|---|---|---|
| 1  Steering knuckle | 4  Pitman arm and steering gear | 7  Spring tie plate |
| 2  Sway bar | 5  Steering damper | 8  Tie-rod |
| 3  Steering connecting rod | 6  Spring | 9  Shock absorber |

11

Fig. 11.2  Typical rear suspension component layout

1  Shock absorber        3  Spring tie plate
2  Spring                4  Spring shackle

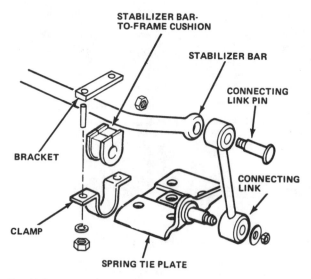

STABILIZER BAR-
TO-FRAME CUSHION

STABILIZER BAR

CONNECTING
LINK PIN

BRACKET

CONNECTING
LINK

CLAMP

SPRING TIE PLATE

Fig. 11.3  Front stabilizer bar components — exploded view
(Sec 2)

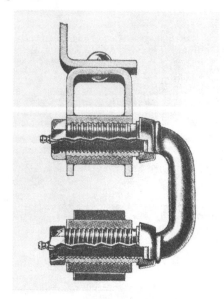

Fig. 11.4  Early model (pre-1957) threaded
bushing-type spring shackle (Sec 4)

4    Install the bushings in the shock absorber eyes, place the shock absorber in position, install the mounting nuts and tighten them to the specified torque.
5    Install the wheels, lower the vehicle and remove the jack.

## 4   Front spring — removal and installation

### Removal

1    Raise the front of the vehicle, support it securely on jackstands and remove the wheels.
2    Raise the axle with a jack just enough to relieve the weight from the spring.
3    Disconnect the stabilizer bar link (if equipped) and remove the U-bolts, nuts and tie plates.
4    Remove the spring shackle and rear spring hanger bolt, then remove the spring. On early models (prior to early 1957), the spring shackles have threaded instead of rubber bushings. These bushings may have either right or left-hand threads. Right-hand thread bushings have plain hex heads and left-hand thread bushings have a groove around the heads or a small forged boss on the lower shank of the shackle.

### Installation

5    Place the spring rear eye in the hanger bracket and install the bolt and nut loosely.
6    On later model rubber bushed shackles, place the rear spring eye in the shackle and install the shackle in the hanger with the nuts finger tight.
7    On early models with threaded bushing shackles, install the grease seal over the threaded end of the shackle up to the shoulder. Insert the shackle through the frame bracket and the spring eye. Hold the U-shackle tightly against the frame and start the upper bushing in the shackle, taking care not to cross thread it. Screw the bushing in about half-way and repeat the procedure on the lower bushing. Turn the upper and lower bushings in alternately until the head is snug against the frame bracket and the spring eye is 1/32-inch away from the inside of the hex head. Lubricate the bushing with oil and make sure the shackle can move freely with no binding.
8    Install the U-bolts and the tie plate, tightening the nuts to the specified torque. Connect the stabilizer bar.
9    Install the wheels, lower the vehicle weight onto the suspension and tighten the spring front and rear mounting bolts and nuts to the specified torque.

## 5   Front hub — removal and installation

### Removal

1    Remove the hub cap or hub assembly cover and loosen the wheel lug nuts. Raise the front of the vehicle, support it securely on jackstands and remove the wheels.
2    Remove the drive flange or axleshaft snap-ring. On drum brake models, remove the axle flange bolts and the flange as described in Chapter 8.
3    On disc brake-equipped models, remove the caliper (Chapter 9).
4    Straighten the lip of the outer locknut washer and remove the outer locknut and washer, followed by the inner locknut and washer.
5    Grasp the hub and brake drum or disc assembly securely and withdraw it from the spindle.

### Installation

6    Install the hub on the spindle.
7    Install the inner locknut and washer and adjust the wheel bearings as described in Section 9.
8    Install the disc brake caliper, outer locknut and washer, snap-ring, gasket and drive flange or hub assembly and hub cap.
9    Install the wheels and lower the vehicle.

## 6   Rear spring — removal and installation

### Removal

1    Raise the rear of the vehicle, support it securely on jackstands and

remove the wheels.
2    Use a jack to raise the vehicle weight off the spring.
3    Remove the U-bolts, nuts and tie plates.
4    Remove the bolt attaching the rear spring eye to the shackle. On very early models (prior to early 1957) which use threaded rather than rubber bushed shackles, the bushings may have either right or left-hand threads. The right-hand threaded bushings have plain hex heads, while the left-hand bushings have a groove around the heads or a small forged boss on the lower shank of the shackle.
5    Remove the front spring-to-frame rail hanger bolt.
6    Remove the spring from the vehicle.

### Installation

7    Place the spring in position and install the front spring-to-hanger bolt with the nut finger tight.
8    On vehicles with rubber bushed shackles, install the spring in the shackle with the nuts and bolts finger tight.
9    On early models with threaded bushing shackles, install the shackle as described in Section 4.
10   Install the U-bolt and tie plate, tightening the nuts to the specified torque.
11   Install the wheels, lower the vehicle weight onto the suspension and tighten the spring front and rear bolts (rubber bushed shackle) to the specified torque.

## 7   Spring bushing — check and replacement

### Check

1    All later models are equipped with silent block type rubber bushings which are pressed into the spring eyes. The bushings should be inspected for cracks, damage and looseness indicating excessive wear. To check for wear, jack up the frame until the weight is removed from the spring bushing. Pry the spring eye up-and-down to check for movement. If there is considerable movement, the bushing is worn and should be replaced.

### Replacement

2    Remove the spring (Section 4 or 6).
3    The bushings are of two different sizes and tools can be fabricated from threaded rod for pressing them out. For small diameter bushings, cut an eight (8) inch length of 3/8-inch diameter threaded rod and, for the large diameter bushings, cut an 11-inch length of 1/2-inch diameter threaded rod.
4    Insert the threaded rod half-way through the bushing.
5    Place a socket over one end of the rod with the open end toward the bushing to serve as a driver. The socket must be large engough to bear against the bushing outer sleeve and small enough to pass through the spring eye.
6    Install a flat washer and hex nut on the rod behind the socket.
7    On the opposite end of the threaded rod, install a 2-inch long (small bushing) or 3-inch long (large bushing) piece of pipe to serve as a receiver as shown in the illustrations. The inside diameter of the pipe

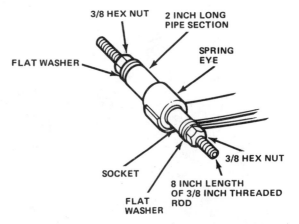

Fig. 11.5   Small diameter spring eye bushing replacement
(Sec 7)

**11**

must be large enough to accommodate the bushing while still seating against the spring eye surface.

8    Secure the pipe section on the rod with a flat washer and hex nut as shown in the illustrations. The washer must be large enough to properly support the pipe section alignment.

9    Tighten the hex nuts finger tight to align the components. The socket must be positioned in the spring eye and aligned with the bushing and the pipe must butt against the eye surface so the bushing can pass through it.

10   Press the bushing out of the spring eye by tightening the nut at the socket end of the rod.

11   Remove the bushing and tool from the spring eye.

12   Install the new bushing on the threaded rod and assemble and align the tools as previously described.

13   Line up the bushing with the spring eye and press the new bushing into position.

14   Loosen the nuts and check to make sure the bushing is centered in the spring eye with the ends of the bushing flush with or slightly below the sides of the eye. If necessary, reinstall the tools and adjust the bushing position.

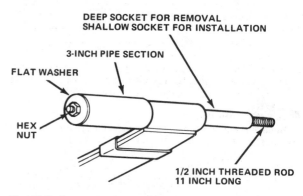

Fig. 11.6   Large diameter spring eye bushing replacement (Sec 7)

## 8   Steering knuckle — removal and installation

1    The steering knuckle on 1949 through 1971 models can only be removed or installed using special tools, so the job should be left to your dealer or a properly equipped shop.

2    To remove the knuckle on later models, raise the front of the vehicle, support it securely on jackstands and remove the front wheels.

3    Remove the front hub (Section 5) and axleshaft (Chapter 8).

4    Remove the brake assembly from the steering knuckle and hang it out of the way with wire.

5    Disconnect the tie-rod end from the steering knuckle arm.

6    Remove the lower ball-stud jam nut as shown in the illustration.

7    Remove the cotter pin from the upper ball-stud and loosen the nut until its top edge is flush with the top of the stud.

8    Use a lead hammer to unseat the upper and lower ball-studs.

9    Remove the upper ball-stud nut and separate the steering knuckle from the axle.

10   Replacement of the ball-studs requires special tools and service techniques. Consequently, if the ball-studs require replacement, the job should be left to a dealer or properly equipped shop.

11   Install the upper ball-stud split ring seat in the axle yoke with the top of the seat flush with the top of the yoke.

12   Install the steering knuckle on the axle yoke and install the lower ball-stud nut finger tight.

13   Use a jack to raise the knuckle into position so the lower ball-stud is held firmly in its seat and tighten the jam nut to the specified torque.

14   Use a split ring nut wrench (such as AMC tool J-25158) to tighten the upper ball-stud split ring seat to the specified torque as shown in the illustration. This will set the preload for the upper ball-stud.

15   Install the upper ball-stud nut, tighten it to the specified torque and install a new cotter pin. If the cotter pin holes do not line up, tighten the nut just enough to allow insertion of the pin. Do not loosen the nut to align the cotter pin holes.

16   Connect the steering rod and install the brake assembly.

17   Install the axleshaft and hub.

18   Install the wheels and lower the vehicle.

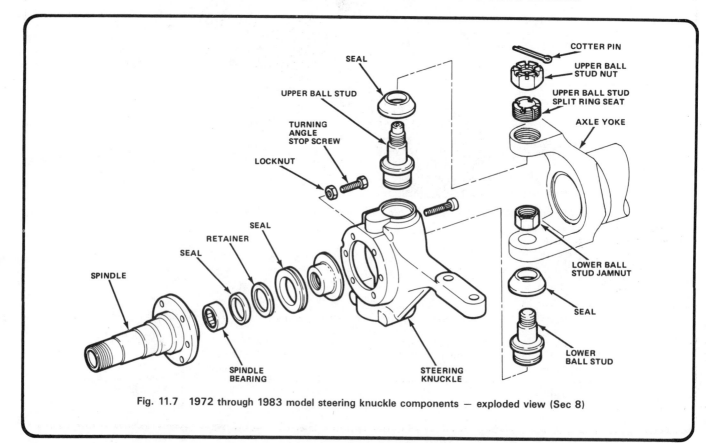

Fig. 11.7   1972 through 1983 model steering knuckle components — exploded view (Sec 8)

## 9  Wheel bearings — adjustment

1    The front wheel bearings on all models and the rear wheel bearings on early CJ-2A models with full-floating axles (Chapter 8) should be adjusted at the specified intervals. Also, the bearings should be adjusted if the check (Chapter 1) indicates excessive drag or play.
2    Raise the vehicle and support it securely on jackstands.

### Front wheel bearings

3    Remove the hub cap, snap-ring, drive flange and gasket and the outer locknut (Section 5). On some models it will be necessary to remove the flange with a tool (Chapter 8).
4    Straighten the outer locknut tabbed washer lip and remove the washer and locknut.
5    Loosen the inner locknut.
6    Rotate the wheel and tighten the locknut until the bearings bind. Alternately, if a torque wrench is available, tighten the locknut while rotating the wheel until a torque of 50 ft-lbs is achieved.

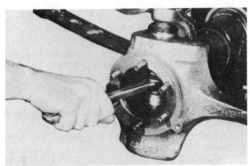

Fig. 11.8  Removing the lower ball-stud jam nut (Sec 8)

Fig. 11.9  Tightening the upper ball-stud split ring with a special nut wrench (Sec 8)

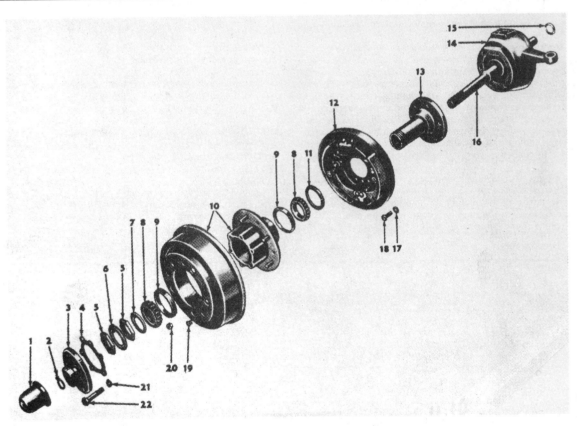

Fig. 11.10  Typical early model front hub and bearing assembly — exploded view (Sec 9)

| | | | |
|---|---|---|---|
| 1   Hub cap | 7   Tabbed washer | 12  Brake assembly | 17  Lock washer |
| 2   Snap-ring | 8   Bearing | 13  Spindle and bushing | 18  Bolt |
| 3   Drive flange | 9   Cup | 14  Steering knuckle | 19  Screw |
| 4   Gasket | 10  Hub and drum assembly | 15  Thrust washer | 20  Nut |
| 5   Locknut | 11  Seal | 16  Axleshaft | 21  Lock washer |
| 6   Tabbed washer | | | 22  Bolt |

11

7    While rotating the wheel, back off the inner locknut approximately 1/6 of a turn. The wheel should turn freely with no looseness or lateral movement.

8    Install the washer and locknut and tighten the nut to the specified torque.

9    Install the gasket, drive flange and hub cap.

### CJ-2A rear wheel bearings

10   Remove the drive flange screws and the axleshaft (Chapter 8).

11   Bend the lock washer lip back and remove the locknut and washer.

12   Rotate the wheel while adjusting the inner adjusting nut until the bearing binds. Back the nut off approximately 1/6 of a turn while rotating the wheel until it turns freely with no lateral movement or looseness.

13   Install the outer washer and locknut and bend the lip of the washer over the nut.

14   Install the axleshaft, using a new flange gasket.

---

### 10   Wheel bearings — inspection and lubrication

1    The front wheel bearings on all models and the rear wheel bearings on early CJ-2A models with full-floating axles should be inspected and lubricated at the specified intervals. The bearings should also be inspected and lubricated if leakage is noted.

2    Raise the vehicle and support it securely on jackstands.

### Front wheel bearings

3    Remove the front hub (Section 5).

4    On the rear side of the hub, use a screwdriver to pry out the inner bearing seal. As this is done, note the direction in which the seal is installed. The inner bearing can now be removed from the hub, again noting how it is installed.

5    Remove the outer bearing from the hub if it has not already been dislodged during hub removal.

6    Use solvent to clean the bearings, hub and spindle.

7    Allow the parts to air dry and inspect the bearings for cracks, heat discoloration, bent rollers, score marks and wear. Check the bearing races inside the hub for cracks, score marks and uneven surfaces. If the bearing races are defective, have them replaced by a repair shop which can press the new races squarely into position.

8    Use wheel bearing grease to pack the bearings. Work the grease completely into the bearings, forcing it between the rollers, race and cage.

9    Place the grease-packed inner bearing into the rear of the hub and put a little more grease outboard of the bearing.

10   Place a new seal over the inner bearing and tap on the seal with a hammer and block of wood until it is flush with the hub.

11   Carefully place the hub assembly onto the spindle and push the grease-packed outer bearing into position.

12   Install the inner locknut and washer and adjust the wheel bearings (Section 9).

13   Install the outer locknut and washer and the remainder of the hub assembly.

### CJ-2A rear wheel bearings

14   Remove the axleshaft and hub (Chapter 8). Drive out the inner wheel bearing and seal with a hammer and *brass* drift. The outer bearing should have been dislodged during hub removal.

15   Clean the bearings, hub and axle housing bearing surfaces with solvent.

16   Inspect the components as described in Step 7.

17   Pack the wheel bearings with wheel bearing grease, forcing it between the rollers, race and cage.

18   Spread a thin (approximately 1/16-inch) layer of grease inside the hub to prevent rust.

19   Position the grease-packed inner bearing in the rear of the hub and place a little more grease outboard of the bearing.

20   Place a new seal over the inner bearing with the lip toward the bearing and tap the seal with a hammer and block of wood until it is flush with the hub.

21   Carefully place the hub assembly onto the spindle and push the grease-packed outer bearing into position.

22   Install the washer and locknut, adjust the bearings (Section 9) and install the axleshaft.

23   Lower the vehicle.

---

### 11   Drag link — removal and installation

### Removal

1    Raise the front of the vehicle, support it securely on jackstands and remove the front wheels.

2    Remove the cotter pins from the ends of the drag link.

3    Use a screwdriver to unscrew the adjusting plugs and remove the ball seat, springs and spring plugs.

4    Remove the drag link, dust covers and dust shield from the vehicle.

### Installation

5    Place the drag link, dust covers and dust shields in position on the bellcrank and steering gear arm.

6    Install the ball seats, springs and spring plugs, as shown in the illustration.

7    Install the adjusting plugs and tighten them to 20 ft-lbs, then back them off one full turn. This will adjust the balljoints so they will be tight enough to prevent end play and still allow free movement. Install a new cotter pin in each end of the link.

8    Install the wheels and lower the vehicle.

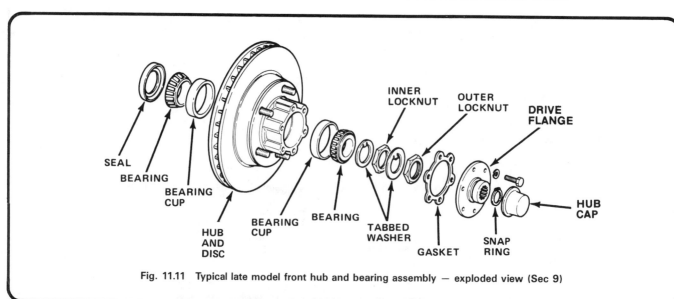

Fig. 11.11  Typical late model front hub and bearing assembly — exploded view (Sec 9)

Fig. 11.12  Typical early model steering
          linkage components (Sec 11)

1  Frame cross tube (CJ-3B)
2  Steering bellcrank bracket (CJ-3B)
3  Steering bellcrank
4  Front axle assembly
5  Drag link
6  Steering gear arm
7  Steering gear
8  Left steering knuckle and arm
9  Left shaft and universal joint
10  Left tie-rod socket
11  Left steering tie-rod
12  Left tie-rod socket
13  Right tie-rod socket
14  Bellcrank nut
15  Washer
16  Bolt
17  Bellcrank bearing
18  Bearing spacer (early model)
19  Washer
20  Bellcrank shaft
21  Bearing seal
22  Nut
23  Lock washer
24  Right steering tie-rod
25  Right shaft and universal joint
26  Right steering knuckle and arm

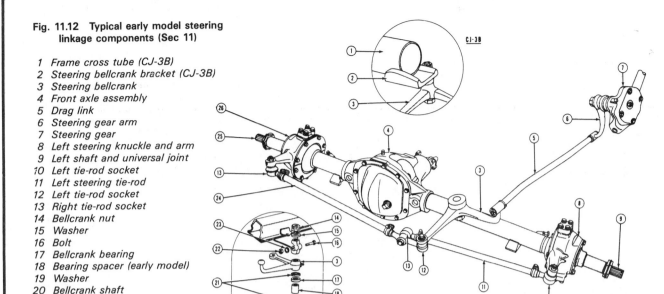

Fig. 11.13  Drag link
components — exploded
view (Sec 11)

1  Cotter pin
2  Large adjusting plug
3  Ball seat
4  Ball seat spring
5  Spring plug
6  Dust cover
7  Dust shield
8  Small adjusting plug
9  Lubrication fitting
10  Drag link

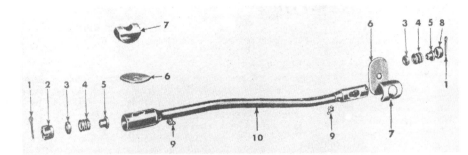

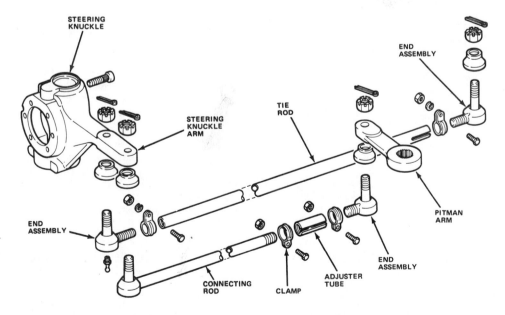

Fig. 11.14  Typical later model steering linkage components (Sec 12)

11

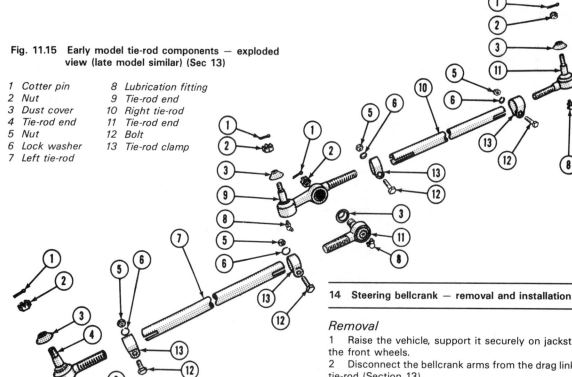

**Fig. 11.15 Early model tie-rod components — exploded view (late model similar) (Sec 13)**

| | |
|---|---|
| 1 Cotter pin | 8 Lubrication fitting |
| 2 Nut | 9 Tie-rod end |
| 3 Dust cover | 10 Right tie-rod |
| 4 Tie-rod end | 11 Tie-rod end |
| 5 Nut | 12 Bolt |
| 6 Lock washer | 13 Tie-rod clamp |
| 7 Left tie-rod | |

## 12  Steering connecting rod — removal and installation

### Removal

1   Raise the vehicle, support it securely on jackstands and remove the front wheels. Place the steering wheel in the straight ahead position with the steering arms parallel to the vehicle centerline.
2   Remove the cotter pins and nuts and disconnect the ends of the connecting rod from the Pitman arm and knuckle with a puller.

### Installation

3   Verify that the steering arm is parallel to the vehicle centerline.
4   Place the connecting rod in position on the Pitman arm and steering knuckle and install the retaining nuts and new cotter pins.
5   Install the wheels and lower the vehicle.
6   Have the front end alignment checked.

## 13  Tie-rod — removal and installation

### Removal

1   Raise the front of the vehicle, support it securely on jackstands and remove the wheels.
2   Remove the cotter pins and retaining nuts at both ends of the tie-rod. On steering damper-equipped models, remove the mounting nut and move the damper aside.
3   Use a puller to disconnect the tie-rod ends and remove the tie-rod assembly.
4   The rod ends can be removed from the tie-rod assembly by loosening the clamp bolts and unscrewing the ends.

### Installation

5   Place the tie-rod in position, install the nuts, tighten them to the specified torque and install new cotter pins.
6   Connect the damper (if equipped) to the tie-rod.
7   Install the wheels and lower the vehicle.
8   Have the front end alignment checked.

## 14  Steering bellcrank — removal and installation

### Removal

1   Raise the vehicle, support it securely on jackstands and remove the front wheels.
2   Disconnect the bellcrank arms from the drag link (Section 11) and tie-rod (Section 13).
3   Remove the clamp bolt and locknut.
4   Remove the bellcrank shaft locknut and the shaft, followed by the bellcrank.
5   Replace any worn or damaged bellcrank assembly components.

### Installation

6   When assembling the bellcrank components, make sure that new bearings are positioned 1/8-inch below the bellcrank face surface as shown in the illustration. The bearings are a light press fit, which will hold them in place. The chamfer on the washer nut must be installed facing the bellcrank.
7   Install the clamp bolt and locknut finger tight and adjust the bellcrank shaft locknut until the bellcrank just begins to rotate freely with no binding.
8   Tighten the clamp nut securely.
9   Connect the drag link and tie-rod to the bellcrank.
10  Install the wheels, lower the vehicle and have the front end alignment checked.

## 15  Steering damper — removal and installation

1   The steering damper should be replaced with a new one if it is damaged or leaking.

### Removal

2   With the front wheels in the straight-ahead position, raise the vehicle and support it securely on jackstands.
3   Remove the damper-to-spring tie plate locknut and lift the damper from the stud.
4   Remove the damper pushrod end-to-tie-rod bracket locknut and separate the damper from the vehicle.

### Installation

5   Attach the rubber bushings to the damper eyes and the pushrod.
6   Place the pushrod on the tie-rod bracket stud and install the remaining components.
7   Install the bushings in the damper mounting eye.
8   Pull back on the damper body to extend the piston and attach the mounting eye to the tie plate bracket stud.
9   Install the locknuts.
10  Lower the vehicle.

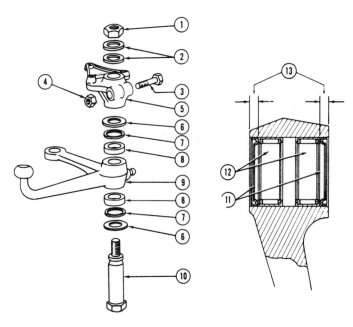

Fig. 11.16   Steering bellcrank components — exploded view (Sec 14)

| | |
|---|---|
| 1  Locknut | 8  Bearing |
| 2  Washer | 9  Bellcrank |
| 3  Clamp bolt | 10  Bellcrank shaft |
| 4  Locknut | 11  Seals |
| 5  Bellcrank support | 12  Bearings |
| 6  Washer | 13  1/8-inch clearance |
| 7  Seal | |

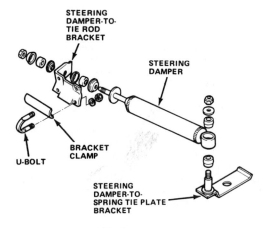

Fig. 11.17   Steering damper components — exploded view (Sec 15)

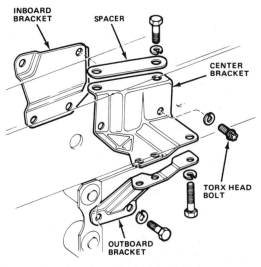

Fig. 11.18   1977 through 1983 model steering gear mounting brackets (Sec 16)

## 16   Steering gear — removal and installation

### Removal

1   On power steering-equipped models, disconnect the hoses from the steering gear housing and plug them. Remove the clamp bolt and nut and disconnect the intermediate shaft from the stub shaft.
2   Paint alignment marks on the steering gear arm and steering arm (early models) or Pitman arm and steering gear Pitman shaft (late models) to simplify installation.
3   Remove the steering gear arm or Pitman arm bolt and washer and remove the arm with a puller (AMC tool J-6632).
4   On early models (through 1976), remove the steering gear-to-frame bolts and separate the steering gear from the frame.
5   On 1977 through 1983 models, raise the left side of the frame just enough to relieve the pressure on the left front spring and support the frame with a jackstand. Remove the crossmember cover (if equipped), followed by the bolts attaching the steering gear lower bracket to the frame. Remove the steering gear upper bracket-to-frame rail bolts and separate the gear from the frame. The brackets can be unbolted from the frame.

### Installation

6   On all models, clean the mounting bolt threads and apply thread-locking compound prior to installation.
7   On 1949 through 1976 models, engage the steering shaft with the steering gear. Place the steering gear in position on the frame and install the mounting bolts. Tighten them to the specified torque.
8   On 1977 through 1983 models, attach the mounting brackets to the steering gear and tighten the bolts to the specified torque.
9   On all models, tighten the steering shaft coupling bolts and nuts to the specified torque.
10   On all models, install the steering gear arm or Pitman arm and tighten the nut to the specified torque.
11   On 1977 through 1983 models, install the crossmember cover (if equipped), remove the jackstand and lower the vehicle.
12   On power steering-equipped models, connect the hoses and bleed the system (Section 18).

## 17   Power steering pump — removal and installation

### Removal

1   Loosen the pump belt adjusting bolts, push the pump toward the engine and remove the belt and (if equipped) the air pump belt.
2   Disconnect the hoses from the pump and plug them and the pump connections to prevent the entry of dirt.
3   On V8 engines, remove the front bracket-to-engine bolts and lift the pump and bracket from the engine compartment.
4   On six-cylinder engines, remove the mounting bolts and nuts and lift the pump away from the engine.

### Installation

5   On V8 engines, install the front mounting bracket on the pump.
6   On all models, place the pump in position in the mounting bracket and install the pump-to-bracket bolts and nuts.
7   Connect the hoses to the pump. Fill the pump reservoir with the specified fluid and rotate the pulley in a counterclockwise direction until no more bubbles are expelled from the fluid.
8   Install the pump and (if equipped) the air pump drivebelt.
9   Adjust the belt tension (Chapter 1) and tighten the bracket adjusting bolts.
10   Tighten all mounting bolts to the specified torque.
11   Fill the reservoir with fluid and bleed the air from the power steering system (Section 18).

11

## 18    Power steering system — bleeding procedure

1    Bleeding air out of the power steering system is accomplished in the following manner. Check the fluid level first, with the engine and pump at normal operating temperature, adding fluid as necessary.
2    Raise and support the front of the vehicle on jackstands.
3    Turn the steering wheel lock-to-lock (without contacting the stops) two or three times and recheck the fluid level. It should be at the Cold or Full cold mark.
4    Start the engine and let it run at a fast idle. Turn the steering wheel lock-to-lock (again, without contacting the stops) and recheck the fluid level to make sure it is above the pump body. Fluid with air in it will be light tan or tan-orange in color.
5    Continue turning the steering wheel lock-to-lock until all air is bled from the system.
6    After bleeding the air from the system, return the wheels to the straight-ahead position, allow the engine to run for two or three more minutes, shut it off and lower the vehicle.
7    Road test the vehicle to check the steering action and response and make sure the fluid is at the Hot mark.

## 19    Steering wheel — removal and installation

### Removal
1    Disconnect the negative battery cable from the battery.
2    Turn the steering wheel until the front wheels are in the straight-ahead position.
3    Remove the horn button. This can be done by grasping it and pulling out or, on some models, rotating the button until the tabs align with the notches and then withdrawing it.
4    Remove the steering wheel nut and washer.
5    Remove the receiver, bushing and contact plate.
6    Scribe or paint alignment marks on the steering wheel hub and shaft for reference during reassembly.
7    Use a puller to remove the steering wheel from the shaft.

### Installation
8    Align the steering wheel and hub marks made during removal and install the wheel on the shaft.
9    Install the contact plate, bushing and receiver assembly.
10   Install the steering wheel washer and nut and tighten the nut to the specified torque.
11   Connect the negative battery cable.

## 20    Wheel alignment — general information

**Note:** *Since wheel alignment equipment is generally out of the reach*

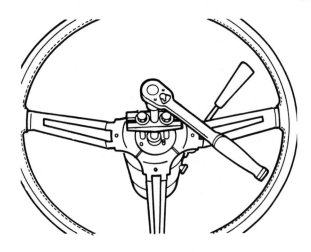

**Fig. 11.19   Removing the steering wheel with a special puller (Sec 19)**

*of the home mechanic, this Section is intended only to familiarize the reader with the basic terms used and procedures followed during a typical wheel alignment job. In the event that your vehicle needs a wheel alignment check or adjustment, we recommend that the work be done by a reputable front end alignment and repair shop.*

The three basic adjustments made when aligning a vehicle's front end are toe-in, caster and camber.

Toe-in is the amount the front wheels are angled in relationship to the centerline of the vehicle. For example, in a vehicle with zero toe-in, the distance measured between the front edges of the wheels is the same as the distance measured between the rear edges of the wheels. The wheels are running parallel with the centerline of the vehicle. Toe-in is adjusted by lengthening or shortening the tie-rods. Incorrect toe-in will cause tires to wear improperly by making them 'scrub' against the road surface.

Camber and caster are the angles at which the wheel and suspension upright are inclined to the vertical. Camber is the angle of the wheel in the lateral (side-to-side) plane, while caster is the angle of the wheel and upright in the longitudinal (fore-and-aft) plane. Camber angle affects the amount of tire tread which contacts the road and compensates for changes in the suspension geometry when the vehicle is traveling around curves or over an undulating surface. Caster angle affects the self-centering action of the steering, which governs straight-line stability.

# Chapter 12   Body

## Contents

Body and frame repairs — major damage . . . . . . . . . . . . . . .   5
Body repair — minor damage  . . . . . . . . . . . . . . . . . . . . .   4
Bumpers — removal and installation . . . . . . . . . . . . . . . . .   11
Front fender — replacement . . . . . . . . . . . . . . . . . . . . . .   7
General information . . . . . . . . . . . . . . . . . . . . . . . . . . . .   1
Hood — removal and installation . . . . . . . . . . . . . . . . . . . .   9
Instrument panel crash pad — removal and installation . . . . .   15
Maintenance — body and frame . . . . . . . . . . . . . . . . . . . . .   2

Maintenance — hinges and latches . . . . . . . . . . . . . . . . . . .   6
Maintenance — upholstery and carpets . . . . . . . . . . . . . . . .   3
Radiator grille — removal and installation . . . . . . . . . . . . . .   10
Seat belts — removal and installation . . . . . . . . . . . . . . . . .   14
Seats — removal and installation . . . . . . . . . . . . . . . . . . . .   13
Tailgate — removal and installation . . . . . . . . . . . . . . . . . .   12
Windshield and frame assembly — removal and installation . .   8

## Specifications

### Torque specifications

| | Ft-lb | Nm |
|---|---|---|
| Seat belt anchor bolts . . . . . . . . . . . . . . . . . . . . . . . . . . . | 25 to 35 | 34 to 47 |

## 1   General information

All models have a separate frame and body. The hood, front fenders, radiator grille, windshield and frame assembly and tailgate can be unbolted and removed in the event of damage.

## 2   Maintenance — body and frame

1   The condition of your vehicle's body is very important, because it is on this that the second-hand value will mainly depend. It is much more difficult to repair a neglected or damaged body than it is to repair mechanical components. The hidden areas of the body, such as the fender wells, the frame, and the engine compartment, are equally important, although obviously do not require as frequent attention as the rest of the body.
2   Once a year, or every 12 000 miles, it is a good idea to have the underside of the body and the frame steam cleaned. All traces of dirt and oil will be removed and the underside can then be inspected carefully for rust, damaged brake lines, frayed electrical wiring, damaged cables, and other problems. The front suspension components should be greased after completion of this job.
3   At the same time, clean the engine and the engine compartment using either a steam cleaner or a water soluble degreaser.
4   The fender wells should be given particular attention, as undercoating can peel away and stones and dirt thrown up by the tires can cause the paint to chip and flake, allowing rust to set in. If rust is found, clean down to the bare metal and apply an anti-rust paint.
5   The body should be washed once a week (or when dirty). Wet the vehicle thoroughly to soften the dirt, then wash it down with a soft sponge and plenty of clean soapy water. If the surplus dirt is not washed off very carefully, it will in time wear down the paint.
6   Spots of tar or asphalt coating thrown up from the road should be removed with a cloth soaked in solvent.
7   Once every six months, give the body and chrome trim a thorough wax job. If a chrome cleaner is used to remove rust from any of the vehicle's plated parts, remember that the cleaner also removes part of the chrome, so use it sparingly.

## 3   Maintenance — upholstery and carpets

1   Every three months, remove the carpets or mats and clean the interior of the vehicle (more frequently if necessary). Vacuum the upholstery and carpets to remove loose dirt and dust.
2   If the upholstery is soiled, apply upholstery cleaner with a damp sponge and wipe it off with a clean, dry cloth.

**12**

## 4  Body repair — minor damage

*See color photo sequence*

### *Repair of minor scratches*

If the scratch is very superficial and does not penetrate to the metal of the body, repair is very simple. Lightly rub the scratched area with a fine rubbing compound to remove loose paint and built-up wax. Rinse the area with clean water.

Apply touch-up paint to the scratch, using a small brush. Continue to apply thin layers of paint until the surface of the paint in the scratch is level with the surrounding paint. Allow the new paint at least two weeks to harden, then blend it into the surrounding paint by rubbing with a very fine rubbing compound. Finally, apply a coat of wax to the scratch area.

If the scratch has penetrated the paint and exposed the metal of the body, causing the metal to rust, a different repair technique is required. Remove all loose rust from the bottom of the scratch with a pocket knife, then apply rust-inhibiting paint to prevent the formation of rust in the future. Using a rubber or nylon applicator, coat the scratched area with glaze-type filler. If required, the filler can be mixed with thinner to provide a very thin paste, which is ideal for filling narrow scratches. Before the glaze filler in the scratch hardens, wrap a piece of smooth cotton cloth around the tip of a finger. Dip the cloth in thinner and then quickly wipe it along the surface of the scratch. This will ensure that the surface of the filler is slightly hollow. The scratch can now be painted over as described earlier in this section.

### *Repair of dents*

When repairing dents, the first job is to pull the dent out until the affected area is as close as possible to its original shape. There is no point in trying to restore the original shape completely as the metal in the damaged area will have stretched on impact and cannot be restored to its original contours. It is better to bring the level of the dent up to a point which is about 1/8-inch below the level of the surrounding metal. In cases where the dent is very shallow, it is not worth trying to pull it out at all.

If the back side of the dent is accessible, it can be hammered out gently from behind using a soft-faced hammer. While doing this, hold a block of wood firmly against the opposite side of the metal to absorb the hammer blows and prevent the metal from being stretched out.

If the dent is in a section of the body which has double layers, or some other factor that makes it inaccessible from behind, a different technique is required. Drill several small holes through the metal inside the damaged area, particularly in the deeper sections. Screw long, self-tapping screws into the holes just enough for them to get a good grip in the metal. Now the dent can be pulled out by pulling on the protruding heads of the screws with locking pliers.

The next stage of repair is the removal of paint from the damaged area and from an inch or so of the surrounding metal. This is easily done with a wire brush or sanding disk in a drill motor, although it can be done just as effectively by hand with sandpaper. To complete the preparation for filling, score the surface of the bare metal with a screwdriver or the tang of a file (or drill small holes in the affected area). This will provide a very good grip for the filler material. To complete the repair, see the Section on filling and painting.

### *Repair of rust holes or gashes*

Remove all paint from the affected area and from an inch or so of the surrounding metal using a sanding disk or wire brush mounted in a drill motor. If these are not available, a few sheets of sandpaper will do the job just as effectively. With the paint removed, you will be able to determine the severity of the corrosion and decide whether to replace the whole panel, if possible, or repair the affected area. New body panels are not as expensive as most people think and it is often quicker to install a new panel than to repair large areas of rust.

Remove all trim pieces from the affected area (except those which will act as a guide to the original shape of the damaged body, i.e. headlight shells, etc.). Then, using metal snips or a hacksaw blade, remove all loose metal and any other metal that is badly affected by rust. Hammer the edges of the hole in to create a slight depression for the filler material.

Wire brush the affected area to remove the powdery rust from the surface of the metal. If the back of the rusted area is accessible, treat it with rust-inhibiting paint.

Before filling is done, block the hole in some way. This can be done with sheet metal riveted or screwed into place, or by stuffing the hole with wire mesh.

Once the hole is blocked off, the affected area can be filled and painted (see the following section on filling and painting).

### *Filling and painting*

Many types of body fillers are available, but generally speaking, body repair kits which contain filler paste and a tube of resin hardener are best for this type of repair work. A wide, flexible plastic or nylon applicator will be necessary for imparting a smooth and contoured finish to the surface of the filler material.

Mix up a small amount of filler on a clean piece of wood or cardboard (use the hardener sparingly). Follow the manufacturer's instructions on the package, otherwise the filler will set incorrectly.

Using the applicator, apply the filler paste to the prepared area. Draw the applicator across the surface of the filler to achieve the desired contour and to level the filler surface. As soon as a contour that approximates the original one is achieved, stop working the paste. If you continue, the paste will begin to stick to the applicator. Continue to add thin layers of filler paste at 20-minute intervals until the level of the filler is just above the surrounding metal.

Once the filler has hardened, the excess can be removed with a body file. From then on, progressively finer grades of sandpaper should be used, starting with a 180-grit paper and finishing with 600-grit wet-or-dry paper. Always wrap the sandpaper around a flat rubber or wooden block, otherwise the surface of the filler will not be completely flat. During the sanding of the filler surface, the wet-or-dry paper should be periodically rinsed in water. This will ensure that a very smooth finish is produced in the final stage.

At this point, the repair area should be surrounded by a ring of bare metal, which in turn should be encircled by the finely feathered edge of good paint. Rinse the repair area with clean water until all of the dust produced by the sanding operation is gone.

Spray the entire area with a light coat of primer. This will reveal any imperfections in the surface of the filler. Repair the imperfections with fresh filler paste or glaze filler and once more smooth the surface with sandpaper. Repeat this spray-and-repair procedure until you are satisfied that the surface of the filler and the feathered edge of the paint are perfect. Rinse the area with clean water and allow it to dry completely.

The repair area is now ready for painting. Spray painting must be carried out in a warm, dry, windless and dust-free atmosphere. These conditions can be created if you have access to a large indoor work area, but if you are forced to work in the open, you will have to pick the day very carefully. If you are working indoors, dousing the floor in the work area with water will help settle the dust which would otherwise be in the air. If the repair area is confined to one body panel, mask off the surrounding panels. This will help minimize the effects of a slight mismatch in paint color. Trim pieces such as chrome strips, door handles, etc., will also need to be masked off or removed. Use masking tape and several thicknesses of newspaper for the masking operations.

Before spraying, shake the paint can thoroughly, then spray a test area until the spray painting technique is mastered. Cover the repair area with a thick coat of primer. The thickness should be built up using several thin layers of primer rather than one thick one. Using 600-grit wet-or-dry sandpaper, rub down the surface of the primer until it is very smooth. While doing this, the work area should be thoroughly rinsed with water and the wet-or-dry sandpaper periodically rinsed as well. Allow the primer to dry before spraying additional coats.

Spray on the top coat, again building up the thickness by using several thin layers of paint. Begin spraying in the center of the repair area and then, using a circular motion, work out until the whole repair area and about two inches of the surrounding original paint is covered. Remove all masking material 10 to 15 minutes after spraying on the final coat of paint. Allow the new paint at least two weeks to harden, then use a very fine rubbing compound to blend the edges of the new paint into the existing paint. Finally, apply a coat of wax.

## 5  Body and frame repairs — major damage

1    Major damage must be repaired by an auto body/frame repair shop with the required welding and hydraulic straightening equipment.

2   If the damage is serious, have the frame checked for correct alignment, as the handling characteristics of the vehicle will be affected. Other problems, such as excessive tire wear and wear in the transmission and steering may also occur.

### 6   Maintenance — hinges and latches

Every 3000 miles or three months, the hood, windshield, tailgate and glovebox hinges, as well as the hood latches, should be lubricated with a few drops of oil. Also, the hood latch mechanism should be given a thin coat of grease to reduce wear and ensure free movement.

### 7   Front fender — replacement

1   Remove or disconnect all components and wire connectors attached to the fender and apron.
2   Remove the rocker panel molding (if equipped) and remove the bolts and washers attaching the fender and brace to the dash panel.
3   Remove the fender-to-radiator grille bolts, nuts and washers.
4   Pull the fender out and separate it from the vehicle.
5   To install the fender, place it in position and install the bolts, washers and nuts attaching it to the radiator grille and dash panel.
6   Install the brace-to-dash and fender attaching bolts and washers.
7   Connect the side marker light and install the components which were previously removed.

### 8   Windshield and frame assembly — removal and installation

1   Disconnect the windshield wiper motor electrical or vacuum hose connector.
2   On early models (through 1975), unlatch the two clamps and fold the windshield forward until the slot lines up with the flat side of the pin in the body hinges. Slide the windshield off the pins and separate it from the vehicle.
3   On later models, remove the Torx-head screws attaching the windshield hinge to the frame. Remove the hold-down knobs and separate the windshield from the vehicle.
4   To install the windshield on early models, slide it onto the pins, swing it to the upright position and latch the clamps.
5   On later models, place the windshield in position and install the Torx-head screws and hold-down knobs.
6   Connect the windshield wiper motor harness or vacuum hose.

### 9   Hood — removal and installation

1   Release the hood latches and safety catch.
2   Mark the position of the hinges on the hood with tape or a wax-type pencil.
3   Remove the bolts attaching the hinges to the hood and, with the help of an assistant, separate the hood from the vehicle.
4   Place the hood in position, align the hinges with the marks made during removal and install the bolts.

### 10   Radiator grille — removal and installation

1   On air-conditioned models, have the system discharged by a qualified technician.
2   Remove the front crossmember cover (if equipped) and the screws and washers retaining the radiator shroud to the grille.
3   Remove the grille-to-fender bolts and washers.
4   Remove the radiator grille-to-frame crossmember hold-down assembly, noting the parts sequence shown in the illustration.
5   Loosen the nuts attaching the radiator support rods to the grille guard support brackets and separate the rods from the brackets.
6   Tilt the grille panel forward and disconnect all wires which would interfere with removal.
7   Disconnect the air-conditioning high-pressure hose at the sight glass and plug the connections to prevent the entry of dirt. **Caution:** *The system must first be discharged by a qualified technician or injury could result.*
8   Disconnect the air-conditioning high-pressure hose at the compressor fitting and plug the connections.

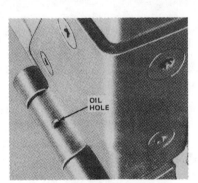

Fig. 12.1   Hood hinge lubrication points (Sec 6)

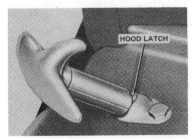

Fig. 12.2   Hood latch lubrication point (Sec 6)

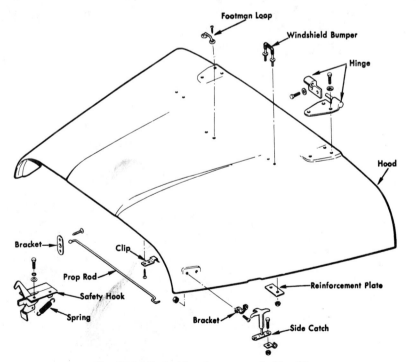

Fig. 12.3   Typical hood components (Sec 9)

These photos illustrate a method of repairing simple dents. They are intended to supplement *Body repair - minor damage* in this Chapter and should not be used as the sole instructions for body repair on these vehicles.

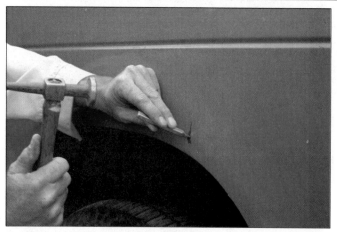

1   If you can't access the backside of the body panel to hammer out the dent, pull it out with a slide-hammer-type dent puller. In the deepest portion of the dent or along the crease line, drill or punch hole(s) at least one inch apart . . .

2   . . . then screw the slide-hammer into the hole and operate i Tap with a hammer near the edge of the dent to help 'pop' the metal back to its original shape. When you're finished, the dent area should be close to its original contour and about 1/8-inch below the surface of the surrounding metal

3   Using coarse-grit sandpaper, remove the paint down to the bare metal. Hand sanding works fine, but the disc sander shown here makes the job faster. Use finer (about 320-grit) sandpaper to feather-edge the paint at least one inch around the dent area

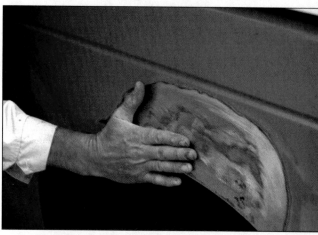

4   When the paint is removed, touch will probably be more helpful than sight for telling if the metal is straight. Hammer down the high spots or raise the low spots as necessary. Clean the repair area with wax/silicone remover

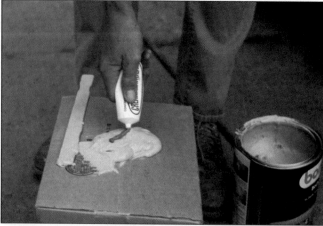

5   Following label instructions, mix up a batch of plastic filler and hardener. The ratio of filler to hardener is critical, and, if you mix it incorrectly, it will either not cure properly or cure too quickly (you won't have time to file and sand it into shape)

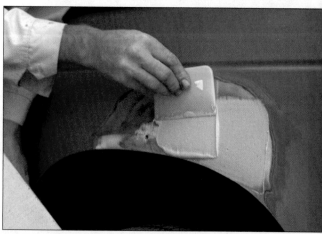

6   Working quickly so the filler doesn't harden, use a plastic applicator to press the body filler firmly into the metal, assuring bonds completely. Work the filler until it matches the original contour and is slightly above the surrounding metal

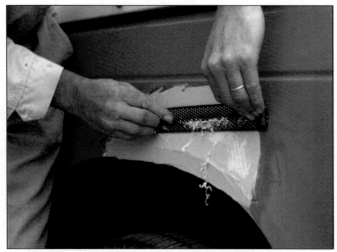

7   Let the filler harden until you can just dent it with your fingernail. Use a body file or Surform tool (shown here) to rough-shape the filler

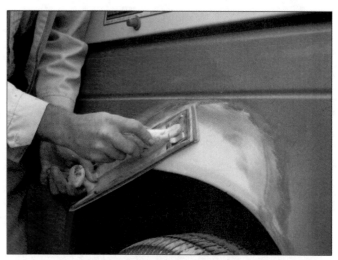

8   Use coarse-grit sandpaper and a sanding board or block to work the filler down until it's smooth and even. Work down to finer grits of sandpaper - always using a board or block - ending up with 360 or 400 grit

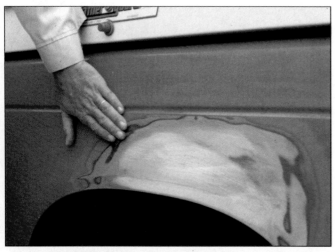

9   You shouldn't be able to feel any ridge at the transition from the filler to the bare metal or from the bare metal to the old paint. As soon as the repair is flat and uniform, remove the dust and mask off the adjacent panels or trim pieces

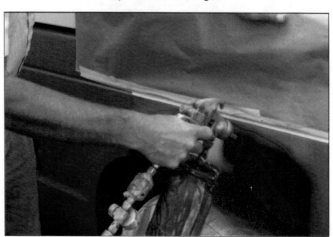

10   Apply several layers of primer to the area. Don't spray the primer on too heavy, so it sags or runs, and make sure each coat is dry before you spray on the next one. A professional-type spray gun is being used here, but aerosol spray primer is available inexpensively from auto parts stores

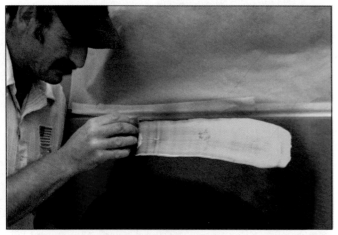

11   The primer will help reveal imperfections or scratches. Fill these with glazing compound. Follow the label instructions and sand it with 360 or 400-grit sandpaper until it's smooth. Repeat the glazing, sanding and respraying until the primer reveals a perfectly smooth surface

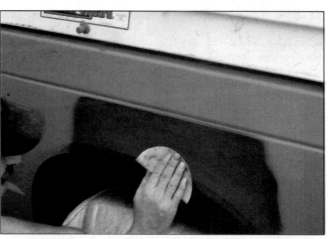

12   Finish sand the primer with very fine sandpaper (400 or 600-grit) to remove the primer overspray. Clean the area with water and allow it to dry. Use a tack rag to remove any dust, then apply the finish coat. Don't attempt to rub out or wax the repair area until the paint has dried completely (at least two weeks)

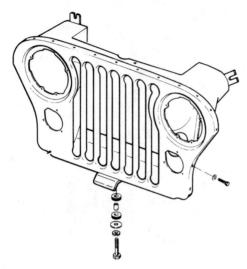

Fig. 12.4  Radiator grille and hold-down
assembly — exploded view (Sec 10)

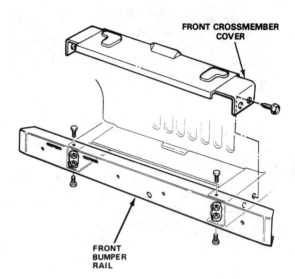

Fig. 12.5  Front bumper and crossmember cover (Sec 11)

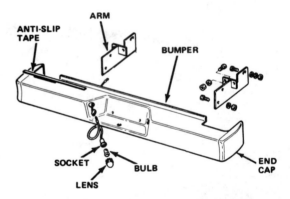

Fig. 12.6  Typical later model step rear bumper components
(Sec 11)

9    Separate the grille from the vehicle.
10   To install the grille, place it in position and connect the wires.
11   Remove the plugs and connect the air-conditioning hoses.
12   Place the radiator support rods in position in the grille support brackets and install the mounting hardware.
13   Attach the grille to the crossmember hold-down assembly.
14   Align the grille panel with the fenders and install the retaining bolts and washers.
15   Install the screws and washers retaining the radiator shroud.
16   Install the crossmember cover (if equipped).
17   Take the vehicle to a properly equipped shop to have the air-conditioning system recharged and checked for leaks.

## 11   Bumpers — removal and installation

1    Disconnect all components which could interfere with removal (such as fog lights and license plate lights).
2    On front bumpers, remove the front crossmember cover (if equipped) from the frame extensions.
3    Remove the mounting bolts and nuts and separate the bumper from the vehicle.
4    To install the bumper, place it in position and install the mounting nuts and bolts.
5    Install or connect all components which were removed.

## 12   Tailgate — removal and installation

1    On most models the tailgate is held in the closed position by hooks which pass through the slotted brackets on the tailgate and body. To remove the tailgate, rotate it approximately 45 degrees from the full up position, disengage the right hinge and then rotate it a few degrees further to disengage the left hinge. Separate the tailgate from the vehicle.
2    On late model CJ-7 and Scrambler models, the tailgate is held in place by Torx-head screws and supported by two cables. Remove the screws and washers retaining the cables and, with the tailgate closed, remove the Torx-head screws and separate the tailgate from the vehicle.
3    To install the slotted bracket-type tailgates, hold the tailgate at approximately 45 degrees from the full up position and engage the right hinge. Rotate the tailgate a few degrees further and engage the left hinge.
4    On late model CJ-7 and Scrambler models, place the tailgate in position and install the Torx-head screws. Install the support cables on the tailgate.

## 13   Seats — removal and installation

1    Remove the bolts attaching the seat assembly brace or support to the floor pan and lift the seat out of the vehicle.
2    Place the seat assembly in position and install the mounting bolts.

## 14   Seat belts — removal and installation

1    Remove the anchor bolts and the seat belts. On later models a Torx-head bolt, requiring a special tool for removal, is used to anchor the seat bolts.
2    Plate the seat belt in position, install the anchor bolts and tighten them to the specified torque.

## 15   Instrument panel crash pad — removal and installation

1    Fold the windshield forward for access.
2    Remove the retaining screws and separate the crash pad from the instrument panel. On earlier models it will be necessary to use a flat blade tool, such as a putty knife, inserted between the frame and the pad to pry the four clips loose.
3    Place the pad in position and snap the clips (if equipped) into the retaining holes. Install the retaining screws.

# Chapter 13 Supplement: Revisions and information on 1984 through 1986 models

## Contents

Introduction . . . . . . . . . . . . . . . . . . . . . . . . . . . . . . . . . . . . 1
Specifications . . . . . . . . . . . . . . . . . . . . . . . . . . . . . . . . . . 2
Tune-up and routine maintenance . . . . . . . . . . . . . . . . . . . 3
  Routine maintenance intervals
  Locking front hub lubrication
  Ignition timing check and adjustment (150 cubic inch
    four-cylinder engine)
Engine — 150 cubic inch four-cylinder . . . . . . . . . . . . . . . . 4
  General information
  Oversize/undersize components
  Removal and installation
  Rocker arm cover removal and installation
  Timing cover, chain and sprocket removal and installation

Oil seal replacement
Cylinder head installation
Intake/exhaust manifold installation
Engine — in-line six-cylinder . . . . . . . . . . . . . . . . . . . . . . 5
  Intake/exhaust manifold installation
Fuel and exhaust systems . . . . . . . . . . . . . . . . . . . . . . . . 6
  General information
  Carter YFA carburetor
Engine electrical systems . . . . . . . . . . . . . . . . . . . . . . . . . 7
  General information
Emissions control systems . . . . . . . . . . . . . . . . . . . . . . . . 8
  General information

## 1 Introduction

This supplement contains specifications and service procedure changes that apply to all Jeep CJ models produced from 1984 through 1986. Also included is information related to previous models that was not available at the time of original publication of this manual.

Where no differences (or very minor differences) exist between 1984 through 1986 models and earlier models, no information is given. In such instances, the original material included in Chapters 1 through 12 should be used. Therefore, owners of 1984 through 1986 vehicles should refer to this Chapter *before* using the information in the original Chapters of the manual.

## 2 Specifications

*Note: The following specifications are revisions of or supplementary to those listed at the beginning of each Chapter of this manual. The original specifications apply unless alternative figures are included here.*

## 150 cubic inch four-cylinder engine

### Tune-up and routine maintenance

| | |
|---|---|
| Engine oil (with filter change) . . . . . . . . . . . . . . . . . . . . . . | 4 US qts |
| Cooling system | |
|   standard . . . . . . . . . . . . . . . . . . . . . . . . . . . . . . . . . . . . | 11 qts |
|   with air conditioning or HD system . . . . . . . . . . . . . . . . . | 14 qts |
| Spark plug type . . . . . . . . . . . . . . . . . . . . . . . . . . . . . . . | Champion RFN14LY or FN14LY |
| Spark plug gap | |
|   1984 | |
|     50-state . . . . . . . . . . . . . . . . . . . . . . . . . . . . . . . . . . | 0.035 in |
|     with high altitude compensation . . . . . . . . . . . . . . . . . . | 0.033 to 0.038 in |
|   1985 and 1986 . . . . . . . . . . . . . . . . . . . . . . . . . . . . . | See *Vehicle Emissions Control Information* label located in the engine compartment |

*Tune-up and routine maintenance (continued)*

| | |
|---|---|
| Distributor direction of rotation | Clockwise |
| Ignition timing | |
|     50-state | 12° BTDC + 1° |
|     high altitude | 19° BTDC + 1° |
| Curb idle settings | See *Vehicle Emissions Control Information* label located in the engine compartment |
| Compression pressure | 155 to 185 psi |
| Maximum variation between cylinders | 30 psi |
| Firing order | 1-3-4-2 |

Cylinder numbers/firing order

## Engine

### General

| | |
|---|---|
| Displacement | 150 cu in (2.46 liters) |
| Bore and stroke | 3.876 x 3.188 in |
| Compression ratio | 9.2:1 |
| Oil pressure | |
|     600 rpm | 13 psi |
|     above 1600 rpm | 37 to 75 psi |

### Engine block

| | |
|---|---|
| Cylinder bore | |
|     diameter | 3.8751 to 3.8775 in |
|     taper limit | 0.001 in |
|     out-of-round limit | 0.001 in |
| Deck warpage limit | 0.002 in over 6 in |

### Pistons and rings

| | |
|---|---|
| Piston-to-bore clearance | |
|     standard | 0.0009 to 0.0017 in |
|     preferred | 0.0012 to 0.0013 in |
| Piston ring side clearance | |
|     compression | |
|         standard | 0.0017 to 0.0032 in |
|         preferred | 0.0017 in |
|     oil control | |
|         standard | 0.001 to 0.008 in |
|         preferred | 0.003 in |
| Piston ring end gap | |
|     compression | 0.010 to 0.020 in |
|     oil control | 0.010 to 0.025 in |

### Crankshaft

| | |
|---|---|
| Main journal | |
|     diameter | 2.4996 to 2.5001 in |
|     taper limit | 0.0005 in |
|     out-of-round limit | 0.0005 in |
| Main bearing oil clearance | |
|     standard | 0.001 to 0.0025 in |
|     preferred | 0.002 in |
| Connecting rod journal | |
|     diameter | 2.0934 to 2.0955 in |
|     taper limit | 0.0005 in |
|     out-of-round limit | 0.0005 in |
| Connecting rod bearing oil clearance | |
|     standard | 0.001 to 0.003 in |
|     preferred | 0.0015 to 0.002 in |
| Connecting rod end play | 0.010 to 0.0019 in |
| Crankshaft end play | 0.0015 to 0.0065 in |

### Camshaft

| | |
|---|---|
| Bearing journal diameter | |
|     number 1 | 2.029 to 2.030 in |
|     number 2 | 2.019 to 2.020 in |
|     number 3 | 2.009 to 2.010 in |
|     number 4 | 1.999 to 2.000 in |
| Bearing oil clearance | 0.001 to 0.003 in |
| Lobe lift | 0.265 in |
| End play | Zero (engine operating) |

### Cylinder head and valve train

| | |
|---|---|
| Head warpage limit | 0.002 in over 6 in |
| Intake valve seat angle | 44° 30' |
| Exhaust valve seat angle | 44° 30' |
| Intake valve seat width | 0.040 to 0.060 in |
| Exhaust valve seat width | 0.040 to 0.060 in |
| Valve seat runout limit | 0.0025 in |

| | |
|---|---|
| Valve guide inside diameter . . . . . . . . . . . . . . . . . . . . . . | 0.313 to 0.314 in |
| Intake valve face angle . . . . . . . . . . . . . . . . . . . . . . . . | 44° |
| Exhaust valve face angle . . . . . . . . . . . . . . . . . . . . . . . | 44° |
| Valve margin width . . . . . . . . . . . . . . . . . . . . . . . . . . | 1/32 in minimum |
| Valve stem diameter . . . . . . . . . . . . . . . . . . . . . . . . . . | 0.311 to 0.312 in |
| Valve stem-to-guide clearance . . . . . . . . . . . . . . . . . . . | 0.001 to 0.003 in |
| Valve spring free length . . . . . . . . . . . . . . . . . . . . . . . | 1.82 in |
| Lifter/tappet type . . . . . . . . . . . . . . . . . . . . . . . . . . . | Hydraulic |
| Valve lash adjustment . . . . . . . . . . . . . . . . . . . . . . . . . | Zero |
| Lifter bore diameter . . . . . . . . . . . . . . . . . . . . . . . . . . | 0.9055 to 0.9065 in |
| Lifter diameter . . . . . . . . . . . . . . . . . . . . . . . . . . . . . | 0.904 to 0.9045 in |
| Lifter-to-bore clearance . . . . . . . . . . . . . . . . . . . . . . . | 0.001 to 0.0025 in |
| Pushrod diameter . . . . . . . . . . . . . . . . . . . . . . . . . . . | 0.312 to 0.315 in |
| Pushrod length . . . . . . . . . . . . . . . . . . . . . . . . . . . . . | 9.640 to 9.660 in |

## Oversize and undersize component code letter definition

| | |
|---|---|
| Code letter | |
| **B** All cylinder bores . . . . . . . . . . . . . . . . . . . . . . . | 0.010 in oversize |
| **M** All crankshaft main bearing journals . . . . . . . . . . . . | 0.010 in undersize |
| **P** All connecting rod bearing journals . . . . . . . . . . . . | 0.010 in undersize |
| **C** All camshaft bearing bores . . . . . . . . . . . . . . . . . | 0.010 in oversize |

| **Torque specifications** | **Ft-lbs** |
|---|---|
| Bellhousing-to-engine bolts . . . . . . . . . . . . . . . . . . . . | 55 |
| Camshaft sprocket bolts . . . . . . . . . . . . . . . . . . . . . . | 50 |
| Connecting rod cap nuts . . . . . . . . . . . . . . . . . . . . . . | 33 |
| Cylinder head bolts . . . . . . . . . . . . . . . . . . . . . . . . . | 85 |
| Crankshaft pulley-to-damper bolts . . . . . . . . . . . . . . . . | 20 |
| Exhaust manifold bolts . . . . . . . . . . . . . . . . . . . . . . . | 23 |
| Fan and hub assembly bolts . . . . . . . . . . . . . . . . . . . . | 18 |
| Flywheel/driveplate-to-crankshaft bolts . . . . . . . . . . . . . | 50 plus an additional 60° |
| Intake manifold bolts . . . . . . . . . . . . . . . . . . . . . . . . | 23 |
| Main bearing cap bolts . . . . . . . . . . . . . . . . . . . . . . . | 80 |
| Oil pump cover bolts . . . . . . . . . . . . . . . . . . . . . . . . . | 6 |
| Oil pump mounting bolts | |
| short . . . . . . . . . . . . . . . . . . . . . . . . . . . . . . . . . | 10 |
| long . . . . . . . . . . . . . . . . . . . . . . . . . . . . . . . . . | 17 |
| Oil pan bolts | |
| 1/4 x 20 . . . . . . . . . . . . . . . . . . . . . . . . . . . . . . | 7 |
| 5/16 x 18 . . . . . . . . . . . . . . . . . . . . . . . . . . . . . . | 11 |
| Bridged rocker pivot bolt . . . . . . . . . . . . . . . . . . . . . . | 19 |
| Vibration damper bolt . . . . . . . . . . . . . . . . . . . . . . . . | 80 |
| Water pump bolts . . . . . . . . . . . . . . . . . . . . . . . . . . | 13 |

## *Carter YFA carburetor*

| | |
|---|---|
| Float level | |
| set to . . . . . . . . . . . . . . . . . . . . . . . . . . . . . . . . | 0.600 in |
| acceptable . . . . . . . . . . . . . . . . . . . . . . . . . . . . . | 0.570 to 0.630 in |
| Float drop | |
| type 1 . . . . . . . . . . . . . . . . . . . . . . . . . . . . . . . . | 1.50 in |
| type 2 . . . . . . . . . . . . . . . . . . . . . . . . . . . . . . . . | 1.250 in |
| plastic float . . . . . . . . . . . . . . . . . . . . . . . . . . . . | 1.375 in |
| Initial choke plate clearance | |
| set to . . . . . . . . . . . . . . . . . . . . . . . . . . . . . . . . | 0.240 in |
| acceptable . . . . . . . . . . . . . . . . . . . . . . . . . . . . . | 0.225 to 0.255 in |
| Choke unloader . . . . . . . . . . . . . . . . . . . . . . . . . . . | 0.370 in |
| Fast idle speed | |
| set to . . . . . . . . . . . . . . . . . . . . . . . . . . . . . . . . | 2000 rpm |
| acceptable . . . . . . . . . . . . . . . . . . . . . . . . . . . . . | 1900 to 2100 rpm |

| **Torque specifications** | **Ft-lbs** |
|---|---|
| Carburetor mounting nuts . . . . . . . . . . . . . . . . . . . . . | 14 |

## All models

| **Torque specifications** | **Ft-lbs** |
|---|---|
| Front locking hub bolts . . . . . . . . . . . . . . . . . . . . . . . | 30 |

---

**3   Tune-up and routine maintenance**

*Routine maintenance intervals*

The following maintenance procedures for later model vehicles are required in addition to the procedures outlined in Chapter 1.

**Every 30,000 miles or 30 months, whichever comes first**      **13**

Drain and refill the automatic transmission (Chapter 1)
Replace the spark plugs (Chapter 1)
Lubricate the locking front hubs (Chapter 13)

## Locking front hub lubrication

1    On later model vehicles equipped with the Type 300 transfer case and model M253 locking hubs, the hubs should be lubricated at the specified intervals.

2    Raise the vehicle and support it securely on jackstands.

3    Remove the bolts and tabbed lockwashers retaining the hub body to the axle hub and remove the hub body, gasket, retaining ring, hub clutch and bearing assembly as shown in the accompanying illustrations. **Caution:** *Do not rotate the hub control dial after removing the hub body. Severe damage to the hub clutch nut and cup can occur if the dial is turned while the hub is off the vehicle.*

4    Clean the hub components with solvent and dry them thoroughly with a clean, lint-free cloth or compressed air. Make sure that all dirt, water and old lubricant has been flushed out.

5    Apply a light coat of EP-type waterproof lithium base chassis grease to the hub internal components. **Note:** *Do not pack the hubs with lubricant — apply a light coat only.*

6    Place the hub clutch and bearing assembly in position on the axleshaft and install the retaining ring.

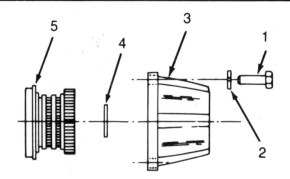

**Fig. 13.1   Locking front hub installation details**

| | |
|---|---|
| 1  Bolts | 4  Retaining ring |
| 2  Tabbed lockwashers | 5  Hub clutch and |
| 3  Hub body |     bearing assembly |

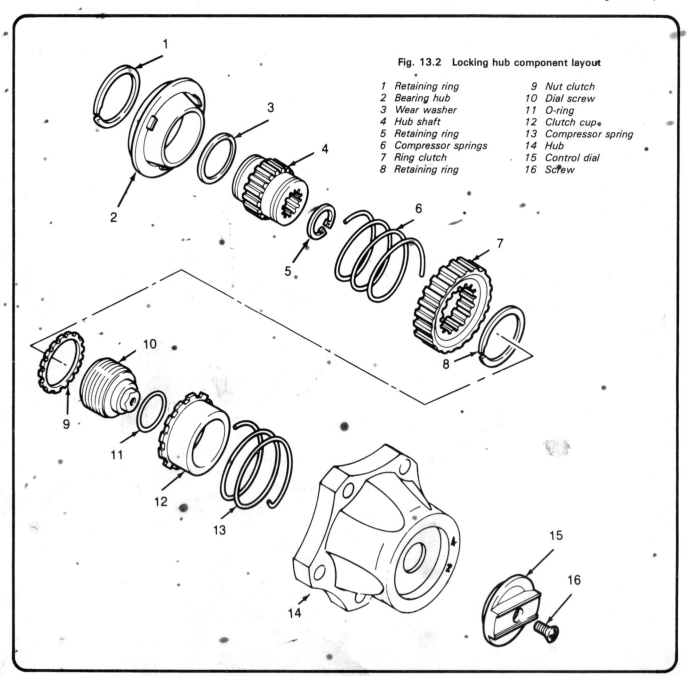

**Fig. 13.2   Locking hub component layout**

| | | | |
|---|---|---|---|
| 1  Retaining ring | | 9   Nut clutch |
| 2  Bearing hub | | 10  Dial screw |
| 3  Wear washer | | 11  O-ring |
| 4  Hub shaft | | 12  Clutch cup |
| 5  Retaining ring | | 13  Compressor spring |
| 6  Compressor springs | | 14  Hub |
| 7  Ring clutch | | 15  Control dial |
| 8  Retaining ring | | 16  Screw |

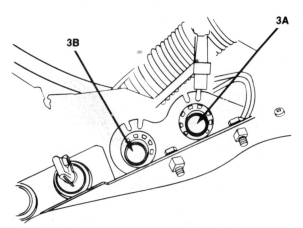

**Fig. 13.3  The vacuum switches (3A and 3B) must be disconnected during the ignition timing procedure**

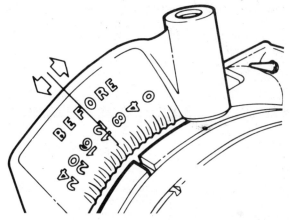

**Fig. 13.4  150 cubic inch four-cylinder engine timing scale and mark location**

7    Using a new gasket, install the hub body.
8    Align the bolt holes and install the tabbed lockwashers and bolts. Tighten the bolts to the specified torque.
9    Turn the hub control dial to the 2X4 position and rotate the front wheel. It should rotate freely. If it does not, check to make sure the control dial is fully engaged and that the hub is properly installed.

## Ignition timing check and adjustment (150 cu in four-cylinder engine)

10  With the engine at normal operating temperature, the parking brake set, the transmission in Neutral and the ignition switch off, disconnect the wires from the vacuum switches. These switches are located on a bracket attached to the center of the firewall in the engine compartment (Fig. 13.3).
11  Disconnect the vacuum hose from the distributor and plug the open end of the hose.
12  Connect a timing light in accordance with the manufacturer's instructions.
13  Locate the numbered timing tag on the front cover of the engine. It is just behind the lower crankshaft pulley. Clean it with solvent, if necessary, to reveal the printing and small grooves.
14  Locate the notched groove across the crankshaft pulley. It may be necessary to have an assistant temporarily turn the ignition Off and On in short bursts without starting the engine to bring this groove into a position where it can easily be cleaned and marked. **Warning:** *Stay clear of all moving engine components if the engine is turned over in this manner.*
15  Use white soapstone, chalk or paint to highlight the groove in the crankshaft pulley. Also put a mark on the timing tag at the point that corresponds to the number of degrees called for in the Specifications or on the *Vehicle Emission Control Information* label in the engine compartment. Each peak or notch on the timing tab represents 2°. The word BEFORE indicates advance and the letter O indicates Top Dead Center (TDC). As an example, if your vehicle specifications call for 12° BTDC (Before Top Dead Center), you will make a mark on the timing tag at the number 12 on the timing tag as shown in the accompanying illustration.
16  Make sure that the wiring for the timing light is clear of all moving engine components, then start the engine.
17  Point the flashing timing light at the timing marks, again being careful not to come in contact with moving parts. The marks you made should appear stationary. If the marks are in alignment, the timing is correct. If the marks are not aligned, turn off the engine.
18  Loosen the bolt at the base of the distributor slightly, just enough to turn the distributor.
19  Restart the engine and turn the distributor until the timing marks are aligned.
20  Shut off the engine and tighten the distributor bolt, being careful not to move the distributor.
21  Start the engine and recheck the timing to make sure the marks are still in alignment.
22  Disconnect the timing light, unplug the vacuum hose and reconnect it to the distributor and reconnect the vacuum switches.

23  Drive the vehicle and listen for "pinging" noises. They will be most noticeable when the engine is hot and under load (climbing a hill, accelerating from a stop). If you hear pinging, the ignition timing is advanced too much. Reconnect the timing light and turn the distributor to move the mark 1 or 2 degrees in the retard direction. Road test the vehicle again to check for proper operation.

## 4    Engine — 150 cubic inch four-cylinder

### General information

Beginning in 1984, the 151 cubic inch four-cylinder engine made by General Motors was replaced by a 150 cubic inch four-cylinder engine manufactured by AMC. This new engine is basically a four-cylinder version of the in-line six-cylinder engine described in Chapter 2. The majority of the engine operations are the same as for the in-line six-cylinder engine. Specifications and information for the four-cylinder engine which differ from those for the in-line six-cylinder engine in Chapter 2 can be found in the appropriate Sections of this supplement.

The main differences between the two engines (other than the obvious ones because there are two less cylinders) are in the rocker arm cover, the slightly different timing chain design, incorporating a tensioner, and the press-in type rear oil seal. Procedures which differ from those in Chapter 2 are noted below.

### Oversize/undersize components

Some components, such as the crankshaft or cylinder bores, may be equipped with oversize or undersize components. If such is the case, an identifying letter code is stamped on a boss between the fuel pump and distributor. refer to the Specifications for the interpretation of various letter codes.

### Removal and installation

**Caution:** *If the vehicle is equipped with air conditioning, have the lines disconnected by an automotive air conditioning mechanic. Do not attempt to do this yourself — serious injury or damage could result.*

**Removal**
1    Remove the hood.
2    Disconnect the cables (negative cable first) and remove the battery.
3    Drain the coolant into a clean container and remove the fan shroud and radiator.
4    Disconnect and tag the wires at the alternator, starter, carburetor, distributor, ignition coil, oxygen sensor and oil pressure sender.
5    Remove and plug the fuel line from the tank at the fuel pump.
6    Detach the engine ground strap.
7    Disconnect the thermostatically controlled air cleaner vacuum hose from the intake manifold and remove the air cleaner.
8    Detach and plug the fuel filter return hose at the fuel filter.
9    Disconnect the ECS system hose at the canister.
10  Detach the throttle cable and disengage it from the bracket.
11  Disconnect the throttle rod at the bellcrank.
12  Remove the radiator hoses.

**13**

13 Disconnect the heater hoses from the intake manifold and thermostat housing.
14 Remove the radiator, shroud and fan.
15 Detach the power brake vacuum hose from the booster.
16 On power steering equipped models, remove the power steering pump and drivebelt and position the pump out of the way. *Do not disconnect the power steering hoses.*
17 Raise the vehicle and support it securely on jackstands.

18 Remove the starter motor (Chapter 5) and the flywheel housing access cover.
19 Disconnect the clutch and transmission linkage.
20 Remove the engine mount nuts.
21 Disconnect the exhaust pipe at the manifold.
22 Remove the upper bellhousing bolts and *loosen* the lower bolts.
23 Lower the vehicle.
24 Attach a chain/cable and hoist to the engine. Raise the engine off

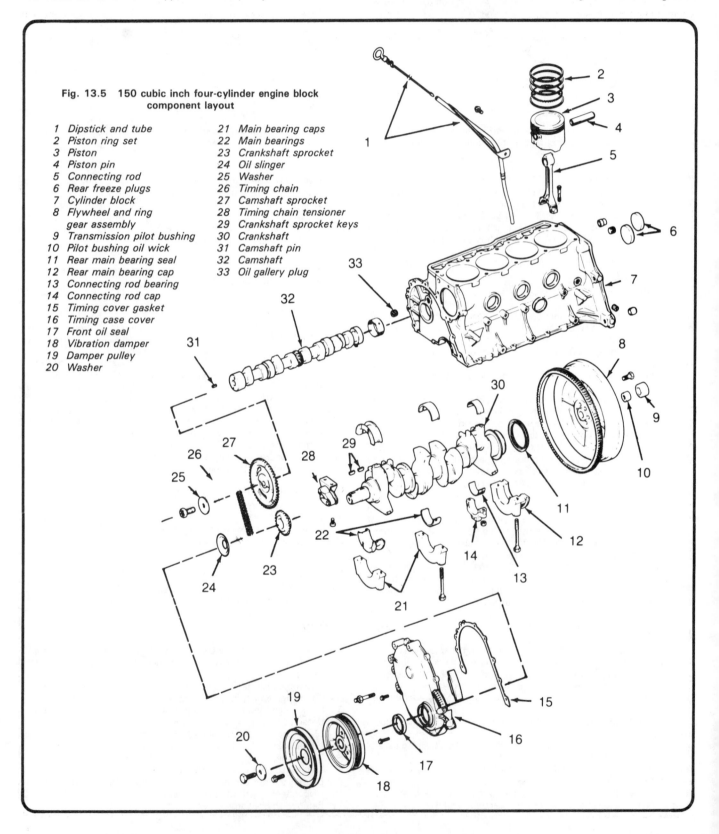

Fig. 13.5   150 cubic inch four-cylinder engine block component layout

1   Dipstick and tube
2   Piston ring set
3   Piston
4   Piston pin
5   Connecting rod
6   Rear freeze plugs
7   Cylinder block
8   Flywheel and ring gear assembly
9   Transmission pilot bushing
10   Pilot bushing oil wick
11   Rear main bearing seal
12   Rear main bearing cap
13   Connecting rod bearing
14   Connecting rod cap
15   Timing cover gasket
16   Timing case cover
17   Front oil seal
18   Vibration damper
19   Damper pulley
20   Washer

21   Main bearing caps
22   Main bearings
23   Crankshaft sprocket
24   Oil slinger
25   Washer
26   Timing chain
27   Camshaft sprocket
28   Timing chain tensioner
29   Crankshaft sprocket keys
30   Crankshaft
31   Camshaft pin
32   Camshaft
33   Oil gallery plug

the front mounts and support the bellhousing with a jack. Remove the remaining bellhousing bolts and move the engine forward carefully to disengage it from the transmission. It may be necessary to raise and lower the engine to separate the engine from the transmission.
25  Lift the engine from the engine compartment.

**Installation**
26  To make the installation job easier it is a good idea to remove the engine mount cushions from the engine mount brackets to aid in align-

ing the engine and transmission. Lower the engine carefully into the engine compartment.
27  Attach the engine to the bellhousing, making sure the input shaft is correctly installed in the pilot bushing and clutch disc.
28  Align the bellhousing with the engine and install the lower bellhousing bolts finger tight.
29  If removed, install the engine mount cushions and remove the jack from under the bellhousing.
30  Make sure the bolt holes are lined up, then lower the engine and

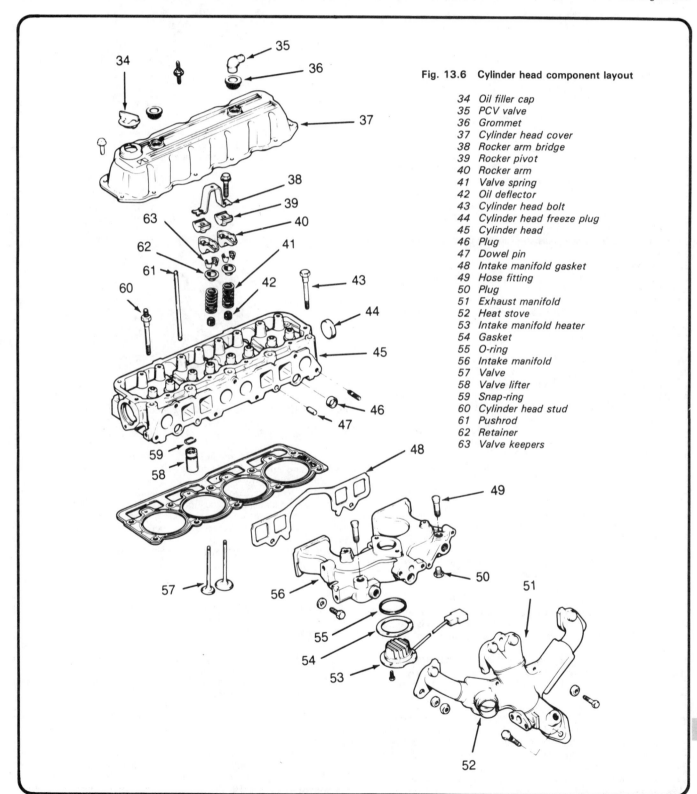

**Fig. 13.6   Cylinder head component layout**

34  Oil filler cap
35  PCV valve
36  Grommet
37  Cylinder head cover
38  Rocker arm bridge
39  Rocker pivot
40  Rocker arm
41  Valve spring
42  Oil deflector
43  Cylinder head bolt
44  Cylinder head freeze plug
45  Cylinder head
46  Plug
47  Dowel pin
48  Intake manifold gasket
49  Hose fitting
50  Plug
51  Exhaust manifold
52  Heat stove
53  Intake manifold heater
54  Gasket
55  O-ring
56  Intake manifold
57  Valve
58  Valve lifter
59  Snap-ring
60  Cylinder head stud
61  Pushrod
62  Retainer
63  Valve keepers

**13**

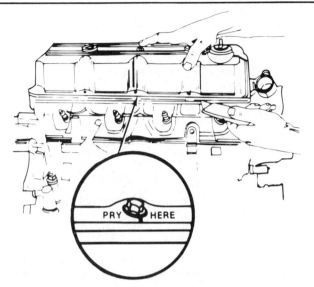

Fig. 13.7  Pry on the 150 cubic inch four-cylinder engine
rocker arm cover only at the marked locations

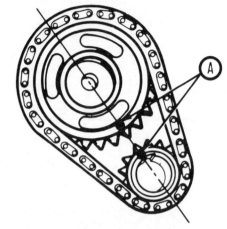

Fig. 13.8  Proper alignment of the camshaft and
crankshaft sprocket timing marks (A) on the
150 cubic inch four-cylinder engine

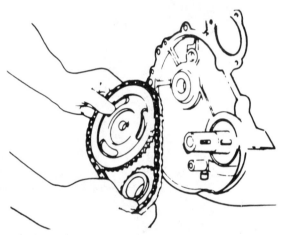

Fig. 13.9  Remove the timing chain and sprockets as a unit

mount cushions onto the brackets. Tighten the cushion mounting nuts securely.

31  Remove the hoist and raise the vehicle. Support it securely on jackstands.

32  Connect the exhaust pipe.

33  Install the upper bellhousing bolts. Tighten all of the bellhousing bolts to the specified torque.

34  Connect the clutch and transmission linkage.

35  Install the starter motor and connect the battery cable and solenoid wires.

36  Install the flywheel access cover.

37  Lower the vehicle.

38  Install the power steering pump and drivebelt.

39  Connect the power brake vacuum hose.

40  Connect the heater and radiator hoses.

41  Place the fan shroud in position over the fan and install the radiator and hoses. Attach the shroud to the radiator and fill the radiator with the specified coolant.

42  Connect the throttle linkage.

43  Connect the ECS and fuel system hoses.

44  Connect the engine ground strap.

45  Install the thermostatically controlled air cleaner vacuum hose on the intake manifold and install the air cleaner assembly.

46  Connect the wires to the alternator, carburetor, ignition system, oxygen sensor and oil pressure sender.

47  Fill the engine to the correct level with the recommended oil.

48  Install the battery and connect the cables (positive first, then negative).

49  Install the hood.

50  On air conditioning equipped models, have the lines hooked up and the system recharged by an air conditioning technician.

### Rocker arm cover removal and installation

51  Remove the air cleaner assembly. Tag each hose to be disconnected with a piece of numbered tape to simplify installation.

52  Disconnect the fuel line from the fuel pump and plug it. Swivel the line out of the way.

53  Pull the PCV valve from the grommet in the rocker arm cover and disconnect the PCV shut off valve vacuum hose.

54  Disconnect and tag all hoses which would interfere with removal of the rocker arm cover.

55  Remove the rocker arm cover retaining bolts.

56  Use a razor blade or putty knife to carefully break the rocker cover-to-cylinder head gasket seal, working around the cover perimeter. Once the gasket seal has been broken, pry the cover up at the ramp locations on the cylinder head marked *Pry Here* as shown in Fig. 13.7. Remove the rocker arm cover.

57  Carefully clean all traces of gasket material and sealant from the cover and cylinder head.

58  Apply a 3/8-inch diameter bead of RTV-type sealant to the cylinder head sealing surface. Make sure the sealant does not come in contact with the rocker arms or valve assemblies.

59  Place the rocker arm cover on the cylinder head while the sealant is still wet and install the bolts. Tighten the bolts in several steps, working from the inside out, until they are all secure.

60  Complete the installation by reversing the removal procedure.

### Timing cover, chain and sprocket removal and installation

61  If these components are being removed with the engine in the vehicle, remember to:

   a)  Remove the drivebelt(s), cooling fan, shroud and damper pulley.

   b)  Remove the vibration damper and key, using a puller.

   c)  Remove the alternator bracket.

62  Remove the timing cover bolts and the bolts retaining the front of the oil pan to the timing cover.

63  Withdraw the timing cover, gasket and oil slinger.

64  If the engine is in the vehicle, turn the crankshaft until the O-degree timing mark on the crankshaft sprocket is closest to and aligned with the timing mark on the camshaft sprocket (Fig. 13.8).

65  Remove the camshaft retaining bolt and withdraw the camshaft sprocket, crankshaft sprocket and timing chain as an assembly as shown in Fig. 13.9.

66  Prior to installation, turn the chain tensioner lever to the Down (unlocked) position, pull the tensioner block toward the lever to compress the spring and then turn the lever to the Up (locked) position as shown in Fig. 13.10.

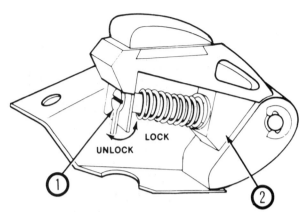

Fig. 13.10   Before installing the timing chain, turn the tensioner lever (1) to the unlocked position, pull the block (2) back and then turn the lever to the lock position

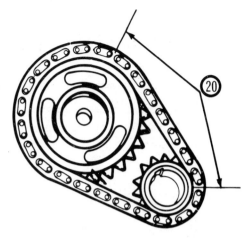

Fig. 13.11   With the camshaft sprocket timing mark at the 1 o'clock position, the timing marks must be 20 pins apart

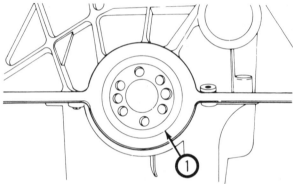

Fig. 13.12   The rear oil seal (1) on the 150 cubic inch four-cylinder engine fits tightly into a groove in the block

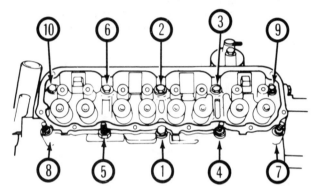

Fig. 13.13   150 cubic inch four-cylinder engine cylinder head bolt *tightening* sequence

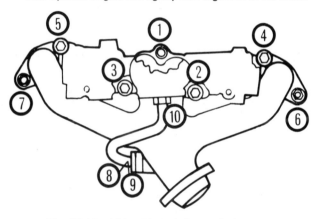

Fig. 13.14   150 cubic inch four-cylinder engine intake/exhaust manifold bolt *tightening* sequence

67  Engage the camshaft and crankshaft sprockets in the timing chain and install them as an assembly with the timing marks aligned as described in Step 64. A line drawn through the sprocket timing marks will also pass through the centers of the sprockets if everything is aligned properly. To achieve this, a certain amount of slight rotating of the camshaft and repositioning of the camshaft sprocket within the loop of the chain may be necessary.

68  Secure the camshaft sprocket and then check the timing. To do this, set the camshaft sprocket timing mark at the one o'clock position. There should be 20 chain pins between the sprocket timing marks as shown in Fig. 13.11.

69  Install the oil slinger.

70  Install a new oil seal in the timing chain cover as described in Chapter 2, Part C, Section 62, then attach the cover to the engine with a new gasket. Tighten the bolts finger tight at this time.

71  Apply grease to the oil seal contact surfaces of the vibration damper and push it into position. If necessary, tap the timing cover from side-to-side (or up-and-down) to center it on the damper shaft.

72  Tighten the timing chain cover bolts securely.

73  Install the damper and tighten the mounting bolt to the specified torque. To keep the crankshaft from turning while tightening the bolt, place two 5/16 x 1-1/2 inch bolts in the damper pulley holes and wedge a bar between them.

## Oil seal replacement

**Timing cover seal**

74  Refer to Chapter 2, Part C.

**Rear main bearing oil seal**

75  The rear main bearing oil seal on these models is a one-piece, single-lip rubber-type seal which fits in a groove in the rear of the block as shown in the accompanying illustration. It can be replaced with the engine in the vehicle after the transmission and flywheel have been removed.

76  Pry the old seal out very carefully with a screwdriver or similar tool. *Do not nick or scratch the crankshaft surface.*

77  Carefully clean the sealing surfaces of the engine block and crankshaft. Inspect the crankshaft for nicks and scratches.

78  Coat the inner lip of the new seal with clean engine oil.

79  Insert the seal squarely into the bore and tap it evenly into place until the outer surface is flush with the engine block.

## Cylinder head installation

80  Follow the procedure in Chapter 2, but tighten the cylinder head bolts in the sequence shown in Fig. 13.13.

## Intake/exhaust manifold installation

81  Follow the procedure in Chapter 2, but tighten the bolts in the sequence shown in Fig. 13.14.

**13**

### 5   Engine — in-line six-cylinder

#### Intake/exhaust manifold installation

On 1984 through 1986 models, follow the procedure in Chapter 2, but tighten the bolts in the sequence shown in Fig. 13.15.

### 6   Fuel and exhaust systems

#### General information

The fuel system on later models is essentially the same as the system covered in Chapter 4. Minor changes were made to the BDD carburetor used on six-cylinder in-line engines. On the 150 cubic inch four-cylinder engine introduced in 1984, a Carter YFA single venturi feedback carburetor is used.

#### Carter YFA carburetor
##### Removal and installation
**Warning:** *Gasoline is extremely flammable, so extra precautions must be taken when working on any part of the fuel system. Do not smoke or allow open flames or bare light bulbs near the work area. Also, do not work in a garage if a natural gas-type appliance with a pilot light is present.*

1    Remove the air cleaner assembly.
2    Mark or tag all hoses and lines connected to the carburetor to simplify installation.
3    Disconnect the control shaft from the throttle lever.
4    Remove the retaining nuts and lift the carburetor from the manifold.
5    Carefully clean the gasket surfaces of the carburetor, spacer or gasket and intake manifold. Inspect them for nicks and damage which could affect carburetor-to-manifold sealing. Replace the gasket or spacer with a new one if it is warped, damaged or distorted.
6    Place the carburetor and spacer or gasket in position and install the retaining nuts. Tighten the nuts evenly and securely in a criss-cross pattern.
7    Connect the throttle linkage, vacuum hoses, fuel lines and other hoses and wires to the carburetor.

##### Overhaul and adjustment
8    Remove the choke cover by drilling out the rivet heads and then using a 1/8-inch punch to drive out the remainder of the rivets. Remove the choke retainer, thermostat spring assembly, housing gasket and

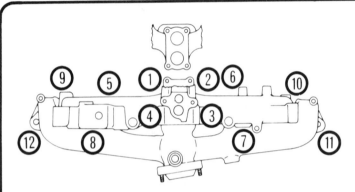

Fig. 13.15   In-line six-cylinder engine intake/exhaust manifold bolt *tightening* sequence (1984 through 1986)

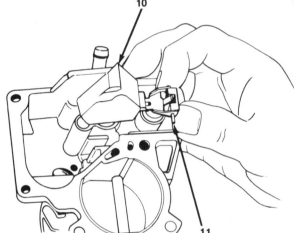

Fig. 13.16   Float (10) and float pin (11) removal details

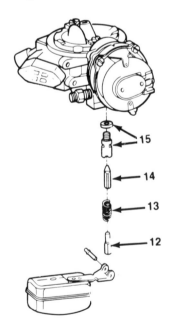

Fig. 13.17   After removing the float and pin invert the air horn and catch the needle pin (12), spring (13) and needle (14), then remove the needle seat and gasket (15)

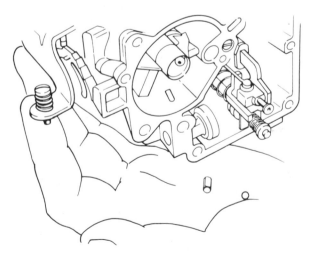

Fig. 13.18   Turn the main body over and catch the pump check ball and weight

locking and indexing plate.

9    Remove the vacuum break diaphragm.

10   Use a screwdriver to disengage the vacuum break connector link and then remove it from the choke shaft lever.

11   Remove the throttle positioner and bracket.

12   Remove the two screws and detach the mixture control solenoid from the air horn.

13   Remove the air horn attaching screws and the fast idle link and then detach the air horn and gasket from the carburetor main body.

14   Separate the float from the air horn by holding the air horn bottom side up and then removing the float and pin as shown in Fig. 13.16.

15   Turn the air horn upside down and catch the needle pin, spring and needle (Fig. 13.17). Remove the needle seat and gasket.

16   Invert the main body casting and catch the pump check ball and weight as shown in Fig. 13.18.

17   Remove the throttle shaft retaining bolt and detach the wide open throttle switch actuator.

18   Loosen the throttle shaft arm screw with an Allen wrench and

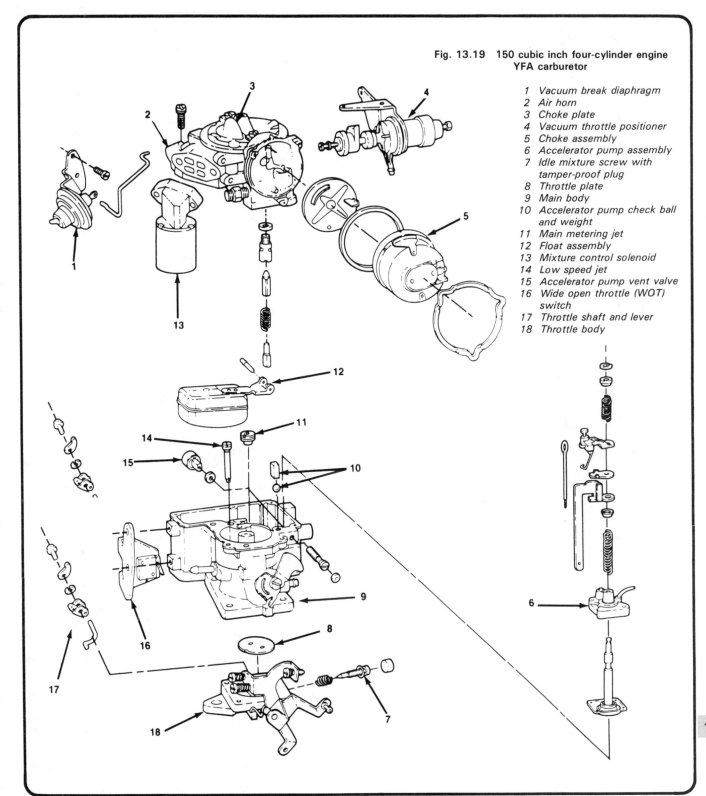

Fig. 13.19   150 cubic inch four-cylinder engine YFA carburetor

1    Vacuum break diaphragm
2    Air horn
3    Choke plate
4    Vacuum throttle positioner
5    Choke assembly
6    Accelerator pump assembly
7    Idle mixture screw with tamper-proof plug
8    Throttle plate
9    Main body
10   Accelerator pump check ball and weight
11   Main metering jet
12   Float assembly
13   Mixture control solenoid
14   Low speed jet
15   Accelerator pump vent valve
16   Wide open throttle (WOT) switch
17   Throttle shaft and lever
18   Throttle body

**13**

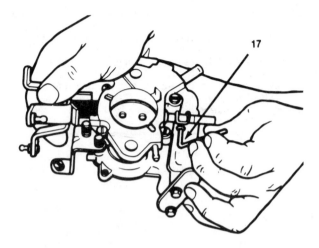

Fig. 13.20   Use an Allen wrench to loosen the throttle shaft arm screw (17)

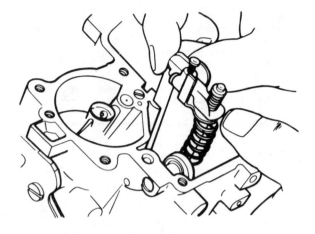

Fig. 13.21   Lift the accelerator pump assembly lifter link and metering rod out as a unit

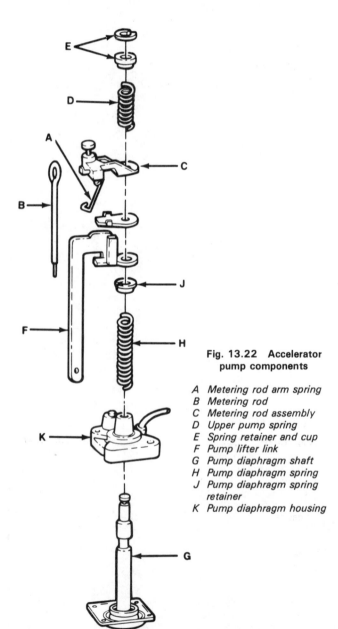

Fig. 13.22   Accelerator pump components

A   Metering rod arm spring
B   Metering rod
C   Metering rod assembly
D   Upper pump spring
E   Spring retainer and cup
F   Pump lifter link
G   Pump diaphragm shaft
H   Pump diaphragm spring
J   Pump diaphragm spring retainer
K   Pump diaphragm housing

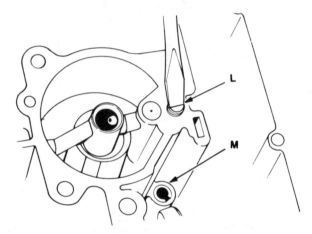

Fig. 13.23   Low speed jet (L) and main metering jet (M) locations

remove the arm and pump connector link as shown in Fig. 13.20.
19   Remove the screws and separate the throttle body from the main body.
20   Remove the wide open throttle switch and mounting bracket.
21   Remove the accelerator pump housing screws and lift out the pump assembly lifter link and metering rod as shown in Fig. 13.21.
22   Referring to Fig. 13.22, disassemble the pump as follows:

    a)   Disengage the metering rod arm spring from the metering rod and remove the rod from the assembly.
    b)   Compress the upper pump spring and then remove the spring retainer and cup.
    c)   Remove the upper spring, metering rod arm assembly and the pump lifter link from the pump diaphragm shaft.
    d)   Compress the pump diaphragm spring and remove the diaphragm spring retainer, spring and housing from the shaft.

23   Use a screwdriver to unscrew the low speed jet and remove the main metering jet (Fig. 13.23).
24   Use a sharp punch to remove the accelerator pump bleed valve plug from the outside of the main body casting, loosen the bleed valve screw and remove the valve (Fig. 13.24).
25   Drill a hole in the tamper-proof plug and lever it out of the bore, then count and record the number of turns required to *lightly* seat the idle mixture screw. Remove the idle mixture screw, O-ring and spring.
26   The carburetor is now completely disassembled and should be cleaned and inspected for wear. After the carburetor components have been soaked in solvent to remove dirt, gum and carbon deposits, they should be rinsed in kerosene and dried, preferably with compressed air. Do not use a wire brush to clean the carburetor and clean all passages with compressed air rather than wire or drill bits, which could

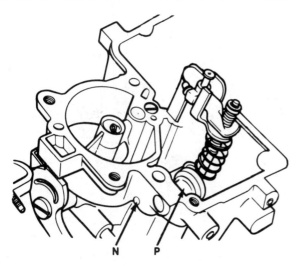

Fig. 13.24   Use a punch to remove the plug (N) so the bleed valve (P) can be removed

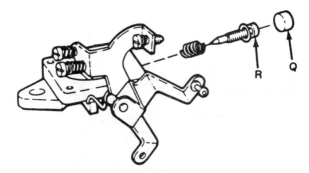

Fig. 13.25   Drill out the plug (Q) for access to the idle mixture screw (R)

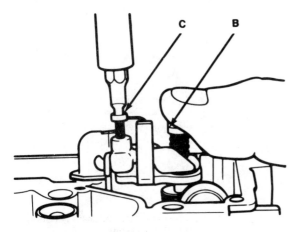

Fig. 13.26   To adjust the metering rod, push down on and hold the pump diaphragm (B) while turning the metering rod (C)

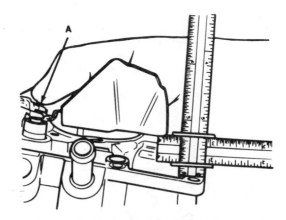

Fig. 13.27   Adjust the float level by bending the float arm (A)

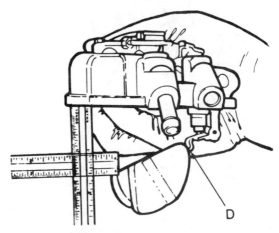

Fig. 13.28   Adjust the float drop by bending the tab (D) at the end of the float arm

enlarge them. Inspect the throttle and choke shafts for grooves, wear and excessive looseness. Check the throttle and choke plates for nicks and smoothness of operation. Inspect the carburetor body and components for cracks. Check the float arm needle contact surface for grooves. If the grooves are light, polish the needle contact surface with crocus cloth or steel wool. Replace the floats if the shafts are badly worn. Inspect the gasket mating surfaces for burrs and nicks. Replace any distorted springs and bolts which have stripped threads.

27  To begin reassembly, attach the throttle body to the main body with the retaining screws. Use thread locking compound on the screw threads.

28  Install the low speed jet, main metering jet, pump bleed valve and plug, accelerator pump assembly and the pump passage tube.

29  Slide the throttle shaft arm onto the shaft and install the retaining screw and pump connector link.

30  Install the wide open throttle switch actuator, the throttle shaft retaining bolt and the switch and bracket.

### Metering rod adjustment

31  With the air horn removed, back out the idle speed adjusting screw until the throttle plate is closed tightly in the bore, then push down on the pump diaphragm until it bottoms.

32  To adjust the metering rod, hold the diaphragm down and turn the adjustment screw counterclockwise until the metering rod lightly bottoms on the main metering jet as shown in Fig. 13.26. Turn the adjustment screw one turn *clockwise* for final adjustment.

33  Install the float assembly needle pin, spring seat and gasket, float and pin.

### Float level adjustment

34  Turn the air horn assembly over and measure the clearance between the top of the float and the bottom of the air horn with a float level gauge or a dial or vernier caliper. The air horn should be held at eye level during this procedure and the float lever should be resting on the needle pin.

35  Bend the float arm as necessary to bring the float level within the specified range (Fig. 13.27).

### Float drop adjustment

36  With the carburetor air horn held upright and the float hanging free, measure the distance from the air horn gasket surface to the top of the float. Compare this float drop measurement to the Specifications. To adjust, bend the tab at the end of the float arm (Fig. 13.28).

**13**

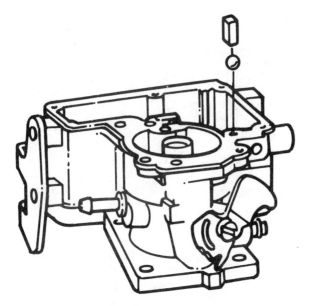

Fig. 13.29   Accelerator pump check ball and weight installation

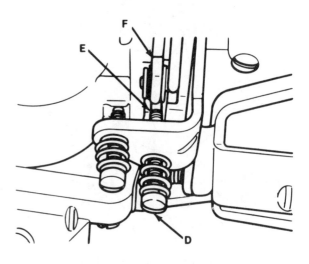

Fig. 13.30   The fast idle adjustment screw (D) should be on the second step (E) of the fast idle cam (F) before adjusting the fast idle cam link

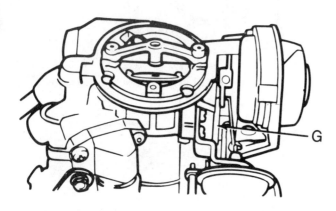

Fig. 13.31   Adjust the fast idle cam index by bending the link (G)

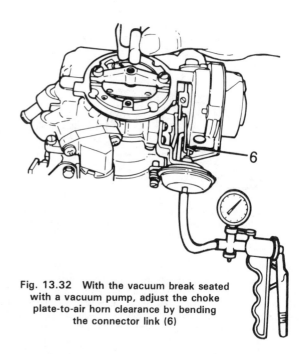

Fig. 13.32   With the vacuum break seated with a vacuum pump, adjust the choke plate-to-air horn clearance by bending the connector link (6)

37  Install the accelerator pump check ball and weight.
38  Install the air horn and gasket on the main body.
39  Install the fast idle cam link, throttle positioner and bracket and mixture control solenoid.
40  Install the choke cover locking and indexing plate, cover and housing assembly and retainer, using screws to replace the rivets.

**Fast idle cam index adjustment**
41  Place the fast idle adjustment screw on the second step of the fast idle cam and against the shoulder of the high step as shown in Fig. 13.30.
42  Check the clearance between the lower edge of the choke plate and the air horn wall using a drill bit as a gauge. Compare this measurement to the Specifications.
43  To adjust the fast idle cam, bend the fast idle cam link as shown in the accompanying illustration until the choke plate clearance is as specified.

**Initial choke plate-to-air horn clearance adjustment**
44  With the fast idle adjustment screw on the top step of the fast idle cam, connect a vacuum pump to the vacuum break, apply vacuum and measure the choke plate lower edge-to-air horn wall clearance with a drill bit shank as shown in Fig. 13.32. Bend the vacuum break link to adjust the clearance.

**Choke unloader adjustment**
45  Hold the throttle wide open while pushing the choke plate toward the closed position. Measure the clearance between the choke lower edge and the air horn wall with a drill bit shank. Compare this measurement to the Specifications.
46  To adjust, bend the unloader tang which contacts the fast idle cam (Fig. 13.33).
47  Install the idle mixture screw and back it out the same number of turns required to seat it.

**Anti-diesel adjustment**
48  Turn the anti-diesel adjustment screw counterclockwise until the throttle plate is closed, then turn it clockwise 3/4-turn as shown in Fig. 13.34.
49  Install the carburetor on the engine.

**Fuel/air mixture adjustment**
50  Because of the special equipment and techniques required, fuel/air mixture adjustment should be left to a dealer service department or properly equipped shop.

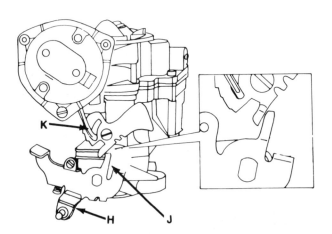

Fig. 13.33   With the throttle (H) held wide open, adjust the choke unloader by bending the unloader tang (J) which contacts the fast idle cam (K)

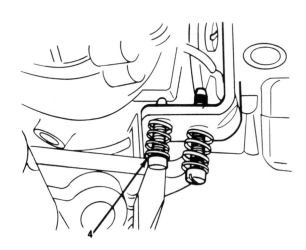

Fig. 13.34   Anti-diesel adjustment screw (4)

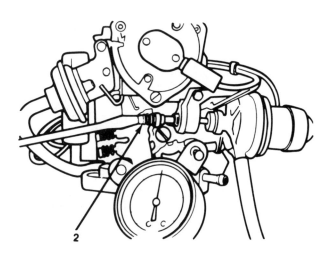

Fig. 13.35   With vacuum applied to the actuator, adjust the idle speed at the actuator adjustment screw (2)

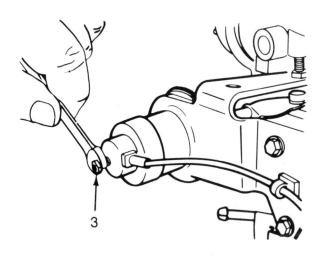

Fig. 13.36   Use a small wrench to adjust the curb idle speed screw (3)

**Idle speed adjustment**

51  Prior to setting the idle speed the following precautions must be taken:

*Parking brake securely set*
*Transmission must be in Neutral*
*Engine at normal operating temperature*
*Air cleaner installed*

52  Following the manufacturer's instructions, attach a tachometer to the ignition coil TACH connector.

53  Prior to idle speed adjustment, the vacuum actuator must be adjusted.

54  With the engine idling, connect a vacuum pump to the vacuum actuator, apply 10 to 15 in-Hg of vacuum and adjust the vacuum actuator until an idle speed of approximately 1000 rpm is achieved as shown in Fig. 13.35.

55  Disconnect and plug the vacuum actuator hose and turn the hex head curb idle speed adjustment screw to obtain an idle speed of 500 rpm as shown in Fig. 13.36.

**Fast idle adjustment**

56  The fast idle adjustment is made with the engine at normal operating temperature, the EGR valve hose disconnected and plugged at the valve and the fast idle screw on the second step of the fast idle cam. Turn the fast idle adjustment screw until a setting of approximately 1500 rpm is reached (Fig. 13.37).

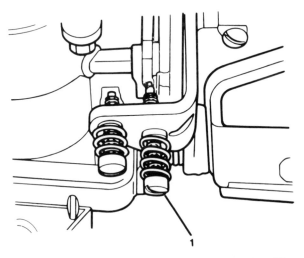

Fig. 13.37   Fast idle adjustment screw location (1)

**13**

## 7   Engine electrical systems

### General information

Later model vehicles are equipped with ignition and starting systems which differ from earlier models only in certain details that do not appreciably affect maintenance and service procedures. Therefore, the material in Chapter 5 can be used in most cases. The distributor used on the 150 cubic inch four-cylinder engine introduced in 1984 is of basically the same design as the unit used on the in-line six-cylinder engine described in Chapter 5.

## 8   Emissions control systems

### General information

The emissions control systems used on 1984 through 1986 models are virtually the same as earlier models. Starting in 1984 all models are equipped with feedback carburetors.

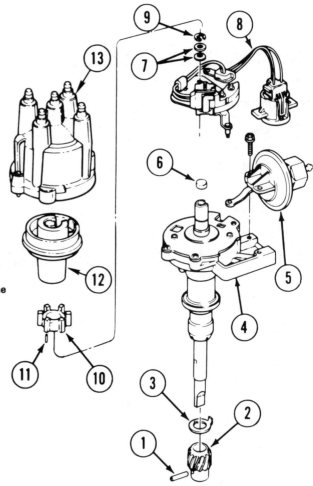

**Fig. 13.38   150 cubic inch four-cylinder engine distributor — exploded view**

 1   Pin
 2   Gear
 3   Washer
 4   Distributor body
 5   Vacuum advance mechanism
 6   Wick
 7   Washers
 8   Pickup coil
 9   Retainer
10   Trigger wheel
11   Pin
12   Rotor
13   Cap

# Conversion factors

## Length (distance)

| | | | | | |
|---|---|---|---|---|---|
| Inches (in) | X | 25.4 | = Millimetres (mm) | X | 0.0394 | = Inches (in) |
| Feet (ft) | X | 0.305 | = Metres (m) | X | 3.281 | = Feet (ft) |
| Miles | X | 1.609 | = Kilometres (km) | X | 0.621 | = Miles |

## Volume (capacity)

| | | | | | |
|---|---|---|---|---|---|
| Cubic inches (cu in; in³) | X | 16.387 | = Cubic centimetres (cc; cm³) | X | 0.061 | = Cubic inches (cu in; in³) |
| Imperial pints (Imp pt) | X | 0.568 | = Litres (l) | X | 1.76 | = Imperial pints (Imp pt) |
| Imperial quarts (Imp qt) | X | 1.137 | = Litres (l) | X | 0.88 | = Imperial quarts (Imp qt) |
| Imperial quarts (Imp qt) | X | 1.201 | = US quarts (US qt) | X | 0.833 | = Imperial quarts (Imp qt) |
| US quarts (US qt) | X | 0.946 | = Litres (l) | X | 1.057 | = US quarts (US qt) |
| Imperial gallons (Imp gal) | X | 4.546 | = Litres (l) | X | 0.22 | = Imperial gallons (Imp gal) |
| Imperial gallons (Imp gal) | X | 1.201 | = US gallons (US gal) | X | 0.833 | = Imperial gallons (Imp gal) |
| US gallons (US gal) | X | 3.785 | = Litres (l) | X | 0.264 | = US gallons (US gal) |

## Mass (weight)

| | | | | | |
|---|---|---|---|---|---|
| Ounces (oz) | X | 28.35 | = Grams (g) | X | 0.035 | = Ounces (oz) |
| Pounds (lb) | X | 0.454 | = Kilograms (kg) | X | 2.205 | = Pounds (lb) |

## Force

| | | | | | |
|---|---|---|---|---|---|
| Ounces-force (ozf; oz) | X | 0.278 | = Newtons (N) | X | 3.6 | = Ounces-force (ozf; oz) |
| Pounds-force (lbf; lb) | X | 4.448 | = Newtons (N) | X | 0.225 | = Pounds-force (lbf; lb) |
| Newtons (N) | X | 0.1 | = Kilograms-force (kgf; kg) | X | 9.81 | = Newtons (N) |

## Pressure

| | | | | | |
|---|---|---|---|---|---|
| Pounds-force per square inch (psi; lbf/in²; lb/in²) | X | 0.070 | = Kilograms-force per square centimetre (kgf/cm²; kg/cm²) | X | 14.223 | = Pounds-force per square inch (psi; lbf/in²; lb/in²) |
| Pounds-force per square inch (psi; lbf/in²; lb/in²) | X | 0.068 | = Atmospheres (atm) | X | 14.696 | = Pounds-force per square inch (psi; lbf/in²; lb/in²) |
| Pounds-force per square inch (psi; lbf/in²; lb/in²) | X | 0.069 | = Bars | X | 14.5 | = Pounds-force per square inch (psi; lbf/in²; lb/in²) |
| Pounds-force per square inch (psi; lbf/in²; lb/in²) | X | 6.895 | = Kilopascals (kPa) | X | 0.145 | = Pounds-force per square inch (psi; lbf/in²; lb/in²) |
| Kilopascals (kPa) | X | 0.01 | = Kilograms-force per square centimetre (kgf/cm²; kg/cm²) | X | 98.1 | = Kilopascals (kPa) |

## Torque (moment of force)

| | | | | | |
|---|---|---|---|---|---|
| Pounds-force inches (lbf in; lb in) | X | 1.152 | = Kilograms-force centimetre (kgf cm; kg cm) | X | 0.868 | = Pounds-force inches (lbf in; lb in) |
| Pounds-force inches (lbf in; lb in) | X | 0.113 | = Newton metres (Nm) | X | 8.85 | = Pounds-force inches (lbf in; lb in) |
| Pounds-force inches (lbf in; lb in) | X | 0.083 | = Pounds-force feet (lbf ft; lb ft) | X | 12 | = Pounds-force inches (lbf in; lb in) |
| Pounds-force feet (lbf ft; lb ft) | X | 0.138 | = Kilograms-force metres (kgf m; kg m) | X | 7.233 | = Pounds-force feet (lbf ft; lb ft) |
| Pounds-force feet (lbf ft; lb ft) | X | 1.356 | = Newton metres (Nm) | X | 0.738 | = Pounds-force feet (lbf ft; lb ft) |
| Newton metres (Nm) | X | 0.102 | = Kilograms-force metres (kgf m; kg m) | X | 9.804 | = Newton metres (Nm) |

## Power

| | | | | | |
|---|---|---|---|---|---|
| Horsepower (hp) | X | 745.7 | = Watts (W) | X | 0.0013 | = Horsepower (hp) |

## Velocity (speed)

| | | | | | |
|---|---|---|---|---|---|
| Miles per hour (miles/hr; mph) | X | 1.609 | = Kilometres per hour (km/hr; kph) | X | 0.621 | = Miles per hour (miles/hr; mph) |

## Fuel consumption*

| | | | | | |
|---|---|---|---|---|---|
| Miles per gallon, Imperial (mpg) | X | 0.354 | = Kilometres per litre (km/l) | X | 2.825 | = Miles per gallon, Imperial (mpg) |
| Miles per gallon, US (mpg) | X | 0.425 | = Kilometres per litre (km/l) | X | 2.352 | = Miles per gallon, US (mpg) |

## Temperature

Degrees Fahrenheit = (°C x 1.8) + 32          Degrees Celsius (Degrees Centigrade; °C) = (°F - 32) x 0.56

*It is common practice to convert from miles per gallon (mpg) to litres/100 kilometres (l/100km), where mpg (Imperial) x l/100 km = 282 and mpg (US) x l/100 km = 235

# Index

**Note:** *Refer to Chapter 13 for information related to 1984 through 1986 models*

## A

About this manual — 4
Acknowledgments — 4
Air conditioning system
    check — 140
    compressor removal and installation — 143
    compressor drivebelt adjustment — 44
Air filter replacement — 46
Air Injection (AI) system — 195
Antifreeze — 141
Automatic transmission
    band adjustment — 232
    diagnosis — 230
    fluid change — 49
    fluid level check — 39
    general information — 229
    removal and installation — 232
    shift linkage adjustment — 230
    throttle linkage adjustment — 230
Automotive chemicals and lubricants — 16

## B

Battery
    charging — 59
    electrolyte level check — 39
    emergency jump starting — 15
    maintenance — 58
    removal and installation — 178
Body
    color body repair photos — 314, 315
    damage
        major repairs — 312
        minor repairs — 312
    general information — 311
    maintenance — 311
Booster battery (jump) starting procedure — 15
Brakes
    bleeding — 259
    brake line inspection and replacement — 259
    brake master cylinder fluid level check — 39
    check — 51
    disc brake inspection — 51
    front disc brakes
        caliper removal — 263
        disc removal and installation — 261
        inspection — 261
        overhaul and installation — 263
        pad removal and installation — 260
    general information — 258
    master cylinder overhaul — 269
    master cylinder removal and installation — 269
    parking brake adjustment — 268
    power brake
        booster assembly removal and installation — 260
        check — 259
    rear brakes
        drum removal, inspection and installation — 264
        inspection — 52
        manual adjustment — 52
        shoe removal and inspection — 264
        wheel cylinder removal, overhaul and installation — 267
    specifications — 30, 258
Bulb replacement — 275
Bumpers
    front removal and installation — 316
    rear removal and installation — 316
Buying parts — 8

## C

Camshaft
    removal and installation
        151 cu in four-cylinder — 83
        in-line six-cylinder — 92, 98
        V8 — 107, 108
        V6 — 118
        F- and L-head four-cylinder — 127, 131
    bearing inspection and replacement
        151 cu in four-cylinder — 83
        in-line six-cylinder — 94
        V8 — 107
        V6 — 118
        F- and L-head four-cylinder — 131
Carburetors *see also* **Fuel system**
    adjustments — 48, 154, 156, 159, 163, 167, 173, 329 to 331
    application — 151, 326
    choke inspection — 47
    cleaning and inspection — 151, 328
    disassembly — 151, 326
    linkage check and adjustment — 150, 329
    mounting torque — 48
    removal and installation — 151, 326
Carpet maintenance — 311
Catalytic converter
    general — 192
    removal and installation — 193
    servicing — 193
Charcoal canister and filter — 58, 191

**Charging system general information** — 178
**Chassis lubrication** — 42
**Choke inspection** — 47
**Clutch**
  general information — 246
  pedal free play check and adjustment — 99, 247
  removal, inspection and installation — 246
  specifications — 29, 245
**Color photos**
  bodywork — 314, 315
  spark plugs — 57
**Compressor drivebelt adjustment** — 44
**Connecting rod side clearance check** — 65
**Cooling system**
  check and servicing — 43, 60
  general information — 136
  temperature sending unit replacement — 141
**Crankcase front cover removal and installation**
  150 cu in four-cylinder — 324
  151 cu in four-cylinder — 79
  in-line, six-cylinder — 92, 98
  V8 — 105, 108
  V6 — 116
  F- and L-head four-cylinder — 127, 133
**Crankshaft removal** — 66
**Crankshaft and bearing inspection** — 68
**Crankshaft main bearings and oil seal installation**
  151 cu in four-cylinder — 84
  in-line six-cylinder — 96
  V8 — 109
  V6 — 120
  F- and L-head four-cylinder — 131
**Cylinder block inspection** — 67
**Cylinder head**
  assembly — 65
  cleaning — 63
  disassembly — 63
  inspection — 63
  installation
    150 cu in four-cylinder — 325
    151 cu in four-cylinder — 79
    in-line six-cylinder — 99
    V8 — 109
    V6 — 117
    F- and L-head four-cylinder — 133
  removal
    151 cu in four-cylinder — 78
    in-line six-cylinder — 92
    V8 — 105
    V6 — 117
    F- and L-head four-cylinder — 127

**D**

**Differential**
  oil change — 51
  oil level check — 39
**Dimmer switch removal and installation** — 277
**Disc brakes** *see* Braking system
**Distributor**
  cap replacement — 53
  check — 189
  general information — 178
  installation — 186
  removal — 186
**Drivebelt check and adjustment** — 44

**E**

**Electrical system**
  battery check and maintenance — 58
  directional switch check and replacement — 279
  fuses — 274
  fusible links — 274

  general information — 273
  headlight dimmer switch removal and installation — 277
  headlight replacement — 275
  headlight switch removal and installation — 277
  horn testing — 279
  ignition switch — 276
  instrument cluster removal and installation — 279
  troubleshooting, general — 273
  specifications — 272
  windshield wiper motor — 272
  wiring diagrams — 280 to 299
**Electronic control module removal and installation** — 186
**Emissions control systems**
  general information — 190, 332
  torque specifications — 190
  troubleshooting — 190
**Engine**
  coolant level check — 38
  disassembly — 63
  drivebelt check and adjustment — 44
  general information — 76, 89, 103, 113, 124, 321
  general overhaul information — 62
  installation
    150 cu in four-cylinder — 323
    151 cu in four-cylinder — 85
    in-line six-cylinder — 99
    V8 — 110
    V6 — 121
    F- and L-head four-cylinder — 134
  major overhaul disassembly sequence — 63
  oil and filter change — 40
  oil level check — 37
  rebuilding alternatives — 62
  removal
    methods and precautions — 62
    150 cu in four-cylinder — 321
    151 cu in four-cylinder — 76
    in-line six-cylinder — 91
    V8 — 104
    V6 — 113
    F- and L-head four-cylinder — 124
  specifications — 73, 86, 101, 111, 122, 318
  start-up after major repair or overhaul — 72
**Evaporative Control System (ECS)**
  checking — 191
  filter replacement — 58
  general description — 191
**Exhaust Gas Recirculation (EGR)**
  checking — 198
  general description — 198
  valve replacement — 199
**Exhaust system**
  check — 43
  component replacement — 176
  general information — 150
  heat valve check — 48
  specifications — 149

**F**

**Fan removal and installation** — 139
**Fender removal and installation** — 313
**Filter and oil change** — 40
**Filter (ECS) replacement** — 58
**Fluid level checks** — 37
**Flywheel removal and installation**
  151 cu in four-cylinder — 82
  in-line six-cylinder — 94, 98
  V8 — 109
  V6 — 120
  F- and L-head four-cylinder — 127, 132
**Front hub removal and installation** — 303
**Front seat removal and installation** — 316
**Front shock absorber testing** — 44
**Front side marker light removal** — 275

**Fuel system**
  check — 45
  filter replacement — 45
  general information — 150, 326
  line repair and replacement — 151
  pump
    check — 150
    removal and installation — 150
  specifications — 146, 319
  tank
    cleaning and repair — 176
    removal and installation — 175
**Fuses** — 274
**Fusible links** — 274

**G**

**Generator**
  brush replacement — 181
  check — 179
  drivebelt adjustment and replacement — 44
  removal and installation — 181
**Grille removal and installation** — 313

**H**

**Headlight**
  removal and installation — 275
  switch removal and installation — 277
**Heating system general information** — 141
**Hood**
  alignment — 313
  latches — 313
**Horn testing** — 279
**Hydraulic lifter removal, inspection and installation**
  151 cu in four-cylinder — 77
  in-line six-cylinder — 92, 94, 99
  V8 — 107, 108
  V6 — 118
  F- and L-head four-cylinder — 129, 131

**I**

**Idle speed adjustment** — 48
**Ignition system**
  coil removal and installation — 185
  distributor removal and installation — 186
  general information — 178
  specifications — 177
  switch removal and installation — 276
  timing — 55, 321
**Instrument cluster removal and installation** — 279
**Intake manifold removal and installation**
  150 cu in four-cylinder — 325
  151 cu in four-cylinder — 77
  in-line six-cylinder — 91, 326
  V8 — 105, 109
  V6 — 121
**Introduction to the Jeep CJ** — 4

**J**

**Jacking and towing** — 15

**L**

**Latches** — 313
**Locking front hub lubrication** — 320
**Lubricants** — 16

**M**

**Main bearings** — 68
**Maintenance techniques, tools and working facilities** — 9
**Manual transmission**
  general information — 205
  oil level check — 39
  overhaul — 207
  removal and installation — 206
  shift linkage adjustment — 207
  specifications — 204
**Master cylinder removal, overhaul and installation** — 269
**Model photographs** — 4, 5
**Muffler removal and installation** — 176

**O**

**Oil**
  change — 40
  filter change — 40
**Oxygen sensor** — 202

**P**

**Parking brakes** *see* Brakes
**Parking light removal and installation** — 275
**PCV filter replacement** — 46
**PCV valve replacement** — 45
**Pistons, connecting rods and bearings**
  cleaning and inspection — 68
  installation — 70
  removal — 65
**Positive Crankcase Ventilation (PCV) system** — 45, 46, 191
**Power brakes** *see* Brakes
**Power steering system**
  bleeding — 310
  pump belt adjustment — 44
  pump removal and installation — 309
**Pressure plate (clutch) removal, inspection and installation** — 246
**Pulse air system**
  checking — 195
  general description — 195
  valve replacement — 197

**R**

**Radiator removal and installation** — 136
**Rear axle assembly removal and installation** — 257
**Rear hub and bearing assembly removal and installation** — 255
**Rear shock absorber removal and installation** — 301
**Rear side marker lights** — 275
**Rear spring removal and installation** — 303
**Release (throwout) bearing** — 246
**Routine maintenance intervals** — 30, 319

**S**

**Safety first** — 17
**Shock absorber**
  removal and installation — 301
  testing — 44
**Spark plugs**
  color chart — 57
  replacement — 52
  wire check — 53
**Speedometer cable removal and installation** — 278
**Speedometer removal and installation** — 278
**Stabilizer bar removal and installation** — 301
**Starting system**
  check — 181
  general information — 178
  specifications — 178

**Starter motor**
  brush replacement — 182
  removal and installation — 182
  solenoid removal, repair and installation — 183
  testing in vehicle — 181
**Steering system**
  bellcrank removal and installation — 308
  check — 44
  connecting rod removal and installation — 308
  drag link removal and installation — 306
  gear removal and installation — 309
  general information — 301
  knuckle removal and installation — 304
  specifications — 300
  tie-rod removal and installation — 308
  wheel removal and installation — 310
**Supplement: Revisions and information on 1984 through 1986 models** — 317
**Suspension system**
  check — 44
  general information — 301
  shock absorber removal and installation — 301
  specifications — 300
  spring bushings — 303
  springs — 303

**T**

**Tail light removal and installation** — 275
**Temperature sending unit** — 141
**Thermo-controlled Air Cleaner (TAC)**
  check — 47, 201
  general description — 200
  switch replacement — 202
  temperature sensor replacement — 202
  vacuum motor replacement — 202
**Thermostat removal and installation** — 139
**Throttle linkage check** — 150
**Timing chain and sprockets**
  150 cu in four-cylinder — 324
  in-line six-cylinder — 92, 94, 98
  V8 — 105, 107, 108
  V6 — 116
  F- and L-head four-cylinder — 127, 133
**Tires**
  removal and installation — 15
  rotation — 49
  pressure checks — 41
**Tools and working facilities** — 9
**Towing** — 15
**Transfer case**
  diagnosis — 235
  general information — 235
  linkage adjustment — 236

  oil change — 50
  oil level check — 39
  overhaul — 237, 239, 241
  removal and installation — 235
  seal replacement — 237
**Transmission**
  band adjustment — 232
  diagnosis — 230
  fluid change — 49
  fluid level check — 39
  general information — 205, 229
  oil level check — 39
  overhaul — 207
  removal and installation — 206, 232
  shift linkage adjustment — 207, 230
  specifications — 204, 229
  throttle linkage adjustment — 230
**Troubleshooting** — 18
**Tune-up and routine maintenance** — 25, 319

**U**

**Upholstery maintenance** — 311

**V**

**Vacuum advance check** — 185
**Vacuum motor replacement** — 202
**Valve clearance adjustment** — 60
**Valve (EGR) replacement** — 199
**Valve spring removal and installation** — 63
**Valves and valve seals inspection and servicing** — 63
**Vehicle identification numbers** — 7

**W**

**Water pump**
  drivebelt adjustment and replacement — 44
  removal and installation — 139
**Wheel bearings**
  check — 49
  adjustment — 305
**Wheels**
  bearing check — 49
  front end alignment — 310
  removal and installation — 15
**Windshield**
  removal and installation — 313
  washer level check — 39
**Wiper blade removal and installation** — 60
**Wiring diagrams** — 280 to 299
**Working facilities** — 9

# HAYNES AUTOMOTIVE MANUALS

NOTE: New manuals are added to this list on a periodic basis. If you do not see a listing for your vehicle, consult your local Haynes dealer for the latest product information.

## ACURA
**1776** **Integra & Legend** '86 thru '90

## AMC
**Jeep CJ** – see JEEP (412)
**694** **Mid-size models,** Concord, Hornet, Gremlin & Spirit '70 thru '83
**934** **(Renault) Alliance & Encore** all models '83 thru '87

## AUDI
**615** **4000** all models '80 thru '87
**428** **5000** all models '77 thru '83
**1117** **5000** all models '84 thru '88

## AUSTIN
**Healey Sprite** – see MG Midget Roadster (265)

## BMW
**276** **320i** all 4 cyl models '75 thru '83
**632** **528i & 530i** all models '75 thru '80
**240** **1500 thru 2002** all models except Turbo '59 thru '77
**348** **2500, 2800, 3.0 & Bavaria** '69 thru '76

## BUICK
**Century (front wheel drive)** – see GENERAL MOTORS A-Cars (829)
**1627** **Buick, Oldsmobile & Pontiac Full-size (Front wheel drive)** all models '85 thru '93
**Buick** Electra, LeSabre and Park Avenue; **Oldsmobile** Delta 88 Royale, Ninety Eight and Regency; **Pontiac** Bonneville
**1551** **Buick Oldsmobile & Pontiac Full-size (Rear wheel drive)**
**Buick** Electra '70 thru '84, Estate '70 thru '90, LeSabre '70 thru '79
**Oldsmobile** Custom Cruiser '70 thru '90, Delta 88 '70 thru '85, Ninety-eight '70 thru '84
**Pontiac** Bonneville '70 thru '81, Catalina '70 thru '81, Grandville '70 thru '75, Parisienne '84 thu '86
**627** **Mid-size** all rear-drive **Regal & Century** models with V6, V8 and Turbo '74 thru '87
**Regal** – see GENERAL MOTORS (1671)
**Skyhawk** – see GENERAL MOTORS J-Cars (766)
**552** **Skylark** all X-car models '80 thru '85

## CADILLAC
**751** **Cadillac Rear Wheel Drive** all gasoline models '70 thru '90
**Cimarron** – see GENERAL MOTORS J-Cars (766)

## CAPRI
**296** **2000 MK I Coupe** all models '71 thru '75
**205** **2600 & 2800** V6 Coupe '71 thru '75
**375** **2800 Mk II** V6 Coupe '75 thru '78
**Mercury Capri** – see FORD Mustang (654)

## CHEVROLET
**1477** **Astro & GMC Safari Mini-vans** all models '85 thru '91
**554** **Camaro** V8 all models '70 thru '81
**866** **Camaro** all models '82 thru '91
**Cavalier** – see GENERAL MOTORS J-Cars (766)
**Celebrity** – see GENERAL MOTORS A-Cars (829)
**625** **Chevelle, Malibu & El Camino** all V6 & V8 models '69 thru '87
**449** **Chevette & Pontiac T1000** all models '76 thru '87
**550** **Citation** all models '80 thru '85
**1628** **Corsica/Beretta** all models '87 thru '92
**274** **Corvette** all V8 models '68 thru '82
**1336** **Corvette** all models '84 thru '91

**704** **Full-size Sedans** Caprice, Impala, Biscayne, Bel Air & Wagons, all V6 & V8 models '69 thru '90
**Lumina** – see GENERAL MOTORS (1671)
**Lumina APV** – see GENERAL MOTORS (2035)
**319** **Luv Pick-up** all 2WD & 4WD models '72 thru '82
**626** **Monte Carlo** all V6, V8 & Turbo models '70 thru '88
**241** **Nova** all V8 models '69 thru '79
**1642** **Nova and Geo Prizm** all front wheel drive models, '85 thru '90
**420** **Pick-ups '67 thru '87** – Chevrolet & GMC, all full-size models '67 thru '87; Suburban, Blazer & Jimmy '67 thru '91
**1664** **Pick-ups '88 thru '92** – Chevrolet & GMC all full-size (C and K) models, '88 thru '92
**1727** **Sprint & Geo Metro** '85 thru '91
**831** **S-10 & GMC S-15 Pick-ups** all models '82 thru '92
**345** **Vans** – Chevrolet & GMC, V8 & in-line 6 cyl models '68 thru '92

## CHRYSLER
**1337** **Chrysler & Plymouth Mid-size** front wheel drive '82 thru '89
**K-Cars** – see DODGE Aries (723)
**Laser** – see DODGE Daytona (1140)

## DATSUN
**402** **200SX** all models '77 thru '79
**647** **200SX** all models '80 thru '83
**228** **B-210** all models '73 thru '78
**525** **210** all models '78 thru '82
**206** **240Z, 260Z & 280Z** Coupe & 2+2 '70 thru '78
**563** **280ZX** Coupe & 2+2 '79 thru '83
**300ZX** – see NISSAN (1137)
**679** **310** all models '78 thru '82
**123** **510 & PL521 Pick-up** '68 thru '73
**430** **510** all models '78 thru '81
**372** **610** all models '72 thru '76
**277** **620 Series Pick-up** all models '73 thru '79
**720 Series Pick-up** – see NISSAN Pick-ups (771)
**376** **810/Maxima** all gasoline models '77 thru '84
**124** **1200** all models '70 thru '73
**368** **F10** all models '76 thru '79
**Pulsar** – see NISSAN (876)
**Sentra** – see NISSAN (982)
**Stanza** – see NISSAN (981)

## DODGE
**723** **Aries & Plymouth Reliant** all models '81 thru '89
**1231** **Caravan & Plymouth Voyager Mini-Vans** all models '84 thru '91
**699** **Challenger & Plymouth Saporro** all models '78 thru '83
**236** **Colt** all models '71 thru '77
**610** **Colt & Plymouth Champ (front wheel drive)** all models '78 thru '87
**556** **D50/Ram 50/Plymouth Arrow Pick-ups & Raider** '79 thru '91
**1668** **Dakota Pick-up** all models '87 thru '90
**234** **Dart & Plymouth Valiant** all 6 cyl models '67 thru '76
**1140** **Daytona & Chrysler Laser** all models '84 thru '89
**545** **Omni & Plymouth Horizon** all models '78 thru '90
**912** **Pick-ups** all full-size models '74 thru '91
**1726** **Shadow & Plymouth Sundance** '87 thru '91
**1779** **Spirit & Plymouth Acclaim** '89 thru '92
**349** **Vans** – Dodge & Plymouth V8 & 6 cyl models '71 thru '91

## FIAT
**094** **124 Sport Coupe & Spider** '68 thru '78

**479** **Strada** all models '79 thru '82
**273** **X1/9** all models '74 thru '80

## FORD
**1476** **Aerostar Mini-vans** all models '86 thru '92
**788** **Bronco and Pick-ups** '73 thru '79
**880** **Bronco and Pick-ups** '80 thru '91
**268** **Courier Pick-up** all models '72 thru '82
**789** **Escort & Mercury Lynx** all models '81 thru '90
**2046** **Escort & Mercury Tracer** all models '91 thru '93
**2021** **Explorer & Mazda Navajo** '91 thru '92
**560** **Fairmont & Mercury Zephyr** all in-line & V8 models '78 thru '83
**334** **Fiesta** all models '77 thru '80
**754** **Ford & Mercury Full-size,** Ford LTD & Mercury Marquis ('75 thru '82); Ford Custom 500, Country Squire, Crown Victoria & Mercury Colony Park ('75 thru '87); Ford LTD Crown Victoria & Mercury Gran Marquis ('83 thru '87)
**359** **Granada & Mercury Monarch** all in-line, 6 cyl & V8 models '75 thru '80
**773** **Ford & Mercury Mid-size,** Ford Thunderbird & Mercury Cougar ('75 thru '82); Ford LTD & Mercury Marquis ('83 thru '86); Ford Torino, Gran Torino, Elite, Ranchero pick-up, LTD II, Mercury Montego, Comet, XR-7 & Lincoln Versailles ('75 thru '86)
**654** **Mustang & Mercury Capri** all models including Turbo '79 thru '92
**357** **Mustang V8** all models '64-1/2 thru '73
**231** **Mustang II** all 4 cyl, V6 & V8 models '74 thru '78
**649** **Pinto & Mercury Bobcat** all models '75 thru '80
**1670** **Probe** all models '89 thru '92
**1026** **Ranger & Bronco II** all gasoline models '83 thru '92
**1421** **Taurus & Mercury Sable** '86 thru '92
**1418** **Tempo & Mercury Topaz** all gasoline models '84 thru '91
**1338** **Thunderbird & Mercury Cougar/XR7** '83 thru '88
**1725** **Thunderbird & Mercury Cougar** '89 and '90
**344** **Vans** all V8 Econoline models '69 thru '91

## GENERAL MOTORS
**829** **A-Cars** – Chevrolet Celebrity, Buick Century, Pontiac 6000 & Oldsmobile Cutlass Ciera all models '82 thru '90
**766** **J-Cars** – Chevrolet Cavalier, Pontiac J-2000, Oldsmobile Firenza, Buick Skyhawk & Cadillac Cimarron all models '82 thru '92
**1420** **N-Cars** – Buick Somerset '85 thru '87; Pontiac Grand Am and Oldsmobile Calais '85 thru '91; Buick Skylark '86 thru '91
**1671** **GM:** Buick Regal, Chevrolet Lumina, Oldsmobile Cutlass Supreme, Pontiac Grand Prix, all front wheel drive models '88 thru '90
**2035** **GM:** Chevrolet Lumina APV, Oldsmobile Silhouette, Pontiac Trans Sport '90 thru '92

## GEO
**Metro** – see CHEVROLET Sprint (1727)
**Prizm** – see CHEVROLET Nova (1642)
**Tracker** – see SUZUKI Samurai (1626)

## GMC
**Safari** – see CHEVROLET ASTRO (1477)
**Vans & Pick-ups** – see CHEVROLET (420, 831, 345, 1664)

(continued on next page)

* Listings shown with an asterisk ( * ) indicate model coverage as of this printing. These titles will be periodically updated to include later model years – consult your Haynes dealer for more information.

**Haynes North America, Inc., 861 Lawrence Drive, Newbury Park, CA 91320 • (805) 498-6703**

NOTE: New manuals are added to this list on a periodic basis. If you do not see a listing for your vehicle, consult your local Haynes dealer for the latest product information.

## HONDA
- 351 **Accord CVCC** all models '76 thru '83
- *1221 **Accord** all models '84 thru '89
- 160 **Civic 1200** all models '73 thru '79
- 633 **Civic 1300 & 1500 CVCC** all models '80 thru '83
- 297 **Civic 1500 CVCC** all models '75 thru '79
- *1227 **Civic** all models '84 thru '91
- *601 **Prelude CVCC** all models '79 thru '89

## HYUNDAI
- *1552 **Excel** all models '86 thru '91

## ISUZU
- *1641 **Trooper & Pick-up**, all gasoline models '81 thru '91

## JAGUAR
- *242 **XJ6** all 6 cyl models '68 thru '86
- *478 **XJ12 & XJS** all 12 cyl models '72 thru '85

## JEEP
- *1553 **Cherokee, Comanche & Wagoneer Limited** all models '84 thru '91
- 412 **CJ** all models '49 thru '86
- *1777 **Wrangler** all models '87 thru '92

## LADA
- *413 **1200, 1300. 1500 & 1600** all models including Riva '74 thru '86

## MAZDA
- 648 **626 Sedan & Coupe (rear wheel drive)** all models '79 thru '82
- 1082 **626 & MX-6 (front wheel drive)** all models '83 thru '91
- 370 **GLC Hatchback (rear wheel drive)** all models '77 thru '83
- 757 **GLC (front wheel drive)** all models '81 thru '86
- *2047 **MPV** '89 thru '93
- **Navajo** – see FORD Explorer (2021)
- *267 **Pick-ups** '72 thru '92
- 460 **RX-7** all models '79 thru '85
- *1419 **RX-7** all models '86 thru '91

## MERCEDES-BENZ
- *1643 **190 Series** all four-cylinder gasoline models, '84 thru '88
- 346 **230, 250 & 280** Sedan, Coupe & Roadster all 6 cyl sohc models '68 thru '72
- 983 **280 123 Series** all gasoline models '77 thru '81
- 698 **350 & 450** Sedan, Coupe & Roadster all models '71 thru '80
- 697 **Diesel 123 Series** 200D, 220D, 240D, 240TD, 300D, 300CD, 300TD, 4- & 5-cyl incl. Turbo '76 thru '85

## MERCURY
*For all PLYMOUTH titles see FORD Listing*

## MG
- 111 **MGB** Roadster & GT Coupe all models '62 thru '80
- 265 **MG Midget & Austin Healey Sprite** Roadster '58 thru '80

## MITSUBISHI
- *1669 **Cordia, Tredia, Galant, Precis & Mirage** '83 thru '90
- *2022 **Pick-ups & Montero** '83 thru '91

## MORRIS
- 074 **(Austin) Marina 1.8** all models '71 thru '80
- 024 **Minor 1000** sedan & wagon '56 thru '71

## NISSAN
- 1137 **300ZX** all Turbo & non-Turbo models '84 thru '89

- *1341 **Maxima** all models '85 thru '91
- *771 **Pick-ups/Pathfinder** gas models '80 thru '91
- *876 **Pulsar** all models '83 thru '86
- *982 **Sentra** all models '82 thru '90
- *981 **Stanza** all models '82 thru '90

## OLDSMOBILE
- **Custom Cruiser** – see BUICK Full-size (1551)
- 658 **Cutlass** all standard gasoline V6 & V8 models '74 thru '88
- **Cutlass Ciera** – see GENERAL MOTORS A-Cars (829)
- **Cutlass Supreme** – see GENERAL MOTORS (1671)
- **Firenza** – see GENERAL MOTORS J-Cars (766)
- **Ninety-eight** – see BUICK Full-size (1551)
- **Omega** – see PONTIAC Phoenix & Omega (551)
- **Silhouette** – see GENERAL MOTORS (2035)

## PEUGEOT
- 663 **504** all diesel models '74 thru '83

## PLYMOUTH
*For all PLYMOUTH titles, see DODGE listing.*

## PONTIAC
- **T1000** – see CHEVROLET Chevette (449)
- **J-2000** – see GENERAL MOTORS J-Cars (766)
- **6000** – see GENERAL MOTORS A-Cars (829)
- 1232 **Fiero** all models '84 thru '88
- 555 **Firebird** all V8 models except Turbo '70 thru '81
- *867 **Firebird** all models '82 thru '91
- **Full-size Rear Wheel Drive** – see Buick, Oldsmobile, Pontiac Full-size (1551)
- **Grand Prix** – see GENERAL MOTORS (1671)
- 551 **Phoenix & Oldsmobile Omega** all X-car models '80 thru '84
- **Trans Sport** – see GENERAL MOTORS (2035)

## PORSCHE
- *264 **911** all Coupe & Targa models except Turbo & Carrera 4 '65 thru '89
- 239 **914** all 4 cyl models '69 thru '76
- 397 **924** all models including Turbo '76 thru '82
- *1027 **944** all models including Turbo '83 thru '89

## RENAULT
- 141 **5 Le Car** all models '76 thru '83
- 079 **8 & 10** all models with 58.4 cu in engines '62 thru '72
- 097 **12 Saloon & Estate** all models 1289 cc engines '70 thru '80
- 768 **15 & 17** all models '73 thru '79
- 081 **16** all models 89.7 cu in & 95.5 cu in engines '65 thru '72
- **Alliance & Encore** – see AMC (934)

## SAAB
- 247 **99** all models including Turbo '69 thru '80
- *980 **900** all models including Turbo '79 thru '88

## SUBARU
- 237 **1100, 1300, 1400 & 1600** all models '71 thru '79
- *681 **1600 & 1800** 2WD & 4WD all models '80 thru '89

## SUZUKI
- *1626 **Samurai/Sidekick and Geo Tracker** all models '86 thru '91

## TOYOTA
- *1023 **Camry** all models '83 thru '91
- 150 **Carina Sedan** all models '71 thru '74
- *2038 **Celica Front Wheel Drive** '86 thru '92
- 935 **Celica Rear Wheel Drive** '71 thru '85
- *1139 **Celica Supra** '79 thru '92
- 361 **Corolla** all models '75 thru '79
- 961 **Corolla** all models (rear wheel drive) '80 thru '87
- *1025 **Corolla** all models (front wheel drive) '84 thru '91
- *636 **Corolla Tercel** all models '80 thru '82
- 230 **Corona & MK II** all 4 cyl sohc models '69 thru '74
- 360 **Corona** all models '74 thru '82
- *532 **Cressida** all models '78 thru '82
- 313 **Land Cruiser** all models '68 thru '82
- 200 **MK II** all 6 cyl models '72 thru '76
- *1339 **MR2** all models '85 thru '87
- 304 **Pick-up** all models '69 thru '78
- *656 **Pick-up** all models '79 thru '92

## TRIUMPH
- 112 **GT6 & Vitesse** all models '62 thru '74
- 113 **Spitfire** all models '62 thru '81
- 322 **TR7** all models '75 thru '81

## VW
- 159 **Beetle & Karmann Ghia** all models '54 thru '79
- 238 **Dasher** all gasoline models '74 thru '81
- *884 **Rabbit, Jetta, Scirocco, & Pick-up** all gasoline models '74 thru '91 & **Convertible** '80 thru '91
- 451 **Rabbit, Jetta & Pick-up** all diesel models '77 thru '84
- 082 **Transporter 1600** all models '68 thru '79
- 226 **Transporter 1700, 1800 & 2000** all models '72 thru '79
- 084 **Type 3 1500 & 1600** all models '63 thru '73
- 1029 **Vanagon** all air-cooled models '80 thru '83

## VOLVO
- 203 **120, 130 Series & 1800 Sports** '61 thru '73
- 129 **140 Series** all models '66 thru '74
- *270 **240 Series** all models '74 thru '90
- 400 **260 Series** all models '75 thru '82
- *1550 **740 & 760 Series** all models '82 thru '88

## SPECIAL MANUALS
- 1479 **Automotive Body Repair & Painting Manual**
- 1654 **Automotive Electrical Manual**
- 1480 **Automotive Heating & Air Conditioning Manual**
- 1762 **Chevrolet Engine Overhaul Manual**
- 1736 **Diesel Engine Repair Manual**
- 1667 **Emission Control Manual**
- 1763 **Ford Engine Overhaul Manual**
- 482 **Fuel Injection Manual**
- 1666 **Small Engine Repair Manual**
- 299 **SU Carburetors** thru '88
- 393 **Weber Carburetors** thru '79
- 300 **Zenith/Stromberg CD Carburetors** thru '76

*See your dealer for other available titles*

Over 100 Haynes motorcycle manuals also available

1-93

* Listings shown with an asterisk ( * ) indicate model coverage as of this printing. These titles will be periodically updated to include later model years – consult your Haynes dealer for more information.

**Haynes North America, Inc., 861 Lawrence Drive, Newbury Park, CA 91320 • (805) 498-6703**